Current Issues in Public Administration

Current Issues in Public Administration

Frederick S. Lane

St. Martin's Press
New York

ACKNOWLEDGMENTS

Frederick C. Mosher, "Public Administration." Reprinted with permission from *Encyclopaedia Britannica*, 15th edition. © 1974 by Encyclopaedia Britannica, Inc.

Joseph L. Bower, "Effective Public Management," reprinted from *Harvard Business Review*, March-April 1977, Copyright © 1977 by the President and Fellows of Harvard College; all rights reserved.

Harold Stein, "Public Administration as Politics." From *Public Administration and Policy Development: A Case Book*, by Harold Stein, copyright 1952 by Harcourt Brace Jovanovich, Inc. Reprinted by permission of the publishers.

James Q. Wilson, "The Rise of the Bureaucratic State." Reprinted with permission of the author from *The Public Interest*, No. 41 (Fall 1975), 77–103. © by National Affairs Inc.

Richard E. Neustadt, "Politicians and Bureaucrats" in *The Congress and America's Future*, Second Edition, edited by David B. Truman.

© 1973 The American Assembly, Columbia University. Reprinted by permission of Prentice-Hall, Inc. Englewood Cliffs, New Jersey.

Richard P. Nathan, "The 'Administrative Presidency.'" Reprinted with permission of the author from *The Public Interest*, No. 44 (Summer 1976), pp. 40–54. © by National Affairs Inc.

Martha Wagner Weinberg, "Managing the State." Reprinted from Chapter 3 of *Managing the State* by Martha Wagner Weinberg by permission of the M.I.T. Press, Cambridge, Massachusetts. Copyright © 1977 by Massachusetts Institute of Technology.

Allen Schick, "Congress and the 'Details' of Administration." Reprinted by permission from *Public Administration Review*, 36 (September/October 1976). Copyright © 1976 by American Society for Public Administration, 1225 Connecticut Avenue N.W., Washington, D. C. 20036. All rights reserved.

Acknowledgments and copyrights continue at the back of the book on page 570, which constitutes an extension of the copyright page.

Preface

Government expenditures in the United States account for 35 percent of the gross national product. There are 78,000 units of government in the United States with 15 million employees. To say the least, public administration is "big business." It is also one of the fastest growing academic fields.

Current Issues in Public Administration provides a comprehensive set of readings that cover, with clarity and depth, all the main topics in this rapidly developing field. As the title suggests, the emphasis is on current issues and problems, and the readings are largely drawn from the recent literature, although some indispensable classics are also included. The readings cover both the political setting of public agencies and the management of large public bureaucracies. State and local as well as federal government issues are given due attention. The readings are organized to correspond as closely as possible to the sequence in which topics are taken up in most public administration survey courses and in most of the two dozen introductory textbooks in the field.

In preparing this book my first debt has been to my teachers. Dwight Waldo and the late Roscoe Martin of the Maxwell School, Syracuse University, and Ruth McQuown and the late Gladys Kammerer of the University of Florida contributed much to my understanding of public administration.

I am also grateful to my colleagues and students at Bernard M. Baruch College of the City University of New York for their willingness to share their ideas and favorite articles, and especially to my colleagues Lewis Friedman and Thomas Halper. I also owe a considerable debt to Matthew Goldstein and Sidney Lirtzman in the academic vice president's office at Baruch College, with whom I practice public administration each day.

The professionalism and commitment to a developing academic field by those in the St. Martin's College Department—especially Thomas Broadbent, Glenn Cowley, Bertrand Lummus, and Edward Cone—are gratefully acknowledged. Only here can I extend my thanks to the six anonymous reviewers commissioned by St. Martin's whose comments helped me in focusing on various key topics and in reducing the size of the original manuscript to manageable proportions.

This book, as so many other things, would not have been possible without the support and assistance of my wife, Lea, and the tolerance of our sons, Cary and Rand.

Frederick S. Lane

TO MY MOTHER
AND THE MEMORY OF MY FATHER

Contents

Introduction

Public policies are the outputs or results of the political system. Governmental agencies, sometimes called bureaucracies, constitute an important set of actors in the public policy-making process. Public administration is the study of the activities and impacts of governmental agencies.

There are eight principals in the national policy system:

1. the citizen
2. the Congress
3. the president
4. the U.S. Supreme Court and the court system
5. political parties
6. interest groups
7. the press
8. the bureaucracy

Figure 1 depicts the national policy system, or policy-making "octagon." The nation's policy system is also its political system because, in the end, the two systems turn out to be one.[1] Social and economic factors are important to policy making but impact on public policies only as they affect the political system.

In this country, state and local levels of government have their own policy systems that interconnect through a federal system. Intergovernmental relations raise some of the most important current issues in the formation of public policy and its implementation.

The lines in Figure 1 represent the interrelationships and interactions among the actors in the policy system. Depending on the given issue at any particular time and the specific participants, these relations range from direct and continuous and intense, to frequent, to indirect and/or intermittent.

Policy making can be conceptualized to occur in five stages:

1. policy initiation
2. policy formulation/articulation/consideration
3. policy legitimation (or formal approval)
4. policy implementation
5. policy evaluation

Figure 1 The National Policy System

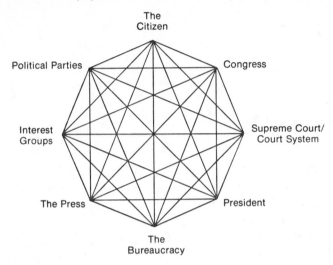

The core of the practice of public administration deals with policy implementation, but public agencies are also deeply involved in the other stages of the policy-making process. This is shown in Figure 2.

In 1887, Woodrow Wilson published "The Study of Administration," from which the study of public administration in America is often dated.[2] In the article, Wilson advocated a distinction between policy formation and implementation, sometimes called the policy-administration dichotomy, through which he attempted to increase the competence and ethics of civil servants. Remember, this was only four years after the formal beginning of the civil service system and not far removed from the "spoils" approach to public personnel management. Also, Wilson's essay on the study of government was in a legally oriented tradition, wherein elected legislators, "lawmakers," made the policy and administrators, greatly oversimplified, carried out the programs developed.

If it was ever true, the policy-administration dichotomy is certainly not valid today. As depicted earlier, public agencies are involved in all stages of public policy making: Agency personnel often initiate an idea for a new public program. Public administrators regularly interact with agency clientele and other interest groups, with appropriate legislative committees and members, and with their staffs. Public executives testify regularly before legislative committees considering a particular policy proposal. And public agencies increasingly evaluate the effectiveness and impact of public policies by obtaining citizen feedback and by employing systematic research techniques.

The power of a public agency derives from (1) the influence of its constituencies or clientele and (2) the character and priority of its activities.[3] If an agency's clients are organized and powerful—business groups, big farming interests, or organized labor, for example—the agency has relatively greater authority and influence. In

Figure 2   Defining Public Administration in Terms of the Public Policy-Making Process

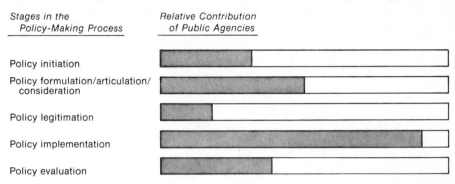

addition, if an agency is concerned with broad-based matters of importance—like national security or economic progress—it is more powerful than other agencies though the relative importance of an agency can change over time, as, for example, is the case currently with the significance of the energy issue.

The technical nature of work (if its function is hard for the average person to understand, much less perform) and its record of accomplishment also influence an agency's power, as does the quality of organizational leadership. The principal administrators' style, skill, personality, experience, and ability to communicate are naturally related to the agency's power. Similarly, organizational morale and commitment are also important. Finally, the agency's size—number of employees, budget, scope, and geographic distribution of its activities—also contributes to its power.

It is impossible to study public administration without including political science because public bureaucracies operate in a political (or policy-making) setting, though public administration draws on a variety of other disciplines as well—economics, psychology, and sociology among others—and readings from these perspectives have been included in this presentation.

The text has been divided into four parts. Part one treats the practice of public administration and how it is studied in the academic community. Parts two and three are the core of the volume: Chapters 2–5 focus on the political environment in which public agencies operate and the interaction among the participants in the policy-making system. Chapters 6–12 look at the process of public administration: although politics and the poltical setting must be considered, the focus here is distinctly managerial. Finally, in part four, we examine the issues and contexts of the practice as well as the study of public administration as it will develop in the future. These chapters again raise the questions with which we will begin:

What is the role of public agencies in American society?
How may bureaucratic power be controlled?
How is public administrative activity likely to develop in the future?

NOTES

1. Figure 1 is adapted from a similar pictorial scheme developed by the late Roscoe C. Martin, Maxwell Professor of political science, Syracuse University.
2. Woodrow Wilson, "The Study of Administration," *Political Science Quarterly*, 2 (June 1887), 197–222.
3. See Francis E. Rourke, *Bureaucracy, Politics, and Public Policy* (Boston: Little, Brown, 1969), esp. Chap. 4.

Current Issues in Public Administration

PART ONE

Introduction to Public Administration

1

WHAT IS
PUBLIC ADMINISTRATION?

When beginning the study of a new subject, the student normally seeks some form of definition of the subject matter, or at least its boundaries, and an overview of its content and importance. The purpose of this chapter is to come to grips with these questions:

What is public administration?

What factors have influenced the development of public administration in America?

What are the key issues in this field?

What are some of the current controversies regarding this important societal activity?

What is unique about public administration as distinct from, for example, business administration?

Public administration is an ancient activity common to just about all countries and all levels of government. But just as economic, social, physical, cultural, and technological factors change with time, so do societies differ from country to country. As a result, public administrative structures and activities also vary from one nation to another. In the first selection, Frederick Mosher outlines the historical development of American public administration. The second article, by Joseph Bower, explores the distinctiveness of public administration. The importance, the complexity, and the challenge of the administrative process in the public context is analyzed .

A variety of terms is often used to identify this field of study. A professor at the Harvard Business School, Bower refers to "public management." Some schools that educate individuals for careers in governmental and nonprofit organizations are labeled "public affairs," "public service," or "public policy." The traditional and most meaningful label, however, remains *public administration.*

Public Administration

FREDERICK C. MOSHER

Public administration, traditionally defined, comprises those activities involved in carrying out the policies and programs of governments. The term is also used today in a broader sense, for public administration is often regarded as including some responsibility—varying widely in degree among governments and departments—in determining what the policies and programs of governments should be, as well as in executing them. But public administration focuses principally on the planning, organizing, directing, coordinating, and controlling of government operations.

As an occupational field, public administration is common to all nations, whatever their system of government. Whether monarchical, totalitarian, socialist, parliamentary, or congressional-presidential, all countries require machinery to put into effect the policies of the government. Within nations public administration is practiced by the central government, by local governments, and, in federal systems, by intermediate provinces and states. The interrelationship of different levels of government within individual nations is in fact a continuing and growing problem for public administration generally.

The professional identity of those engaged in public administration has been strengthened in European countries, and, by colonial imposition or diffusion, in most of the rest of the world, through the establishment of more or less elite administrative, executive, or directive classes in civil services. In the United States and a few other countries, the elitist class connotation was consciously abandoned or avoided, with the result that professional recognition has come slowly and only partially.

Public administration, as well as being a profession, is also a distinct field of study, and the middle decades of the 20th century have seen a considerable increase in research and in the education and training of public administrators.

Historical background.   Public administration is an ancient activity. It must have existed for as long as there have been organized societies, for few group determinations in society are self-executing. The earliest records of civilization in south Asia, China, and Egypt contain references to what one would now call public administration.

Modern public administration is a by-product of the emergence of nation-states from the feudal societies of Europe. With the growth and centralization of power and responsibility in monarchical courts came the need for a full-time, stable, and qualified corps of public administrators, who became increasingly specialized in different fields of national activity. One of the earliest systematic manifestations of public administration was known as cameralism, which developed during the 17th and 18th centuries in Prussia and Austria. Cameralism was designed to provide efficient management of highly centralized, paternalistic states characterized by mercantilist economies. It required university training in such fields as public finance and its administration, police science, economics, and agriculture and forestry. The 18th century also witnessed the development in France of a high degree of emphasis and proficiency in technical and engineering activities and saw the establishment of national professional schools, primarily to provide qualified technicians for the public service.

Though some of the elements of cameralism and French technology have had significant impact on public administration in various countries down to the present time, the emphases upon them could not survive the French Revolution and the Napoleonic era. The weight given to the rights of individuals and the obligation of states to protect those rights, the introduction of laissez-faire economics, the codification of law, and other developments led to a quite different view of the state and of its administration. The essence of the latter came to be obligation and loyalty to the state through the interpretation and fair-handed application of law, legitimately enacted to express the will of the state. Such a view suggested that senior permanent officers should be trained in law. The nation-state was sovereign, centralized, and durable; and the legally oriented bureaucracy served the function of providing permanence and stability and of expressing and preserving its "will," despite changes of government and even systems of government. This legalistic view of the state and its bureaucracy persists in much of western Europe and, to a lesser degree, in parts of eastern Europe, as well as in many of the newer countries that were once colonies of continental powers.

Great Britain and the United States followed paths quite different from each other and from continental Europe in the development of their systems of public administration. Neither adopted the somewhat mystical European view of the state, and neither abandoned its common-law tradition for codification. Britain had long entrusted the administrative responsibilities of its government to representatives drawn from its aristocracy of unspecialized, often well-educated gentlemen. Until the Industrial Revolution of the late 18th and early 19th centuries, most of the aristocracy came from rural estates. Following the reform of the civil service in the 19th century, most administrators came to be drawn from the growing mercantile and business classes of the cities. For the last century, they have been selected primarily on the basis of stiff competitive examinations of university graduates, mainly from Oxford and Cambridge. These examinations tested neither administrative law, as on the continent, nor any other specialization directly related to public administration but concentrated on the classics and humanities. This method of recruitment to the British administrative class persisted, with only temporary changes during periods of crisis, into the late 1960s. It was designed to produce generalist administrators—intelligent, broadgauged men free of parochial, professional perspectives. They would learn administration and the activities they were administering on the job. Administration was perceived more in terms of providing policy advice to ministers and less in terms of internal management than in most other countries. In general, British administrative practice was highly centralized, with controls over the system itself largely concentrated in the Treasury. In 1968 a committee of inquiry into the civil service under the chairmanship of Lord Fulton made recommendations that would result in much broader recruitment into the upper reaches of the civil service.

Through the Indian and other colonial civil services, the British concepts of administration were conveyed to the colonies, and they continue to have impact, though with varying force, in the Commonwealth.

Public administration in the American colonies and in the states and national government that succeeded them also began on the model of the mother country. Administration was by the gentry or landed aristocracy in the South, and by the increasingly commercial and industrial gentry in the North. Public administration was not perceived as a distinct and separable kind of activity or occupation, and the term was not used in the U.S. Constitution. There were three basic structural differences from the British system. One was the federal system and particularly the limited powers of the national government. Second was the separation of executive from legislative powers at the national, state, and city level of government. Third, growing out of the fear and distrust of concentrated executive powers over which the American Revolution had been fought was the tendency to scatter executive power among a wide variety of commissions, boards, or elected or appointive officials who were either autonomous or responsible to the legislative body. Among other consequences of these structural differences are that to this day, the primary problems of American public administration are these: bridging the separation of executive and legislative powers; establishing more effective and cooperative relationships between and among the national government, the states, and a vast array of local governments; and integrating executive powers in single executives at each level.

Since the Revolution three major developments have significantly affected American public administration. One has been the two-party political system and, especially during the middle decades of the 19th century, the invasion by political parties of the administrative offices of governments under the patronage system. This practice of rewarding political service with public office effectively thwarted the development of stable administrative systems and made the career prospects of administrators uncertain, for with each change in political control a new group of officeholders would replace the old. Party affiliation, rather than merit or ability, was the criterion for appointment. But the so-called spoils, or patronage, system had a corollary and more wholesome effect: it was a sweeping expression of egalitarianism in its weakening of the hold of the gentry on public offices and its opening of public service to the common man. This move toward egalitarianism preceded by more than a century steps in the same direction that were underway in many European and other countries in the 1970s. The depredations of the spoils system gave rise in the late 19th century to a second development: a fervent movement to reform the civil service on the basis of merit and without regard to political affiliation or to social class background. Civil service reform is still far from complete, but it has given rise to many of the features and developments of public administration throughout much of the 20th century. American civil service reform was originally molded on the British pattern, but its effects were entirely different, for it prevented the development of an elite administrative class.

The third development affecting the character of American public administration was the accelerating specialization, diversification, and professionalization of occupations that began about the turn of the 20th century in the United States and within its governments. This development took place all around the world, but its impact in the United States on public administration has been somewhat different. The public agencies of the United States had no entrenched amateur, gentlemen administrators as in Britain, nor administrative lawyers, as in continental Europe. Specialists assumed substantial control over the agencies appropriate to their skills: engineers for public works, agriculturists for agriculture, doctors for public health, lawyers for regulatory programs, and so forth.

Russia inherited some of the legal tradition associated with the Napoleonic era, acquired in its case largely through international osmosis rather than occupation. The Russian Revolution of 1917 superimposed a very different set of values and institutions in public administration: subordination of the individual citizen in favour of dominance of the state; a high degree of concentration of power; the one-party system and party control not only of basic policy but of administrative and industrial agencies at every level. The goals of the state are determined by the Communist Party, and these have been primarily concerned with the expansion of political, economic, and military power. The means toward this end are seen as rapid industrialization, high productivity, discipline, and the suppression of elements in society that might retard or endanger such development. The Soviet Union has thus moved in the direction of a technocratic administration. Its administrative leadership consists increasingly of engineers, production managers, and scientists. They are usually party members, but of a distinctly different type from the older revolutionaries. The Soviet Union may thus be regarded as providing a fourth main source of administrative thought and practice, its system of public administration contrasting strongly with the British, American, and continental patterns. The importance of these four patterns of public administration has been greatly increased as a result of their impact on many other governments of the world.

An important factor in the spread of particular approaches to public administration is the education and training of future leaders in foreign countries. Many Communist political, as well as administrative, leaders around the world were trained in the Soviet Union. A good many public administrators in Africa, Latin America, and Asia were trained in Britain, the United States, and France. Finally, and related to such educational activity, is the conscious imitation of the administrative systems of other countries, often coupled with a request for assistance in establishing such a model. During the 19th century, for example, Japan imitated, and was assisted by, Germany; Thailand was aided similarly by Britain and France. Since World War II, most of the former colonies have been assisted and influenced by their erstwhile mother countries. The United States has had the largest technical assistance program, and American practices are consequently becoming increasingly prevalent. This may be due in part to the greater ability of the United States to provide such assistance and in part to a belief that the United States is most advanced in this field. Public administration is one of the major fields of technical assistance of the United Nations, and such assistance is also provided by a number of other international organizations and by some private foundations.

Current efforts to improve public administration, which seem to be common to almost every country in the world, take different forms in different lands. Improvement is everywhere identified with greater effectiveness or productivity in responding to public needs, but particular facets of the different administrative systems retard such improvement in a variety of ways. The continental legal psychology, for example, is more conducive to stability than to innovation, and the dominance of a legal class has not encouraged the employment of other kinds of specialists and scientists. To a considerable extent the same is true of the British administrative-class generalists. Insofar as both groups are drawn principally from established upper class minorities, their domination is not conducive to what has been called "democratization" of the public services. By way of contrast, a major problem of public administration in the United States is to coordinate the efforts of numerous separate departments at the federal, state, and local levels, each dominated by its particular brand of specialists. In addition, the long-standing American orientation toward business, free enterprise, and economics has discouraged the development of integrating mechanisms for social planning. And the severity and discipline of the single party in most of the Communist states has, according to many observers, provided disincentives toward either innovation or productivity.

Basic approaches.   A central theme of public administration throughout the 20th century has been reform. That is, it has been assumed that current administrative processes can and should be improved. The study and practice of public administration has been essentially pragmatic and normative rather than theoretical and value free. This may explain why public administration, unlike some social sciences, developed without much concern about an encompassing theory. Not until the middle decades of the 20th century and the dissemination of the German sociologist Max Weber's theory of bureaucracy was much interest stimulated concerning a theory of public administration. Most of the recent development of bureaucratic theory, however, has been addressed to organizations in the private sector, and, with a very few exceptions, there has been little effort to relate organizational theory with political theory. The main emphasis remains upon pragmatic reform.

A second theme of public administration has been economy and efficiency; that is, the provision of public services at the minimum cost. This has usually been the stated objective of administrative reform. Despite growing concern about other kinds of values such as responsiveness to public needs, justice and equal treatment, and citizen involvement in government decisions, efficiency continues to be a major goal.

A third feature of public administration has been its emphasis on the structure of formal organization. Most efforts at administrative reform have included as their central element the modification of organizational structures. They reflect a basic faith, held by administrators, politicians, and the educated public, that administrative ills can be at least partly corrected by reorganization guided by logical rules or "principles." Many of the principles were initially borrowed from the military, a few from private business. They include, for example:(1) organizing departments, ministries, and agencies on the basis of common or closely related purposes; (2) grouping like activities in single units; (3) equating responsibility with authority; (4) ensuring unity of command (only one supervisor for each group of employees); (5) limiting the number of subordinates reporting to a single supervisor; (6) differentiating line (operating or end-purpose) activities from staff (advisory, consultative, or support) activities; (7) employing the principle of management by exception (only the unusual problem or case is brought to the top); (8) having a clear-cut chain of command downward and of responsibility upward.

Some critics have maintained that these and other principles of public administration are useful only as rough criteria for given organizational situations. They hold that organizational problems differ, and that the applicability of rules to different situations differs, too. Nonetheless, and despite much more sophisticated analyses of organizational behaviour in recent decades, such principles as those enumerated above continue to carry force.

A fourth feature of public administration has been its stress upon personnel. In most countries, administrative reform has been preceded or accompanied by civil service reform. Historically, the direction of such reform has been toward what has been labelled "meritocracy"—the best man for each job, competitive examinations for entry, and selection and promotion on the basis of merit. Recently, greater attention has been given to factors other than merit, including personal attitudes, incentives, personality, personal relationships, and collective bargaining.

A fifth feature of public administration has been the development of the budget as a principal tool in planning future programs, in making decisions as to program priorities and the allocation of resources, in managing current programs, in linking executive with legislature, and in developing control and accountability. The public budget and the contests for its control have a long history in the Western world, a history that began with centuries of struggle between monarchs and representatives of their subjects for control over public finances. The modern executive budget system, in which the executive develops and recommends and the legislature reviews and legitimizes expenditures, originated in 19th-century Britain. In the United States during the 20th century, the budget became the principal vehicle for legislative surveillance of administration, for executive control of departments, and for departmental control of subordinate programs. It is now assuming a similar role in many of the developing countries of the world.

Recent developments. The classical approach to public administration sketched above probably reached its furthest development in the United States during the 1930s. Since that time, through educational and training programs, technical assistance, and the work of international organizations, it has become standard doctrine in many countries, although some of its elements have been resisted by governments oriented to the British or the continental-legal perspectives. It was also during the 1930s that this rather simplistic, mechanistic approach was challenged from a number of different directions. The field, in practice and in study, has since been greatly enlarged and enriched by new perspectives and insights.It has also been somewhat confused as a result of certain inconsistencies in approach.

The orthodox doctrine rested on the premise that administration is simply the carrying out of public policies determined by others. According to this view, administrators should seek maximum efficiency but should be otherwise neutral about values and goals. But during the Depression of the 1930s, and even more so during World War II, it became increasingly evident that most new policies originated within the administration; that policy and value judgments were implicit in most significant administrative decisions; that many administrative officials worked on nothing except policy; and that, insofar as public policies were controversial, such work inevitably involved administrators in politics. The presumed separation of administration from policy and politics was seen to be artificial. Since the 1930s there has thus been increasing concern in public administration about the determination of policies and the development and use of techniques to improve policy decisions. The concept of a value-free, neutral administration is regarded by many as a thing of the past, but no fully satisfactory substitute has been offered. How to ensure that responsible and responsive policy decisions are made by career administrators, and how to coordinate their work with the policies of politically elected or appointive officials, remain vital problems, especially in democratic states.

A second challenge to the old concepts of public administration was a result of a direct response to the Depression and the accompanying responsibility of national governments to restore, stimulate, and stabilize their economies. With these responsibilities came new informational devices, including the whole system of national income accounting, and the emergence of gross national product as the supreme index of economic health. The practices of fiscal and monetary policy are now established specializations of public administration. Economists now occupy key posts in the administrations of most nations, and many other administrators must have at least elementary knowledge and awareness of the economic implications of government operations. Among the leaders in the development of tools and techniques for economic planning were Great Britain, Sweden and other Scandinavian nations, and the United States. Economic planning is a dominating concern of public administration in many of the developing countries.

More recently economists have introduced new methods of analyzing the costs and benefits of government programs. A refinement of simple cost-benefit analysis known as Planning Programming Budgeting System (PPBS) was officially introduced in the United States Department of Defense in 1961. Later, PPBS was made mandatory for most of the civilian programs of the national government and is in varying stages of development in many American states and cities. PPBS has proven internationally infectious. Most of the nations of western Europe, Japan, and some of the developing nations have introduced it or some aspects of it, although sometimes under a different name.

Under a PPBS system long-range objectives are defined as specifically as possible, and alternative programs for the attainment of such objectives are analyzed and compared from the standpoint of their predicted costs and benefits. PPBS is objective, quantitative, and economic in its orientation. Whether or not it will survive as a "system" is conjectural. But its emphasis upon concrete evaluation and analysis of programs has already made a significant contribution to decision making in the administrative sphere, and it seems likely that this influence will continue to grow.

PPBS is likely to prove a forerunner of a more profound shift in emphasis in public administration toward systems and systems analysis and away from structures and processes. As indicated above, public administration has traditionally been concerned with the legitimacy and efficiency of the organizations and procedures by which public decisions are reached and executed. In the emerging systems approach, public problem areas—such as weapons systems, housing, employment, and education—are perceived and analyzed as systems that consist of interacting parts and that are responsive in predictable ways to influences and "inputs" from outside. Public administrators require more and different kinds of data from those customarily available to governments, and new kinds of information systems providing data on the condition of society are therefore being developed.

Most of the domestic activities of governments are directed to the betterment of society and of the quality of life. Quantitative economic measurement is useful to a certain extent in this respect, but the value of human life, of freedom from sickness and pain, of safety on the streets, of clean air, and of opportunity for achievement are hardly measurable in monetary terms. Public administration is thus increasingly concerned with finding and developing better social indicators, quantitative and qualitative—that is, better indexes of the effects of public programs, and new techniques of social analysis.

A concurrent, but entirely different, development in public administration is the movement known generally as human relations. Its seeds were also planted in the 1930s when research was conducted over a period of several years concerning the workers and management of an industrial plant near Chicago. The research brought out, among other things, the importance of social or informal organization, of good communications, of individual and group behaviour, and of attitudes (as distinct from aptitudes). Concurrent and subsequent studies, especially in Britain and America, explored group dynamics, the process of attitude change, and differing styles of leadership and their effects.

The human relations movement was initiated by interest among the "human" scientists—psychologists, social psychologists, sociologists, cultural anthropologists, and psychiatrists. During the middle decades of the 20th century their views had increasing impact upon business management, and somewhat less but a still significant influence upon public administration. The human relations approach raised questions concerning many of the oldest dogmas of administration: hierarchy; directive styles of leadership; clear and set definitions of duties; treatment of employees as impersonal "units" of production; and monetary incentive systems.

By the early 1970s the human relations approach had developed into a field known as "organization development." Its primary goal and orientation is toward change: change in the attitudes, values, and structures of organizations so as to better adapt them to rapid change in their environment and in the demands placed upon them. Its tools include the use of trained consultants, usually from outside the organization, intensive interviewing of managers and employees, sensitivity training, and confrontation meetings among employees. Unlike the rationalistic PPBS approach, organization development stresses the identification of personal with organizational goals; the "self-actualization" of workers and managers; effective interpersonal communication; and broad participation in decision making. Its direct use within governmental agencies has been limited and is not always successful. But it has had considerable indirect influence upon the way administrators think and behave.

Another current movement in public administration, which is at least philosophically related to organization development, is directed toward the greater participation of citizens in governmental decision making and action. It was stimulated during the 1950s and 1960s by a growing feeling that governments were not responding to the needs of their citizens, particularly minority groups and the poor. This disaffection contributed to widening protests against public agencies and institutions. During the 1960s were begun a variety of experiments to involve citizens or their representatives in governmental decision processes. These involved delegation of decision-making power from central to local offices and, at the local level, sharing of authority with citizen groups. This challenge to governmental bureaucracy could lead to fundamental changes in the nature and style of public administration. At the least it will probably contribute to greater concern on the part of administrators over the effects of their actions on citizens.

Comparative public administration.   Until World War II there was rather little cross filtration or even communication of public administration across national boundaries except, as noted earlier, within the confines of imperial systems. There was established as early as 1910 a professional organization now known as the International Institute of Administrative Sciences (IIAS). Its membership, however, at first consisted principally of scholars and practitioners of administrative law in the countries of continental Europe. In the early 1970s the IIAS had a membership drawn from about 70 countries. Its congresses range over all aspects of the field.

But the period since World War II has witnessed an extraordinary burst of interest in the administrative systems of other countries. This was precipitated by the necessity of cooperation among the allied countries during the war; by the formation of international organizations; by the occupation of conquered nations and the administration of economic recovery programs for Europe and the Far East; and by aid and technical assistance programs for developing countries. One by-product of aid and assistance programs was a renewed appreciation of how crucial effective administration is to national development. Another by-product was a realization of how parochial and culture-bound public administration thinking and practice had often remained within individual countries.

Another effect of this international communication and sharing of experiences has been the realization that development is not exclusive to the so-called underdeveloped countries. Hopefully, all countries are developing, and public administration is increasingly perceived as the administration of planned change in societies that themselves are undergoing rapid change, not all of it planned. No longer is government merely the keeper of the peace and the provider of basic services. In the postindustrial era government has become a principal innovator, a determinant of social and economic priorities, and an entrepreneur on a major scale. On virtually every significant problem or challenge—from unemployment to clean air—people look to the government for solutions or assistance. The tasks of planning, organizing, coordinating, managing, and evaluating modern government are awesome in both dimension and importance.

Education and training for public administration.   It is probably a safe judgment that every nation in the world suffers a shortage of well-trained public administrators. European universities have been producing administrative lawyers for their governments for more than a century and a half, but legal skills are hardly adequate for handling contemporary problems. American universities almost half a century ago began graduate programs, and there are now more than sixty university programs in public administration. Their total output is, however, insufficient to meet the needs of government, and very few of the scientists and other specialists who will later become administrators in their fields attend such programs.

There has been a burgeoning of training programs around the world since World War II, many of them set up or sponsored by national governments, and some of them attached to universities. As one of its civil service reforms of 1946–47, France established an Ecole Nationale d'Administration, which provides an extensive course for recruits to the higher civil service. It was not until 1969 that Britain established a Civil Service College under the new Civil Service Department. In the United States the government established a variety of educational and training programs during the 1960s, including the Federal Executive Institute and two Executive Seminar Centers. Many of the developing countries have established one or more schools or training institutes, and by 1970 centres for the training of public administrators existed in over 100 countries.

Effective Public Management

JOSEPH L. BOWER

Political scientists, legislators, educators, business executives, lawyers, consumerists—practically everyone, it sometimes seems—is calling for better public management. For businessmen, the need is especially important because they feel surrounded by government institutions with which they are legally required to interact.

But enthusiasm for good government is one thing; understanding the nature of it, to say nothing of achieving it, is another. Often we seem to assume that effective management in the public sector has the same basic qualities as effective management in the private sector.

Yet, several years after Watergate, Americans are still chafing at the acts of a president who claimed to have taken considerable care to keep his office businesslike. To him, that meant no leaks, absolute loyalty to the organization, tight hierarchy in structure and operations, and a single coordinated voice in relations with other organizations and the public. Some observers have taken the consequences of the Nixon White House to be evidence not merely of the personal failure involved but also of the inherent weakness of applying a business model to government activity.

If indeed good business management is qualitatively different from good government management, we need to rethink some of our expectations of public servants as well as many common notions of managerial performance and training in government. As both individuals and agents of their companies, business people should operate under no illusions about there being similarities between their work and the tasks of public administrators.

To compare management in the two sectors, let us begin with a common definition and an example that businessmen will readily recognize. Management is commonly defined in some such terms as "the accomplishment of purpose through the organized effort of others." A business executive carries out the corporation's purpose by building and modifying organization structures, systems, and relationships through the efforts of the men and women whom he (or she) recruits. As Chester Bernard, former president of New Jersey Bell Telephone Co., pointed out years ago, the effectiveness of a corporation can be measured by the degree to which it accomplishes its purpose.[1] Its efficiency can be measured by whether individuals are willing to serve as workers, shareholders, bankers, and/or customers.

A very good measure of efficiency, as we all know, is profit. The fact that the first thing we expect business managers to do is manage profitably colors our expectations of them—of what they do as well as of how soon they do it.

For instance, it took IBM about ten years to conceive and build the 360 series of computers. The effort began after Thomas Watson, Jr. became chief executive officer in 1956, when IBM was predominantly a marketer and an assembler of computers. The concept of the 360 series was revolutionary. It meant formulating a new corporate strategy. It led to major reorganization, the breaking of the power

of IBM world trade (so that development could proceed on a worldwide, integrated basis), the entry of IBM into component manufacturing (to protect its proprietary circuitry), the crash introduction of "time sharing" capability, and the
rise of a young, talented generation of managers committed to the notion of compatibility among computers.

From 1956 to 1966, IBM did just what a well-managed corporation is supposed
to do. It achieved its purpose—gaining leadership in the industry. Therefore, it
met the test of effectiveness. In addition, during that decade its executives, other
employees, and shareholders profited. Therefore, it met the test of efficiency.
Having managed to meet both tests, management was above challenge for its
choice of a new strategy and the time required to carry out the strategy.

The IBM example typifies our expectations of business in general. But what of
management in the public sector? The late Professor Wallace S. Sayre of Columbia University once suggested that "business and government administration are
alike in all unimportant respects." On the basis of the previous discussion, it is
relatively easy to show that he was right.

Sayre was correct in the first half of his aphorism, for it is true that we can talk
usefully about the public executive's role in terms of purpose, organization, and
people. But when we get to the content of those words, the similarity ends. Like a
business, a public organization is expected to serve society. But without a market
to determine effectiveness, the process of measuring becomes diffuse and complex. Moreover, if the executives of an effective public organization distribute the
surplus resources they control (that is, the excess of revenues over expenditures)
among the executives whose skills produce the surplus, the officials are put in jail
when apprehended.

Moreover, any good Tammany politician will tell you what a few "social scientists" have just discovered: namely, that the most important results of activity may
be related not to the stated purposes of the organization but rather to *how* that
purpose is accomplished—in particular, to how the revenues called "cost of operation" are distributed. To put the point in the extreme, one could conceive of an
effective welfare program in which 85% of the funds received would go toward
operating expenses. If the operators themselves would be on welfare but for the
program, it would not matter so much that outside recipients would get only 15%
of the funds.

What does *purpose* mean in the public sector? As in the private sector, the administrative motive is self-interest; but the stated organizational motive is *not*.
The neat relationship between the external view of an organization in terms of its
accomplishments and the internal view of administrative arrangements is shat-
tered. The administrator who finds a "product" to keep the Rural Electrification
Administration alive is criticized as a recalcitrant bureaucrat, a preserver of un-
needed jobs. Though it may motivate administrative success, self-interest is considered venal. Moreover, the chief executive in a public organization may have no
presumptive right to set purpose; it may be given by legislation.

Still more difficult to cope with is the fact that the changes in formal organization and systems that are the principal sources of managerial influence in large corporations are only marginally available to the public executive and can only be
used at considerable political cost. The structure of public agencies is usually dictated by legislation. Furthermore, the selection and compensation of people, an
important business tool, is almost universally controlled by a civil service system.

PUBLIC MANAGEMENT VS. PRIVATE MANAGEMENT

However management in the public sector is defined and delineated, it differs from corporate management in several important ways. Public sector managers frequently must:

Accept goals that are set by organizations other than their own.

Operate structures designed by groups other than their own.

Work with people whose careers are in many respects outside management's control.

Accomplish their goals in less time than is allowed corporate managers.

Let us examine some realities of public management and see how important these differences can be.

One Public Manager's Plan of Action

To begin, consider the contrast in behavior of public and private executives on assuming office. The private manager is usually promoted from within the organization. He (or she) knows that in order to alter the direction of the corporation he needs to change the organization's structure and its people. Doing so is customarily his first move. Almost without exception, he makes changes among the key people reporting to him and modifies their jobs.

In contrast, one can describe public officials as outsiders who enter office with cherished policy objectives, accomplish little, and leave office with unfulfilled desires for structural reform; for, in order to accomplish important political objectives having to do with due process and responsiveness to the electorate, the United States has very nearly denied the public executive the tools of management. It is almost true that the business executive's enabling resources—structure and people—are the public executive's *constraints*.

How, then, can the public manager accomplish his (or her) ends? First, we must remember what his goals are: like the private manager, he seeks a share of the rewards generated by his organization's activity. Since this share cannot include the profits of government, he usually seeks such goals as salary, the perquisites of office, and the intangible rewards of serving the public. The intangible rewards may be ephemeral or real, but ideologically they are as important in the public sector as the profit motive is in business. The intangibles include influencing policy, changing the direction of events, and helping others. Common to all of them is the pleasure of exercising power usefully. Power is a necessary element of effectiveness and a reward for efficiency. Thought of as the ability to influence outcomes, power has both short-term and long-term dimensions. Like money, it can be spent for today's results or invested for tomorrow's.

The goal of the public manager on taking office is to "get things done" in such a fashion that when he (or she) leaves office, he will have the satisfaction of accomplishment as well as the prospect of the office becoming higher or more useful in the future. This prospect will be the result of increased respect for his personal capability or of his participation in important coalitions.

But how does he get things done when the usual sources of managerial influence in the private sector are not available? Part of the answer is illustrated by the comments of Gordon Chase, the widely respected former administrator of the New York City Health Service Administration. Reflecting on his approach to that task, Chase said:

"My own view, after talking with a lot of people and thinking about it a long while, is that there were roughly four kinds of problems in the city pertaining to health care. Some of them I could have a large impact on; others I could not change.

"The first set of problems was a series of social and environmental dangers that affected enormous numbers of people—lead poisoning, drug addiction, alcoholism, hypertension, and so on. One characteristic of these types of problems is that they have usually been ignored by the health establishment. One of my first objectives was to fix that deficiency or begin to fix it, and in fixing it, to drag in by some means the health establishment. Eventually, that was done through the contract mechanism.

"There were a couple of reasons for employing this method. One was our conscious decision to try to involve the whole medical establishment. While roughly one-third of all the health services in New York are delivered by the public sector, the largest part is still provided by the voluntary hospitals or private sector. I very much wanted to get that voluntary sector involved in the city's problems to a greater degree, and the contract approach allowed me to do that. Involving the voluntary sector also gave me a basis to measure the performance of the municipal sector with.

"Another important reason for going the contract route was time. When we started the methadone program, we wanted to get under way very fast. It was clear to me that if we had run it as a city operation, it would have been impossibly slow to set up. We would have to go to the Bureau of the Budget and the Department of Purchasing for everything. We would run into problems like not being able to pay doctors enough to do the job. We would encounter the usual incredible amount of red tape.

"The second major thing that struck me was a whole series of irrationalities in the system. There was a bad distribution of hospitals and doctors. I could do something about this problem but not much.

"Third, a whole series of gross social inefficiencies existed in the system. They affected enormous numbers of people, directly and indirectly, but the medical establishment in the past had often ignored them. These inefficiencies affected mostly poor people.

"The fourth category of things connected with the second and third This was the whole problem of rising health care costs."[2]

At the very beginning, Chase's comments seem to be describing a situation that a private sector manager would find familiar. The system for delivering health care in New York City had the wrong goals, functioned irrationally and inefficiently, and was becoming very costly. But the problem on which Chase had to operate lay substantially beyond the boundaries of his agency, large as it was. He had to "drag in the health establishment." And to do that, he had to bypass the city administration and in the end use the contract mechanism.

Compressed in Chase's words is a significant point. The time horizon of the public administrator is far shorter than that of the traditional corporate manager.

IBM had about a decade to establish the 360 computer series, as we saw earlier. In 1963, George Romney, then president of American Motors, admitted that it had taken him seven years working within his company and seven years selling in the market to make the idea of a Detroit-made compact car acceptable. Fourteen years! (In retrospect, we see that even more time was needed.)

Chase sought to improve the delivery of care for lead poisoning, drugs, and alcoholism as well as traditionally defined disease in "very fast" time—how fast is not clear but certainly less than 14, 10, or even 5 years. Why so little time for such complex tasks? In part, because the public executive doesn't have more time. Our system of appointed administrators gives the chief executive responsibility in operating agencies to men and women whose tenure is tied to the elected executive who appointed them.

A Manager with an Early Deadline to Meet

We will come back to Chase later. Now let us consider the reflections of another former government executive.

William Ruckelshaus, appointed the first head of the U.S. Environmental Protection Agency (EPA) in November 1970, began his administration as Chase did, talking to a great many people and trying to get a sense of direction. Similarly, he found many of the operations inappropriately focused. In an interview, he spoke sharply of the importance of his time horizon:

"The automobile emission problem was obviously something we were going to have to deal with. There was going to come a time—if you read the Clean Air Act, this was in January 1971, right after it passed—that [the auto companies] were going to come ask me for some more time [to comply with the emission standards]. I was going to have to decide whether or not they had made a 'good faith' effort. If this whole situation wasn't going to be completely farcical, the first thing I had to do was convince the automobile industry that we were serious about enforcement. That was immediately clear to me. Otherwise, there would be no way, two years hence or whenever they asked for an extension of time, that I could conceivably make a judgment that they had made this good faith effort. So, we had to figure out how we were going to convince them that we were serious. Every 30 days we had deadlines to meet involving very complicated matters on the Clean Air Act."[3]

In other words, 60 days after taking office, Ruckelshaus had to take steps that would influence the behavior of the entire U.S. auto industry. And there would be further decisions every 30 days. Ruckelshaus pointed out that his goals were complicated by legislative and other acts:

"The agenda was, in the first place, spelled out in terms of the inheritance in the reorganization plan, in terms of the agencies we inherited. Secondly, we inherited, along with those agencies, a lot of implementing legislation that, like the Clean Air Act, just rapidly came on and didn't give us a lot of leeway in terms of setting not only the goals but also the method by which they were to be achieved.

"The Council on Environmental Quality had been in existence since January of that year and had in its first report laid out a very extensive environmental agenda for the administration. There had been a lot of work done on that. The president, in his message of February 1970, had also laid out 37 separate goals that he wanted to achieve in the next year and to translate into legislation."

Goals were also set by pressure groups and elected superiors. Ruckelshaus had to concern himself with the Sierra Club, the Audubon Society, and the Earth Day movement, not to mention General Motors, Ford, Chrysler, and (if jobs were threatened), the AFL-CIO.

The resource allocation process is fragmented precisely so that it can be responsive to local wants. As long as these wants are expressed as needs or demands in a way that makes good press or good politics, they find their way onto the administrator's agenda. Sometimes these local goals make good sense; sometimes they are an obstacle and a burden.

Pressure from the Press

For top executives in the public sector, the press is a vital consideration—much more so than for corporate management. The press has an important bearing on goals and time horizons. Here is what Chase had to say:

"My view is that in New York you're always going to get a certain amount of bad press because you can't avoid it. The media are very tough here, they have a lot of access. Good press is very important. You should try to build up some 'press capital'—it's good to have money in this bank for a lot of reasons. One reason is that it's good for your programs. If you get good press on what you've done and what your programs have done, it makes recruiting easier, it makes getting money easier, it makes all sorts of things easier. It also does another thing. It tends to keep people off your back. If your press is reasonably good, it will keep people from hounding you. President Harry Truman once said something to this effect: 'In Washington they *sometimes* hit a man when he's down. In New York, they *always* hit a man when he's down.'

"The people in government who have a tough life with regard to the press are those people who run programs and who are responsible for pieces of the budget. You get caught if you aren't truthful, and then you're really in trouble.

"One other thing I learned was that you have, in the media, stars and nonstars. My advice to any official is that you should know with whom you are dealing. If you are dealing with a star, whether a reporter from the *New York Times* or a TV guy, remember that he knows he's a star and what he's interested in is looking very good. The way that he's going to look good is, usually, to make you look bad. What some guys are interested in is looking good on the six o'clock news. Other reporters, probably the vast majority, really seem to be interested in what is going on."

As opposed to the business executive, who can function with near anonymity, the public executive must manage the flow of information about his (or her) agency so that he can get on with the task of achieving goals. When McGeorge Bundy was special assistant to President Johnson, he once commented on what he considered the pernicious impact on policy of the media's treatment of issues, especially television's.[4] Press stars must produce news that sells daily. They do not want stories about the slow, careful turnaround of an organization or about the delicate conversion of an establishment to new ideas.

RESTRAINTS ON THE PUBLIC MANAGER'S POWER

In the corporation, purpose, organization, and people are central themes of top management. In government, the same themes appear—but with what a difference!

Business strategy has been called the art of imbalance—the application of massive resources to limited objectives. In contrast, a public institution's strategy might be called the art of the imperfect—the application of limited resources to massive objectives. The point is not that a business has more money at its command relative to its objectives than government. Usually the opposite is true. But a business is allowed to limit its objectives to a set of tasks consistent with its resources.

If Chase's time horizon of a few years seems very short in comparison with Romney's 14 and IBM's 10, what about Ruckelshaus's? He had to set emission standards for the U.S. auto industry in 60 days!

Compounding the difficulty is the lack of control of key resources. Consider Chase's situation again. Responsible in principle for the health of New York, his agency dealt with only a fraction of the organizations and activities responsible for health. The organizations he could control were seen as so slow to respond to his efforts that he worked around them rather than through them.

Why did he not take the slower, more direct approach? Because he would be out of office long before the consequences of such an approach might work themselves out. An extreme example of the impact of time horizons is the case of Jerome Miller, youth services commissioner in Massachusetts from 1969 to 1973. Having discovered that facilities for incarceration and correction of youthful offenders were destructive as well as filthy and cruel, and having concluded that he could not make permanent improvements during his tenure, he closed all the facilities rather than let them slip backward after he left office.

One reason, then, that public sector executives find it hard to mobilize resources in order to achieve objectives is that time horizons are short but institutional response times are long. It is true that agencies can be reorganized. But as Chase, Ruckelshaus, and many other government leaders have found out, the agency head is unlikely to have the time, the information, or the ready control of incentives to redirect the efforts of operating levels of the organization.

But this is not all. Partly because measures of progress are hard to devise (in Ruckelshaus's case, for instance, what is a good measure of "clean air"?), partly because public accounting systems tend to be designed to control expense and not to support management and planning, partly because the civil service protects personnel from the immediate desires of political leaders, and partly because it is virtually impossible to change any organization's behavior quickly—for all these reasons, public managers seldom find it possible to make the changes they would like.

Operating Managers

Both Chase and Ruckelshaus were able to bring talented people in to staff their new organizations. In some ways, these two were lucky. New leaders of old organizations are often quite constrained. But the odd fact is that public managers seldom complain about the quality of their immediate subordinates. It is at operating and middle management levels that complaints arise.

Compare the situation in private business. The heads of a company can alter the size of the management cadre at any level. They can pay a limited number of managers well, and—perhaps most important—they can take time and money to invest in management education. But outside of the military and a very few civilian career services (like the forest service and the foreign service), there is no tradition in the United States of training public managers, perhaps because it has usually been thought more important for managers to be responsive than skillful. After all, if a public manager has the time and power to build a smoothly running organization, his successor does not necessarily benefit. For the successor, that very organization may be an obstacle to the achievement of newly chosen social objectives.

This point is critical, for it may well be that, with enough time and persistence, a public administrator can move structure and people to produce the ends he wishes. The organization then becomes as efficient a producer of a well-defined product as any private organization. Examples of this sort of public manager are Claude Shannon of the National Institutes of Health, J. Edgar Hoover of the F.B.I., Robert Moses of the Triborough Bridge Authority and the New York State Park Commission, and Edward King of the Massachusetts Port Authority. Each of these men was able to maneuver himself into a position where his control over the personnel and structure of his organization and of the organization's access to funds was immune to political intervention.

Measurements of Performance

To list these names is to reveal a new problem. When efficient public managers achieve political monopolies that enable them to ignore market pressures, the costs to society can be much greater than the costs of a business monopoly violating the Sherman Act. The question of the costs and benefits of politically immune managers needs to be studied further, but part of the answer is likely to be found in the way we measure top managers.

In the private sector, as mentioned earlier, we rely on the market to test the purposes of private managers. If the market wants what they produce, the purposes are accepted. If a company wants its managers' efforts, it rewards the managers. In contrast, in the public sector we ask whether there is due process in the *way* a manager has accomplished his task. And in judging the substance of a program, we debate whether it is an efficient use of resources, given *promised* results.

But due process is a political end. What can it mean that we use a political end to judge the means of management and use an efficiency criterion, applied before the fact, to judge the ends of a promised program? Back in the 1960s, was Head Start a "waste of funds," as often alleged, because it was a poor idea (this was the conventional view) or because it was implemented at the operating level by inadequately skilled people (an alternative view)?

Everything we have learned about the technology of managing large organizations suggests that when the stakes of administrators are tied to short-term, intermediate outcomes rather than to the broad, long-term consequences of their action, the results are often pathological for the organization.[5] Effort is distracted from and often becomes subversive of purpose.

What can the public manager do to be constructive when it is given that (1) his time horizon must be short, and (2) his elected boss—and, therefore, he—are politically vulnerable? Direction toward an answer may be found in the record of how Chase and Ruckelshaus managed organizational purpose, the problem of structure, and the selection of people.

To begin with, both men were willing to lead. Each found a simple goal that helped orient his organization and that protected his political flanks. Chase's comments are instructive:

"Basically, I felt my job was making people healthy and that politics—whether with a big *P* or with a little *p*—would not, even if I handled it well, necessarily make people healthy. However, it was very important to handle those situations as skillfully as I could because, if I didn't, I could have a lot of trouble and the work wouldn't get done. So what I tried to tell myself, and also my staff, was that the way they had to measure themselves was to ask, 'Whom did we make healthy today?' That was the output. Having a meeting with this councilman or that community group per se was not an output."

In the same vein, Ruckelshaus explained why he chose pollution abatement as a goal for the EPA. Everyone in the organization could understand and relate his or her activity to that goal. In the administrative terms we have discussed, they stated purpose in terms of outputs that could be measured. Chase's looser deadlines permitted him a second step that was denied Ruckelshaus. He noted:

"In my view, politics happens very often when there is a vacuum, when there is no real analysis. Then the resource allocation decision is usually based on who has more clout or who screams louder. I feel very strongly that if you don't have the analytic talent and if important decisions are up, they'll be made, but they'll be made by another process than analysis."

As a consequence, Chase moved early to build his own analytic capability. Ruckelshaus also created a staff for analysis, but he could not bring it to bear on the early decisions the EPA had to make.

Each man was responsible for managing a new agglomeration of previously independent agencies. Ruckelshaus moved to integrate his subunits by reorganizing from programmatic lines toward functional lines and by grouping the headquarters staffs in a single building. Perhaps because Chase's analysis indicated that he would not operate directly through his own organization, he made no structural changes in the operating agencies.

Chase did, however, make important changes in operating personnel. Most notably, he brought in professional managers as number-two men in programs traditionally run by doctors. Chase's choices for top jobs reflected his concern for the lack of analysis and inefficiency that he believed characterized the health delivery system. His choices reflected also his political sensitivity to the role of doctors in the health establishment. In contrast, Ruckelshaus drew new managers for EPA from within the traditional regulatory and federal administration structure. Forced to work through rather than around the organizations he inherited, he needed managers familiar with the intricacies of Washington and with the capabilities of his subunits.

Ruckelshaus was ingenious in the use he made of the political pressure from environmentalists and Senator Edmund Muskie. With environmental goals under debate, Ruckelshaus used the environmental lobby in effect to measure his organization's position and accomplishments. The lobby's measures—and its ability to get them publicized—helped keep pressure on Congress and the White House to support further efforts of his organization. In contrast, Chase took an approach characteristic of the private sector: he built reporting systems to provide quantitative control over operations.

In sum, it would seem that both Chase and Ruckelshaus made progress because they managed to influence the purpose, structure, and people of their organizations. But they were able to do this because each was able to devise a politically acceptable way of phrasing the goals of his organization. Also, each was able to move his organization toward the goals with actions that were politically acceptable. Both were good politicians, but neither "played politics" in the pejorative sense of that phrase.

This presumably is the message toward which Richard E. Neustadt and other political scientists have directed our attention. To be effective in the public sector, you must be a politician. But (perhaps contrary to what they have argued is wise) you must not play for political power. Rather, it is through use of analytic and operating skills, supported by staff, that a substantive program can be developed and implemented.

Because direct access to administrative influence is limited, this task is extremely difficult. Progress comes not from revolutionary turnarounds or purging of established agencies but from adjustments in the perspective, manning procedures, and measures of the existing framework. It is precisely because time is short, the tools limited, and the political context consuming that good public managers are so hard to find. The management job is staggering.

DISCARDING AN OLD ANALOGY

I have tried to show that American business is an inappropriate analogy for discussing and evaluating public management. In the public sector, *purpose, organization,* and *people* do not have the same meaning and significance that they have in business. The differences would become even greater and more complicated if we could take space to recognize the contrasts among public organizations—regulatory agencies as opposed to military and paramilitary organizations, for example, or cabinet secretaries as opposed to elected officials.

Although we know enough about management in the public sector to know that it is different from corporate management, we do not know nearly as much as we should. There is enormous promise in some of the university courses in public management that have been developed around the country. They are building the base of understanding we need. If we accept as inevitable that legislatures will legislate the Second Coming at least once a sitting, and that the press will proclaim the arrival of messiahs and devils with weekly regularity; if we understand that efficiency of certain sorts implies monopoly of power in a way that we do not tolerate even in the making and selling of plastic, appliances, or food; and if we can accept these phenomena as human and not pathological; then perhaps we can systematically observe how public organizations behave and learn how to manage them better.

NOTES

1. Chester Bernard, *The Functions of the Executive* (Cambridge, Mass.: Harvard University Press, 1938).
2. Unpublished interview with Andrew Kerr in connection with the New York City Charter Study.

3. "William D. Ruckelshaus and the Environmental Protection Agency," Harvard Business School Case 4-375-083, prepared by Peggy Wiehl under the direction of Professor Joseph L. Bower and distributed by the Intercollegiate Case Clearing House, Soldiers Field, Boston, Mass. 02163 (copyright 1974 by the President and Fellows of Harvard College).
4. McGeorge Bundy, "Damn the Absolute: Notes on Authority and Autonomy," address delivered November 11, 1970 to The Scottish Council.
5. See, for example, my article, "Planning in the Firm," *American Economic Review,* May 1970, p. 186, and Chapter 7 of the book, *The Corporate Society,* Robin Marris, editor (New York: John Wiley & Sons, 1974).

PART TWO
Public Administration and Politics

2

PUBLIC AGENCIES AS POLITICAL ACTORS

As was suggested in the introduction and in Frederick Mosher's article, public administration today is most commonly viewed as a political process. Public agencies and public administrators are important actors in the public policy-making process.

Few have understood the political aspects of public administration better than Harold Stein. In his well-known discussion that follows, Stein demonstrates how public administrative activity is, at least in part, inherently political.

Different agencies have different levels of power. Perhaps most important in determining the degree of power has been agency "clientelism"—the influence of an agency's constituencies and the relationship between the agency and its constituencies. James Wilson explains the place of clientelism in the historic growth of bureaucratic authority in the policy-making system. Wilson points out that this need not be inevitable and that a strong legislative branch could alter the current balance of power. This topic is discussed in the next two chapters and then again in chapter 14.

Public Administration as Politics

HAROLD STEIN

Many, perhaps most, of the insights gained from an understanding of public administration as process are insights that are also applicable to private administration as well. Yet there are differences between these two kinds of administration, the most important of which are derived, of course, from the political environment and purpose of the former.

In the United States, the study of public administration has been, and still is occasionally, confused by an attempt to define public administration in terms of the constitutional separation of powers. This has led to a series of meaningless and misleading generalizations, such as: "Congress creates policy, administrators carry it out," "the good public administrator pays no attention to politics," and so forth. Such artificial divisions (and other parallel ones) were, of course, not exclusively the result of treating public administration as a branch of public law; they were also in part the product of other intellectual currents, an over-simplified concept of a "neutral" civil service, for example. And these awkward conclusions were likewise supported by a parallel line of interpretation applied to business, involving a formal and strict separation of powers between stock holders, directors, and management. But the unreality of this doctrine as a definition of actual corporate behavior has become increasingly obvious, and the appeal to the supposed example of business no longer carries weight when used in an attempt to interpret the nature of public administration.

There were various reasons why the establishment of water-tight compartments for "administration" and "politics" persisted so long. Perhaps the most important is to be found in the ambiguities of the word "politics" itself. Naïvely, but honestly, it has occasionally been assumed, for example, that to admit the political nature of public administration is to abandon faith in a non-partisan civil service. "Politics," "politician," "political" are all slippery words. In the United States all of them tend to be used in a pejorative sense, though the connotation of the phrase "political science," if not universally enlivening, is at least honorable. In this situation the dictionary fails to enlighten.

Without attempting a formal definition, it can be said that the concept of public administration as politics as used here is designed particularly to refer to the administrator's understanding and pursuit of his objectives and his relations with the social environment outside his agency that affects or is capable of affecting its operations. This is obviously a rather special use of the phrase; the administrator also deals with the distribution of power and other political problems within his organization. But in this brief sketch, these matters are treated as part of public administration as process, so that the phrase "public administration as politics" in this particular context is given an essentially external orientation. The two concepts are, of course, complementary, and refer to two aspects of the same basic process.

It is in its political character that public administration tends to differ most decisively from private administration, and to vary most notably from one country, or even one jurisdiction within a country, to another. These differences are perhaps matters of degree not kind. All business is sensitive to a sort of constituency—its customers and prospective customers—and many businesses show an increasing tendency to give conscious thought to trade union, public, and governmental relations. Adaptations of this character are political in the sense in which the term is used here. Nevertheless, public administrators as a group are far more deeply affected than private administrators in making decisions by large, complex, often vaguely defined, social objectives and by the need for adjusting effectively to a highly complex environment composed of many forces, frequently conflicting—individuals, private associations, and the government itself.

A moment's reflection will show that variations in the tasks of public administrators are greatest in this area of external relations and final goals. While the British civil servant cannot be insensitive to public needs and desires, his formal line of responsibility is comparatively simple and direct, and his immediate relations with the outer world carefully defined. How different the problem of the administrator in our own national government. The Constitution, our customs and traditions, the size and complexity of our land and our society, produce cumulatively centrifugal pressures. Every executive agency, and many of its top administrators, have responsibilities to or toward the President, to a variety of control agencies either only partially or not at all under the President's discretionary supervision, ordinarily to at least four congressional committees, to Congress more generally, and to an indeterminate number of individual Congressmen and Senators; to the organized and unorganized constituencies of the agency; to pressure groups, public and private, local and national, powerful or merely persistent; frequently to the courts, and occasionally to a political party.

It is in this atmosphere that the administrator makes his decisions. It is perhaps arguable that all this is not as it should be, that while the administrator should be sensitive to public needs and desires, his direct line of responsibility should be reasonably clear and simple and he should be fairly free from the direct impact of the organized forces of American society. But that is another question. The individual administrator can do very little about changing the rules of the game; his task is to carry on his job under the rules as they exist, and the rules require him to deal with the forces that seek to deal with him.

Purely for purposes of discussion, it may be useful to distinguish two aspects of the administrator's adjustment to his political environment: the problem of survival and the problem of values. The problem of survival is omnipresent, though in fact the word "survival" tends to over-dramatize what occurs. In theory, an administrator who fails politically by antagonizing powerful groups may live to see the legislature repeal the law and thereby prevent the fulfillment of the public function he has been endeavoring to execute; but in practice this painful denouement, or even the anticipation of this painful denouement, is rare. Survival with disabilities is more usual. The administrator's job may be at stake—in some positions the job-holder may not even expect to be able to hold on very long—or some modification of the program (or curtailment of funds) may be involved, or both: on occasion the danger may lie in the possibility of transfer of function to another agency. And all these possible threats to what may be loosely called survival may come from a legislature such as Congress, for instance, or from an administrative superior such as the President, frequently acting on pressure from the general public or some specialized public.

Administrator, agency, program—all are subject to attack. But the reader should note that to phrase the question of survival in this way tends to assume the virtue of the administrator. For obvious reasons, most administrators normally assume their own virtue; but here the student must go his own way; for him, the virtue of the administrator cannot be assumed; it must be examined and evaluated.

Sometimes administrative survival is undermined by acts that clearly do the administrator no credit. There is no virtue in endangering person, agency, or program by clumsiness or tactlessness; there is no virtue (save perhaps for some special cases where the executive fulfills inescapable constitutional responsibilities in a way that incurs legislative disfavor) in cleaving to a policy that lacks any formal legislative sanction and meets with explicit legislative repugnance. But the usual case in this country is much harder: explicit legislative sanction and actual legislative repugnance—a law still on the books, but active objection to its energetic enforcement. What should the administrator do under such circumstances? (Throughout this discussion, opposition between administrator and superior can be substituted for the legislative-executive antithesis.)

No formula can provide the right answer to questions like this. Analysis and answer must follow two paths—tactics and values. Living with chief executive, legislature, pressure groups, and other elements in the political environment is a constant challenge to the administrator's tactical skill, and the components of that skill—timing, public relations, ability to mobilize friends, and the rest—are subject to analysis and evaluation.

The other aspect of survival—values—is also basic to the whole concept. For politics involves ethics and benefits and power; it is the resolution of the contending forces in society. In this light we see the administrator as an agent of society making choices that affect the well-being of society. With the increasing scope of government activity, the range of administrative discretion is enormously broadened. Pre-determined answers become increasingly less appropriate, and self-explanatory and self-executing standards more and more elusive. The administrator must rely on his own system of values—his feeling for what is right—his judgment of what to emphasize, or what to play down—his sense of justice and fair play. The fundamental safeguard against an administrator's arbitrary and unethical conduct is the fact that public administration, especially in a democracy, circumscribes the range of values which the administrator can observe. For the making of value judgments by the administrator is part and parcel of the whole system; every act of political response that can be weighed in terms of its significance for survival has value connotations as well. In our society and particularly in our national government, it is doubtful that any administrator can long survive, no matter how adroit a manipulator, if his decisions reflect values that are sharply at variance with the general standards of society or the goals which society seeks.

The consideration of values in administrative behavior is thus no mere academic exercise. Students of public administration must be concerned with values. They are observers and they should be capable of dispassionate observation: but ultimate neutrality with respect to administrative decisions is self-defeating. A lack of concern for the values of public administration is indicative of a lack of sensitivity; and an insensitive observer can never attain to more than a limited insight.

The Rise of the Bureaucratic State

JAMES Q. WILSON

During its first 150 years, the American republic was not thought to have a "bureaucracy," and thus it would have been meaningless to refer to the "problems" of a "bureaucratic state." There were, of course, appointed civilian officials: Though only about 3,000 at the end of the Federalist period, there were about 95,000 by the time Grover Cleveland assumed office in 1881, and nearly half a million by 1925. Some aspects of these numerous officials were regarded as problems—notably, the standards by which they were appointed and the political loyalties to which they were held—but these were thought to be matters of proper character and good management. The great political and constitutional struggles were not over the power of the administrative apparatus, but over the power of the President, of Congress, and of the states.

The Founding Fathers had little to say about the nature or function of the executive branch of the new government. The Constitution is virtually silent on the subject and the debates in the Constitutional Convention are almost devoid of reference to an administrative apparatus. This reflected no lack of concern about the matter, however. Indeed, it was in part because of the Founders' depressing experience with chaotic and inefficient management under the Continental Congress and the Articles of Confederation that they had assembled in Philadelphia. Management by committees composed of part-time amateurs had cost the colonies dearly in the War of Independence and few, if any, of the Founders wished to return to that system. The argument was only over how the heads of the necessary departments of government were to be selected, and whether these heads should be wholly subordinate to the President or whether instead they should form some sort of council that would advise the President and perhaps share in his authority. In the end, the Founders left it up to Congress to decide the matter.

There was no dispute in Congress that there should be executive departments, headed by single appointed officials, and, of course, the Constitution specified that these would be appointed by the President with the advice and consent of the Senate. The only issue was how such officials might be removed. After prolonged debate and by the narrowest of majorities, Congress agreed that the President should have the sole right of removal, thus confirming that the infant administrative system would be wholly subordinate—in law at least —to the President. Had not Vice President John Adams, presiding over a Senate equally divided on the issue, cast the deciding vote in favor of Presidential removal, the administrative departments might conceivably have become legal dependencies of the legislature, with incalculable consequences for the development of the embryonic government.

THE "BUREAUCRACY PROBLEM"

The original departments were small and had limited duties. The State Department, the first to be created, had but nine employees in addition to the Secretary. The War Department did not reach 80 civilian employees until 1801; it commanded only a few thousand soldiers. Only the Treasury Department had substantial powers—it collected taxes, managed the public debt, ran the national bank, conducted land surveys, and purchased military supplies. Because of this, Congress gave the closest scrutiny to its structure and its activities.

The number of administrative agencies and employees grew slowly but steadily during the 19th and early 20th centuries and then increased explosively on the occasion of World War I, the Depression, and World War II. It is difficult to say at what point in this process the administrative system became a distinct locus of power or an independent source of political initiatives and problems. What is clear is that the emphasis on the sheer *size* of the administrative establishment—conventional in many treatments of the subject—is misleading.

The government can spend vast sums of money—wisely or unwisely—without creating that set of conditions we ordinarily associate with the bureaucratic state. For example, there could be massive transfer payments made under government auspices from person to person or from state to state, all managed by a comparatively small staff of officials and a few large computers. In 1971, the federal government paid out $54 billion under various social insurance programs, yet the Social Security Administration employs only 73,000 persons, many of whom perform purely routine tasks.

And though it may be harder to believe, the government could in principle employ an army of civilian personnel without giving rise to those organizational patterns that we call bureaucratic. Suppose, for instance, that we as a nation should decide to have in the public schools at least one teacher for every two students. This would require a vast increase in the number of teachers and school rooms, but almost all of the persons added would be performing more or less identical tasks, and they could be organized into very small units (e.g., neighborhood schools). Though there would be significant overhead costs, most citizens would not be aware of any increase in the "bureaucratic" aspects of education—indeed, owing to the much greater time each teacher would have to devote to each pupil and his or her parents, the citizenry might well conclude that there actually had been a substantial reduction in the amount of "bureaucracy."

To the reader predisposed to believe that we have a "bureaucracy problem," these hypothetical cases may seem farfetched. Max Weber, after all, warned us that in capitalist and socialist societies alike, bureaucracy was likely to acquire an "overtowering" power position. Conservatives have always feared bureaucracy, save perhaps the police. Humane socialists have frequently been embarrassed by their inability to reconcile a desire for public control of the economy with the suspicion that a public bureaucracy may be as immune to democratic control as a private one. Liberals have equivocated, either dismissing any concern for bureaucracy as reactionary quibbling about social progress, or embracing that concern when obviously nonreactionary persons (welfare recipients, for example) express a view toward the Department of Health, Education, and Welfare indistinguishable from the view businessmen take of the Internal Revenue Service.

POLITICAL AUTHORITY

There are at least three ways in which political power may be gathered undesirably into bureaucratic hands: by the growth of an administrative apparatus so large as to be immune from popular control, by placing power over a governmental bureaucracy of any size in private rather than public hands, or by vesting discretionary authority in the hands of a public agency so that the exercise of that power is not responsive to the public good. These are not the only problems that arise because of bureaucratic organization. From the point of view of their members, bureaucracies are sometimes uncaring, ponderous, or unfair; from the point of view of their political superiors, they are sometimes unimaginative or inefficient; from the point of view of their clients, they are sometimes slow or unjust. No single account can possibly treat of all that is problematic in bureaucracy; even the part I discuss here—the extent to which policial authority has been transferred undesirably to an unaccountable administrative realm—is itself too large for a single essay. But it is, if not the most important problem, then surely the one that would most have troubled our Revolutionary leaders, especially those that went on to produce the Constitution. It was, after all, the question of power that chiefly concerned them, both in redefining our relationship with England and in finding a new basis for political authority in the Colonies.

To some, following in the tradition of Weber, bureaucracy is the inevitable consequence and perhaps necessary concomitant of modernity. A money economy, the division of labor, and the evolution of legal-rational norms to justify organizational authority require the efficient adaptation of means to ends and a high degree of predictability in the behavior of rulers. To this, Georg Simmel added the view that organizations tend to acquire the characteristics of those institutions with which they are in conflict, so that as government becomes more bureaucratic, private organizations—political parties, trade unions, voluntary associations—will have an additional reason to become bureaucratic as well.

By viewing bureaucracy as an inevitable (or, as some would put it, "functional") aspect of society, we find ourselves attracted to theories that explain the growth of bureaucracy in terms of some inner dynamic to which all agencies respond and which makes all barely governable and scarcely tolerable. Bureaucracies grow, we are told, because of Parkinson's Law: Work and personnel expand to consume the available resources. Bureaucracies behave, we believe, in accord with various other maxims, such as the Peter Principle: In hierarchical organizations, personnel are promoted up to that point at which their incompetence becomes manifest—hence, all important positions are held by incompetents. More elegant, if not essentially different, theories have been propounded by scholars. The tendency of all bureaus to expand is explained by William A. Niskanen by the assumption, derived from the theory of the firm, that "bureaucrats maximize the total budget of their bureau during their tenure"—hence, "all bureaus are too large." What keeps them from being not merely too large but all-consuming is the fact that a bureau must deliver to some degree on its promised output, and if it consistently underdelivers, its budget will be cut by unhappy legislators. But since measuring the output of a bureau is often difficult—indeed, even *conceptualizing* the output of the State Department is mind-boggling—the bureau has a great deal of freedom within which to seek the largest possible budget.

Such theories, both the popular and the scholarly, assign little importance to the nature of the tasks an agency performs, the constitutional framework in which it is embedded, or the preferences and attitudes of citizens and legislators. Our approach will be quite different: Different agencies will be examined in historical perspective to discover the kinds of problems, if any, to which their operation gave rise, and how those problems were affected—perhaps determined—by the tasks which they were assigned, the political system in which they operated, and the preferences they were required to consult. What follows will be far from a systematic treatment of such matters, and even farther from a rigorous testing of any theory of bureaucratization: Our knowledge of agency history and behavior is too sketchy to permit that.

BUREAUCRACY AND SIZE

During the first half of the 19th century, the growth in the size of the federal bureaucracy can be explained, not by the assumption of new tasks by the government or by the imperialistic designs of the managers of existing tasks, but by the addition to existing bureaus of personnel performing essentially routine, repetitive tasks for which the public demand was great and unavoidable. The principal problem facing a bureaucracy thus enlarged was how best to coordinate its activities toward given and noncontroversial ends.

The increase in the size of the executive branch of the federal government at this time was almost entirely the result of the increase in the size of the Post Office. From 1816 to 1861, federal civilian employment in the executive branch increased nearly eight-fold (from 4,837 to 36,672), but 86 per cent of this growth was the result of additions to the postal service. The Post Office Department was expanding as population and commerce expanded. By 1869 there were 27,000 post offices scattered around the nation; by 1901, nearly 77,000. In New York alone, by 1894 there were nearly 3,000 postal employees, the same number required to run the entire federal government at the beginning of that century.

The organizational shape of the Post Office was more or less fixed in the administration of Andrew Jackson. The Postmaster General, almost always appointed because of his partisan position, was aided by three (later four) assistant postmaster generals dealing with appointments, mail-carrying contracts, operations, and finance. There is no reason in theory why such an organization could not deliver the mails efficiently and honestly: The task is routine, its performance is measurable, and its value is monitored by millions of customers. Yet the Post Office, from the earliest years of the 19th century, was an organization marred by inefficiency and corruption. The reason is often thought to be found in the making of political appointments to the Post Office. "Political hacks," so the theory goes, would inevitably combine dishonesty and incompetence to the disservice of the nation; thus, by cleansing the department of such persons these difficulties could be avoided. Indeed, some have argued that it was the advent of the "spoils system" under Jackson that contributed to the later inefficiencies of the public bureaucracy.

The opposite is more nearly the case. The Jacksonians did not seek to make the administrative apparatus a mere tool of the Democratic party advantage, but to purify that apparatus not only of what they took to be Federalist subversion but also of personal decadence. The government was becoming not just large, but lax. Integrity and diligence were absent, not merely from government, but from social institutions generally. The Jacksonians were in many cases concerned about the decline in what the Founders had called "republican virtue," but what their successors were more likely to call simplicity and decency. As Matthew Crenson has recently observed in his book *The Federal Machine,* Jacksonian administrators wanted to "guarantee the good behavior of civil servants" as well as to cope with bigness, and to do this they sought both to place their own followers in office and—what is more important—to create a system of depersonalized, specialized bureaucratic rule. Far from being the enemies of bureaucracy, the Jacksonians were among its principal architects.

Impersonal administrative systems, like the spoils system, were "devices for strengthening the government's authority over its own civil servants"; these bureaucratic methods were, in turn, intended to "compensate for a decline in the disciplinary power of social institutions" such as the community, the professions, and business. If public servants, like men generally in a rapidly growing and diversifying society, could no longer be relied upon "to have a delicate regard for their reputations," accurate bookkeeping, close inspections, and regularized procedures would accomplish what character could not.

Amos Kendall, Postmaster General under President Jackson, set about to achieve this goal with a remarkable series of administrative innovations. To prevent corruption, Kendall embarked on two contradictory courses of action: He sought to bring every detail of the department's affairs under his personal scrutiny and he began to reduce and divide the authority on which that scrutiny depended. Virtually every important document and many unimportant ones had to be signed by Kendall himself. At the same time, he gave to the Treasury Department the power to audit his accounts and obtained from Congress a law requiring that the revenues of the department be paid into the Treasury rather than retained by the Post Office. The duties of his subordinates were carefully defined and arranged so that the authority of one assistant would tend to check that of another. What was installed was not simply a specialized management system, but a concept of the administrative separation of powers.

Few subsequent postmasters were of Kendall's ability. The result was predictable. Endless details flowed to Washington for decision but no one in Washington other than the Postmaster General had the authority to decide. Meanwhile, the size of the postal establishment grew by leaps and bounds. Quickly the department began to operate on the basis of habit and local custom: Since everybody reported to Washington, in effect no one did. As Leonard D. White was later to remark, "the system could work only because it was a vast, repetitive, fixed, and generally routine operation." John Wanamaker, an able businessman who became Postmaster General under President Cleveland, proposed decentralizing the department under 26 regional supervisors. But Wanamaker's own assistants in Washington were unenthusiastic about such a diminution in their authority and, in any event, Congress steadfastly refused to endorse decentralization.

Civil service reform was not strongly resisted in the Post Office; from 1883 on, the number of its employees covered by the merit system expanded. Big-city postmasters were often delighted to be relieved of the burden of dealing with hundreds of place-seekers. Employees welcomed the job protection that civil service provided. In time, the merit system came to govern Post Office personnel almost completely, yet the problems of the department became, if anything, worse. By the mid-20th century, slow and inadequate service, an inability technologically to cope with the mounting flood of mail, and the inequities of its pricing system became all too evident. The problem with the Post Office, however, was not omnipotence but impotence. It was a government monopoly. Being a monopoly, it had little incentive to find the most efficient means to manage its services; being a government monopoly, it was not free to adopt such means even when found—communities, Congressmen, and special-interest groups saw to that.

THE MILITARY ESTABLISHMENT

Not all large bureaucracies grow in response to demands for service. The Department of Defense, since 1941 the largest employer of federal civilian officials, has become, as the governmental keystone of the "military-industrial complex," the very archetype of an administrative entity that is thought to be so vast and so well-entrenched that it can virtually ignore the political branches of government, growing and even acting on the basis of its own inner imperatives. In fact, until recently the military services were a major economic and political force only during wartime. In the late 18th and early 19th centuries, America was a neutral nation with only a tiny standing army. During the Civil War, over two million men served on the Union side alone and the War Department expanded enormously, but demobilization after the war was virtually complete, except for a small Indian-fighting force. Its peacetime authorized strength was only 25,000 enlisted men and 2,161 officers, and its actual strength for the rest of the century was often less. Congress authorized the purchase and installation of over 2,000 coastal defense guns, but barely six per cent of these were put in place.

When war with Spain broke out, the army was almost totally unprepared. Over 300,000 men eventually served in that brief conflict, and though almost all were again demobilized, the War Department under Elihu Root was reorganized and put on a more professionalized basis with a greater capacity for unified central control. Since the United States had become an imperial power with important possessions in the Caribbean and the Far East, the need for a larger military establishment was clear; even so, the average size of the army until World War I was only about 250,000.

The First World War again witnessed a vast mobilization—nearly five million men in all—and again an almost complete demobilization after the war. The Second World War involved over 16 million military personnel. The demobilization that followed was less complete than after previous engagements, owing to the development of the Cold War, but it was substantial nonetheless—the Army fell in size from over eight million men to only half a million. Military spending declined from $91 billion in the first quarter of 1945 to only slightly more than $10 billion in the second quarter of 1947. For the next three years it remained relatively flat. It began to rise rapidly in 1950, partly to finance our involvement in the Korean conflict and partly to begin the construction of a military force that could counterbalance the Soviet Union, especially in Europe.

In sum, from the Revolutionary War to 1950, a period of over 170 years, the size and deployment of the military establishment in this country was governed entirely by decisions made by political leaders on political grounds. The military did not expand autonomously, a large standing army did not find wars to fight, and its officers did not play a significant potential role except in wartime and occasionally as Presidential candidates. No bureaucracy proved easier to control, at least insofar as its size and purposes were concerned.

A "MILITARY-INDUSTRIAL COMPLEX"?

The argument for the existence of an autonomous, bureaucratically-led military-industrial complex is supported primarily by events since 1950. Not only has the United States assumed during this period world-wide commitments that necessitate a larger military establishment, but the advent of new, high-technology weapons has created a vast industrial machine with an interest in sustaining a high level of military expenditures, especially on weapons research, development, and acquisition. This machine, so the argument goes, is allied with the Pentagon in ways that dominate the political officials nominally in charge of the armed forces. There is some truth in all this. We have become a world military force, though that decision was made by elected officials in 1949–1950 and not dictated by a (then nonexistent) military-industrial complex. High-cost, high-technology weapons have become important and a number of industrial concerns will prosper or perish depending on how contracts for those weapons are let. The development and purchase of weapons is sometimes made in a wasteful, even irrational, manner. And the allocation of funds among the several armed services is often dictated as much by inter-service rivalry as by strategic or political decisions.

But despite all this, the military has not been able to sustain itself at its preferred size, to keep its strength constant or growing, or to retain for its use a fixed or growing portion of the Gross National Product. Even during the last two decades, the period of greatest military prominence, the size of the Army has varied enormously—from over 200 maneuver battalions in 1955, to 174 in 1965, rising to 217 at the peak of the Vietnam action in 1969, and then declining rapidly to 138 in 1972. Even military hardware, presumably of greater interest to the industrial side of the military-industrial complex, has often declined in quantity, even though per unit price has risen. The Navy had over 1,000 ships in 1955; it has only 700 today. The Air Force had nearly 24,000 aircraft in 1955; it has fewer than 14,000 today. This is not to say the combat strength of the military is substantially less than it once was, and there is greater firepower now at the disposal of each military unit, and there are various missile systems now in place, for which no earlier counterparts existed. But the total budget, and thus the total force level, of the military has been decided primarily by the President and not in any serious sense forced upon him by subordinates. (For example, President Truman decided to allocate one third of the federal budget to defense, President Eisenhower chose to spend no more than 10 per cent of the Gross National Product on it, and President Kennedy strongly supported Robert McNamara's radical and controversial budget revisions.) Even a matter of as great significance as the size of the total military budget for research and development has proved remarkably resistant to inflationary trends: In constant dollars, since 1964 that appropriation has been relatively steady (in 1972 dollars, about $30 billion a year).

The principal source of growth in the military budget in recent years has arisen from Congressionally-determined pay provisions. The legislature has voted for more or less automatic pay increases for military personnel with the result that the military budget has gone up even when the number of personnel in the military establishment has gone down.

The bureaucratic problems associated with the military establishment arise mostly from its internal management and are functions of its complexity, the uncertainty surrounding its future deployment, conflicts among its constituent services over mission and role, and the need to purchase expensive equipment without the benefit of a market economy that can control costs. Complexity, uncertainty, rivalry, and monopsony are inherent (and frustrating) aspects of the military as a bureaucracy, but they are very different problems from those typically associated with the phrase, "the military-industrial complex." The size and budget of the military are matters wholly within the power of civilian authorities to decide—indeed, the military budget contains the largest discretionary items in the entire federal budget.

If the Founding Fathers were to return to review their handiwork, they would no doubt be staggered by the size of both the Post Office and the Defense Department, and in the case of the latter, be worried about the implications of our commitments to various foreign powers. They surely would be amazed at the technological accomplishments but depressed by the cost and inefficiency of both departments; but they would not, I suspect, think that our Constitutional arrangements for managing these enterprises have proved defective or that there had occurred, as a result of the creation of these vast bureaus, an important shift in the locus of political authority.

They would observe that there have continued to operate strong localistic pressures in both systems—offices are operated, often uneconomically, in some small communities because small communities have influential Congressmen; military bases are maintained in many states because states have powerful Senators. But a national government with localistic biases is precisely the system they believed they had designed in 1787, and though they surely could not have then imagined the costs of it, they just as surely would have said (Hamilton possibly excepted) that these costs were the defects of the system's virtues.

BUREAUCRACY AND CLIENTELISM

After 1861, the growth in the federal administrative system could no longer be explained primarily by an expansion of the postal service and other traditional bureaus. Though these continued to expand, new departments were added that reflected a new (or at least greater) emphasis on the enlargement of the scope of government. Between 1861 and 1901, over 200,000 civilian employees were added to the federal service, only 52 per cent of whom were postal workers. Some of these, of course, staffed a larger military and naval establishment stimulated by the Civil War and the Spanish-American War. By 1901 there were over 44,000 civilian defense employees, mostly workers in government-owned arsenals and shipyards. But even these could account for less than one fourth of the increase in employment during the preceding 40 years.

What was striking about the period after 1861 was that the government began to give formal, bureaucratic recognition to the emergence of distinctive interests in a diversifying economy. As Richard L. Schott has written, "whereas earlier federal departments had been formed around specialized governmental functions (foreign affairs, war, finance, and the like), the new departments of this period—Agriculture, Labor, and Commerce—were devoted to the interests and aspirations of particular economic groups."

The original purpose behind these clientele-oriented departments was neither to subsidize nor to regulate, but to promote, chiefly by gathering and publishing statistics and (especially in the case of agriculture) by research. The formation of the Department of Agriculture in 1862 was to become a model, for better or worse, for later political campaigns for government recognition. A private association representing an interest—in this case the United States Agricultural Society—was formed. It made every President from Fillmore to Lincoln an honorary member, it enrolled key Congressmen, and it began to lobby for a new department. The precedent was followed by labor groups, especially the Knights of Labor, to secure creation in 1888 of a Department of Labor. It was broadened in 1903 to be a Department of Commerce and Labor, but 10 years later, at the insistence of the American Federation of Labor, the parts were separated and the two departments we now know were formed.

There was an early 19th-century precedent for the creation of these client-serving departments: the Pension Office, then in the Department of the Interior. Begun in 1833 and regularized in 1849, the Office became one of the largest bureaus of the government in the aftermath of the Civil War, as hundreds of thousands of Union Army veterans were made eligible for pensions if they had incurred a permanent disability or injury while on military duty; dependent widows were also eligible if their husbands had died in service or of service-connected injuries. The Grand Army of the Republic (GAR), the leading veterans' organization, was quick to exert pressure for more generous pension laws and for more liberal administration of such laws as already existed. In 1879 Congressmen, noting the number of ex-servicemen living (and voting) in their states, made veterans eligible for pensions retroactively to the date of their discharge from the service, thus enabling thousands who had been late in filing applications to be rewarded for their dilatoriness. In 1890 the law was changed again to make it unnecessary to have been injured in the service—all that was necessary was to have served and then to have acquired a permanent disability by any means other than through "their own vicious habits." And whenever cases not qualifying under existing law came to the attention of Congress, it promptly passed a special act making those persons eligible by name.

So far as is known, the Pension Office was remarkably free of corruption in the administration of this windfall—and why not, since anything an administrator might deny, a legislator was only too pleased to grant. By 1891 the Commissioner of Pensions observed that his was "the largest executive bureau in the world." There were over 6,000 officials supplemented by thousands of local physicians paid on a fee basis. In 1900 alone, the Office had to process 477,000 cases. Fraud was rampant as thousands of persons brought false or exaggerated claims; as Leonard D. White was later to write, "pensioners and their attorneys seemed to have been engaged in a gigantic conspiracy to defraud their own government." Though the Office struggled to be honest, Congress was indifferent—or more accurately, complaisant: The GAR was a powerful electoral force and it was ably and lucratively assisted by thousands of private pension attorneys. The pattern of bureaucratic clientelism was set in a way later to become a familiar feature of the governmental landscape—a subsidy was initially provided, because it was either popular or unnoticed, to a group that was powerfully benefited and had few or disorganized opponents; the beneficiaries were organized to supervise the administration and ensure the funding of the program; the law authorizing the program, first passed because it seemed the right thing to do, was left intact or even expanded because politically it became the only thing to do. A benefit once bestowed cannot easily be withdrawn.

PUBLIC POWER AND PRIVATE INTERESTS

It was at the state level, however, that client-oriented bureaucracies proliferated in the 19th century. Chief among these were the occupational licensing agencies. At the time of Independence, professions and occupations either could be freely entered (in which case the consumer had to judge the quality of service for himself) or entry was informally controlled by the existing members of the profession or occupation by personal tutelage and the management of reputations. The latter part of the 19th century, however, witnessed the increased use of law and bureaucracy to control entry into a line of work. The state courts generally allowed this on the grounds that it was a proper exercise of the "police power" of the state, but as Morton Keller has observed, "when state courts approved the licensing of barbers and blacksmiths, but not of horseshoers, it was evident that the principles govern- ing certification were—to put it charitably—elusive ones." By 1952, there were more than 75 different occupations in the United States for which one needed a license to practice, and the awarding of these licenses was typically in the hands of persons already in the occupation, who could act under color of law. These licens- ing boards—for plumbers, dry cleaners, beauticians, attorneys, undertakers, and the like—frequently have been criticized as particularly flagrant examples of the excesses of a bureaucratic state. But the problems they create—of restricted entry, higher prices, and lengthy and complex initiation procedures—are not primarily the result of some bureaucratic pathology but of the possession of public power by persons who use it for private purposes. Or more accurately, they are the result of using public power in ways that benefited those in the profession in the sincere but unsubstantiated conviction that doing so would benefit the public generally.

The New Deal was perhaps the high water mark of at least the theory of bureau- cratic clientelism. Not only did various sectors of society, notably agriculture, be- gin receiving massive subsidies, but the government proposed, through the Na- tional Industrial Recovery Act (NRA), to cloak with public power a vast number of industrial groupings and trade associations so that they might control production and prices in ways that would end the depression. The NRA's Blue Eagle fell be- fore the Supreme Court—the wholesale delegation of public power to private in- terests was declared unconstitutional. But the piecemeal delegation was not, as the continued growth of specialized promotional agencies attests. The Civil Aero- nautics Board, for example, erroneously thought to be exclusively a regulatory agency, was formed in 1938 "to promote" as well as to regulate civil aviation and it has done so by restricting entry and maintaining above-market rate fares.

Agriculture, of course, provides the leading case of clientelism. Theodore J. Lowi finds "at least 10 separate, autonomous, local self-governing systems" lo- cated in or closely associated with the Department of Agriculture that control to some significant degree the flow of billions of dollars in expenditures and loans. Local committees of farmers, private farm organizations, agency heads, and com- mittee chairmen in Congress dominate policy-making in this area— not, perhaps, to the exclusion of the concerns of other publics, but certainly in ways not power- fully constrained by them.

"COOPERATIVE FEDERALISM"

The growing edge of client-oriented bureaucracy can be found, however, not in government relations with private groups, but in the relations among governmen- tal units. In dollar volume, the chief clients of federal domestic expenditures are state and local government agencies. To some degree, federal involvement in local affairs by the cooperative funding or management of local enterprises has always existed. The Northwest Ordinance of 1784 made public land available to finance local schools and the Morrill Act of 1862 gave land to support state colleges, but what Morton Grodzins and Daniel Elazar have called "cooperative federalism," though it always existed, did not begin in earnest until the passage in 1913 of the 16th Amendment to the Constitution allowed the federal government to levy an income tax on citizens and thereby to acquire access to vast sources of revenue.

Between 1914 and 1917, federal aid to states and localities increased a thousand-fold. By 1948 it amounted to over one tenth of all state and local spending; by 1970, to over one sixth.

The degree to which such grants, and the federal agencies that administer them, constrain or even direct state and local bureaucracies is a matter of dispute. No general answer can be given—federal support of welfare programs has left considerable discretion in the hands of the states over the size of benefits and some discretion over eligibility rules, whereas federal support of highway construction carries with it specific requirements as to design, safety, and (since 1968) environmental and social impact.

A few generalizations are possible, however. The first is that the states and not the cities have been from the first, and remain today, the principal client group for grants-in-aid. It was not until the Housing Act of 1937 that money was given in any substantial amount directly to local governments, and though many additional programs of this kind were later added, as late as 1970 less than 12 per cent of all federal aid went directly to cities and towns. The second general observation is that the 1960's mark a major watershed in the way in which the purposes of federal aid are determined. Before that time, most grants were for purposes initially defined by the states—to build highways and airports, to fund unemployment insurance programs, and the like. Beginning in the 1960's, the federal government, at the initiative of the President and his advisors, increasingly came to define the purposes of these grants—not necessarily over the objection of the states, but often without any initiative from them. Federal money was to be spent on poverty, ecology, planning, and other "national" goals for which, until the laws were passed, there were few, if any, well-organized and influential constituencies. Whereas federal money was once spent in response to the claims of distinct and organized clients, public or private, in the contemporary period federal money has increasingly been spent in ways that have *created* such clients.

And once rewarded or created, they are rarely penalized or abolished. What David Stockman has called the "social pork barrel" grows more or less steadily. Between 1950 and 1970, the number of farms declined from about 5.6 million to fewer than three million, but government payments to farmers rose from $283 million to $3.2 billion. In the public sector, even controversial programs have grown. Urban renewal programs have been sharply criticized, but federal support for the program rose from $281 million in 1965 to about $1 billion in 1972. Public housing has been enmeshed in controversy, but federal support for it rose from $206 million in 1965 to $845 million in 1972. Federal financial support for local poverty programs under the Office of Economic Opportunity has actually declined in recent years, but this cut is almost unique and it required the steadfast and deliberate attention of a determined President who was bitterly assailed both in the Congress and in the courts.

SELF-PERPETUATING AGENCIES

If the Founding Fathers were to return to examine bureaucratic clientelism, they would, I suspect, be deeply discouraged. James Madison clearly foresaw that American society would be "broken into many parts, interests and classes of citizens" and that this "multiplicity of interests" would help ensure against "the tyranny of the majority," especially in a federal regime with separate branches of government. Positive action would require a "coalition of a majority"; in the process of forming this coalition, the rights of all would be protected, not merely by self-interested bargains, but because in a free society such a coalition "could seldom take place on any other principles than those of justice and the general good." To those who wrongly believed that Madison thought of men as acting only out of base motives, the phrase is instructive: Persuading men who disagree to compromise their differences can rarely be achieved solely by the parceling out of relative advantage; the belief is also required that what is being agreed to is right, proper, and defensible before public opinion.

Most of the major new social programs of the United States, whether for the good of the few or the many, were initially adopted by broad coalitions appealing to general standards of justice or to conceptions of the public weal. This is certainly the case with most of the New Deal legislation—notably such programs as Social Security—and with most Great Society legislation—notably Medicare and aid to education; it was also conspicuously the case with respect to post-Great Society legislation pertaining to consumer and environmental concerns. State occupational licensing laws were supported by majorities interested in, among other things, the contribution of these statutes to public safety and health.

But when a program supplies particular benefits to an existing or newly-created interest, public or private, it creates a set of political relationships that make exceptionally difficult further alteration of that program by coalitions of the majority. What was created in the name of the common good is sustained in the name of the particular interest. Bureaucratic clientelism becomes self-perpetuating, in the absence of some crisis or scandal, because a single interest group to which the program matters greatly is highly motivated and well-situated to ward off the criticisms of other groups that have a broad but weak interest in the policy.

In short, a regime of separated powers makes it difficult to overcome objections and contrary interests sufficiently to permit the enactment of a new program or the creation of a new agency. Unless the legislation can be made to pass either with little notice or at a time of crisis or extraordinary majorities—and sometimes even then—the initiation of new programs requires public interest arguments. But the same regime works to protect agencies, once created, from unwelcome change because a major change is, in effect, new legislation that must overcome the same hurdles as the original law, but this time with one of the hurdles—the wishes of the agency and its client—raised much higher. As a result, the Madisonian system makes it relatively easy for the delegation of public power to private groups to go unchallenged and, therefore, for factional interests that have acquired a supportive public bureaucracy to rule without submitting their interests to the effective scrutiny and modification of other interests.

BUREAUCRACY AND DISCRETION

For many decades, the Supreme Court denied to the federal government any general "police power" over occupations and businesses, and thus most such regulation occurred at the state level and even there under the constraint that it must not violate the notion of "substantive due process"—that is, the view that there were sharp limits to the power of any government to take (and therefore to regulate) property. What clearly was within the regulatory province of the federal government was interstate commerce, and thus it is not surprising that the first major federal regulatory body should be the Interstate Commerce Commission (ICC), created in 1887.

What does cause, if not surprise, then at least dispute, is the view that the Commerce Act actually was intended to regulate railroads in the public interest. It has become fashionable of late to see this law as a device sought by the railroads to protect themselves from competition. The argument has been given its best-known formulation by Gabriel Kolko. Long-haul railroads, facing ruinous price wars and powerless to resist the demands of big shippers for rebates, tried to create voluntary cartels or "pools" that would keep rates high. These pools always collapsed, however, when one railroad or another would cut rates in order to get more business. To prevent this, the railroads turned to the federal government seeking a law to compel what persuasion could not induce. But the genesis of the act was in fact more complex: Shippers wanted protection from high prices charged by railroads that operated monopolistic services in certain communities; many other shippers served by competing lines wanted no legal barriers to prevent competition from driving prices down as far as possible; some railroads wanted regulation to ease competition, while others feared regulation. And the law as finally passed in fact made "pooling" (or cartels to keep prices up) illegal.

The true significance of the Commerce Act is not that it allowed public power to be used to make secure private wealth but that it created a federal commission with broadly delegated powers that would have to reconcile conflicting goals (the desire for higher or lower prices) in a political environment characterized by a struggle among organized interests and rapidly changing technology. In short, the Commerce Act brought forth a new dimension to the problem of bureaucracy: not those problems, as with the Post Office, that resulted from size and political constraints, but those that were caused by the need to make binding choices without any clear standards for choice.

The ICC was not, of course, the first federal agency with substantial discretionary powers over important matters. The Office of Indian Affairs, for a while in the War Department but after 1849 in the Interior Department, coped for the better part of a century with the Indian problem equipped with no clear policy, beset on all sides by passionate and opposing arguments, and infected with a level of fraud and corruption that seemed impossible to eliminate. There were many causes of the problem, but at root was the fact that the government was determined to control the Indians but could not decide toward what end that control should be exercised (extermination, relocation, and assimilation all had their advocates) and, to the extent the goal was assimilation, could find no method by which to achieve it. By the end of the century, a policy of relocation had been adopted *de facto* and the worst abuses of the Indian service had been eliminated—if not by administrative skill, then by the exhaustion of things in Indian possession worth stealing. By the turn of the century, the management of the Indian question had become the more or less routine administration of Indian schools and the allocation of reservation land among Indian claimants.

REGULATION VERSUS PROMOTION

It was the ICC and agencies and commissions for which it was the precedent that became the principal example of federal discretionary authority. It is important, however, to be clear about just what this precedent was. Not everything we now call a regulatory agency was in fact intended to be one. The ICC, the Antitrust Division of the Justice Department, the Federal Trade Commission (FTC), the Food and Drug Administration (FDA), the National Labor Relations Board (NRLB)—all these *were* intended to be genuinely regulatory bodies created to handle under public auspices matters once left to private arrangements. The techniques they were to employ varied: approving rates (ICC), issuing cease-and-desist orders (FTC), bringing civil or criminal actions in the courts (the Antitrust Division), defining after a hearing an appropriate standard of conduct (NRLB), or testing a product for safety (FDA). In each case, however, Congress clearly intended that the agency either define its own standards (a safe drug, a conspiracy in restraint of trade, a fair labor practice) or choose among competing claims (a higher or lower rate for shipping grain).

Other agencies often grouped with these regulatory bodies—the Civil Aeronautics Board, the Federal Communications Commission, the Maritime Commission—were designed, however, not primarily to regulate, but to *promote* the development of various infant or threatened industries. However, unlike fostering agriculture or commerce, fostering civil aviation or radio broadcasting was thought to require limiting entry (to prevent "unsafe" aviation or broadcast interference); but at the time these laws were passed few believed that the restrictions on entry would be many, or that the choices would be made on any but technical or otherwise noncontroversial criteria. We smile now at their naïveté, but we continue to share it—today we sometimes suppose that choosing an approved exhaust emission control system or a water pollution control system can be done on the basis of technical criteria and without affecting production and employment.

MAJORITARIAN POLITICS

The creation of regulatory bureaucracies has occurred, as is often remarked, in waves. The first was the period between 1887 and 1890 (the Commerce Act and the Antitrust Act), the second between 1906 and 1915 (the Pure Food and Drug Act, the Meat Inspection Act, the Federal Trade Commission Act, the Clayton Act), the third during the 1930's (the Food, Drug, and Cosmetic Act, the Public Utility Holding Company Act, the Securities Exchange Act, the Natural Gas Act, the National Labor Relations Act), and the fourth during the latter part of the 1960's (the Water Quality Act, the Truth in Lending Act, the National Traffic and Motor Vehicle Safety Act, various amendments to the drug laws, the Motor Vehicle Pollution Control Act, and many others).

Each of these periods was characterized by progressive or liberal Presidents in office (Cleveland, T. R. Roosevelt, Wilson, F. D. Roosevelt, Johnson); one was a period of national crisis (the 1930's); three were periods when the President enjoyed extraordinary majorities of his own party in both houses of Congress (1914-1916, 1932-1940, and 1964-1968); and only the first period preceded the emergence of the national mass media of communication. These facts are important because of the special difficulty of passing any genuinely regulatory legislation: A single interest, the regulated party, sees itself seriously threatened by a law proposed by a policy entrepreneur who must appeal to an unorganized majority, the members of which may not expect to be substantially or directly benefitted by the law. Without special political circumstances—a crisis, a scandal, extraordinary majorities, an especially vigorous President, the support of media—the normal barriers to legislative innovation (i.e., to the formation of a "coalition of the majority") may prove insuperable.

Stated another way, the initiation of regulatory programs tends to take the form of majoritarian rather than coalitional politics. The Madisonian system is placed in temporary suspense: Exceptional majorities propelled by a public mood and led by a skillful policy entrepreneur take action that might not be possible under ordinary circumstances (closely divided parties, legislative-executive checks and balances, popular indifference). The consequence of majoritarian politics for the administration of regulatory bureaucracies is great. To initiate and sustain the necessary legislative mood, strong, moralistic, and sometimes ideological appeals are necessary—leading, in turn, to the granting of broad mandates of power to the new agency (a modest delegation of authority would obviously be inadequate if the problem to be resolved is of crisis proportions), or to the specifying of exacting standards to be enforced (e.g., *no* carcinogenic products may be sold, 95 per cent of the pollutants must be eliminated), or to both.

Either in applying a vague but broad rule ("the public interest, convenience, and necessity") or in enforcing a clear and strict standard, the regulatory agency will tend to broaden the range and domain of its authority, to lag behind technological and economic change, to resist deregulation, to stimulate corruption, and to contribute to the bureaucratization of private institutions.

It will broaden its regulatory reach out of a variety of motives: to satisfy the demand of the regulated enterprise that it be protected from competition, to make effective the initial regulatory action by attending to the unanticipated side effects of that action, to discover or stretch the meaning of vague statutory language, or to respond to new constituencies induced by the existence of the agency to convert what were once private demands into public pressures. For example, the Civil Aeronautics Board, out of a desire both to promote aviation and to protect the regulated price structure of the industry, will resist the entry into the industry of new carriers. If a Public Utilities Commission sets rates too low for a certain class of customers, the utility will allow service to those customers to decline in quality, leading in turn to a demand that the Commission also regulate the quality of service. If the Federal Communications Commission cannot decide who should receive a broadcast license by applying the "public interest" standard, it will be powerfully tempted to invest that phrase with whatever preferences the majority of the Commission then entertains, leading in turn to the exercise of control over many more aspects of broadcasting than merely signal interference—all in the name of deciding what the standard for entry shall be. If the Antitrust Division can prosecute conspiracies in restraint of trade, it will attract to itself the complaints of various firms about business practices that are neither conspiratorial nor restraining but merely competitive, and a "vigorous" antitrust lawyer may conclude that these practices warrant prosecution.

BUREAUCRATIC INERTIA

Regulatory agencies are slow to respond to change for the same reason all organizations with an assured existence are slow: There is no incentive to respond. Furthermore, the requirements of due process and of political conciliation will make any response time consuming. For example, owing to the complexity of the matter and the money at stake, any comprehensive review of the long-distance rates of the telephone company will take years, and possibly may take decades.

Deregulation, when warranted by changed economic circumstances or undesired regulatory results, will be resisted. Any organization, and *a fortiori* any public organization, develops a genuine belief in the rightness of its mission that is expressed as a commitment to regulation as a process. This happened to the ICC in the early decades of this century as it steadily sought both enlarged powers (setting minimum as well as maximum rates) and a broader jurisdiction (over trucks, barges, and pipelines as well as railroads). It even urged incorporation into the Transportation Act of 1920 language directing it to prepare a comprehensive transportation plan for the nation. Furthermore, any regulatory agency will confer benefits on some group or interest, whether intended or not; those beneficiaries will stoutly resist deregulation. (But in happy proof of the fact that there are no iron laws, even about bureaucracies, we note the recent proposals emanating from the Federal Power Commission that the price of natural gas be substantially deregulated.)

The operation of regulatory bureaus may tend to bureaucratize the private sector. The costs of conforming to many regulations can be met most easily—often, *only*—by large firms and institutions with specialized bureaucracies of their own. Smaller firms and groups often must choose between unacceptably high overhead costs, violating the law, or going out of business. A small bakery producing limited runs of a high-quality product literally may not be able to meet the safety and health standards for equipment, or to keep track of and administer fairly its obligations to its two employees; but unless the bakery is willing to break the law, it must sell out to a big bakery that can afford to do these things, but may not be inclined to make and sell good bread. I am not aware of any data that measure private bureaucratization or industrial concentration as a function of the economies of scale produced by the need to cope with the regulatory environment, but I see no reason why such data could not be found.

Finally, regulatory agencies that control entry, fix prices, or substantially affect the profitability of an industry create a powerful stimulus for direct or indirect forms of corruption. The revelations about campaign finance in the 1972 presidential election show dramatically that there will be a response to that stimulus. Many corporations, disproportionately those in regulated industries (airlines, milk producers, oil companies), made illegal or hard to justify campaign contributions involving very large sums.

THE ERA OF CONTRACT

It is far from clear what the Founding Fathers would have thought of all this. They were not doctrinaire exponents of laissez faire, nor were 18th-century governments timid about asserting their powers over the economy. Every imaginable device of fiscal policy was employed by the states after the Revolutionary War. Mother England had, during the mercantilist era, fixed prices and wages, licensed merchants, and granted monopolies and subsidies. (What were the royal grants of American land to immigrant settlers but the greatest of subsidies, sometimes—as in Pennsylvania—almost monopolistically given?) European nations regularly operated state enterprises, controlled trade, and protected industry. But as William D. Grampp has noted, at the Constitutional Convention the Founders considered authorizing only four kinds of economic controls, and they rejected two of them. They agreed to allow the Congress to regulate international and interstate commerce and to give monopoly protection in the form of copyrights and patents. Even Madison's proposal to allow the federal government to charter corporations was rejected. Not one of the 85 *Federalist* papers dealt with economic regulation; indeed, the only reference to commerce was the value to it of a unified nation and a strong navy.

G. Warren Nutter has speculated as to why our Founders were so restrained in equipping the new government with explicit regulatory powers. One reason may have been the impact of Adam Smith's *Wealth of Nations,* published the same year as the Declaration of Independence, and certainly soon familiar to many rebel leaders, notably Hamilton. Smith himself sought to explain the American prosperity before the Revolution by the fact that Britain, through "salutary neglect," had not imposed mercantilist rules on the colonial economy. "Plenty of good land, and liberty to manage their own affairs in their own way" were the "two great causes" of colonial prosperity. As Nutter observes, there was a spirit of individualistic venture among the colonies that found economic expression in the belief that voluntary contracts were the proper organization principle of enterprise.

One consequence of this view was that the courts in many states were heavily burdened with cases testing the provisions of contracts and settling debts under them. In one rural county in Massachusetts the judges heard over 800 civil cases during 1785. As James Willard Hurst has written, the years before 1875 were "above all else, the years of contract in our law."

The era of contract came to an end with the rise of economic organizations so large or with consequences so great that contracts were no longer adequate, in the public's view, to adjust corporate behavior to the legitimate expectations of other parties. The courts were slower to accede to this change than were many legislatures, but in time they acceded completely, and the era of administrative regulation was upon us. The Founders, were they to return, would understand the change in the scale and social significance of enterprise, would approve of many of the purposes of regulation, perhaps would approve of the behavior of some of the regulatory bureaus seeking to realize those purposes, but surely would be dismayed at the political cost resulting from having vested vast discretionary authority in the hands of officials whose very existence—to say nothing of whose function—was not anticipated by the Constitutional Convention, and whose effective control is beyond the capacity of the governing institutions which that Convention had designed.

THE BUREAUCRATIC STATE AND THE REVOLUTION

The American Revolution was not only a struggle for independence but a fundamental rethinking of the nature of political authority. Indeed, until that reformulation was completed the Revolution was not finished. What made political authority problematic for the colonists was the extent to which they believed Mother England had subverted their liberties despite the protection of the British constitution, until then widely regarded in America as the most perfect set of governing arrangements yet devised. The evidence of usurpation is now familiar: unjust taxation, the weakening of the independence of the judiciary, the stationing of standing armies, and the extensive use of royal patronage to reward office-seekers at colonial expense. Except for the issue of taxation, which raised for the colonists major questions of representation, almost all of their complaints involved the abuse of *administrative* powers.

The first solution proposed by Americans to remedy this abuse was the vesting of most (or, in the case of Pennsylvania and a few other states, virtually all) powers in the legislature. But the events after 1776 in many colonies, notably Pennsylvania, convinced the most thoughtful citizens that legislative abuses were as likely as administrative ones: In the extreme case, citizens would suffer from the "tyranny of the majority." Their solution to this problem was, of course, the theory of the separation of powers by which, as brilliantly argued in *The Federalist* papers, each branch of government would check the likely usurpations of the other.

This formulation went essentially unchallenged in theory and unmodified by practice for over a century. Though a sizeable administrative apparatus had come into being by the end of the 19th century, it constituted no serious threat to the existing distribution of political power because it either performed routine tasks (the Post Office) or dealt with temporary crises (the military). Some agencies wielding discretionary authority existed, but they either dealt with groups whose liberties were not of much concern (the Indian Office) or their exercise of discretion was minutely scrutinized by Congress (the Land Office, the Pension Office, the Customs Office). The major discretionary agencies of the 19th century flourished at the very period of greatest Congressional domination of the political process—the decades after the Civil War—and thus, though their supervision was typically inefficient and sometimes corrupt, these agencies were for most practical purposes direct dependencies of Congress. In short, their existence did not call into question the theory of the separation of powers.

But with the growth of client-serving and regulatory agencies, grave questions began to be raised—usually implicitly—about that theory. A client-serving bureau, because of its relations with some source of private power, could become partially independent of both the executive and legislative branches—or in the case of the latter, dependent upon certain committees and independent of others and of the views of the Congress as a whole. A regulatory agency (that is to say, a truly regulatory one and not a clientelist or promotional agency hiding behind a regulatory fig leaf) was, in the typical case, placed formally outside the existing branches of government. Indeed, they were called "independent" or "quasi-judicial" agencies (they might as well have been called "quasi-executive" or "quasi-legislative") and thus the special status that clientelist bureaus achieved *de facto,* the regulatory ones achieved *de jure.*

It is, of course, inadequate and misleading to criticize these agencies, as has often been done, merely because they raise questions about the problem of sovereignty. The crucial test of their value is their behavior, and that can be judged only by applying economic and welfare criteria to the policies they produce. But if such judgments should prove damning, as increasingly has been the case, then the problem of finding the authority with which to alter or abolish such organizations becomes acute. In this regard the theory of the separation of powers has proved unhelpful.

The separation of powers makes difficult, in ordinary times, the extension of public power over private conduct—as a nation, we came more slowly to the welfare state than almost any European nation, and we still engage in less central planning and operate fewer nationalized industries than other democratic regimes. But we have extended the regulatory sway of our national government as far or farther than that of most other liberal regimes (our environmental and safety codes are now models for much of Europe), and the bureaus wielding these discretionary powers are, once created, harder to change or redirect than would be the case if authority were more centralized.

The shift of power toward the bureaucracy was not inevitable. It did not result simply from increased specialization, the growth of industry, or the imperialistic designs of the bureaus themselves. Before the second decade of this century, there was no federal bureaucracy wielding substantial discretionary powers. That we have one now is the result of political decisions made by elected representatives. Fifty years ago, the people often wanted more of government than it was willing to provide—it was, in that sense, a republican government in which representatives moderated popular demands. Today, not only does political action follow quickly upon the stimulus of public interest, but government itself creates that stimulus and sometimes acts in advance of it.

All democratic regimes tend to shift resources from the private to the public sector and to enlarge the size of the administrative component of government. The particularistic and localistic nature of American democracy has created a particularistic and client-serving administration. If our bureaucracy often serves special interests and is subject to no central direction, it is because our legislature often serves special interests and is subject to no central leadership. For Congress to complain of what it has created and it maintains is, to be charitable, misleading. Congress could change what it has devised, but there is little reason to suppose it will.

3

THE CHIEF EXECUTIVE
AND THE BUREAUCRACY

Elected chief executives play an important role in the American governmental tradition. More and more, citizens are judging chief executives by their managerial ability and accomplishment.

Other governmental officials, especially the members of legislative bodies, are also important in the public policy-making process. Indeed, those in Congress as well as those in state and local legislatures often view themselves as "co-directors" along with the chief executives of the bureaucracy. In the first article in this chapter, Richard Neustadt surveys the relations of legislators and chief executives with public agencies. His focus is on the various perspectives, expectations, and vehicles for influence.

In the second reading, Richard Nathan carefully analyzes the evolution of the "administrative presidency" and its relationship to the conduct of the Nixon administration. Nixon's presidency and the incidents associated with Watergate (broadly defined) have forced many scholars into a careful examination of the place of the chief executive in American government.

Next Martha Wagner Weinberg examines these issues as they relate to state government. She assesses the relationship between the governor and a state's agencies, and she weighs the difficulties associated with leading and supervising a wide variety of agencies and functions. Many of the problems common at the federal level also manifest themselves in state and local government. In other ways, states and localities confront unique issues.

Politicians and Bureaucrats

RICHARD E. NEUSTADT

In the decade of the 1940s an extraordinary element was added to the government of the United States: an executive establishment, a body of officials, which for size, scale, and corporate survival was a new creation, unlike anything our governmental system knew before. This was the institutional deposit of a series of events: New Deal, World War, the Bomb, Cold War, Fair Deal, Korea. The events are irreversible, the deposit is permanent. For decades our system has been struggling to assimilate it. This chapter deals with aspects of that struggle.

A few figures help to indicate what happened in the forties and thereafter. By 1939, before the Nazis marched on Poland, federal civilian personnel, professional and clerical (excluding postal and industrial workers), numbered a half-million, which then appeared a staggering total. Since 1942 their number never has been less than twice that size, not even at the low point of retrenchment between V-J Day and the Korean War. Before World War II our military forces had an active officer corps of some thirty-five thousand. Since 1945 the number never has been less than ten times that size, save briefly just before Korea when it fell to a mere two hundred thousand. The change has been both lasting and profound.

CONGRESS AND THE NEW EXECUTIVE ESTABLISHMENT

According to the literary theory of the Constitution, Congress as the "legislative branch" makes policy and a President as head of the "executive branch" administers it. If this theory squared with constitutional practice, or even with the Constitution's plain prescription, our new officialdom would be a corporate entity, collectively accountable to Congress through the President and otherwise subordinate to him. But theory is deficient (as it always has been), and bureaucratic structure is a very different thing, the product of a much more complicated context.

Congress, constitutionally, has at least as much to do with executive administration as does an incumbent of the White House. "The executive power" may be vested in his office, but four tangible, indispensable administrative powers rest with Congress: organization, authorization, financing, and investigation. Departments and agencies—the operating arms of the "executive branch"—are created by acts of Congress. They gain operational authority, programmatic jurisdiction, from laws passed by Congress. They gain funds to pay for personnel and programs from congressional appropriations. And their use of both authority and money is subject to "oversight," to inquiry in Congress.

Executive Reflection of Congress

Had Congress been a unit tightly organized and centrally directed, its employment of these powers might have brought us something comparable at the other end of Pennsylvania Avenue: a unified executive establishment. But actually, and naturally, what was produced "downtown" reflects congressional *dis*unity. As preceding chapters show, Congress is not one entity but many, mainly the committees and the subcommittees of each House. "Congress," as Clem Miller once wrote, "is a collection of committees that come together in a Chamber periodically to approve one another's actions."[1] In the administrative sphere, as elsewhere, congressional prerogatives adhere most of the time—and most concretely all the time—to these committees and are exercised by them, piecemeal, on the executive establishment downtown. Its character is shaped accordingly.

Our national bureaucracy expanded in a range of separate agencies, corresponding roughly to traditional departments, each dependent on particular congressional committees for its life-blood: laws and funds. These agencies owed little more to Congress as an entity than chairmen of committees owe, which is not much. And they owed almost nothing to each other. Operational authority ran to the heads of agencies, or to subordinates, not to a collectivity. Personnel systems were built up inside agencies, not among them. Even the general career system, "the" civil service—to say nothing of uniformed or diplomatic services—is "general" in name only. For most intents and purposes it functions as a set of departmental services. Most careerists everywhere live out their lives inside a single agency; their loyalties and perspectives are centered there.

Both organizationally and in terms of personnel the new bureaucracy is a projection of congressional committee jurisdictions—or, more precisely, since 1946, of standing subcommittee jurisdictions. And most committees guard, with jealousy and pride, the separations among agencies downtown. Why, for example, is the Small Business Administration independent of the Department of Commerce? The answer lies in the committee structure of the House. Of course, committee jurisdictions have been influenced, in turn, by organizational developments downtown. Unification of the armed services was matched by unification on the Hill of the committees which had dealt with War and the Navy. Still, the pattern remains one in which particular committees deal with given agencies, and thereby keep the agencies distinct from one another.

Executive Competition with Congress

Yet in their operations day by day, agencies are much more than "projections" of Congress. They also are competitors with congressmen. Their work defines and embodies public policy, enlisting clients and arousing opposition. They weigh and balance interests while they work. Their regulations have the force of law. Their decisions make news. Their jobs interest partisans. Their expertise helps to get legislation drafted (and committee reports written, speeches prepared, tactics devised). Also, their actions matter at the "grass roots." They carry government into the lives of voters; their "field" officials are in touch with voters. Thirty years ago, aside from postmen and tax collectors (for the well-to-do), the federal presence rested lightly on most citizens. Congressmen could claim to be—and often were—*the* local representatives of "Washington." That time is gone.

Defense contracts and installations underpin the economic growth of many regions. Federal grants-in-aid support the major undertakings of state governments. Federal funds are crucial in the redevelopment of cities. Federal subsidies, direct or indirect, support whole sectors of our industry and commerce—not least commercial agriculture—and become the hope of higher education, private as well as public. And day-to-day decision-making in such spheres as these—on the details of programming and execution which affect constituents concretely—this is done downtown, not on the Hill, and by agency officials, not by congressmen.

This goes hard with the elective politicians who are charged in theory to direct the government and who have won their places through the tests of nomination and election, tests officials do not take. Particularly for new members of the House—among the lowest of the low in Washington's real power structure—it is frustrating to find that their effectiveness in such decision-making matches neither their own expectations nor the expectations of constituents at home. Oftener than not, the pressures of constituents run to the things that only agencies can do, and congressmen perforce become petitioners downtown, a role which often adds humiliation to frustration.

Frustration is compounded by the fact that members of Congress have not only their entitlement to a great voice in government, legitimated by their popular election, they also have wills of their own, views of their own, ideas of their own. Quite naturally these seem to them at least as worthy of attention in detailed administration as are those of any agency official. There is something to be said for this position; congressional ideas are often apt. But as a practical matter, the officials with immediate authority to act, and the necessity, are bound to make decisions day-by-day which reflect their conceptions and their reading of the issues—and which violate the values of some congressmen. This is understood in Congress but it grates. Repetitive experience of offering advice without material result is likelier to make advisers scornful than humble, especially if they are certain of their right to offer. So it seems to be for many congressmen.

Congressional Devices for Control

Frustration with an overture of scorn has brought a strong reaction from both houses of Congress, a reaction which amounts to vigorous assertion of administrative powers held by Congress. For years entrenchment of the new bureaucracy has given rise to efforts aimed at tightening congressional control over the details of administrative operations. These efforts have been cumulative for a generation, growing in intensity and ingenuity from year to year. New techniques, almost unknown in prior practice, have been devised to meet the new condition of a vast machine downtown. Congress has not been passive in the face of competition from officialdom. It actively attempts to control its competitors.

The reach for control has taken many forms, but there are three in particular. First is a quite traditional device, the patronage, with special reference nowadays to top appointive posts and to those sensitive subordinate positions—so-called Schedule C positions—which are in the civil service but not subject to its tenure rules. Congressional pressure on the President and on department heads is nothing new, but where postmasterships were once the aim, assistants to assistant secretaries and the like are now a natural target, with good reason. And where "senatorial courtesy" was once the means of putting teeth into congressional desires, hints of trouble in the legislative and appropriation processes now take their place alongside that time-honored technique.

A second device is untraditional, a novelty, a postwar innovation, rapidly expanding in the fifties and the early sixties, leveling off since. This is the device of annual authorization for agencies themselves and for their programs. About $50 billion of the federal budget now is subject every year not only to appropriations but to prior legislation authorizing a continuation of existing agencies and programs. Among these are the Agency for International Development with foreign aid, the National Aeronautics and Space Administration with space exploration, and the Office of Economic Opportunity with its poverty programs.

A third device for control also is a postwar innovation: the "committee clearance." In recent years we find numerous statutory provisions—some enacted, some rejected, some enforced without enactment—which require that an agency report particular administrative actions in advance to a committee, or, stronger still, which require that an agency "come into agreement" with committee personnel before action is taken or, strongest of all, which require that an agency respect committee veto in a fixed time-period after the fact. These clearances, whatever their strength, have been asserted in the main by Agriculture, Armed Services, Interior, and Public Works Committees, and by the Joint Committee on Atomic Energy, which has a special statutory right of supervision over the Atomic Energy Commission. Taken together, these assertions seem to aim at giving legislative committees (and their members) a hold on bread-and-butter for home districts: site locations, purchase contracts, surplus sales. The impulse is entirely understandable.

Such devices for congressional control have often made an impact on the details of particular administrative operations, and also on the detailed distribution of administrative powers in Congress. Indeed the latter impact may, in sum, be greater than the former. Annual authorization and committee clearance are, among other things, devices whereby legislative committees gain a share in the surveillance always open to appropriations committees. This frequently redounds to the advantage of the agencies concerned, and probably has often been encouraged by them. For legislative committees often champion "their" agencies against economizers in appropriations committees.

From the standpoint of good management as understood in private corporations or as preached by the apostles of administrative rationality, devices of this sort create a host of troubles for an agency official and for his executive superiors. Annual authorization causes turmoil every year, especially in personnel administration. "Agreement" and "veto" mean delay, uncertainty. (Moreover these requirements are constitutionally dubious.) And "reporting" is a nuisance at the very least. Yet in administrative practice it is far from clear that agency officials are net losers.

On balance, these assertions of control have compensations for officialdom. They sometimes produce good ideas and sensible improvements: congressmen are capable of being very helpful. They may produce a measure of political protection, which is never to be slighted by an agency official. Moreover, they permit an able operator to play his committee "masters" off against each other. Control by two committees of each House can mean control by none, while serving at the same time to dilute direction from above, from the administration.

Limitations on Congressional Control

It is significant that the most heartfelt arguments against these new devices have come from central, presidential agencies, such as the Office of Management and

Budget and its predecessor, the Bureau of the Budget, especially in Lyndon Johnson's time. Congressional assertions of control are bound to complicate attempts at central management in presidential terms. It does not follow that they have made Congress an effective manager. "Congress" is not involved. Nor are most congressmen.

The competition agency officials offer congressmen is not dispelled by control through congressional committee. Net gainers from this sort of enterprise are likely to be limited in number and are never found exclusively on Capitol Hill. The gainers, ordinarily, are of two sorts: on the one hand, effective agency careerists; on the other hand, well-placed committee members, especially seniority leaders (or their staffs). Control devices can produce a merger, in effect, between particular committees and "their" agencies. Some segments of officialdom are held under the thumb of a strong chairman; others suffer close surveillance by committee staff. Conversely, some staffs are accustomed to take cues from key officials; some chairmen have been known to act as agents of "their" agencies. Either way, there may result a tight relationship between affected agencies and congressmen, restraining competition in the interest of stability for policy and personnel alike. If clients and constituents are brought into the combine to the satisfaction of all sides, so much the better. The outcome then is a monopoly, a true "subgovernment," to adapt Douglass Cater's term, as in the sphere of sugar. Cater writes:

> . . . consider the tight little subgovernment which rules the nation's sugar economy. Since the early 1930s, this agricultural commodity has been subjected to a cartel arrangement sponsored by the government. By specific prescription, the sugar market is divided into the last spoonful. . . .
>
> Political power within the sugar subgovernment is largely vested in the chairman of the House Agricultural Committee who works out the schedule of quotas. It is shared by a veteran civil servant, the Director of the Sugar Division in the U.S. Department of Agriculture, who provides the necessary "expert" advice for such a complex marketing arrangement. Further advice is provided by Washington representatives of the . . . producers.[2]

But congressmen in general gain no measurable benefit from mergers on these terms, no special hold of policy or personnel, no special claims with clientele. The benefits accrue to members of particular committees and their friends (both on and off the Hill). For all the rest, officialdom becomes more powerfully competitive than ever, buttressed by its links to "Congress" *in committee.*

Moreover, the executive establishment is only ripe for "merger" at the margins of its policy concerns. In central spheres of policy, committees rarely serve the needs of agencies sufficiently to nurture true subgovernments. Bureaucratic organizations may be molded in the image of committee jurisdictions. But agency operations are not. For the very causal factors which brought forth the new officialdom, the same events both foreign and domestic, mix and mingle operations among agencies. Neither in military spheres, nor in diplomacy, nor in domestic welfare, nor in economic management can one agency pursue its statutory mandates independently of aid or acquiescence from others, usually many others. Programmatic purposes and operating problems spill across dividing lines on organization charts, entangling jurisdictions in the process. This always was the case to a degree; it now is markedly more so. Thirty years ago the Departments of State and Agriculture worked in separate worlds. So did the Department of Justice and the Office of Education. Now even these cross wires often, while the operations of the

Departments of Defense and State are always intertwined, to say nothing of such Lyndon Johnson legacies as "poverty" and "model cities" programs. These continuously entangle half the government. Indeed continuous entanglement is characteristic of the hundreds of new ventures in education, health care, housing, transportation, welfare passed by Congress during the triumphant part of Johnson's term.

Committee "domination" of an agency is constantly imperiled by these jurisdictional entanglements. "Mergers" do not flourish in the midst of mingled programs. Overlapping operations force entangled agencies to deal with one another day by day, and to appeal over each other's heads when bargaining breaks down. The need for bargaining arenas is endemic; so is the need for arbitrators. But in central spheres of policy, the spheres of greatest overlap, congressional committees rarely offer either adequate arenas or authoritative arbitrators. Committee jurisdictions usually are too confined for that. And bargaining *between* committees rarely meets the needs of daily work downtown. As a forum for administrative bargaining, our legislative process has its uses in securing and defending fixed positions, not in reaching or applying operational accommodations suited to a job in hand.

Thus even for the privileged few, controls exerted through committee may break down just when and where their use becomes most interesting. For operators with a job to do will sidle out from under the committees and will deal with one another or appeal against each other in executive arenas at the other end of Pennsylvania Avenue—the White House end—where congressional seniors, however potent in their own committee bailiwicks, have limited access and a (relatively) weak voice.

In general then, the politicians on the Hill reach for control of their competitors downtown without securing a surcease from competition. On the contrary, these efforts at control have rather helped than hindered agency officials—and indeed have spurred them on—to play committees off against each other. For most intents and purposes, much of the time, detailed decision-making with direct impact on voters still eludes the politicians, while their agency competitors still flourish as before. Who controls whom is a nice question. Perhaps officials are as often the manipulators of committees as congressional seniors are the managers of agencies.

Congressmen continue to have reason for frustration. When they compare their nominal administrative powers with the actualities of who-does-what in Washington, the fact that their committees can assert control of relatively marginal affairs is little comfort. When they look down the Avenue toward the White House and perceive the Presidency, with its own officialdom, asserting the prerogatives of central management—as any President has done since Franklin Roosevelt's time—their comfort grows the less. And when they add what they are bound to see, and so to feel, that policy initiatives are centered in the White House too, the pain in their position grows severe. Constituents rub salt into the wound. So does a proper pride in the traditions of a parliamentary body.

When the elective politicians on the Hill voice their frustration they are likelier than not to pass over its source, competitive officialdom, in favor of a target more traditional and easier to watch: their constitutional competitor, that Man in the White House. Yet he, an elective politician in his own right, struggles with officialdom no less than they. He too is in a competition with their new competitor.

THE PRESIDENT AND THE EXECUTIVE AGENCIES

The Presidency's character shapes what there is of unity in the executive establishment. Every agency is headed by a presidential appointee (Senate consenting). These appointees are not immune to the old charge of Charles G. Dawes that "members of the Cabinet are a President's natural enemies." But they and their immediate associates do have some things in common with each other and the President which their career subordinates do not: temporary tenure and a stake in his success. Our terminology acknowledges their semblance of community; we speak of them collectively as "the administration," something wider than "the White House," looser than "the Presidency," but different from "officialdom," an intermediate layer neither truly presidential nor wholly bureaucratic.

Within limits, these distinctions have reality behind them: presidential appointees are men-in-the-middle, owing loyalty at once to the man who put them there, to the laws they administer, and to the body of careerists, backed by clientele, whose purposes they both direct and serve. They also owe some loyalty to their own careers, which may make for dependence on each other. And being similarly placed they may have fellow-feeling for each other. All these are two-edged swords. In many circumstances these induce a "scatteration" rather than community-of-interest. But insofar as this exists, the Presidency lies back of it.

The Presidency is a binding force in other ways as well. In many spheres of action the executive establishment can scarcely move except as it invokes the President. One such sphere is a traditional "royal prerogative" where Presidents are heirs to English kings: command of the armed forces and the conduct of foreign relations. A second sphere is of more recent origin, a modern prerogative: the initiative in legislation, authority and funds alike. A third sphere, rooted in our politics, has been transformed by our technology: the appeal to the people, the defense of new departures. In each sphere presidential acts, or delegations, or approvals (as a matter of form at least) are vital for official action, legitimating it as nothing else can. Thus each sphere weaves a bond around all those concerned in action—the bond of common need.

Defense and Diplomacy

The President's place in defense and diplomacy turns on his role as commander-in-chief, a role created by the Constitution, deepened by history, confirmed by modern practice. The Vietnam War, part of that practice, has made this role more controversial lately than at any time since 1940, but like FDR before him Richard Nixon is constrained only by prudence. The excuse is that no one else can make him use the nation's troops—or its nuclear weapons for that matter—and no one else can stop him except (in theory) Congress if it cares to intervene after the fact by changing force-levels or cutting funds; hard to do. A President's place in foreign policy has other sources also, but they pale by comparison with this. The same thing can be said of his authority, long since acknowledged by the Supreme Court, to guard the "peace of the United States" *internally*. Again, the fact that *he* commands the troops is paramount. So, when the use or threat or possibility of force comes into play, officials of all sorts in every agency concerned will keep the President in mind because they must, and each will seek his sanction for the course of action each prefers. The twenty years *since* the Korean War are marked by Dien

Bien Phu, Suez, Quemoy, Lebanon, Berlin, Congo, Cuba, Santo Domingo, Laos, Vietnam, Thailand, Cambodia, where troops were either sent or quite deliberately withheld—to say nothing of Little Rock, Arkansas, or Oxford, Mississippi, or Detroit, Michigan. From the standpoint of government agencies there is no need to labor the point.

Legislative Initiative

The President's initiative in legislation is a rather different matter, more a product of convenience, of pragmatic adaptation, than a constitutional imperative. Presidents have always had a role in legislation: the veto power and the right to recommend stem from the Constitution. But the process of enlarging these foundations to support initiative across-the-board began only with the Budget and Accounting Act of 1921. Congress then imposed upon the White House—having nowhere else to put it—the duty to propose an executive budget, a statement of financial need for every agency, in the President's judgment, not theirs. This was conceived by its sponsors as a way to cut expenditures. It also proved a way to make the White House matter more to agencies than it had done before. No other single innovation has so markedly enlarged the practical importance of the Presidency to the whole executive establishment; those sponsors got more than they bargained for. Nevertheless, once done the thing was irreversible. Congressional committees remained ultimately "in control": witness the successes of an Otto Passman, terror of the foreign aid program. But the Presidency held an intermediate control; oftener than not this proved conclusive for the agencies, always, at the least, a problem to them; the starting line for Congress was the *President's* proposal. So it has remained.

In the years of FDR and Harry S. Truman, the initial years of our contemporary "big government," White House initiative spread from the sphere of money to the sphere of substance.[3] Ultimately it encompassed the full range of measures coming before Congress. By 1939 the central clearance of all agency proposals and reports on pending measures—whether money bills or not—had been established in the Bureau of the Budget. By 1949 the legislative "program of the President" had come to be a fixed, defined, and comprehensive entity, laid down by annual messages and spelled out in a set of special messages in each session. Continuation of both practices through subsequent administrations has accorded to both the sanction of long usage, "ancient custom." There are not many civil servants left who can recall when things were different. In the forties some agencies habitually evaded central clearance. This is rare today. In the fifties the White House still stopped short of sending bill-drafts with its messages; these went instead from a department head to a committee chairman for introduction "by request"; the fiction was preserved that Presidents themselves did not send bills to Congress. By 1961, however, "John Kennedy" became the signature on draft bills sent with messages directly to the Speaker and the President of the Senate, very much as though the White House were Whitehall. While this has not been the invariable practice since, the fiction disappeared—and no one noticed.

The fact that "no one noticed" is suggestive of the character of this entire half-century development. It has been among the quietest pragmatic innovations in our constitutional history. The reason for the quiet is that it has proved at every stage to have advantages for all concerned, not least for Congress. What Congress gains is a prestigeful "laundry-list," a starting order-of-priority to guide the work of each committee in both houses in every session. Since it comes from downtown, committee and house leaders—and all members—can respond to or react against it at *their* option. But coming from downtown it does for them what they, in their disunity, cannot do for themselves: it gives them an agenda to get on with, or depart from.

The President's initiative in legislation is accepted on the Hill because it serves a purpose there. And since it serves a purpose there it is respected by officialdom downtown. Inclusion of their own aims in "the program of the President" matters to most agencies—and to their clientele—for reasons both of prestige and of practical advantage. Exclusion is distasteful, at the least, sometimes disastrous. In consequence, both budgeting and program-making are among the binding forces fostered by the Presidency.

So in recent years is "legislative liaison," a matter not of setting the congressional agenda but of keeping up relations between houses and with agencies in the pursuit of presidential programs on the Hill. The White House has become, long since, a place—almost the only place—where Senate and House party leaders meet with one another on the tactics and prospects of congressional action. The White House telephone has been for many years a major weapon in the hunt for votes, especially when it conveys the President's own voice. But more than this, since Eisenhower's time a special staff for legislative liaison has been established in the White House to monitor the progress of all presidential bills and to assist in rounding up the votes. This staff makes claims on congressmen, and they in turn assert their claims on operating programs in the agencies. The staff attempts to harness agency resources, and the agencies respond by claiming White House help for *their* congressional concerns. Agencies will often have the better of that bargain: a President's connections with the leadership will often serve their purposes more nearly than their help serves his. Because they stand to gain from White House liaison—and liaisoners—this is still another binding tie.

Appeal to the People

A President's preeminence as spokesman *for* the government and *to* the country is again a different matter, a compound of many things: Madison's Constitution, Washington's propriety, Jackson's politics, Lincoln's martyrdom, TR's energy, Wilson's earnestness, FDR's voice—all mingled with the human need to personalize "government," a need which grows the greater as the government enlarges and its work becomes arcane. Since the thirties, first radio then television fed that need by offering the *President* at work and play for everyone to hear or see directly, through a form of personal encounter which by now becomes a settled expectation, a matter of course.

After FDR, all Presidents have felt impelled to go before the country, into people's homes (and bars), at every time of gravity in national affairs and at each major turn in governmental policy, to soothe, explain, defend, or urge, as circumstances required. The public expectation is so clear—or seems so—that a Kennedy, who had no native taste for "fireside chatting," nevertheless put himself through these encounters gamely, while elaborating televised press conferences as a congenial form (for him) of partial substitute. A Nixon shuns the Kennedy-style press conference while reaching for new forms of media exposure. But he too follows the "fireside" format, with radio and television talks at appropriate moments. So did LBJ (who reportedly liked such set pieces no better than Kennedy). Almost certainly their successors will feel bound by the tradition.

For agency officials who have new departures to espouse, or risky courses to pursue, or clients in deep trouble, it seems natural and proper, often indispensable, to make the President their television spokesman. Presidents may demur, and often do, but their presumed utility is none the less for that. Accordingly, officials never cease to urge. The net effect is still another force for unity originating in the White House—again a force of need.

THE PRESIDENT AND THE "INSTITUTIONALIZED PRESIDENCY"

These spheres of presidential primacy give every part of the executive establishment the shared experience, the mutuality of interest (such as it may be), which stems from common claims upon the President. The claims have grown the stronger as officialdom has grown. The same events fed both. But if, while this was happening, the White House had proved institutionally incapable of dealing with these claims, then shared experience would have been sheer frustration, and those spheres would have become bone-yards for agency contention, dog-eat-dog. Actually, White House capabilities have kept pace just enough to counter separations of that aggravated sort.

It is the "Institutionalized Presidency," another constitutional innovation of our time, which gives concreteness to the elements of unity in our "Executive." The Presidency began to change from man to institution while our bureaucratic apparatus still was relatively small and still in flux, during the New Deal years. The change was guided by a President whose grasp of office and whose continuity in office were extraordinary: FDR. Both timing and guidance appear providential in the light of what came after: stabilized, entrenched officialdom. The Brownlow Report of 1937 and its sequel "The Executive Office of the President" established not alone an organization, but a doctrine: the rightness of a "President's Department," the need for staff resources of his own. These were established in the nick of time. The organization changes, but the doctrine remains. Otherwise, the Presidency as we know it scarcely could have weathered the subsequent years. By now it would have been a hollow shell.

Conflicting Demands

Yet having said this much, it remains to be said that the institutionalized Presidency has not proved an unmixed blessing for the President. In its evolution since the second Roosevelt's years, this institution vividly suggests a basic conflict, probably irreconcilable, between bureaucratic claims upon the White House and a President's own claims upon officialdom. Agencies need decisions, delegations, and support, along with bargaining arenas and a court of last resort, so organized as to assure that their advice is always heard and often taken. A President needs timely information, early warning, close surveillance, organized to yield him the controlling judgment, with his options open, his intent enforced. In practice these two sets of needs have proved quite incompatible; presidential organizations rarely serve one well without disservice to the other.

The National Security Council is a case in point. This Cabinet committee got its statutory start in 1947, as a product of reaction against FDR's secretiveness and "sloppiness" and "meddling" with the conduct of the war and its diplomacy. Yet barring some extraordinary lapses—German zonal agreements above all—he had managed by his methods to maintain a high degree of personal control during the war, which is what *he* was after. That heightened the reaction. Its ultimate results were seen in Eisenhower's NSC, which came to have a formalized and "paperized" procedure, buttressed by an elaborate interagency substructure. This produced a counterreaction. In 1961 Kennedy abolished both procedure and substructure to escape bureaucratization of his business. He replaced them, in effect, with a handful of personal aides enjoined to do no business but his own. In the main they gave him what he wanted, and the Cuban missile crisis served to vindicate his whole approach, at least in White House eyes. But outside White House precincts in the great departments, especially at levels twice removed from Cabinet rank, memories of those Eisenhower regularities—and of the access they provided—grow fonder every year. By 1966 senior officials had succeeded in persuading Lyndon Johnson to restore the forms of regularized procedure: the SIG-IRG system, so-called, with the State Department nominally at the center. This never worked to anybody's satisfaction, partly because Johnson's operating style was incompatible with it. In 1969 Richard Nixon replaced it by a still more formal system manned by a larger staff, avowedly intended to eliminate Johnsonian "disorder." Ostensibly this was a move back toward the Eisenhower regularities. Officialdom, however, found in it cold comfort. For the Nixon system's center was removed from State to White House more decisively than ever in the past. The NSC became a peg on which to hang not Kennedy's few staffers but a massive White House agency headed by a single, presidential confidant, Henry Kissinger. At second levels of Defense and State, officials now yearn to dismantle Nixon's system.[4]

Presidential vs. Agency Judgment

What this instance suggests has pertinence beyond the realm of staffing: not only is officialdom competitive with Congress; it also is in competition with the President. Granted that officials need his sanction, he needs their resources; the dependence being mutual is no bar to competition.

Agency officials, seized by a given problem, rarely seem unequal to the task of making judgments for the government. Nor do they seem inclined to seek a presidential judgment, their's aside, for any other reason than because they cannot help it. The White House would be treated to a novelty if bureaucrats began to ask the President's opinion out of nothing but respect for his good sense. Most careerists see authority as hierarchical—such is the world they live in—and consider that the President is nominally at the top. Because he is on top they can accept his *right* to judge, at least when he asserts it with a show of real authority or when they find it a useful thing to assert against their colleagues. But this is not because they think his judgment better than their own. That thought seems a stranger in officialdom. The usual official view of Presidents is rather like the academic view of businessmen: respect for power, a degree of resignation, a tinge of contempt. Given any chance to work the government without the President, officials will proceed to do so in good conscience, except as they may want his voice or acquiescence for their purposes.

If this does not seem quite the disciplined official style respectful of authority à *la* Max Weber, ours is not a European civil service. In certain other well-established governments, relationships are rigged to minimize, as far as possible, the personal and institutional insecurities of everyone in public life. This seems to be the situation in Great Britain, for example. Not so with us. With us it is almost the opposite: we maximize the insecurities of men and agencies alike. Careerists jostle in-and-outers (from the law firms, business, academic life) for the positions of effective influence; their agencies contend with the committees on the Hill, the Office of Management and Budget, other agencies for the prerequisites of institutional survival, *year by year*. Pursuit of programs authorized in law can be a constant struggle to maintain and hold support of influential clients, or the press. And seeking new authority to innovate a program can be very much like coalition warfare. Accordingly, most agencies have need for men of passion and conviction—or at least enormous powers of resistance—near the top. American officialdom may generate no more of these than other systems do, but it rewards them well: they rise toward the top. And there they tend to set the tone of bureaucratic views about all comers from "outside," not least the President.

Yet any modern President will see things very differently. It is routine for White House aides to seethe with irritation at the unresponsiveness of "them," the almost-enemy, officialdom. And aides are but more royalist than the King. Their principals tend to become resigned, but not less irritated. For a President combines in his own person a unique perspective with unique responsibility. Naturally he will consider that the one is relevant to the other, that his own outlook has bearing on the issues which invoke his own official obligations. Moreover, he is not himself an "office" but a human being, eager to make marks upon events, conscious of *his* place in the republic's history, and mindful—now that ICBM's are held in Moscow too—of a shared capability to terminate that history. Besides, the human being sees himself in office as the outcome of his own career, topped off by national nomination and election. Ordinarily this is the hardest course to run in our political system. He has run it; in his first term he faces it again; in his second term he faces it at one remove, for a successor (he will hope) of his own choosing. So at least have our Presidents seen things up to now.

To an observer from outside, this seems a reasonable vision of the President's own place. Indeed, our governmental system sanctions it, what we have called "democracy" requires it, the system is legitimated by it, and our history confirms its practical utility—which is with us no small consideration. Despite the present failures-in-particular recorded by our history, not least recent history, too many of our Presidents have done too well in exercising judgment for observers to dismiss their claims upon the role. Historically, the averages still seem to support them.

In exercising judgment, Presidents quite often have contributed themselves what none of their executive associates could offer with an equal skill: a first-hand feel for feasibilities across the board of politics, from publics, interests, partisans, to Congress, and officialdom, and governments abroad—a feel for current prospects of support, indifference, toleration, opposition, with respect to lines of action wherever they lead.

This contribution is the province of elective politicians, those who bear the burdens, take the heat, and face the risks of sudden death by ballot box, especially when they share in administrative power and have learned the risks peculiar to that line of work as well. But in the whole executive establishment there are no such risk-takers, short of the White House. Aside from the Vice-President, whose role is bound to be ambiguous at best, the President stands quite alone. Officials cannot make his contribution for him. Few can help him very much to make it. For no one stands on a spot like his, with comparable duties, facing comparable risks. A Lincoln in the months before emancipation, a Franklin Roosevelt in the years after his "quarantine" address, a Kennedy in the weeks after Birmingham, or in the days of his climactic confrontation with Khrushchev, a Johnson in the early months of 1968—all these men were engaged in calculating feasibilities, and it is not of record that associates could have been counted on to come up with their answers for them. In this trade there is no reliable apprentice system.

A President does have some fellow journeymen, of course, but they are far away, a long mile down the Avenue on Capitol Hill.

THE COMMON STAKES OF ELECTIVE POLITICIANS

The separations between President and congressmen are partly constitutional, partly political, partly attitudinal, and in no small degree a matter of semantics. The Constitution's barriers look higher than they are. The barriers of politics may soon start to decline. But differences in attitude may still be on the rise, fed by the connotations of our words.

Executive vs. Legislative

Constitutionally the President and Congress share each other's powers, from the veto, to appointments, to administrative "oversight," and so down the list. Practically this is a sharing between one man at the White House and a scattering of others who hold key positions in the two congressional "bodies"; they share powers with each other even as they share with him. Politically, these sharers are kept separate by their differing dependence upon different electorates. These differences are sharpest at the stage of nomination: senators and congressmen will owe their seats to separate sets of nominators; chairmen owe their powers to seniority acquired by repeated nomination. The President, by contrast, owes his place and powers to a nominating contest of another order, as far removed from theirs, in timing and geography and personnel alike, as theirs are separated from each other. The fact that nominators everywhere would like to win elections has not served to produce like-minded party candidates—far from it. Terms of party competition and conditions of survival and electoral arithmetic have differed far too much. Realignment of congressional districts, reapportionment of legislatures, and Republican gains in the once "solid South" *may* now combine to change this situation, to reduce those differences, to force more uniformity on nominators, and hence on candidates. If so, then there will be a narrowing of separations among senators and congressmen and Presidents—a narrowing, at least, of gaps induced by politics. But that time is not yet.

Even if it comes, there will remain the gaps induced by attitudes of mind, by habit, custom, way of life, and ways of doing work. In some respects our Constitution and our politics tell less about what separates the Presidency from Congress than our architecture does. For the White House and the Capitol as structures almost perfectly express these underlying differences of attitude: the former has an exterior which at first glance looks simpler than it is, and inside all seems orderly:

rectangular rooms mostly, connected by straight corridors, as neat-appearing as an organization chart. The latter is almost rococo in externals, appearing more complex at first than on long knowledge, and within it seems all twists and turns: passages which lead in circles, little-known connections, sudden detours, hidden treasures, obscure sanctuaries, walls in curves. The men who work inside these buildings literally work in different worlds. Their attitudes are shaped accordingly.

The Senate and the House, of course, are not identical workplaces. For most of its inhabitants the Senate is a pleasant place, possessed of quite enough prestige and power (or its semblance), and amenities of staff and space, and time to enjoy them (six years at a crack), so that it alone remains what much of government once was, a refuge for the spirit of political free-enterprise, unfettered either by undue responsibility or the restraints of size. The House, however, offers comparable enjoyments only to a few, the men of great seniority or great good luck. The rest either content themselves with marginal existences or scramble for political and personal identity amidst the ruck and ruckus of large numbers, rigid rules, demanding lobbyists, disdainful agencies, unheeding press, importunate constituents, and pitifully short tenure. No wonder that the House is seen by many of its members as a stepping stone, a place to be endured on the way up and out. It may well be the most frustrating place to work in Washington. It certainly ranks high among such places.

Even so, the contrasts between houses pale compared to those between the work of either and of men downtown. Tiber Creek is gone, but there remains a great dividing line across the Avenue.

This is the product not alone of work-ways but of substance, not merely who-works-how but who-does-what. So much of the decision-making critical for all of us is centered nowadays in the executive establishment that congressmen and senators feel cheated of a birthright. They are, for the most part, men of seriousness, intelligence, and patriotism, to say nothing of experience. They also are men of elections, voted into office by a portion of the citizens and sharing with the President the risk of death by ballot box. Yet others have a greater voice than they in numbers of decisions, day by day, which touch the lives of citizens. They may accept this, but they cannot like it.

For instance, the most critical of government decisions, the war-or-peace decisions, have been snatched away from Congress by technology, at least where nuclear war is risked, despite the plain words of the Constitution. As for limited war, Congress may now vote itself authority to do what it always could have done anyway, namely stop hostilities once started. But while the threat of legislative veto might deter a President, the evidence of history makes it appear remote that Congress actually would call a halt once troops had been engaged. No congressman disputes the fact that Congress has lost hold of war-making. Few have any eagerness to take upon themselves the heat of presidential choices. But many, perhaps most, dislike to draw the corollary that they have no choice at all and not even a voice, except by presidential courtesy, in presidential prudence. When it comes to lesser instances, where courtesy and prudence are prerogatives of a mere appointee or even of a careerist, then their sense of deprivation will be stronger still, and for good reason.

Hurts like these are rendered the more painful by the press, which centers its attention on the President. Publicity is far too great a prize for politicians to make this a happy outcome for most members of Congress. Only elders can remember when the Hill was the best-covered part of town. Franklin Roosevelt's Presidency put an end to that. But even juniors are impelled by sheer professional concern to nurse their disadvantage as a grievance.

Such feelings are returned with interest from downtown. In executive eyes, Congress is at best a necessary nuisance and at worst a great conspiracy against efficient government. All Presidents will wish they could make Congress serve them as a rubber-stamp, converting their agendas into prompt enactments, and most Presidents will try to bring that miracle about, whenever and as best they can. Most presidential appointees will grow despairing about drains upon their time, skill, energy, and ingenuity—to say nothing of reputation—occasioned by the legislative (and investigative) process with its "endless" repetitions in committee hearings, correspondence, phone calls. Most careerists, even if their agencies show profit, will grow sick, or cynical, at seeing "rational" solutions twisted out of recognition by committee compromise. And most of them, reacting in anticipation, become do-it-yourself types, compromisers-in-advance, despite the risks of amateurish outcomes. (Amateur careerists, in turn, sicken the politicians; some, however, do acquire near-professional standing.) Underlying all of this is a persistent puzzle: why should "they" be so blind to imperatives of good administration? It is the obverse of a question constantly occurring on the Hill: what makes "them" so obtuse about the necessities of the legislative process and of political survival?

"They" and "them" are optical illusions, but these make the sense of separation all the sharper. Administrators may know well, from personal experience and frequent exploitation, how disjointed is the power structure on the Hill. Yet most of them would say and feel with Kennedy:

> . . . the Congress looks more powerful sitting here than it did when I was there in Congress. But that is because when you are in Congress you are one of a hundred in the Senate or 435 in the House, so that power is so divided. But from here I look at a Congress, and I look at the collective power of the Congress, particularly the bloc action, and it is a substantial power.[5]

And most members of Congress may be quite aware that any one of them, with influence enough, can penetrate or even dominate the programs of some agency or other. Yet looking down the Avenue at the array of agencies—the rows of office buildings, the outpouring of officials, the interminable corridors, the bustle of department heads departing for the White House from their grandiose office-suites—these legislators see an entity of monolithic aspect, the executive branch, apparently commanded by one man, the President: that other and more grandly placed elective politician whose hold upon the agencies seems mighty in comparison with theirs.

These visual impressions are confirmed by our semantics, reinforced by words in common use: *the* Congress, *the* Executive, "legislation," "administration." Decades ago the coming of the "Institutionalized Presidency" was justified by experts outside government (and by officials near the White House) as essential to the role of "Chief Administrator," a presidential role read into constitutional provisions by analogy with private corporations. The analogy has stuck, and with it the suspicion that all efforts to enlarge a President's resources threaten the prerogatives of *Congress,* striking at committee rights to authorize, finance, investigate, and "oversee." Presidents in fact are merely fighting for their rights as independent operators, threatened with engulfment by official claims upon them.

This is a fight which should enlist the sympathy of fellow politicians on the Hill. But phrases twist the fact into a contest between President and Congress.

Politicians vs. Bureaucrats

This is symptomatic of a great confusion about who is fighting whom and who is winning in our government. Bureaucracy has brought a new contestant into play: the great prospective struggle is between entrenched officialdom and politicians everywhere, White House and Hill alike. Officialdom already is competitive with both. Its strength is sapped by institutional disunity, the gift of Congress. Temporarily, at least, this shields the politicians from the consequences of their own disunity. But it seems far from certain that the bureaucrats will not learn how to close their ranks in better order, faster, than their showing up to now. What then would happen to the politicians separated as they are by all the factors just described?

The first edition of this essay written during LBJ's first year as President took that last question as a peg on which to hang three final paragraphs. These follow:

> We now are entering our second generation of experience with an executive establishment in modern dress. Even now, experienced officials tend to work across their lines of jurisdiction with an ease and understanding little known some twenty years ago. Relations between the Departments of Defense and State exemplify the trend. Their disputation still remains incessant, as before, but temperature and tempo are decidedly below the levels of, say, 1949. If this trend should continue and accelerate, encompassing domestic agencies as well, a President and congressmen might confront competition too intense for them to meet in isolation from each other. If so, they either must array their own ranks or our government will risk losing what they uniquely bring to public policy; the feel for feasibility of men who take the heat from an electorate. It is a risk not only to their power but also to our polity.
>
> Fortunately for the politicians, there is little likelihood that bureaucrats will soon be tightly united. The separations among agencies, induced by separations on the Hill, run far too deep. The risk lies not in an official unity but simply and more subtly in a heightened sense of official community. And nowadays not only are there signs of fellow-feeling among "second-generation" bureaucrats, there also are great efforts being made by private sources to induce community spirit through enhanced professionalization. Our schools, foundations, and study groups make no such efforts for our politicians.
>
> The moral is plain. To paraphrase Karl Marx: Politicians at the two ends of the Avenue unite! You have nothing to lose but your pieces of power—and even now these may be slipping out of reach. To call for unity in form would be absurd. To call for sheer subservience of Congress to the President, or *vice versa,* would be futile. But to urge some change of attitudes at both ends of the Avenue, to urge awareness of joint stakes and common risks is not perhaps to ask too much of our established system. This might induce a unity sufficient for the purpose. Moreover, politicians might enjoy it when they thought about it. Opportunities to think, however, will come hard unless outside observers—academic and other—set about repairing our semantics. We might begin now.

Recent Developments

So much for commentary circa 1964. Like all else dating from that year those words convey an atmosphere often curiously remote. "Prewar" we probably will start to call it soon. A lot has happened since.

Three developments especially affect the near-term prospects for relations among Congress, Presidency, and officialdom.

One of these developments is the spread of congressional mistrust, of grievance nurtured by deprivation, into the realms of defense and diplomacy. These are realms where presidential leadership was relatively uncontested for the generation from Truman to Johnson. On Capitol Hill, as well as outside Washington, a legacy of Vietnam's long-drawn course becomes frustration tinged with fear. Such feelings are not universal, but are widespread and in some minds deep. The sense of separation between President and congressmen deepens accordingly. Snarls at "they" and "them" are heard on every hand. In Nixon's time, of course, these are abetted by the lack of party ties between the White House and congressional majorities.

A second development is what appears to be progressive diminution in the relative positions of most Cabinet officers, a weakening of the traditional "Administration." These men and their immediate associates are caught between a burgeoning White House staff—enlarged four-fold in Nixon's time alone—and ever more entangled departmental jurisdictions consequent upon the outpouring of laws in Johnson's time.

Departmental heads now seem distinctly more subordinate to Presidents than twenty years ago, or even ten. Presidents do not seem to have profited thereby, not anyway in their own estimations. Johnson seriously considered and Nixon has proposed a sweeping scheme of departmental reorganization, meant to produce fewer but more potent Cabinet members tied to one another and the White House in such fashion as to strengthen central management of Federal agencies.[6] Whether structural reform along these lines is possible congressionally, and if so whether it could actually induce the benefits now claimed for it, are both uncertain quantities. Meanwhile, presidential staff grows at a frantic rate, as does the burden of coordination thrust upon it. Every entanglement means more work up top.

The third development is an appearance, possibly deceptive, of progressive loss of confidence, morale, assurance, perhaps also of quality, in many different parts of the executive establishment. Public and congressional suspiciousness of soldiers—for the first time in a generation—plays some part. So does White House suspiciousness of diplomats. So does Republican suspiciousness of career staffs. So do the suspicions in reverse of some careerists, especially among professionals, for example lawyers. Party separation of the White House from congressional committee chairmanships no doubt feeds such suspicions on all sides. So does the vocal discontent of many publics.

Deeper down, the operational experiences of the sixties have left bafflement, confusion, apprehension, in a lot of minds not only at the Pentagon, not only in response to ineffectual warfare, but also at HUD, OEO, some parts of HEW, and other "home" departments in response to ineffectual administration. The massive task of turning legislative mandates into actual results, implemented in the field, often under budgetary stringency, has proved far harder, more demanding, less assuredly achievable, than was foreseen in the initial years of LBJ when all those laws poured in. Discouragement and disillusionment—and often bafflement—accompany the implementation struggle.

What these developments portend for the long run is hard to say, possibly nothing. In the short-run, however, they assuredly defer the day when bureaucrats cohere sufficiently to confidently reach for governmental leadership. They also reduce reasons for the politicians to cohere among themselves. Their electorates, of course, may force them to it. Television, crime, and race, combined with war, may have profound effects upon the separations between President and Congressmen by reducing the separations of their electorates. But consciousness of bureaucratic challenge will not do it, not anyway in the short run.

NOTES

1. Clem Miller, *Member of the House* (New York; Scribners, 1962), p. 110.
2. Douglass Cater, *Power in Washington* (New York: Random House, 1964), pp. 17–18.
3. For details on this development see my "Presidency and Legislation," *American Political Science Review* (Sept. 1954 and Dec. 1955).
4. For a further statement of the issues in the national security sphere see my *Afterword* (written jointly with Graham T. Allison) to Robert F. Kennedy's classic *Thirteen Days* (New York: Norton, 1971), esp. pp. 130–6.
5. Television and radio interview, December 17, 1962, *Public Papers of the President: John F. Kennedy* (1962), p. 893.
6. See Executive Office of the President, Office of Management and Budget, *Papers Relating to the President's Departmental Reorganization Program, Revised, February, 1972.*

The "Administrative Presidency"

RICHARD P. NATHAN

While he was President, John F. Kennedy reportedly once told a caller, "I agree with you, but I don't know if the government will." Whether true or not, Kennedy's remark illustrates a difficulty that has challenged modern Presidents: Should the President control the bureaucracy? And if so, how?

Clinton Rossiter speculated 20 years ago in *The American Presidency* that many a President would consider his hardest job was ". . . not to persuade Congress to support a policy dear to his political heart, but to persuade the pertinent bureau or agency—even when headed by men of his own choosing—to follow his direction faithfully and transform the shadow of the policy into the substance of the program." A number of modern Presidents have wrestled with this problem with varied motives, diverse strategies, and mixed results. The Budget and Accounting Act of 1921, the Brownlow Committee of 1936-37, and a succession of Presidential committees and task forces on executive management have all been part of their effort to give specific meaning to the general statement in Article II, Section 1, of the Constitution that "the Executive power shall be vested in a President of the United States of America."

Among recent Presidents, Richard M. Nixon stands out for the typically intense and—for a President—reasonably systematic attention that he gave to this problem. Before the fall, Nixon had devised an elaborate plan for Presidential control over the domestic bureaucracy for his second term—a strategy that can be called the "Administrative Presidency."

FROM OPERATIONS TO POLICY

The idea that the President *should* manage the bureaucracy has long been favored by public administration experts. Franklin D. Roosevelt's Brownlow Committee emphasized the strong executive—in the Hamiltonian model—as the unique contribution of the Founding Fathers. "Those who waver at the sight of needed power," the Committee said, "are false friends of modern democracy. Strong executive leadership is essential to democratic government."

This classical public administration position, now dismissed by some as naive and outdated, has been replaced in the literature for many contemporary students of the Presidency by the more pessimistic interpretation offered by Richard Neustadt. Corresponding with Kennedy's statement quoted above, Neustadt's view downgrades the President's ability to be the chief executive of the bureaucracy: He can persuade and he can dramatize, but he cannot run the show—or at least it is very difficult for him to try to do so.

Another view of the President's relationship to the bureaucracy that has gained momentum since Watergate embodies the concept of "participatory bureaucracy," a sort of "moveable feast" of power rather than the traditional hierarchial model. This is what might be called the "democracy-inside-of-technocracy" theory, or the "blow-the-whistle" code of bureaucratic behavior, in which the President's role is commensurately downgraded. According to this view, the career official should provide not just competent staff work, but also his judgments concerning the right decisions and proper course of action for his agency and program area, about which he presumably has much more expertise than his political superiors.

What is significant about Nixon's idea for an "Administrative Presidency"—an idea shared by his Advisory Council on Executive Organization, headed by Roy L. Ash—is that it was clearly based on the traditional public administration model. Toward the close of his first term, Nixon increasingly came to believe that the President *should* manage, that as the chief elected official of the nation, he had every right—indeed, had a responsibility—to adopt measures that would have the federal bureaucracy carry out his policy preferences. To do so, there were essentially two courses of action available to the President: relying upon strong, Presidentially-appointed domestic-program managers assigned to various executive agencies, or working through the White House and Executive Office staffs to see to it that the President's policy preferences were put into effect. From time to time, the Nixon Administration considered adopting—and, in fact, eventually did adopt—both strategies, only to come to the conclusion at the end of the first term that they could not be pursued together: Strong agency managers, closely tied to the President, are bound to have difficulty functioning effectively if a powerful White House staff is monitoring their every move. The President had to make a choice; Nixon decided to go with strong agency managers as his second term got underway in 1973.

Reduced to its essentials, his plan involved putting his own trusted appointees in positions to manage directly key elements of the bureaucracy without elaborate White House or Executive Office machinery to encumber their efforts. New appointees for the Nixon second term would be arranged so that there would be clear lines of authority. The bureaucracy would report to them; they would be held accountable.

This plan for an "Administrative Presidency" helps to explain Nixon's entire domestic policy. The roots of this plan were in the experience of the first term. The President and John D. Ehrlichman, his chief domestic advisor, came to the conclusion sometime in late 1971 or early 1972 that, in most areas of domestic affairs, operations constitute policy. Much of the day-to-day management of domestic programs—regulation writing, grant approval, personnel deployment, agency organization and reorganization, program oversight, and budget apportionment—can involve high-level policy-making. Getting control over these processes was the aim of the President's strategy; and, judged against the lack of legislative success on domestic issues in the first term, there are grounds for concluding that this was a rational objective. Among Nixon's various domestic proposals, only revenue sharing cleared Congress in his first term, despite the fact that Nixon had advocated from 1969 through 1971 a wide-ranging legislative agenda for domestic affairs—revenue sharing, welfare reform, health insurance, and block grants for manpower, community development, education, and transportation. In this setting of legislative non-achievement, there are grounds for concluding that a conservative/centrist President facing a considerably more liberal Congress was well-advised to eschew legislative action and concentrate instead on administrative measures.

Existing domestic legislation, typically leaving many decisions to administrative discretion, offers an experienced President wide-ranging opportunities for managerial initiatives as an alternative to seeking Congressional action. But again, a President cannot have it both ways. If he does opt for an energetic managerial strategy, there are sure to be instances where the Congress will dig in and resist legislative initiatives he puts forward; as a result, prospects for his legislative program will be reduced.

PRESIDENT VERSUS BUREAUCRAT

The strong management strategy, set in motion in 1973, was to be implemented by a new set of Cabinet and sub-Cabinet officials, along with a corresponding deemphasis of major domestic legislative initiatives. Nixon and Ehrlichman were no doubt aware of the problems they faced in carrying out this plan. At the same time that the experience of the first term indicated the pitfalls of legislative initiatives, White House aides frequently warned of an uncooperative—even unfriendly—domestic bureaucracy. According to Hugh Heclo, writing in *The Public Interest,* No. 38 (Winter 1975), the Nixon Administration's view was that it "faced not only an opposition Congress but also an opposition executive, a collection of agencies and departments with a vested interest in the ways of the past." A study forthcoming in *The American Political Science Review* bears out this interpretation. In 1970, Joel D. Aberbach and Bert A. Rockman interviewed 126 supergrade-level administrators of federal domestic programs and found them "ideologically hostile" to the domestic policies of the Nixon Administration:

> Our findings document a career bureaucracy with very little Republican representation but most pointedly picture a social service bureaucracy dominated by administrators ideologically hostile to many of the directions of the Nixon Administration in the realm of social policy.

Concern about bureaucratic subterfuge, widespread among White House aides at this time, was often expressed in situations where less partial observers would have judged the Administration's intentions to be so unclear that agency officials could not have been expected even to know what the President wanted. It was common, nevertheless, for Nixon staffers at White House meetings to discuss at length cases where program managers, without authorization, went to the Congress to plead for help in reversing Administration decisions or attended meetings of interest groups around the country to drum up support for their subversive activities. Close ties between executive branch agencies and Members of the Congress often made it possible for agencies to resist White House policies.

A remark by a White House aide, quoted in *The Wall Street Journal* (June 21, 1971), summed up the attitude of the Nixon staff members toward the bureaucracy:

> President Nixon doesn't run the bureaucracy; the civil service and the unions do. It took him three years to find out what was going on in the bureaucracy. And God forbid if any President is defeated after the first term, because then the bureaucracy has another three years to play games with the next President.

Even Nixon's own Cabinet and sub-Cabinet officials were portrayed by Nixon's aides in White House strategy sessions as too easily tempted by the lures and snares of the permanent bureaucracy. Late in 1972, Ehrlichman remarked in his often acerbic way that after Cabinet and sub-Cabinet officials were appointed, they were only seen at Christmas parties: "They go off and marry the natives."

Observing this tendency for Nixon appointees to "go native," one agency official, a political appointee and former Republican Congressional staffer, developed in this period his own law of bureaucratic decision making. He noted: *"No decision in government is made only once"*—if at first you don't get your way, keep trying, reopen the question, try another channel, use a different approach. In large agencies, there are sure to be many opportunities for locating a political—that is, appointed—official whose vantage point (Congressional relations, public relations, the budget, substantive concerns, or policy analysis) is such that he will be willing to go back to the Secretary, to the Office of Management and Budget (OMB), or to the White House in an effort to overturn or change a given policy decision.

On occasion, Nixon officials would visit the office of a Congressional committee to explain an Administration legislative proposal, only to be told that the committee had already been briefed by career agency officials known to have reservations about the Administration's plans. This led to the establishment in the Department of Health, Education, and Welfare (HEW) of a system of chaperones to accompany career officials on visits to Capitol Hill, along with a clearance system for all such outings. (An indignant response from Senate Finance Committee Chairman Russell B. Long, however, resulted in the demise of HEW's chaperonage plan.)

NEW TEAM, NEW STRATEGY

Nixon unveiled his strategy for an "Administrative Presidency" on the morning after his reelection. At a hastily called meeting, he told Cabinet members and their chief subordinates that they should submit their resignations immediately. The instruction was given in a spirit very different from the *pro forma* manner of the past; it was clear that a new team would be named for the second term. One of their essential tasks would be to take charge of the domestic bureaucracies. Key members of Nixon's new team were James T. Lynn at Housing and Urban Development, Caspar W. Weinberger at HEW, Earl L. Butz at Agriculture, along with a second line of sub-Cabinet officials, primarily made up of former White House aides with close ties to Ehrlichman. The new team was to *take on* the Congress and *take over* the bureaucracy. New legislation would be eschewed in deference to this administrative strategy. A system of "Super-Secretaries" was established—Lynn for Community Development, Weinberger for Human Resources, Butz for Natural Resources, and George P. Shultz (then Secretary of the Treasury) for Economic Affairs. The White House staff, which Nixon complained had grown "like Topsy" in his first term, was to be pared down. Haldeman, Ehrlichman, Henry Kissinger, Ash (the new Director of the Budget), and Shultz (doubling as a White House aide for economic affairs) were to be the "starting five" among White House assistants. Other Executive Office personnel would be cut so that the trusted lieutenants appointed as agency heads could have frequent and direct access to the President and these chief aides.

It is ironic that, in the midst of Watergate, this decision in favor of strong, loyalist Cabinet and sub-Cabinet officials appeared to involve a deliberate attempt to reduce the power and importance of the White House staff. It may be that there was such a connection in the President's mind. However, there was not even a clue at the time that this was so. To the contrary, it was Haldeman and Ehrlichman who emerged at the top of the new structure, and it was quite clear, as noted earlier, that Ehrlichman was the principal architect of the new plan, which had four principal facets.

1. *Personnel shifts:* The balanced Cabinet, customary in American politics, which Nixon himself had relied on in his first term, was dropped. A new Cabinet and sub-Cabinet of lesser luminaries was largely in place when the tide of Watergate crested and the "Administrative Presidency" strategy, together with other plans for the second term, had to be put aside. Commenting on Nixon's decision to retool the Cabinet and put trusted lieutenants in the top agency posts, *New York Times* reporter John Herbers contrasted the independent, national political figures in Nixon's first-term Cabinet with the new breed of the second: "But now high posts, with rare exceptions, are held by little-known Nixon loyalists who can be dismissed or transferred at will without creating a ripple in public opinion" (March 6, 1973).[1] The personnel shifts involved not only Cabinet and sub-Cabinet officials and appointed agency heads, but many other top policy posts as well. Within their new agency homes, it was expected that Nixon's new team would also redeploy career program managers, selecting the most cooperative, sympathetic, and talented officials for top posts.

2. *Budget impoundments and reductions:* President Nixon's budget for fiscal year 1974 (submitted in January 1973) involved the strong use of fiscal powers as an essential part of his new management strategy. Few more direct ways could be

imagined to take on the bureaucracy. Whole programs were to be stopped by impoundment. Important constitutional issues were raised by these decisions: Can a President use his executive authority to curtail or nullify programs that the Congress had previously enacted? The courts eventually had something to say about these executive actions, but in the early months of 1973 these and other such aggressive uses of fiscal tactics appeared to be immensely powerful.

3. *Reorganization:* The third element of the "Administrative Presidency" was the use of reorganization powers to give the President's trusted lieutenants authority and leverage to act. In some cases, whole activities were reorganized out of existence, and in others, there were significant changes in reporting relationships. An example of the former was the attempt to abolish the Office of Economic Opportunity (OEO) in early 1973. Although OEO was established in the Executive Office under Lyndon Johnson, it was not anticipated at the time that a future President would have greater authority over OEO than over other agencies. But instead of following the procedure of the formal Reorganization Act (whereby the Congress has 60 days to disapprove an organizational change), President Nixon's lawyers argued that since OEO was within the Executive Office, the President alone controlled its fate. With this rationale, in 1973 Nixon assigned as the new director of OEO a young conservative, Howard Phillips, an assistant director of OEO and formerly president of the Young Americans for Freedom. The President stipulated that when Phillips had completed his task of dismantling OEO, in part by devolving its functions to other agencies, he would be assigned some other post. Phillips' exuberance in his new task appeared to exceed even White House expectations: In one statement, he was quoted as saying he would do his job so rapidly, before Congress had a chance to react, that no one would be able to put "Humpty-Dumpty" together again. In a more restrained fashion, the special offices in the White House for Consumer Affairs and Science and Technology were devolved to new agency homes and eliminated as Executive Office units. The establishment of the "Super-Secretaries" also constituted an important use of reorganization as a tool for the President to get a firmer hold over the machinery of domestic government.

According to the new "game plan," the reorganization approach was not to be limited to the Executive Office and the Cabinet: Within their respective agencies, Nixon's new appointees were expected to take advantage of opportunities to rearrange their agencies in ways that would enable them to obtain stronger managerial control.

4. *Regulation:* The fourth component of the "Administrative Presidency" was regulation-writing—another exercise of federal authority that had not been thought of in the past as a method by which a President could achieve major policy goals. Two illustrations of how this authority could be used were revealed in conjunction with the federal budget for fiscal year 1974. In the field of social services (where this tactic eventually floundered because of strong Congressional opposition) new rules were issued early in 1973 that restricted the way in which funds to aid the poor through social services could be expended. The new rules, among other steps, required that these funds be used only for persons with specifically defined conditions of need, and then only under a system of detailed accounting for the services provided. Here the aim was to reduce the options available to social-work professionals, long subject to Administration disdain, and strongly entrenched in the welfare bureaucracy of HEW. On the other hand, in

the manpower field, the regulatory power was to be used not to introduce federal government controls, but to reduce them. The aim in this case was to decentralize by implementing Nixon's plan for manpower special revenue sharing through administrative action in the form of changed regulations under existing statutory authority.

Although in retrospect these four elements of the "Administrative Presidency" fit together in a fairly neat package, it is not likely that anyone in the White House systematically identified and defined this framework in preparing for the second term. In any event, it was all for naught: On April 30, 1973, John Ehrlichman, the driving force behind these various measures, was gone. Soon, too, the designations of the "Super-Secretaries" were removed. As the new White House staff was assembled in the late spring and summer of 1973, it came into being in a far different setting. The mandate of 1972 had dissipated, and decisive action, including unnecessary fights with program bureaucracies and Congressional committees, could not now be undertaken. General Alexander Haig, Jr., as Haldeman's successor, called for "an open Presidency" with activist, independent roles for Cabinet officers. The wheel had turned a full revolution.

MANAGEMENT AS POLICY

It must be emphasized that the abortive "Administrative Presidency" strategy for Nixon's second term was much more than a managerial plan: It was closely tailored to the President's policy ideas. The two main elements of the "New Federalism" agenda, which Nixon had advanced in August 1969, were welfare reform and revenue sharing. Both moved away from the "Great Society" approach of attempting to solve a wide range of social problems by establishing new programs and agencies of the federal government. Instead, the aim was to rely on the community through revenue-sharing programs, and on individuals through a welfare-reform strategy that provided welfare recipients with adequate resources so they could make their own decisions. In his White House Food Conference address, on December 2, 1969, Nixon said:

> The task for Government is not to make decisions for you or for anyone. The task of Government is to enable you to make decisions for yourselves. Not to see the truth of that statement is fundamentally to mistake the genius of democracy. We have made too many mistakes of this type—but no more. Our job is to get resources to people in need and then to let them run their own lives.

Both of these themes—localism and individualism—were closely in line with the anti-big-government, anti-bureaucracy mood of the 1970's.

Just as in physics, if the aim is to shift power, it is necessary to take it away from somewhere else. Nixon's advisers realized that they would have their hands full in attempting to assign more responsibility to state and local governments and individual citizens under his "New Federalism" domestic program, because these policy changes involved reducing the power of strongly entrenched bureaucracies of the national government. In short, having had only limited success with the legislative route to the "New Federalism" in his first term, Nixon decided in his second term to take on the bureaucracy directly, using the "Administrative Presidency" approach.

Although decentralization remained a major aim, it should be noted that Nixon's "New Federalism" domestic program frequently shifted in tone and content. In particular, the President's ardor for welfare reform cooled as the time for reelection neared. It dropped off completely following the controversy over George McGovern's "demogrant" plan in 1972. After the election, there was in addition an across-the-board shift to the right in the President's budget and related messages for 1973.

The post-Watergate notion of the "Imperial Presidency" and similar views warning of the dangers of a strong Presidency caution against any attempt, such as Nixon's, to have the President be a strong manager. Yet Franklin D. Roosevelt sought similar goals, and many students of the Presidency credit him for doing so. In the present day, there are good arguments to the effect that we need a force to counter strongly entrenched bureaucracies and interest groups. In *The End of Liberalism,* Theodore J. Lowi warns against just such a concentration of power in centers of technical expertise that are not subject to the give-and-take of democratic political processes.

In addition to such theoretical concerns about the power of bureaucracies, the memoirs of public officials offer abundant examples of the frustrations involved in challenging the functional fiefdoms of Washington. There is reason to think that managerial tasks are harder to perform in Washington than at other levels of our political system. Political appointees with state and local experience frequently commented during the Nixon years that they found it more difficult to tackle Washington bureaucracies than those at the state level, which tended to be more responsive to policy decisions by political officials.

The essential question is whether we need to have more and stronger checks and balances *within* the federal executive branch. Nixon's notion that the only way to take on the bureaucracy was to assemble like-minded political appointees strongly committed to his program and policy ideas raises questions of political behavior similar to those raised by Watergate. In the case of Watergate, like-minded associates, strongly devoted to the President, developed a warped and unbalanced perspective where excesses reinforced and fed upon each other. The result was catastrophic for Nixon and for the country. Would this same behavior have occurred in the area of domestic policy if the "Administrative Presidency" had been played out in the absence of Watergate? Would the orientation of Nixon's trusted lieutenants for domestic affairs have caused men to yield to the same temptation to put ends before means? Or would our traditions of public service have been sufficient in these substantive policy areas to assure responsible conduct?

It must be remembered that the key figures of the "Administrative Presidency" were men of character and ability, untainted by Watergate (with one exception, Ehrlichman). George Shultz (economic policy), Caspar Weinberger (human resources), Earl Butz (natural resources), and James Lynn (community development) are all men of centrist or moderately conservative views who, in one capacity or another, have proved themselves to be skillful public-policy managers. It was in the campaign arena, not in the arena of domestic policy, that Nixon's choice of unprincipled subordinates produced his ultimate crisis.

The intriguing question whether the "Administrative Presidency" could have succeeded in the absence of Watergate may not be answered for a long time. For Watergate has had a deep impact on political morality in the United States. With a new and heightened concern for political ethics, it is possible that a President with a coherent program could organize his administration to navigate a course similar to Nixon's plan but, at the same time, adhere to high standards of public service and personal conduct. Yet Watergate may have made the "Administrative Presidency" impossible for some time. Its aftertaste will no doubt discourage a future President from soon again attempting this kind of a domestic strategy; such a firm grabbing of the reins with an emphasis on administrative accomplishment may now be unacceptable. If the domestic bureaucracies have acquired too much power, a solution in terms of a Presidential strategy may now be very hard to implement. Clearly, President Ford is not disposed, or does not seem to be disposed, in this direction.

FORD AND THE FUTURE

By the time of Nixon's departure, much of the "New Federalism" agenda was in place.[2] It might be argued that President Ford, who appears to hold to a philosophy of domestic policy similar to Nixon's, could have advanced goals closely in line with the "New Federalism" without adopting a management plan specifically designed to do so.

Ford's domestic strategy initially involved a shift back to the traditional concept of a balanced Cabinet. He named to the Cabinet a group of distinguished citizens—some of whom he had not previously known—who apparently were selected without much concern for their political or philosophical orientation. As of this writing, the Ford Cabinet for domestic affairs consists of a Southerner at HEW (a Democrat, considered by many a liberal), a woman at HUD (also with an essentially liberal track record), a black at Transportation, a Harvard man at Labor, a Westerner at Interior. Balanced according to religion, sex, race, and region, the Ford Cabinet in many ways resembles Nixon's first Cabinet. Can such a group be loyal to the Administration's conservative, decentralist domestic policies? The answer in part depends on the importance which the President and his advisers attach to these objectives: Preoccupied with other tasks, the Ford White House has shown little disposition so far to highlight domestic affairs.

Nevertheless, there were signs in late 1975 that the new President, in international affairs at least, was learning the lessons of Nixon's experience—perhaps learning them all too well. Explaining his decision to fire Secretary of Defense James R. Schlesinger in November 1975, Ford said he wanted to avoid "growing tensions" in his Administration. "I need a feeling," said the President, "of comfort with an organization: no tension, complete cohesion." Hugh Sidey, writing in *Time* magazine (November 3, 1975), called attention to what he saw as the need for a stronger interest in management in the Ford White House. Although "Ford has repeatedly attacked the bureaucracy," said Sidey, his aides have made "no reliable assessments of how some of the huge Government programs are working." Noting that although Ford had promised to cut federal payrolls, they had increased during his 14-month tenure, Sidey urged that the President "come out from behind the microphone and grapple with the problem himself."

Others have argued that the Congress should give managerial direction to the federal bureaucracy. But even though we may decide that coherent management of the federal bureaucracy is needed, I do not believe that the Congress can fulfill this role. Its oversight role, however, in this area is an essential one.

Aaron Wildavsky has written, "The weakening of the Presidency is about as likely as the withering away of the state" (*The Public Interest,* No. 41, Fall 1975). There was, as might be expected, a strong tendency to think otherwise in the aftermath of Watergate. The long-held belief in the strong Presidency, favored by public-administration groups since the mid-1930's, was abandoned. In a report prepared in 1974 for the Ervin Committee of the United States Senate, a panel of the National Academy of Public Administration rejected the tactics being developed for the Nixon second term: "The federal executive is necessarily pluralistic." Although made up of the ideological descendants of the authors of the Brownlow and Hoover reports, the Academy panel, referring to Nixon's management strategy for his second term, breathed a sigh of relief that Watergate had stemmed the tide of Presidential power:

> The United States Government [under Nixon] would be run like a corporation—or at least a popular view of the corporate model—with all powers concentrated at the top and exercised through appointees in the President's office and loyal followers placed in crucial positions in the various agencies of the Executive Branch. . . . No one can guess how close the American government would be to this closed hierarchical model had not Watergate exposures halted the advance towards it—at least temporarily.

There were many who believed when Nixon resigned in 1974 that his plan for a managerial takeover of domestic government in his second term constituted a threat to our political system. Maybe so; but, as often happens after periods of great emotion, there is likely yet to be a revision of attitudes. When this happens, I predict that Nixon's strategy for his second term—not necessarily for *the* "Administrative Presidency," but for a *more* administrative Presidency in domestic affairs—will be seen to have raised basic questions for our political system. In more immediate terms, whoever is elected President in 1976, and whatever his major objectives for domestic affairs (decentralization, reduction of the bureaucracy, fiscal responsibility, full employment, equal opportunity), he would do well, at the outset of his term, to study carefully the President's role as Chief Executive.

THE MANAGERIAL AGENDA

Assuming the next President is so disposed, the key to the establishment of some measure of managerial control over the executive establishment is in one word—*appointments.* The predominant tradition in American government is for a new administration to name a balanced Cabinet, to use this first step for binding and healing, selecting men and women who represent the various streams of opinion, regions, and races that the new President wishes to have represented on his team. Unfortunately, this honeymoon mood often exceeds real prospects for political harmony. As a result, it can exacerbate the normal adversarial relationship between the President and his Cabinet.

Despite the fact that this adversarial relationship is built into our system, the essential point is that it can be ameliorated by naming sympathetic men and women to Cabinet and sub-Cabinet posts, appointees clearly pointed in the same policy direction as the new President in their assigned areas of responsibility. Only with such persons can the President hope to get a handle on running the government. Unless his top appointees share his substantive goals, the normal politics of Washington mitigate strongly against even a semblance of managerial cohesion in government. Managerial experience and interests are additional important qualifications, but basic substantive agreement is the essential ingredient.

If this diagnosis is correct, the next President (unless it is Gerald Ford) will not have time to learn in the caldron of Presidential experience. Once the wrong Cabinet is appointed, the managerial agenda becomes unfeasible. This is the lesson of Nixon's Watergate-aborted "Administrative Presidency."

To conclude, I believe a managerial strategy or emphasis is appropriate for the American Presidency. Even if we assume that the next President is successful in establishing some measure of managerial cohesion and control over the federal bureaucracy, there still exist an abundance of ways in which his power in this area and in others can be checked and balanced. It can be argued, in fact, that a managerial emphasis on the part of the President enhances popular control, given the tendency of industrialized states to become increasingly controlled from bureaucratic and technocratic power centers. The exercise of a greater measure of civilian control over the Executive branch of the American national government—properly reflective of legal and Constitutional requirements—is fully consistent with democratic values.

NOTES

1. From Nixon's original Cabinet, all had exited but Shultz. Among the more prominent and outspoken members of the original group for the domestic agencies were George Romney at HUD, John Volpe at Transportation, Walter Hickel at Interior, and Robert Finch at HEW (whose outspokenness was somewhat of a surprise to his mentor).
2. General revenue-sharing, and block grants for manpower and community development. Enactment of the latter two measures, in 1973 and 1974 respectively, came as something of a surprise to most Nixon Administration domestic strategists.

Managing the State

MARTHA WAGNER WEINBERG

In the common parlance of politics, the descriptions of chief executives as "managers" and as "leaders of large organizations" often are used interchangeably. In fact they imply quite different things. All governors have to perform certain management functions, but they perform these functions according to their own preferences and styles. Just as it is important to identify what the management functions are that they perform, it is also necessary to understand the dimensions along which they vary in carrying them out and the kinds of choices they make that determine their individual styles of leadership.

Leadership in any large organization is a highly personalized commodity. Implicit in any definition of leadership is some notion of uniqueness of style or attributes that distinguish and identify both the leader and those who are led. Every governor develops his own leadership style. This style does not depend as much on the formal powers that he has or on the number of orders that he gives as it does on how he chooses to spend his time, what resources he uses, and whose advice and pleas for support he heeds.

Understanding the kinds of variation in gubernatorial leadership style is essential to drawing conclusions about the overall effectiveness of a chief executive's management and about how he compares with other chief executives. How he chooses to use his resources in managing agencies and how many of these resources he chooses to devote to management may be a legitimate criterion for judging his performance. In addition, a governor's leadership style may be important in defining the nature of his relationship with agencies. The mesh or clash between his style and the particular style of the agency with which he is dealing may be as important as the substance of policies he espouses in determining his success or failure at controlling the agency's behavior.

This chapter will look at how [Massachusetts Governor Francis] Sargent's own leadership style and the choices he made affected his management of state government. Sargent's relationship to the agencies was often directly influenced by the obligations he had as governor, by how management issues got on his agenda, and by how he used the resources available to him. By looking at these questions it is possible to understand not only some of the determinants of Sargent's own particular style of management but also some of the dimensions along which all chief executives may vary in their personal leadership styles.

HOW DO THE OTHER ROLES THAT A GOVERNOR HAS TO PLAY AFFECT HIS JOB AS MANAGER?

A governor, even if he wants to, cannot manage all the time. The extent to which he is able to spend time and energy managing his agencies is dependent on the other functions he has to perform and on their importance to him. Perhaps the most significant thing that can be said about Francis Sargent in this respect is that he did not especially enjoy the detailed work of agency management and therefore did not accord it a favored position among his duties. His job as "manager of the bureaucracy" and the demands it imposed on him for his time, attention, and resources had to be balanced against other demands. His own preference to stay clear of the particulars of agency management was reinforced by the fact that his ability to appear a credible manager was heavily dependent on his success at building resources and power in performing his other functions. This was especially true of his ability to remain a successful political figure because his legitimacy as an elected executive depended on his maintaining, or appearing to maintain, electoral support. It is therefore worthwhile to look briefly at the other roles Sargent had to perform and at the importance and attention he accorded them.

An analysis of Sargent's calendar indicates that he spent well over half of his time performing what generally might be labeled the "ceremonial" functions of the governor.[1] These include proclamation signings, swearing-in of public officials, and, especially, large numbers of public appearances. Appearances at ceremonial occasions are intimately tied to any ongoing campaigning a governor does and are often his best way of staying in the public eye. In Sargent's case, the jobs of ceremonial head of government and of campaigner were especially tightly linked and took large amounts of his time. There were two primary reasons for this. First, he was an ebullient and skilled campaigner who enjoyed public appearances. Unlike many governors who neither relish the role of ceremonial head of the government nor perform it with polish, Sargent thrived on it. In addition, to a large extent the Sargent political organization revolved around him personally. Although he is a Republican, Sargent's relationship with the state Republican party was strained to the point of involving Sargent in public disputes with the Massachusetts party leadership. The Republican state committee regarded him with suspicion because of his liberal policies, his appointment of many Democrats to positions in his administration, his refusal to back unilaterally all party candidates, and his lukewarm response to the candidacy of Richard Nixon and Spiro Agnew. Sargent, in turn, did not rely heavily on the state Republican party organization but instead built "Governor Sargent Committees" in each county in the state. Although several times he attempted to purge the Republican State Committee of his opponents, he relied on his own organization to attract the Independents and Democrats whom he needed to survive in Massachusetts, where a large majority of registered voters are Democrats and Independents. His organization was personally based, so public appearances were extremely important to his money-raising and general campaign efforts. Responding to these combined duties as ceremonial head of state, candidate, and head of his own electoral organization not only was more pleasant personally for him than spending time managing the agencies but also kept him out of his office and used up one of his most valuable resources, his own time.

Sargent's role as spokesman to other branches and levels of government did not greatly interest him or his staff, and consequently they devoted little time to it. Although any governor must deal with the legislature, for several reasons Sargent did not mobilize an especially effective or lively effort to do this. First, during the six years Sargent was governor the General Court of Massachusetts was overwhelmingly Democratic, and partisan resistance to Sargent programs and initiatives was steady. In addition even the Republican minority had no strong loyalty to Sargent as party leader and often balked at his initiatives. His chances of being able to work closely with such a legislature and at the same time appear to be a forceful executive were low. Instead, Sargent's strategy was often to avoid the costs of dealing with the General Court and to portray himself and his policies as the "victims" of a partisan and parochial legislature.

In addition to the fact that the setting for dealing with the legislature was not favorable to Sargent, he did not devote an enormous amount of time to it because his staff was neither especially interested in it nor especially talented at dealing with it. His legislative liaison was a pleasant and mild ex-legislator who had limited interest in or taste for lobbying and arm-twisting bills through the legislature. Sargent's staff kept no records of favors they had done for particular legislators and they made few attempts to change votes or to lobby on any issues except those that seemed within their grasp.

The governor's unwillingness to deal with the legislature can also be explained by the fact that neither the governor nor his staff members showed any particular fondness or respect for the legislature as an institution. Sargent had not served as a legislator. Two of his staff members (Kramer and Morrow) were former representatives, but when members of the governor's staff dealt with the legislature, they characteristically did so with a good deal of arrogance and in a manner that indicated they felt they were dealing from a superior position.[2] This combination of overwhelming partisan opposition and lack of staff interest and skill at dealing with the legislature meant that Sargent did not devote much time or energy to it. The importance of legislative support or opposition to agency budgets and policies also affected Sargent's ability to influence the outcomes of individual agencies' interactions and dealings with the legislature. This was true both in his enforcing his own policy preferences and in his preventing agency personnel from dealing directly with the legislature and paying little attention to him.

Sargent also took only a limited number of initiatives in dealing and cooperating with the state's other constitutional officers. Perhaps the main reason for this was that during the six years he was in office the other constitutional officers were Democrats. The job of attorney general has always been one potential stepping stone to the governor's office in Massachusetts. Sargent chose to ignore the attorney general as much as possible rather than to attempt to bargain or to joust with him over issues of concern to both of them. Attorney General Robert Quinn was not nearly so aloof from Sargent. He ran for governor in the Democratic primary in 1974, emphasizing in his campaign his investigations of the legality of many actions of Sargent's agencies.

Sargent did not devote much of his own time to dealing with other government jurisdictions, and he did not organize his staff so that the job fell naturally to any one of them. He had a representative in Washington who attempted to keep track of the Massachusetts congressional delegation and to serve as a liaison to large federal agencies, but his ties to the Nixon administration were neither strong nor close. As the Republican governor of the only state in the union in which Richard Nixon did not receive a majority of the popular vote cast in the 1972 election, he was not in a good bargaining position with the Nixon administration. He exacerbated his isolation from the national administration by being a spokesman for the liberal wings of the New England and national Republican governor's organizations, particularly on such issues as welfare, corrections, and the environment. In addition, he did not hold a prominent place in the hierarchy of the national Republican party. This meant that the little time he spent dealing with the federal government was as an advocate for a specific cause or as a supplicant, begging for funds.

The consequences for this for his management of the agencies were twofold. First, he had no easy or special access to federal monies to supplement state appropriations. Second, many of the agencies that built up special relationships with their federal counterparts did it without his help and therefore had access to funding and expertise that allowed them independence from him.

Sargent had no formal ongoing relationship or channel of communications with the cities and towns of Massachusetts, including Boston. Robert Wood argued in 1949 that the City of Boston and its problems are so influential for any governor of Massachusetts that "the organization of the executive branch is best discussed in terms of aids or deterrents to the governor's representation of the Boston interest."[3] The major movement of population to suburbs outside the Boston city limits made this not as true during the Sargent administration as it had been in 1949. But because of the overlap of government services as well as the location of the electorate in the state, cities in general and Boston in particular were important to Sargent. Despite this fact, however, neither the governor nor any staff person attempted to keep track of Boston's activities on a day-to-day basis or to work on a series of joint programs or policy plans. Kevin White, the mayor of Boston, had been Sargent's opponent in the 1970 gubernatorial campaign. Sargent kept himself informed of White's activities to the extent that they made him a potential rival and cooperated with him on issues on which both men could gain. However, neither in Sargent's own office nor in his administrative agencies was there a formalized liaison to the City of Boston. Kramer left his job as urban affairs advisor to become chief of the policy staff, and his old job was never filled. The major crises involving the City of Boston and other municipalities were handled on an issue-by-issue basis through informal channels of negotiation.

Sargent, like most other chief executives, devoted enormous amounts of time and personal resources to the duties of a governor that traditionally would not be regarded as "management." Most of his attention had to be directed to one primary objective: ensuring his political survival. Even when he "managed," he often did so because handling a crisis involving the agencies was important to his political future. Much of his ability to manage the agencies depended on his success at being able to perform these other roles credibly and to build up his resources with other institutions of government and with the electorate. These resources useful in managing the agencies could have been built up in a variety of different places with different results. Sargent's choice of investing his time primarily in his electoral organization, in campaigning, and in public appearances was the result both of his need to preserve his political constituency and of his own personal style.

For Sargent, the job of performing the managerial functions commonly associated with running a large organization often had to be forgone in favor of more pressing matters. If they were done at all, they had to be carried out by staff members or administrators in line agencies acting in behalf of the governor. The irony of this kind of management is that precisely because a political executive draws his legitimacy from being the single person elected to fill the job of governor, his managerial authority is difficult to delegate. Though Sargent supported his chief staff personnel in their policy decisions, there were many management issues on which he was legally and formally the final authority. Even if disputes were resolved or policies handled by virtue of his having delegated them to a staff member, he was often viewed as a weak executive by his agency personnel precisely because it was known that he had not made the final decision himself.

HOW DOES A MANAGEMENT ISSUE GET ON THE GOVERNOR'S AGENDA?

One important dimension along which governors differ is the importance they accord obligations other than management and the capital or leverage their performance of these obligations gives them in the political and administrative system. Equally important in understanding how chief executives manage and how they differ from each other is the question of how issues involving agencies get on their agendas in the first place. There is great variation among executives on this point. The way an issue gets on the governor's agenda and the extent to which a governor can control it may vary because of the differences in states. For example, one might speculate that a governor of a heavily populated, highly industrial state like Massachusetts or New York might have to spend more time dealing with issues put on his agenda by well-organized constituencies than the governor of a state like Wyoming or Idaho, where the population is less dense and where crises are likely to occur less frequently. In addition, how issues get on a chief executive's agenda may vary because of the style and interests of the person who holds the office. For example, in this respect Francis Sargent was extremely different from Richard Ogilvie of Illinois. Though both Sargent and Ogilvie were Republican governors of large industrial states, their agendas often consisted of very different kinds of issues. Ogilvie was fascinated by the question of how well the bureaucracy was working. He spent a great deal of time trying to measure the efficiency and effectiveness of agencies and working to improve the performance of large organizations he felt were not doing well. Sargent, on the other hand, when given a choice rarely put this kind of issue on the top of his agenda and, in fact, actively avoided working on questions of this kind as much as possible. Differences of this kind may indicate a good deal both about a particular governor's personal commitment and style and about the reasons for the autonomy or control with which individual agencies operate.

There are three distinctly different ways in which an issue can get on a chief executive's agenda. The first involves issues put on the agenda by the governor himself. A governor may take a firm stand on an issue or set of issues that he wants implemented, changed, or handled in the agencies because of his own personal commitment to them. The hallmark of the group of governors who might be labeled "activists" is the large number of these kinds of issues they publicly place on their agencies. This may involve overseeing a single set of issues during a limited period of time or it may involve a governor's "adoption" of a policy area or agency that becomes his pet project throughout his administration. In either case, he becomes closely identified with the management of this particular issue or agency because he has chosen it, because he has taken a strong stand on which his position is known from the outset, and because his own credibility is tied up with how it fares.

The second way a management issue may get onto the governor's agenda is if the public or some large group of the electorate puts it there. This kind of issue is similar in many ways to the first kind. Though the chief executive may not have been deeply involved with a particular department or agency, he must take a strong stand on the issue immediately because the electorate as a whole or some important segment of it may *see* him as responsible.[4] As on the first kind of issue, he becomes personally involved at the outset and his ability, real or perceived, to deal with the agencies involved and to convince or coerce them to respond to him becomes crucial. These are often "crisis" situations, such as a prison revolt or discovery of major fraud or errors in a welfare department. In instances of this sort, where his own credibility is at stake, his role as manager of the agencies may take on overwhelming importance and may force him to become intimately involved with the agencies. Even if one single issue is not important enough to determine his electoral future, the cumulative "box score" of how many issues with which he was closely identified he won or lost may become extremely important.

The third distinct kind of management issue that may get on the governor's agenda is different from the first two because of its visibility, its implications, and the demands that are made on the governor. These issues could be labeled "technocratic" or "bureaucratic" issues and are characterized by the fact that they first surface within the administrative agencies or because of a highly technical problem with which the agencies deal.[5] They may be the result of a clash between agencies over jurisdiction, method of operation, or allocation of scarce resources. They may involve highly technical issues that because of their complexity or because of the expertise required to understand them have little potential for arousing immediate public concern or public pressure. At least in its initial stage, this kind of issue may work its way up the administrative hierarchy to be dealt with by agency heads, commissioners, or division directors. Though the issue may become publicly visible, the individuals held responsible by those following the situation are likely to be administrators identified with one particular agency or substantive area of the bureaucracy. For example, a commissioner of public health may be perceived as the immediately responsible official in a controversy over whether a hospital should be allowed to expand. The first contact the governor's office has with such an issue is through a staff person. If the issue cannot be resolved, it may work its way up to the governor for a decision. Unlike issues on which he is personally involved, however, in this situation his major role is as mediator, not as advocate. His job is to be above the fray, to listen to arguments made by both staff and line personnel, and to hand down a decision. Although he may eventually end up with credit for such a policy or program, he does not involve himself initially either by visibly taking a strong stand or by going to war with or exerting strong pressure on the agency or agencies involved. In this situation, unlike those in which the governor is involved from the beginning, the advocates tend to be agency or staff personnel and it is their credibility, not the governor's, that is tied up with resolving or winning the issue.[6]

Technocratic issues are not immediately public, but a chief executive may sustain "losses" on them that may affect his ability to manage. He may become known for taking no initiatives at all on technical issues or for having an incompetent group of people working for him. Or he may "lose" because by deciding in favor of one advocate or another he may destroy the morale, effectiveness, or goodwill of a staff person or agency head who in day-to-day activities is supposed to speak for him. It is also possible to find out a good deal about the nature of the long-term strength and responsiveness of the relationship between the governor and any particular set of agencies by looking at whether the governor attempts to manage and maintain an interest in an agency only at a time when his personal credibility is at stake or whether he takes a more active interest in the day-to-day workings and activities of the agency.

Though it is possible to find individual examples of all three kinds of issues getting onto Sargent's agenda, it is clear that his own style and personal preferences dictated that most of the time he spent on management issues involved those he dealt with because he perceived a public demand that he manage or avert a crisis. When Sargent took office, he had no strong personal commitments to particular agency policies. His natural inclination was toward being a mediator rather than an activist, and this personal preference caused him to wait for technocratic issues to surface on their own rather than to rummage around the bureaucracy searching them out. Because his own and his staff's temperamental preferences were to deal with crisis issues, often resulting in the "crisis of the day" receiving enormous amounts of attention, most of Sargent's management effort was directed toward dealing with a few highly visible issues. The kinds of bureaucratic issues that had little potential for ballooning to crisis proportions often went unnoticed. Whether there was any initiative taken on them at all depended heavily on the strength and imagination of the staff person assigned responsibility for that functional area, of the cabinet secretary, or of agency personnel.

Policy areas in which the Sargent administration became known for taking initiatives included health regulation, environmental policy, provision of children's services, right to privacy legislation, transportation policy, "deinstitutionalization," welfare management, and correctional reform. Sargent took firm stands on environmental management, correctional reform, and deinstitutionalization after specific possibilities for policy in these areas were presented to him by his staff. He associated himself closely with bold policies in these areas and had to take an on-going interest in the agencies that dealt with them. When he had to fire his radical and highly controversial commissioner of corrections, John Boone, public response focused on the governor personally and on his ability to handle the situation. The issue became a crisis as well as a question of personal commitment for the governor and caused him to become intimately involved with the Department of Corrections.

The governor's initiatives in welfare made him equally visible and vulnerable. Like his concern over correctional issues, Sargent's interest in managing the welfare issue was the result not of a strong set of beliefs about welfare management but of the chronic sense of public dismay about the Department of Public Welfare. Sargent asked that the state assume control of the welfare system and made major administrative changes in department operations because of the system's high cost and because of the public's anger over the issue. He as governor was seen as responsible for the welfare issue, so he *had* to take initiative and *had* to familiarize himself with the department and with the most controversial of its policies.

Sargent's moratorium on highway building was not as clear cut a response to crisis, but it was a response to crisis just the same. His announcement of the highway moratorium was precipitated both by public outcry and by his having been persuaded by Kramer and a series of allies from a variety of anti-highway constituencies that the issue had reached crisis proportions.[7]

On all of these issues involving an immediate and highly visible position taken by the governor, control of the agencies involved became an important issue for the governor and his staff. These agencies were often closely scrutinized and constantly had broad (and sometimes strict) parameters of action laid down for them by someone close to the governor, if not by the governor himself. Their performance was closely watched, and commissioners or high-ranking agency personnel were removed from office or resigned at a far greater rate than those of other agencies.[8]

Some of the policy positions for which Sargent was known did *not* involve immediate action on his part initially but instead surfaced first at lower levels of the government. These included protection of the public from large-scale data gathering by government and limitation of access to data-gathering facilities, creation of an Office for Children to extend the state's network of children's services, and initiation of a strong health regulatory mechanism. These issues differed markedly from the crisis issues both in the governor's treatment of them and in the consequences of that treatment for the state's agencies. They involved problems that normally would have been considered "technicalities" of running a bureaucracy and as such might have escaped public notice indefinitely. They usually surfaced because of the particular preferences, interests, and talents of someone in an agency or a junior "functional specialist" on the governor's staff or a combination of both. For example, the emphasis on children's services (particularly on foster care and adoption) came from Elton Klebanoff, a lawyer who by adopting a child had become involved with the state's array of children's service agencies. Andrew Klein, who initiated the effort to block massive accumulation of data on individuals by the state and federal governments, had picked the issue as a non-threatening one with which to deal with the agencies for which he had been designated the governor's liaison and in order to focus his job beyond the amorphous assignment of being a special assistant for welfare, law enforcement, and public safety.

The staff member from the governor's office worked closely with agency personnel on each of these issues, providing support for and receiving support from the agency involved. Both Klebanoff and Stephen Weiner, the staff person most responsible for initiating the state's health regulatory legislation, made an effort to spend much time in the agencies assigned to them and based their opinions of what should be done more on the views of the personnel working in the agencies than on the guidance of the senior staff in the governor's office. The circumstances under which Weiner secured cooperation within the Executive Office of Human Services and the Department of Public Health were among the most fortuitous of any experienced by any functional specialist on the governor's staff. He knew the agencies and personnel involved in health regulation well and enjoyed the goodwill and confidence of the agency staffs. He began to work for the state at the same time that the secretariat's leading expert on health did, and he helped recruit and hire the commissioner of public health. He showed himself to be willing to work on the details of health regulatory policy and functioned at times as if he were a staff member of the agency. Finally, he enjoyed the confidence of both Kramer and the governor and was known in the governor's office as a person who asked for attention only when it was absolutely necessary.

The crisis orientation of Sargent's style was not without its costs, particularly as it affected the relationship between the governor and his agencies. There was intense competition among staff members and between staff members and agency personnel to provide a solution in a crisis. Because Sargent liked to hear all sides of an issue and then decide it, there tended to be losers and winners. Agency heads and agency personnel resented getting attention from the governor's office only in times of crisis, when they were often at their most disorganized. This style also promoted competition for the governor's time between the staff and the secretariats and agencies. The staff was concerned with and liked "managing crisis," even if the issue involved was simply the "crisis of the day." The agency and secretariat personnel, on the other hand, did not tend to see the major issues that concerned them as potential electoral crises for the governor but, rather, as issues that affected their working conditions and the capacity of the agencies to deal with policy. Finally, although there were some unspectacular policy initiatives on which agency personnel worked closely with members of the governor's staff, there was a certain randomness about these. They were highly dependent on whether anyone on the governor's staff was assigned to their agency and on the personality, talent, and personal preferences of the governor's staff member who was assigned.

WHAT MANAGEMENT RESOURCES DOES A GOVERNOR HAVE?

Having looked at variations in executive agendas, it is important to ask, once an item gets on a governor's agenda, what influences how it is managed and the success or failure of an executive's intervention? A governor's ability to manage a particular incident or to control an agency over a sustained period of time depends, more than on anything else, on the resources he is able to mobilize. Resources vary in kind and in importance. A resource is any identifiable set of goods, services, or skills that help someone reach a desired end. Political resources may be useful in only one situation or may be used continuously over a period of time. Political resources are often highly personalized—a resource for one political executive may not necessarily be a resource for another. For purposes of analysis, political resources important in management may be divided into three categories: personal resources, situational resources, and enabling resources.

Personal Resources

"Personal resources" include personal traits such as intelligence, humor, verbal facility, and personal political skill. They are the resources most difficult to generalize about because they are highly dependent on the individual manager's particular personality. Richard Neustadt has argued that the most important power a chief executive has is "the power to persuade," describing the chief executive's main task as "to induce them [those agencies with which he is dealing] to believe that what he wants of them is what their own appraisal of their own responsibilities requires them to do in their interest, not his."[9] One could argue that it is in exercising this "power to persuade" that personal resources are especially important, though difficult to identify or catalog from one situation to the next.

Sargent's personal appeal was considerable. Though he was not overwhelmingly articulate, even his detractors conceded that Sargent's charm and humor were among his strongest political assets. He was especially effective at using the media both in campaigns and during crises in his administration because of his ability to project a likeable, easy-going quality. For example, in his debates in 1970 with his Democratic rival for governor, Kevin White, the general consensus of the press was that though White had made his arguments more sharply and more articulately, Sargent had "won" the debates by appearing to be the nicer, more easy-going, less "political" of the two. The fact that he was not an "arm-twister" had both negative and positive implications for his ability to manage. He did not like "horsetrading" and bargaining with political favors, which meant that he did not exercise as much leverage with the legislature, other jurisdictions, his party, and even his own agencies as he might have. On the other hand, he was not negatively perceived as a "politician" who would sell his soul for a vote by either the other branches of the government or by the electorate in general.

Situational Resources

"Situational resources" are those highly diverse sources of help in managing particular situations that vary according to the particular combination of circumstances of an agency and the issues with which it deals. They are not constant in their value. For example, having a close and well-informed relationship with the chairman of the Committee on Ways and Means may be an extremely valuable resource for a governor when he wants to prevent cuts in the state's welfare budget, but it may not necessarily be a resource to him in attempting to pass a measure to change the process of judicial selection. Of all the kinds of resources a governor uses, situational resources are the most variable in their applicability and importance within any single administration. There are four especially salient kinds of situational resources: knowledge of the jurisdiction and of the political climate, technical expertise, clear authority, and the ability to define the management task or objective clearly. In dealing with one agency or situation he is trying to control, a governor may have to rely on his ability to manipulate and master only one of these resources; but in dealing with another situation, he may need to summon several or all of them.

Knowledge of the Jurisdiction and of the Political Climate. One resource that is important to any public manager, especially to a governor, is a detailed knowledge of the particular political environment in which he operates. For a governor whose jurisdiction is broad, this may involve detailed knowledge of the personalities and particular quirks of the other governmental institutions with which he has to deal. It also involves having enough experience to be able to identify key actors in any given political situation and to understand the composition and size of the pool of those politically talented or active in a given area. This kind of knowledge may be particularly important in making management decisions on issues with a long or controversial history or in selecting personnel for new jobs or to fill vacancies.

Sargent, like most governors, had spent most of his life in his native state, Massachusetts. Unlike many other governors, however, his career in Massachusetts government had been confined to jobs in the state bureaucracy in natural resources and public works and did not include service in the legislature, in any other constitutional offices, or in local government. He was familiar with the workings of two state agencies but not with the agencies of administrative oversight like the Executive Office of Administration and Finance. Although as governor he had to deal with a variety of governmental institutions, his only "apprenticeship" had been in an administrative agency. The result of this was that his knowledge of the important actors and of relevant information about the political process was largely confined to the general political climate of Massachusetts and did not include in-depth familiarity with or fondness for such institutions as the legislature or the lower levels of the bureaucracy.

Technical Expertise. Another crucial resource in any managerial situation may be technical expertise. Understanding a particular situation fully may require knowledge of one technical area. This may be especially crucial to a public manager at a level below that of the governor because the governor's responsibility is so broad that he could not possibly be an expert in all substantive areas falling under his jurisdiction. Even for a governor, however, technical expertise, or access to someone possessing that expertise who is also loyal to him, may be a crucial management resource. The resource of technical expertise may also involve knowledge of how highly complex general government functions such as personnel systems or resource allocation mechanisms work. It may include an understanding of certain techniques for operations research, capital budgeting, or accounting. On questions that are so highly technical that how the question is put and what choices are outlined may determine the answer, trusted technical expertise may be a crucial management resource.

Sargent was an architect by training and, except in the fields of natural resources and engineering, he had had no formal academic or management training in any of the highly technical fields for which he was responsible. Because he took great pains to recruit competent professionals for high-level government jobs, his access to trusted technical expertise in such areas as transportaion, housing, and welfare was good. His own grasp of the details of these particular areas or of the general complexities of administrative management such as budgeting or financial transactions was limited. His style of management was not to be a "details man." This meant that his access to the resources of technical expertise was not based on his own understanding of many issues, that it was highly dependent on the ability of his own appointees in those areas, and that it was extremely variable from one functional area to another.

Clear Authority. A third kind of situational resource is presence of clear authority. This authority may stem from the formal legal authority granted by the consitution or by law. It may also be informal and may be the result of a chief executive's ability to convince everyone that he is and should be in control of a situation or an agency. For an elected public manager such as the governor, this authority may come from an electoral victory widely interpreted as a "sweeping mandate." It may also come from the appearance of general support within agencies. In any case, the resource consists of being able to assume control of a situation in a context in which everyone involved believes that the governor has the legitimate right to do so.

The Massachusetts governor's formal authority is broad compared with that of governors in many other states.[10] The governor has a four-year term, can submit his own budget to the legislature, and can hire and fire his cabinet and most commissioners at will. Although Sargent submitted a budget to the legislature each year, he did not have the staff, the expertise, or the personal inclination to develop his budgetary power to be a significant resource and to use it as a mechanism to maintain day-to-day control over his agencies. He was less reluctant to use the power to hire and fire and to make it clear that he had the authority to do this.

Sargent was less adept at establishing his authority where there was no formal grant of power than he was at exercising his constitutional authority. Although he occasionally made policy by use of administrative fiat, he seldom used his budgetary power as a carrot or a stick in asserting his authority over the agencies. Similarly, he made little effort to use his legal staff to interpret agency statutes or regulations to give him leverage with the agencies. Finally, although he did often appeal directly to the electorate for support, very seldom did he use the argument that his decision should be final because of his popular mandate to govern.

Ability to Define the Management Task Clearly. A fourth situational resource that may be the most crucial in determining how well an executive is able to manage a problem is his ability to define the job to be accomplished in such a way that it is capable of being reduced to a clear, simple, straightforward task. Whether this resource is present or absent may depend on the governor's ability to reduce a highly complex management situation to be a single task or to define the task in such a way that this becomes possible. It may also depend on the nature of the task itself, which may be so complex that it cannot be simplified without being distorted out of proportion.

Because it varies so much from situation to situation and from agency to agency, it is difficult to generalize about Sargent's use of this resource during his administration. To define the task of the Divison of Employment Security ("to mail out unemployment checks'') is less difficult than to define the task of the Department of Public Welfare. However, it is true that Sargent's temperament and style did not lead him to want to set fixed goals, especially arbitrary ones, for agencies. He did not deal frequently enough or closely enough with the agencies so that he could constantly measure or evaluate their performance according to any definition of their tasks. This meant that he did not make the effort to state or to simplify the complex goals of most agencies and then to take credit or blame for their performances or failures based on those goals. This was especially true of those agencies whose tasks were difficult to define. Sargent was more likely to ignore these agencies than to insist that they meet any goals set by him.

Enabling Resources

A third set of resources on which any governor draws might be called "enabling resources." These resources are much less likely to vary within any executive's term of office than situational resources and often allow a governor to develop his situational resources. Perhaps the most important of these enabling resources is staff assistance.[11] Also included among these resources are funding for the governor's office, time, and easy access to information. Although these resources are not always separable from situational resources, what distinguishes them from other kinds of resources is that they are not as valuable in and of themselves as they are for *enabling* a governor to build up other kinds of resources. For example, a large and well-funded staff may not by virtue of its existence be valuable to a chief executive but may only become important when it is used to build up other resources. Like all political resources, enabling resources have no inherent value, and their importance depends on whether and how they are used.

Sargent was aided in developing some of the resources necessary to control the agencies by several factors. Compared with many other governors, he had a large, well-financed staff.[12] Perhaps the greatest single determinant of how he was or was not able to utilize resources to manage was the way he designed his staff, which in turn often determined the other resources to which he had the best access. Sargent recognized his own penchant for being a mediator and built into his staff a variety of political views. By ensuring representation of a variety of views along the political spectrum, he made it possible for agencies with extremely diverse interests and for groups outside the government to find allies on his staff. He had some functional policy specialists on his staff who were willing to work as closely with the agencies with which they dealt as with their peers in the governor's office and who knew a great deal about the resources and information necessary to make the agencies behave as they wished. In addition, Sargent received a special bonus by being able to appoint all ten of the first cabinet secretaries to take office. The secretaries were to be "deputy-governors," appointed by the governor to manage clusters of agencies in particular functional areas. By deciding what individuals he was going to appoint, he was able to shape the expectations of both the agencies and the public of what the job of secretary should be and at the same time command personal loyalty from the individuals who took the jobs because they were *his* appointees.

Although the way he constructed his staff and the style with which it operated provided him with access to one set of resources, it also had its costs. The fact that

he and his staff opted to concentrate most of their scarce resource of time on maintaining and polishing the governor's electoral image and on managing crises, coupled with the size of the job of running state agencies with a budget of more than
$2.5 billion, meant that his attempts at dealing with complicated day-to-day
issues were uneven. Particularly because he himself did not devote personal attention to agency matters, his "control" of the administration often depended on
the agility with which his staff was able to perform in the difficult "minister-
without-portfolio" role. They often had to speak "for the governor" in situations
about which the governor, and often the staff member, knew nothing. This difficult role was especially complicated in the Sargent administration for two
reasons. First, the incentives for any staff member to want to devote his time to
dealing with the big issues, the "crises," were powerful because those issues were
high on Sargent's own agenda. But the greater the competition to propose the solution to a crisis, and the more extremely and visibly a staff member stated his own
position, the less likely he was to be seen as "speaking for the governor" by the
agencies, especially if his solutions "lost" frequently. Second, not only did
Sargent create a large number of situations for ministers-without-portfolio, but he
also filled these positions, particularly those of "functional specialists," with
young inexperienced generalists. An agency that wished to be intractable could
mask what it was doing with technicalities and complexities totally unfamiliar to
the staff person with responsibility. Also, because few of the members of the governor's staff aspired to holding down their position after the governor was gone,
the agency personnel could count on simply outliving the generalists.

The secretaries and commissioners were appointed by the governor, but because
of the Sargent style of operating they were often pitted in deadly competition with
the governor's own staff. The staff, busy with dealing with the issue of the day,
had little time to focus on any but the most spectacular problems arising in the
agencies. The secretaries and commissioners, on the other hand, were hired as full-
time administrators and generally concerned themselves with issues different from
those with which the staff dealt. Though to a certain extent this meant that responsibility was divided and delegated, it led to bloody battles and extreme competition between the staff and the agencies when each had to compete for the
governor's time and attention or when the issue on which the governor had to
focus lay in the agencies themselves. Often this competition, coupled with the
governor's own reluctance to deal with the legislature, led some agency personnel
to negotiate directly with members of the legislature, end-running the governor.

The style and quality of gubernatorial leadership of public agencies varies from
governor to governor along several dimensions including the personal temperament of the chief executive, the kind of management he is called on to do, and
the resources he can mobilize. But even within one administration, gubernatorial
leadership and control can vary greatly from one agency to another. A governor's
control and an agency's responsiveness depend not only on conscious decisions on
the part of the governor but also on the nature of individual agencies. Different
kinds of agencies demand different kinds of management. It is useful briefly to
differentiate among kinds of agencies according to the kinds of circumstances in
which a governor may deal with them.

The typology of these agencies corresponds roughly to that used to describe how
particular issues get on a governor's agenda. Certain agencies require constant

scrutiny because the public perceives the issues with which they deal to be on the governor's agenda. Other agencies require constant scrutiny because the governor has dictated that the issues with which they deal be given priority. A third kind of agency receives a governor's attention only when it is responsible for a crisis issue. Finally, some agencies handle matters that seldom if ever get on the governor's agenda.

Those Agencies Requiring Constant Scrutiny

The agencies that demand constant scrutiny may vary from one state to another and from one governor to another, depending on the governor's priorities and his own personal style. These agencies are of two kinds. The first kind is one in which a crisis would be so spectacular or in which the cost of a malfunction would be so high that the governor under no circumstances could afford not to attempt to anticipate it. In Massachusetts, for example, despite the limitations under which he operated in dealing with the bureaucracy, Sargent had to be familiar with the Department of Public Welfare and the Department of Corrections.

The second kind of agency a chief executive must constantly watch differs subtly but significantly from the first kind. It is an agency that must be monitored because it involves such heavy commitment of state money or personnel or such well-organized interests that a problem can cause an outcry or a response from some important constituency or constituencies and, potentially, from the public as a whole. The response to an error or a crisis may not be as clearly immediate as that to the volatile first category, but it may be equally important, either because of the implications for the long-run service provided or because of the importance of the constitutencies involved. In Massachusetts one might cite the Department of Public Works or the Department of Public Health as examples of this second sort of agency. It is also important to point out that for these agencies in Massachusetts the more imminent the threat of crisis, the more likely it is that they will get the kind of attention that the agencies threatening constant spectacular crisis receive.

Those Agencies That Receive Constant Scrutiny Because of the Personal Preferences of the Governor

Some agencies receive attention not because of their size or importance or because they bristle with political bombshells but because the governor has some other interest in them. They may represent a substantive policy area in which he is interested or they may offer a particular resource on which he can capitalize, such as patronage jobs.

Francis Sargent came into office with no strong interest in how any one substantive area or agency of government ran. He was more interested in dealing with agencies on the basis of the seriousness of issues raised within their boundaries than in consistently following any agency or group of agencies that dealt with a substantive policy area of personal interest to him. Perhaps the closest he came to this sort of personal interest was his emphasis on the deinstitutionalization of persons in state facilities. However, he was not a governor like Paul Dever, a Massachusetts chief executive who during his term adopted mental health as his pet issue and chose to keep close track of the Department of Mental Health.

Those Agencies That Receive Gubernatorial Attention Because of a Single Crisis

Every governor has a series of agencies that he generally ignores but that may suddenly become very important because of an unanticipated crisis. For example, in Massachusetts, until the time of the controversy over whether or not to develop the large section of downtown Boston known as Park Plaza, the governor and his staff had no idea who worked in the Department of Community Affairs or what went on there. As a consequence, during the crisis they had to act quickly on the basis of very little previous knowledge of how the agency worked or who in the agency could handle some of the decisions that had to be made. The fact that an agency is the source of a crisis does not necessarily ensure that it can be "crisis-managed," especially if neither the governor nor his staff has invested any resources in it before.

Those Agencies the Governor Leaves Alone

Finally, there is always a series of agencies that a governor makes no effort to control and that he deals with in a limited way or ignores. These agencies fall into two categories: those he leaves alone because of some calculated consideration on his part and those he leaves alone because of the nature of the agencies themselves.

There are several reasons a governor may make a deliberate choice to ignore an agency. First, he may not attempt to exert control over an agency because it performs as he would like. He does not have to use his scarce resources to persuade its personnel to behave as he would like or to make policies he wants because the agency personnel share the chief executive's goals for the agency. During the Sargent administration, the Massachusetts Housing Finance Agency was an example of this kind of agency.

A governor also may not intervene because he realizes that he does not have the resources or the authority to control an agency and may therefore be unwilling to go to battle with it and lose. Even in what may normally be regarded as a crisis, he may hold back from dealing with the issue (as Sargent did, for example, on issues involving higher education in Massachusetts) because he may not be certain of appearing to "win." Or a governor may not deal with an agency because he wants it to be known publicly that he is not fully responsible or in control of that agency. For example, Sargent often made it known that he did not go to battle with the Massachusetts Port Authority because he had no legal control over it.

Finally, a governor may not deal with an agency at all purely because of the nature of the agency. The governor or his staff may see it as having no potential for crisis. For example, in Massachusetts, most governors have assumed that the Massachusetts Department of Agriculture is an agency of this type. An agency may also be left alone because of the highly technical nature of its work. Or it may be ignored because it serves easily identifiable, single, specialized goals. In Massachusetts during the Sargent administration the job of the Division of Employment Security was to send out checks for unemployment compensation, a procedure that varied little from one month to the next.

This chapter has looked at gubernatorial leadership and style and at the characteristics of and limitation on it that affect how the governor manages his agencies and holds them accountable. It has also examined the variation in the kinds of response a governor may make to these agencies and has attempted to explain some general reasons for this variation. . . .

NOTES

1. In order to find out how Sargent spent his time, I looked at his daily schedules, divided into fifteen-minute intervals, from 1970 until 1974. This analysis was obviously a rough one because often the calendar was changed at the last minute to meet a crisis and the issues considered at appointments with individuals or "staff time" often were not detailed. Still, over the period of four years, such an analysis of the calendar made it possible to arrive at a gross approximation of how the governor spent his time.
2. For documentation of two specific instances of this, see my papers on "Reorganization of Government: the Massachusetts Case" and "Correctional Reform in Massachusetts."
3. Robert Wood, "The Metropolitan Governor," p. 112.
4. Though the leadership styles of political leaders to a certain extent are the result of conscious choices by political executives, it is clear that the issues with which they deal and the style with which they deal with them are often heavily influenced by the publics that are important to them. Leadership style is not only the result of the executive's personal traits but also of his perceptions of public expectations. As Murray Edelman points out in *The Symbolic Uses of Politics* on p. 188:
   Through taking the roles of publics whose support they need, public officials achieve and maintain their positions of leadership. The official who correctly gauges the response of publics to his acts, speeches and gestures makes those behaviors significant symbols, evoking common meanings for his audience and for himself and so shaping his further actions as to reassure his public and in this sense "represents" them.
5. The term "technocratic politics" is Samuel H. Beer's, and much of the discussion that follows is based on a helpful conversation with him. The distinction between a "public" issue and a "technocratic" one is not always clear cut. The number of para-governmental groups in society makes it difficult to enforce this definition strictly. For example, technical advisors who work for government but who advise citizen groups may use their technical skills to clarify a public issue. However, the distinction is useful in trying to determine whether an issue reaches the governor's desk because of immediate public pressure or because it first surfaced within a technical elite and was "translated" into public business.
6. This is one of the points at which the distinction between a governor and his staff becomes obvious. In such a situation, when a staff person is operating as a "minister-without-portfolio" and/or as an advocate, he cannot sustain a large number of losses and still be closely identified as speaking for the governor.
7. For fine documentation of the whole highway moratorium incident, see Alan Lupo, Frank Colcord, and Edmund P. Fowler's *Rites of Way: The Politics of Transportation in Boston and the U.S. City.*
8. For example, the commissioner of public works, Edward Ribbs was fired in the middle of the highway crisis. Robert Ott was replaced by Steven Minter as commissioner of public welfare immediately before the initiation of the flat grant system in the Department of Public Welfare. John Fitzpatrick was replaced by John Boone as commissioner of corrections after the first major uprising at the Massachusetts Correctional Institution at Walpole. Boone was subsequently removed when the prisons continued to flare up.
9. Richard Neustadt, *Presidential Power,* p. 53. Although it is difficult to generalize about personal resources, most students of executive management of large organiza-

tions, both public and private, stress their importance. See, for example, James Sterling Young's *The Washington Community 1800-1828,* p. 157ff and Kenneth Andrews' *The Concept of Corporate Strategy,* p. 227ff.

10. For a comparative analysis of the limitations on gubernatorial power see Douglas Fox, *The Politics of City and State Bureaucracy* p. 26ff. It is important to note, however, that Thomas Dye has concluded that "there is little evidence that a governor's formal powers significantly affect policy outcomes in the fifty states." See Thomas Dye, "Executive Power and Public Policy in the United States" in Richard Leach and Timothy O'Rourke, eds., *Dimensions of State and Urban Policymaking,* p. 128.

11. For an excellent analysis of how several presidents arrayed and used their staffs and of the consequences for public policy, see Richard T. Johnson's "Management Styles of Three U.S Presidents." One of the points Johnson makes well is that there is no single "best" way to design a political staff, that each style has its costs and benefits.

12. Of all the governors or ex-governors attending the 1974 John F. Kennedy Institute of Politics seminar on "The Governor's Office"—including Hoff of Vermont, Peterson of New Hampshire, Holton of Virginia, Ogilvie of Illinois, and Evans of Washington—only Ogilvie had had a staff of comparable size.

4

THE LEGISLATURES, COURTS, AND THE BUREAUCRACY

In the wake of the Watergate scandals and nearly two decades of forceful presidents, Congress appears to be in the process of reasserting its policy-making authority. State and local legislatures are also challenging chief executives who have become more and more dominant in the American policy system.

Allen Schick analyzes the relationships between Congress and the federal bureaucracy. He points out the importance of "details" when congressional dealings are with the executive branch, and he surveys recent developments in this regard.

Attention to details is increasing at the state level as well. State Senator Richard Marvel and his associates from Nebraska next present their approach to this issue in an area with which we all have some familiarity—higher education. Even in this difficult policy area, the experience described in Nebraska is increasingly discernible in other state and local legislative bodies throughout the country, albeit in a variety of forms.

The American constitutional tradition also emphasizes judicial review and control of bureaucratic power. Courts are increasingly involved in review of administrative action (after administrative remedies have been exhausted), assuring due process and providing a point of access in the policy-making system for disadvantaged groups. Roger Cramton looks at prevailing trends in the link between the courts and public agencies and concludes with a discussion of the long-term effects of this relationship.

Congress and the "Details" of Administration

ALLEN SCHICK

A former President once wrote of Congress: "it has entered more and more into the details of administration until it has virtually taken into its own all the substantial powers of government."[1] This protest was not composed by a recent President railing against the renascent assertiveness of Congress in the post Vietnam-Watergate era. It was written by Woodrow Wilson in 1885, almost 30 years before he attained the presidency,[2] and only two years before the publication of his influential essay "The Study of Administration" which demarked public administration as an activity and discipline separate from politics.

There is a certain ambivalence in Wilson's complaint, one which has persisted through 200 years of American government and which helps to account for disparities in legislative and executive views about control of administration. Wilson refers to the "details of administration" as if these everyday matters were unworthy of legislative attention. Congress, the phrase suggests, should not be distracted from the big and important affairs of state by the minutiae of public administration. But Wilson clearly recognizes that control of these very details of administration could give Congress "all the substantial powers of government." Administration, Wilson implies, is the source of power in modern governments; hence, control of administration means control of the government. This view of administration and statecraft dominated his 1887 essay.[3]

Throughout American history, the Executive Branch has tended to advance the first interpretation while intending the second. (Nobody bothered to explain why, if administration is indeed merely a matter of details, executives should be concerned by legislative intrusions.) For its part, Congress has instinctively realized that loss of the details would diminish its political role. It is not that every small detail brings big power, but that the accumulated loss of control over administrative details unquestionably aggrandizes executive power at the expense of Congress. From the perspective of administrative reform, this has not been an unintended or unwanted outcome. There was no place for Congress in the new discipline of public administration, nor has Congress been given much attention in the subsequent development of the field. Hyneman's *Bureaucracy in a Democracy* is a distinguished (and still relevant) exception,[4] but "if we simply assume that public administration is what students of public administration study, the executive is clearly the solid center of their special concern."[5] For 100 years, American public administration has functioned in the service of executive power, an arrangement that has accommodated this discipline to the realities of American politics.

THE QUIESCENCE OF CONGRESS

The Wilsonian division of government labor (and power) has had its ups and downs in the course of American history. At the start, as Leonard White noted in his administrative history of the United States, the Federalists sought a national government "which left substantial freedom of action to high officials and kept Congress out of most administrative details."[6] This preference for executive power was successfully challenged by the Jeffersonians who "were more energetic in their effort to control administration than had been their predecessors. . . . They emphasized the responsibility of the executive branch and the administrative system to Congress."[7] The Legislative Branch generally was dominant through most of the 19th century (wartime was an exception), though the particular control exercised by Congress over administration varied with changes in the presidency. Congress fashioned a variety of controls over administration centered, as Wilson protested, in its increasingly specialized and powerful committee system.

The trend began to change, however, shortly after Wilson wrote, about the time that public administration was emerging as a distinct and important discipline. War, economic expansion, and a host of other influences (including public administration itself) bolstered the claim for administrative independence from detailed legislative control. But the dominant factor was the huge expansion of the national government and its administrative structure. During the half century between 1871 and 1921, civilian employment in the Executive Branch multiplied elevenfold, from 50,000 to 550,000; during the same period, federal expenditures soared from $292 million to more than $5 billion, although they dropped to about $3 billion later in that decade. Big government weakened the ability of Congress to govern by controlling the details and it vested administrators with more details over which to govern. In the face of bigness, Congress could master the small things only by losing sight of the important issues.

Nowhere has the congressional abandonment of administrative details been as visible as in the shift from line item to lump sum appropriations. The specificity of appropriations was one of the great issues over which Congress and the Executive Branch fought during the early years of nationhood, and it was the triumph of itemized appropriations which assured legislative supremacy during the 19th century. But as the federal government expanded, the lines were merged into bigger and bigger appropriation units in a process which still is going on.[8] There are substantially fewer "lines" in the $375 billion budget for 1976 than there were in the $265 million of expenditures for 1876. A single appropriation act in 1876 for the Military Academy had about 40 lines (a number of which were subdivided into discrete items) for an appropriation totalling perhaps $200,000. There are only about 50 appropriation accounts in the 1976 budget for the Defense Department's nearly $100 billion of new budget authority. In fact, although the 1976 budget has about 1,000 accounts, fewer than 100 of these amount to more than $300 billion.

Why did Congress let control slip from its grasp? The details were too numerous to be comprehended; each detail was too small to be of consequence. Congress could not line itemize a $400 billion budget in the same manner as it had detailed the 19th century appropriations. Moreover, Congress harbored the expectation that the President would function as its agent of control over the administrative agencies. In the same year that Wilson left the White House, the Budget and Accounting Act empowered the President to establish budget control over government agencies. Control by executive direction was substituted for control by legislative means.

This was exactly what the new discipline of public administration advocated. The persistent message that a legislature should not trespass on administrative matters inevitably registered on congressional thinking about its appropriate role, especially because the theme was so attractively laced with the promise of order and efficiency in the public service and carried the warning that legislative intervention would be injurious to good government. In the course of decades, Congress became a grudging subscriber to the notion that it should refrain from most administrative entanglements. Some of its retreats were comprehensive and truly significant, such as the establishment of the executive budget system. More commonly, however, congressional withdrawal was piecemeal, such as the extension of civil service coverage to additional federal employees. Inch by inch Congress gave ground until it no longer was a dominant participant in the conduct of administration.

However, the extent of congressional withdrawal from administration was clouded by its incompleteness. When it wanted, Congress (or its members or committees) continued to meddle in administrative particulars, intervening in behalf of interests, writing restrictions into legislation, using its investigatory powers to spotlight an administrative problem, holding on to old administrative prerogatives. At will, Congress could penetrate to the smallest administrative detail, but these usually were pinpricks, mere nuisances compared to the countless matters which escaped legislative control. Appropriation bills might still limit the number of cars that could be procured, but the constrained agency could function with little hindrance in everyday administrative matters. With the growth of big administration, the zone of indifference (or perhaps more accurately, of ignorance) came to encompass most of the business of administration.

But the congressional retreat never has been sufficiently complete to satisfy administrative reformers. Congress was always stepping over the line, intruding on matters beyond its legitimate sphere of action. This failure to achieve administrative purity has sustained the reformist ethic of public administration for several generations.

In addition to the sway of administrative doctrine and governmental necessity, two ideological factors influenced Congress to expand the scope of administrative discretion. One was the spell of nonpartisanship in international affairs; the other was the dominance of pluralism in domestic politics. Nonpartisanship conveyed the assurance that unchecked executive power would be applied benevolently in the national interest of the United States; pluralism suggested that administrative discretion would be used to the advantage of the salient interests. Nonpartisanship normally escalates during wartime (Vietnam was a notable exception), so that the protracted cold war extended the influence of this ideology over a considerable period of time. Whatever the virtues of nonpartisanship, it effectively diminished the ability and inclination of Congress to superintend executive actions. Pluralism, always a presence in American politics, came to be regarded as its democratic linchpin in mid 20th century. With the blossoming of what Lowi has termed "interest group liberalism," the use of government power to provide benefits to powerful interests, the great bureaucracies of the federal government functioned as dispensaries of the "who gets what" of American politics. But since this distributive politics depended on administrative performance, an overly obstructive Congress would have hindered the flow of public goods and services to the intended beneficiaries. Interest groups were the political link between a Congress that authorized and a bureaucracy that delivered benefits. Rather than viewing one another as adversaries, these two power centers forged a political symbiosis that enabled the interest group state to flourish. Congressmen might still rail against bureaucrats or intervene to influence the award of a grant or contract, but administrators were given, as Kenneth Culp Davis has shown, enormous discretion to run their own operations.[9]

THE RESURGENCE OF CONGRESS

Congress is chronically ambivalent about the limited role into which it has been cast, and it episodically rears up to assert its control over administration. These spasms can be very discomfitting to the administrators who must cope with legislative intervention or harassment, but they cannot adequately assure that the overall conduct of administration is faithful to legislative interests. The spasms miss much more than they hit, leaving wide gaps in the coverage of administration by Congress. Nor have the regularized means of securing legislative control sufficed. Administrators have to supply more reports to Congress, are subject to more legislative investigations, and are monitored by more congressional staff, but, at least from the perspective of congressmen, these are not enough.

Nowadays Congress seems to expect more control over administration. Vietnam robbed nonpartisanship of its seductive hold on the loyalty of Congress; Watergate stripped much of the allure from executive dominance of domestic politics. Even before these shocks, revisionist scholars had begun to question the intellectual foundations of nonpartisanship and pluralism. Many other mini-shocks registered on congressional consciousness and contributed to dissatisfaction with a political arrangement which legitimized dominance by the Executive Branch. President Nixon overreached in the constitutional gray areas between the two branches such as executive privilege and the impoundment of funds. Disillusionment with the Great Society initiatives of the 1960s impacted on Congress, along with concern about the size and direction of the federal government.[10] Regulations poured from executive offices in record quantities as did complaints about the efficacy and fairness of regulatory policies. More and more of the budget was beyond effective congressional control, and deficit spending became a perennial practice. Congress underwent some destabilizations of its own as a result of unusually high turnovers in membership and an erosion of party and committee leaderships.

In the 1970s, the Congress has sought new methods for holding administrators to account and has applied old controls more extensively. While Congress has not perfected a comprehensive or consistent set of controls—most have been improvised or applied for particular problems—the cumulative effect of the congressional initiatives has been at least a temporary halt in the growth of administrative independence from the Legislative Branch. Examples of the recent congressional interventions in the "details" of administration include the following:

(1) The requirement of Senate confirmation has been extended to a number of presidential officials in recent years. The executive director of the Council on International Economic Policy was made subject to Senate confirmation in 1972 and the director and deputy director of the Office of Management and Budget were covered in 1973.[11]

(2) Congress also has moved to obtain more direct influence over the appointment of government officials. The Congressional Budget Act of 1974 established one of the first legislative offices to be filled solely by de-

termination of Congress—the director of the Congressional Budget Office.[12] Older Legislative Branch positions such as the Comptroller General, the Librarian of Congress, and the Public Printer still are appointed by the President with the advice and consent of the Senate.

(3) Perhaps the most direct attempt to enlarge the role of Congress in the selection of government officials was the original composition of the Federal Elections Commission, established in 1974. Two members each were to be appointed by the President, the Speaker of the House, and the President pro tem of the Senate. All of the appointments were to be subject to confirmation by both Houses of Congress. In addition, the Secretary of the Senate and Clerk of the House were to be ex officio members of the Commission. This arrangement was ruled unconstitutional in a 1976 decision of the Supreme Court, which held that appointments of "officers of the United States" cannot be made by Congress.[13]

(4) Congress has taken a number of steps to assure its and the public's access to administrative information and to open administrative proceedings to the public. The Freedom of Information Act has replaced the "need to know" test of the 1946 Administrative Procedures Act with a general presumption in favor of disclosure. Certain exemptions were permitted in the 1967 FOI Act, but these were tightened in 1974 Amendments.[14] The Federal Advisory Committee Act of 1972 opened most of the meetings of these organizations to the public. "Sunshine" legislation moving toward possible enactment in the 94th Congress would open up the meetings of most administrative agencies.

(5) The Budget and Accounting Act of 1921 barred federal agencies from submitting their budget estimates to Congress except at the request of the House or Senate. But a number of recently established agencies are required to furnish Congress with their estimates at the same time that they are submitted to the Office of Management and Budget. The Consumer Product Safety Commission, the Federal Elections Commission, and the Commodity Futures Trading Commission, among others, are required to make concurrent submissions of their budget estimates. Legislation to extend this requirement to all federal agencies has been considered in both the 93rd and the 94th Congresses, and though none has passed, many agencies now supply their original budget estimates at the requests of congressional committees.

(6) The 1973 War Powers Resolution requires the President "in every possible instance" to consult with Congress before military forces are entered into hostilities and to "consult regularly" with Congress while such forces are engaged in hostile situations. The Resolution intends that "the collective judgment" of both branches be applied before forces are committed to combat.

(7) The Congressional Budget Act of 1974 establishes a legislative process for determining national programs and priorities. This new process begins with much less involvement by executive officials than has been customary in the authorization and appropriation processes.

(8) Finally, Congress has broken new ground in the legal representation of its interests. The Impoundment Control Act authorizes the Comptroller General to bring court action to enforce the new impoundment procedures. In 1975, the Comptroller General sued to secure the release of $264

million impounded by the Department of Housing and Urban Development. The Justice Department moved to dismiss the action, noting that "it is apparently the first suit ever brought in the Judicial Branch by the Legislative Branch in its official capacity against the Executive Branch in its official capacity."[15] On a broader front, the 94th Congress is considering a Watergate Reform Act which would establish an Office of Congressional Legal Counsel to represent Congress in certain legal matters.

The above list is necessarily incomplete, but it suggests the range of congressional efforts to control the Executive Branch. In the sections that follow, three additional types of control are considered in detail. Each affects a different stage of the administrative process. (1) Legislative oversight and evaluation occurs after the administrative action has been completed. (2) The congressional veto relates to pending administrative matters. (3) Congressional authorization of programs and agencies enables Congress to shape government policy before agencies act.

LEGISLATIVE OVERSIGHT AND EVALUATION

The dominant feature of legislative oversight is review after the fact. The main form of oversight is investigatory activity by congressional committees or other reviews (such as appropriations hearings) of past administrative actions.

Official policy with regard to legislative oversight is not in doubt; its practice is another matter. The Legislative Reorganization Act of 1946 charged each standing committee with responsibility "to exercise continuous watchfulness of the execution by the administrative agencies concerned of any laws, the subject matter of which is within the jurisdiction of such committee."[16] The 1970 Reorganization Act restated the review functions of legislative committees and required most of them to submit biennial reports on their review activities.[17] The legislative commitment to oversight was further elaborated by the House Committee Reform Amendments of 1974, which tasked each House Committee "to establish an oversight committee, or require its subcommittees, if any, to conduct oversight in the area of their respective jurisdiction."[18] To assure compliance with their oversight duties, House Committees are to develop oversight plans at the start of each Congress.[19]

This official commitment to legislative oversight thus goes back 30 years (although some oversight functions were established in the early 1800s); the theory on which it is based is much older, as we shall soon note. But despite increased investigations by congressional committees, such oversight still is not practiced in a regular or comprehensive fashion. At best, Congress gets oversight by exception in the sense that a small number of matters that provoke legislative attention are subjected to review. At worst, Congress persists in an arrangement in which most of what the administrative branch does is beyond legislative cognizance.

There appears to be general agreement that regular oversight ought to be conducted, but is not. Walter Oleszek has identified seven factors that inhibit legislative oversight of bureaucracy.[20] In perhaps the first book-length examination of oversight, Morris Ogul draws a dismal conclusion:

There seems to be consensus in the Congress on the principle that extensive and systematic oversight *ought* to be conducted.

That expectation is simply not met. . . . The plain but seldom acknowledged fact is that this task, at least as defined above, is impossible to perform. No amount of congressional dedication and energy, no conceivable increase in the size of committee staffs, and no extraordinary boost in committee budgets will enable the Congress to carry out its oversight obligations in a comprehensive and systematic manner. The job is too large for any combination of members and staff to master completely.[21]

Something even more fundamental is awry in the expectation that Congress will become an overseeing branch. This expectation is grounded on executive presumptions about how Congress ought to behave, not on the preferences manifested by Congress in its own actions and priorities. Even as it has embraced the theory of legislative oversight, Congress has refused to subscribe to the division of labor implicit in the theory. One of the earliest statements of that theory appears in *Congressional Government,* the book in which Woodrow Wilson castigated congressional intervention in administrative matters. "Quite as important as legislation," Wilson insisted, "is vigilant oversight of administration." Wilson conceived of oversight as a counter to the excesses of legislation. "There is no similar legislature in existence which is so shut up to the one business of lawmaking as is our Congress."[22] Laws constrain administrative discretion in advance; oversight has the advantage of allowing full scope to administration, with legislative scrutiny occurring afterwards. The oversight role renders broad administrative discretion legitimate by making it accountable to legislative authority.

The contemporary significance of oversight derives entirely from the enormous growth of administrative discretion. As Arthur Macmahon noted in a 1943 article on the subject, "the need for such oversight increases with executive initiatives in policy and the delegation of discretion under the broad terms of statutes."[23] The theory of legislative oversight, however, is more than a de facto accommodation to the enlargement of administrative power. It welcomes that development and seeks the recasting of Congress from a lawmaking to an overseeing body. As argued by Huntington,

Explicit acceptance of the idea that legislation was not its primary function would, in large part, simply be recognition of the direction which change has already been taking. It would legitimize and expand the functions of constituent service and administrative oversight, which, in practice, already constitute the principal work of most congressmen.[24]

Much of the literature on oversight views Congress from an executive perspective. Congress is told to oversee more and legislate less. But Ogul and others conclude that Congress cannot handle the comparatively modest oversight chores it now has. Congress is asked to trade away its historic role for one which it cannot perform the way the theory expects it to perform.

The deal simply won't wash. There is an important place for oversight in the spectrum of congressional functions, but not as the dominant activity, and certainly not one that is preemptive of lawmaking interests. Expectations about oversight must be scaled down to accord with Congress' own preferences about its place in the political system. Congress is incurably ambivalent about the amount of control and independence it is willing to invest the administrative branch with. But its 200-year history demonstrates that Congress prefers making laws to overseeing their execution. If oversight is to flourish on Capitol Hill, it will not be at the expense of more traditional legislative activities.

Much the same can be said of program evaluation, which is a specialized form of oversight. Evaluation focuses on the results rather than the processes of administration. Unlike legislative oversight, it does not scatter its attention to the details of administration, except to the extent that these affect the costs or effectiveness of programs.

Judging from recent developments, legislative interest in evaluation is on the upswing. The 1970 Legislative Reorganization Act directs the General Accounting Office to make cost-benefit studies of government programs on its own initiative or at the request of congressional committees.[25] Title VII of the Congressional Budget Act of 1974 authorizes congressional committees to conduct evaluations on their own or by contract and it directs the GAO to assist committees, at their request, in formulating statements of legislative objectives. GAO also is authorized to develop program evaluation methods for Congress and to establish an Office of Program Review and Evaluation.[26] In addition to these general mandates, Congress in recent years has prescribed, or earmarked funds for, the evaluation of particular programs.[27]

Unlike oversight, which is clearly a legislative responsibility, evaluation does not operate with a differentiation of legislative and executive roles. Both branches can evaluate, and there is no *prima facie* expectation for a legislative evaluation to differ in form or content from one conducted under executive auspices. For both, evaluation is supposed to be an objective activity, meaning that it is to be divorced from the interests and constraints of the organization conducting it. Perhaps for this reason, the GAO has been assigned the lead role in legislative evaluations of programs.

If there is no distinctively legislative type of evaluation, why consign this responsibility to Congress at all? An obvious but compelling answer is that administrative organizations cannot be trusted to evaluate themselves objectively. Self-evaluating organizations are administrative aberrations and they rarely rank among the more successful or durable executive agencies.[28] From time to time organizations invest in stocktaking and retrospection, but not at the risk to their security and growth.

The exceptions shed some light on the normal impulse for self-promotion. During its sad and brief existence, the Office of Economic Opportunity excelled in its sponsorship and utilization of program evaluations, even to the extent of terminating some of its most promising initiatives (such as performance contracting for education) when they proved to be ineffective. In OEO, evaluation came to be a substitute for action, a manner of existence appropriate for a mendicant rather than an affluent organization. Well-supported agencies tend to move into action before they have evaluative confirmation of their program innovations, and they often continue what they are doing even if the results are unfavorable.

There are a number of reasons why agencies do not genuinely evaluate their own performance. One has to do with the annual budget process. Agencies are not neutrals in the recurring budgetary wars; they are budget maximizers. The language of budgeting is geared to advocacy and justification, not to an objective search for truth. A truly objective evaluation can damage an agency's budget position by arming outsiders (such as OMB or Congress) with reasons to reduce spending below previously authorized levels. For this reason, evaluators quickly become outsiders within their own organization, with their views and loyalties suspect. Organizations probably would be more receptive to evaluations if they consistently upheld the worthwhileness of programs. But in recent years it has appeared that for every evaluation highlighting program success there have been handfuls pronouncing failure or uncertain results. The market for evaluation dries up when evaluation becomes an anti-organization weapon.

The role of Congress, therefore, is to assure objectivity in the conduct of evaluation, sometimes by superintending the executive activity, sometimes by doing the job itself. But Congress has its own incentives for non-objectivity, its own reasons for dragging its feet on evaluation. A keen participant in the legislative process for many years recently wrote of congressional committees: "Those who are program advocates in the beginning become program protectors along the way."[29] The very factors which constrain executive commitment to evaluation also dampen congressional enthusiasm. Many committees are "captured" by the agencies they are charged to oversee, a predicament which is induced by the close and continuing contact between committee and agency staffs. Some authorizing committees consider it advantageous to inflate authorizations in order to protect their favored programs at the later appropriations stage. Like agencies, committees can behave as budget maximizers for the agencies under their jurisdiction.

Congress has no inherent advantage *vis à vis* the executive in terms of objectivity, though there surely are instances in which legislative committees do a better job of program evaluation. Both branches are prey to the same tendencies to see things their way, to close off potentially threatening avenues of inquiry, and to seek evidence in support of positions already staked out. But evaluation by Congress assures that the biases are legislative rather than executive ones, that Congress is not "snowed" by the mass of data and findings thrust upon it by administrative agencies in the name of program evaluation. There is much to be said for this subjective use of evaluation. Tainted evaluation competes against tainted evaluation and though the truth might not emerge from this process, it is less likely to be suppressed than if only one side of the story were told. Evaluation thus serves as a means of increasing congressional independence from administrative influence.

Program evaluation still is the exception, but it has been applied much more extensively in recent years, particularly by GAO, than in the past. However, before rallying to this new banner, a few caveats ought to be admitted. First, Congress cannot possibly acquire sufficient staff or resources to evaluate more than a small fraction of the programs subject to its review. The bulk of evaluation efforts always will have to come from the executive side, and these can make Congress even more beholden to administrative persuasion. Second, Congress cannot effectively conduct evaluations as after-the-fact inquiries in the manner of its general oversight functions. Evaluations which lack some sense of legislative intent are open to interminable confusion and conflict over their meaning and validity. If Davis is right that much contemporary legislation implies that "We the Congress don't know what the problems are; find them and deal with them,"[30] then the evaluators can only respond, "And we don't know the solution." Finally, the quantity of evaluation should not be taken as a measure of legislative (or executive, for that matter) commitment to the cause. As difficult as it is to evaluate, it is even more difficult to apply the findings to government programs, especially when client support is established and benefits are flowing to advantaged interests. Few evaluations offer such compelling findings as to lead inexorably to legislative action. Almost all evaluations are vulnerable to challenge and conflicting interpretations.[31] A decade later, for example, scholars and practitioners still are quarrelling over the soundness and policy implications of the Coleman report.

As long as each evaluation is an "event," a special accomplishment that commands notice and applause, we can be sure that progress on Capitol Hill is inadequate. Only when it becomes a regular feature of the legislative process—with congressmen behaving as consumers of evaluations done by their own staffs and outsiders—will program evaluation impact on public choice. By this test, Congress still has a long way to go.

CONGRESSIONAL VETO OF ADMINISTRATIVE ACTIONS

Oversight and evaluation are forms of congressional activity after an administrative action has occurred. A second type of control is activated by Congress in the course of the administrative process. The leading control in this category is the congressional veto of proposed executive actions.

As used here, "congressional veto" covers a variety of statutory provisions which authorize either or both Houses of Congress (or one or more committees) to review and overturn executive actions. The congressional veto is generally regarded to have made its debut in the Economy Act of 1932 which authorized the President to reorganize federal agencies by executive order. A proposed reorganization could not take effect for 60 days, during which period it could be disapproved by resolution of the House or Senate. This new device had a slow beginning, with another 23 laws containing 25 congressional veto provisions enacted between 1932 and 1950.[32] The number of review requirements increased during the next two decades, with 34 laws (embodying 36 provisions) enacted during the 1950s and 49 laws (with 70 provisions) enacted during the 1960s. But there has been an astounding rise in the adoption of congressional review procedures during the first half of the 1970s. At least 89 laws and 163 provisions for the review of administrative actions were enacted between 1970 and the end of 1975. Approximately half of all the congressional veto requirements have been established in just half a dozen years. This expanded use undoubtedly has been provoked by congressional concern over recent excesses by the Executive Branch.

The congressional power to disapprove or defer a proposed executive action rests on the principle that the administrative authority derives from a delegation of power by Congress and that Congress, therefore, can set the terms and limitations under which administrative action is to be taken.[33] The constitutionality of congressional review has been questioned from time to time, but the Supreme Court has never ruled on the issue.[34]

There are many variations on the congressional veto concept. Almost all require the Executive Branch to notify Congress of the proposed action. Some merely authorize review by Congress without providing specifically for disapproval of the action. Others provide special procedures for committee and floor consideration of disapproval resolutions. Most establish a fixed period within which Congress must act if it is to disapprove or defer the executive action. The most popular waiting period is 30 days, but some are as brief as five days and one is as long as three years. Some provide for two-House review; others permit review by the House or the Senate; still others provide for review by the committee of jurisdiction.

The actual effects of these veto procedures on legislative-executive relations depend on how they are applied by the two branches. Delegations of power by Congress to the Executive Branch can vastly expand the authority of the President (or other executive officials) to act without advance legislative approval. But the veto process offers Congress an expeditious way to intervene and overrule executive actions. Both possibilities are latent in the impoundment controls enacted into law during the last month of the Nixon presidency. The Impoundment Control Act of 1974 establishes different review procedures for rescissions (repeal of appropriations) and deferrals (delays in the expenditure of funds). Proposed rescissions lapse, and the funds must be released, unless a rescission law is enacted within 45 days (as defined by the statute). Deferrals, however, can remain in effect until the end of a fiscal year unless they are disapproved by either the House or the Senate. This arrangement is generally more advantageous to the President in the case of deferrals than for rescissions. If Congress does nothing, proposed rescissions terminate while deferrals continue in force. The Impoundment Control Act concedes the de facto authority of the President to impound funds, but the Act also establishes, for the first time, a legislative means of controlling and overturning executive impoundments.

The statistical evidence is that with the exception of impoundment control, the hundreds of congressional veto provisions have not induced wholesale interventions by Congress in the conduct of administration. Clark Norton of the Congressional Research Service has examined congressional veto activities during the 16 years between 1960 and 1975. For this period, Norton identified 351 House or Senate resolutions that were introduced pursuant to congressional review authority, and more than 100 of these were duplicates. Only 63 resolutions became effective through passage by one or both Houses as required by law, and almost two-thirds of these adoptions occurred in 1975. During the 16-year period, most of the congressional veto provisions generated no legislative action whatsoever, not even the introduction of a resolution. Only one in six of the introduced resolutions was passed.[35]

These statistics do not cover committee-level actions, nor do they address the possible effects of the congressional review process on Executive Branch behavior. But they show that congressional reviews have been selectively applied to particular concerns; they have not been across-the-board challenges to executive power.

When Congress is disturbed by the exercise of executive power, it can utilize the review process more forcefully. This has been the experience thus far with the new impoundment controls. Despite their potential for enlarging presidential power, the impoundment controls definitely have curbed administrative discretion. Although they have been in effect for less than two years, the controls account for almost two-thirds of the congressional vetoes since 1960. The congressional controls have been applied with varying effect to rescissions and deferrals.

During fiscal 1975, the President proposed 87 rescissions totalling $2,732,678,218.[36] In addition, the Comptroller General notified Congress of two rescission actions not reported by the President and he reclassified seven reported deferrals as rescissions, raising the total during fiscal 1975 to $4,292,500,218. Congress enacted three rescission bills during the fiscal year, rescinding less than 15 per cent of the amount proposed by the President and only about 9 per cent of the adjusted amount reported by the Comptroller General.

During fiscal 1976, the President proposed 44 rescissions totalling $3,274,602,655. An additional $26.3 million in rescissions were reported by the

Comptroller General. Three rescissions—totalling $138.3 million— were enacted, so that during fiscal 1976 the enactment rate dropped below 5 per cent.

In responding to rescission proposals, Congress appears to have drawn a fairly clear distinction between routine and policy impoundments. With few exceptions, Congress has approved routine rescissions involving no change in government policy, such as when funds no longer are needed to accomplish the purposes for which they were appropriated. In cases of policy rescissions, when the President has sought to eliminate funds appropriated in excess of his budget requests, Congress has not wanted to give the President a ''second chance'' to accomplish by means of the new impoundment process that which it has denied to him only weeks or months earlier in the course of the appropriations process. The very high rejection rates indicate that the President was repeatedly rebuffed in his efforts to convert impoundment control into an opportunity to reorder the budget priorities established by Congress. However, most of the enacted rescissions did not involve substantial questions of policy. Most of these routine cases concerned comparatively small amounts of money, while the policy impoundment often dealt with very large amounts. The median amount proposed for rescission in the approved cases was less than $3 million; in the rejected rescissions the median was $14 million.

During fiscal 1975, President Ford submitted 161 deferral messages to Congress, seven of which were subsequently reclassified as rescissions by the Comptroller General. These deferrals totalled approximately $25.3 billion, with two-thirds of the funds concentrated in federal grants to states for the construction of highways and water pollution control facilities. During the fiscal year, 82 impoundment resolutions were introduced in Congress and 16 were adopted. The deferrals disapproved by the House or the Senate totalled $9.3 billion, and an additional $9 billion of water pollution funds were released by the Administration.

During the 1976 fiscal year, the President submitted 111 deferral messages totalling approximately $8.8 billion to Congress and the Comptroller General notified Congress of a failure to report the deferral of $10 million of youth conservation funds. During the year, 22 deferrals of 1976 funds were disapproved by the House or the Senate, compelling the President to release $388 million.

The distinction between routine and policy impoundments also applies to deferrals. In various reports to Congress, the Comptroller General identified approximately half of the deferrals as being routinely authorized by the Anti-deficiency Act.

Congressional activity in the form of impoundment resolutions has been concentrated on policy deferrals. The 82 resolutions filed during fiscal 1975 related to only 30 impoundments, almost half of which attracted resolutions in both the House and the Senate. In virtually every instance that impoundment resolutions were introduced in both the House and Senate, the deferral was disapproved. The vast majority of deferrals permitted to continue in effect did not generate any congressional action because they were routine financial transactions involving no change in governmental policy.

The veto provisions of the Impoundment Control Act are coupled to new legislative enforcement procedures. The Comptroller General must inform Congress if the President has failed to report a proposed rescission or deferral or if an impoundment has been improperly classified. The congressional veto can then be applied ''in the same manner and with the same effect'' as if it were reported by the President. Congress can veto an executive action which has not been reported to it by the Executive Branch. Moreover, as was noted earlier, the Comptroller General is empowered to bring suit to secure compliance with the new impoundment controls.

When Congress feels that the delegation of power to the Executive Branch is not sufficiently constrained by the congressional veto, it can terminate the arrangement altogether. This has happened with regard to executive reorganization, the first area to which the veto device was applied. During the decades that the President was authorized to propose reorganizations, Congress disapproved about one out of every five plans that were submitted to it. Harvey Mansfield found that:

> the reorganization plan method has provided a compromise procedure for safeguarding congressional interests while permitting presidential initiatives on matters where considerable stakes of power and prestige are at issue and in situations where deadlock might otherwise prevail.[37]

However, shortly after Mansfield drew this judicious conclusion, President Nixon used his reorganization authority in a way that aggrandized presidential power at the expense of Congress. Reorganization Plan No. 2 of 1970 transferred the functions and powers of the Bureau of the Budget to the President, who in turn delegated these by executive order to the new Office of Management and Budget and the Domestic Council. The effects of this two-step procedure were to enable the President to make future changes in the Executive Office without going through the reorganization process and to weaken the accountability of presidential subordinates to Congress. A resolution of disapproval was considered in the House, but it failed by a small margin. However, in 1973 Congress permitted the reorganization power of the President to expire, thereby foreclosing its future use to disadvantage the Legislative Branch.

AUTHORIZING LEGISLATION

Congressional oversight and vetoes are directed at past and current administrative actions. The authorization process gives Congress an opportunity to control future administrative behavior. The extent to which Congress avails itself of this opportunity depends on the use of annual or multi-year as opposed to permanent authorizations.

At one time, permanent authorizations—without limit of time and usually without limit of money as well—were the standard practice. At the end of World War II, as much as 95 per cent of the federal budget (exclusive of one-time projects) was under permanent authorization. The usual formula was, "There are hereby authorized to be appropriated such funds as may be necessary." In effect, Congress would set up an agency or program and authorize it to continue in operation until further notice. These permanent activities would be considered by the Appropriations Committees; there would be no routine review by the substantive committees of Congress.

During the past 25 years there has been a trend toward fixed authorization periods. In the case of annual authorizations, Congress usually is motivated by a desire to bolster its control over executive agencies or by a desire of its authorizing committees to expand their legislative influence over the programs within their jurisdiction. But regardless of the original motive, a shift to limited-term authorizations enhances the ability of Congress to intervene in administrative matters.

The list of agencies and programs now operating under annual authorization includes the National Science Foundation, the Maritime Administration, the National Aeronautics and Space Administration, and the Energy Research and Development Administration. In dollar terms, the largest annual authorizations apply to certain programs of the Defense Department. Section 412 of Public Law 86-149 (enacted in 1959) requires annual authorization for the procurement of aircraft, missiles, and naval vessels. In subsequent legislation annual authorizations were extended to virtually all of the procurement, construction, and research activities of the Defense Department.

An important recent addition to the list is the State Department which, together with the United States Information Agency, was placed under annual authorizations by the Foreign Assistance Act of 1971. The State Department thus became the first Cabinet department to be subject to annual authorizations for its entire appropriation.

Multi-year authorizations range in most instances from two to five years and have been popular for many of the grant-in-aid programs established during the past two decades. In seeking a middle course between permanent and annual authorizations, Congress apparently has been unwilling to accord permanent status to new and untried programs, but it also has been sensitive to the needs of state and local governments for some advance indication as to the amounts of federal aid that may be forthcoming in future years.

In dollar amounts, permanent authorizations still dominate the federal scene. Most of the major entitlement programs such as social security, veterans benefits, public assistance, and medicare are permanently authorized. Less than one-quarter of the federal budget requires authorization in a particular year. Like the congressional veto, Congress has used its authorization process selectively, to bolster its intervention in those policy areas where it wishes to maintain closer control over the Executive Branch. When Congress no longer feels it necessary to give such close attention to a program, the reauthorization process becomes a *pro-forma* exercise. Such now is the case with regard to the annual authorization of the saline water program.

But when Congress wishes to exploit its authorization process to control executive activities, it can write specific conditions into authorizing legislation. This has been the case in recent years for the authorization bills dealing with foreign policy. The 1976 Foreign Relations Authorization Act,[38] for example, bars the State Department from developing a machine-readable passport system; declares that political contributions should not be criteria for the award of ambassadorial positions; urges the reopening of a consulate at Gothenburg, Sweden; instructs the Arms Control and Disarmament Agency to study the effects of arms limitations on military expenditures; modifies statutory requirements with regard to security investigations for contractors; limits United States contributions to certain international organizations and activities; calls for the temporary assignment of foreign service officers to congressional, state and local, and other public organizations; establishes detailed grievance procedures for foreign service personnel; and authorizes certain government employees to carry firearms. This is just one law's list of congressional actions affecting the conduct of foreign policy. Each of these controls piggybacked the annual authorization process to enactment.

The foreign relations area is vastly different from the policy areas in which permanent authorizations prevail. In the latter cases, an agency can escape detailed review by its authorizing committee for many years and the legislation under which it operates often is cast in broad terms, with few specific controls or restraints. Even if considerable annual review comes through the appropriations process, it is likely to focus on financial rather than on other substantive issues and it is not likely to occasion as thorough an inquiry into the agency activities as can be provided by a dual authorizations-appropriations process.

In the 94th Congress more than half of the Senators have sponsored "sunset" legislation to require the periodic termination of all but a few federal programs and agencies.[39] Substantive laws would not be directly affected; only authorization provisions would terminate. But Congress would be able to use its consideration of reauthorizing legislation to review all activities of a program and agency and to attach new conditions to substantive laws. The sunset concept has attracted considerable support in a brief period of time, but if it were enacted, Congress probably would continue in its selective ways. Not every corner of federal activity can be reexamined every four or five years; sudden death will not become a Washington routine. The periodic sunset of government agencies will enable Congress to focus on particular programs and make changes as it deems desirable.

BACK TO THE DETAILS OF ADMINISTRATION?

Details are important and control over the details is important. Congressional control over the details means conflict and confrontation, for it clashes directly with the Executive Branch's preference for freedom of action. Control runs to the particulars of policy; to its manner of implementation, not just to its general shape. Moreover, the emphasis in Congress is on controlling current activities: telling the President "No" when he wants to act.

Shortly after Woodrow Wilson complained about congressional meddling in the details of administration, the Executive Branch embarked on a major expansion of its power and administrative discretion. Thirty years ago, Arthur Macmahon complained that "Congress seeks in sundry ways to claim what it gave; it asserts the right of continuous intervention."[40] Once again the Executive Branch enlarged its power and discretion.

Congressional attempts to reassert its control have characterized legislative-executive relationships during the 1970s. Divided political leadership and pervasive mistrust of executive power have whetted the congressional appetite for control. But neither Congress nor the Executive Branch relishes perpetual collision. When the passions of recent times have cooled, we may look to a more balanced relationship which combines reasonable executive discretion with congressional involvement in the important details of American policy.

NOTES

1. Woodrow Wilson, *Congressional Government* (New York: Meridian Books, 1956), p. 49.
2. But when he became President, Wilson carried his old views with him, as reflected in the following argument in one of his veto messages: "The Congress and the Executive should function in their respective spheres. Otherwise, efficient and responsible management will be impossible and progress impeded by wasteful forces of disorganiza-

tion and obstruction." Quoted in Louis Fisher, *Presidential Spending Power* (Princeton: Princeton University Press, 1975), p. 258.

3. For a critical analysis of the Wilsonian theory of public administration, see Vincent Ostrom, *The Intellectual Crisis in American Public Administration* (University, Ala.: University of Alabama Press, 1974), especially pp. 23-29.

4. Charles S. Hyneman, *Bureaucracy in a Democracy* (New York: Harper & Brothers, 1950). Significantly, Hyneman devotes six chapters to direction and control of bureaucracy by Congress, and these appear before the chapters on presidential control.

5. Martin Landau, *Political Theory and Political Science* (New York: The Macmillan Company, 1972), p. 188.

6. Leonard D. White, *The Federalists* (New York: The Macmillan Company, 1948), p. 512.

7. Leonard D. White, *The Jeffersonians* (New York: The Macmillan Company, 1951), p. 552.

8. For example, the 1977 budget proposes to merge into a single appropriation five previously separate accounts for the Supreme Court. Salaries, printing and binding, miscellaneous expenses, an automobile for the Chief Justice, and books are to be consolidated into a "salaries and expenses" appropriation. See The Budget of the United States Government, Fiscal Year 1977, *Appendix*, p. 49.

9. Kenneth Culp Davis, *Discretionary Justice* (Baton Rouge: Louisiana State University Press, 1969).

10. This writer has believed for some years that the accomplishments of the 1960s have been underrated. For recent support of this view, see Sar A. Levitan and Robert Taggart, *The Promise of Greatness* (Cambridge: Harvard University Press, 1976).

11. Congress first passed a bill abolishing and reestablishing the offices of director and deputy director, but this was vetoed by the President and Congress failed to override. Congress then passed, and the President signed, a bill to require Senate confirmation of future holders of these offices.

12. The director of the Congressional Budget Office is appointed by the Speaker of the House and President pro tem of the Senate after considering the recommendations of the House and Senate Budget Committees.

13. *Buckley v. Valeo*, decided January 30, 1976. Congress subsequently reestablished the Commission with all members appointed by the President.

14. The 1967 Freedom of Information Act contains nine exemptions. Two of these—relating to classified national security information and investigatory records— were tightened in the 1974 Amendments.

15. *Staats v. Ford*, et al. (Civ. Action No. 75-0551), District Court, District of Columbia. Points and Authorities in Support of Defendants Motion to Dismiss.

16. 60 *Stat.* 832.

17. 84 *Stat.* 1156.

18. H. Res. 988, 93d Congress, as adopted on October 8, 1974.

19. See House Committee on Government Operations, *Oversight Plans of the Committees of the U.S. House of Representatives*, H. Rept. No. 94-61 (March 14, 1975).

20. Walter J. Oleszek, "Toward a Stronger Legislative Branch," in *The Bureaucrat*, Vol. 3 (January 1975), p. 457.

21. Morris S. Ogul, *Congress Oversees the Bureaucracy* (Pittsburgh: University of Pittsburgh Press, 1976), p. 5.

22. Wilson, *op. cit.*, p. 195.

23. Arthur Macmahon, "Congressional Oversight of Administration: The Power of the Purse: I," *Political Science Quarterly*, Vol. LVIII (June 1943), p. 161.

24. Samuel P. Huntington, "Congressional Responses to the Twentieth Century," in David B. Truman (ed.), *The Congress and America's Future* (Englewood Cliffs, N.J.: Prentice-Hall Inc., 1965), p. 30.

25. 84 *Stat.* 1168.
26. 88 *Stat.* 325.
27. See Joseph S. Wholey and others, *Federal Evaluation Policy* (Washington, D.C.: The Urban Institute, 1970).
28. For a perceptive critique of why organizations do not ordinarily evaluate their own activities, see Aaron Wildavsky, "The Self-Evaluating Organization," *Public Administration Review,* Vol. 32 (1972), pp. 509-520.
29. Herbert Roback, "Program Evaluation by and for the Congress," *The Bureaucrat,* Vol. 5 (April 1976), p. 27.
30. Quoted in Theodore J. Lowi, *The End of Liberalism* (New York: W.W. Norton & Company, 1969), p. 303.
31. See Allen Schick, "From Analysis to Evaluation," *Annals of the American Academy of Political and Social Science,* March 1971, pp. 57-71.
32. The data in this paragraph are derived from Clark F. Norton, *Congressional Review, Deferral and Disapproval of Executive Actions: A Summary and an Inventory of Statutory Authority* (Washington, D.C.: Congressional Research Service, April 30, 1976). Norton does not use the term "veto" in his study which comprehends some review activities which do not provide for congressional veto.
33. See Edward S. Corwin, *The President: Office and Powers,* 4th ed. rev. (New York: New York University Press, 1957), p. 130 for a succinct defense of the congressional veto as a proper use of congressional power.
34. In *Buckley v. Valeo,* decided January 30, 1976, dealing with the constitutionality of the Federal Election Campaign Act of 1971, the U.S. Supreme Court stated that "because our holding that the manner of appointment of the members of the [Federal Elections] Commission precludes them from exercising the rule-making powers in question, we have no occasion to address this separate challenge here." The challenge was to the constitutionality of congressional veto provisions of rules promulgated by the Federal Elections Commission. However, in a concurring opinion, Justice White indicated that in his judgment the congressional veto device in that case would not violate the Constitution.
35. The author is indebted to Clark F. Norton for making available to him unpublished statistics on the exercise of the congressional review power during the 1960-75 period.
36. The data and analysis in this part are adapted from Allen Schick, *The First Years of the Congressional Budget Process* (Washington, D.C.: Congressional Research Service, June 30, 1976).
37. Harvey C. Mansfield, "Federal Executive Reorganization: Thirty Years of Experience" *Public Administration Review,* Vol. 29 (1969), p. 341.
38. 89 *Stat.* 756.
39. The leading bill is S. 2925 which would establish a five-year cycle for the termination and review of most federal programs. At this writing, S. 2925 is under consideration by the Senate Government Operations Committee.
40. Macmahon, *op. cit.,* p. 163.

Legislative Intent and Oversight

RICHARD MARVEL
ROBERT J. PARSONS
WINN SANDERSON
N. DALE WRIGHT

Legislative oversight traditionally has been concerned with broad programs to be instituted, a careful examination of budgetary items (whether line-item or program), and a legal or financial audit to determine if there has been compliance with procedures. There has been a focus on items of expenditure and especially on categorical increases over the prior years' appropriations. The outcome of expenditures and programs often has been ignored or bypassed.

During 1974, the Legislative Appropriations Committee of Nebraska's unicameral Legislature implemented a model for expressing intent and facilitating oversight which differs from these traditional concepts. The budgetary process provides the skeleton for the model. Nebraska uses a basic performance budgeting process. To this is added, in the appropriations bill, a clear, detailed statement of legislative intent. Oversight is facilitated by the submission of a series of reports on the status of elements prescribed in legislative intent. These reports are prepared by the executive agencies. In addition, the legislative staff monitors and evaluates executive action and reports to the Appropriations Committee.

The purpose of this system is to provide the legislature with a tool to express intent and to provide a means of oversight and evaluation to ensure that intent is being met. As a side benefit, it also assists legislators in thinking about the present status of state programs and whether legislative goals are being achieved.

LEGISLATIVE INTENT

An important part of this system is the expression of legislative intent through the budget. The appropriations bills in a majority of States are primarily a list of funds for each agency. The appropriations bill of the 1974 Nebraska Legislature included policy statements as well as the listing of financial figures. Legislative intent is spelled out within the program budget for each agency of state government. As a result, the appropriations bill has more narrative than numbers. An example of the legislative intent is found in the portion relating to the university system.

> It is the expressed intent of the Nebraska Legislature that the University of Nebraska . . . accomplish certain objectives in the expenditure of the funds appropriated in this section.

The act then contains 12 pages of directives relating to programs, management systems, and instructional quality. For example:

In developing the "Areas of Excellence—1974-75," the University of Nebraska-Lincoln shall have developed a preliminary model for the implementation of a systematic process which shall:

(a) Develop a budgetary concept which identifies and organizes its activities in terms of objectives, identifies the cost of these activities, and relates these activities and the cost of the outputs associated with the achievement of the objectives;

(b) Develop an organized systematic review and evaluation of the present institutional effort to mold effective instruction at all levels in the institution.

This model stresses output rather than input and keeps the Legislature at a policy level rather than an administrative level. It also emphasizes accountability on the part of the university administration and facilitates evaluation of administrative performance.

The development of policy calls for the analysis of alternatives for establishment or continuation of a program. In order to conduct such an analysis, there needs to be evaluation of existing programs to determine if they are fulfilling expectations. Legislatures frequently establish programs and assume that the executive branch will evaluate program accomplishments. This places the responsibility of evaluation on the same branch of government which is administering the program. Because legislative bodies have not concerned themselves with evaluation, expressions of legislative intent have not been made in a manner to facilitate evaluation.

HOW TO FORMULATE INTENT

The area of higher education provides a good example of how intent is formulated in Nebraska. Higher education was facing many problems in Nebraska in the early 1970s. Enrollments were declining and costs were increasing. The State had a large investment in physical facilities, especially in teacher colleges which were facing the greatest decrease in enrollment. Enrollments were affected because of the elimination of the military draft, the declining demand for teachers, and increasing student interest in vocational training.

The Legislative Committee on Higher Education directed the Legislative Fiscal Office to prepare a series of issues affecting higher education in Nebraska. The staff conferred with national organizations and the various Nebraska institutions of higher education and compiled a list of 15 issues.

The committee decided to focus on the two highest priority issues and attempt to develop and implement solutions to meet these problems. Experience had shown that an attempt by the Legislature to address many complex problems had not been productive. As stated in a position paper presented to the Nebraska Appropriations Committee:

It is recommended that the Legislature be encouraged to accept the fact that the complexity of the problems facing the State's agencies hinders the Legislature and the agencies from solving all of the immediate problems during the given fiscal year.[1]

The determination of which programs to analyze was not done randomly. Guidelines such as the list of 15 issues in higher education on which analysis could be significant helped in the decision process.

The legislative committee decided that decreasing enrollments and a lack of data for policy-making were the highest priority items of the 15 suggested. The staff was directed to begin research on the two issues so that information would be available for preparation of the appropriations bill.

The policy committee of legislative and institutional staff was formed. The institutional representatives, through negotiation, encouraged the substitution of an issue which they viewed as more significant—the quality of education. The legislative committee concurred and quality of education was substituted for the problem of decreasing enrollment.

The committee's work led to measurements, both quantitative and qualitative, of educational quality. Agreement was reached that part of an evaluation of quality education was to be conducted by a peer review committee composed of academic representatives from institutions outside Nebraska. The Legislature, in the appropriations bill, instructed the institutions to determine the academic areas in which it would be desirable and feasible to increase quality and to have the improvement assessed by the peer review committee.

CRITERIA FOR MEASUREMENT

Criteria to assess the second issue—what data was significant for policy-making—and a timetable for the implementation of an information system to develop and process this data were likewise written into the bill. For example, the bill states that institutional management is charged to develop a preliminary model for the implementation of a systematic process which shall:

(a) Develop an organized systematic review and evaluation of the present institutional effort to mold effective instruction at all levels in the institution;

(b) Develop a systematic process of programmatic review which shall:
   (i) Evaluate current level of quality of course;
   (ii) Evaluate each academic course offering;
   (iii) Evaluate the current academic organizational structure;
   (iv) Evaluate faculty teaching performance; and
   (v) Evaluate student learning ability;

(c) Develop a uniform process of instructional cost analysis which will develop direct programmatic costs, unit cost per FTE (full-time equivalent) student and unit cost per student major.

It was difficult, as would be expected, to agree on criteria with which to measure quality of education. The committee and members of the two staffs, through compromise, agreed on these processes. As the institutions carried out these processes they would be compelled to look for criteria which would then be used in evaluation.

The role of the institution in setting the goals which were incorporated into the legislative intent expressed in the appropriations bill is an important feature of the process. The agency was encouraged to review the bill prior to printing. Representatives reviewed priority of items and the time frame for activities stipulated in the bill. This is important as the agency has the data available to determine if the goals, evaluation methods, and time frames are realistic.

The Appropriations Committee also decided to expand the budgeting time frame from one to three years to accomplish the goals. It wanted to allow a sufficient, realistic period to accomplish the elements contained in the act.

LEGISLATIVE OVERSIGHT

The appropriations bill emphasized the policy decision in higher education rather than focusing solely on the money to be expended. Legislative oversight was, thereby, directed to policy objectives rather than budgetary control.

This orientation of an emphasis on legislative policy-making was initiated by a survey conducted by the staff in 1971. The purpose of the study was to gather information on formulas used in budgeting for higher education. It was noted that each State had a different means of conveying to state agencies the decisions made during the appropriations process. While all States called it "legislative intent," the format was not universal.

All 11 States surveyed indicated that legislative intent was mandatory for effective legislative post-audit. However, only five of the States' Legislatures publicly expressed intent and only three States had a formal means of transmitting a statement to various state agencies. None of the States wrote any intent into the appropriations act. All of the 11 States, paradoxically, noted that post-audit would be based on legislative intent. The result was that legislative staffs were being directed to conduct performance audits without adequate guidance from the Legislature.

Conventional post-audits primarily review financial and other legal compliance rather than what the programs have accomplished. It, therefore, is not evaluation. Such post-audits emphasize inputs rather than outputs. The Nebraska legislative post-audit is not of this type. It is an evaluation of program plans, goals, and accomplishments. The Nebraska Legislature has begun to deal with the accomplishment of program objectives rather than focusing solely on line-item budget entries such as personnel services, operating expenses, or travel.

Likewise, Nebraska's method of evaluating program accomplishments has replaced "workload" measurements such as student-teacher ratios and patient days per year. Such measures have been used because outputs are difficult to determine in many public enterprises. These measures are very tempting to use because they are quantitative. They fail, however, to measure program effectiveness and, therefore, have weaknesses in evaluation.

The Nebraska Legislature facilitates performance or program auditing by clearly indicating intent. This enables the staff to use intent as a "guidepost" against which to review program accomplishment.

In the case of higher education, for example, legislative oversight was facilitated by the intent written in the appropriations bill. Oversight of higher education was accomplished in several phases. First, a series of reports was required of and subsequently issued by the executive agency. These reports described the procedures established by the institution to meet the intent in the appropriations bill. They also delineated the accomplishments in meeting various aspects of the intent. The legislative staff monitored these reports and the programs described.

Second, the legislative staff performed its own studies of the problems involved in the two issue areas. A survey was made of other midwest universities which compared faculty-student ratios, faculty salaries, cost per student by discipline, and the overall institutional role. The latter point was highly subjective. It did, however, allow comparisons between schools with similar primary missions.

A second study compared the three higher education systems within Nebraska—the university system, the state college system, and the vocational/technical system. Comparisons were made on the total appropriations to each system, the total appropriations per student, and data on local expenditures for higher education.

Third, evaluations were conducted by the peer evaluation group on the quality of educational programs within the Nebraska institutions. These three activities served as a basis of evaluation and provided some basic data for policy decisions in higher education.

Goal-setting and priorities for attaining excellence were begun on the departmental level and were aggregated at the college and, finally, university level. Decisions were made in which areas to achieve excellence and methods were devised to determine the measurement of excellence. The peer review committee was used to ascertain whether the means for determination of quality were acceptable and to what extent the programs had been successful. The legislative staff then evaluated the organizational mechanism established to carry out this aspect of legislative intent.

The staff analyzed the budgetary requests which were aimed at meeting these goals. Funding recommendations were made on the basis of what the university system had accomplished. This was basically a reward system focusing on accomplishments rather than deficiencies. The entire atmosphere surrounding the decision process was changed. Participants from both the legislative and executive branches had an attitude of cooperation and responsibility for meeting the problems facing higher education in Nebraska.

During the second year it was determined, through the evaluation process, that progress was being made on the management information system and that the next step should be expanded implementation. The legislative committee, with input from the two staffs, decided that student enrollment and university productivity was the area to be addressed. The choice of this issue grew out of the self-evaluation involved in setting priorities for areas of excellence and two legislative staff reports. This issue was one of the two originally identified by the legislative committee.

CONCLUSIONS

Two observations should be made about the process. One of the strengths in the Nebraska experience is the process of program goal formulation. It is a joint activity of the legislative committee and the executive agency. It is important that both parties be involved. The process is a valid exercise of the legislative role while the executive agency provides the expertise developed from daily confrontation with problems.

One of the weaknesses of the Nebraska experience was that the Governor's budget office was not highly involved in the process. Nebraska recently changed from a legislative to an executive budget format. A lack of experience with the new executive budget system probably led to this omission. Legislative committees had a tradition of dealing directly with institutional staffs and apparently overlooked the need to involve the Governor's staff.

In Nebraska, there is a strong feeling that the Legislature should develop the system described above as a budget tool. This includes:

(1) Establishing a performance bugeting system for legislative decision-making;

(2) Incorporating in the general appropriations act a statement of legislative performance intent;

(3) Developing intent that is policy-setting in nature rather than administrative;

(4) Transferring the evaluation process from the executive to the legislative branch; and

(5) Creating within the legislative staff the capability to evaluate program performance based on legislative intent.

Rather than limiting legislative oversight to input controls, emphasis is now placed on output measures which are, in many instances, more elusive and less understood. Evaluation has not proven to be simple. It is costly, time-consuming, and the methodology in many instances is not well developed. It has, however, proven to be a useful approach for formulating and expressing policy and determining if legislative intent is being met in Nebraska.

NOTES

1. Winn Sanderson, "Model of Measurement of Instructional Quality: A Report to the Nebraska Legislative Appropriations Committee." Office of Legislative Fiscal Office, State of Nebraska, April 1974. HE 74-008.

Judicial Law Making and Administration

ROGER C. CRAMTON

Seventy years ago in St. Paul, Roscoe Pound gave a famous speech on "The Causes of Popular Dissatisfaction with the Administration of Justice." Recently, a prestigious group of lawyers and judges, assembled by Chief Justice Burger, reconvened in St. Paul to reconsider Pound's theme. A surprising conclusion was that, although the professionals—the lawyers and judges themselves—have many problems with the administration of justice, the tide of popular dissatisfaction is at a relatively low ebb.

In contrast to other agencies of the government, the people have confidence in the fairness and integrity of the courts. True, there is continuing complaint over the law's cost and delay. But, apart from this perennial complaint, popular dissatisfaction appears to stem from two perceptions: first, that decisions in criminal cases turn too often upon procedural technicalities rather than upon the guilt or innocence of the offender; and second, that some judges, and especially the federal judiciary, have been too actively engaged in lawmaking on social and economic issues that are better handled by other institutions of government. The layman, on scanning his newspaper or viewing the television screen, discovers to his surprise that judges are running schools and prison systems, prescribing curricula, formulating budgets, and regulating the environment.

Causation is a tricky matter. A student theme has reported that, since Smokey the Bear posters were displayed in the New York subways, forest fires have disappeared in Manhattan. Despite the risks, I hazard the generalization that several fundamental changes in the nature of our society may have altered the role of the judiciary.

Foremost among those changes is that suggested by the title of this article. The Leviathan is upon us, and it has implications for all branches of government, including the judiciary. Government now attempts so much! Every technical, economic, and social issue seems to end up in the hands of government; and the demand for further government action is combined with charges that existing government is inefficient, heavy-handed, and ineffective. This is one field in which the appetite for nostrums does not fade with the demonstrated failure of prior cures. Each reformer, after criticizing the failure and inefficiency of government, then concludes that the remedy is—more of the same!

But our attitudes about ourselves and about conflict have also changed. The confrontational style of contemporary America assures that social conflict will increase. "Doing your own thing" is the central value of a hedonistic, self-regarding society; and patience is a nearly extinct virtue. Nowadays no one takes "no" for an answer, whether it is a job aspirant or a welfare claimant or a teacher who has been denied tenure. We perceive our society as having grown old; the enthusiastic and venturesome spirit that prompted the uncharted growth of the American past is now suffering from hardening of the arteries. As we experience slower economic development and approach zero population growth, organized groups contend with each other with increasing ferocity for larger shares of a more static pie. There is a declining sense of a common purpose; the prevailing attitude is "what's in it for me?"

These trends give lawyers and judges an even more central role in our society than they have had in the past. The decline of moral consensus and of institutions of less formal control, such as the family and the church, places much more strain on the law as an instrument of conflict resolution and social control. And the increasing contentiousness of groups organized for their own advantage has made conflict resolution a growth industry. If you could buy stock in law firms, I would advise you to do so. Lawyers have a legal monopoly on the conflict resolution industry, and it is the boom industry of today.

To these developments—the increasing reliance on law as an instrument of social control and the rapid growth of group conflict—must be added another factor: the failure of the executive and the legislature to meet the challenge of today's inflated expectations. The public perception that these branches of government have failed—a perception greatly abetted by the debacles of Vietnam and Watergate—has led the people to turn increasingly to the courts for solutions to their problems.

MODELS OF JUDICIAL REVIEW

Consider in the context of the Leviathan State two models of judicial review of administrative action. The traditional model is one of a restrained and sober second look at what government has done that adversely affects a citizen. The controversy is bipolar in character, with two parties opposing each other; the issues are narrow and well-defined; and the relief is limited and obvious. Has a welfare recipient been denied a benefit to which he is entitled by statute? Was fair procedure employed by the agency? Were constitutional rights violated?

Judicial review in this model serves as a window on the outside world, a societal escape valve which tests the self-interest and narrow vision of the specialist and the bureaucrat against the broader premises of the total society. Every bureaucracy develops its own way of looking at things and these belief patterns are enormously resistant to change. In time an agency acquires a tunnel vision in which particular values are advanced and others are ignored. An independent judiciary tests agency outcomes against the statutory framework and the broader legal context.

Judicial review in this form is an absolute essential, especially in a society in which the points of contact between officials and private individuals multiply at every point. The impartial and objective second look adds to the integrity and acceptance of the administrative process rather than undermining it. If the administrator is upheld, as usually is the case, citizen confidence in the fairness and rationality of administration is enhanced. In the relatively small number of cases in which the administrator is reversed, the administrator is forced to readjust his narrower view to the larger perspective of the total society.

During the last 20 years the pace of constitutional change, especially in judicial review of government action, has been astounding. The values implicit in general constitutional provisions such as due process, equal protection, and free speech have been given expanded content and new life. Even more important, constitutional rights have been extended to persons who were formerly neglected by the legal system—blacks, aliens, prisoners, and others. One can disagree with the merits of particular decisions. But the general trends—implementation of fundamental values by the courts and the inclusion of previously excluded groups in the application of these values—constitute a great hour in the long struggle for human freedom.

There is, however, a second model of judicial review that is growing in acceptance and authority. This model of the judicial role has characteristics more of general problem-solving than of dispute resolution. Simon Rifkind speaks of a modern tendency to view courts as modern handymen—as jacks of all trades available to furnish the answer to whatever may trouble us. "What is life? When does death begin? How should we operate prisons and hospitals? Shall we build nuclear power plants, and if so, where? Shall the Concorde fly to our shores?"[1]

Thoughtful observers believe that controversies of this character strain the capacities of our courts and may have debilitating effects on the self-reliance of administrators and legislators. At the risk of appearing more reactionary than I am, let me focus not on the achievements of the past but on the possible dangers that arise when the judiciary succumbs to pressures to attempt too much.

THE COURT AS ADMINISTRATOR

The traditional judicial role, earlier described, envisions a lawsuit which is bipolar in character, seeks traditional relief (usually damages), and applies established law to a relatively narrow factual situation. The relief given is backward-looking and does not order government officials to take positive steps in the future.

The traditional model still persists in much private litigation and in many routine cases challenging official action, but in many other constitutional and statutory controversies radical changes have occurred. The changes have led Abram Chayes to argue that the basic character of public litigation has changed.[2] In today's public litigation, a federal judge often is dealing with issues involving numerous parties; indeed, everyone in the community may be affected. Moreover, the issues are complex, interrelated, and multi-faceted; and they turn less on proof concerning past misconduct than on complex predictions as to how various social interests should be protected in the future. Since the remedy is not limited to compensating named plaintiffs for a past harm, the judge gets drawn, for example, into coercing school officials to close schools, bus pupils, change curricula, and build new facilities. The federal judge becomes one of the most powerful persons in the community; on the particular issue, he is the one who decides.

Consider the role of one man, Frank Johnson, in the governance of the once sovereign State of Alabama. Johnson, a distinguished United States District Judge in Alabama, is supervising the operation of the prisons, mental hospitals, highway patrol, and other institutions of the state. His decrees have directed the state to hire more wardens with better training, rebuild the prisons, and even extend to such details as the length of exercise periods and the installation of partitions in the men's rooms.

What is the authority of a federal judge to take such far-reaching actions? Why isn't the Alabama legislature the proper body to determine what prison or hospital care should be provided, and at what cost, through agencies administered by the state's executive branch? The answer is that all of these actions are designed to remedy violations of the constitutional rights of prisoners, mental patients, and others. And the Alabama legislature and executive have defaulted on their obligation to remedy these violations.

We are caught on the horns of a terrible dilemma. It is unconscionable that a federal court should refuse to entertain claims that state officials have systematically violated the constitutional rights of prisoners, mental patients, or school children. On the other hand, the design of effective relief may draw the court into a continuing role as an administrator of complex bureaucratic institutions. The dangers of the latter choice are worth brief exploration.

First, the judge who assumes an administrative role may gradually lose his neutrality, becoming a partisan who is pursuing his own cause. In one recent class action, a federal judge not only appointed expert witnesses, suggested areas of inquiry, and took over from the parties a substantial degree of the management of the case, but also went so far as to order that $250,000 from an award required of the defendants be paid for social science research on the effectiveness of the decree. That may be good government, but is it judicial justice?

A further problem arises from the tentativeness of our knowledge about such matters as minimum standards in operating a prison or mental hospital. We fervently hope that civilized and humane treatment will be provided to all of those who are confined to public institutions. But is it desirable to take the view of the current generation of experts, especially those self-selected by the plaintiffs or the judge, and to give their views of acceptable standards the status of constitutional requirements, with all that implies concerning their fixed meaning and difficulty of change?

Here as elsewhere, our capacity to anticipate the future or to discern all relevant facets of polycentric problems is limited. Thus, for example, when a federal judge ordered New York City to close the Tombs as a city jail or to rebuild it, the City, faced with an extraordinary financial crisis, opted to close it and prisoners confined to the Tombs were transferred to Riker's Island. The crowded conditions of the Tombs were immediately duplicated on Riker's Island. But a further result was not anticipated: Riker's Island is much less accessible to the families and attorneys of prisoners; and there is reason to believe that the vast majority of prisoners prefer the convenience of the Tombs, despite its problems, to the inaccessibility of Riker's Island.

The underlying truth is that court orders cannot by judicial decree achieve social change in the face of the concerted opposition of elected officials and public opinion. In a representative democracy, the consent of the people is required for lasting change.

The impulse to reform, moreover, is not limited to courts nor to constitutional law. A vigilant press, an informed populace, and the leadership of a committed minority have mobilized forces of change and reform throughout our history. A representative democracy may move slowly, but if we lack patience we may undermine the self-reliance and responsibility of the people and their elected officials.

The danger of confrontation between branches of government is yet another concern. What happens, for example, if Alabama refuses to fund its mental hospitals or prisons at the level required to achieve the standards specified in Judge Johnson's decrees? The next step, Judge Johnson has said, is the sale of Alabama's public lands in order to finance, through court-appointed officers, the necessary changes.

A degree of tension is a necessary concomitant of the checks and balances of a federal system. But in our urge to check we should not forget that balance is involved as well. One of the lessons of the Watergate era is that cooperation, restraint, and patience among the various branches and levels of government is necessary if our system is to survive in the long run. As Ben Franklin said many years ago, we must hang together or we will hang separately.

PRESSURES FOR JUDICIAL ACTION

Why have the courts undertaken these more expansive functions? They have not done so as volunteers desirous of expanding their own powers, but reluctantly and hesitantly in response to public demands for effective implementation of generally held values.

The American people today have little patience or restraint in dealing with social issues. An instant problem requires an instant solution that provides instant gratification. Playing this game under those rules, the executive and legislature have done their best—grinding out thousands of laws and regulations, many of them ineffective and some of them intrusive and harmful. The public, while demanding even more action from legislators and administrators, perceives these bodies as inept, ineffective, and even corrupt. Moreover, issues on which there is a deep social division, such as school busing or abortion, are avoided by elected officials, who view them as involving unacceptable political risks.

Nature abhors a vacuum and the inaction of the executive and lawmaking branches creates pressures for judicial action. A prominent federal judge put it succinctly at the recent St. Paul conference: "If there is a serious problem, and the legislature and executive don't respond, the courts have to act."

And they have done so on one after another burning issue. The mystery is that they have been so successful and that there has been so little popular outcry. The desegregation of Southern schools, of course, is a success story of heroic proportions. Legislative reapportionment is also generally viewed as a success despite the mathematical extreme to which it was carried in its later years. Organs of opinion, especially the TV networks and major newspapers, support the Court's actions in general and especially in such areas as civil rights and criminal procedure. There is no institution in our society that has as good a press as the Supreme Court. Judicial activism, it appears, has the approval of the intellectual elite who have become disillusioned with the effectiveness of social change by other means. It is more doubtful, however, whether the common man concurs either in the elite's support of judicial lawmaking or of its substantive results.

LONG-TERM EFFECTS

Neither popular acclaim nor criticism, of course, can answer the long-term question of the appropriate lawmaking role of the judiciary and the desirable limits on the scope of judicial decrees. More fundamental considerations must be decisive.

First, the practical question of comparative qualifications. Do judges, by training, selection, or experience, have an aptitude for social problem solving that other officials of government lack? And are the techniques of adjudication well designed to perform these broader policy-making functions? Professor Abram Chayes of the Harvard Law School has answered these questions with a confident affirmative.[3] I am inclined to disagree.

Second, what will be the long-term effects of this trend on the credibility of the courts and on the sense of responsibility of administrators and legislators?

After completion of this article, my fears on this score received support from an unlikely source—Anthony Lewis in the *New York Times*. After acknowledging, as I do, that the Boston School Case "presented exceptional difficulties," that "a judge could [not] in conscience remit the complaining black families to their political remedy," and that District Judge Garrity's lonely efforts should be viewed with sympathy, Lewis nevertheless concludes that Garrity's involvement in the day-by-day administration of school affairs "has not worked well" and "is a serious philosophical error:"

> American judges have to handle many controversial problems with political implications—redistricting, prisons and the like. Their object should always be to nudge elected officials into performing their responsibility. [Excessive intervention by the judge] tends to take responsibility away from those who ought to be seen to bear it.[4]

And finally, as Simon Rifkind has put it, there is "the ancient question, *quo warranto?* By what authority do judges turn courts into mini-legislatures?"[5]

The critical question in a republic is how government by nonelected, lifetime officials can be squared with representative democracy. The magic of the robe, the remnants of the myth that law on these matters is discovered by an elaboration of existing rules (rather than by personal preference), and the prudence of the judiciary in picking issues on which it could command a great deal of popular support—perhaps these factors explain why the judges have been as successful as they have.

I fear, however, that the judiciary has exhausted the areas where broad majoritarian support will sustain new initiatives and that the tolerance of local communities for "government by decree" is fast dissipating. If so, caution is in order lest a depreciation of the esteem in which we hold the courts undermines their performance of the essential tasks that are indisputably theirs and that other institutions cannot perform.

The authority of the courts depends in large part on the public perception that judges are different from other policy makers. Judges (but not elected officials) are impartial rather than willful or partisan; judges utilize special decisional procedures; and they draw on established general principles in deciding individual cases. In short, traditional ideas concerning the nature, form, and functions of adjudication as a decisional technique underlie popular acceptance of judicial outcomes.

While the precise boundaries of the adjudicative technique are flexible rather than fixed, if they are abandoned entirely the judge loses credibility as a judge. He becomes merely another policy maker who, in managing prisons or schools or whatnot, is expressing his personal views and throwing his weight around. When that point is reached, the judge's credibility and authority is no greater than that of Mayor White in Boston or Mayor Rizzo in Philadelphia.

With the credibility of the legislature and executive branches of government in such disrepair, we cannot afford any further depreciation in the judicial currency. General acceptance of the authority of law is a necessary bulwark of our otherwise fragile social order. If it disappears, the resulting collapse of order may put the American people in the mood for that "more effective management" which is likely to characterize any distinctly American brand of authoritarianism.

Opportunities for charismatic and authoritarian leadership, it has been said, derive in considerable measure from the ability to "accentuate [a society's] sense of being in a desperate predicament." If the courts, by overextension and consequent failure, contribute to our growing sense of desperation, our liberties may not long survive. When a people despair of their institutions, force arrives under the masquerade of ideology.

NOTES

1. Simon H. Rifkind, "Are We Asking Too Much of Our Courts?" paper prepared for the National Conference on the Causes of Popular Dissatisfaction with the Administration of Justice, St. Paul, Minn., April 8, 1976, p. 5.
2. Abram Chayes, "The Role of the Judiciary in a Public Law System," *Harvard Law Review* (May 1976).
3. *Op. cit.* n. 2, *supra.*
4. *New York Times*, May 24, 1976, p. 29.
5. Rifkind, *op. cit.* n. 1, *supra*, p. 20.

5

ADMINISTERING FEDERALISM

In a federally structured policy system, intergovernmental relations play a critical part, especially in policy formation and policy implementation. Monetary transfers are often involved, hence the widespread use of the term "fiscal federalism."

Our discussion of the federal principle begins with James Fesler's review of the broad basic approaches to organizing governmental functions. He demonstrates the differences between area and function orientations and examines their implications for public administration.

Deil Wright continues this discussion by tracing the development of American intergovernmental relations from conflict to cooperation to competition. In practice, federalism is increasingly "administrative," relying on the administration of intergovernmental grants and recognizing the necessity of managing the complexity brought about by increasing intergovernmental activity in public programs.

The Basic Theoretical Question: How to Relate Area and Function

JAMES W. FESLER

The conflict between area and function has manifested itself in so many countries, at so many levels of government, and over so many centuries, that this problem may be one that we simply must live with rather than go around desperately wondering why we cannot solve it. To recognize this is no minor achievement. If you understand when you confront a problem that it has no real, stable solution, you then know that it must be lived with, you may appreciate why a solution proves so elusive, and you may be prepared for the tensions that are going to arise. At the minimum, such an understanding can remove the guilt feelings of many administrators who feel that it is some personal inadequacy that prevents them from devising a solution for their particular government or agency. At the maximum, such understanding may lead to measures that, while they won't solve the problem, will moderate the costs of persistent conflict.

We begin with a simple and basic proposition—that area and function are competing bases of organization, which is to say that they are strikingly different ways of defining the parts into which the whole can be divided. Notice they do not differ on the need for dividing up the whole. They agree on the need for specialization whether it be specialization by area or specialization by function; they do not differ on the need for delegation of authority or, on the other hand, for the exercise of that authority within boundaries specified by constitutions, statutes, or regulations. On either basis, the fragmentation of authority may lead to parochialism, which by one definition is a passion for autonomy and a disregard for the whole. It is precisely because they share these characteristics that they must be fundamentally thought of as alternative ways of organizing rather than as complementary ways that can easily be blended.

The heart of our problems, though, is that both the claims of area and the claims of function are so immensely persuasive that political and administrative systems persistently seek ways to reconcile the irreconcilable.

All except the tiniest countries have a national government and local governments and most have an intermediate tier of states, provinces or regions. At all three levels, except for the smallest towns and villages, the administrative work is organized by function. We digress to note that this has not always been the case and that there are even exceptions today. In seventeenth and eighteenth century England two men shared the office of the King's Principal Secretary of State (one of those British anomalies in that it was a single office although two people occupied it) and, with their staffs, constituted the northern and southern divisions of the office. The southern division dealt with France, Italy, Portugal, Spain, and the colonies (Britain tended to choose colonies that were in tropical climes); while the northern division of the office concerned itself with such areas as Germany, the Netherlands, and the Baltic. Domestic affairs were divided between the two at random and, one might say, at "scrandom" because they scrambled over who might get to do these things, the intensity of the scramble depending upon the fees associated with the business they might gain. It was only in 1782 that the Home Office came into existence, gathering domestic business under one of the secretaries of state, while the other secretary became head of the Foreign Office. This, of course, constituted no triumph of function over area, for a division between foreign affairs and domestic affairs is geographically based.

In the sixteenth century, France had attempted another solution. There, each of the four secretaries of state had both a functional and a geographical responsibility. The secretaries of state for foreign affairs and for war had not only the appropriate functional responsibilities but also a set of border (frontier) provinces to oversee. The interior provinces were entrusted to the Secretary of State for the King's Household who also had functional responsibilities even then—veteran's pensions and other pensions, religious affairs, etc. The Secretary of State for the Marine handled not only naval affairs, consulates, and fishing, but also the French colonies—an areal concept again.

In our own national government today, the Department of State is area-based, constituting in effect, although State Department people might not like it, our

Office of Field Operations and Intergovernmental Relations beyond the water's edge. The Tennessee Valley Authority is clearly area-based and some years ago I lost some friendships in the Department of the Interior when I puckishly suggested that since most of its business is west of the 100th meridian, Interior might have its name changed to Department of the West and perhaps move its headquarters to Denver.

These of course are merely some curiosities—historical bumblings, a reflection of the simple fact that foreign affairs concern relations with other sovereign territorial units, or lonely experiments whose apparent success has not led to their replication, as for instance a multiplication of valley authorities. Not only have the major federal departments of government been function-based; each department in turn has divided and subdivided and sub-subdivided by activities on the functional basis. The major set of exceptions is again in the field of foreign affairs. In the State Department, AID, and USIA, the traditional organization has been by region and by country. Significantly, though, function-based offices have arisen and quite predictably, have proved difficult partners of the area-based offices and bureaus.

It will be convenient now to think principally of a national government's problems in relating area to the functional organization at the center. But let me emphasize that every government serving a sizable population confronts a problem of outreach from the center to where the people are, from the state capital to all parts of the state, and from the city hall to the neighborhoods, police precincts, health districts, and the rest.

A national government has two ways to get its responsibilities discharged outside of the capital city. One is to delegate authority to independently based political power holders that in the aggregate cover the country geographically. This includes not only such obvious areally-based independent political centers as state and local governments in the United States, but also counts with their counties and dukes with their duchies in the Frankish kingdom between the fifth and tenth centuries (with the exception of Charlemagne's reign) and later the feudal lords in France whose domains for some time were states within the state. The connection is not so remote as you might think.

The medieval city of western Europe typically obtained its autonomy—its municipal franchise (which is another word for freedom)—from the king on the understanding that the city corporation, much as a feudal lord, would serve as exclusive agent for enforcement of royal ordinances and collection of royal revenues within its boundaries. It was "contracting out," in a way, by the king. It should not astonish you that 500 to 1,000 years ago some of these territorial dukes, counts, barons, and municipal oligarchs were conservatives and some were liberals; some were nationally minded but many put local interests first; some had sufficient political power to refuse to administer national programs in their areas; some that had the political willingness to perform according to national expectations did not have staffs of sufficient administrative competence to fulfill those expectations in practice; and a very few, perhaps about a fifth of the subnational centers, were the instruments on which the national government had to depend in order to reach over half the country's population, for fiefdoms varied greatly in size. But, of course, that was all very long ago.

The other way a national government can solve its outreach problem is to set up its own field administration system, staffed with national government officials, not with provincial and local magnates. This, of course, has been the preferred way of all nation builders and empire builders. They knew that feudal and confederal arrangements trapped them into dependency on often disloyal and unqualified men of provincial power. They wanted instead to have king's men in the field, not men who might march to a different drummer. Nothing stands out more in administrative history than the determination of strong rulers that the key agents recruited should be "nobodies," men "raised from the dust," with no power in their own persons or family connections, but holding power and an assured income only while serving as the king's administrators.

Only slightly less prominent in the administrative history of nations is the concern for assuring that the core of field agents continued to evince the loyalty that was a prerequisite to "the faithful execution of the laws." In fifteenth century England, Henry III's orders to his sheriffs often read: "As you cherish your life and all that you have, see to it that . . .," and in eighteenth century Siam, the king three times specified in one set of instructions to his provincial governors that for disobedience, "punishment ranges up to death." For good measure, he added that "men in positions of trust who betray that trust shall be heavily punished by molten silver being poured down their throats." More sophisticated measures than these were common to many nations. Field agents could not be assigned to their native districts. Normally, they could not serve in any district longer than three or four years lest they "go native"; they and their families could not marry into local families during their time in a district; and they could not acquire local property. Lest these prohibitions did not work, most national rulers (Charlemagne is the principal example) regularly sent out men from the capital on tour as itinerant investigators and correctors of the field agent's performance.

This kind of field administration system was not only a preferred alternative to use of the feudal hierarchy and other provincially oriented arrangements. The national system was often deliberately used as a counterweight to, and an underminer of local power. Historians credit France's royal bailiffs and seneschals, for example, with gnawing away at the foundations of feudalism and so contributing significantly to its eventual collapse and to the rise of the modern nation-state. This means, of course, that the king's field agents were not only administrative instruments, but political instruments. The political role of field agents under this type of system remains the characteristic feature to this day.

France's prefectoral system as instituted by Napoleon and as it has performed to the present, has required the prefect to play a political role in his assigned district and in relation to Paris. It is no wonder that the prefect has at times been characterized as "a little Napoleon." Nor is it surprising that Britain, which does not have a prefectoral system at home has used the prefectoral system for the government of its colonies (as do all imperial powers). That means not only having a governor of the colony, but having district officers stationed throughout the colony.

National field administration systems come in two principal models: one we may call the *prefectoral* where a single official is in charge of all national government activities in his field area; the other we shall call the *functional* and is the one familiar to you in the United States and in Britain. In the functional system, each national functional department or bureau establishes its own field administration system—with regions it chooses, with staff it chooses, and with direct supervision from departmental or bureau headquarters in the capital. One looks in vain for a broadly empowered official like the prefect; one even looks in vain for a representative of the Executive Office of the President. In the pure prefectoral model, the conflict between area and function has been won by area, while, as its name indicates, the functional model represents the triumph of function.

Between these two models there are many variants. The Italian prefect has never had the dominant role enjoyed over considerable periods by the French prefect. And in a functional system in which a department's regional directors have strong authority over bureau programs in the region, the regional director shares some of the role characteristics and problems of a prefect. On the other hand, if we find, as we do in the current U.S. Government Organization Manual, 26 maps of regional systems of Department of Agriculture sub-units, and 10 regional maps of The Geological Survey, we may wonder if functionalism has not gone to extremes.

The prefectoral system has always survived best when the central government itself was not functionally differentiated; that is, when all significant business was handled by the king-in-court or the king-in-council rather than distributed among departments that had "gone out of court," which is to say that they had institutionalized and, in a sense, set up business for themselves. The prefectoral system has worked best when the key functions to be performed in the field were the maintenance of law and order, collection of revenue, and road and bridge construction and repair. None of these duties was highly technical; none was a positive program of economic or social development and service. It has worked best when the prefect's staff was small, well below him in social status, and differentiated, if at all, by sub-districts, rather than by functions within the area. It is a system found mostly in countries whose populations lack consensus and may be actively or latently hostile, rebellious, or anarchic as in the case of colonies and those countries whose governments tend to instability, forceful seizure of power, and absolutism. A national prefectoral system is rarely found in countries that have accepted a federal system of government, though the component states themselves may adopt a prefectoral system. Finally, a prefectoral system seems not to tempt countries such as England that are of moderate size and have a strong tradition of local self-government. Even in France, the major cities apparently escape the prefect's control and deal directly with Paris.

The most important phenomenon to observe is the recurrent corruption of the pure prefectoral system by the pressures of functionalism. This is today in France, as it was in the thirteenth and fourteenth centuries. Between 1220 and 1320 A.D. three kings developed a model prefectoral system whose area directors, the bailiffs, reported directly to the king-in-court. But soon at the center the judicial function was assigned to a special body called the *Parlement* and financial supervision moved to another special body called the Court of Accounts. The bailiff out in the field had to report to each of these. Indeed, a new bailiff took an oath before each of the bodies, in addition to one before the King's Great Council before he was sent out to his bailiwick. So the bailiffs became subject to multiple supervision from the capital, with orders flowing from the King's Great Council and his Chancellery, from the judicial Parlement, and from the Chamber of Accounts. But worse yet, the bailiff was furnished with functionally specialized subordinates; or he thought them subordinates. But his tax collector subtly won his independence. For a while only the bailiff's name continued to appear on the regular report of tax collections for the area. Then the tax collector prepared the accounts and submitted them to Paris under the legend, "for such and such bailiff" and then the heading became "in the time of such and such bailiff," or "so and so being the bailiff.'' Then the bailiff's name wholly disappears and only the collector's name is shown. Finally, the tax collector, not the bailiff, is the one who appears personally at the Chamber of Accounts in Paris for the formal audit.

The same thing happened with the judicial function. The bailiff initially held court, but as men acquired legal training at the new law schools, they were assigned to assist the bailiff in judging. Before long they were the ones holding court and the bailiff had lost another function. Lastly, prosecutors were assigned to the bailiff's staff and they too became formally independent as time passed. By the sixteenth century, the bailiffs had become only ornamental figures. American regional directors may discern cautionary parallels in this medieval progress of multiple supervision and functional subordinates' independence.

However, in monarchical France, enfeeblement of the bailiff was not the end; you get recurrent resurgence of the other doctrine; there followed other prefectoral systems. First arose a system of governors, and as they became ornamental and locally oriented, the famous system of ''intendants'' was instituted and they were the real field administrators.

French doctrine since Napoleon's time is very explicit on the dominant role of the prefect in each of the approximately 90 *departements* (areas). To convey a sense of this, we quote a 1964 decree:

> The prefect, depository in the departement of the authority of the State sees to the execution of the laws, regulations, and governmental decisions. He is the delegate of the Government and the direct representative of each of the ministers.
>
> [He] animates and coordinates the organizational units of the various civilian administrations of the State operating in the departement . . . .
>
> In each departement, only the prefect has the capacity to receive either delegations of power from ministers in charge of civilian administrations or newly established powers of decision for authorities operating within the departement. . . .
>
> Communications between the central . . . administrations on the one hand and the organization units of ministries operating in the departement . . ., on the other hand, are addressed in care of the prefect.

Some American administrators who have participated in the drafting of departmental definitions of the role of a regional director may admire the typical French clarity of this decree. But something has been lost in translation into practice. Indeed, this 1964 decree reads very much like one of 1953 signed by the whole cabinet of ministers, most of whom apparently went back to their offices and ignored it. In the last several decades, the ministries have eagerly sought ways to bypass the prefect. A number of them, for instance, have established their own regional systems, and since each region is larger than any prefect's *departement,* men in the ministries' regional offices clearly cannot be subjected to any single prefect's oversight.

That functional specialists at the capital and in the field make common cause in seeking to evade control by a generalist area administrator, whether the government-wide prefect or the department-wide regional director, should help you perceive the patterned nature of the area-function conflict. Britain is like the United States in its adherence to the functional model in field administration. Yet, during World War II England had ten regions, each under a regional commissioner. After the war the Treasury designated standard regions to which each department was required to conform unless it could demonstrate its need for an exception. In this framework of similar regions, regional coordinating committees grew luxuriantly. This, however, was all relaxed in the 1950's and standard regions, coordinating committees, even some departments' field offices all vanished or contracted greatly. In the 1960's the direction reversed again, but only with respect to planning regions. In each such region a planning board brings together regional departmental officials and an appointed advisory planning council addresses itself to problems of regional planning. This British on-again, off-again cycle may also remind you of patterns closer to home.

Let us now abandon what may have seemed an oddly roundabout approach to our problem. If we have succeeded in our direction though, you should have sensed that field administration problems are neither merely contemporary nor peculiar to this continent; that some nations in some periods have affirmed and reaffirmed an area basis of coordination for all the national government functions (which makes one suppose that our simpler problem of intra-departmental coordination of bureaus should be more easily solved than it is); and that area and function never seem to come to rest long in harmony, for if area dominates, the claims of function clamor for recognition, and if function dominates, the need for area coordination reasserts itself.

If we think of area as on a horizontal plane and of the hierarchy of areas as a series of such planes, we can think of function as a set of vertical channels, cutting through the areal planes. In this image, a field administration region is not different from a state government's or city government's area. In a modern intergovernmental system where national, state, and city governments share the same functions, each of these areal tiers will have roughly corresponding functional agencies and each will have a general legislative body and a chief executive. Officials concerned with the same functional spheres at the three governmental levels will have shared interests, value orientations, professional training, and any other clubby characteristics. One shared interest is protection of their functional programs from the meddling of the chief executives. One wonders why chief executives at the three levels have not themselves made common cause in mutual defense against the functionalists. One guess is that political differences, Republican and Democratic, liberal and conservative, together with substantial turnover in office, account for much of this failure.

In the case of field administration, one clear lesson is that the strength of a regional director mirrors the strength of his department head in Washington. If the department head cannot run his bureaus in Washington, the regional director certainly cannot run them in the field. It is conceivable that governors and mayors might gain strength from a presidency so instrumented as to give effective direction to the domestic departments, and, through them, the bureaus.

Let us attempt some more legerdemain with area and function. It is a commonplace that the natural scope of a problem, its natural boundaries, should be encompassed by the governmental jurisdiction that is expected to deal with it. This is true of area for we keep telling one another that the problems of metropolitan-area scope cry for a government of at least metropolitan-area dimensions, and that problems of multi-state regional scope cry for some regional government instrumentality. The commonplace is also part of our lore about functional organization: A functional problem or program we say should be the responsibility of a single functional agency, not be morselized among several agencies. Whether these "shoulds" and "oughts" are persuasive is not immediately relevant, for they have been ignored in the real world. It seems that the more it becomes apparent that everything is a part of everything else, the less capable we are of marking out broad fields of competence. So, paradoxically, we continue to deal in fragments of a puzzle; functional and areal parochialisms persist.

Cosmetic non-solutions are adopted for both kinds of parochialism. Among adjoining local government areas, a vast multitude of intergovernmental contracts, agreements, councils, and special districts has been spawned, the bulk of them adding up to what can be termed cooperation, not coordination. Cooperation is horizontal i.e., cooperation among equals; coordination involves a coordinator. Among federal functional agencies in Washington that share pieces of problems or programs, the parallels to the metropolitan-area case are almost exact, with inter-agency agreements (sometimes known as treaties), inter-agency committees, lead agencies, special task forces, and other devices all amounting to horizontal cooperation efforts. This intricate web then gets extended into the field with across-the-board councils and boards and with committees, commissions, and boards of particular sets of agencies. Finally, all these functional and area cooperation efforts come together in joint federal-state or federal-state-local commissions and boards.

A curiosity may be worth noting. Most of the effective cooperation efforts to overcome area parochialism tend to reinforce functional parochialism. We have already seen the by-passing of federal, state and local areas' chief executives through vertical functional relations among the several tiers of governmental areas, and you are aware that most special districts that ignore general governmental boundary lines are, as their names suggest, unifunctional. In fact, they subtract the particular function from the scope of each government that might effect coordination among functions for its territorial area. The converse of this proposition is that most of the cooperative efforts to overcome functional parochialism tend to reinforce area parochialism. As we examine the landscape we see a number of horizontal, intergovernmental efforts to interrelate functional program concerns as well as areas. But these turn out to be mostly limited to research, plan formulation, and advisory services. In other words, the individual area governments have not given up their particularistic control of action; they have merely gone along with jointness of effort at the pre-action stage and remain relatively free to act without regard to the research, the plans, or the advice.

We know a good deal about horizontal cooperation among area governments and cooperation among functional agencies. We have certainly had enough experience; a good deal of that experience consisted of repeating the same errors. One of the lessons learned from both sets of experience is the baleful fact that the least cooperative local government or functional agency is the one that fixes the threshold level of cooperation for all participants. An obvious corollary is that the participant least free to speak authoritatively for his government or agency at meetings, for example the field representative of the agency with the least degree of delegation of authority to the field, will delay joint agreement because he still must get central approval before he makes a commitment for his principal.

There is yet another corollary, again entirely familiar. An intergovernmental or interagency council or commission that begins with the state governors and the departmental regional representatives attending for their agencies is likely to move down to attendance by second and third string subordinates as time passes. Simultaneously, you may lose the capacity of participants to negotiate authoritatively at the table and may also have fewer spacious minds for perception of broader interests and the desirability of mutual accommodation.

There are other lessons to be learned from these experiences. First, "general-specialist" appears to be the clue to the problem of relating a multi-functional or supra-functional area chief to the functional specialists below and above such an area official. This is an easy way of phrasing the problem. It is the old conflict between generalist and specialist; the regional director is the generalist, the functional field men are specialists, as are their counterparts at the capital. But who is a generalist and who is a specialist is not a simple definitional question; what we find is a repeated pattern or interface regardless of what level we are talking about. This is illustrated by Herbert Kaufman's case study of New York City health districts. The district directors there were M.D.'s whom we would not consider to be generalists. Nonetheless, the sub-specialists within the health department regarded those district directors as mere amateurs dabbling in business they shouldn't get into. The sub-specialists therefore opposed the establishment of area directors with power over functional subordinates, even though everyone involved was a public health specialist.

In other words, everything is relative and relational patterns are recurrent. So we circle back to the remarkable fact that the same set of problems arise regardless of the breadth or narrowness of the functional scope of the key field agent. The prefect for all the government, the regional director for a large federal department, the regional director for a single bureau where the department does not have a departmental field organization, all face much the same issue of how to make a bundle of functions make sense *vis-a-vis* a single geographic area, and how to survive between the upper millstone of functional units at the capital and the nether millstone of functional counterparts in the region. It appears that the triumph of area over function in this country would require that functional bureaus in Washington be converted to staff rather than line agencies. That is, the functional bureaus would simply be advisory to the central, general line administrators—secretary, to the under secretary, etc.—and second, possibly, such bureaus might issue advisories to the field, such advisories not to have any compelling force. And indeed, the Ash Council came out quite strongly for virtually this kind of solution. In its wisdom the President's Executive Office then concluded that this might be fine for the housing and community development kind of activity, but wasn't appropriate for human resources, natural resources, and economic affairs.

This may not be wrong because one of the real problems is the number of field problems that must go back to the capital because that is where the real solutions lie. If a department is a hodge-podge of functions, you really don't have a rational basis for saying that it must be integrated in the field. If there is no sense of its being integrated in Washington, if it's just a convenient assemblage of bureaus, all you do is make it look as if fewer people are reporting to the President by putting them into one little square on the chart. On the other hand, any department whose components do have a strong common purpose provides a basic rationale for organizing in the field the way it is done in Washington. This is a consideration that precedes the resolution of which kind of field system you should adopt.

Now many people naturally are unhappy with that kind of triumph of area over function—converting all the bureaus in Washington into staff agencies—and this again is a recurrent pattern. A solution is triumphantly found—we will have a dual supervision system; we will have the best of both worlds, with both function and area as lines of supervision. What is done then is to decree that the regional director or the governor of the state shall provide administrative supervision, often qualified to read "general" or "overall" administrative supervision. This means the opposite of what it says, of course. The broader the term, the less content it has in those circumstances. And then, the order goes on to say that the technical bureaus in Washington are only to provide "technical" supervision. We are talking here about the counterpart functional people below the regional director and the relations of them to the regional director, and their relations to their counterpart bureaus in Washington. Oddly, there you have a precise term and a rationale—obviously technical people ought to supervise technical things, not let amateurs get into the act. It turns out that "technical" means "program substance and policy" and it does not mean a plumber's or chemist's technical competence or anything of that nature. "Administrative," in this setting, turns out to be processing of personnel forms for lower and intermediate grades only, approval of travel vouchers, and operation of a stenographic pool. Often the regional director is accorded an ornamental function, making speeches to the Rotary Club, keeping on good terms with the press, and, relatedly, a promotional function.

The promotional role is vested by orders that say, "He shall promote cooperation among the functional units under his jurisdiction." Or they even use the word "coordination." But that, happily, is one of those ambiguous terms, particularly if they say "he shall promote coordination." Then you know where the power lies. But even if the orders say "he shall coordinate," it may still have a "kicker" reading something like this:

"Nothing in this Order shall be construed as subjecting any department, establishment, or other instrumentality of the executive branch of the Federal Government or the head thereof, or any function vested by law in or assigned pursuant to law to any such agency or head, to the authority of any other such agency or head or as abrogating, modifying, or restricting any such function in any manner."

That is the conclusion of the February 1972 Executive Order for Federal Regional Councils.

Intergovernmental Relations: An Analytical Overview

DEIL S. WRIGHT

William Anderson, one of the intellectual parents of the intergovernmental relations field, once claimed that "intergovernmental relations is, I believe, a term indigenous to the United States, of a relatively recent origin, and still not widely used or understood."[1] Since Anderson's assertion in 1960, the phrase intergovernmental relations (IGR) has experienced wider usage, but whether the term is clearly or adequately understood remains questionable. Brief attention to the definition and features of IGR is therefore appropriate if not mandatory.

GAINING FORCE BY UNUSUALNESS:
THE DISTINCTIVE FEATURES OF IGR

We need look no further than the author quoted above for a starting point in clarifying IGR. Professor Anderson says that IGR is a term intended "to designate an important body of activities or interactions occurring between governmental units of all types and levels within the [United States] federal system."[2] It is possible to use his general definition as a starting point to elaborate the concept of IGR.

First and foremost, IGR occurs within the federal system. American federalism is the context, not the totality, of IGR. IGR encompasses more than is usually conveyed by the concept of federalism, where the emphasis is chiefly on national-state relationships with occasional attention to interstate relationships. IGR recognizes not only national-state and interstate relations, but also national-local, state-local, national-state-local, and interlocal relations. In short, IGR includes as proper objects of study all the permutations and combinations of relations among the units of government in the American system.

Anderson also assists us in making a second important point about IGR. "It is human beings clothed with office who are the real determiners of what the relations between units of government will be. Consequently the concept of intergovernmental relations necessarily has to be formulated largely in terms of human relations and human behavior . . ."[3] Strictly speaking, then, there are no intergovernmental relations, there are only relations among officials in different governing units. Individual interactions among public officials is at the core of IGR. In this sense it could be argued that federalism deals with the anatomy of the system, whereas IGR treats its physiology.

A third notion implicit in IGR is that relations are not one-time, occasional occurrences, formally ratified in agreements or rigidly fixed by statutes or court decisions. Rather, IGR is the continuous, day-to-day pattern of contacts, knowledge, and evaluations of government officials. A major concern is with the informal as well as with the formal, the practices as well as with the principles, pursued in both competitive and cooperative interjurisdictional patterns. This third facet of IGR reads into the concept those activities—as well as research studies—that have previously gone under the title of cooperative federalism, which the late E. S. Corwin defined as one in which governmental units "are regarded as mutually complementary parts of a single governmental mechanism all of whose powers are intended to realize the current purposes of government according to their applicability to the problem at hand."[4] These words from a constitutional law scholar provide the desirable emphasis on the working, problem-oriented informalities of IGR and at the same time are a reminder of the formal, legal, institutional context within which those relationships originate and flourish.

It has been shown that IGR recognizes multiple unit relationships, that it respects the primacy of public officials acting in an interjurisdictional context, and that it is concerned with informal working relationships in institutional contexts. A fourth distinguishing characteristic of IGR is its awareness of the role played by all public officials. Automatically assumed as integral and important to IGR are mayors, councilmen, governors, state legislators, members of Congress and others. But in recent years more attention has been paid to the actions, attitudes and roles of appointed administrators. The increased focus on administrators as relevant

IGR participants is a natural outgrowth of the increasingly important role played by public bureaucracies in government. The concern for the administrative aspects of IGR also arises, however, from attention to informal working relationships and from the academic leanings of most of the writers who have staked out claims to the IGR field. A majority of these persons have been oriented toward public administration and have also held a strong interest in state and local government.

A fifth and final distinctive feature of IGR is its policy component. Federalism has, to a large extent, translated questions of policy into questions of law and relied upon the courts for their resolution. Economic and political complexities, combined with rapid rates of social and technological change, have greatly reduced the capacity of courts—and legislatures—to deal with continuous pressures for policy change. The secular shift from regulatory politics to distributive and redistributive politics signaled new power relationships and configurations to which the term federalism could be applied only with awkward and ambiguous modifiers, such as direct, private, functional, economic. From its origins in the 1930s, IGR was recognized as anchored in politics and suffused with policy. It retains those features in the 1970s.

IGR cut its teeth on the massive political and policy issues that remained following the Supreme Court decisions on the social welfare legislation of the New Deal. It reached early adolescence in grappling with federal aid to education, urban development and civil rights. It is now attempting to claim maturity on issues related to citizen participation and effective services delivery systems. Near the policy core of IGR have been fiscal issues. These have been dominated by allocational issues: Who shall raise what amounts by what method from which citizens, and who shall spend how much for whose benefit with what results? This "fiscal fixation" has sometimes skewed diagnoses of and prescriptions for IGR problems, but the main point stands: IGR is centrally concerned with policy. As the Kestenbaum Commission noted in 1955, "The crucial questions now are questions of policy: What level ought to move? Or should both?"[5] These questions, the commission added, are ones on which the criteria for judgment "are chiefly political, economic, and administrative rather than legal."[6]

The five distinctive features of IGR are summarized in table 1. These characteristics combine and interact to produce new directions, vectors, and results in the conduct of public affairs in the United States. A new term or phrase to describe these special features therefore seems amply justified. The term IGR alerts one to the multiple, behavioral, continuous and dynamic exchanges occurring between various officials in the political system. It may be compared to a different, novel and visual filter or concept that can be laid on the American political landscape. It permits one to observe, classify and cumulate knowledge without obscuring other relevant data which prior political concepts have provided.

PHASES OF IGR

> To follow still the changes of the moon,   *Shakespeare*

To say that the American political system has evolved and changed is trite. The significant questions in dealing with change are ones centering on the frequency, mechanisms, direction, and effects of change. It is possible, for example, to understand aspects of the solar system by studying carefully the phases of the moon.

TABLE 1
DISTINCTIVE FEATURES OF INTERGOVERNMENTAL RELATIONS

1.	All Units (Multiple entities)		4.	All Public Officials (Administrators)
	National	Municipalities		Elected officials
	States	Special districts		a. legislators
	Counties	School districts		b. executives
				c. judges
2.	Interactions of Officials (Informal)			Appointed administrators
	Behavior	Perceptions		a. generalists
	Beliefs	Preferences		b. functional specialists or program professionals
3.	Continuous and Cumulative (Regularities)		5.	Policy Emphasis (Fiscal focus)
	Day-to-day contacts			Financial issues
	Working relationships			Anchored in politics
	Cumulative patterns			Suffused with policy

Similarly, a better grasp of the American political system may hopefully be gained by identifying and analyzing five phases of IGR.

In each of the five IGR phases, three main components are considered. First, what were the main problems dominating the public agenda during each phase? Second, what were the perceptions held by the main participants that seemed to guide or direct their behavior in each phase? Third, what mechanisms and techniques were used to implement intergovernmental actions and objectives during each period? Additional elements will help describe each phase, orient the reader, and reveal the effects of changing intergovernmental behavior patterns. These elements are a one-word descriptor, a metaphoric or graphic characterization, and an indication of the approximate dates in which each IGR phase peaked or climaxed.

The five phase descriptors employed here, together with rough date designations are: (1) conflict (pre–1937); (2) cooperative (1933–1953); (3) concentrated (1945–1960); (4) creative (1958–1968); and (5) competitive (1965–?). A condensed and summary chart of the successive phases is offered in table 2. Added to that overview are verbal and graphic expositions of the phases with important caveats. The phases are clearly indicated as successive ones with some overlapping of dates among the periods. While the dates have been selected with deliberateness, they are not sharp and arbitrary cutting points. Forces and tendencies bringing one or another phase to its climax were present or had antecedents in prior periods. Also, caution is necessary on terminal dates. None of the phases ends in any exact or literal sense. Each phase produces carryover effects beyond the years designated in table 2. Indeed, it is probably most accurate to think of the current state of intergovernmental affairs as resulting from overlaps of the cumulative and successive effects of each IGR phase.

Conflict (Pre-1937)

The chief concern of the conflict phase of IGR was the effort to identify and implement "proper" spheres of governmental jurisdiction and neatly defined

TABLE 2
PHASES OF INTERGOVERNMENTAL RELATIONS (IGR)

Phase Descriptor	Main Problems	Participants Perceptions	IGR Mechanisms	Federalism Metaphor	Approximate Climax Period
Conflict	Defining boundaries Proper spheres	Antagonistic Adversary Controversy Exclusivity	Statutes Courts Regulations	Layer cake federalism	Pre–1937
Cooperative	Economic stress International threat	Collaboration Complementary Mutuality Supportive	Policy planning Broad formula grants Open-ended grants Tax credit	Marble cake federalism	1933–1953
Concen- trated	Program needs Capital works	Professionalism Objectivity Neutrality Functionalism	Categorical grants Service standards	Focused or channelled federalism (water taps)	1945–1960
Creative	Urban-metro- politan Disadvantaged clients	National goals Great society Grantsmanship	Program planning Project grants Participation	Fused-foliated federalism (prolifer- ated)	1958–1968
Competitive	Coordination Program effectiveness Delivery systems Citizen access	Disagreement Tension Rivalry	Revenue sharing Reorganization Regionalization Grant consolidation	Picket fence federalism (frag- mented)	1965– ?

boundaries for officials' actions. This emphasis operated at the state-local level as well as between national and state governments. Dillon's rule, as a principle for interpreting narrowly the powers of local governments, was not only an assertion of state supremacy but also a consequence of the search for the exact limits of local power. Guiding this search was an expectation of exclusive powers. Public officials' perceptions reflected these adversary and antagonistic patterns of interaction.

These conceptions and attitudinal postures by participants were anchored in deeper societal values of competition, corporate organizational forms, profit and efficiency. Residual elements of this phase remain today on the urban-metropolitan scene in the so-called market models of metropolitanism and in the search for the political jurisdiction to perform most efficiently a particular function—for example, should an activity be assigned to a city or to an areawide body?

The manner in which problems of jurisdiction were resolved in the conflict model of IGR was through statutes and the courts. Growing social and economic complexity subsequently brought regulatory agencies and commissions into being to referee jurisdictional boundary disputes. The Interstate Commerce Act of 1887 created the first of the great regulatory commissions and was a major breach in the century-old "administrative settlement" between the national government and the states.[7] It broke the long-standing presumption against the creation and growth of a national administrative establishment. Attempts to locate the scope of federal regulatory power under the commerce clause and other authority have persisted to the point that under a recent court ruling *all* electric generating and transmission companies fall under the rate-making authority of the Federal Power Commission.

Other illustrations of the continued adversary, conflict-oriented pattern of national-state relations abound. Environmental and health concerns recently precipitated a jurisdictional dispute over the spheres of national and state power to regulate the safety levels of a nuclear generating plant in Minnesota. National standards set by the Atomic Energy Commission (AEC) specified one level of allowable millirems of radiation escaping from the reactor into the atmosphere. The Minnesota Pollution Control Agency set the permissible level of millirems at only two percent of that sanctioned by the AEC. The Northern States Power Company brought suit in the federal court challenging the state standards and requesting permission to construct the nuclear power plant without regard for the Minnesota regulations. At issue in the case was the application and intent of federal statutes dealing with atomic energy. The court ruled in favor of the exclusive jurisdiction of the national government and invalidated the more restrictive state regulations.[8]

These recent court decisions probably come as close to reflecting current economic realities, social interdependencies, and technological necessity as pre-1937 courts and legislatures thought they were reflecting economic, social and technological separatism. That supposed separatism—however limited, qualified or restricted in practice—gave credence to the metaphor of "layer cake federalism" as a crude means of describing national, state and local disconnectedness.

Cooperation (1933–1953)

Several authors have ably argued and amply demonstrated that intergovernmental collaboration in the United States existed throughout the 19th and 20th centuries.[9] That such collaboration was of major significance or the dominant fact of our political history is less clear. It does seem possible, however, to point to one period in which complementary and supportive relationships were most prominent and had high political significance. That period is the cooperative phase from 1933–1953. The prime elements of national concern during those two decades were the alleviation of widespread economic distress and response to international threats. It seems logical and natural that internal and external challenges to national survival would bring us closer together.

The means by which increased collaboration occurred were several and varied. Most pertinent for our concerns were such approaches as national policy planning, tax credits, and categorical grants-in-aid. Most of the dozen or so grant programs enacted during the depression period were broad formula grants, with a few being open-ended. Special emergency funding arrangements were instituted during the depression years and repeated in selected federally-impacted areas in wartime. As one observer noted in 1943:

> Cooperative government by federal-state-local authorities has become a byword in the prodigious effort to administer civilian defense, rationing, and other war-time programs. . . . Intergovernmental administration, while it is a part of all levels of government, is turning into something quite distinct from them all.[10]

The IGR collaboration that persisted during these years was present on such unusual occasions as the 1952 steel seizure confrontation; prior to his seizure effort, President Truman polled state governors for their views.

The prime IGR mechanism, as well as the major legacy of this cooperative period, was fiscal. Substantial and significant fiscal links were firmly established. These established conduits were harbingers of more to come. They also served as important illustrations of a new and differently textured model of intergovernmental patterns, the well-publicized "marble cake" metaphor. The marble cake characterization appears to have been coined by Professor Joseph McLean of Princeton University in the early 1940s for the visual or contrast effect with the layer cake conception. Professor Morton Grodzins probably had the greatest impact in popularizing and elaborating the marble cake concept.

Concentrated (1945–1960)

The descriptor employed for this IGR phase stands for the specific, functional, highly focused nature of intergovernmental interaction that evolved and dominated the Truman-Eisenhower years. From 1946 to 1960, twenty-nine major new grant-in-aid programs were established, a number that doubled the total number of programs enacted before and during the depression and wartime eras. The expanded use of categorical grant programs was accompanied by increased attention to service standards and program measurement.

Guiding this growing functional emphasis were corps of program professionals in each of the specialized grant fields, such as airport construction, hospital construction, slum clearance and urban renewal, urban planning, waste treatment facilities, library construction, and so on. The pervasiveness of professionalism enhanced the service standards emphasis by covering the domain with a cloak of objectivity and neutrality. These fit comfortably into Professor Herbert Kaufman's conception of the autonomy accompanying "neutral competence" in public administration contrasted with the control over policy by a strong executive leader.[11] The professionalism, specialized grants and growing insulation also coincided neatly in time, as well as thematically, with Professor Frederick Mosher's view that the 1950s confirmed the triumph of the "professional state" in the public service.[12]

What aims or ends guided and provided the rationale for this surge of activity? Two appear to be most prominent. One was a capital works, public construction push. Between 1946 and 1960, state and local capital outlays increased twelvefold while current operating expenses rose by a multiple of four. Federal grants for highways, hospitals, sewage plants, and airports underwrote much of the state-local effort to meet deferred wartime needs and respond to changing technology and population configurations, especially its suburbanization.

A second motive force propelling intergovernmental action in this period was the political realization that government generally, and IGR especially, was capable of responding to particularistic middle class needs. The New Deal may have had its most telling political effect in making the American middle class acutely aware of the positive and program-specific capabilities of governmental action. Effective political action based on this awareness came after World War II and was reinforced by several conditions.

One condition already mentioned was suburbanization. It constituted the urban frontier and reinforced the myth of Jeffersonian ward republics. Another was the predisposition for using intergovernmental mechanisms because they also meshed with the historical political tradition of localism. In addition, IGR techniques fitted middle class values of professionalism, objectivity and neutrality. It appeared that objective program needs rather than politics were being served. Like reform at the turn of the century, IGR appeared to take a program out of politics.

Those political values coincided with an important structural change at the national level: the legislative reorganization of Congress in 1946. The most significant result of this event for IGR was the creation and stabilization of standing committees with an explicit program emphasis. These congressional committee patterns soon became the leverage points and channels through which influence on program-specific grants flowed. Furthermore, the committees developed their own cadre of professional staff members with functional and programmatic inclinations.

The flow of influence combined with the concentrated or focused flow of funds in the 1946–1960 period prompts one to employ a hydraulic metaphor in depicting this phase of IGR. The national government had become an established reservoir of fiscal resources to which a rapidly increasing number of water taps were being connected. The functional flows of funds could be facilitated by those knowledgeable at turning on the numerous spigots, that is, the program professionals. Cooperation was prominent during this period, but it occurred in more concentrated and selectively channeled ways.

A crude effort to express the water tap phase of IGR is made in figure 1. The intergovernmental flow of funds for 1950 is shown by the lines connecting the national-state and state-local spending sectors. This phase of IGR confirmed the interconnected and interdependent nature of national-state-local relations.

Creative (1958–1968)

The foundations for the creative phase of IGR were formed and filled in the cooperative and concentrated periods. The dates delimiting this phase are again somewhat arbitrary, but they mark a decade of moves toward decisiveness rather than drift in American politics and public policy. The election of a heavily Democratic Congress in 1958 and the 1964 presidential results were the political pegs to which this phase of IGR was attached. An added input that contributed to direction and cohesiveness, if not decisiveness, was the report of the Eisenhower-appointed President's Commission on National Goals. The commission, appointed partially in response to the Russian challenge of Sputnik, was created in 1959 and reported in 1961.[13]

The term Creative Federalism is applied to this decade because of presidential usage and because of the novel and numerous initiatives in IGR during the period. Three mechanisms are prominent: (1) program planning, (2) project grants, and (3) popular participation. The sheer number of grant programs alone is sufficient to set this decade apart from the preceding periods. In 1961 the Advisory Commission on Intergovernmental Relations (ACIR) identified approximately 40 major grant programs in existence that had been enacted prior to 1958. By 1969 there were an estimated 160 major programs, 500 specific legislative authorizations, and 1,315 different federal assistance activities, for which money figures, application deadlines, agency contacts, and use restrictions could be identified. Federal grants jumped in dollar magnitude from $4.9 billion in 1958 to $23.9 billion in 1970. At the state-local level, state aid to local governments rose from $8.0 billion to $28.9 billion over the 1958–1970 span.

FIGURE 1   PUBLIC EXPENDITURES BY TYPE AND BY LEVEL OF GOVERNMENT
AND THE INTERGOVERNMENTAL FLOW OF FUNDS, FISCAL YEAR 1950
(in billions of dollars)

Total Expenditures (all governments): 70.3*

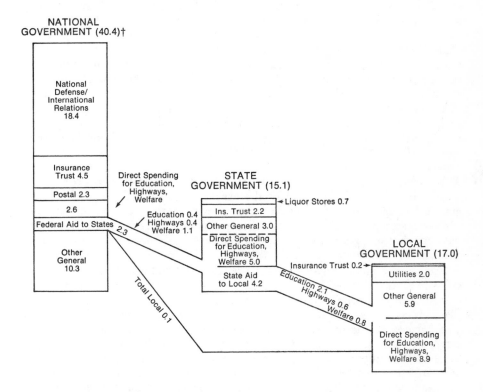

*Excludes duplicate transfers.
†Excludes interest on the national debt ($4.4 billion).

Numbers and dollars alone are insufficient to distinguish the creative phase. Planning requirements, for example, were attached to 61 of the new grant programs enacted between 1961 and 1966. The tremendous growth in project grants as contrasted with formula grants increased the diversity of activities supported by federal funds and increased further the autonomy and discretion of program professionals. Project grant authorizations grew from 107 to 280 between 1962 and 1967, while formula grants rose from 53 to 99 in the same period. Finally, the public participation requirements tied to some grants increased the complexity, the calculations, and occasionally the chagrin of officials charged with grant allocation choices.

To what ends or aims were these federal initiatives directed? What were the chief problems addressed by this activism? At the risk of great oversimplification, two major policy themes are identified: (1) an urban-metropolitan emphasis and (2) attention to disadvantaged persons in the society through the anti-poverty programs and aid to education funds. The latter problem needs little documentation.

Only one supporting item is mentioned for the former. Between 1961 and 1969 the percentage of all federal aid that went to urban areas increased from 55 percent to 70 percent, as total dollar amount so allocated went from $3.9 billion to $14.0 billion.[14]

Supporting the urban and disadvantaged emphases of this phase were selective but significant views held by important actors. President Johnson's speech first mentioning Creative Federalism also contained a phrase of larger and more popular political importance, that is, "The Great Society." As one observer has noted: "The Great Society was, by definition, one society; the phrase was singular, not plural."[15] How much this consensus politics push owed to the popularity of national goals efforts in the late 1950s and early 1960s is unknown. The unitary emphasis was evident, however. The president's preference on the need for centralized objective-setting made his 1965 moves toward planning- programming-budgeting a natural offshoot of views which held that our governmental system was a single system. Indeed, the basis for such revisionary thinking had been spelled out in a 1961 speech by Senator Joseph Clark entitled "Toward National Federalism."[16]

Accompanying these national and unitary sets of participants' perspectives was a subsidiary theme. It grew out of the expansion and proliferation of federal grants. This was the grantsmanship perspective that formed around the poverty and project grant programs. Playing the federal grant game became a well-known but time-consuming activity for mayors, managers, governors, universities, and, of course, for the program professionals.

This creative phase of IGR contains a paradox. Federal grants expanded massively in number, scope, and dollar magnitudes. The diversity that accentuated grantsmanship tendencies, however, moved from political and policy assumptions that were common—if not unitary—in their conception about the aims of society. The paradox is one of proliferation, participation, and pluralism amid convergence, consent, and concord. The prominence of the latter set suggests that "fused" is an appropriate metaphor by which this IGR phase can be characterized. An effort to show visually the coalesced character of IGR at the end of the creative period is provided in figure 2. The ties between national-state and state-local sectors are broad and weld the segments into a closely linked system. The visual contrast between figures 1 and 2 helps confirm the shift from a focused to a fused model of the IGR system.

The contrasting component present in this creative phase has not yet been noted. Figure 2 conveys the impression of intense interconnectedness and interdependence. What it does not convey is the diversity, proliferation, and fragmentation of the national-state fiscal links. There may be a superficial appearance of fusion, but the scores of specific and discrete categorical grants require additional adjectives to describe this period, such as the fused-foliated or proliferated phase.

Other, more crude metaphors that could be used are flowering federalism and spaghetti federalism. Both terms attempt to capture the elaborate, complex, and intricate features of IGR that developed in this phase.

Competitive (1965–?)

The proliferation of grants, the clash between professionals and participation-minded clients, the gap between program promises and proven performance, plus

FIGURE 2 PUBLIC EXPENDITURES BY TYPE AND BY LEVEL OF GOVERNMENT
AND THE INTERGOVERNMENTAL FLOW OF FUNDS, FY 1970
(in billions of dollars)

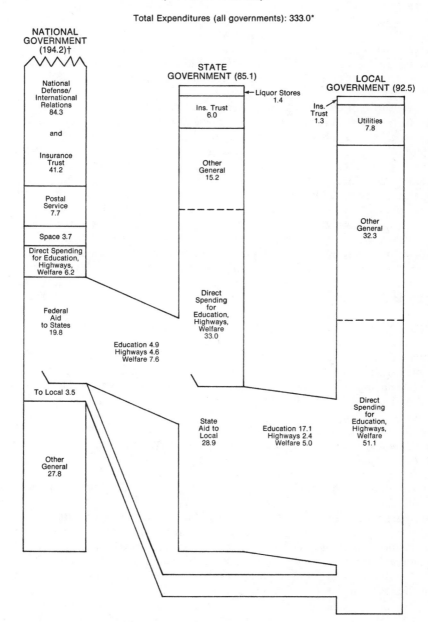

Source: Bureau of the Census, *Governmental Finances in 1969-70*.

*Excludes duplicate transfers.

†Excludes interest on the national debt ($14.0 billion).

the intractability of domestic urban and international problems, formed a malaise in which IGR entered a new phase.

A different statement of central problems emerged when the administrative consequences of prior legislative whirlwinds became the center of attention. Issues associated with bureaucratic behavior and competence came to the forefront. One talisman earnestly sought was coordination. Others in close association were program accomplishment, effective service delivery systems and citizen access. Attention shifted to administrative performance and to organizational structures and relationships that either hindered or helped the effective delivery of public goods and services.

A sharply different tack was taken regarding appropriate IGR mechanisms. Pressure grew to alter and even reverse previous grant trends. Grant consolidation and revenue sharing were mentioned, popularized, and ultimately proposed by a Republican president on the basis of both program effectiveness and strengthening state and local governments. Some progress was made in the grant consolidation sphere, but as of 1973 the ACIR reported 69 formula grants and 312 project grants in existence. On the federal administrative scene, moves were made toward regionalization and reorganization. With the strong support of mayors, governors and county officials, general revenue sharing slipped through a divided Congress.

A flood of other developments in the late 1960s and early 1970s underscored the competition present in the system and also signaled efforts to reduce it. Perhaps the more visible actions and initiatives came at the national level, but in numerical terms and potential significance, important policy shifts occurred at the state and local levels. It is impossible to compress the numerous trends that were competition-inducing and to acknowledge some that eased competitive tendencies. Only three policy patterns will be mentioned as illustrations of tension-promoting developments: (1) economic opportunity programs and their chief implementation mechanisms—community action agencies; (2) "white flight" and the polarization of central city-suburban relationships, especially along racial lines; and (3) elimination or funding reductions in several grant programs by the Nixon administration in 1973—some of which were achieved by the impounding of funds.

Countervailing tendencies in the direction of reduced tensions and increased cooperation appeared during this competition-dominated phase. At the local level, prompted and supported by national action, councils of governments sprang into existence in large numbers. One major aim was to foster metropolitan and regional coordination, especially through the A-95 grant review process. At the state level, herculean tax efforts were made to: (1) expand state services, (2) greatly increase state aid to local governments, and (3) meet the enlarged state-level funding requirements to match the vastly expanded federal grant monies.[17] Tension-reducing aims can also be attributed to such national-level actions as new departures with interstate compacts, the Partnership for Health Act (P.L.89–749), the Intergovernmental Cooperation Act of 1968 (P.L.90–577) and the Intergovernmental Personnel Act of 1970 (P.L.91–648).

The developments noted above reflected contrasting sets of perspectives that old as well as new participants brought to IGR. A statement by Senator Edmund Muskie—Democrat, Maine—in 1966 will serve as one example: "The picture, then, is one of too much tension and conflict rather than coordination and cooperation all along the line of administration—from top Federal policymakers and administrators to the state and local professional administrators and elected officials.''[18] Similar views about the unwarranted degree of disagreement, tension, and rivalry among and between officials prompt the use of ''competitive'' for this phase of IGR.

The competition, however, is different in degree, emphasis, and configuration from the interlevel conflict of the older, layer cake phase. It is more modulated, and it acknowledges the lessons learned from the intervening periods of cooperation, concentration and creativity. For example, the current competitive phase appears reasonably realistic about the interdependencies within the system and the inability to turn the clock back in IGR. The three statutory enactments cited above bear witness to reasoned and reality-oriented approaches to IGR.

The nature of the competition in the present IGR phase is indicated in part by Senator Muskie's remarks. He mentions professional program administrators and state-local elected officials. It is the tension betweeen the policy generalist, whether elected or appointed, and the program-professional-specialists that currently produces great static and friction in IGR. This cleavage is another reason for describing this phase of IGR as competitive. A visual representation of the fractures and rivalry characterizing this phase is offered in figure 3. The metaphor of the picket fence, referred to in former Governor Sanford's book, *Storm Over the States,*[19] was the original stimulus for this formulation. The seven public interest groups, often called the Big Seven, have parted ways from the functional specialists. Their common interest in revenue sharing, grant consolidation and similar proposals represents a reassertion of the executive leadership doctrine and a challenge to the program professionals' doctrine of neutral competence.

A second type of competition can also be discerned from figure 3: the competition between the several functional program areas. Each vertical picket represents an alliance among like-minded program specialists or professionals, regardless of the level of government in which they serve. As early as the mid-1950s these interlevel linkages of loyalties were identified and criticized as ''vertical functional autocracies.''[20] Other epithets used against these patterns are: balkanized bureaucracies, feudal federalisms and autonomous autocracies. These terms emphasize not only the degree of autonomy that the program specialists have from policy control by political generalists, but also the separateness and independence that one program area has from another. This lack of horizontal linkage prompts interprogram, interprofessional and interagency competition. The cross-program competition combined with the generalist-specialist split helps confirm the contention that the competition depicted by the picket fence model best describes the current and most recent phase of IGR.

Both competitive patterns were captured in the words of local officials as quoted by James Sundquist. Speaking in the late 1960s, the director of a local model cities program contended that ''Our city is a battleground among federal Cabinet agencies.''[21] Similar sentiments came from mayors and city managers whose limited control and coordination powers over federal programs caused them to feel like spectators of the governmental process in their own cities. If, in fact, this competitive model is applicable to IGR today, then a recognition of these tensions and cleavages would seem to be the first-order task of those seeking changes and improvements in IGR.

FIGURE 3   PICKET FENCE FEDERALISM: A SCHEMATIC REPRESENTATION

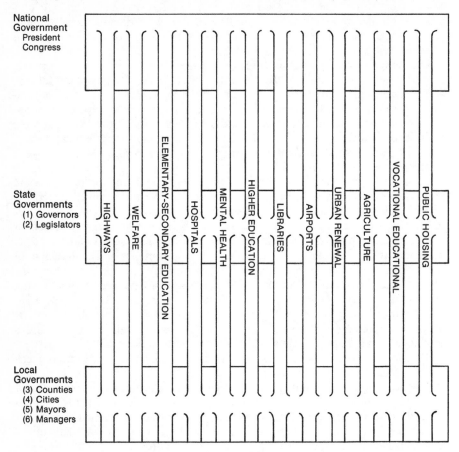

THE BIG SEVEN

(1) National Governors Conference   (4) National Association of County Officials
(2) Council of State Governments   (5) National League of Cities
(3) National Legislative Conference   (6) U.S. Conference of Mayors
                                           (7) International City Management Association

CONCLUDING COMMENT

IGR has become a distinctive dimension of activities in the American political system. It refers to a significant domain of political, policy and administrative actions by public officials. An acknowledged emphasis was made in this discussion on the meaning, features and trends in IGR (as a term or phrase). Concept explication and clarification have their uses; but they also have limits. There is much more to be said about the realities, practices and problems of IGR. Subsequent articles are appropriately addressed to these types of concerns.

One concluding comment on this exposition is offered in anticipation of the analyses that follow. This is an era when the *management* of IGR is a matter of major moment. James Sundquist observes that "The federal system is too important to be left to chance."[22] His book can be seen as an effort to critique and reconstruct the organizational philosophy undergirding effective intergovernmental action. Sundquist's treatment and the mood of this essay move toward a similar conclusion: intergovernmental achievements hinge on coping successfully with complexity. Complexity is an inherent and persistent characteristic of the several features of IGR. Accomplishments in the intergovernmental arena therefore depend on the successful management of complexity.

NOTES

1. William Anderson, *Intergovernmental Relations in Review* (Minneapolis: University of Minnesota Press, 1960), p. 3.
2. Ibid., p. 3.
3. Ibid., p. 4.
4. E. S. Corwin, *The Passing of Dual Federalism*, VIRGINIA LAW REVIEW 36 (February 1950), p. 19.
5. Commission on Intergovernmental Relations, *A Report to the President for Transmittal to the Congress* (Washington, D.C., June 1955), p. 33.
6. Ibid., p. 33.
7. Leonard D. White, *The States and The Nation* (Baton Rouge: Louisiana State University Press, 1953), pp. 9–10.
8. *Northern States Power Co. v. State of Minnesota*, 447 F. 2nd 1143 (1971); *see also, Science* 171 (8 January 1971), p. 45, and Harry Foreman, ed., *Nuclear Power and the Public* (Minneapolis: University of Minnesota Press, 1970).
9. Morton Grodzins, *The American System: A New View of Government in the United States* (Chicago: Rand McNally, 1966); Daniel J. Elazar, *The American Partnership: Intergovernmental Cooperation in the Nineteenth Century United States* (Chicago: University of Chicago Press, 1962).
10. Arthur W. Bromage, "Federal-State-Local Relations," *American Political Science Review* 37, no. 1 (February 1943), p. 35.
11. Herbert Kaufman, "Emerging Conflicts in the Doctrines of Public Administration," *American Political Science Review* 50, no. 4 (December 1956), pp. 1057–1073.
12. Frederick Mosher, *Democracy and the Public Service* (New York: Oxford University Press, 1968), esp. ch. 4, "The Professional State."
13. Report of the President's Commission on National Goals, *Goals for Americans* (Englewood Cliffs, N.J.: Prentice-Hall, Spectrum Series and the American Assembly of Columbia University, 1960).
14. *Special Analyses, Budget of the United States, Fiscal Year 1971* (Washington, D.C., 1970), pp. 228–229.
15. James L. Sundquist, *Making Federalism Work: A Study of Program Coordination at the Community Level* (Washington, D.C.: The Brookings Institution, 1969), p. 12.
16. George Washington University, *The Federal Government and the Cities: A Symposium* (Washington, D.C.: George Washington University, 1961), pp. 39–49.
17. For example, state funds to match federal aid increased from $5.1 billion in 1964 to an estimated $18.4 billion in 1972; *see,* Deil S. Wright and David E. Stephenson, "The States as Middlemen: Five Fiscal Dilemmas," *State Government* 47, no. 2 (Spring 1974), pp. 101–107.
18. U.S., Congress, Senate, *Congressional Record,* 89th Cong., 2nd sess., 1966, 112, p. 6834.
19. Terry Sanford, *Storm Over the States* (New York: McGraw-Hill, 1967), p. 80.
20. Advisory Committee on Local Government, *An Advisory Committee Report on Local Government* (submitted to the Commission on Intergovernmental Relations, Washington, D.C., June 1955), p. 7.
21. Sundquist, *Making Federalism Work*, p. 27.
22. Ibid., p. 31.

PART THREE

The Management of Governmental Agencies

6

ORGANIZATIONAL
THEORIES AND BEHAVIOR

So far our emphasis has been on the *external* political environment in which public agencies operate. Part three focuses on the *internal* politics of public organizations—administrative behavior and management processes. Of course these can
never be separated completely, as will be obvious in future chapters.

Historically there have been two principal and contending schools of organization theory: (1) the classical school, which emphasizes the formal organization, its
structure, and the authority vested in individuals according to the positions they
hold in the organizations; and (2) the neoclassical school, which rejects the assumptions about human beings implicit in the theories of the classicists on the
grounds that informal organization was believed more important to an organization's performance than formal structure. Those associated with the human relations approach frequently stressed the importance of participative management.

The first two selections in this chapter summarize the debate between the classicists and neoclassicists. First, Peter Blau and Marshall Meyer summarize the ideas
about bureaucracy of the great German sociologist Max Weber, who concentrated
on the formal organization and hierarchy in administration. Then, Douglas
McGregor focuses on the informal aspects of human behavior in organizations.

Scholars have increased our sophistication about organizational behavior, and it
is generally thought now that modern organization theory requires input from
both the classical and neoclassical schools. Much research also suggests that the behavior of an effective administrator must be task-oriented as well as people-ori-
ented. In the next two articles, Melvin Kohn and Fred Fiedler summarize their
extensive research. Kohn reports on a study of "bureaucrats" to see whether they
resemble their popular stereotype. Fiedler analyzes the nature of organizational
leadership under a variety of circumstances.

Significant changes are underway in public organizations, and the last two selections in this chapter assess their significance. First, Robert Denhardt and Jan
Perkins discuss the impact of women and the feminist movement on public agencies. Next, Adam Herbert examines the status of the minority administrator in
government. Both cases represent more than simple personnel changes; they suggest new attitudes toward and expectations for the behavior of public agencies.

The Concept of Bureaucracy

PETER M. BLAU
MARSHALL W. MEYER

The main characteristics of a bureaucratic structure (in the "ideal-typical" case[1]), according to Weber, are the following:

1. "The regular activities required for the purposes of the organization are distributed in a fixed way as official duties."[2] The clear-cut division of labor makes it possible to employ only specialized experts in each particular position and to make every one of them responsible for the effective performance of his duties. This high degree of specialization has become so much part of our socioeconomic life that we tend to forget that it did not prevail in former eras but is a relatively recent bureaucratic innovation.

2. "The organization of offices follows the principle of hierarchy; that is, each lower office is under the control and supervision of a higher one."[3] Every official in this administrative hierarchy is accountable to his superior for his subordinates' decisions and actions as well as his own. To be able to discharge his responsibility for the work of subordinates, he has authority over them, which means that he has the right to issue directives and they have the duty to obey them. This authority is strictly circumscribed and confined to those directives that are relevant for official operations. The use of status prerogatives to extend the power of control over subordinates beyond these limits does not constitute the legitimate exercise of bureaucratic authority.

3. Operations are governed "by a consistent system of abstract rules . . . [and] consist of the application of these rules to particular cases."[4] This system of standards is designed to assure uniformity in the performance of every task, regardless of the number of persons engaged in it, and the coordination of different tasks. Explicit rules and regulations define the responsibility of each member of the organization and the relationships among them. This does not imply that bureaucratic duties are necessarily simple and routine. It must be remembered that strict adherence to general standards in deciding specific cases characterizes not only the job of the file clerk but also that of the Supreme Court justice. For the former, it may involve merely filing alphabetically; for the latter, it involves interpreting the law of the land in order to settle the most complicated legal issues. Bureaucratic duties range in complexity from one of these extremes to the other.

4. "The ideal official conducts his office . . . [in] a spirit of formalistic impersonality, 'Sine ira et studio,' without hatred or passion, and hence without affection or enthusiasm."[5] For rational standards to govern operations without interference from personal considerations, a detached approach must prevail within the organization and especially toward clients. If an official develops strong feelings about some subordinates or clients, he can hardly help letting those feelings influence his official decisions. As a result, and often without being aware of it himself, he might be particularly lenient in evaluating the work of one of his subordinates or might discriminate against some clients and in favor of others. The

exclusion of personal considerations from official business is a prerequisite for impartiality as well as for efficiency. The very factors that make a government bureaucrat unpopular with his clients, an aloof attitude and a lack of genuine concern with them as human beings, actually benefit these clients. Disinterestedness and lack of personal interest go together. The official who does not maintain social distance and becomes personally interested in the cases of his clients tends to be partial in his treatment of them, favoring those he likes over others. Impersonal detachment engenders equitable treatment of all persons and thus equal justice in administration.

5. Employment in the bureaucratic organization is based on technical qualifications and is protected against arbitrary dismissal. "It constitutes a career. There is a system of 'promotions' according to seniority or to achievement, or both."[6] These personnel policies, which are found not only in civil service but also in many private companies, encourage the development of loyalty to the organization and esprit de corps among its members. The consequent identification of employees with the organization motivates them to exert greater efforts in advancing its interests. It may also give rise to a tendency to think of themselves as a class apart from and superior to the rest of the society. Among civil servants, this tendency has been more pronounced in Europe, notably in Germany and France, than in the United States, but among military officers, it may be found here too.

6. "Experience tends universally to show that the purely bureaucratic type of administrative organization . . . is, from a purely technical point of view, capable of attaining the highest degree of efficiency."[7] "The fully developed bureaucratic mechanism compares with other organizations exactly as does the machine with non-mechanical modes of production."[8] Bureaucracy solves the distinctive organizational problem of maximizing organizational efficiency, not merely that of individuals.

The superior administrative efficiency of bureaucracy is the expected result of its various characteristics as outlined by Weber. For an individual to work efficiently, he must have the necessary skills and apply them rationally and energetically; but for an organization to operate efficiently, more is required. Every one of its members must have the expert skills needed for the performance of his tasks. This is the purpose of specialization and of employment on the basis of technical qualifications, often ascertained by objective tests. Even experts, however, may be prevented by personal bias from making rational decisions. The emphasis on impersonal detachment is intended to eliminate this source of irrational action. But individual rationality is not enough. As noted above, if the members of the organization were to make rational decisions independently, their work would not be coordinated and the efficiency of the organization would suffer. Hence there is need for discipline to limit the scope of rational discretion, which is met by the system of rules and regulations and the hierarchy of supervision. Moreover, personnel policies that permit employees to feel secure in their jobs and to anticipate advancements for faithful performance of duties discourage attempts to impress superiors by introducing clever innovations, which may endanger coordination. Lest this stress on disciplined obedience to rules and rulings undermine the employee's motivation to devote his energies to his job, incentives for exerting effort must be furnished. Personnel policies that cultivate organizational loyalty and that provide for promotion on the basis of merit serve this function. In other words, the combined effect of bureaucracy's characteristics is to create social conditions which constrain each member of the organization to act in ways that, whether they appear rational or otherwise from his individual standpoint, further the rational pursuit of organizational objectives.

Without explicitly stating so, Weber supplied a *functional* analysis of bureaucracy. In this type of analysis, a social structure is explained by showing how each of its elements contributes to its persistence and effective operations. Concern with discovering all these contributions, however, entails the danger that the scientist may neglect to investigate the disturbances that various elements produce in the structure. As a result, his presentation may make the social structure appear to function more smoothly than it actually does, since he neglects the disruptions that do in fact exist. To protect ourselves against this danger, it is essential to extend the analysis beyond the mere consideration of functions, as Robert K. Merton points out.[9] Of particular importance for avoiding false implications of stability and for explaining social change is the study of *dysfunctions,* those consequences that interfere with adjustment and create problems in the structure.[10]

A reexamination of the foregoing discussion of bureaucratic features in the light of the concept of dysfunction reveals inconsistencies and conflicting tendencies. If reserved detachment characterizes the attitudes of the members of the organization toward one another, it is unlikely that high esprit de corps will develop among them. The strict exercise of authority in the interest of discipline induces subordinates, anxious to be highly thought of by their superiors, to conceal defects in operations from superiors, and this obstruction of the flow of information upward in the hierarchy impedes effective management. Insistence on conformity also tends to engender rigidities in official conduct and to inhibit the rational exercise of judgment needed for the efficient performance of tasks. If promotions are based on merit, many employees will not experience advancements in their careers. If they are based primarily on seniority so as to give employees this experience and thereby to encourage them to become identified with the organization, the promotion system will not furnish strong incentives for exerting efforts and excellent performance. These illustrations suffice to indicate that the same factor that enhances efficiency in one respect often threatens it in another; it may have *both* functional and dysfunctional consequences.

Weber was well aware of such contradictory tendencies in the bureaucratic structure. But since he treats dysfunctions only incidentally, his discussion leaves the impression that administrative efficiency in bureaucracies is more stable and less problematical than it actually is. In part, it was his intention to present an idealized image of bureaucratic structure, and he used the conceptual tool appropriate for this purpose. Let us critically examine this conceptual tool.

Weber dealt with bureaucracy as what he termed an "ideal type." This methodological concept does not represent an average of the attributes of all existing bureaucracies (or other social structures), but a pure type, derived by abstracting the most characteristic bureaucratic aspects of all known organizations. Since perfect bureaucratization is never fully realized, no empirical organization corresponds exactly to this scientific construct.

The criticism has been made that Weber's analysis of an imaginary ideal type does not provide understanding of concrete bureaucratic structures. But this criticism obscures the fact that the ideal-type construct is intended as a guide in empirical research, not as a substitute for it. By indicating the characteristics of bureaucracy in its pure form, it directs the researcher to those aspects of organizations that he must examine in order to determine the extent of their bureaucratization. This is the function of all conceptual schemes: to specify the factors that must be taken into consideration in investigations and to define them clearly.

The ideal typical model of bureaucracy, however, is not simply a conceptual scheme. It includes not only definitions of concepts but also implicit generalizations about the relationships among them, and specifically the hypothesis that the diverse bureaucratic characteristics increase administrative efficiency. If certain attributes (for example, specialization, hierarchy, rules, and impersonality) are distinctive of bureaucracy compared to other forms of administration, and if bureaucracy is the most efficient form of administration, then at least some of the attributes of bureaucracy must be conducive to efficient operations. Whereas conceptual definitions are presupposed in research and not subject to verification by research findings, hypotheses concerning relationships among factors are subject to such verification. Whether strict hierarchical authority, for example, indeed furthers efficiency is a question of empirical fact and not one of definition. But as the scientific construct Weber intended it to be, the ideal type cannot be refuted by empirical evidence. If a study of several organizations were to find that strict hierarchical authority is not related to efficiency, this would not prove that no such relationship exists in the ideal-type bureaucracy; it would show only that these organizations are not fully bureaucratized. Since generalizations about idealized states defy testing in systematic research, they have no place in science. On the other hand, if empirical evidence is taken into consideration and generalizations are modified accordingly, we deal with prevailing tendencies in bureaucratic structures and no longer with a pure type.

Two misleading implications of the ideal-type conception of bureaucracy deserve special mention. The student of social organization is concerned with the patterns of activities and interactions that reveal how social conduct is organized, and not with exceptional deviations from these patterns. The fact that one official becomes excited and shouts at his colleague, or that another arrives late at the office, is unimportant in understanding the organization, except that the rare occurrence of such events indicates that they are idiosyncratic, differing from the prevailing patterns. Weber's decision to treat only the purely formal organization of bureaucracy implies that all deviations from these formal requirements are idiosyncratic and of no interest for the student of organization. Later empirical studies have shown this approach to be misleading. Informal relations and unofficial practices develop among the members of bureaucracies and assume an organized form without being officially sanctioned. Chester I. Barnard, one of the first to call attention to this phenomenon, held that these "informal organizations are necessary to the operations of formal organizations."[11] These informal patterns, in contrast to exceptional occurrences, . . . are a regular part of bureaucratic organizations and therefore must be taken into account in their analysis.

Weber's approach also implies that any deviation from the formal structure is detrimental to administrative efficiency. Since the ideal type is conceived as the perfectly efficient organization, all differences from it must necessarily interfere with efficiency. There is considerable evidence that suggests the opposite conclusion; informal relations and unofficial practices often contribute to efficient operations. In any case, the significance of these unofficial patterns for operations cannot be determined in advance on theoretical grounds but only on the basis of empirical investigations. . . .

NOTES

1. The "ideal type" is discussed later in this chapter (in Blau and Meyer's original work).
2. H.H. Gerth and C. Wright Mills (eds.), *From Max Weber: Essays in Sociology* (New York: Oxford University Press, 1946), p. 196. By permission.
3. Max Weber, *The Theory of Social and Economic Organization*, translated by A. M. Henderson and Talcott Parsons (New York: Oxford University Press, 1947), p. 331.
4. *Ibid.*, p. 330.
5. *Ibid.*, p. 340.
6. *Ibid.*, p. 334.
7. *Ibid.*, p. 337.
8. Gerth and Mills, *op. cit.*, p. 214.
9. Robert K. Merton, *Social Theory and Social Structure*, 3rd ed. (New York: Free Press, 1968), pp. 73–138.
10. For a general discussion of functional analysis, see Ely Chinoy, *Sociological Perspective* (New York: Random House, 1968), Chap. 5.
11. Chester I. Barnard, *The Functions of the Executive* (Cambridge: Harvard University Press, 1948), p. 123.

The Human Side of Enterprise

DOUGLAS M. McGREGOR

It has become trite to say that industry has the fundamental know-how to utilize physical science and technology for the material benefit of mankind, and that we must now learn how to utilize the social sciences to make our human organizations truly effective.

To a degree, the social sciences today are in a position like that of the physical sciences with respect to atomic energy in the thirties. We know that past conceptions of the nature of man are inadequate and, in many ways, incorrect. We are becoming quite certain that, under proper conditions, unimagined resources of creative human energy could become available within the organizational setting.

We cannot tell industrial management how to apply this new knowledge in simple, economic ways. We know it will require years of exploration, much costly development research, and a substantial amount of creative imagination on the part of management to discover how to apply this growing knowledge to the organization of human effort in industry.

MANAGEMENT'S TASK: THE CONVENTIONAL VIEW

The conventional conception of management's task in harnessing human energy to organizational requirements can be stated broadly in terms of three propositions. In order to avoid the complications introduced by a label, let us call this set of propositions "Theory X":

1. Management is responsible for organizing the elements of productive enterprise—money, materials, equipment, people—in the interest of economic ends.
2. With respect to people, this is a process of directing their efforts, motivating them, controlling their actions, modifying their behavior to fit the needs of the organization.
3. Without this active intervention by management, people would be passive—even resistant—to organizational needs. They must therefore be persuaded, rewarded, punished, controlled—their activities must be directed. This is management's task. We often sum it up by saying that management consists of getting things done through other people.

Behind this conventional theory there are several additional beliefs—less explicit, but widespread:

4. The average man is by nature indolent—he works as little as possible.
5. He lacks ambition, dislikes responsibility, prefers to be led.
6. He is inherently self-centered, indifferent to organizational needs.
7. He is by nature resistant to change.
8. He is gullible, not very bright, the ready dupe of the charlatan and the demagogue.

The human side of economic enterprise today is fashioned from propositions and beliefs such as these. Conventional organization structures and managerial policies, practices, and programs reflect these assumptions.

In accomplishing its task—with these assumptions as guides—management has conceived of a range of possibilities.

At one extreme, management can be "hard" or "strong." The methods for directing behavior involve coercion and threat (usually disguised), close supervision, tight controls over behavior. At the other extreme, management can be "soft" or "weak." The methods for directing behavior involve being permissive, satisfying people's demands, achieving harmony. Then they will be tractable, accept direction.

This range has been fairly completely explored during the past half century, and management has learned some things from the exploration. There are difficulties in the "hard" approach. Force breeds counter-forces: restriction of output, antagonism, militant unionism, subtle but effective sabotage of management objectives. This "hard" approach is especially difficult during times of full employment.

There are also difficulties in the "soft" approach. It leads frequently to the abdication of management—to harmony, perhaps, but to indifferent performance. People take advantage of the soft approach. They continually expect more, but they give less and less.

Currently, the popular theme is "firm but fair." This is an attempt to gain the advantages of both the hard and the soft approaches. It is reminiscent of Teddy Roosevelt's "speak softly and carry a big stick."

IS THE CONVENTIONAL VIEW CORRECT?

The findings which are beginning to emerge from the social sciences challenge this whole set of beliefs about man and human nature and about the task of management. The evidence is far from conclusive, certainly, but it is suggestive. It comes from the laboratory, the clinic, the schoolroom, the home, and even to a limited extent from industry itself.

The social scientist does not deny that human behavior in industrial organization today is approximately what management perceives it to be. He has, in fact, observed it and studied it fairly extensively. But he is pretty sure that this behavior is *not* a consequence of man's inherent nature. It is a consequence rather of the nature of industrial organizations, of management philosophy, policy, and practice. The conventional approach of Theory X is based on mistaken notions of what is cause and what is effect.

Perhaps the best way to indicate why the conventional approach of management is inadequate is to consider the subject of motivation.

PHYSIOLOGICAL NEEDS

Man is a wanting animal—as soon as one of his needs is satisfied, another appears in its place. This process is unending. It continues from birth to death.

Man's needs are organized in a series of levels—a hierarchy of importance. At the lowest level, but pre-eminent in importance when they are thwarted, are his *physiological needs.* Man lives for bread alone, when there is no bread. Unless the circumstances are unusual, his needs for love, for status, for recognition are inoperative when his stomach has been empty for a while. But when he eats regularly and adequately, hunger ceases to be an important motivation. The same is true of the other physiological needs of man—for rest, exercise, shelter, protection from the elements.

A *satisfied need is not a motivator of behavior!* This is a fact of profound significance that is regularly ignored in the conventional approach to the management of people. Consider your own need for air: Except as you are deprived of it, it has no appreciable motivating effect upon your behavior.

SAFETY NEEDS

When the physiological needs are reasonably satisfied, needs at the next higher level begin to dominate man's behavior—to motivate him. These are called *safety needs.* They are needs for protection against danger, threat, deprivation. Some people mistakenly refer to these as needs for security. However, unless man is in a dependent relationship where he fears arbitrary deprivation, he does not demand security. The need is for the "fairest possible break." When he is confident of this, he is more than willing to take risks. But when he feels threatened or dependent, his greatest need is for guarantees, for protection, for security.

The fact needs little emphasis that, since every industrial employee is in a dependent relationship, safety needs may assume considerable importance. Arbitrary management actions, behavior which arouses uncertainty with respect to continued employment or which reflects favoritism or discrimination, unpredictable administration of policy—these can be powerful motivators of the safety needs in the employment relationship *at every level,* from worker to vice president.

SOCIAL NEEDS

When man's physiological needs are satisfied and he is no longer fearful about his physical welfare, his *social needs* become important motivators of his behavior—needs for belonging, for association, for acceptance by his fellows, for giving and receiving friendship and love.

Management knows today of the existence of these needs, but it often assumes quite wrongly that they represent a threat to the organization. Many studies have demonstrated that the tightly knit, cohesive work group may, under proper conditions, be far more effective than an equal number of separate individuals in achieving organizational goals.

Yet management, fearing group hostility to its own objectives, often goes to considerable lengths to control and direct human efforts in ways that are inimical to the natural "groupiness" of human beings. When man's social needs—and perhaps his safety needs, too—are thus thwarted, he behaves in ways which tend to defeat organizational objectives. He becomes resistant, antagonistic, uncooperative. But this behavior is a consequence, not a cause.

EGO NEEDS

Above the social needs—in the sense that they do not become motivators until lower needs are reasonably satisfied—are the needs of greatest significance to management and to man himself. They are the *egoistic needs,* and they are of two kinds:

1. Those needs that relate to one's self-esteem—needs for self-confidence, for independence, for achievement, for competence, for knowledge.
2. Those needs that relate to one's reputation—needs for status, for recognition, for appreciation, for the deserved respect of one's fellows.

Unlike the lower needs, these are rarely satisfied; man seeks indefinitely for more satisfaction of these needs once they have become important to him. But they do not appear in any significant way until physiological, safety, and social needs are all reasonably satisfied.

The typical industrial organization offers few opportunities for the satisfaction of these egoistic needs to people at lower levels in the hierarchy. The conventional methods of organizing work, particularly in mass-production industries, give little heed to these aspects of human motivation. If the practices of scientific management were deliberately calculated to thwart these needs, they could hardly accomplish this purpose better than they do.

SELF-FULFILLMENT NEEDS

Finally—a capstone, as it were, on the hierarchy of man's needs—there are what we may call the *needs for self-fulfillment*. These are the needs for realizing one's own potentialities, for continued self-development, for being creative in the broadest sense of that term.

It is clear that the conditions of modern life give only limited opportunity for these relatively weak needs to obtain expression. The deprivation most people experience with respect to other lower-level needs diverts their energies into the struggle to satisfy *those* needs, and the needs for self-fulfillment remain dormant.

MANAGEMENT AND MOTIVATION

We recognize readily enough that a man suffering from a severe dietary deficiency is sick. The deprivation of physiological needs has behavioral consequences. The same is true—although less well recognized—of deprivation of higher-level needs. The man whose needs for safety, association, independence, or status are thwarted is sick just as surely as the man who has rickets. And his sickness will have behavioral consequences. We will be mistaken if we attribute his resultant passivity, his hostility, his refusal to accept responsibility to his inherent "human nature." These forms of behavior are *symptoms* of illness—of deprivation of his social and egoistic needs.

The man whose lower-level needs are satisfied is not motivated to satisfy those needs any longer. For practical purposes they exist no longer. Management often asks, "Why aren't people more productive? We pay good wages, provide good working conditions, have excellent fringe benefits and steady employment. Yet people do not seem to be willing to put forth more than minimum effort."

The fact that management has provided for these physiological and safety needs has shifted the motivational emphasis to the social and perhaps to the egoistic needs. Unless there are opportunities *at work* to satisfy these higher-level needs, people will be deprived, and their behavior will reflect this deprivation. Under such conditions, if management continues to focus its attention on physiological needs, its efforts are bound to be ineffective.

People *will* make insistent demands for more money under these conditions. It becomes more important than ever to buy the material goods and services which can provide limited satisfaction of the thwarted needs. Although money has only limited value in satisfying many higher-level needs, it can become the focus of interest if it is the *only* means available.

THE CARROT-AND-STICK APPROACH

The carrot-and-stick theory of motivation (like Newtonian physical theory) works reasonably well under certain circumstances. The *means* for satisfying man's physiological and (within limits) his safety needs can be provided or withheld by management. Employment itself is such a means, and so are wages, working conditions, and benefits. By these means the individual can be controlled so long as he is struggling for subsistence.

But the carrot-and-stick theory does not work at all once man has reached an adequate subsistence level and is motivated primarily by higher needs. Management cannot provide a man with self-respect, or with the respect of his fellows, or with the satisfaction of needs for self-fulfillment. It can create such conditions that he is encouraged and enabled to seek such satisfactions for *himself,* or it can thwart him by failing to create those conditions.

But this creation of conditions is not "control." It is not a good device for directing behavior. And so management finds itself in an odd position. The high standard of living created by our modern technological know-how provides quite adequately for the satisfaction of physiological and safety needs. The only significant exception is where management practices have not created confidence in a "fair break"—and thus where safety needs are thwarted. But by making possible the satisfaction of low-level needs, management has deprived itself of the ability to use as motivators the devices on which conventional theory has taught it to rely—rewards, promises, incentives, or threats and other coercive devices.

The philosophy of management by direction and control—*regardless of whether it is hard or soft*—is inadequate to motivate because the human needs on which this approach relies are today unimportant motivators of behavior. Direction and control are essentially useless in motivating people whose important needs are social and egoistic. Both the hard and the soft approach fail today because they are simply irrelevant to the situation.

People, deprived of opportunities to satisfy at work the needs which are now important to them, behave exactly as we might predict—with indolence, passivity, resistance to change, lack of responsibility, willingness to follow the demagogue, unreasonable demands for economic benefits. It would seem that we are caught in a web of our own weaving.

A NEW THEORY OF MANAGEMENT

For these and many other reasons, we require a different theory of the task of managing people based on more adequate assumptions about human nature and human motivation. I am going to be so bold as to suggest the broad dimensions of such a theory. Call it "Theory Y," if you will.

1. Management is responsible for organizing the elements of productive enterprise—money, materials, equipment, people—in the interest of economic ends.
2. People are *not* by nature passive or resistant to organizational needs. They have become so as a result of experience in organizations.
3. The motivation, the potential for development, the capacity for assuming responsibility, the readiness to direct behavior toward organizational goals are all present in people. Management does not put them there. It is a responsibility of management to make it possible for people to recognize and develop these human characteristics for themselves.
4. The essential task of management is to arrange organizational conditions and methods of operation so that people can achieve their own goals *best* by directing *their own* efforts toward organizational objectives.

This is a process primarily of creating opportunities, releasing potential, removing obstacles, encouraging growth, providing guidance. It is what Peter Drucker has called "management by objectives" in contrast to "management by control." It does *not* involve the abdication of management, the absence of leadership, the lowering of standards, or the other characteristics usually associated with the "soft" approach under Theory X.

SOME DIFFICULTIES

It is no more possible to create an organization today which will be a full, effective application of this theory than it was to build an atomic power plant in 1945. There are many formidable obstacles to overcome.

The conditions imposed by conventional organization theory and by the approach of scientific management for the past half century have tied men to limited jobs which do not utilize their capabilities, have discouraged the acceptance of responsibility, have encouraged passivity, have eliminated meaning from work. Man's habits, attitudes, expectations—his whole conception of membership in an industrial organization—have been conditioned by his experience under these circumstances.

People today are accustomed to being directed, manipulated, controlled in industrial organizations and to finding satisfaction for their social, egoistic, and self-fulfillment needs away from the job. This is true of much of management as well as of workers. Genuine "industrial citizenship"—to borrow again a term from Drucker—is a remote and unrealistic idea, the meaning of which has not even been considered by most members of industrial organizations.

Another way of saying this is that Theory X places exclusive reliance upon external control of human behavior, while Theory Y relies heavily on self-control and self-direction. It is worth noting that this difference is the difference between treating people as children and treating them as mature adults. After generations of the former, we cannot expect to shift to the latter overnight.

STEPS IN THE RIGHT DIRECTION

Before we are overwhelmed by the obstacles, let us remember that the application of theory is always slow. Progress is usually achieved in small steps. Some innovative ideas which are entirely consistent with Theory Y are today being applied with some success.

Decentralization and Delegation

These are ways of freeing people from the too-close control of conventional organization, giving them a degree of freedom to direct their own activities, to assume responsibility, and, importantly, to satisfy their egoistic needs. In this connection, the flat organization of Sears, Roebuck and Company provides an interesting example. It forces "management by objectives," since it enlarges the number of people reporting to a manager until he cannot direct and control them in the conventional manner.

Job Enlargement

This concept, pioneered by I.B.M. and Detroit Edison, is quite consistent with Theory Y. It encourages the acceptance of responsibility at the bottom of the organization; it provides opportunities for satisfying social and egoistic needs. In fact, the reorganization of work at the factory level offers one of the more challenging opportunities for innovation consistent with Theory Y.

Participation and Consultative Management

Under proper conditions, participation and consultative management provide encouragement to people to direct their creative energies toward organizational objectives, give them some voice in decisions that affect them, provide significant opportunities for the satisfaction of social and egoistic needs. The Scanlon Plan is the outstanding embodiment of these ideas in practice.

Performance Appraisal

Even a cursory examination of conventional programs of performance appraisal within the ranks of management will reveal how completely consistent they are with Theory X. In fact, most such programs tend to treat the individual as though he were a product under inspection on the assembly line.

A few companies—among them General Mills, Ansul Chemical, and General Electric—have been experimenting with approaches which involve the individual in setting "targets" or objectives *for himself* and in a *self*-evaluation of performance semiannually or annually. Of course, the superior plays an important leadership role in this process—one, in fact, which demands substantially more competence than the conventional approach. The role is, however, considerably more congenial to many managers than the role of "judge" or "inspector" which is usually forced upon them. Above all, the individual is encouraged to take a greater responsibility for planning and appraising his own contribution to organizational objectives; and the accompanying effects on egoistic and self- fulfillment needs are substantial.

APPLYING THE IDEAS

The not infrequent failure of such ideas as these to work as well as expected is often attributable to the fact that a management has "bought the idea" but applied it within the framework of Theory X and its assumptions.

Delegation is not an effective way of exercising management by control. Participation becomes a farce when it is applied as a sales gimmick or a device for kidding people into thinking they are important. Only the management that has confidence in human capacities and is itself directed toward organizational objectives rather than toward the preservation of personal power can grasp the implications of this emerging theory. Such management will find and apply successfully other innovative ideas as we move slowly toward the full implementation of a theory like Y.

THE HUMAN SIDE OF ENTERPRISE

It is quite possible for us to realize substantial improvements in the effectiveness of industrial organizations during the next decade or two. The social sciences can contribute much to such developments; we are only beginning to grasp the implications of the growing body of knowledge in these fields. But if this conviction is to become a reality instead of a pious hope, we will need to view the process much as we view the process of releasing the energy of the atom for constructive human ends—as a slow, costly, sometimes discouraging approach toward a goal which would seem to many to be quite unrealistic.

The ingenuity and the perseverance of industrial management in the pursuit of economic ends have changed many scientific and technological dreams into commonplace realities. It is now becoming clear that the application of these same talents to the human side of enterprise will not only enhance substantially these materialistic achievements, but will bring us one step closer to "the good society."

Bureaucratic Man

MELVIN L. KOHN

It is often said that bureaucracy makes for unthinking, literal conformity. So self-evidently correct does this view seem that Webster's *Third New International Dictionary* defines bureaucracy as, among other things, "a system of administration marked by . . . lack of initiative and flexibility, by indifference to human needs or public opinion, and by a tendency to defer decisions to superiors or to impede action with red tape." What is more, there are plausible, theoretical reasons why bureaucracy should have such effects. As Robert Merton pointed out, the social psychological corollary of the efficiency, rationality and predictability that Max Weber prized in bureaucratic organisational practice, must be a certain "over-conformity" in the behaviour of bureaucrats.

But does working in a bureaucracy merely make automatons of men, or are there some compensating features that encourage individualistic qualities? Surprisingly, there has been little empirical study of how bureaucracy affects those who spend their working hours engaged in it. Is the stereotype true? We are not sure *how* bureaucracy exerts its social psychological impact, whatever that impact may be. The overall structure of the organisation can matter, for those who work there, only through its impact on job conditions that bear directly on men's lives—such as closeness of supervision, time pressure, and the complexity of the work. Bureaucratisation affects many of these themes, but most discussions seem to have arbitrarily focused on only one. In this inquiry, I am going to look at the many occupational effects of bureaucracy to see which ones contribute to its impact. I shall deliberately limit my attention to how (and why) the experience of working in a bureaucracy affects men's values, social orientation, and intellectual functioning.

The research is based on interviews with 3,101 men, representative of all men throughout the United States employed in civilian jobs. The interviews were conducted for me by the National Opinion Research Centre in the spring and summer of 1964. For the full interview schedule, and further information on sample and research design, see my book, *Class and Conformity: a study in values.* That book also provides more complete information in the index construction than can be incorporated here.

My conception of bureaucracy is derived from Weber's classic analysis summarised by Robert Merton: "Bureaucracy involves a clear-cut division of integrated activities which are regarded as duties inherent in the office. A system of differentiated controls and sanctions is stated in the regulations. The assignment of roles occurs on the basis of technical qualifications which are ascertained through formalised, impersonal procedures, such as examinations. Within the structure of hierarchically arranged authority, the activities of the 'trained and salaried experts' are governed by general, abstract, clearly defined rules, which preclude the necessity for the issuance of specific instructions for each specific case."

In this study, I am able to index only one of these several dimensions of bureaucracy, the hierarchical organisation of authority. This limitation is the price we pay for a sample sufficiently large and diverse to permit a systematic assessment of the occupational conditions attendant on bureaucratisation. In studying a multitude of organisations, we cannot assess their structure at first hand, but must rely on reports by the men who work there, some of whom know little about their employing organisation except insofar as it directly affects them. The one facet that necessarily affects all men is authority.

I treat the hierarchical organisation of authority as equivalent to the number of formal levels of supervision. Although many men do not have a comprehensive view of the authority structure of the firm or organisation in which they work, even the man at the bottom of the hierarchy knows whether his boss has a boss and whether that man is the ultimate boss. So I asked my subjects: "Is this [an organisation] where everyone is supervised directly by the same man, where there is one level of supervision between the people at the bottom and the top, or where there are two or more levels of supervision between the people at the bottom and the top?"

To distinguish further, I assumed that when an organisation reaches at least three levels of formal authority, greater differentiation of structure is very roughly proportional to size, at least in organisations of about 100 to 1,000 employees. (I cannot make the same assumption about organisations of more than 1,000 employees; neither would I even trust respondents' estimates of size when the number surpasses 1,000.) Thus, the index of bureaucratisation is as follows: (i) one level of supervision; (ii) two levels of supervision; (iii) three or more levels of supervision, fewer than 100 employees; (iv) three or more levels of supervision,

100-999 employees; and (v) three or more levels of supervision, 1,000 or more employees.

This index makes explicit what is, in any case, implicit: that it is impossible to index hierarchical structure without also indexing size—their correlation is too great. For now, I simply accept as empirical fact that bureaucratisation implies large size; later I shall try to separate the consequences of bureaucratic structure, as such, from those of size.

I also constructed indices of values, social orientation, and intellectual functioning.

First, valuation of conformity. By values, I mean standards of desirability—criteria of preference. Specifically pertinent here, because of the argument that bureaucracy breeds conformism, is men's relative valuation of self-direction or of conformity to external authority. The index is based on a factor analysis of the men's rankings of the relative desirability of a number of generally valued characteristics. Self-direction, as thus indexed, means regarding as most desirable such characteristics as curiosity, good sense and sound judgment, and the ability to face facts squarely; valuing conformity means giving priority to respectability.

Second, social orientation. What is at issue here is whether bureaucratisation makes for intolerance of nonconformity, literalism in moral positions, and resistance to innovation and change. I attempted to measure all three by means of the following indices:

1. "Authoritarian conservatism," that is, men's definition of what is socially acceptable—at one extreme, rigid conformance to the dictates of authority and intolerance of nonconformity; at the other extreme, open-mindedness. It is indexed by agreement or disagreement with such assertions as: "The most important thing to teach children is absolute obedience to their parents." "Young people should not be allowed to read books that are likely to confuse them." "There are two kinds of people in the world: the weak and the strong." "People who question the old and accepted ways of doing things usually just end up causing trouble."

2. "Criteria of morality," by which we mean a continuum of moral positions—from believing that morality consists of strict adherence to the letter of the law, to holding personally responsible moral standards. This dimension is indexed by answers to the question, "Do you believe that it's all right to do whatever the law allows, or are there some things that are wrong even if they are legal?" and by agreement or disagreement with such assertions as: "It's all right to do anything you want as long as you stay out of trouble." "If something works, it doesn't matter whether it's right or wrong." "It's all right to get around the law as long as you don't actually break it."

3. "Stance toward change," that is, men's receptiveness or resistance to innovation and change. It is indexed by responses to the questions: "Are you generally one of the first people to try out something new, or do you wait until you see how it's worked out for other people? Are you the sort of person who takes life as it comes, or are you working toward some definite goal?" and by agreement or disagreement with: "It generally works out best to keep on doing things the way they have been done before."

Third, intellectual functioning. The most serious charge against bureaucracy is that it inhibits men's readiness to think for themselves. As one test of this assertion, I have measured men's intellectual flexibility, as evidenced in several appraisals of actual performance deliberately built into the interview. These include cognitive problems that require weighing both sides of an economic or a social issue; a test involving the differentiation of figure from ground in complex colour designs; and a test of men's ability to draw a recognisably human figure whose parts fit together in a meaningful whole. I also asked interviewers to evaluate each respondent's "intelligence"; and did a simple count of the respondent's tendency to agree with agree-disagree questions. All these I take to reflect, in some substantial part, intellectual flexibility.

As a single index, I used scores based on a factor analysis of these diverse measures. I also extracted from these same data two rotated factors, which provide measures of two distinct aspects of intellectual functioning. One is "perceptual," based primarily on inferences from the figure-drawing and form perception tests. The other one is "ideational," showing primarily in problem-solving and in impressing the interviewer as being an intelligent person.

One final index examines the demands men put on their intellectual resources, no matter how great or limited those resources may be. This index, based on a factor analysis of questions about a wide range of leisure-time activities, focuses on how intellectually demanding are those activities. The relevant factor contrasts spending a large amount of one's leisure time watching TV, and reading popular magazines, with engaging in such intellectually active pursuits as going to museums and plays, reading books, and working on hobbies. Some of the latter activities are facilitated by education and income; that will be taken into account in my analysis.

The most difficult problem in assessing the social psychological impact of bureaucratisation is deciding who to compare with whom. Who are bureaucrats? The narrowest definition would be that they are the higher, non-elective officialdom of government. But there is reason and ample precedent to expand that definition to include all employees of all organisations that are bureaucratic in structure—blue-collar as well as white-collar workers, employees of profit-making firms and non-profit organisations as well as government. To whom should bureaucrats be compared—entrepreneurs, employees of non-bureaucratic organisations, or both?

Rather than make *a priori* decisions, I prefer to deal with these questions empirically. I began at the simplest descriptive level, seeing what relationship there might be between bureaucratisation, as I indexed it, and those aspects of values, orientation, and intellectual functioning on which it has been thought to bear. No man employed in a civilian occupation is excluded from this analysis, whether he is employee or entrepreneur, whether he works in a profit-making firm, a non-profit organisation, or a governmental agency.

The correlations of bureaucratisation with values, orientation, and intellectual functioning are small. They are nonetheless impressive, because they consistently contradict preconception. Men working in bureaucratic firms or organisations tend to value, not conformity, but self-direction (see table 1). They are more open-minded, have more personally responsible standards of morality, and are more receptive to change than are men who work in non-bureaucratic organisations. They show greater flexibility in dealing both with perceptual and with ideational problems. They spend their leisure time in more intellectually demanding activities. In short, the findings belie critics' assertions.

Now I can consider what difference it makes if the definitions of bureaucrat and non-bureaucrat be altered.

Table 1
Mean Scores for Values, Social Orientation, and Intellectual Functioning by Index of Bureaucracy (Total Sample)

Index of Bureaucracy:	Values and Orientation				Intellectual Functioning				Number of Cases
	Valuation of Self-Direction/Conformity (+ = conformist)	Authoritarian Conservatism (+ = authoritarian)	Criteria of Morality (+ = personally responsible)	Stance Toward Change (+ = receptive)	Perceptual Component of Intellectual Flexibility (+ = flexible)	Ideational Component of Intellectual Flexibility (+ = flexible)	Overall Index of Intellectual Flexibility (+ = flexible)	Intellectual Demandingness of Leisure-Time Activities (+ = demanding)	
One level of supervision	1.01	0.91	−0.59	−0.57	−1.47	−0.74	−2.17	−0.49	(840)
Two levels	−0.12	0.16	−0.63	0.01	−0.69	−1.06	−2.34	−1.22	(121)
Three or more levels:									
Under 100 employees	0.23	0.12	0.50	0.33	0.68	−0.03	0.15	−0.32	(307)
100–999 employees	−0.97	−0.36	0.08	0.13	0.26	1.07	0.54	−0.07	(466)
1,000 + employees	−0.61	−1.29	0.66	0.68	1.20	1.82	1.78	1.35	(1,023)

Ownership

Many discussions of bureaucracy assume or assert that the antithesis of the bureaucrat is the entrepreneur. But I find, to the contrary, that entrepreneurs are remarkably similar to bureaucrats, particularly to bureaucrats of comparable occupational status. (The one notable difference is that bureaucrats are more intellectually flexible—another refutation of the stereotype.) The real contrast is not between bureaucrats and entrepreneurs, but between both these groups and the employees of non-bureaucratic organisations.

To properly assess the effects of bureaucratisation, I must limit the analysis to employees, comparing the employees of bureaucratised organisations to those of non-bureaucratic organisations. Thus limiting the analysis strengthens the contrast between bureaucrats and non-bureaucrats. Most of the correlations are stronger. The picture of the bureaucrat as self-directed and intellectually flexible becomes a little more sharply etched.

Sector of the Economy

Just as the entrepreneur has been thought to be the antithesis of the bureaucrat, the government official is usually thought to be its prototype. In fact, employees of government (and of non-profit organisations) do exemplify the social psychological characteristics associated with bureaucratisation: they are more tolerant of non-conformity, have more personally responsible moral standards, evidence greater flexibility in dealing with ideational problems, and make more intellectually demanding use of their leisure-time than do employees of equally bureaucratised profit-making firms.

In order to examine the impact of bureaucratisation separately from that stemming from employment in the public or the private sphere, I further limited the analysis to profit-making firms—the one sector of the economy where there is a substantial variation in conditions of bureaucratisation. I then found that the correlations of bureaucracy with values, orientation, and intellectual functioning, to be nearly the same for employees of profit-making firms as for all employees. Thus, my earlier findings do not simply reflect the bureaucratisation of the public sector of the economy, for bureaucracy's influence extends to the private sector as well.

Occupational Position

Many discussions of bureaucracy have been addressed only to its salaried, its white-collar, or its professional staff. It is, therefore, necessary to see if bureaucratisation bears the same relationship to values, orientation, and intellectual functioning for blue-collar as for white-collar employees. To do this, I examined the two groups separately, recognising that in so doing I partially controlled variables correlated with occupational positions, such as education, the substantive complexity of the work, and job protections.

Even so (see table 2), bureaucracy's social psychological effects are similar for blue-collar and for white-collar workers. Moreover, the link is as strong for blue-collar as for white-collar workers. Thus, any explanation of the social psychological impact of bureaucracy must apply to the entire work force, not just to the white-collar portion. It is true, of course, that the explanation need not be the same for both groups.

Table 2
The Psychological Effects of Bureaucracy—With Allowances Made for Personal Background (Limited to Employees of Profit-Making Firms and Expressed as a Correlation)

Psychological Effects Measure	Overall Correlation with Bureaucracy	Partial Correlation with Bureaucracy Allows for	
		Education	Education plus region, size of community, race, national background, religion, and whether childhood was urban or rural
Valuation of self-direction/conformity	0.08**	0.07**	0.06*
Authoritarian conservatism	0.07**	0.00	0.01
Criteria of morality	0.11**	0.09**	0.07**
Stance toward change	0.10**	0.07**	0.06*
Perceptual component of intellectual flexibility	0.08**	0.05	0.03
Ideational component	0.18**	0.11**	0.10**
Overall index of intellectual flexibility	0.19**	0.11**	0.09**
Intellectual demandingness of leisure-time activities	0.15**	0.08**	0.09**

*Chances of this result occurring by chance are less than 1:20.
**Chances of this result occurring by chance are less than 1:100.

I concluded that bureaucratisation bears essentially the same relationship to values, orientation, and intellectual functioning, wherever and to whomever it occurs. Why? What is there about working in a bureaucratic organisation that makes men more self-directed, open to change, and intellectually flexible?

I must also ask: why should the correlations be so small? The comparable correlations for several other aspects of occupation are much stronger. Does the small size of bureaucracy's correlations imply that I have used an inadequate index, or does bureaucratisation have a weaker impact than had been supposed?

Bureaucrats and non-bureaucrats are drawn from different segments of the American population. Bureaucrats necessarily live where large firms are located: disproportionately in big cities. Not only are they now urban, but they grew up in urban places. Few are black, few are Jews. They are disproportionately Catholic. Those who are Protestant are a little more likely to be members of large, and established denominations than of smaller sects. Most notable of all, bureaucrats are more highly educated than are non-bureaucrats.

Out of all these differences in the composition of bureaucratic and non-bureaucratic work forces, only education seems to matter in explaining why bureaucrats differ from non-bureaucrats in values, orientation, and intellectual functioning. That is, statistically controlling education markedly reduces bureaucracy's impact. Additionally controlling any, or all, of the other measures of social background, reduces the correlations little more than does controlling education alone.

Important though education may be, it can provide only a partial explanation of the differences between bureaucrats and non-bureaucrats. That is, even with education statistically controlled, bureaucrats are found to value self-direction more highly than do non-bureaucrats, to have more personally demanding moral standards, to be more receptive to change, to be intellectually more flexible (especially in dealing with ideational problems), and to spend their leisure-time in more intellectually demanding activities. The explanation of these differences must lie either in bureaucracies somehow recruiting more self-directed, intellectually flexible people, or in bureaucracies subjecting their employees to occupational conditions that foster these social psychological attributes.

Bureaucratisation does make for widespread, and in some instances substantial, differences in the conditions of occupational life—few of them attributable to educational disparities and most of them applicable (although not always in equal degree) to both the white-collar and blue-collar work forces. These are, principally, that the employees of bureaucracies tend to work at more complex jobs than do other men of comparable educational level, but under conditions of somewhat closer supervision; to work under an externally-imposed pressure of time that results in their having to think faster; to work a shorter week; to work in company of, but not necessarily in harness with, co-workers; to face greater competition; to enjoy much greater job protection; and to earn more than other men who are of similar educational background (even when in jobs that are of comparable occupational status).

In assessing the possible explanatory relevance of these occupational conditions, I statistically controlled education throughout and limited the analysis to those social psychological effects of bureaucracy that remain significant, even with education controlled. From one point of view, this procedure gives undue weight to education, which may matter primarily because it is a precondition for certain types of jobs—substantively complex jobs, for example. But since most men come to their jobs only after completing their education, I need to show that occupational conditions matter above and beyond any effect that might be attributed to education.

Three of the occupational effects of bureaucracy—job protection, income, and substantive complexity, prove to be relevant (see table 3). The combined effect of controlling all three is to reduce the overall correlation of bureaucracy with values, orientation, and intellectual functioning by two thirds and to render this, and all individual correlations, statistically nonsignificant.

Further analysis shows that all three occupational conditions contribute independently to bureaucracy's social psychological impact. Job protection contributes notably to the relationship between bureaucracy and men's orientation to morality and to change, and even to the relationship between bureaucracy and intellectual flexibility. It thus appears that men who are protected from some of the dangers that change might bring are less fearful of the new and the different, are better able to accept personal responsibility for their acts, and are even able to make fuller use of their intellectual talents. Substantive complexity is more specifically pertinent for explaining bureaucrats' flexibility in dealing with ideational problems, and their making intellectually demanding use of leisure-time. The experience of working at complex jobs thus appears to have direct carry-over to the use of one's intellectual resources in non-occupational endeavours. And job income is most pertinent for explaining bureaucrats' high valuation of self-direction; the higher income enjoyed by employees of bureaucracies appears to facilitate their feeling sufficiently in control of their lives to think self-direction an attainable goal.

I concluded, then, that job protection, complexity, and income all contribute to, and together may largely explain, the social psychological impact of bureaucratisation. Separate analyses of the white-collar and blue-collar work forces do indicate, however, that job protection contributes more to bureaucracy's impact on blue-collar workers; complexity, to its impact on white-collar workers. It would seem that the job protections afforded by bureaucracy matter most for men in occupations that do not already enjoy a substantial measure of security; complexity comes to the fore only when some degree of security has been attained.

There are four issues that my results do not fully resolve. The first is whether the effects I have attributed to the experience of working in a bureaucratic organisation might really be an artifact of what types of people bureaucracies recruit. I have found that the educational disparities between bureaucratic and non-bureaucratic work forces cannot provide a sufficient explanation, and that other disparities in the social and demographic compositions of the work forces have little relevance. But there remains the possibility that bureaucracies may hold a special attraction for self-directed, intellectually flexible men who are receptive to innovation and change. Perhaps, for example, intellectually active people seek jobs in bureaucratic organisations because that is where more challenging work is to be found.

This interpretation cannot be tested, because there is no information about the men's values, orientation, and intellectual functioning prior to their employment in bureaucratic (or in non-bureaucratic) organisations. There are, however, two good reasons to doubt that "self-selection" can explain my findings.

The interpretation assumes that men have more complete and accurate knowledge of working conditions in bureaucratic organisations, before starting to work

Table 3
Psychological Effects of Bureaucracy—With Allowance Made for These Aspects of the Job That Tend to Change with an Increase in Bureaucratisation (Limited to Employees of Profit-Making Firms)

Percentage Reduction in this Particular Correlation when Controlling

Psychological Effects	Partial Correlation with Bureaucracy with Education Controlled	Job Protection	Job Income	Substantive Complexity	Amount of Competition	Time Pressure	Hours of Work	Inter-personal Setting	Closeness of Supervision and Positional Disparity	Job Protections, Income, and Complexity
Valuation of self-direction/conformity	0.07*	17%	20%	14%	−06%	08%	20%	−03%	06%	44%
Criteria of morality	0.09*	50	24	25	−02	05	12	00	−08	85
Stance towards change	0.07*	39	19	08	21	10	−19	10	12	80
Ideational component of intellectual flexibility	0.11*	24	21	29	05	03	01	−06	−03	64
Overall index of intellectual flexibility	0.11*	32	12	16	05	−05	−07	−01	−05	66
Intellectual demandingness of leisure-time activities	0.08*	11	35	33	00	05	01	−01	05	71

*The chances of this result occurring by chance are less than 1:100.

there, than is usually the case—especially in the light of the widely-held stereotypes about bureaucracy. The interpretation also assumes that men have a fuller range of choice in deciding on jobs than is usually the case—particularly when one remembers that my findings apply to men of all educational and skill levels and that many types of job can be found only in bureaucratic or only in non-bureaucratic settings. It would be more in line both with our broader knowledge of occupational realities, and with the specific results of this study, to conclude that bureaucrats differ from non-bureaucrats primarily because they have experienced different conditions of occupational life.

The second issue is why the correlations are so small. I may have underestimated their size by limiting this investigation to just one dimension of bureaucracy or by employing an inadequate index of that dimension. The results, however, suggest an alternative explanation: that bureaucracy really does have a smaller social psychological impact than has been assumed. The psychologically most potent occupational conditions are those that maximise men's opportunities for self-direction in their work: freedom from close supervision, complex work, and a varied array of activities. Bureaucracies do provide substantively complex work. But they conspicuously fail to provide freedom from close supervision. And although they provide a wide variety of complexly interrelated jobs to their white-collar workers, they tend to entrap their blue-collar workers in a routinised flow of simply-organised tasks. It is ironic and probably self-defeating that bureaucracies hire educated men, give them complex jobs to perform, and then fail to give them as much opportunity for occupational self-direction as their educational attainments and the needs of the work allow.

The third issue is whether my findings reflect bureaucratisation or only size. Two out of the three occupational conditions that have come to the fore in my analyses—income and complexity—may be only ancillary features of bureaucracy. It is not, in fact, intrinsic to bureaucratic organisation that it pays its employees more, or even that its work be more complex.

These are, instead, products of the very conditions that give rise to bureaucracy itself—large size, technology, the need for highly skilled employees, and the problems of coordination, planning, and record-keeping that result from size and technology. Job protection, though, is an essential feature of bureaucracy. As Weber long ago recognised, it is necessary to bureaucratic organisation that its authority be circumscribed. The principal findings of this research—that job protection is central to the impact of bureaucratisation on its employees—cannot be attributed to size alone; they reflect the structural essentials of bureaucracy.

Last, and most important, is the issue of whether my focus on one dimension of bureaucratic structure—the hierarchical organisation of authority—produces so partial a picture as to be misleading. Had I also studied such facets of bureaucracy as impersonality of procedures or specificity of rules, other factors, might have come to the fore. The picture I have presented may be seriously incomplete.

Even if this be true, my findings are so different from common presuppositions as to require a rethinking of how bureaucracy affects its employees. Many writings about bureaucracy assert that a system based on the hierarchical organisation of authority necessarily imposes tight discipline, leaving little leeway for initiative. My results do indicate a tendency in this direction—employees of bureaucratic firms are supervised a little more closely than are other men of their educational levels, and close supervision does have the constricting effects ascribed to it. But the tendency of bureaucracies to supervise employees too closely is more than off-set by the protections it affords from the arbitrary actions of superordinates.

Bureaucracies must ensure that superordinate officials are limited in what facets of their subordinates' behaviour they are allowed to control and how they may exercise that control; superordinates cannot dismiss subordinates at will, and questionable actions can be appealed to adjudicatory agencies. The power of non-bureaucratic organisations over their employees is more complete and may be more capricious.

Thus, the alternative to bureaucracy's circumscribed authority is likely to be, not less authority, but personal, potentially arbitrary, authority. What is notable about bureaucratic practice is not how closely authority is exercised, but how effectively it is circumscribed.

Style or Circumstance: The Leadership Enigma

FRED E. FIEDLER

What is it that makes a person an effective leader?

We take it for granted that good leadership is essential to business, to government and to all the myriad groups and organizations that shape the way we live, work and play.

We spend at least several billions of dollars a year on leadership development and executive recruitment in the United States. Leaders are paid 10, 20 and 30 times the salary of ordinary workers. Thousands of books and articles on leadership have been published. Yet, we still know relatively little about the factors that determine a leader's success or failure.

Psychologists have been concerned with two major questions in their research on leadership: How does a man become a leader? What kind of personality traits or behavior makes a person an *effective* leader? For the past 15 years, my own work at the University of Illinois Group-Effectiveness Research Laboratory has concentrated on the latter question.

Psychologists used to think that special personality traits would distinguish leaders from followers. Several hundred research studies have been conducted to identify these special traits. But the search has been futile.

People who become leaders tend to be somewhat more intelligent, bigger, more assertive, more talkative than other members of their group. But these traits are far less important than most people think. What most frequently distinguishes the leader from his co-workers is that he knows more about the group task or that he can do it better. A bowling team is likely to choose its captain from good rather than poor bowlers, and the foreman of a machine shop is more likely to be a good machinist than a poor one.

In many organizations, one only has to live long in order to gain experience and seniority, and with these a position of leadership.

In business and industry today, the men who attain a leadership position must have the requisite education and talent. Of course, as W. Lloyd Warner and James C. Abegglen of the University of Chicago have shown, it has been most useful to come from or marry into a family that owns a large slice of the company's stock.

Becoming a leader, then, depends on personality only to a limited extent. A person can become a leader by happenstance, simply by being in the right place at the right time, or because of such various factors as age, education, experience, family background and wealth.

Almost any person in a group may be capable of rising to a leadership position if he is rewarded for actively participating in the group discussion, as Alex Bavelas and his colleagues at Stanford University have demonstrated. They used light signals to reward low-status group members for supposedly "doing the right thing." However, unknown to the people being encouraged, the light signal was turned on and off at random. Rewarded in this unspecified, undefined manner, the low-status member came to regard himself as a leader and the rest of the group accepted him in his new position.

It is commonly observed that personality and circumstances interact to determine whether a person will become a leader. While this statement is undoubtedly true, its usefulness is rather limited unless one also can specify how a personality trait will interact with a specific situation. We are as yet unable to make such predictions.

Having become a leader, how does one get to be an effective leader? Given a dozen or more similar groups and tasks, what makes one leader succeed and another fail? The answer to this question is likely to determine the philosophy of leader-training programs and the way in which men are selected for executive positions.

There are a limited number of ways in which one person can influence others to work together toward a common goal. He can coerce them or he can coax them. He can tell people what to do and how to do it, or he can share the decision-making and concentrate on his relationship with his men rather than on the execution of the job.

Of course, these two types of leadership behavior are gross oversimplifications. Most research by psychologists on leadership has focused on two clusters of behavior and attitudes, one labeled autocratic, authoritarian and task-oriented, and the other as democratic, equalitarian, permissive and group-oriented.

The first type of leadership behavior, frequently advocated in conventional supervisory and military systems, has its philosophical roots in Frederick W. Taylor's *Principles of Scientific Management* and other early 20th Century industrial engineering studies. The authoritarian, task-oriented leader takes all responsibility for making decisions and directing the group members. His rationale is simple: "I do the thinking and you carry out the orders."

The second type of leadership is typical of the "New Look" method of management advocated by men like Douglas McGregor of M.I.T. and Rensis Likert of the University of Michigan. The democratic, group-oriented leader provides general rather than close supervision and his concern is the effective use of human resources through participation. In the late 1940s, a related method of leadership training was developed based on confrontation in unstructured group situations where each participant can explore his own motivations and reactions. Some excellent studies on this method, called T-group, sensitivity or laboratory training, have been made by Chris Argyris of Yale, Warren Bennis of State University of New York at Buffalo and Edgar Schein of M.I.T.

Experiments comparing the performance of both types of leaders have shown that each is successful in some situations and not in others. No one has been able to show that one kind of leader is always superior or more effective.

A number of researchers point out that different tasks require different kinds of leadership. But what kind of situation requires what kind of leader? To answer this question, I shall present a theory of leadership effectiveness that spells out the specific circumstances under which various leadership styles are most effective.

We must first of all distinguish between leadership style and leader behavior. Leader behavior refers to the specific acts in which a leader engages while directing or coordinating the work of his group. For example, the leader can praise or criticize, make helpful suggestions, show consideration for the welfare and feelings of members of his group.

Leadership style refers to the underlying needs of the leader that motivate his behavior. In other words, in addition to performing the task, what personal needs is the leader attempting to satisfy? We have found that a leader's actions or behavior sometimes does change as the situation or group changes, but his basic needs appear to remain constant.

To classify leadership styles, my colleagues and I have developed a simple questionnaire that asks the leader to describe the person with whom he can work least well:

LPC—Least-Preferred Co-worker

Think of the person with whom you can work least well. He may be someone you work with now, or he may be someone you knew in the past. Use an X to describe this person as he appears to you.

helpful	8 7 6 5 4 3 2 1	frustrating
unenthusiastic	1 2 3 4 5 6 7 8	enthusiastic
efficient	8 7 6 5 4 3 2 1	inefficient

From the replies, a Least-Preferred-Co-worker (LPC) score is obtained by simply summing the item scores. The LPC score does not measure perceptual accuracy, but rather reveals a person's emotional reaction to the people with whom he cannot work well.

In general, the high-scoring leader describes his least-preferred co-worker in favorable terms. The high-LPC leader tends to be "relationship-oriented." He gets his major satisfaction from establishing close personal relations with his group members. He uses the group task to gain the position of prominence he seeks.

The leader with a low score describes his least-preferred co-worker in unfavorable terms. The low-LPC leader is primarily "task-oriented." He obtains his major satisfaction by successfully completing the task, even at the risk of poor interpersonal relations with his workers.

Since a leader cannot function without a group, we must also know something about the group that the leader directs. There are many types of groups, for example, social groups which promote the enjoyment of individuals and "counteracting'' groups such as labor and management at the negotiating table. But here we shall concentrate on groups that exist for the purpose of performing a task.

From our research, my associates and I have identified three major factors that can be used to classify group situations: (1) position power of the leader, (2) task structure, and (3) leader-member personal relationships. Basically, these classifications measure the kind of power and influence the group gives its leader.

We ranked group situations according to their favorableness for the leader. Favorableness here is defined as the degree to which the situation enables the leader to exert influence over the group.

Based on several studies, leader-member relations emerged as the most important factor in determining the leader's influence over the group. Task structure is rated as second in importance, and position power as third. *(See illustration.)*

Under most circumstances, the leader who is liked by his group and has a clear-cut task and high position power obviously has everything in his favor. The leader who has poor relationships with his group members, an unstructured task and weak position power likely will be unable to exert much influence over the group.

The personal relationships that the leader establishes with his group members depend at least in part upon the leader's personality. The leader who is loved, admired and trusted can influence the group regardless of his position power. The leader who is not liked or trusted cannot influence the group except through his vested authority. It should be noted that a leader's assessment of how much he is liked often differs markedly from the group's evaluation.

Task structure refers to the degree the group's assignment can be programmed and specified in a step-by-step fashion. A highly structured task does not need a leader with much position power because the leader's role is detailed by the job specifications. With a highly structured task, the leader clearly knows what to do and how to do it, and the organization can back him up at each step. Unstructured tasks tend to have more than one correct solution that may be reached by any of a variety of methods. Since there is no step-by-step method that can be programmed in advance, the leader cannot influence the group's success by ordering them to vote ''right'' or be creative. Tasks of committees, creative groups and policy-making groups are typically unstructured.

Position power is the authority vested in the leader's position. It can be readily measured in most situations. An army general obviously has more power than a lieutenant, just as a department head has more power than an office manager. But our concern here is the effect this position power has on group performance. Although one would think that a leader with great power will get better performance from his group, our studies do not bear out this assumption.

However, it must be emphasized that in some situations position power may supersede task structure (the military). Or a very highly structured task (launching a moon probe) may outweigh the effects of interpersonal relations. The organization determines both the task structure and the position power of the leader.

In our search for the most effective leadership style, we went back to the studies that we had been conducting for more than a decade. These studies investigated a wide variety of groups and leadership situations, including basketball teams, business management, military units, boards of directors, creative groups and scientists engaged in pure research. In all of these studies, we could determine the groups that had performed their tasks successfully or unsuccessfully and then correlated the effectiveness of group performance with leadership style.

Group Situation Model. Task-oriented groups are classified in a three-dimensional model using the three major factors affecting group performance.

The Effective Leader. Directive leaders perform best in very favorable or in unfavorable situations. Permissive leaders are best in mixed situations. Graph is based on studies of over 800 groups.

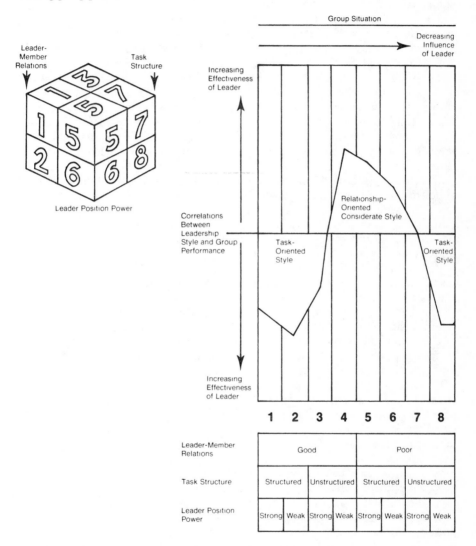

Now by plotting these correlations of leadership style against our scale of group situations, we could, for the first time, find what leadership style works best in each situation. When we connected the median points on each column, the result was a bell-shaped curve. *(See illustration.)*

The results show that a task-oriented leader performs best in situations at both extremes—those in which he has a great deal of influence and power, and also in situations where he has no influence and power over the group members.

Relationship-oriented leaders tend to perform best in mixed situations where they have only moderate influence over the group. A number of subsequent studies by us and others have confirmed these findings.

The results show that we cannot talk about simply good leaders or poor leaders. A leader who is effective in one situation may or may not be effective in another. Therefore, we must specify the situations in which a leader performs well or badly.

This theory of leadership effectiveness by and large fits our everyday experience. Group situations in which the leader is liked, where he has a clearly defined task and a powerful position, may make attempts at nondirective, democratic leadership detrimental or superfluous. For example, the captain of an airliner can hardly call a committee meeting of the crew to share in the decision-making during a difficult landing approach. On the other hand, the chairman of a voluntary committee cannot ask with impunity that the group members vote or act according to his instructions.

Our studies also have shown that factors such as group-member abilities, cultural heterogeneity and stressfulness of the task affect the degree to which the leader can influence members of the group. But the important finding and the consistent finding in these studies has been that mixed situations require relationship-oriented leadership while very favorable and very unfavorable job situations require task-oriented leaders.

Perhaps the most important implication of this theory of leadership is that the organization for which the leader works is as responsible for his success or failure as is the leader himself.

The chances are that *anyone* who wants to become a leader can become one if he carefully chooses the situations that are favorable to his leadership style.

The notion that a man is a "born" leader, capable of leading in all circumstances, appears to be nothing more than a myth. If there are leaders who excel under all conditions, I have not found them in my 18 years of research.

When we think of improving leadership performance, we tend to think first of training the leader. Personnel psychologists and managers typically view the executive's position as fixed and unchangeable and the applicant as highly plastic and trainable. A man's basic style of leadership depends upon his personality. Changing a man's leadership style means trying to change his personality. As we know from experience in psychotherapy, it may take from one to several years to effect lasting changes in a personality structure. A leader's personality is not likely to change because of a few lectures or even a few weeks of intensive training.

It is doubtful that intensive training techniques can change an individual's style of leadership. However, training programs could be designed to provide the opportunity for a leader to learn in which situations he can perform well and in which he is likely to fail. Laboratory training also may provide the leader with some insights into his personal relationships with group members.

Our theory of leadership effectiveness predicts that a leader's performance can be improved by engineering or fitting the job to the leader. This is based, at least in part, on the belief that it is almost always easier to change a leader's work environment than to change his personality. The leader's authority, his task and even his interpersonal relations within his group members can be altered, sometimes without making the leader aware that this has been done.

For example, we can change the leader's position power in either direction. He can be given a higher rank if this seems necessary. Or he can be given subordinates who are equal or nearly equal to him in rank. His assistants can be two or three ranks below him, or we can assign him men who are expert in their specialties. The leader can have sole authority for a job, or he may be required to consult with his group. All communications to group members may be channeled through the leader, making him the source of all the inside information, or all members of the group can be given the information directly, thus reducing the leader's influence.

The task structure also can be changed to suit the leader's style. Depending upon the group situation, we can give the leader explicit instructions or we can deliberately give him a vague and nebulous goal.

Finally, we can change the leader-member relations. In some situations it may be desirable to improve leader-member relations by making the group homogeneous in culture and language or in technical and educational background. Interdisciplinary groups are notoriously difficult to handle, and it is even more difficult to lead a group that is racially or culturally mixed. Likewise, we can affect leader-member relations by giving a leader subordinates who get along well with their supervisor or assign a leader to a group with a history of trouble or conflict.

It may seem that often we are proposing the sabotaging of the leader's influence over his group. Although common sense might make it seem that weakening the leader's influence will lower performance, in actuality our studies show that this rarely happens. The average group performance (in other words, the leader's effectiveness) correlates poorly with the degree of the leader's influence over the group.

In fact, the findings from several studies suggest that a particular leader's effectiveness may be improved even though the situation is made less favorable for him.

The leader himself can be taught to recognize the situations that best fit his style. A man who is able to avoid situations in which he is likely to fail, and seek out situations that fit his leadership style, will probably become a highly successful and effective leader. Also, if he is aware of his strengths and weaknesses, the leader can try to change his group situation to match his leadership style.

However, we must remember that good leadership performance depends as much upon the organization as it does upon the leader. This means that we must learn not only how to train men to be leaders, but how to build organizations in which specific types of leaders can perform well.

In view of the increasing scarcity of competent executives, it is to an organization's advantage to design jobs to fit leaders instead of attempting merely to fit a leader to the job.

The Coming of Death of Administrative Man

ROBERT B. DENHARDT
JAN PERKINS

Contemporary theories of organization are largely theories about men in organizations, by men, and for men. For this reason, it should not be surprising (nor considered coincidental) that the key paradigmatic commitment of organizational analysis is expressed by the concept of administrative *man*. Nor should it be surprising that the behavior of most organizational practitioners is well characterized by this idea. Administrative *man* provides not only a starting point from which all major components of the rational model of organization flow, but also a model for the culturally dominant version of how people in organizations should act.

In marked contrast to this view of organizational life, some feminist theorists are developing alternative models of organization, based primarily on their experience in the women's movement. Both women's rights groups and radical feminists are experimenting with new patterns of group activity which substantially depart from the rational model of administration. In this article, we will ask how these new patterns may affect the way individuals think about and consequently behave in complex organizations. After describing the concept of administrative *man*, we will focus on alternative theories of organization developed in the women's movement. We will then consider the implications of these ideas for the future of organizations.

CONCEPT OF ADMINISTRATIVE MAN

The concept of administrative *man* can be traced to a series of writings appearing in the late '40s and early '50s, involving most prominently the organization theorist, Herbert Simon. In his now classic work, *Administrative Behavior*, Simon suggests that "the theory of administration is concerned with how an organization should be constructed and operated in order to accomplish its work efficiently."[1] Since the skills, values, and knowledge of the individual organizational member are limited, these attributes become the scarce means which must be maximized to attain organizational ends. When this occurs, the "bounded rationality" of the single organizational member is transcended by the rationality involved in the efficient utilization of organizational resources. "The administrative man takes his place alongside the classical 'economic man.'"[2]

In the organization's pursuit of rationality, administrative *man* is hardly an active participant. By accepting the goals of the organization as his own, administrative *man* loses his distinctiveness and becomes an instrument to be used in the pursuit of organizational rationality. In a passage from *Public Administration,*

Simon et al. describe administrative *man* in terms more reminiscent of organization man:

> Administrative man accepts the organization goals as the value premises of his decisions, is particularly sensitive and reactive to the influences upon him of the other members of his organization, forms stable expectations regarding his own role in relation to others and the roles of others in relation to him, and has high morale in regard to the organization's goals. What is perhaps most remarkable and unique about administrative man is that the organizational influences do not merely cause him to do certain specific things (e.g., putting out a forest fire, if that is his job), but induce in him a habit pattern of doing *whatever* things are appropriate to carry out in cooperation with others the organization goals. *He develops habits of cooperative behavior* (emphasis added).[3]

Indeed, such patterns of behavior are absolutely essential in order for rationality to be achieved by social institutions. "Since these institutions largely determine the mental sets of the participants, they largely set the conditions for the exercise of docility, and hence of rationality in human society."[4]

Having chosen to emphasize the rational achievement of purpose, Simon is led inevitably to an instrumental view of the organizational member. As Dahl and Lindblom point out,

> A bias in favor of a deliberate adaptation of organizational means to ends requires that human relationships be viewed as instrumental means to the prescribed goals of organization not as sources of direct prime goal achievement. Joy, love, friendship, pity, and affection must all be curbed—unless they happen to foster the prescribed goals of the organization.[5]

As we will see, this depersonalization of the organizational member is in considerable contrast to much contemporary feminist thought.

The means-end dilemma faced by administrative *man* suggests another component of the rational view of organization, the inevitability of hierarchy. As Simon points out, "Ends themselves, however, are often merely instrumental to more final objectives."[6] These intermediate levels become ends with reference to levels below, but means with reference to levels above. Following this chain, one is forced to conclude that the only sensible way of ordering the complex process of achieving goals is through a hierarchical structure in which various sub-units contribute their limited goals as means toward the ultimate goal of the total organization. As Vincent Ostrom notes in *The Intellectual Crisis in Public Administration*, Simon chose to confine his analysis to organizations in action rather than to develop a broader theory of rational choice. In doing so, he was forced to focus primarily on institutions "characterized by hierarchical ordering."[7]

From the top of the resulting organizational hierarchy flow the directives that govern the behavior of administrative *man*. Simply put, "the values and objectives that guide individual decisions . . . are usually imposed in the individual by the exercise of authority."[8] Authority is basically a relationship between a superior and a subordinate in which it is expected that the superior will issue directives which will be followed by the subordinate under normal circumstances. In Simon's formulation, orders are accepted only when they fall within the individual's "zone of acceptance." However, when one recalls that administrative *man* develops "habits of cooperative behavior," which greatly expand the zone, this hardly presents a serious problem.

The rational organization requires that individuals accept (1) a view of organization as a method or instrument for achieving rational efficiency, and (2) patterns of superior domination through hierarchical patterns of authority. In the world of administrative *man,* these elements have assumed the proportions of "cultural traits," adopted through a process of social learning at an early age.[9] Indeed, the pressure to conform to the standards of the rational model is so strong that the concept of administrative *man* is no longer an abstraction helpful in developing a theory of rational choice, but is now a model for the behavior of people in complex organizations. We are all socialized to adopt the character of administrative *man,* efficient but also joyless.

MORE HOPEFUL ALTERNATIVES

In contrast to the dismal picture of administrative *man* drawn by the rational theory of organization, certain elements of the current women's movement are developing more hopeful alternatives. While differences are apparent in the way in which divergent feminist groups conceptualize the primary problem confronting women, there are developing similarities in approaches to organization. In this section, we will discuss the emerging organizational concerns of two types of feminist groups, women's rights feminists and radical feminists. Women's rights feminists, probably comprising a majority of women in the movement, are those seeking expansion of women's rights within the existing social structure. Radical feminists, on the other hand, see the social structure itself as the problem and thus are seeking radical alteration of the system.

National *women's rights* organizations with local chapters such as the National Organization for Women, National Women's Political Caucus, and Women's Equity Action League accept "the basic structure of the society and social relationships, but (seek) to improve the status of women through legal, economic, and political means."[10] For example, NOW has as its original and stated goal to "take action to bring women into full participation in the mainstream of American society *now,* exercising all the privileges and responsibilities thereof in truly equal partnership with men."[11] Accordingly, little is considered wrong with current institutions beyond the fact that women are excluded from them.

The formal structure of NOW consists of a well-defined hierarchy of authority, with a national board at the top and statewide organizations serving as bridges from the national level to the local chapters. National NOW has written rules, bylaws, procedures, and membership dues requirements which are to be followed by all state and local NOW organizations. On the local level, like the national, a complex division of labor with specified job assignments is found; for instance, most local chapters have the positions of president, membership chairperson, treasurer, fund-raiser, and anywhere from one to 15 task force chairpersons.

Although the formal structure is fairly traditional, increasingly the top leadership and local chapters are informally adopting an anti-authoritarian stance, with aspirations of a participatory ideal. The developing ideal is that

> all participants should be able to express their personal needs and to develop their individual talents in a sympathetic social environment. . . . Implicitly and explicitly such members adopt a consensus model of decision-making in contrast to the adversary model of the "male world."[12]

In this view, leaders are considered facilitators, persons with special talents in helping the group reach decisions. All members have the responsibility to fully participate in the process and let the leader know their feelings. Conversely, the officers must "learn to grasp the sense of a meeting and to present this in a way that emphasizes everyone's responsibility."[13] NOW has adopted consciousness raising as a means to bring its members into active participation in the organization.

The *radical feminist* branch of the women's movement consists of local or regional feminist groups, such as Female Liberation in Boston, the N.Y. Radical Feminists, Redstockings, and WITCH. Radical feminists see their mission as going to the root of social phenomena to criticize and to seek changes in power relationships and social institutions. Radical feminists may agree to the need for some reforms sought by women's rights groups, but reforms are not considered the ultimate solution. Indeed, some feel that to accept reform constitutes the greatest danger for the feminist movement, for to engage in reform is to accept the present structure and risk being co-opted by it, thereby preventing in the future fundamental change in the structure.[14] Furthermore, by accepting reform and thus an immediate increase in opportunities for participation in economic and political institutions, many radical feminists fear that women end up trading off positive aspects of the traditional female role for less attractive aspects of the male role.[15]

Female Liberation of Boston, a radical feminist group, has articulated its struggle with these issues in its quarterly, *The Second Wave*. In one issue of the magazine its members discussed the organization's split into two groups: socialist feminists and radical feminists. The root difference was the socialist emphasis upon end product as opposed to the radical insistence on the "importance of process-consciousness."[16] The socialists contended that so-called personal change must wait until "after the revolution"; the other group argued that if feminists are not developing new ways of relating to each other and the world around them along the way then there will be no revolution.

> If we have not developed new forms, the same types of structure will supplant the old with only a change in content. That is no revolution. Power must be shared, not controlled by a few at the top of the pyramid.[17]

Female Liberation began to understand that work on interpersonal relations and projects go together, with one enhancing the other, and that women "have been conditioned to be receptive to each others' needs and feelings, and we must *not* lose this quality."[18] The group felt that a major difficulty in its organization was equalizing the desire to be a supportive group for its members, with the goal of bringing about social change in the environment. "We recognize that the integration of internal and external, or personal and political, is a classic problem in our schizoid society and that the attempt itself is revolutionary."[19] Indeed the foundation of their feminism has been the integration of "male and female" principles: female-principle qualities of inner growth and nurturing and male-principle qualities of action and outreach (not to be confused with women and men).[20]

In their third year, Female Liberation found that the division of labor issue was central, so they set out to (1) uncover the covert informal structure and examine its destructive effects, (2) discover why they had drifted into that structure, and (3) develop an alternative structure and the means to get there.[21] They found that although they held the ideal of collective effort, their process was in fact not collective. Secondly, the process was found to be physically and emotionally oppressive to the person in charge, while the interrelationships of the staff were not enhanced. They felt that because they had all been socialized to operate in hierarchical structures they naturally fell into that pattern. Consequently, the organization periodically consciously evaluated its efforts in light of its ideology and goals.

BASIS FOR CHALLENGE

The organizational challenges posed by the women's groups described in the preceding section go to the heart of the rational theory of organization—the concept of administrative *man*. Specifically, parts of the women's movement extol alternative values which contrast sharply with the traditional concerns for (1) organization as a method for achieving rational efficiency, and (2) superior domination through hierarchical patterns of authority. In this section, we will examine the basis for this challenge, suggesting that these alternatives may eventually help change the way we think about organizations and the way we behave as members of organizations.

As noted earlier, the traditional view of organization as a method for achieving rational efficiency leads directly to an instrumental conception of the organizational member. To the extent that the organization is conceived as devoted to the efficient utilization of resources, including human resources, the individual organizational member is simply a tool in the organizational process, not a part of the process itself. The focus of administrative *man* is on the completion of tasks (e.g., putting out the forest fire); therefore, he needs little involvement in the process of determining organizational operations.

A significant challenge to this view is coming from radical feminists in their insistence upon fluid, temporary structures in which process is as important as tasks. Emphasis in these groups is upon consensual decision making for the purpose of enhancing both creativity and group solidarity.[22] Personal development of members' skills and insights is aided by the flexible structure of feminist groups. This concept of self-realization, developing full human potential both intellectually and emotionally,[23] is clearly inconsistent with the bureaucratic emphasis upon task efficiency. Radical feminists believe that it is only after members feel they have had an opportunity to develop their personal ideology and understand the views of others that they can effectively work towards common goals. Indeed, once a goal is formulated, tasks are then divided upon the basis of skill and interest in the particular situation.

The rational view of organization suggests that it is only through his participation in organized endeavor that administrative *man* can approximate full rationality. "The rational individual is, and must be, an organized and institutionalized individual."[24] The rationality of the organizational member is not defined in terms of the full range of the individual's interests, but only in terms of a contribution to the accomplishment of organizational purpose. The notion of rationality does not extend to the individual's life-work outside the organization. The direction for administrative *man* is clear—full rationality requires complete commitment to the pursuit of organizational goals.

This degree of commitment is unacceptable to feminists who wish to balance various life interests. Women participating in the workforce are more conscious of the competing demands of marriage and family than previously had been the case among male workers.[25] Traditionally career success for men has meant that if conflict arose between work and family roles, the conflict would be resolved in favor of work.[26] Career in this sense connotes a demanding, pre-ordained life pattern, to which everything else is subordinated. Success for men has been traditionally measured in terms of upward mobility, status, and monetary rewards; there have been no predetermined standards against which to measure "success" for women if one removes marriage and motherhood as role indicators. A number of new strategies are aimed at developing a new concept of increased occupational flexibility, through part-time work, flexible work hours, longer leaves of absence without pay, educational leaves, and alternative retirement options.[27]

The feminist challenge to the second major theme suggested by administrative *man* is even more explicit; it argues that superior domination through hierarchical patterns of authority is not essential to the achievement of important goals but in fact is restrictive of the growth of the group and its individual members. All feminists agree that women should have the right to control their own lives, which necessarily precludes continued male domination. The issue is carried further by radical feminists in their stance that domination by males should not simply be replaced by domination by leaders. Where women's rights feminists largely operate within formal hierarchical organizations, some (e.g., NOW) have recently adopted more flexible and egalitarian forms at the local level. All along most radical feminist groups have sought equality of members within an anti-elitist structure.

As the notion of superior domination relates to the more general issue of power, feminists are struggling with what they see as the root of their oppression. Women's rights feminists feel that if they are given a significant amount of power, particularly in economic and political institutions, then the essential problems facing women will generally be solved. Radical feminists too realize that feminist visions can only be obtained if women gain some control or power in society. The problem as they see it is to redefine power so that there is not simply a substitution of a female elite for the present male elite, a situation which would still maintain the oppression of men and most women. Such a redefinition of power would include such questions as the following:

> What kind of organizations must [feminists] develop to support a different kind of power and decision making? Must women dominate or might it be possible to share power with men once [women] have obtained it? Will a feminist society have leaders at all? If so, how will they be chosen? Is it possible to envision a society in which there is not power, where there are no leaders? Are women ready to work collectively? With men?[28]

One response is the belief that it is impossible to significantly develop one's own ideology and personhood if one accepts the authority of leaders and thereby abdicates personal responsibility. Operationalization of this strategy has sometimes led to "structureless" and "leaderless" groups, with structurelessness "a natural reaction against the overstructured society" in which feminists find themselves.[29] Others have found that the informal structure allows formation of elites, who have, in effect, control over the group and exclude other members from participation in decision making.[30] However, effectiveness in achieving group goals is undermined where there is no structure within which expectations can become explicit and egalitarian decisions can be made.

This is not to say that traditional organizational forms are being adopted by radical feminist groups. Indeed these groups are finding that "temporary" structures are often best suited to their needs. These structures usually last "only as long as the activity and then dissolve, leaving no permanent leaders or organizational apparatus.''[31] Another form of structuring to accomplish goals is through focusing of certain groups on particular problems.[32] For example, there may be one group conducting classes on women's history and another one teaching self-defense within one particular region or locality. Similarly, other groups (such as the Michigan Women's Liberation Coalition) are experimenting with the use of coalitions which serve to provide flexible coordination of groups and activities while preserving the autonomy of members. The structure is nonhierarchical—one of diffused leadership and responsibility.[33]

POTENTIAL IMPACT

The feminist challenge to the concept of administrative *man* has not yet been fully articulated; however, the basic elements of that challenge are clear. In contrast to the dependence of administrative *man* on a view of organization as a method for achieving rational efficiency, a growing number of feminists view group activity as also valuable in terms of personal growth and are therefore interested in *both* task and process. In such a view, the inevitable passivity and impersonality of administrative *man* is replaced by activity and self-disclosure on the part of the organizational member. In contrast to the traditional domination of administrative *man* through hierarchical systems of authority, feminists are experimenting with alternative forms of organizational structure and alternative patterns of leadership. The emphasis in such experiments is on the development of individual capacities as well as feminist ideology in a more open and supportive environment.

We can anticipate that feminist theories of organization will continue to be refined and more clearly articulated, especially as they are consistent with and encouraged by other organizational humanists.[34] However, it remains an open question as to whether such theories will have any major impact on the structure of public and private organizations in the future. Increasing numbers of women will be entering such organizations in the coming years; however, larger numbers of women in these organizations will not in itself bring about the demise of administrative *man.* As noted earlier, there are powerful social forces which act to maintain the existing model of organization. Women entering traditionally structured organizations will be subject to substantial pressures to adopt the model of administrative *man;* they may be socialized into traditional patterns of behavior.

In order for alternative beliefs to develop in traditional organizations, it will be necessary for feminists to counter the pressures to conform. For those feminists who are willing to undertake this task, several activities may be useful. Among these, feminists must develop appropriate systems of support among others in the organization for the purpose of sharing information, mutually resolving emerging difficulties, and aiding one another in resisting the forces of socialization. A related activity is the formation of consciousness-raising groups, which encourage independent thinking concerning the central issues of feminist thought. Consciousness-raising activities may bring about changes in the way women view themselves, developing new images which may deviate from the traditional view of organizational life. Such groups could develop a close connection between personal development and organizational change.

The key to the potential impact of feminist thinking on organizations of the future may finally come in the radical feminist rejection of the notion of superior domination—either by men or other elites—and their adoption of the concept of the authority of personal experience.[35] Rejecting the traditional acceptance of "expert" opinions, ideology, or structure, radical feminists believe they must develop an ideology and a structure from their experience of being female in a male-dominated society. They are therefore unwilling to give up personal responsibility for their own actions by submitting to the authority of some accepted theory or structure. To the extent that individuals follow this admonition and accept personal responsibility for their actions, even in the face of powerful pressures to conform to the model of administrative *man*, we may expect more and more people to become aware of the values of a feminist and ultimately humanist organization. And we may expect the coming death of administrative *man*.

NOTES

1. Herbert A. Simon, *Administrative Behavior* (New York: The Free Press, 2nd ed., 1966), p. 38.
2. *Ibid.*, p. 39.
3. Herbert A. Simon, Donald W. Smithburg, and Victor A. Thompson, *Public Administration* (New York: Alfred A. Knopf, 1950), p. 82.
4. Simon, *op. cit.*, p. 104.
5. *Ibid.*, p. 252.
6. *Ibid.*, p. 62.
7. Vincent Ostrom, *The Intellectual Crisis in American Public Administration* (University, Ala.: University of Alabama Press, 1974), p. 46.
8. Simon, *Administrative Behavior, op. cit.*, p. 198.
9. See Herbert G. Wilcox, "The Cultural Trait of Hierarchy in Middle Class Children," *Public Administration Review*, Vol. 28 (May/June 1968), pp. 222-235; and Robert B. Denhardt, "Bureaucratic Socialization and Organizational Accommodation," *Administrative Science Quarterly*, Vol. 13 (December 1968), pp. 441-450.
10. Barbara Bovee Polk, "Women's Liberation: Movement for Equality," in Constantina Safilios-Rothschild (ed.), *Toward a Sociology of Women* (Xerox Corp., 1972), p. 321.
11. Nancy Reeves, *Womankind* (Chicago: Aldine Publishing Co., 1973), p. 119.
12. Maren Lockwood Carden, *The New Feminist Movement* (New York: Russell Sage Foundation, 1974), p. 128.
13. *Ibid.*, p. 129.
14. Jo Freeman, *The Politics of Women's Liberation* (New York: David McKay Co., 1975), p. 241.
15. See Jessie Bernard, *Women and the Public Interest* (Chicago: Aldine Publishing Co., 1971), p. 41; and Caroline Bird's "old feminists," in *Born Female* (New York: McKay, 1970), p. 161.
16. "From Us," *The Second Wave*, Vol. 2, No. 2, p. 2.
17. *Ibid.*
18. *Ibid.*
19. "From Us," *The Second Wave*, Vol. 2, No. 4, p. 2.
20. Linda Thurston, "On Male and Female Principle," *The Second Wave*, Vol. 1, No. 2.
21. "From Us," *The Second Wave*, Vol. 3, No. 1, p. 2.
22. See Reeves, *op. cit.*, p. 182; and Alice Rossi, "Sex Equality: The Beginnings of Ideology," in Safilios-Rothschild, *op. cit.*, p. 352.
23. Carden, *op. cit.*, p. 86.
24. Simon, *Administrative Behavior, op. cit.*, p. 102.
25. See Rhona Rapoport and Robert N. Rapoport, "The Dual-Career Family: A Variant Pattern and Social Change," in Safilios-Rothschild, *op. cit.*, p. 236.

26. Bernard, *op. cit.*, p. 192; also see Philip Slater, *The Pursuit of Loneliness* (Boston: Beacon Press, 1971), p. 73.
27. Constantina Safilios-Rothschild, *Women and Social Policy* (Englewood Cliffs, N.J.: Prentice-Hall, Inc., 1974), p. 73.
28. Jane Dolkart and Nancy Hartsock, "Feminist Visions of the Future," *Quest*, Vol. II, No. 1 (Summer 1975), p. 6.
29. Joreen (Jo Freeman), "The Tyranny of Structurelessness," in Anne Kordt, Ellen Levine, and Anita Rapone (eds.), *Radical Feminism* (New York: New York Times Book Co., 1973), p. 285.
30. *Ibid.*
31. Polk, *op. cit.*, p. 329.
32. Carden, *op. cit.*, p. 73.
33. Polk, *op. cit.*, p. 326.
34. Wendell L. French and Cecil H. Bell, *Organization Development* (Englewood Cliffs, N.J.: Prentice-Hall, Inc., 1973), pp. 65-66.
35. Carden, *op. cit.*, p. 86.

The Minority Administrator: Problems, Prospects, and Challenges

ADAM W. HERBERT

The first National Conference on the Role of Minorities in Urban Management and Related Fields was held in Washington, D.C., on June 10 and 11, 1973. The significance of this conference was three-fold: (1) it was the first organized national meeting of non-elected minority public administrators and educators held to discuss the problems, education, responsibilities, and needs of minority public sector professionals; (2) it represented a symbolic acknowledgement that the quest of minority groups for more responsive government must, and does now, include a sophisticated concentration on the political and administrative affairs of government; and (3) its theme suggested, quite appropriately, that minority administrators do have an important and unique role to play in the public management field, which they must accept if the plight of minority (if not all) people in America is to be improved.

Since this Conference, a number of major developments around the country suggest that minority administrators, however small in number, are increasingly gaining positions from which they can respond to the universal cry for more responsive government. Five cities as diverse as Compton, California, and East Lansing, Michigan, have selected black city managers to administer their governments. Black elected administrators are leading 108 cities in all regions of the nation, including Los Angeles, Atlanta, Raleigh, and Detroit. Another 62 serve as vice mayors.[1] Data from the 1973 State and Local Information Survey (EEO-4) reveal that 18.2 per cent of the total labor force in state and local governments represent minority groups (Blacks, Spanish-Surnamed Americans, Asian, American Indian, and Other). While only 6.8 per cent of this group is labeled "Professional," on the surface these figures do suggest growing influence on local government policy implementation and formulation.[2]

Recent federal employment data as reflected in Table I reveal that despite the continued decline in total federal employment, minority employment has continued to increase. Total minority employment (20.4 per cent of the federal work force) expanded 1.9 per cent for the period May 1972-May 1973.[3] While the increase in the number of GS 14-15, and supergrade administrators is not significant, current hiring practices will result in greater opportunities for minorities to make inputs into agency decision-making and policy execution.

TABLE I

Net Change in Employment Under the General Schedule and Similar Pay Plan, by Grade Grouping from May 31, 1972 to May 31, 1973

Grade Grouping	Total Employment Change	Minority Group Employment Change					
		Total Minority	Negro	Spanish Surnamed	American Indian	Oriental	All Other
Total, General Schedule or Similar	− 173	+ 11,210	+ 8,756	+ 1,913	+ 200	+ 341	− 11,383
GS 1- 4	+ 9,159	+ 3,704	+ 2,797	+ 869	− 45	+ 83	+ 5,455
GS 5- 8	− 6,906	+ 3,952	+ 3,538	+ 348	+ 48	+ 18	− 10,858
GS 9-11	− 4,298	+ 2,169	+ 1,518	+ 434	+ 130	+ 87	− 6,467
GS 12-13	+ 1,133	+ 961	+ 697	+ 173	+ 45	+ 46	+ 172
GS 14-15	+ 805	+ 416	+ 199	+ 84	+ 24	+ 109	+ 389
GS 16-18	− 66	+ 8	+ 7	+ 5	− 2	− 2	− 74

Source: U.S. Civil Service Commission, *Minority Group Employment in the Federal Government* (Washington, D.C.: U.S. Government Printing Office, 1973).

Although there has been a conscious movement toward equal employment opportunity and affirmative action in the field of public administration since the late '60s, the nature of these public sector efforts continues to be questioned in many circles. Indeed a major finding of the aforementioned Conference was that:

Minority persons are still skeptical about the willingness of governmental systems to accept them as trained professionals with the knowledge and ability to perform in administrative positions of increasing responsibility and authority.[4]

This finding appears to coincide with several conclusions reached by the Civil Rights Commission in its 1969 survey of cities in seven SMSAs. While employment rates have improved for minority group administrators since this 1969 survey, some of the Commission's conclusions are worth mentioning, particularly in light of the skepticism felt by many minority group members relative to the good will of government agencies. The Commission found that:

Minority group members are denied equal access to State and local government jobs.
(a)   Negroes, in general, have better success in obtaining jobs with central city governments than they do in State, county, or suburban jurisdictions and are more successful in obtaining jobs in the North than in the South.

(b) Negroes are noticeably absent from managerial and professional jobs even in those jurisdictions where they are substantially employed in the aggregate. In only two central cities, out of a total of eight surveyed, did the overall number of black employees in white-collar jobs reflect the population patterns of the cities.

(c) Access to white collar jobs in some departments is more readily available to minority group members than in others. Negroes are most likely to hold professional, managerial, and clerical jobs in health and welfare and least likely to hold these jobs in financial administration and general control.

(d) Negroes hold the large majority of laborer and general service worker jobs—jobs which are characterized by few entry skills, relatively low pay, and limited opportunity for advancement.[5]

Related to these conclusions (particularly point "C") are data from the aforementioned EEO-4 survey which indicate that while minorities do hold a number of administrative positions outside *social* agencies, most continue to work in these areas. Table II provides a summary of current local government hiring practices by functional areas. As the Civil Rights Commission indicated in 1969, minorities continued in 1973 to be assigned primarily to departments that have a "social" orientation. It is particularly significant to note that police and fire departments continue to employ significantly lower percentages of minority group

TABLE II

State/Local Government Employment Rates by Functional Areas, 1973

		Percentage of		
	Group	Non-White Employment	Officials/ Administrators	Professionals
I	Sanitation and sewage	38.8%	12.4%	8.9%
	Housing	34.6	20.7	24.2
	Hospitals and sanitariums	30.4	9.1	18.6
II	Public welfare	23.6	11.0	15.4
	Utilities and transport	22.7	9.4	10.6
	Other	18.9	7.9	10.0
	Employment security	18.7	8.2	13.5
	Corrections	18.7	9.8	14.7
	Health	17.8	3.2	11.6
	Natural resources	15.9	6.2	8.9
	Community development	15.1	7.9	13.2
III	Streets and highways	11.8	3.8	6.0
	Financial administration	11.4	5.3	7.9
IV	Police	9.3	4.4	5.5
	Fire	5.0	2.2	2.8

Source: Compiled from data cited in the Equal Employment Opportunity Commission, *State and Local Government Information, EEO-4, National Statistical Summaries* (Washington, D.C.: FEOC, Office of Research, 1974).

people than do other governmental agencies. Financial administration also continues to be an area in which minority people have been unable to make significant inroads, although employment rates in this area are higher than in police and fire departments. It is also important to note that with the exception of housing, the percentage of professionals and officials/administrators (white collar jobs) continues to be low in all functional areas.

At the federal level, a similar pattern of minorities being hired by some agencies at much higher rates than others is evident, as reflected in Table III. Three disting-

TABLE III
Federal Government Minority Group Employment Rates, 1972–1973

Agencies	Total Employment Rates of Agency GS 9-18	Total Minority Employment of Agency GS 9-18	Minority Employment as a Percentage of			
			Total GS 9-18	Total GS 9-11	GS 12-15	GS 16-18
OEO	1,234	385	31.2%	46.3%	26.6%	40.9%
ACTION	946	220	23.3	30.3	19.6	18.8
State	2,491	456	18.3	32.2	8.5	2.5
Labor	7,568	1,336	17.6	27.3	14.3	6.8
HEW	40,178	5,796	14.4	18.0	10.9	9.3
HUD	9,912	1,304	13.2	15.9	11.0	9.4
OMB	383	47	12.3	22.1	10.0	9.0
Interior	27,883	2,646	9.5	12.7	5.9	3.2
Commerce	16,108	1,434	8.9	11.7	7.3	2.3
Treasury	45,133	3,004	6.7	8.3	5.0	2.1
Defense	262,726	16,797	6.4	8.2	4.2	1.1
Transportation	46,337	2,578	5.6	7.9	4.3	7.0
Justice	20,041	1,109	5.5	7.4	3.6	3.3
Agriculture	41,725	2,110	5.1	6.2	3.3	2.4

Source: Compiled from data cited in the U.S. Civil Service Commission, *Minority Group Employment in the Federal Government* (Washington, D.C.: U.S. Government Printing Office, March 1974).

uishable groups of agencies seem to be evident with reference to the percentage of minority group members employed. The first group contains four agencies, three of which—Action, OEO, and Labor—might be labeled as "traditional." The presence of the State Department in this first group reflects a deviation from the usual governmental pattern related to minority employment. The Office of Economic Opportunity and ACTION stand out above all other federal agencies as the employers of both the greatest percentage of minority professionals at the GS 9 levels or above, and the greatest percentage of supergrade administrators. The Departments of State and Labor also have relatively high rates of minority employment overall, and particularly at the GS 9-11 levels. At the supergrade levels, however, both departments have much lower minority employment rates.

The second cluster of agencies contains three departments, two of which might be labeled as "social" or "traditional" in the sense referred to by the Civil Rights

Commission—Health, Education, and Welfare; and Housing and Urban Development. To some observers it may be surprising to note the presence of the Office of Management and Budget in this second group. The OMB employment figures are especially significant because of that agency's overall importance in the governmental process.

The third cluster of agencies includes Interior, Commerce, Treasury, Defense, Transportation, Justice, and Agriculture. None of these agencies are usually regarded as being social service agencies: as a consequence, the lack of substantial minority employees is not surprising. It is significant that at the federal level, as in the case of state and local governments, the percentage of minority employees decreases rapidly as decision-making responsibility (GS level) increases. The one exception to this trend is the Office of Economic Opportunity, where the percentage of supergrade administrators (40.9 per cent) is at a level comparable to those at the GS 9-11 levels (46.3 per cent) within that agency.

Although we in the public affairs field have given little attention in our literature to these data and the resulting debate, it is important to recognize that, as the number of minority professionals and administrators at all levels of government increases, the expectations of minority people for more responsive government will probably expand simultaneously. As will be argued later, the powers possessed by minorities employed in the public sector in most cases seldom are adequate to meet these expectations. As a consequence, short of a commitment on the part of administrators generally (white and non-white) to become responsive to the needs of "all" citizens, governmental agencies will continue to address on a priority basis the demands of the more powerful and affluent in our society. Where public agencies do not manifest a change in programmatic efforts which might be interpreted by minority communities as being more responsive to their needs, the tasks of minority administrators within those agencies, particularly at the local level, will become increasingly more difficult.

These difficulties will arise, in part, because of the collective perception that minority administrators understand the nature and magnitude of the problems confronting those from lower socio-economic backgrounds. Indeed, whether one is black, brown, or red, the visible presence of an administrator with whom he/she can identify causes at least greater initial security that someone is listening who can understand the needs, realities, and perceptions being described, and who will help if at all possible.

Another factor creating the expectation among minority groups that the system will change as a result of greater "integration" of public agencies is the belief that many of these positions were made possible through community efforts. It is expected, therefore, that minority administrators and professionals will be spokesmen for other minorities out of an inherent *obligation* to speak out in their best group interest.

Perhaps the most critical factor, however, relates to bureaucratic promises made as the number of minority group members working for an agency or jurisdiction increases. In far too many cases, hiring practices are utilized to demonstrate efforts to be responsive to minority community needs. Because many agencies or governmental jurisdictions equate programmatic commitment or effort with the employment of a larger number of minorities, governmental employees from those groups can become convenient targets of protest when expectations and/or promises to the community groups are unfulfilled.

These and many other related demands and expectations create a number of major dilemmas for minority administrators to which most agencies are insensitive. In some respects many of the dilemmas and forces mentioned in this article confront all administrators, but the minority administrator seems to be subject to their weight more than most. For ultimately, every minority administrator and professional must consciously or otherwise respond to two basic and difficult questions: (1) "What responsibility do I have to minority group peoples?" (2) "What role should I attempt to play in making government more responsive to the needs of all people?"

ROLE DETERMINANTS

In addressing these questions, it is useful to consider six forces which confront the minority administrator, and which influence significantly his/her potential effectiveness and perhaps perceptions of responsibility to both the governmental agency and minority peoples more generally. Graphically these forces might be viewed as indicated in Figure 1.

FIGURE 1   ROLE DEMANDS ON MINORITY ADMINISTRATORS

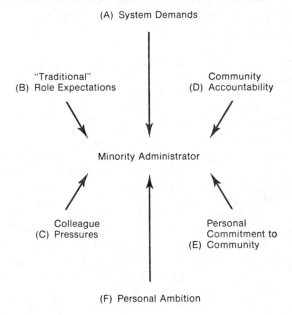

(A) System Demands

"Traditional"
(B) Role Expectations

Community
(D) Accountability

Minority Administrator

Colleague
(C) Pressures

Personal
Commitment to
(E) Community

(F) Personal Ambition

A. System Demands. The first force, "system demands," refers to those expectations of public employees that a governmental system reinforces through a range of sanctions and rewards. Bureaucratic systems are perpetuated because they demand and receive obedience to orders. The traditional model of hierarchy as described by Weber suggests that decisions are made at the top and implemented by those at lower levels within the organization. For political appointees, a failure to respond to demands made by those at the top may mean harassment, dismissal, and embarrassment. Similarly, in a civil service system, pressures are applied "to do as ordered." In cases where the civil servant "bucks" authority, intensive pressures and/or sanctions are applied (e.g., the Fitzgerald vs. Department of Defense case, as well as political pressures recently applied on the IRS, CIA, and FBI).

With regard to blacks, the system has successfully enforced its demands through a careful "weeding out" process. Only the "very best" minority group members could advance as illustrated in Sam Greenlee's novel, *The Spook Who Sat by the Door*. The techniques utilized by agencies to assure the hiring and advancement of these "outstanding" and, as Greenlee suggests, "safe" minority group members include: high education requirement, experience, oral examinations, performance tests, arrest records, probationary periods, general requirements related to residency, etc. Again, if the minority administrator is able to meet these requirements, the ongoing test that remains is that of the willingness to respond to the demands of higher-ups *without question*. Because of their historical difficulties in obtaining employment, some minority public administrators placed job security over program content or impact, and thus have become impediments to efforts to address the needs of their communities.

B. "Traditional" Role Expectations. A conventional wisdom in public administration has been that certain people do particular kinds of jobs well. Tables I and II, as well as the aforementioned Civil Rights Commission report, revealed that a large percentage of minority administrators work in specialized areas. The Civil Rights Commission noted that:

> Access to white-collar jobs in some departments is more readily available to minority group members than in others. Among the seven metropolitan areas studied, the same general pattern of employment in white-collar jobs was discernable in both the North and the South. Negroes were most likely to hold jobs in health and welfare and least likely to hold them in financial administration and general control.[6]

The Commission went on to point out that:

> In addition to the "old traditional jobs" for Black Americans, "new traditional jobs" appear to be emerging. These are usually jobs as staff members of human relations councils, civil rights commissions, or assistants to ranking administrators. They are status jobs carrying major responsibilities and usually bring excellent salaries. But they remain almost exclusively related to minority group problems.[7]

Many of the jobs given minority administrators at both the federal and local levels have been "flack-catching" positions. As Tom Wolfe has indicated in *Radical Chic and Mau-Mauing the Flak Catcher,* during the 1960s in particular, black and brown administrators were often placed in their positions only to become sacrificial lambs in the face of community unrest.

With regard to the future, it is important that minority group members not be herded into "traditional" departments only, nor should they blindly allow themselves to be so directed. Important decisions which affect minority people are made in agencies throughout a governmental jurisdiction or agency. Minority group participation and contributions in all these decision-making processes are becoming increasingly more critical.

C. Colleague Pressures. One of the greatest dangers to the quest for governmental responsiveness remains the pressures imposed by one's peers. Peter Maas' recent book and the adapted movie, *Serpico,* clearly document the pressures which can and frequently are brought to bear on public administrators. The pressures on minority group members take many forms:

1. The minority group policeman who wants to be accepted by his peers may be forced to "bust heads" to gain acceptance, and promotions;
2. The minority welfare worker may be forced to "get tough" with welfare recipients to be regarded as a competent professional;
3. The minority school teacher is placed in the position of "blaming the victims" of the educational process to retain a place of acceptance among his/her colleagues. It is not allowed that these professionals begin to question the quality of the educational experiences of the children supposedly being served, or the unions which represent them in the quest for working conditions which may not be in the best interest of the children.

As social animals, we desire to be accepted as peers by our colleagues. It is difficult, therefore, to ward off these peer pressures. Clearly the task for the minority administrator is that of placing such collegial pressures into a perspective that does not allow them to overshadow broader program objectives and community needs.

D. Community Accountability. In recent years we have heard growing demands for greater community control, coupled with a cry for more minority group professionals who will be responsive to the needs of their people.[8] The problem historically confronting black communities in this latter regard is well described by Piven and Cloward:

> Much Negro leadership exists largely by the grace of white institutions: white political parties and government agencies, white unions and businesses and professions, even white civil-rights organizations. Everything in the environment of the Negro politician, civil servant, or professional makes him attentive to white interests and perspectives.[9]

The demand is clear. Minority people want and need administrators who will listen to them, who can communicate with them, who care about them. If this is not manifested, community control becomes the ultimate demand, and perhaps a necessity.

E. Personal Commitment to Community. Of critical importance in this context is personal commitment to the community. The degree to which the administrator feels that there are obligations to fulfill and a role to be played which only he/she can fulfill can make a critical difference in public policy discussions, decisions, and ultimately, service output. It is my belief that as the number of minority administrators increases, commitment to addressing community needs will increase if only because there is more security in numbers. Equally important is the fact that a growing number of committed young minority administrators are gradually assuming more responsible positions in public agencies. They appear able to address the difficulties of balancing agency objectives with client expectations and their own personal ambitions far better than many of those who have preceded them.

F. Personal Ambition. People want to advance their careers. It is my belief that all administrators weigh important decisions not only in terms of possible programmatic consequences, but also with regard to implications for their own careers. As employment opportunities for minority group people have expanded, personal ambitions among this group have also increased. Until the early 1960s, the bureaucratic system was very effective in minimizing this desire for advancement, basically because it was clear that few opportunities for promotions into professional positions existed. As positions became more available in the 1960s, the initial result was greater competition for an apparently large but actually limited number of high-level appointments. Although employment opportunities have expanded, as mentioned above, it is still argued by some that most agencies do place limits on the numbers of minorities who will fill these positions. The challenge to minority administrators is that of seeking personal security, while simultaneously manifesting a commitment to urge greater efforts to meet governmental responsibilities more effectively.

DILEMMAS OF THE MINORITY ADMINISTRATOR

In light of the above discussion, several dilemmas stand out as being of particular significance for the minority administrator. The effective minority administrator will be one who can respond to the challenges of leadership in the quest for more responsive government in light/in spite of these obstacles:

• Governmental role expectations of minority administrators do not necessarily coincide with the minority administrator's own perceptions, goals, or expectations.

• Unresponsive public policies put minority administrators in extremely tenuous positions *vis-à-vis* the agency, himself/herself, and the community of which he/she is a part.

• Frequently the minority administrator is put into flack-catching positions without the capacity to make meaningful decisions, but is expected to accept the responsibilities of programmatic failures and "keep the natives calm."

• Advancement within the governmental system is generally a function of adherence to established organizational norms; one of these norms historically has been that one need not be concerned about the needs or priorities of minority communities.

• Informal pay and promotional quotas still seem to exist for minority administrators; moreover, it is assumed that they can only fill certain types of positions, usually related to social service delivery or to communication with other minority group members.

• Minority communities sometimes expect much more of the minority administrator than he/she can provide; and in most cases demand a far faster response to their demands than these administrators have developed the capacity to deliver.

• Agencies seem to search for the "super" minority administrator; and even these are frequently hired as show pieces. In other cases there has been evidence of agencies hiring individuals who clearly would be unable to do a job with the intent of showing that an effort was made but "they just can't do this kind of work."

While other dilemmas might be identified, this brief listing seems to reenforce the argument that the task of being a minority administrator within public agencies is not an easy one. Moreover, in the short run the challenges reflected in these dilemmas may become greater in magnitude as governments at all levels fail to address in a meaningful fashion such quality of life problems as hunger, health, housing, etc.

CONCLUSION

For almost two centuries, minority groups have been systematically excluded from making inputs into the administrative processes of government as both decision makers and policy implementors. In the final analysis, it is now the responsibility of governmental leaders generally to expand opportunities for the perspectives of minority administrators to be articulated and acted upon. This responsibility derives not only from executive orders and congressional mandates, but also from the reality that there frequently is a minority perspective on public problems which policy makers should understand if public programs are to be truly responsive and effective.

Schools of public affairs also have a major charge to educate more minority administrators to assume these critical positions. The frequently criticized decrease in foundation monies previously utilized to provide financial assistance to these students must not be utilized as a cop-out to explain away lack of effort in this regard. The minority academic also has a role to play in supporting these efforts to provide the kind of professional training essential to the development of the number and caliber of top-flight minority administrators so critically needed in public agencies. They must also begin to work more closely with both minority elected officials and administrators in continuing education, and in policy research and analysis if some of the major problems facing minority group communities are to be effectively described, understood, and attacked.

Finally, to the minority administrator goes the challenge of accepting the obligation of working for the development and operation of public programs which more effectively meet the needs of *all* people. In some cases this may require an advocacy position. It may demand that the minority group perspective on public policy questions be researched, developed, and articulated. It will frequently demand the capacity and willingness to discuss policy options, directions, and needs with those who have expressed a lack of faith in the governmental process. It will demand a rejection of the argument that administrators are/must be value free and completely neutral in implementing policy decisions. Simultaneously, however, there exists the reality that public employees do work within a bureaucratic context with established procedures, job requirements, and program objectives. These neither can, nor should be ignored. Nor should minority public administrators be *expected* to present minority views, or be given positions solely because they are black, red, or brown. Public agencies, however, must begin to recognize and accept the reality that, in light of the problems confronting our society, it is in the public interest that minority administrators not forget who they are, or from whence they have come.

NOTES

1. Joint Center for Political Studies, *National Roster of Black Elected Officials* (Washington, D.C.: Joint Center, April 1974).
2. Equal Employment Opportunity Commission, *State and Local Government Information, EEO-4 National Statistical Summaries* (Washington, D.C.: Office of Research, 1974).
3. U.S. Civil Service Commission, *Minority Group Employment in the Federal Government* (Washington, D.C.: U.S. Government Printing Office, March 1974), pp. i, ii.
4. *Summary of the First National Conference on the Role of Minorities in Urban Management and Related Fields* (Washington, D.C.: Metropolitan Washington Council of Governments, 1973), p. 19.
5. U.S. Commission on Civil Rights, *For All the People . . . By All the People* (Washington, D.C.: U.S. Government Printing Office, 1969), p. 118.
6. *Ibid.*, p. 2.
7. *Ibid.*, p. 3.
8. For a representative sample of the literature describing these attitudes, see: Alan Altshular, *Community Control* (New York: Pegasus, 1970); Charles E. Wilson, "Year One at I.S. 201," *Social Policy* (May/June 1970), pp. 10-17; Sherry R. Arnstein, "Maximum Feasible Manipulation," *Public Administration Review*, Vol. XXXII (September/October 1972), pp. 377-390; and Mario Fantini and Marilyn Gittell, *Decentralization: Achieving Reform* (New York, Praeger, 1973).
9. Francis Fox Piven and Richard A. Cloward, "Black Control of Cities," in Edward S. Greenburg, et al. (eds), *Black Politics* (New York: Holt, Rinehart and Winston, Inc., 1971), pp. 128-129.

7

PATTERNS OF
ADMINISTRATIVE
ORGANIZATION

Despite increasing recognition of the importance of the human relations approach and of the psychological factors in organizational behavior, patterns in the organizational structure of public agencies remain quite important. In the first of three selections here, Rufus Miles explains why organizational structure is so important.

Jimmy Carter's campaign for the presidency frequently included statements about reorganizing the federal government to increase its productivity and effectiveness. New governors and mayors and new agency administrators often talk about the need for reorganization. In the second article, Herbert Kaufman takes a careful look at what is known about the results of administrative reorganization. Reorganization can often be highly political and problematic. Kaufman raises an important question too often neglected: Is it worth it?

Government chief executives and other administrators often seek rational, clear patterns of organization within agencies that are given exclusive jurisdiction over a particular function, but this rarely occurs in reality. In the last article in this chapter, Martin Landau suggests that this may not be so bad and that the unanticipated consequences of such patterns may actually be desirable.

Considerations for a President Bent on Reorganization

RUFUS E. MILES, JR.

President Carter spoke often during his campaign of his intention to reorganize the federal government. Previous Presidents, especially Lyndon Johnson and Richard Nixon, carried with them into the White House similar convictions that the effectiveness of the United States Government could be substantially improved through reorganization. Each appointed study commissions with sweeping mandates. Two such commissions were appointed by Johnson and one by Nixon; all recommended major regroupings of federal functions.[1] Yet most of such restructuring never occurred.

President Johnson was successful in 1965 and 1966 in gaining congressional approval of two new departments—Housing and Urban Development, and Transportation—but when he tried to combine the Departments of Commerce and Labor into a single department in 1967, it was a fiasco. Thereafter, he recommended no more consolidations to Congress. In 1971, President Nixon built his State of the Union message around sweeping reorganization proposals that would have created Departments of Community Development, Human Resources, Natural Resources, and Economic Affairs, replacing the Departments of Agriculture, Interior, Commerce, Labor, Housing and Urban Development, and Health, Education, and Welfare. These sweeping changes were also pigeon-holed by Congress. The natural inference was that it was much easier to gain congressional approval for the creation of new departments than for the consolidation and abolition of existing departments.

Since neither President succeeded in bringing about any of the major consolidations their advisers counselled, was it faulty advice, congressional obstinacy, or presidential ineptitude and lack of "follow-through" that blocked their purposes? Or was it that the President and his advisers look at the subject of organization in a very different way than does Congress? None of the three advisory commissions, it should be noted, had members with congressional experience. In any event, President Carter and his advisers would do well to ponder the lessons of this experience.

The principles of organization that should guide a President in considering how to structure the federal government differ in many respects from those that normally guide the head of a huge industrial corporation, and even in some respects from those that should guide governors of states. The organization of the federal government affects and reflects many of the purposes and values of the body politic and should be thought of as one of the dynamics that shapes the future of our national society. Organization is especially important at the federal level in expressing the nation's priorities, in allocating resources, in attracting its most competent leader-executives to key positions, and in accomplishing the purposes of the President, the Congress, and the body politic. It may be useful at the outset of a new administration to offer a number of criteria—not an exhaustive list—that the President and his advisers might do well to take into account in considering major reorganization proposals. Following are 13 such criteria.

1. *Organization is an important expression of social values; are the values that deserve greatest emphasis at this stage of the nation's development given appropriate organizational recognition?*

The act of elevating the organizational status of a function, especially when it involves creating an organization that is directly answerable to the President, is, first and foremost, an expression of the importance that the President, the Congress, and the public attach to the purposes of that organization. When Congress enacted the Employment Act of 1946, creating the Council of Economic Advisers and requiring the submission to the Congress of an Annual Economic Report of the President, this represented a new expression of national concern for the management of the economy so as to achieve balanced economic growth and full employment.

A decade later, when the nation was startled by the Russian sputnik in 1957, there was a strongly expressed desire that the United States should promptly do its best to regain the lead in the space race. This led to the creation of the National Aeronautics and Space Administration, with a clearcut mission, directly answerable to the President.

When the country became increasingly distressed over the deterioration of its cities, the President decided to create a Cabinet-level Department of Housing and Urban Development (which, incidentally, had a mission that exceeded its capacity) to reflect the importance that the society attached to the purposes assigned to the Department. The same was true when a Department of Transportation was created. In declaring his war against poverty, President Johnson created the Office of Economic Opportunity and put it in the Executive Office of the President.

When the American people became deeply concerned in the late 1960s over the deterioration of the environment, two new agencies were created, both directly answerable to the President: the Council on Environmental Quality and the Environmental Protection Agency. When the energy crisis descended on the world, the Federal Energy Agency was created, again directly answerable to the President. *Each of these new agencies was created to reflect a new national priority.*

Expression of national priority is the foremost purpose for creating a new Cabinet department or agency directly answerable to the President. It is the first criterion by which any major organizational proposal should be judged: Does the function to be elevated deserve a higher national priority than it has had, or conversely, do functions that are to be submerged deserve relatively lower priority than they have had? Submergence may sometimes be a worthwhile price for improved coordination, but the costs need to be carefully weighed in relation to the benefits.

In the pre-election period, President Carter expressed himself as being strongly in favor of a new Cabinet-level department to consolidate energy functions and develop a coherent energy policy for the nation. He also said, though with less emphasis, that he favored a Cabinet-level Department of Education,[2] presumably to reflect what he believes to be the high level of importance that the country now accords, and should continue to accord, to education. These are the only two functions so far identified as deserving the kind of emphasis that only Cabinet status can give. The first will almost certainly come into being in the near future. It will be a matter of major interest to see whether President Carter will continue to hold to his high valuation of education and elevate its organizational status to the Cabinet level.

2. *Organizations should be placed in a favorable environment for the performance of their central missions.*

Accidents of history, or the vagaries of politics have resulted in placing various organizations in settings hostile to them, or where their major problems are not treated with suitable understanding and emphasis. One major purpose of government reorganization is to correct such conditions and place agencies where they can perform more effectively. This was a major reason why the Office of Education was taken out of the Department of the Interior in 1939 and placed in the newly formed Federal Security Agency (the forerunner of the current Department of Health, Education, and Welfare).

It was why the Public Health Service was moved in the same year from the Treasury Department to the Federal Security Agency. It was the reason for moving the Food and Drug Administration from the Department of Agriculture to the Federal Security Agency. It was the rationale for the removal from the Atomic Energy Commission of the responsibilities for overseeing the safety of the nuclear industry which conflicted with its responsibilities for the development and promotion of the multiple uses of nuclear energy. In the process, the Atomic Energy Commission was abolished and the Nuclear Regulatory Commission was created, directly answerable to the President, separate from a newly created Energy Research and Development Administration. Numerous other examples could be adduced.

The fact that an agency is suitably placed in one decade may not mean that it is appropriately placed one or two decades later. Conditions can change rapidly, and when they do, organizational shifts may become logical and desirable. The water pollution control function that was vested in the Public Health Service in the 1950s and was elevated briefly to agency status within the Department of HEW in the mid-1960s was transferred in the late 1960s to the Interior Department, and was finally made a major component of the new Environmental Protection Agency when it was created at the beginning of the 1970s. Agencies should be placed in settings that are most conducive to the achievement of their central missions.

3. *Organization affects the allocation of resources.*

Other factors equal, the higher the organizational level of any agency, the stronger the voice of its chief in advocating its cause and its fiscal needs in the highest councils of government. A third echelon official rarely can plead his case before the President, and does not often swing much weight with the Office of Management and Budget. The fact of being low in the hierarchy tends unconsciously to establish in the minds of those who make budget recommendations to the President an assumption that the function deserves a smaller share of the nation's fiscal resources than if it were organizationally directly answerable to the President.

Not only does the organizational *level* influence resource allocation, but so does organizational *placement*. The most conspicuous example of this is the effect of the "uncontrollable" parts of the HEW budget on the "controllable" parts. The "uncontrollable" increases in the HEW budget (the term "relatively uncontrollable" is defined in the President's 1977 budget as meaning those expenditures that are required by law and cannot be reduced without changes in law) have risen from $45 billion in 1970 to $132 billion in the 1977 budget. This is an average annual increase of approximately 15 per cent, primarily to cover needs for Social Security, Medicare, Medicaid, and public assistance. *These annual increases are greater than the total budgetary allocation for education programs administered by HEW.* Most of the education programs fall within the controllable category, the small part of HEW's budget. When uncontrollable requirements are increasing so rapidly, the pressures are unavoidably great to hold down or cut back the controllable parts of the department's budget. Organizational setting and status inescapably affect budget allocations.

4. *Organization by reasonably broad purpose serves the President best, not so narrow as to be overly responsive to specific clientele groups, nor so broad as to be unmanageable.*

The President and the public are usually best served when Cabinet officers are put in charge of organizations whose purposes are sufficiently broad so that they exceed the span of concern of any single clientele group. One of the functions of Cabinet officers should be to aid the President in his always difficult task of making all clientele groups understand that resources are limited, that not all programs can be of highest priority, or of equal priority, and that governance is the process of making hard choices in a manner that will enlist confidence in the fairness of the decision-making process and the decision makers themselves, even when the clienteles do not agree with the decisions. This role can be better performed when the portfolio of a Cabinet officer is broad enough to encompass a substantial range of programs and clientele groups, some of which are competing with one another for attention and resources.

On the other hand, a President is poorly served when the portfolio of assignments to a Cabinet officer is so broad as to exceed the capacity of all but a Superman (or perhaps even him) to perform them effectively. If the scope of a Department is excessively broad, certain responsibilities that the President and the nation may wish to treat as being of first order of importance will inescapably slip to second or third order and effective leadership of these functions will then become virtually impossible. The advantage gained by breadth of perspective is then more than offset by failure of effective performance. Emphasis should therefore be placed on a *reasonably* broad set of purposes and responsibilities, *not the broader the better.*

5. *Wide span of control has significant advantages in improving administration and reducing unnecessary layers of bureaucracy.*

While Presidents may prefer Cabinet departments that are few in number, broad in scope, and large in size, there are various advantages to having a dozen or more of lesser size and range. An organizational structure that is in the form of a steep pyramid, with narrow spans of control at each echelon, requires long lines of communication causing distortions of purpose, and it escalates administrative costs. It also increases problems of coordination. Anthony Downs in his *Inside Bureaucracy*[3] illuminates this point forcefully. His principles are worth quoting:

> The foregoing analysis underlies our statement of three principles of organizational control. The first is the Law of Imperfect Control: *No one can fully control the behavior of a large organization.* The second is the Law of Diminishing Control: *The larger any organ-*

ization becomes, the weaker is the control over its actions exercised by those at the top. The third is the Law of Decreasing Coordination: *The larger any organization becomes, the poorer is the coordination among its actions.*

These principles argue for avoiding gigantic departments, unless there is an overriding reason for their existence, as is true in the case of the Department of Defense. A Department of Human Resources (the Nixonian model that would greatly enlarge the existing Department of Health, Education, and Welfare) and even HEW in its present form have no such compelling rationale. No other country in the world, and no state in the United States, groups so many important functions together in a single department. HEW is now the dinosaur of the federal establishment; it has grown too large to survive long in its present form.

Span of control also has important political implications. Wide span of control satisfied many constituencies; narrow span of control satisfies few. Wide span of control puts more key program administrators organizationally close to the President, thus making the program constituencies feel that their cases are being heard and understood by the President. Depending on the President, this may or may not be an advantage. If he wishes to fend off as many officials as possible who might be classified as special pleaders, he is likely to prefer a small number of officials directly answerable to him; if he can take the time and wants to hear what they have to say, he will enlarge the range of important membership in his official family. But from the standpoint of the Congress and its constituencies, there is no question but that wide span of control is preferable.

✓ 6. *Organizational form and prestige are especially important at the federal level in attracting and retaining first-rate leader-managers.*

The principal attraction high government posts have to offer is the combination of prestige and power (opportunity to influence outcomes and be of service to the nation). Both prestige and power diminish rapidly as the number of echelons between the President and any official increases. Frustration sets in when opportunities to influence outcomes become disappointing. Since many are making a financial sacrifice to come to Washington, the psychic rewards must be substantial (or the appointees have independent means, or both) in order to keep them at their posts very long.

In large business corporations, salaries and other benefits can be scaled in such a way as to attract and hold the high quality talent needed to run the company. In government, this is not possible. At the beginning of 1977 the salary of a Cabinet officer was $63,000 and the next highest level was $44,600. The salary of lower level officials, such as the Commissioner of Education, was $37,800, well under that of many large city school superintendents. The practical upper limit upon all executive salaries except those of the President and Cabinet Secretaries is the salary paid to congressmen. This level is not likely to be adjusted upward for inflation for a number of years. With the exception of Cabinet positions (and even these are not an exception for some people), federal salaries have been a negative inducement to many first-rate, potential appointees. Other factors must be sufficiently attractive to offset the negative inducement.

Holding on to the services of first-rate officials is harder than attracting them in the first place. The turnover of officials below the Cabinet level should be cause for greater concern than it is. Assistant Secretaries and other comparable officials average between 18 months and two years. It takes six months to a year for most such officials to learn to perform their jobs reasonably well. About half the time, therefore, the typical presidential appointee is performing below an acceptable level of performance. Often, too, there are long gaps between the departure of one official and the arrival of his replacement. This is an unhealthy situation. It is important, therefore, to make as many officials as possible feel they are a part of the President's team, close enough to feel the aura of the White House and loyalty to the President and his program.

Because of these factors, it is in the President's interest and in the public interest to have a rather large number of Cabinet posts. A small number of Cabinet positions would sharply diminish the attractiveness of the lower positions to the nation's ablest people. Cabinet posts have a magnetic appeal, which lower level positions cannot come close to matching. A comparatively wide span of control is, therefore, in the President's interest and in the public interest because it enables the President to attract and hold more first-rate appointees than any other form of organization.

Increasing the number of Cabinet officers need not be inconsistent with a reduction in the number of organizational entities directly answerable to the President. There are now 11 Cabinet departments; increasing the number by one or two (or more if the need be) could be more than offset by reducing the number of small independent agencies under the President. Some of these could be incorporated within existing or future departments.

7. *Balance is important in government organization: excessive concentration of important responsibilities in one agency diminishes the effective performance of most of them.*

Balance is an underrated criterion by which to judge the merit of organizational proposals. An organization like HEW that has over 300 programs and expenditures of $145 billion (with a projection for 1977 of $165 billion), which is well over half of the federal expenditures for domestic programs, is inherently suspect as an organizational model, and as earlier mentioned, would be made even more unbalanced with the rest of the government by converting it into a Department of Human Resources. Such overconcentration produces a situation in which some parts of the Secretary's responsibilities are bound to be given short shrift and conducted in a less than distinguished manner, to say the least.

The Department of Health, Education, and Welfare—the Department that is most conspicuously out of balance with the others—is also the fastest growing department and the one most in need of major legislative leadership in respect to extremely complex issues. Two such issues, alone, are among the most difficult challenges of legislative design and effective administration ever faced by the federal government: welfare reform and health insurance. Each is incredibly complex in its economic, political, and administrative ramifications. It is vital that in respect to each, mistakes be reduced to a minimum. Once made, mistakes of legislative design that affect the ''uncontrollable'' parts of the budget are both extremely costly and hard to rectify. There are also such pressing matters as tightening up the administration by state governments of the Medicaid program—no easy task—and the downward revision of the benefit formula under Social Security to keep future costs from going through the roof. With such complicated and vital responsibilities in the lap of the Secretary, how is it possible for him to give appropriate attention to dozens of other issues in the fields of education; food, drug, and vaccine regulation; mental health; the aging; child abuse; and on and on?

Administering so huge an array of programs is also complicated by the nature of congressional relationships. The Congress would not tolerate a concentration of power in one substantive committee that would parallel the concentration of responsibilities vested in HEW. Congress is much more mindful of the principle of balance and divides power and responsibility more evenly among its committees. Consequently, HEW must deal with many different committees, a fact that markedly complicates the congressional relationships of HEW. A coordinated approach to the manifold problems and programs of HEW is virtually impossible because of both volume and proliferation among congressional committees and subcommittees.

Finally, balance is important in dealing with the organized groups of society that have a strong interest in the outcomes of the various federal programs. The greater the number of groups, the less access they have to the Secretary. They must concentrate their communications and lobbying on lower level officials. And the greater the number of lower level officials with little or no access to the Secretary, the more unmanageable the Department becomes.

8. *When purposes overlap, one must be designated as dominant; otherwise responsibility is unclear.*

No matter what principles of organization are followed, it is inevitable that programs and purposes will overlap. The concerns of the Department of State overlap with those of the Department of Defense. The concerns of the CIA overlap with both. The responsibilities of the Treasury Department in collecting Social Security taxes and writing checks overlap with those of the Social Security Administration of HEW that keeps all the records and deals with the public. Similar overlaps occur throughout the government. Many are inevitable because purposes cannot be defined so as to put them in tight compartments.

Whenever a program function cuts across two or more major purposes, it is necessary to decide, first, which purpose is dominant in order to decide where to put the unit, organizationally, and second, how to coordinate such cross-cutting functions. For example, there are scores of fellowship programs throughout the government that have been created to develop the skilled manpower needed to assure the success of the mission-oriented agencies such as Defense, NASA, Agriculture, the new Energy Research and Development Administration, the National Institutes of Health, etc. These are obviously educational programs as well as being defense, space, energy, and health programs. But the decision has been made that these are primarily mission-oriented programs, and only secondarily educational programs. They are placed organizationally, therefore, in the mission agencies.

It could be administratively disastrous to remove these programs (and the veterans educational benefit programs) from their respective agencies and put them in a centralized educational agency or department simply because they channel funds to educational institutions and their students. It would soon be found that such a centralized "education" agency was an administrative bottleneck between the mission agencies and the educational institutions and their students, causing unnecessary delays and marked increases in the number of administrative employees and consequent costs, all because the secondary purpose had been mistaken for the dominant purpose. The clarity with which the dominant purpose is identified and the function placed accordingly has much to do with the efficiency of governmental administration.

9. *When purposes overlap, a system of coordination must be established.*

The most difficult task of public management is not deciding how the functions of government should be divided among organizational units, but how the functions can and should be effectively coordinated after they have been divided. All government is a complex set of matrices; if work is divided on one set of principles or axes, it must be coordinated on another. This is the basic reason for the classic organization by line and staff, a useful, almost indispensable method of coordination but not the full answer to the need for coordinating related functions.

A discussion of the various means of achieving coordination would be beyond the purview of this article. It is one area of public administration which has often baffled the experts. One new attempt to cope with this problem is contained in Chapter IX of *A Cabinet Department of Education: Analysis and Proposal* (1976), published by the American Council on Education, from which this article is adapted.

10. *Programs should be grouped on the basis of their affinity or the potential for cross-fertilization.*

The grouping of programs within an organization should depend, in part, on the importance of the actual and potential interrelationships between them. If there are or should be numerous such interrelationships, the argument for putting them together in the same department is strong. If a bureau has few important relationships within the setting where it currently is located, and if its relationships with bureaus that are currently located in another department are far more important, and should be developed and encouraged, then it is a good candidate for transfer. The food stamp program, now in the Department of Agriculture, is a good example of a program that should be administered by the same department that is responsible for welfare and income maintenance, namely, HEW. Yet this would run into the problem of further enlarging an already gargantuan department. The answer to this may be to split off whatever portion of HEW may now have few relations with the rest of the Department, and group it with other organizational units with which it has affinity. The Education Division of HEW would seem to meet this criterion.

11. *Reorganizations have traumatic effects which should be carefully weighed.*

Reorganizations vary widely in the degree to which they disrupt the skein of human relationships that are the communications and nerve networks of every organization. Some reorganizations cause little or no disruption, while others are traumatic. The creation of the Department of Health, Education, and Welfare in 1953, out of what had previously been the Federal Security Agency, was one of the easiest reorganizations ever performed. Only the name was changed, the administrator was made a Cabinet Secretary, and three new positions were added. The cost, in administrative disruption, was close to zero. Other reorganizations have involved much reshuffling of people from one organizational and physical location to another, necessitating a whole new set of human relationships, superiors getting acquainted with new subordinates and vice versa, old habits and trusted communications patterns terminated and new ones initiated. Such were the reorganizations of the Office of Education in 1965, and the Public Health Service in 1968. Reorganizations of the latter type require much time for healing.

Traumatic reorganizations may be analogized to surgical operations. It is important that their purposes be carefully assessed and a thoughtful judgment reached that the wielding of the surgical knife is going to achieve a purpose that, after a period of recuperation, will be worth the trauma inflicted. And the surgical knife should not be wielded again and again before the healing process from earlier incisions has been completed. Yet this is what sometimes happens in government reorganizations. Agencies are kept in a constant state of disruption by having presidential appointees who may average two years of service, or less, conclude that the organizational structure left by their predecessors is not sound because the results being produced are not satisfactory. Hence, they feel they must reorganize. The problem may not be organizational at all, or not primarily organizational, and it may be partly a problem of too much reorganization. Repetitive reorganization without proper initial diagnosis is like repetitive surgery without proper diagnosis: obviously an unsound and unhealthy approach to the cure of the malady.

It is essential, therefore, that the initial diagnosis of any malfunctioning be carefully made, that reorganizations be designed to achieve clearly defined purposes, and that they be no more disruptive than they need to be to accomplish their overriding purpose. In medicine this is known as minimal or conservative surgery.

12. *Reorganizations that require congressional approval or acquiescence should be carefully weighed to make sure that they are worth the expenditure of political capital required and have a reasonable chance of approval.*

By no means the least of the criteria for judging the desirability of a reorganization proposal is the assessment of its political costs and its likelihood of approval by Congress. Congress and the President (and the President's advisers) have different perspectives on the subject of organization. Power is divided differently in Congress than it is in the Executive Branch, and reorganizations that would shift power from one committee to another, or that would demote, relatively speaking, an organizational unit in which powerful committee chairmen and members have a special interest run the hazard of being defeated, ignored, or amended in a manner that would seem unacceptable to the President. Even though the President presides over the Executive Branch, the Constitution gives Congress a significant role in the design of the executive structure. The President must respect the congressional role and the interests of Congress as he considers his own priorities in the matter of reorganization.

A few reorganizations may have low political costs. There are a number of such reorganization options open to the President. The more difficult problem arises when the political costs begin to rise because of the pressure groups that would be offended and the congressmen and their staffs whose bailiwicks would be adversely affected. When the political costs are substantial, the President should be appraised of this fact in advance and, obviously, should not seek reorganizations that will be politically expensive unless he is prepared to spend a substantial amount of political capital in gaining their approval. Reorganization plans submitted and turned down or ignored (if they require affirmative legislation) are humiliating, the more so if the President's own party controls Congress. It is important, therefore, before drawing a trial balance on a series of models of reorganization to examine the positions that the key interest groups and congressmen (and staffs) are likely to take on the various models, and cast them into the balance in arriving at judgments as to both desirability and feasibility.

13. *Economy as a ground for major reorganization is a will-o'-the-wisp.*

Last and least important among the criteria for judging among reorganization models is the matter of whether dollar savings can be accomplished. It is extremely difficult to predict how much, if anything, can be saved by a major reorganization, and it is impossible to prove, after the fact, how much, if any, has been saved. The comparison that must be made in a continually shifting context is the amount that a new organizational pattern will cost compared to what would have been required under the former organization. Since it is never possible to know what costs would have been without the reorganization, such calculations are close to meaningless. The rationale that lies behind most reorganizations is that the new structure will increase the *effectiveness* of government, not reduce its costs.

Almost invariably, reorganizations that elevate the status of a subordinate organization to a higher level, especially those that create new Cabinet Departments or new agencies directly answerable to the President, result in larger staffs for the new Secretary or agency head, and those staffs are more highly paid than when the organization was at a lower level. Indeed, that is one of the purposes of such elevation. If a function needs stronger leadership, one important way in which such leadership can become effective is by creating higher and more prestigious positions and providing such leaders with the opportunity to surround themselves with first-rate staff. It would be a mistake to pretend or predict that these officials are going to be so competent, managerially speaking, that they will be able to reduce the costs of the subordinate units of the organization in sufficient degree to more than offset the added costs of the larger and higher paid staff at the top. It *could happen;* the likelihood is great that it will not. *The officials in such an organization have far greater interest in accomplishing more effectively the missions assigned to their agencies than they do in reducing the staff.*

Even more unlikely is that savings will be made by creating larger aggregations of agencies and putting a new superstructure over them. The additional layer is almost certain to cost more money. To the extent that savings are achievable in the federal government through improved management, they are likely to be made through changes in policies and procedures, not organization.

Thus, it would be a mistake to place the subject of economy high on a list of important criteria for judging the desirability of any proposed reorganization. It is, of course, necessary to consider estimated costs in relation to possible benefits, but these estimates should rarely, if ever, be a controlling consideration.

Obviously, almost no reorganization proposal is likely to rank high in respect to all of these criteria. Some of the criteria pull in opposite directions. But all deserve to be thought about as various reorganization plans are being considered.

NOTES

1. The two Johnson Task Forces were headed by Don K. Price (report submitted in November 1964 and declassified by the Lyndon Baines Johnson Library in 1976) and by Ben W. Heineman (report submitted in sections during 1967 and declassified by

the Lyndon B. Johnson Library in 1976). The Nixon task force, chaired by Roy Ash, reported in 1970 (its full report has not yet been made public, but its basic recommendations were converted into a broad set of reorganization proposals made by President Nixon in 1971). For a full explication of the Nixon proposals see *Papers Relating to the President's Departmental Reorganization Program* (Washington, D.C.: U.S. Government Printing Office, 1971). A revised version of this document was also issued in 1972.

2. Candidate Carter took this position in a statement of his position on a wide variety of issues, published by his campaign headquarters, and also in specific response to a questionnaire sent to all candidates by the National Education Association.

3. See Anthony Downs, *Inside Bureaucracy,* the Rand Corporation (Boston: Little Brown and Co., 1967), p. 271.

Reflections on Administrative Reorganization

HERBERT KAUFMAN

Reorganization of the executive branch is a commonly advocated weapon against inefficiency and complexity, but it is not the only one. Changes in public policy can also be effective. Improvements in administrative management, budgeting, personnel administration, standard operating procedures, methods of purchasing, incentive systems, and other techniques of handling the day-to-day business of the executive branch can increase efficiency and simplify operations. But compared to reorganization—the creation of new administrative organizations on a grand scale, the regrouping of old ones, the termination of outmoded units and the redistribution of their functions among others, changes in the degree of autonomy enjoyed by existing bodies, and other such transformations of structure—they are often seen as superficial, trivial, and politically unrewarding. Thus, when reformers strive to make government simpler, more efficient, and less costly—to get it "under control"—they tend to go the reorganization route. Yet reorganization is not self-evidently the most promising means to achieve efficiency, simplicity, and reduced cost.

THE FRUSTRATING QUEST FOR EFFICIENCY

The standard reorganization strategies for rationalizing and simplifying the executive branch often clash with one another. Many consequences of reorganization, it must be admitted, cannot be tracked; some claims made for specific strategies, and some of the charges against them, rest on nothing more than faith or prejudice or self-interest. Logically and empirically, however, various strategies appear to contribute as much to exacerbation of the problems of executive organization as to their solution. The probabilities of net gains, if any, seem very small. Reviewing the list of standard prescriptions for organizational improvement explains why.

Standard Prescriptions

Although myriad detailed proposals have been advanced to make the executive branch more orderly, symmetrical, and efficient, they all turn out to be variations on one or another of the following seven basic prescriptions.

1. Limit the number of line subordinates over whom any executive is assigned jurisdiction (commonly referred to as "the span of control"). This practice presumably avoids the dilution of leadership and keeps the executive from losing touch with what his subordinates are doing simply because there is too much to keep track of. It also allows immediate subordinates to check in with the boss as frequently as they feel they must in order to find out whether they are in compliance with his or her wishes. And it frees executive time for reflection about broad policy matters and for coping with external relations.

2. Group related functions under a common command. Otherwise, coordination is difficult to achieve and redundancies cannot be eliminated. Moreover, leaders with responsibility for a diversity of functions frequently find themselves at the mercy of their more specialized nominal subordinates.

3. Furnish executives with ample staff assistance so that they are provided with evaluations of subordinates' performance apart from those supplied by the subordinates themselves, with personal sources of information other than the formal hierarchy, and with capacity to work up their own programs and policies. They also need close, trusted, personal emissaries to interpret and expand on policy statements and orders because executives are usually too preoccupied with other demands to perform this function themselves. Forty years ago, the President's Committee on Administrative Management proclaimed emphatically, "The President needs help."[1] At least from that time forward, it has been an axiom of public administration that staff assistance lets an executive multiply his influence in his organization. Executive reorganizations at all levels have consistently increased such staff.

4. Authorize executives to reorganize fairly freely the agencies and units under their command. With such authority, executives would be able not only to take the initiative to rationalize the structures they head, but also to negotiate from positions of strength with the officers below them. In a pluralistic governmental system, bureau chiefs often effect political alliances that make them quite independent of their nominal superiors. Under these conditions, superiors generally need all the implements they can gather to exert the power of their offices.

5. On the other hand, *reduce* the vulnerability and obligations of certain agencies and agency heads to political leaders. Stability of policy is often considered vital to investment and advance planning; if policies were to be reversed every time there was a change of parties or of leaders within parties, the uncertainty could have depressing effects on economic development and growth. Furthermore, politicians are vulnerable to demands for special consideration and special advantages by constituents whom they hesitate to offend. To impede political os-

cillation and favoritism, many public servants have been granted security in office, permitting them to resist political pressures more readily than easily removable personnel can. Organizational designs are often fashioned with this end in view.

6. Decentralize administration. This strategy is sometimes adopted to promote efficiency, effectiveness, and responsiveness by empowering field officers to take action on their own, and thus to deal quickly with matters in their bailiwicks. Because of their knowledge of local circumstances, their judgments are said to stand a better chance of fitting local requirements and of convincing residents that local interests have been respected. Decentralization thus combines speed and adaptability and the possibility of controlled experimentation. It is therefore commonly recommended by critics of governmental cumbersomeness, coldness, and delay.

7. Increase public participation in the administrative process. Underlying this strategy is the premise that if people affected by governmental decisions and actions take part in the formulation of such measures, no interest will be overlooked or neglected and no significant consequence unanticipated. Few claims are made for the efficiency of such procedures, but responsiveness and, to a lesser extent, effectiveness can allegedly be improved in this fashion, thus diminishing the feeling that government is out of control.

Most of the techniques of reinforcing public participation in administrative decisionmaking are procedural rather than organizational. That is, decisionmakers are obliged at various points to afford opportunities to the public to express views on pending matters and to challenge judgments and policies already adopted. But there is also a structural means to this end—namely, giving an interest group an agency of its own, with a chief having a central role in government decisions affecting that group. It may be an entirely new agency or an older one elevated in status after separation from another organization in which it occupied a subordinate position. In either case, it provides the group with a representative in higher circles and a defender of its interests.

All these measures have been recommended as steps on the road to a better administrative system. They are meant to enable leaders to simplify structure, streamline procedure, coordinate action, build cohesive work forces, reward the diligent, expel the deadwood, motivate the staff, rationalize their organizations, and stay attuned to the populace, thus lifting government to higher levels of efficiency, accomplishment, and humanity. They have therefore had considerable influence on federal structure.

The Prescriptions Have Been Followed

These doctrines of administration lie behind some familiar features of the federal executive branch.

1. Limiting the President's span of control and grouping related functions were among the principal reasons for establishing the Department of Defense, the prototypal "superdepartment" ecompasssing two ordinary departments previously at the cabinet level (War and Navy) and a new one of the same rank (Air Force). Similar considerations also gave rise to the Housing and Home Finance Agency, later to become the Department of Housing and Urban Development, which pulled together some of the scattered operations constituting the government's urban and housing programs and policies. Within departments, corresponding developments took place, with new administrative levels, such as the National

Oceanic and Atmospheric Administration and the short-lived Social and Economic Statistics Administration in the Department of Commerce, interposed between
secretaries and groups of bureaus.

2. Staff assistance for executives resulted not only in the Executive Office of the
President, which was created in 1939 and experienced very rapid growth almost
continuously from that time on, but in corresponding multiplication of deputy
secretaries, under secretaries, assistant secretaries; assistants and deputies to all
these new lieutenants; and staff units (legal counsel, public relations, congressional relations, personnel, administrative management, housekeeping services,
budgeting, policy planning, and others) in virtually all departments. There are
reasons why the Congress might sometimes feel uneasy about this trend. For one
thing, it means increases in the size and cost of the executive branch. More importantly, it interposes officials oriented toward the President between congressional committees and "their" bureaus. Nevertheless, the doctrines of administration have been honored; the growth of staff has proceeded steadily.

3. Reorganization authority for executives at the presidential level was granted
in generous measure during both world wars and the Great Depression[2] and in
more circumscribed grants at other times. The first Reorganization Act was passed
in 1939, was superseded by the First War Powers Act during World War II, then
reappeared with some modifications in 1945, and was reenacted regularly thereafter until it was allowed to lapse in 1973. Reinstating it was one of the first things
President Carter requested of the Congress.

The reorganization acts of the past enhanced presidential managerial power by
reversing the roles of the Congress and the President. They provided for the executive to submit reorganization plans that would automatically take effect with
the force of law unless the Congress, which could not amend them, vetoed the
proposals by voting them down within sixty days. They permitted the President
"to appeal directly to the full membership of either house for support in a floor
vote within a stipulated time on the package as he put it together, bypassing both
the leadership and the legislative committee seniors if they are unsympathetic."[3]
As a result, 86 of the 109 plans submitted from 1939 on succeeded.[4]

The Congress was always cautious about this delegation of power. It never made
the legislation permanent, instead granting the authority only for limited periods,
after which it had to be reenacted. Every act since 1964 excluded from the delegation authority to create or eliminate cabinet-level departments, thereby requiring
regular statutes for these purposes. Some also restricted the number of plans to a
maximum of one every thirty days, confined each one to a single subject, and for-
bade the establishment of new legal authority by means of plans. Early versions required negative votes in both houses to defeat a plan; later, a negative vote in
either house was made sufficient. Despite the restraints, however, an eminent student of the reorganization process, Harvey C. Mansfield, concluded that "reorganization plans have proved a serviceable device for shifting bureaus, realigning
jurisdictions, regrouping activities, and upsetting some ties of influence."[5]

President Carter requested not only restoration of the 1971 law that had been
permitted to lapse, but some additional powers as well. He proposed a four-year
life for the legislation instead of a two-year authorization. He sought to eliminate
the requirement that each reorganization plan treat only one subject. He called for
omission of any limitation on the number of plans that could be submitted in a
given period. And he asked for authority to amend a plan within thirty days after

submission, to let him respond to congressional objections. A challenge by the chairman of the House Government Operations Committee requiring an *affirmative* vote by both houses to turn a plan into a law was easily turned back, but the President did not get everything he requested. The enacted bill contains only a three-year life span, the restriction on subject matter, legislative procedures to facilitate floor votes (thus preventing committees from bottling up resolutions of disapproval), exclusion of independent regulatory commissions from the executive's reorganization power, and a provision limiting to three the number of plans pending in the Congress at one time. Still, the President got the main authority he wanted.[6]

At the cabinet level, most department heads already enjoyed broad legal authority to redesign their organizations. Following the recommendations of the first Hoover Commission, a series of successful reorganization plans and some statutes vested in these and a few other officials all the authority given by law to the bureaus and subordinates under them, authorized them to redelegate those powers at will, and permitted them to transfer records, property, personnel, and, to a limited extent, funds within their own departments. Indeed, the logic of reorganization was pushed even further at this level than at the presidential level.

4. Insulating administrative agencies from politics was the major premise behind the original "independent" regulatory commissions, the autonomy of the Federal Reserve Board, and the merit system and job protection for the civil service. More recently, members of the Civil Service Commission, who originally served at the pleasure of the President, were given staggered terms of six years; a professor of administrative law suggested new protections for the commissions;[7] some experts called for the transformation of certain administrative tribunals into full administrative courts;[8] and a reorganization committee recommended that the merit system be expanded "upward, outward, and downward."[9] Even with added protections, none of these institutions can be made totally immune to political pressure. But because of the safeguards around them, they are in a better position to resist such pressures when they want to than they would be without their special shields. Few architects of government expect more than that.

5. Decentralization has had a spotty record within the executive branch (as distinguished from intergovernmental relations, where, through revenue sharing and block grants, the federal government recently returned to states and localities some of the discretion over their affairs it had acquired).[10] Executives have not been disposed to delegate power freely to their subordinates, nor have subordinate administrators been any more generous with *their* subordinates. In any case, citizens applying for agency benefits or other actions do not ordinarily accept adverse decisions at lower levels, but push their cases upward through administrative and political channels in the hope of securing favorable judgments. Still, students of government continue to urge administrative decentralization with great regularity, and now and then a modest step in this direction is taken by this agency or that.[11]

6. Participation by the public in administrative decisionmaking became such a rallying cry in recent years that many people do not realize it has a long history in our government.[12] There are agencies that represent specific groups (the Departments of Labor, of Agriculture, and of Commerce, for instance, and the Veterans' Administration). There have been administrative boards made up of representatives of various interests, and advisory boards that give interests a voice in policy

making. Even prior to enactment of the Administrative Procedure Act in 1946, but more so since then, provisions were made to obtain the views of people affected by impending administrative legislation and adjudications before these decisions became final. To be sure, unorganized interests, which for a long time included such large groups as consumers, the poor, and women, were comparatively ineffectual in pressing their views on administrative actions, and recent efforts to redress the balance may well begin a new chapter in the history of administrative organization and procedure. If so, however, it will be a chapter in a very long book; organizing for interest-group participation is nothing new.

The structure of the federal executive branch is thus in large part the product of the standard prescriptions for better administration. Abstract doctrine has been established in practice.

General Contradictions in the Prescriptions

One of the first things close examination discloses is that the standard prescriptions for reorganization tend in opposite directions. The first four standard prescriptions push power upward in hierarchies, building leadership strength and exerting a centralizing thrust. The last three impel power outward and downward; theirs is an impulse toward dispersal of authority.

Some people maintain that the tendencies are not opposed at all. The making of broad policies, they say, can be centralized while the administration (or "execution" or "implementation") of those policies can be decentralized and dispersed. Although the old distinction between policy and administration, argued most cogently by Frank Goodnow early in this century,[13] had fallen on hard times by the third quarter of the century, it has never been invalidated. There are still many who subscribe to the view that an organization can concentrate policy formulation while devolving administrative responsibility.

On the other hand, if policy is defined as what is actually done rather than what is said or intended, policy and administration cannot be separated in practice, and the contradictory thrusts cannot, by this definition, be reconciled. Theorists of this persuasion[14] hold that leaders who stay aloof from the nitty-gritty of their organizations' operations soon find themselves exercising less and less influence over the actions of those below them. If, however, they endeavor to shape policy in practice by controlling the administrative behavior of their subordinates, they obviously are directing things from the center. Thus, policy and administration being closely intertwined, centralization and decentralization cannot be pursued simultaneously. To get control of policy, it is necessary to get control of administration. If administrative discretion is decentralized, policy follows close behind. Organizations cannot have it both ways, and it would be futile to attempt to apply all seven techniques of organizational improvement at once to a given set of circumstances. Choices must be made. Difficult trade-offs cannot be avoided.

Specific Mutual Negations and Hidden Costs

To be more specific, grouping related functions under a common command wars with the separation of agencies from the hierarchy of the executive branch in order to protect them from political pressures. Coordination and control are increased by hierarchy, but political favoritism and other forms of special consideration are facilitated when organizational barriers to these practices are removed. Some students of administration are so appalled by disclosures of such abuses that they advocate making the barriers around many agencies higher and stronger. Each standard prescription has advantages, but it is impossible to get the advantages of both at the same time.

Similarly, increasing participation by agency clientele in agency decisionmaking opens the way for narrow political interests to exert powerful influence on administration. Indeed, if it is coupled with separation from the executive hierarchy and resolute decentralization, it can be tantamount to turning important sectors of the government over to special interests. It is certainly at the opposite end of the scale from taking politics out of administration and keeping administration out of politics. And it also conflicts with the implications of keeping the span of control narrow.

Reinforcing agency autonomy so as to stiffen resistance to efforts at improper intervention by politicians likewise runs afoul of the strategy of allowing executives to reorganize fairly freely. Independence and its benefits come at the expense of reorganization authority and *its* advantages, and vice versa. There is no way to avoid this trade-off.

And so it goes. Limiting the span of control in a large organization produces a "steeper" hierarchy with more administrative layers, thereby insulating leaders from front-line realities and slowing the process of reaching decisions. It also contributes to the emergence of superdepartments, and of superagencies within departments, which impedes capture of the superadministrators by a single set of narrow interests, but imposes on them such a wide array of responsibilities that they are often at a disadvantage in dealing with their more specialized subordinates. At the same time, superdepartments are created by downgrading ordinary departments, making departmental leadership posts less attractive to many prospective heads.

Grouping agencies or activities by common purpose renounces the advantages of grouping them by target clientele, by area, or by process (not to mention by other purposes). Decentralizing by delegating discretion to lower echelons jeopardizes coordination and consistency, and risks entrapment of field offices by local private and political interests.

The insulation devised to exclude politics from administration at all levels itself entails some significant costs. Government officers and employees with substantial job security sometimes come to regard elected officials and political executives as amateurs, birds of passage, and opportunists compared to career public servants who know their programs and dedicate their lives to them. Under these circumstances, it would be natural for some careerists to feel that instead of bending to every shift in political winds, they should occasionally use their staying power to outlast their political superiors and make their own policies prevail.

Even building up executive staff assistance, once regarded as self-evidently beneficial, can impose heavy charges on the system if allowed to proceed unchecked. In the Watergate inquiries and their aftermath, it became clear that platoons of staff assistants can isolate an executive from currents of opinion and discontent in the country, from the rest of the government, and from his own line lieutenants, the members of the cabinet. Meanwhile, staff members often muddy the waters of administration by intervening in the operation of departments and agencies in the name of their chief, who may know nothing of their adventures.

It was more than thirty years ago that Herbert A. Simon pointed out that administrative principles are like proverbs in that they come in mutually contradictory pairs.[15] "Look before you leap," but "he who hesitates is lost." "Haste makes waste," but "strike while the iron is hot." "Absence makes the heart grow fonder," but "out of sight, out of mind." "Clothes make the man," but "all is not gold that glitters" or "don't judge a book by its cover." The analogy is still apt. There is wisdom and truth in both parts of each pair. The genius of the reorganizer is to know which trade-off to make at a given time.

REAL PAYOFFS

Obviously, no reorganization is inherently right or wrong. No given administrative pattern will invariably increase efficiency, effectiveness, or responsiveness. In particular circumstances, identical organizational arrangements may produce diametrically opposite effects while radically different arrangements may produce identical effects. *It All Depends,* declared Harvey Sherman in his book by that title.[16] One can hardly quarrel with that.

None of this means, however, that there is no point to reorganizing. On the contrary, the consequences of reorganization are frequently profound. But the profound, determinable consequences do not lie in the engineering realm of efficiency, simplicity, size, and cost of government. Rather, the real payoffs are measured in terms of influence, policy, and communication.

Effects on Influence

For example, reorganization redistributes influence. If the Arms Control and Disarmament Agency had been set up in the Department of Defense instead of as an independent unit, it seems likely that the advocates of arms limitations would have had less impact on policy than they did. Policy recommendations to the President and the Congress filtered through the armed services community would almost certainly have been unlike the proposals emerging from an agency with a different perspective on the world, a different mission, and a different set of priorities. Moreover, the conduct of negotiations over disarmament and arms limitations would probably not have been as vigorous, patient, or perseverant under exclusive Defense Department auspices.

Similarly, if environmental protection were scattered among environmental protection units in other agencies instead of being lodged in the Environmental Protection Agency, chances are the views of environmentalists would have been swamped by oil interests in the Federal Energy Administration, air and highway interests in the Department of Transportation, coal interests in the Department of the Interior, and so on. Within the policymaking councils of the government, the environmentalists' voices would have been muffled, if not silenced.

Consumer groups are demanding a separate consumer agency for the same reason. Consumer units dispersed among producer-oriented agencies, they are convinced, would not carry much weight; they want a body beholden to them in the top levels of the government. Not only would they expect to acquire strength directly; central agencies also serve as rallying points for previously dispersed pressure groups with overlapping interests.

People will argue over the effect of such differences in structure on efficiency, and over the danger of needless complexity, and will come to different conclusions according to the goals they favor. They will commonly agree, however, that different structures strengthen the hands of some officials and interest groups and reduce the ability of others to get what they want. The effects are not precisely measurable or completely predictable, but their general thrust is usually discernible.

Effects on Policy

Who acquires power and who is deprived of power would be of interest only to the people involved were it not for the implications of such redistributions for governmental policy; what the government *does* is determined by the distribution of influence. For example, if an overarching energy agency is given access to the inner councils of government and power over sister agencies, energy conservation is likely to be stressed even if it slows economic growth, inhibits the rise in the standard of living or even reduces the level of convenience and comfort, and perhaps even increases unemployment. At the same time, intensified striving after increases in energy production might lead to relaxation of environmental safeguards and uncontrolled prices for energy producers that are passed on to consumers. If the energy agency's powers are split up, lodged in hostile parent organizations, placed at low administrative levels, and given scant authority, other values will probably take precedence over energy considerations, with the result that vulnerability to political pressures by oil producing countries, to severe trade imbalances, and to recurrent domestic shortages will increase steadily.

If preferred status is accorded those who believe the economic marketplace is the best promoter of the manifold interests in our society, government regulation of economic activity will be reduced while efforts to break up industry-dominating combinations and competition-suppressing agreements are emphasized. If stronger positions are given to those who believe there are benefits in large-scale operations, and that the way to protect the public interest is to control them rather than to try to dissolve them in a vain quest to preserve a market through government power, then more and more industries will be treated as public utilities and subjected to surveillance and regulation by specialized government agencies.

To take still another example, the Occupational Safety and Health Administration was placed in the Department of Labor and its regulations were addressed heavily to mechanical hazards and to worker comfort. Had it been put under the assistant secretary for health in the Department of Health, Education, and Welfare, there is reason to surmise that chemical and biological dangers to workers probably would have received higher priority in the regulations.

Organizational arrangements in government, in short, affect not only the leaders and members of the organizations established or moved or redesigned; they impinge on the lives of millions of other people in this generation and the future.

Signals

Organizational arrangements are also a means of communicating the government's intentions. They signal people inside the government, people throughout the country, and, indeed, people and governments throughout the world what this government's emphases will be. Such signals often influence the behavior of those who receive them. All too often, they are misconstrued, so the architects of administration would be mistaken to let the symbolic considerations dominate their designs. At the same time, however, administrative designers would be remiss if they did not take into account the interpretations that may be placed on their handiwork. How well their designs work depends in part on the designers' success in selecting organizational patterns that evoke from everyone concerned the kind of behavior the patterns are meant to produce. The symbolic component is a useful and, indeed, a powerful tool.

Thus, a leader who transfers, combines, and splits organizations in government for engineering purposes will usually find that nobody can be sure whether any progress has been made toward those goals. All too often, the effects on efficiency, simplicity, and cost cannot be determined at all. When they can be assessed, what is successful by one standard may be a failure by another; what improves things in one way makes them worse in another. Real political capital is thus consumed in the pursuit of phantom goals. In contrast, a leader who shifts organizations around to confer power on selected people or remove it from others in order to mold government policies, and to impress on everyone what his or her values and priorities are, will more often be rewarded with a sense of having expended political resources for significant accomplishments. The calculus of reorganization is essentially the calculus of politics itself.

A Case in Point

Despite President Carter's emphasis on efficiency, simplicity, and reduction of government size and cost, the first major reorganization step by his administration seemed to be based on the real payoffs rather than on the standard prescriptions. Within six weeks after his inauguration, the President sent to the Congress draft legislation for the creation of a new, cabinet-level Department of Energy in which most of the economic regulatory functions of the government with respect to energy were to be consolidated.

The proposal certainly concentrated power at a high level (and thus made the position attractive to an administrator of stature and drive). It signaled the President's intentions forcefully. It was a longer stride to formulation of a comprehensive energy policy than the government had previously considered. But its consequences for efficiency and simplicity were quite ambiguous.

To be sure, it called for the abolition of three independent agencies (the Federal Energy Administration, the Energy Research and Development Administration, and the Federal Power Commission) and the vesting of their powers in the new secretary. It also provided for the termination of a coordinating body, the Energy Resources Council. It placed under the command of the secretary units transferred from at least eight other departments and agencies with jurisdiction over parts of the energy field. And it centralized in bodies located in the new department the collection and analysis of energy information and the making of rules on economic regulation of energy.

But if it were adopted as formulated, it would stretch the President's span of control, create as many new structures as it abolishes, and generate fresh problems of coordination. The new department would be the twelfth at the cabinet table.

In addition to the department itself, two new administrations with heads appointed by the President (the Energy Information Administration and the Energy Regulatory Administration) would be established and housed in the department, and the presidential message accompanying the draft statute expressed the intention of establishing by executive order an interdepartmental coordinating body chaired by the Secretary of Energy to "manage government-wide concerns involving energy." Health, safety, and environmental regulation (as distinguished from economic regulation) were not included within the department's purview; these would remain under the administration of untouched existing agencies. "Because public concerns about the safety of nuclear power are so serious," the President said in his message accompanying the bill, "we must have a strong, independent voice to ensure that safety does not yield to energy supply pressures. Therefore, the Nuclear Regulatory Commission will remain as an independent body. For similar reasons, the Environmental Protection Agency should remain independent to voice environmental concern." Under these arrangements, he acknowledged, "problems of interdepartmental coordination will remain, since virtually all government activity affects energy to some extent."[17] Clearly, the standard prescriptions for reorganization gave the President little helpful guidance, so he set them aside. Power, policy, and symbolic factors were the crucial elements in the decision to recommend the Department of Energy.

The public record contains few clues to other structural options President Carter may have weighed and rejected. Certainly, there are other organizational arrangements that might have been considered. In World War II, for instance, the need to draw together all the resources of the government for the conduct of the war led to the creation of the Office of War Mobilization, a unit with powers second only to the President's. When the war ended, it also took charge of the adjustment to peace under the expanded title, Office of War Mobilization and Reconversion. A comparable pattern might have been adapted for energy problems. OWM, however, was probably suitable for difficulties of relatively short duration, during which all values could be subordinated to one overriding objective. Energy problems, on the other hand, are likely to be with us for a long time. To deal with problems of this nature, the OWM format, had it been considered at all, would doubtless have been ruled out as inappropriate.

Conceivably, the National Security Council might also have served as a model. When a matter is both urgent and interagency in scope, a collegial organ is the logical structure for decisionmaking. Chances are, however, that another deliberative body consisting of the President and key cabinet officers, making demands on the already scarce time of top officials, would also have been judged unlikely to succeed.

Another model that might have been considered is the Office of Economic Opportunity, a command post in the Executive Office of the President to supervise and stimulate existing agencies where coordination and innovation are needed, and to undertake some new operations on its own. But OEO's function did not consist of controlling economic activity and technological exploration. Furthermore, justly or unjustly, OEO became a highly controversial agency. It, too, would not have commended itself as a promising prototype for energy administration.

Thus, none of the immediately evident alternatives to an executive department could have had as much appeal to the President as the Department of Energy. Other options do not seem even to have been in the running at all. But they were not ruled out by the ambiguous conventional lore of reorganization; what defeated them were the hard realities of national needs and power politics.

ORGANIZING THE REORGANIZERS

The hard realities can shape the President's reorganization agenda for him, and perhaps push him in directions he may not want to go. Already in the wings, no doubt heartened by the proposal for a Department of Energy, stand groups seeking (and perhaps, on the basis of their reading of campaign oratory, expecting) elevation of the Office of Education, now in the Department of Health, Education, and Welfare, to full department status. Meanwhile, the secretary of HEW, with presidential approbation, ordered major structural changes in his department, shifting, abolishing, and creating components to handle health care financing, cash assistance payments, student financial assistance, human development and social services programs, and departmental management. Other secretaries have similarly embarked upon, or at least have been contemplating, changes of corresponding magnitude. A consumer protection agency is in the works. How such developments will fit into larger plans for the executive branch remains to be seen; clearly, however, some attractive organizational strategies may be foreclosed unless the administration is prepared to undo a number of ad hoc actions now being taken. If it is, great elements of uncertainty and turbulence would pervade the administrative system. To deal systematically with this risk, and to seize and hold the initiative, the President will doubtless strive to formulate a general scheme of reorganization. If so, he will have to make some hard choices with respect to the approach, scope, and form of the reorganization effort.

As regards the approach, the broad options are to commission a grand design for the whole executive branch and delay all large-scale changes until the design is complete or to begin at once to work on selected problem areas one after the other and introduce changes as each one is resolved. The options on scope are to restrict organizational considerations to existing governmental programs and levels of operation or to direct reorganizers to suggest changes in policy as well as modifications of structure. The options on form are to employ some kind of special committee to draw up recommendations or to use the expertise and resources of existing bodies and units within the government. Within each strategic option, additional choices must be made, but they are just variations on the major themes.

Neither of the broad strategies in each pair is inherently superior to the other. As with everything else, evaluations depend on the objectives sought. But each has consequences associated with it that can be outlined in advance.

Approaches to Reorganization

Commissioning a grand design, for example, gains the President breathing space; waiting for the finished product provides him with a justification for declining to act on proposals from other politicians, from interest groups, from the bureaucracies, and from other sources when his mind is not made up, and it temporarily suspends the complaints about administrative shortcomings from many of his critics. It also permits a comprehensive examination of a system in which everything impinges on everything else, and in which piecemeal remedies for ills in one part may therefore engender even worse ailments in other parts. On the other hand, if the President does wish to change a part of the system, the opponents of his alterations might also plead persuasively for delay until the full design is at hand. And incremental reforms often turn out to be more successful than global efforts.[18] The sword is double-edged.

Strategists also have to estimate what sort of reception each reorganization approach will enjoy. Grand designs frequently mobilize all the defenders of the status quo at once; each defender usually opposes only a small bit of the total plan and is indifferent to the rest, but presenting the whole thing in one package brings all of them out simultaneously and can doom the package before it has a chance to gather support. Taking things one step at a time permits supporters to deal individually, and more effectively, with the opponents. Eschewing the grand design, though, may deprive reorganizers of a banner under which to rally all their backers, a device to build enthusiasm and a sense of accomplishment, and a vision of the way the parts fit together. Thus, supporters may be reduced to a small band rushing from battlefield to battlefield on which numerous special interests protecting their respective sectors of the status quo have the advantage. The choice of approach depends on the President's assessment of the political weather and the breadth of his aspirations.

How Much Scope for the Reorganizers?

With regard to scope, forbidding reorganization planners to suggest changes in policies and in the levels of government activity may reduce them to tinkering with marginal adjustments in the prevailing system. The big opportunities for organizational change are often tied to elimination or contraction of certain services or regulatory functions, and to expansion of others. But linking discussions of reorganization with debates over the role of government in society and other fundamental philosophical issues invites divisions among the structural planners likely to preclude even the limited consensus on administrative arrangements possible in a more circumscribed sphere of responsibility. It imposes on organizational designers obligations as broad as the entire political system. It can involve every proposed organizational change, no matter how innocuous, in bitter controversy. The decision on scope therefore depends on whether the President regards reorganization as a means to develop proposals for policy changes or purely as a managerial tool.

Forms of Reorganization Leadership

The options with respect to form diverge widely. Some reorganization plans drawn up under past reorganization acts seem to have been formulated primarily by government officers and employees in the executive branch. When Presidents wanted to make changes in especially sensitive areas or of sweeping effect, however, they usually appointed a body for the specific purpose of offering recommendations. The two Hoover Commissions[19] were the most elaborate, their compositon being specified by statute; the President, the Speaker of the House, and the President pro tempore of the Senate each appointed four, two of each group coming from the executive branch, the House, and the Senate, respectively, and two from private life. In the case of the first commission, not more than one of each pair could be from the same major political party, a restriction not imposed on the composition of the second.

In contrast, bodies appointed by Presidents Roosevelt, Johnson, and Nixon were not established by legislation, and their members were the President's personal choices.[20] President Eisenhower also had such a group, in addition to his Hoover Commission.[21] Roosevelt's committee had only three members, none of whom was in full-time federal service at the time, though all were experienced in government. Eisenhower's also consisted of only three members, of whom two were in high government positions and one was from private life. Each of Johnson's two task forces had ten members, including high federal officials, former officials, state and local officers, and private citizens. Nixon's was composed of five, all from outside the federal government, though one had been a bureau chief and one had been a governor who developed strong Washington ties.

The main reason for setting up special bodies rather than using the regular instrumentalities of government is probably that Presidents are loath to seek advice on change from people with heavy stakes in existing institutions and arrangements. They may also want diversity of viewpoint so that no major problem areas are overlooked and no proposals advanced that are unacceptable to a diverse audience. Moreover, the prestige of the members of a carefully picked body can lend authority to their findings that the same findings put forth from inside the government would not enjoy.[22]

But prestigious committees sometimes bring out reports that a President opposes. Admittedly, the same thing can happen when work is done inside the government. The chances of shaping things more closely to the President's liking, however, are at least a little higher when they are within his own official family. That is probably why Roosevelt and Nixon kept their groups small and nonstatutory, why Johnson treated his task forces' proceedings and reports as submissions to him personally (they still have not been released officially), and why Eisenhower's committee likewise did not produce formal, public studies (even though its recommendations did get into the news from time to time and some were translated into reorganization plans).

Most of the smaller groups brought in relatively short reports and comparatively few recommendations, and concentrated especially on the broad outlines of the executive branch and the problems of the presidency. The larger, more formal commissions delved more deeply into specifics at all levels of management, producing long reports and hundreds of recommendations. It appears that the smaller bodies tended to view the executive branch primarily from the President's standpoint, while the larger ones, reflecting their diversity of origin and interest, ranged more widely.

Of course, it is possible to strengthen and expand the managerial resources of the Office of Management and Budget and use *them* as the core and driving force in a reorganization campaign. Indeed, the renaming and restructuring of the Bureau of the Budget by President Nixon were intended in part to restore the emphasis on administrative management that many observers felt had been allowed to decline over the years.[23] If this thrust were maintained, it could produce groups of specialists with an ongoing concern for organizational and procedural improvements, a governmentwide view of the implications of individual changes, a steadily accumulating body of experience in planning and administering administrative change, a commitment to administrative change as a continuing process rather than as a single, instantaneous measure, and sufficient detachment from the program responsibilities of line agencies to escape their reluctance to rock any boats. But this mechanism generates a steady stream of incremental adjustments rather than a massive, dramatic rearrangement of the whole executive branch to which leaders can point with a sense of pride and accomplishment. It can gradually acquire the perspectives and values of agencies and programs it was meant to improve, and thus become a high-level impediment to change. If it avoids this pitfall, its continuous proposals for organizational change will be perceived as harassment by many line officers and their constituencies, and as endless niggling by busy legislators. And it lacks the potential prestige and symbolic stature of blue-ribbon panels.

Thus, like everything else associated with reorganization, the options for organizing the reorganizers entail trade-offs. No matter which choices are made, something valuable will be given up as well as gained.

Straws in the Wind

Because the advantages of each option are attractive, a new administration may elect to remain as flexible as possible, perhaps experimenting with several options in the course of its period in office. It would therefore be rash to conclude from moves made in the first months of a term that irrevocable commitments have been made, particularly if the initial steps do not preclude shifts and changes later on.

The Carter team has announced that it will proceed in an incremental fashion rather than waiting for the formulation of a comprehensive design before beginning to reorganize. The prompt initiation of legislation for the Department of Energy, the reorganization of the Department of Health, Education, and Welfare, and the announcement that additional "crash programs" are contemplated reflects this choice. Furthermore, the declaration by Harrison Wellford, the executive associate director for reorganization and management of the Office of Management and Budget, that the administration has a long-range perspective on reorganization confirms that it will be handled one step at a time.[24]

There are also signs that the operation will be conducted primarily by regular government staff. A request for $2.6 million for thirty-two added employees for Wellford's reorganization group was submitted to the Congress and advanced smoothly, and Wellford said the effort would depend largely on career personnel in both OMB and other agencies, with the possibility of assistance from volunteers in private business. He told the House Appropriations Committee that the group would be divided into six teams dealing with natural resources and energy, economic development, human development, national security and international affairs, general government, and government regulation.[25] Public pronouncements about reducing the number of federal agencies from 1,900 to 200, made repeatedly during the election campaign, are apparently to be taken as directional guideposts rather than as literal, ironclad guarantees.

Things may change as experience accumulates. For the time being, however, this is the course the administration has set.

NONSURGICAL TREATMENTS

Many of the irritations that reorganization of the executive branch is intended to alleviate, however, may not demand anything so drastic to relieve them. Much distress and resentment can be alleviated by relatively limited correctives. Minor remedies can sometimes bring more relief to more people than more radical therapy does.

The federal information centers recently established in three dozen places throughout the country, with toll-free lines to still more places, are an illustration. Set up to guide people needing help through the complexities of the federal administrative system to the officers and documents that can answer their questions or solve their problems, they are still too new to be evaluated definitively. But they could conceivably take care of one problem that accounts for a good deal of the anger and despair and feelings of helplessness and convinces some critics of government that the system has gotten out of hand.

In like fashion, experience with ombudsmen—that is, complaint- and grievance-handling officers with power to investigate citizens' charges against agencies and to initiate redress where warranted—has been building up in various governments throughout the country.[26] Some version of this institution might also salve specific sore points, and thus reduce much discontent, with minimum disruption of existing arrangements at the federal level.

Part of the outcry against government is linked to paperwork thrust on the public by tax-collection agencies and government information-gathering services. The Commission on Federal Paperwork has been working to ease these burdens, taking aim in particular at the individual forms that generate the bulk of the outcries.[27] Perhaps permanent machinery to seek out and lighten specific paperwork burdens can be devised, thereby removing a major source of current dissatisfaction.

Survey research among the clients of agencies could add a dimension to the assessment of administrative performance. Volunteered complaints do not always tell the whole story because the grievously offended or the easily outraged are usually the ones to take the initiative. Their accusations give an inescapably one-sided impression, which is often discounted on these very grounds by the officials to whom they are addressed. Splendid service may go undetected; so may injustices too small individually to justify expense by the victims to correct them, yet numerous enough to amount to significant deprivation in the aggregate. There are possibilities here for altering incentives within the public service in ways leading to higher client satisfaction.

Modest steps of this kind are not substitutes for reorganization, nor do they cut the size and cost of government. But at least some of the demands for reorganization of the executive branch are spawned by hope for relief from the oppressive weight of government requirements and constraints. Often, that weight can be lifted for thousands of citizens by a pinpointed rather than by a blanket remedy. All too often, limited, attainable remedies are neglected when more visible, glamorous, and exciting grand designs tempt reformers.

NO MIRACLE CURES

Those, however, who cling to the belief that any combination of means will instantaneously transform the character, image, or performance of the executive branch are doomed to disappointment.

The civilian work force of the government grew only modestly over two decades, while the budget as a whole was doubling in constant dollars (increasing fivefold in current dollars).[28] There is not much opportunity for cutbacks here, which is one reason why both the President and the secretary of Health, Education, and Welfare assured civil servants that reorganization would not mean loss of jobs for them. Perhaps the *rate* of growth of federal employment can be held down (though this rate depends on whether new federal initiatives are undertaken in the years ahead, which is a distinct possibility); even if the rate is limited, however, the effects will be felt in the remote rather than in the near future. In any case, the monetary savings through control of civilian personnel growth cannot be more than a small fraction of federal outlays, since all the compensation and benefits of the civilian work force come to under 11 percent of the total, so that marginal reductions in this area would hardly change the overall budget at all.

Reorganizers have also grown wary of claiming massive savings in operations for their reforms. For the most part, they assert that their changes will produce more output per dollar spent rather than the expenditure of fewer dollars; thus, even if the changes end up increasing total outlays, they contend that the total will be lower than it would have been without the reforms.[29] Whether or not such claims are eventually justified, the *immediate* effect on budgets is almost sure to be indiscernible. In this context, the recent statement by Secretary of Health, Education, and Welfare Califano that the reorganization of his department would yield savings of $2 billion in the first two years and at least $2 billion annually by 1981[30] is surprising. He placed particular emphasis on the elimination of fraud and abuse in various benefit programs, but it is not clear whether the costs of intensified enforcement have been included in his estimates. Furthermore, it is not self-evident how regrouping units in the departments, as opposed to changing procedures or adding auditors and investigators, will contribute to prevention of fraud and abuse.

In short, nobody should expect sudden, swift, dramatic diminishment in the size and cost of the executive branch of the federal government as a result of reorganization. Indeed, the upward trend will probably persist for a long time—possibly more gradually than might otherwise have been the case, but upward all the same.

Even if anticipated structural revisions succeed, they will be slow in coming. The executive branch is very big, and the specific faults that need correcting keep changing. "Our confused and wasteful system that took so long to grow," President Carter told the American people in his first informal address to the nation, "will take a long time to change."[31] His staff member spearheading reorganization testified that it would be "a four-year effort at least."[32] The administration harbors no illusions about the length of the campaign on which it is embarked. The 1977–78 controversies over government organization are only the opening skirmishes in what promises to be a long, hard, and frequently futile endeavor.

NOTES

1. The President's Committee on Administrative Management, *Administrative Management in the Government of the United States* (Government Printing Office, 1937), p. 5.
2. In World War I, sec. 2 of the "Lever Act" of 1917 (40 Stat. 276) and the "Overman Act" of 1918 (40 Stat. 556) conferred on the President broad powers of agency creation and reorganization for the duration of the war plus a period afterward. In the Great Depression, Title IV of the Economy Acts of 1932 (47 Stat. 382, 413–15) and 1933 (47 Stat. 1489, 1517–20) authorized extensive transfers, consolidations, and redistributions of executive agencies by executive order of the President (subject in the earlier statute to veto by either house of the Congress) for a limited period of time. In World War II, Title I of the First War Powers Act, 1941 (55 Stat. 838) similarly authorized sweeping reorganizations of "any executive department, commission, bureau, agency, governmental corporation, office, or officer" during and shortly after the war.
3. Harvey C. Mansfield, "Federal Executive Reorganization: Thirty Years of Experience," *Public Administration Review,* vol. 29 (July–August 1969), p. 341.
4. Office of Management and Budget, "President's Reorganization Authority" (OMB, April 1977; processed), app. 3, p. 4.
5. Mansfield, "Federal Executive Reorganization," p. 341.
6. For a comparison of the various proposals for the reorganization act, see American Enterprise Institute for Public Policy Research, *The Executive Reorganization Act: A Survey of Proposals for Renewal and Modification* (The Institute, 1977). The statute is Public Law 95–17, April 6, 1977.
7. Bernard Schwartz, *The Professor and the Commissions* (Knopf, 1959), chap. 7 and pp. 266–69. For a contrasting view, see Emmette S. Redford, "The President and the Regulatory Commissions," *Texas Law Review,* vol. 44 (1965–66), pp. 288–321.
8. Commission on Organization of the Executive Branch of the Government, *Legal Services and Procedure: A Report to the Congress* (Government Printing Office, 1955), pp. 87–88. See also its Task Force report on the same subject and of the same date, pp. 246–56.
9. President's Committee on Administrative Management, *Administrative Management,* p. 7.
10. See James A. Maxwell and J. Richard Aronson, *Financing State and Local Governments* (3rd ed., Brookings Institution, 1977), chap. 3, esp. pp. 71–76.
11. The Department of Housing and Urban Development, for example, adopted a plan of reorganization in 1969 and 1970 that called for decentralization to field offices and established new area offices within regions to carry out the plan. Decentralization was also among the reasons for establishment of common regional boundaries and common headquarters cities for many departments and agencies; see Harold Seidman, *Politics, Position, and Power: The Dynamics of Federal Organization* (Oxford University Press, 1970), pp. 59–61, and *United States Government Manual, 1976/77* (GPO, 1976), app. D. See also Martha Derthick, *Between State and Nation: Regional Organizations of the United States* (Brookings Institution, 1974), chap. 7.
12. Avery Leiserson, *Administrative Regulation: A Study in Representation of Interests* (University of Chicago Press, 1942).
13. Frank J. Goodnow, *Politics and Administration: A Study in Government* (Macmillan, 1900), esp. chap. 4. The distinction had been drawn earlier, though not argued so fully, in Woodrow Wilson, "The Study of Administration," *Political Science Quarterly,* vol. 2 (June 1887), pp. 197–222; reprinted in vol. 56 (December 1941), pp. 481–506.
14. Luther Gulick, for example: "Much of the actual discretion used in administration is used at the very bottom of the hierarchy, where public servants touch the public. The

assessor who walks into the home and sees the furniture and the condition of the house, the policeman who listens to the motorist's story, the health inspector who visits the dairy, the income tax auditor who sees the return and interviews the taxpayer—all these people are compelled to exercise more discretion, and more important discretion from the point of view of the citizen, than many other functionaries much farther up in the organization. While this is the actual situation in badly organized and poorly directed administrative units, it cannot be completely eliminated even in the best." "Politics, Administration, and the 'New Deal,' " *Annals of the American Academy of Political and Social Science*, vol. 169 (September 1933), p. 62.

15. Herbert A. Simon, "The Proverbs of Administration," *Public Administration Review*, vol. 6 (Winter 1946), p. 53.
16. *It All Depends: A Pragmatic Approach to Organization* (University of Alabama Press, 1966), esp. chap. 2. See also Seidman, *Politics, Position, and Power;* Peri E. Arnold, "Reorganization and Politics: A Reflection on the Adequacy of Administrative Theory," *Public Administration Review*, vol. 34 (May–June 1974), pp. 205–11; and Herbert A. Simon, Donald W. Smithburg, and Victor A. Thompson, *Public Administration* (Knopf, 1950), chap. 7.
17. "Energy Reorganization Message," President Carter's Message to Congress, *Congressional Quarterly*, vol. 35 (March 5, 1977), p. 404.
18. David Braybrooke and Charles E. Lindblom, *A Strategy of Decision: Policy Evaluation as a Social Process* (Free Press, 1963), esp. chap. 6; Charles E. Lindblom, *The Intelligence of Democracy: Decision Making through Mutual Adjustment* (Free Press, 1965), esp. pp. 303–09.
19. The first of these, officially named the Commission on Organization of the Executive Branch of the Government, was established in 1947 (61 Stat. 246) and reported in 1949. The second, bearing the same name, was established in 1953 (67 Stat. 142) and reported in 1955.
20. Roosevelt's group was the President's Committee on Administrative Management (the "Brownlow Committee," after its chairman, Louis Brownlow). Johnson's first Task Force on Government Reorganization (the "Price Task Force," after its chairman, Don K. Price) was one of eleven task forces on various issues appointed just before Johnson's election; his second, a couple of years later, was also called the President's Task Force on Government Organization (the "Heineman Task Force," after its chairman, Ben W. Heineman). Nixon's was the President's Advisory Council on Executive Organization (the "Ash Council," after its chairman, Roy L. Ash).
21. Eisenhower's group was the President's Advisory Committee on Government Organization (Executive Order 10432, January 24, 1953), consisting of the chairman, Nelson A. Rockefeller (then Under Secretary of Health, Education, and Welfare), Arthur S. Flemming (Director of the Office of Defense Mobilization), and Milton S. Eisenhower.
22. But, according to Mansfield, "Federal Executive Reorganization," p. 335, "The appointment of a mixed public commission is likely to be read as a sign of weakness or irresolution on his [the President's] part."
23. Nixon's message accompanying Reorganization Plan Number 2 of 1970 (March 12, 1970) said in part, "creation of the Office of Management and Budget represents far more than a mere change of name for the Bureau of the Budget. It represents a basic change in concept and emphasis, reflecting the broader management needs of the Office of the President.

    ". . . The budget function is only one of several important management tools that the President must now have. He must also have a substantially enhanced institutional staff capability in other areas of executive management. . . . Under this plan, strengthened capability in these areas will be provided partly through internal reorganization, and it will also require additional staff resources."

This emphasis on better in-house management capabilities had been strongly urged on the President by the Ash Council, which went so far as to recommend that the agency be named simply Office of Management; Richard P. Nathan, *The Plot that Failed: Nixon and the Administrative Presidency* (Wiley, 1975), pp. 59–60, and 77, n. 1. Roy Ash was later named director of the Office of Management and Budget.

24. OMB, "President's Reorganization Authority," pp. 9–14; see also, David S. Broder, *Washington Post*, March 12, 1977.
25. OMB, "President's Reorganization Authority."
26. See Walter Gellhorn, *When Americans Complain* (Harvard University Press, 1966), and Gellhorn, *Ombudsmen and Others: Citizens' Protectors in Nine Countries* (Harvard University Press, 1966); Roy V. Peel, ed., "The Ombudsman or Citizen's Defender: A Modern Institution," *Annals of the American Academy of Political and Social Science*, vol. 377 (May 1968); Stanley V. Anderson, ed., *Ombudsmen for American Government?* (Prentice-Hall for The American Assembly, 1968); Alan J. Wyner, ed., *Executive Ombudsmen in the United States* (University of California, Berkeley, Institute of Government Studies, 1973).
27. The Commission on Federal Paperwork began operations in 1975. It will submit its final report in 1977, and has already submitted a number of interim reports and recommendations to the President.
28. From 1956 to 1976, civilian employment in the federal government, including postal workers, went from 2.4 million to 2.8 million, an increase of 17 percent. In the same interval, total federal outlays rose from $70.5 billion to $366.5 billion in current dollars, and from $133.0 billion to $264.4 billion in constant (fiscal year 1972) dollars.
29. See, for example, Harry S. Truman's classic statement accompanying Reorganization Plan Number 5, 1950 (March 13, 1950): "The taking effect of the reorganizations included in this plan may not in itself result in substantial immediate savings. However, many benefits in improved operations are probable during the next years which will result in a reduction in expenditures as compared with those that would be otherwise necessary. An itemization of these reductions in advance of actual experience under this plan is not practicable." Similarly, Franklin D. Roosevelt remarked that the transfer of agencies would not save much money. "It is awfully erroneous," he said, "to assume that it is in the reorganization of Departments and Bureaus that you save money;" Richard Polenberg, *Reorganizing Roosevelt's Government:The Controversy over Executive Reorganization, 1936-1939* (Harvard University Press, 1966), p. 8.
30. U.S. Department of Health, Education, and Welfare, *HEW News*, March 8, 1977, p. 2.
31. "The President's Address to the Nation," in *Weekly Compilation of Presidential Documents*, vol. 13 (February 7, 1977), p. 141.
32. Broder, *Washington Post*, March 12, 1977.

Redundancy, Rationality, and the Problem of Duplication and Overlap

MARTIN LANDAU

Not so long ago I experienced an emergency landing. We had been aloft only a short time when the pilot announced some mechanical failure. As we headed toward the nearest airport, the man behind me, no less frightened than I, said to his companion, "Here's where my luck runs out." A few minutes later we touched down to a safe landing amidst foam trucks and asbestos-clad fire fighters.

On the ground I ran into the pilot and asked him about the trouble. His response was vague, but he did indicate that something had been wrong with the rudder. How, then, was he able to direct and land the plane? He replied that the situation had not really been as ominous as it had seemed: the emergency routines we had followed were necessary precautions and he had been able to compensate for the impairment of the rudder by utilizing additional features of the aircraft. There were, he said, safety factors built into all planes.

Happily, such matters had not been left to chance, luck, as we say. For a commercial airliner is a very redundant system, a fact which accounts for its reliability of performance; a fact which also accounts for its adaptability.

A PARADOX

The English language presents us with a striking curiosity. Its lexicons establish an instance of *redundancy* as a "liability" and yet it is precisely the liberal use of redundancy that provides linguistic expression with an extraordinary measure of "reliability."

THE DEFINITION

In the context of ordinary language, redundancy is said to exist whenever there is an excess or superfluity of anything. The excess may be of parts, of rules, of words, . . . of anything. *Excess,* as defined lexically, is something which is more than the normal, the required, the usual, the specified. It is useless, superfluous, needless—terms which are variously employed to define redundancy.

This linguistic habit directs a negative judgment. It points to features of a situation which are of no value, which are wasteful, which are bad. The force of this habit is immediately to be seen by noting that the synonyms for the adjective "excessive" are: immoderate, intemperate, inordinate, extravagant, exorbitant, and extreme. If we need a time scale here, we can note that excessive has been used to define redundancy for some 400 years.

Accordingly, to say of a person's speech that it is redundant is not to extend a compliment. To observe an excess of parts is to observe an unnecessary duplication which, almost automatically, is seen as waste. To confront an excess of rules is, naturally, to make unhappy contact with red tape. And so on. In each case, more than is necessary is apparent, a condition which is sometimes regarded as affluent but more often as profligate. It is rarely regarded as economic and even less often as efficient. Indeed, there are many who seem to make *zero redundancy* the measure of both economy and efficiency. And if this condition is not fully realizable in practice, it nevertheless stands as the optimal state to be attained.

So powerful is this convention, that when Harry Nyquist introduced "redundancy" as a technical term in information theory, it referred to the useless portions of a message—those which could be eliminated without any loss of information. Nyquist sought a nonredundant system, one which would permit the transmission of information with the absolutely minimal number of signs that could possibly be employed.[1] Today, however, this goal is no longer entertained. It has been set aside: not because it is impossible of achievement, but because its realization would, in fact, increase the probability of failure—of false, misleading, and distorted messages.

THE USE OF REDUNDANCY

Consider this essay. I write it because I have a statement to make, one which I think is deserving of interest. And, as befalls anyone who wishes to send a message of this kind, several doubts assail me. To begin with, it is possible that my statement is not worth sending, but upon reflection I think it is. Then, I may not be able to make myself understood. My thoughts and/or my phraseology may be quite unclear and I know that to be understood requires a clarity of expression. I am also aware that I know most about what I want to say, but I am not sure that I can present my position in such a way as to enable the reader to receive it exactly as I want him to. Nor am I any more certain of my reader who, for many reasons beyond my control, may misinterpret what I write and receive an erroneous impression.

These are some of the uncertainties which face me as I seek to communicate. The possibility of misunderstanding, of an inability to make contact, of breakdown, is inescapable. I anticipate this and I work to lessen the risk all along the line. It would be helpful, of course, if I could deploy a decision system specifically designed to do so; statistics perhaps. It does, after all, permit the making of decisions under conditions of uncertainty with the least possible error.[2] But I have not ordered this paper, nor can I, in such a manner as to make use of its powers. Happily, however, I am not without other resources.

Notice that the paragraphs I have written are quite repetitious. I repeat directly and indirectly, and I did this in all similar circumstances before I "knew" that simple repetition is the easiest way to introduce redundancy and that redundancy is a powerful device for the suppression of error. I employ more words than the "absolute minimum" and I arrange them according to a larger number of grammatical rules than are ideally necessary, all of this not to waste space but to insure reliability of communication.[3] If the overall uncertainty factor could be eliminated, I would (theoretically) write with zero redundancy. But then, strangely enough, there would be no way to detect error should one arise.[4] This, of course, is an idle speculation, because no language is without redundancy.[5] Even our most precise scientific languages contain redundancies, and this statement is true for purely formal languages as well.[6]

It is, thus, virtually impossible to eliminate all duplication. And given the state of my knowledge at this point, it is rather fortuitous that the language I must employ is loaded with both a semantic and syntactical redundancy that comes naturally to me. In time I may be able to communicate on this problem with more certainty, with a more logical and precise syntax, with less multiplicity of meanings; then, the type of redundancy needed would change, the amount would diminish, and the risk of inconsistency would lessen. Now, however, a resort to the vernacular and I need not apologize for this. On the contrary, "the rules we call grammar and syntax . . . supplement and duplicate each other, providing a great margin of safety."[7] While I must exercise care so as not to be incoherent, I can nevertheless break some of these rules without destroying or critically damaging the communication process itself. Nor need it be stressed that the redundancy of both our grammar and lexicon are sources of great creativity and innovation.

PUBLIC ADMINISTRATION AND REDUNDANCY

It is, however, the lexical evaluation of redundancy which prevails in public administration. Indeed, this view is to be seen as programmatic in such revitalization movements as Taylorism and scientific management. These demanded the wholesale removal of duplication and overlap as they pressed for "streamlined organizations" that would operate with the absolutely minimal number of units that could possibly be employed in the performance of a task. Zero redundancy constituted the measure of optimal efficiency and this ideal, fortified by a scarcity of resources and an abundance of precedent, has informed both the theory and practice of public administration since the earliest days of the reform movement. Now, of course, we possess new vocabularies, direct our attention to management control systems, and seize upon such new technologies as PPBS. But our perspective remains fully as Utopian as it was a half-century ago.[8]

For the plain fact is that no amount of effort has yet been able to produce, even for limited time-spans, the precise mutually exclusive differentiation of activity that administrative integrationists long for and that PPBS *requires*. In the last 30 years we have observed massive efforts to reduce duplication: we have moved from the radical reconstructions which followed upon the Roosevelt and Hoover commissions to the institution of continuous executive reorganization—only to find that duplication and overlap are as conspicuous today as they have ever been.

Nor will the introduction of PPBS alter this condition to any appreciable extent—if we follow the statements of its advocates (many of which, it must be said, could use a good dose of redundancy). Testimony varies from an unrestrained hyperbole to a caution that is tinged with pessimism, but it remains clear "that the functioning of a program budget will reveal wasteful duplications, overlaps and inconsistencies created or permitted by the scatter of related activities through numerous executive departments, agencies and bureaus."[9] Redressing this grievance, though necessary to effective program budgeting, is not likely to be an easy task and the proponents of PPBS know this. They fully anticipate that they will be unable to withstand the combined resistance of counterpart congressional committees and special-interest groups, "all mortgaged to the existing administrative structure."[10] Anshen then writes,

One may conclude that the program budget could not function effectively in such an environment. Because *wholesale revision of the federal structure in accordance with the logic of a program budget* is clearly not going to be brought about in the near future, this judgment would be definitely negative for the budget's near term prospects.[11]

With such language before us, it is tempting to pursue Wildavsky's proposal that program budgeting is "an integral part of system politics,"[12] a contention that is unassailable. Engaged as we are, however, in an exploration of redundancy, it may suffice to suggest that the nation is not going to allow engineers to order its fundamental decision system "in accordance with the logic of program budgeting" now, or in the long term. That is, the probability that PPBS technicians will be given the authority to rewrite the constitution is zero. Hence they will have to settle for less—much less. And Anshen salvages what he can in the only way that he can; a compromise between the demands of the existing system and the requirements of program budgeting.[13] But if only such complication did not attend this scene: the nation's entire administrative complex could be transformed into one magnificent means-end chain with not an excess link in it.

Thus it is that the removal of redundancy is rarely, if ever, challenged in the technology of public administration. It is an article of faith, a commanding precept: and if its injunctions cannot be followed today, one can always dream of tomorrow. Those controversies that do arise generally concern the manner in which repair is to be effected and are not expressed any more differently than when Francis W. Coker cast a skeptical eye on the dogmas of administration. The doubts he raised turned on whether more might be accomplished through an incremental strategy than by a process of radical integration. But with respect to the need to "eliminate duplication and overlapping,"[14] he felt obliged to state, "No serious exception can be taken to this principle."[15]

In what follows, I shall exercise a theoretical option and take such exception. I cannot argue the case in full here, but I shall try to show that there are good grounds for suggesting that efforts to improve public administration by eliminating duplication and overlap would, if successful, produce just the opposite effect. That so many attempts have failed should perhaps alert us to what sociologists would call the "latent function" of this type of redundancy. This possibility alone is sufficient warrant for transforming a precept into a problem.

REDUNDANCY AND ERROR SUPPRESSION: RELIABILITY

There is, however, an additional reason for doing so.

The reader will observe that the phenomenon of "duplication" is no longer left to chance in the study of language. Nor is it overlooked in the design of automobiles, computers, and aircraft; the latter are reliable to the extent that they are redundant—and we have all had occasion to note that a good deal of the controversy over "safe cars" has had to do with the introduction of this feature as a standard element of design, as with the dual braking system, for example. That is, there is now a developing theory of redundancy, and while it was originally conceived of in the domains of information science (including computer technology) and natural automata (neural networks), it appears to have very wide application. In many areas, therefore, "over-engineering," "reserve power," and "safety-factors" of all sorts need no longer be dealt with intuitively.

But what of large-scale formal organization: can it be engaged in terms of this theory? The answer, of course, cannot be had *a priori,* but the attempt to do so is well under way, precipitated quite naturally by our propensity to draw from such cognate languages as systems analysis, cybernetics, and information theory—in particular, the latter. Fashion aside, however, "this comparison need not be a sterile metaphorical analogy," as Rapoport and Horvath note, for all organizations have "neural physiologies" in the sense that they are unthinkable "without internal communication, integration and control."[16] Marschak, in the same vein, proposes that an organization is to be defined by the rules which determine the sets of messages that can be received by its different members. Any given system, thus, "states who should do what in response to what."[17]

Upon reflection, it makes a good deal of sense to regard a large-scale organization as a vast and complicated information system. It is, after all, necessarily and continuously engaged in the transmission and reception of messages. But it is an awfully noisy system. Its codes, classification rules, are not unambiguous; its internal arrangements are not perfect; the course of its messages are neither consistent nor constant—nor are the messages themselves. Error occurs at the point of origin, where a message is selected from a whole ensemble of signs (stimuli), and at the point of reception. The language which is employed is notoriously vague and the "variable human,"[18] acting both as sender and receiver, often transforms the relation between a sign and its referent into a mystery. In an organizational system one can never be sure that either members or clientele can be reached without error or distortion. The transmission of information is, indeed, a very risky business.[19] Against this backdrop, the demand for control by central officers can clearly be seen as a demand for increased reliability (predictability) of response—and this means a reduction of uncertainty.

In public administration the standard policy for improving the performance characteristics of an administrative agency has rested upon the classical axiom that the reliability and efficiency of an operating system, man or machine, is dependent on the reliability and efficiency of each of its parts, including linkages. Improvement, therefore, calls for a system to be broken down (decomposed or analyzed) into its most basic units, these to be worked on to the point of infallibility. So much success has attended this procedure, especially as regards machine-based systems, that it not only constitutes a sound problem-solving paradigm, but is often generalized into a good commonsense rule. About the only limitations which are imposed on its application are those which derive from market conditions, the law of diminishing returns, and the state of the art.

Yet it is doubtful that the risk of failure can be removed in this manner even in the most advanced technologies. No matter how much a part is perfected, there is always the chance that it will fail. In some cases, many in fact, this is a tolerable risk—the unit involved may not be a basic component and the consequences of failure may be minimal. But where a system is important, and where it is made dependent upon operating parts that are organized into a tight means-end chain, the problem becomes acute. In such systems, especially when large, there is a tendency for even minor errors to be so amplified along the length of the chain as to make the end-result quite unreliable. In formal organizations this tendency can be expressed in terms of "the absorption of uncertainty."[20] The failure, then, of a single part can mean the failure of the entire system: as when the breakdown of a switching circuit blacks out an entire region or the failure of a duty officer to heed radar readings permits a force of unidentified aircraft to attack Pearl Harbor with devastating success. The latter case, it will be recognized, constitutes a stark illustration of the uncertainty principle. Here it was not the *evidence* which was transmitted, only the *inferences*. [21] In complex and tightly ordered systems the cost of error can run very high.

This is the context in which the theory of redundancy bulks so large. For it sets aside the doctrine that ties the reliability of a system to the perfectability of parts and thereby approaches the pragmatics of systems in action much more realistically. That is, it accepts the inherent limitations of any organization by treating any and all parts, regardless of their degree of perfection,[22] as risky actors. The practical implications of this shift in orientation are immediately to be seen when the following question is asked: Is it possible to take a set of individually unreliable units and form them into a system "with any arbitrarily high reliability"?[23] Can we, in other words, build an organization that is more reliable than any of its parts?

The answer, *mirabile dictu,* is yes. In what is now a truly classical paper, Von Neumann demonstrated that it could be done by adding sufficient redundancy.[24] Developments in this domain move swiftly and where before we could only resort to an intuitive and rather pragmatic redundancy, there now exist powerful theorems which can be applied with far greater certainty and much less waste.[25] This, it can be said, is a cardinal feature of "systems analysis"—all too often overlooked.

The theory itself is a rather complicated set of formulations and it serves no purpose to dwell upon it in any great detail. Yet there is one theorem that must be indicated because of the profound effect it can have on organizational design: that the probability of failure in a system decreases exponentially as redundancy factors are increased. Increasing reliability in this manner, of course, raises the price to be paid and if fail-safe conditions are to be reached, the cost may be prohibitive. But an immediate corollary of the theorem eases this problem for it requires only arithmetic increases in redundancy to yield geometric increases in reliability. Costs may then be quite manageable.

The application of this formula, however, depends upon the ability to construct a system so that it satisfies those conditions which permit the laws of probability to apply, in this case, the multiplication theorem or the product rule for independent events: alternatively, the failure of parts must be random and statistically independent (unrelated). In practical terms, therefore, a system must be so arranged that when parts fail, they do so unpredictably and in such manner *that they cannot and do not impair other parts,* as in the dual braking system of a car. If each braking assembly is not completely separated from the other, the redundancy is not only waste, it becomes a very dangerous addition: when it fails it is likely (perhaps certain) to damage the other assembly. So much for a theorem which has to do with duplication. We turn now to "overlapping."

"OVERLAPPING"

Generally employed to denote biological organisms (neural physiologies, in particular), "self-organizing systems" command fully as much attention in the study of redundancy as computing machines and communication networks. There is nothing surprising about this since the theory of redundancy is a theory of system reliability. And self-organizing systems exhibit a degree of reliability that is so far superior to anything we can build as to prompt theorists to suggest "that the richly redundant networks of biological organisms must have capabilities beyond anything our theories can yet explain."[26] In Von Neumann's phrasing, they "contain the necessary arrangements to diagnose errors as they occur, to readjust the organism so as to minimize the effects of errors, and finally to correct or to block permanently the faulty component." Error refers here to malfunction, and Von Neumann states that there is now little doubt that they are "able to operate even when malfunctions set in . . . [while] their subsequent tendency is to remove them."[27] Pierce adds that they are able to improve reliability when errors are common even as they improve their capabilities when errors are infrequent.[28]

EQUIPOTENTIALITY

How, precisely, this works remains an object of inquiry. But it seems clear that such systems possess a fantastic number of parallel hookups of many different types. McCulloch, in commenting on the reliability of biological organisms, speaks of redundancies of codes, of channels, of calculation, and of potential command, noting that each serves differently. "The reliability you can buy with redundancy of calculation cannot be bought with redundancy of code or channel."[29] To these we can add the property of "equipotentiality" which provides the system with an extraordinary adaptive power.

Equipotentiality, interestingly enough, is often referred to as "overlapping."[30] It denotes the tendency of neural networks to resist that kind of precise differentiation of function which is mutually exclusive. Even in the case of highly specialized subsystems the tendency is restricted but not lost. There appears to be some "overlap" at all times which enables residual parts or subsidiary centers to "take over," though somewhat less efficiently, the functions of those which have been damaged. It is this overlap[31] that permits the organism to exhibit a high degree of adaptability, i.e., to change its behavior in accordance with changes in stimuli.

DUPLICATION AND OVERLAP: POLITICS

And this is why it may be quite *irrational* to greet the appearance of duplication and overlap by automatically moving to excise and redefine. To unify the defense departments, or the several independent information-gathering services of the government, or the large number of agencies engaged in technical assistance, or the various antipoverty programs, or the miscellany of agencies concerned with transportation, or the great variety of federal, state, and local administrations that function in the same areas may rob the system of its necessary supports. It can be hypothesized that it is precisely such redundancies that allow for the delicate process of mutual adjustment, of self-regulation, by means of which the whole system can sustain severe local injuries and still function creditably.

Hypothesis?—perhaps it is more than that. If, of course, "men were angels," the systems they constitute would be foolproof. But they are not; and this is the fact that stands at the foundation of the organization created in Philadelphia. For the charter of the national system is a patent illustration of redundancy. Look at it:

separation of powers, federalism, checks and balances, concurrent powers, double legislatures, overlapping terms of office, the Bill of Rights, the veto, the override, judicial review, and a host of similar arrangements. Here is a system that cannot be described except in terms of duplication and overlap—of a redundancy of channel, code calculation, and command.

These are the redundancies which prompt public administration theorists to regard this system as quite inefficient—if not irrational. Where they wish one unambiguous code, there are many and these are hardly unequivocal; where they seek a unity of command, there is a redundancy of command; and so on. As a decision system, the organization of government certainly appears to be inferior to that which underlays program budgeting—which is why we see an expressed longing for a "wholesale revision of the federal structure." After all, as some programmers see it, the objectives of the architects of the Constitution were as much political as economic, and their economics "had a philosophic rather than managerial or operational character. The decision-making structure came . . . under the influence of objectives other than rationality of choice."[32] And, as Smithies has noted, "It is fundamental to our culture that rational choice is better than irrational choice."[33]

It is not possible, however, to determine whether a choice is rational except in terms of systemic context and goal. A course of action may be perfectly rational in one sphere and perfectly silly in another. It is only when context and goal are rendered nonproblematical that objective evaluations of competing decision systems can be had. If these factors cannot be bracketed, then assessments of decision systems are of necessity assignments of priority to specific sets of values. To say, therefore, that rational choice is fundamental to our culture is either to say nothing or, as in the context of administration, to urge that economic rationality is intrinsically superior to political rationality. In this case it should be clear, economic rationality is equated to scientific rationality and we are being told, without restriction, that the rules of scientific decision making are not simply different, they are best. We need not wonder why scientific management programs have always had the appearance of an ideology.

But there is more than one kind of "rationality," including the rationality of redundancy. Theoretically, there can be as many rationalities as there are systems—which is why phenomenologists have urged that rationality not be treated solely as a methodological principle but as "empirically problematical material" as well. In this respect Garfinkle has demonstrated that there are profound differences between "common sense" and "scientific" rationalities—of such an order that the two cannot be ranked. Indeed, it might give us all pause to observe what happens when the maxims of ideal scientific procedure are introduced willy-nilly into the everyday situation; what they do is to disrupt its continuities and multiply its anomic features.[34] In short, they disorganize an organized state.

Moreover, there is an element of paradox in the effort to extend these maxims to government at large. Most of us are influenced, if not absorbed, by the notion of "system," and this statement obviously includes economizers. Among the most fundamental elements of systems analysis, however, is the concept of systemic relevance. And the criteria which establish relevance are the criteria which mark boundaries. This means that any methodology is to be valued only to the extent that it achieves systemically relevant goals and such goals, to be at all sensible, must be desired state conditions which are in reach and which are field determined. Otherwise, they are idle fantasies or simply Utopian. If, of course, boundaries enlarge so as to permit what was heretofore irrelevant, this can only be learned by experience. Under such an expansion, methodologies which were once inappropriate may become extremely valuable. As Hamilton was wont to say, "means ought to be proportional to the end."[35]

AUXILIARY PRECAUTIONS

The constitution-makers, it appears, were eminently "rational." They chose wisely and they did so under hazardous conditions. They knew that they were "organizing" a system in the face of great uncertainty. We need not list the profound and abiding cleavages which existed nor the intense fears which were displayed: *The Federalist* alone makes this clear. But it also instructs that in fabricating the constitution, the architects were ever mindful of the grave possibility of failure and sought a system which could perform in the face of error—which could manage to provide a stable set of decision rules for an exceedingly unstable circumstance. And they found their answer in Newton's Third Law.[36] Experience, Madison wrote, has taught mankind the necessity for *auxiliary precautions:* these were to be had "by so contriving the internal structure of government so that its several constituent parts, may by their mutual relations, be the means of keeping each other in their proper places."[37] The principle of action and reaction, of checks and balances, turns out to have been, in organization terms, the principle of interwoven and competing redundancies.

"That which is redundant is, to the extent that it is redundant, stable. It is therefore reliable."[38] One hundred and seventy-nine years have passed since the original design, and save for one massive failure, the system has withstood the severest of shocks—and may well continue to do so even in the face of today's unprecedented problems. We like to say that it is the oldest constitutional government in the world, yet it remains a novelty. It seems to have worked like a "self-organizing" system exhibiting both the performance reliability and adaptability that such systems display. Marked by a redundancy of law, of power and command, of structure and linkage—*the whole has appeared as more reliable than any of its parts.* Where one part has failed another has taken over, and even when duplicates were not there to be employed, the presence of equipotentiality, of overlapping functions, permitted the load to be assumed elsewhere, however imperfectly. Scholars have for years spoken of the "cyclical character" of intragovernmental arrangements, of a "pendulum of checks and balances," frequently pointing to this phenomenon as an adaptive response. The "uncertain content" (jurisdiction) of the various parts of government just will not allow it to sit still and the hyphenated phrases we are forced to use in describing government are indicative of the extent of its equipotentiality. Even when such reference is pejorative, as often happens in the instance of "judicial-legislation," such a concept points to an overlap which enables adaptation. *Baker v. Carr* is a recent illustration of this kind of self-regulation.[39] The boss, the historical master of an "invisible government," was a redundancy that developed to offset the failures of local government,[40] and this would not have been possible but for the redundancy of party. Senator Mike Mansfield, speaking on the floor of the Senate, warns his colleagues that if they do not act, other branches of government will:

It is clear that when one road to this end fails, others will unfold as indeed they have unfolded. If the process is ignored in legislative channels, it will not necessarily be blocked in other channels—in the executive branch and in the courts.[41]

And the President has been severely criticized because he has radically curtailed the number of channels, formal and informal, that are employed for purposes of control. Richard Neustadt, after describing the extraordinary redundancy which marked FDR's administration, concludes the presidency cannot function effectively without competing information sources.[42]

Nor need any of this be gainsaid by the compelling movement toward centralization. Although this is an empirical problem which I have only begun to investigate, there is some basis for suggesting that this trend constitutes a replacement of historically accepted types of redundancies by those which may be more appropriate to the existent task environment. Because such changes involve command or control, they do not occur without sharp and often protracted conflict—as can be seen in the bitter controversy between the Senate Foreign Relations Committee and the President. This, to be sure, is exacerbated by differences over Vietnam policy, but it necessarily involves competing redundancies. However this is settled, the organization of government in this country, at least until now, demands attention: it seems to have brought an extraordinary amount of reliability and adaptability through its extensive parallel networks (duplication) and equipotential parts (overlap).

Indeed, it is a curiosity to observe the extent to which redundancy theorists resort to political metaphor. Their designs eschew single-line arrangements and they employ a system of multiplexing (multiple lines in parallel) which operates in accordance with the principle of "majority rule." Such devices are known as "vote-takers" which abide by the rules of "democratic suffrage." As Von Neumann put it, they are "majority organs." And Pierce remarks that, "It is as though there were a nation in which no citizen could be trusted, and accordingly, several citizens were required to act together in making decisions, executing orders or delivering messages."[43] But there are times when equally weighted votes are not as effective as one might desire. Under such circumstances, redundancy theorists provide for an "aristocratic suffrage" by assigning unequal weights to decision makers. What is most interesting here is that this assignment is made in proportion to a decision maker's reliability as tested under performance conditions and is adjusted continuously in accordance with the record.[44] More immediately, however, the use of such metaphor bespeaks an implicit grasp of the power of redundancy in politics.

PUBLIC ADMINISTRATION

Not so for public administration, however.

Its prevailing notions of organizational rationality are built upon contrary assumptions. Where the 'rationality' of politics derives from the fact that a system can be more reliable (more responsive, more predictable) than any of its parts, public administration has postulated that a system can be no more than the sum of its parts: reliable components, thus, add up to a reliable system and *per contra*.

The logic of this position, to iterate, calls for each role to be perfected, each bureau to be exactly delimited, each linkage to articulate unfailingly, and each line of communication to be noiseless—all to produce one interlocking system, one means-end chain which possesses the absolutely minimum number of links, and which culminates at a central control point. For the public administration rationalist, the optimal organization consists of units that are wholly compatible, precisely connected, fully determined, and, therefore, perfectly reliable. The model which represents this dream is that of a linear organization in which everything is arrayed in tandem.[45] It is as if the entire house is to be wired in series.

If the analogy holds, and it does to a considerable extent—especially as regards communication processes, organizational systems of this sort are a form of administrative *brinksmanship*. They are extraordinary gambles. When one bulb blows, everything goes. Ordering parts in series makes them so dependent upon each other that any single failure can break the system. It is the old story of "For want of a nail . . . the battle was lost." Other illustrations: each of us can supply any number of instances of rather serious disruptions because of a faulty part, a malfunctioning actor, a noisy channel. Serial arrangements have the property of intensifying error.

In fact, they may be conducive to error—and to all sorts of problems. For they presuppose the human actor is a linear element and can, therefore, produce outputs in proportion to inputs, and on schedule. There is no doubt, of course, that the human actor can perform "indifferently" over a very wide task environment and under very diverse conditions: otherwise, large-scale formal organization as we know it would not be able to maintain itself.[46] But we have come to learn, and at sad cost, that even if serial demands fall within an actor's "zone of acceptance," there are limits to his linearity. The strains imposed can be too much, the burden of error can be too great—in short, he can be overloaded. A ready resort to a "rational calculus," which places actors in serial interdependence on the assumption of linearity, courts trouble. As against optimum performance, it may beget even less than a satisficing one. Indeed, it is more likely to breed a "resistance" which ultimately results in a sharply reduced zone of acceptance. And this reduction may be so severe as to constitute a direct challenge to organizational authority. In this circumstance, organizational expenditures to secure compliance may be far more than the cost of parallel hookups which do not require perfectability to increase reliability and which, thereby, reduce strain.

There are additional risks as well—not the least of which is an intensification of the "displacement of goals."[47] Because each part assumes so weighty a responsibility in the system, exacting controls are required. Rules, therefore, assume even more importance than they ordinarily do. And the more precise they are, the better the control. There is, then, an even greater possibility that strict and slavish adherence to regulations will obtain. The burden of error is sufficient to prompt a refusal to exercise discretion when an untoward situation arises. This holds *a fortiori* in a government organization which is bound by rules that have the force of law: for a mistake in interpretation may place action outside the limits of the rule and render it *ultra vires.* Under such strictures there will neither be the "taking advantage of a technicality" or of a "loophole"—and it is a practice such as this one which often constitutes an adaptive response to an urgent problem.

But, beyond this, the "rationality of redundancy" assumes considerable praxiological force when it is noted that the typical organizational pattern which the administrative rationalist proposes is invariably the ideal organizational structure for synoptic or programmed decision making.[48]

To be sure, this type of decision process stands as the perfect form of problem solving. It is, on analysis, modeled on the deductive chain of a fully axiomatized theory. Where it holds, all that is needed to "decide" is to compute the solution—the correct course of action. It can only obtain, however, under conditions of certainty, in a circumstance that Herbert Simon has called a "closed set of variables."[49] For public administration, this means that the environment has been fully and correctly described, that preferred state conditions are unequivocal, and that the instruments necessary to produce preferred states are at hand. Said alternatively, certainty exists as to fact and value, instrumentation and outcome, means and ends. All that needs to be known is known and no ambiguities prevail. If there is any doubt on either side of the equation, then a forced programmed process is no more than an instance of "Gresham's Law." It will drive out the very activity which is needed to produce knowledge: in organizational terms, operational agencies that have not mastered their task environment will be sealed off from it.[50]

Now there are many areas of administration which admit of the logic of programming, with respect to which we can apply the rather powerful "closed decision systems" we already possess. Not to do so is a witless act, for it is an absurdity to refuse to deploy knowledge which is at hand. But there is a question as to how much of the domain of public administration can be covered in this manner.[51] Conditions of certainty, or near certainty, appear to be rare facts in the life of a public agency, and when they exist, their scope is likely to be severely restricted. If so, it is not very rational to design organizations to pursue decision strategies that can comprehend only a small portion of their activities. On the contrary, it is a very sensible rule to construct organizations so that they can cope with uncertainty as to fact and disagreement over values.

If facts are in question, then we simply do not have knowledge of the appropriate means to use in seeking an outcome. We may have hunches and rules of thumb and we may write elaborate plans which anticipate all conceivable outcomes, but these are only hypotheses. It is, therefore, an obvious and "rational calculus" to employ a pragmatic and experimental procedure: that is, a policy of redundancy which permits several, and competing, strategies to be followed both simultaneously and separately. Separately, because the moment a plan is put into effect it constitutes an experiment, and unless we introduce "controls" we cannot determine which course of action is best. And as difficult as it may be to apply this policy in an ongoing agency, so is it necessary. It can be seen, then, that any attempt to "program" solutions prematurely is the height of folly. Managements may do this in the interest of economy and control, but the economy will be false and the control a ritual—for we are acting, and organizing, as if we "know" when we do not. It is a striking phenomenon of organizational life (and elsewhere, of course) that we often present the appearance of "rationality" when we do not know what we are doing or why. Operating personnel will not find this last statement amiss.

ALTERNATIVES

If the value side is open, we can either fight, slam it shut, or negotiate. It would take us too far afield to discuss conflict here, and we can dispatch the arbitrary closure of value differences by suggesting that it breeds conflict—up to and including "administrative sabotage"—a possibility that programmers must always be alert to. But if there exist differences as to preferences, and the parties involved value the existence of the organization, it makes good sense to compromise, to negotiate differences, to be "political" (a course of action, as noted earlier, that some PPBS spokesmen have had to urge upon their colleagues). This process, we know, is a widespread practice in public administration. The Inter-University Case Program, if it has demonstrated anything, points up "the intricate process of negotiation, mutual accommodation, and reconciliation of competing values . . ." which mark all of the agencies thus far studied.[52] As a decision system, negotiation avoids the precise, mutually exclusive definitions of value that are necessary to any synoptic procedure. This cardinal rule of bargaining has been generated by years of extensive experience, especially in labor-management relations, and is based upon the fact that such clarification of values serves only to extend and intensify disagreement.[53] It, therefore, requires the redundancy of ambiguity, surplus meaning, for it is precisely such surplus that permits values to overlap the parties in dispute providing thereby some common ground for agreement.

There are, then, a number of decision systems,[54] each of which calls for a different organizational perspective. None, however, can do without redundancy. Whatever claims are made for programmed decision making, it is to be recognized that if its organizational structure consisted only of the "absolutely minimal number of parts," error could not be detected. As against pragmatics and negotiation, there is little doubt that reliable performance requires lesser amounts of redundancy. But the task remains to learn to distinguish between inefficient redundancies and those that are constructive and reinforcing—and this includes the kind of knowledge which will permit the introduction of redundancies so that they can work to increase both reliability and adaptability. This task, needless to say, attends pragmatics and negotiation as well, for they are redundant by their nature.

A FINAL NOTE

The appearances, therefore, of duplication and overlap in administrative agencies are not necessarily signs of waste and inefficiency. On the contrary, it is becoming increasingly evident that large-scale organizations function as self-organizing systems and tend to develop their own parallel circuits: not the least of which is the transformation of such "residual" parts as "informal groups" into constructive redundancies. Where we are sometimes prone to regard such groups as sources of pathology, they may be compensating for the deficiencies of the formal organization in the same way that the "boss" once did.

At one and the same time, thus, redundancy serves many vital functions in the conduct of public administration. It provides safety factors, permits flexible responses to anomalous situations, and provides a creative potential for those who are able to see it. If there is no duplication, if there is no overlap, if there is no ambiguity, an organization will neither be able to suppress error nor generate alternate routes of action.[55] In short, it will be most unreliable and least flexible, sluggish, as we now say.

"Streamlining an agency," "consolidating similar functions," "eliminating duplication," and "commonality" are powerful slogans which possess an obvious appeal. But it is just possible that their achievement would deprive an agency of the properties it needs most—those which allow rules to be broken and units to operate defectively without doing critical injury to the agency as a whole. Accordingly, it would be far more constructive, even under conditions of scarcity, to lay aside easy slogans and turn attention to a principle which lessens risks without foreclosing opportunity.

NOTES

1. J. R. Pierce, *Symbols, Signals and Noise* (New York: Harper, 1961), pp. 35–39. Also, see chapters 7 and 8.
2. Irwin D. J. Bross, *Design for Decision* (New York: Macmillan, 1953).
3. So, too, we repeat observations. The more observations, the less the uncertainty.
4. See Pierce, *op. cit.*, chapters 7 and 8. Also, see Colin Cherry, *On Human Communication* (New York: Science Editions, 1961), pp. 180–185.
5. The English language is estimated to be between 50 to 65 per cent redundant. The language employed in control tower-pilot communication is about 95 per cent redundant.
6. It suffices to note that it is precisely the property of redundancy in a formal logic that permits deductive inference. Given a set of algebraic equations, e.g., we can deduce the solution by acting in accordance with the appropriate syntactical rules. This solution is *implicit* in the set of equations and can thereby be deduced. It contains "no more information" than the original equations and constitutes a redundancy (repetition) that is present but not obvious. See Cherry, *op. cit.*, pp. 221–231. Also, see Herbert A. Simon, "The Architecture of Complexity," *Proceedings of the American Philosophical Society*, Vol. 106 (1962), pp. 478–479.
7. *Ibid.*, p. 19.
8. Dwight Waldo, *The Administrative State* (New York: Ronald Press, 1948), pp. 37–38.
9. Melvin Anshen, "The Program Budget in Operation," in *Program Budgeting*, David Novick (ed.) (Cambridge, Mass.: Harvard University Press, 1965), p. 359. Anshen's essay summarizes the sense of the various papers in this volume.
10. *Ibid.*
11. *Ibid*, emphasis added.
12. Aaron Wildavsky, "The Political Economy of Efficiency," *Public Administration Review*, Vol. 24 (December 1966), pp. 304–305.
13. Anshen, *op. cit.*, p. 359.
14. Once again this is a goal of the newly proposed "Hoover Commission" see *Public Administration News* (August 1967), p. 2.
15. "Dogmas of Administrative Reform," *American Political Science Review*, Vol. 16 (August 1922).
16. Anatol Rapoport and William J. Horvath, "Thoughts on Organization Theory and a Review of Two Conferences," *General Systems Yearbook*, Vol. IV (1959), p. 91.
17. Jacob Marschak, "Economic Planning and the Cost of Thinking," *Social Research*, Vol. 33 (Summer 1966), pp. 157–158. Also, see John T. Dorsey, Jr., "The Information-Energy Model," in F. Heady and S. Stokes (eds.), *Papers in Comparative Public Administration* (Ann Arbor: Institute of Public Administration, 1962).
18. The phrase is James D. Thompson's. *Organizations in Action* (New York: McGraw-Hill, 1967), see chapter 8.

19. This, incidentally, is a redundant sentence.
20. James G. March, Herbert A. Simon, and Harold Guetzkow, *Organizations* (New York: John Wiley, 1958), pp. 164–166. I am indebted to Aaron Wildavsky for this suggestion.
21. *Ibid.*, p. 165.
22. It is assumed, of course, that any component meets a specified standard of performance.
23. Jagjit Singh, *Information Theory, Language and Cybernetics* (New York: Dover Publications, 1966), p. 173.
24. John Von Neumann, "Probabilistic Logics and the Synthesis of Reliable Organizations from Unreliable Components," in C. E. Shannon and J. McCarthy (eds.), *Automata Studies* (Princeton: Princeton University Press, 1956). Also, see C. E. Shannon and W. Weaver, *The Mathematical Theory of Communication* (Urbana: University of Illinois Press, 1949). And see Pierce, *op. cit.*, chapter 8; Singh, *op. cit.*, chapters 4 and 5; and Cherry, *op. cit.*, chapter 5.
25. W. H. Pierce, "Redundancy in Computers," *Scientific American*, Vol. 210 (February 1964). Also, see W. S. McCulloch, "The Reliability of Biological Systems," in M. G. Yovitz and S. Cameron (eds.), *Self-Organizing Systems* (New York: Pergamon Press, 1960); and Singh, *op. cit.*, chapters 10–12. And see Robert Gordon, "Optimum Component Redundancy for Maximum System Reliability," *Operations Research*, Vol. 5 (1957).
26. Pierce, *op. cit.*, p. 112.
27. John Von Neumann, "The General and Logical Theory of Automata," in James R. Newman, *The World of Mathematics* (New York: Simon and Schuster, 1956), Vol. IV, pp. 2085–2086.
28. Pierce, *op. cit.*
29. McCulloch, *op. cit.*, p. 265.
30. Singh, *op. cit.*, pp. 246–247, 323.
31. It is interesting to note that learning machines, machines which "interpret their environment," are built upon this principle. They are much more flexible than computers and "can rise to occasions not foreseen by programmed instructions." *Ibid.*, p. 225.
32. Roland N. McKean and Melvin Anshen, "Limitations, Risks and Problems," in Novick, *op. cit.*, p. 287.
33. Arthur Smithies, "Conceptual Framework for the Program Budget," *ibid.*, p. 24.
34. Harold Garfinkle, "The Rational Properties of Scientific and Common-Sense Activities," *Behavioral Science*, Vol. 5 (1960), and *Studies in Ethnomethodology* (Englewood Cliffs, N.J.: Prentice-Hall, 1967), chapter 2.
35. *The Federalist*, No. 31.
36. Martin Landau, "On the Use of Metaphor in Political Analysis," *Social Research*, Vol. 28 (Autumn 1961).
37. *The Federalist*, No. 51, emphasis added; see also Nos. 47 and 48.
38. McCulloch, *op. cit.*, p. 265.
39. See Martin Landau, "Baker v. Carr and the Ghost of Federalism," in G. Schubert (ed.), *Reapportionment* (New York: Scribners, 1964).
40. Robert K. Merton, "Manifest and Latent Functions," in *Social Theory and Social Structure* (Glencoe, N.Y.: The Free Press, 1957).
41. Quoted by Marquis Childs, *New York Post*, May 10, 1962.
42. Richard E. Neustadt, *Presidential Power* (New York: John Wiley, 1960), chapter 7.
43. Pierce, *op. cit.*, p. 105–106. Also, see Singh, *op. cit.*, p. 176.
44. Which appears as a sound principle for constituting "elites."
45. Thompson refers to this organizational pattern as the "long-linked technology" involving "serial interdependence," *op. cit.*, pp. 18–19.

46. *Ibid.*, pp. 105–106. Also, see Herbert Simon, *Administrative Behavior* (New York: Macmillan, 1947).

47. Robert Merton, "Bureaucratic Structure and Personality," in Merton *et al.* (eds.), *Reader in Bureaucracy* (Glencoe, N.Y.: The Free Press, 1952).

48. I take both terms as synonyms for the same concept. See David Braybrooke and Charles E. Lindblom, *A Strategy for Decision* (New York: The Free Press, 1963), and Herbert Simon, *The New Science of Management Decision* (New York: Harper, 1960). "Computation decision is still another name employed by James Thompson and Arthur Tuden; see "Strategies, Structures, and Processes of Organizational Decision" in *Comparative Studies in Administration* (Pittsburgh: University of Pittsburgh Press, 1959).

49. If the situation is one in which we do not have certainty but we are able to measure (accurately) the probability distributions of the outcomes of each alternative course of action, the situation can be treated as "closed."

50. This is especially so with respect to serial designs, since they can only operate under closure. See Thompson, *op. cit.*, p. 19, Prop. 2.1: Under norms of rationality, organizations seek to seal off their core technologies from environmental influences.

51. The history of science and technology indicates that as we gain more knowledge we open new areas of uncertainty. Which is why, I suspect, that Simon says that "many, perhaps most" of the problems that have to be handled at middle and high levels of management" will probably never be amenable to mathematical treatment. Herbert Simon, *The New Science of Management Decision, op. cit.*, p. 21.

52. Herbert Kaufman, "The Next Step in Case Studies," *Public Administration Review*, Vol. 18 (Winter 1958), p. 55.

53. Charles Lindblom offers an appropriate maxim in this regard: Do not try to clarify values if the parties can agree on policies. "Some Limitations on Rationality" in Carl J. Friedrich (ed.), *Rational Decision* (New York: Atherton Press, 1964).

54. The system of classification that I have employed is based upon Thompson and Tuden, *op. cit.* My own explication of their formulations is to be found in "Decision Theory and Comparative Public Administration," *Comparative Political Studies*, Vol. 1 (July 1968).

55. As an immediate illustration, an agency often encounters situations which require prompt and necessary action. Where rules duplicate and overlap, safety factors exist. If one set of rules fails or does not cover the situation, an alternate route can be found or rules can be stretched—broadly interpreted. The problem, again, is to eliminate an inefficient profusion and to provide efficient redundancy.

8

PUBLIC
PERSONNEL SYSTEMS

Perhaps no area of public administration is undergoing so much turbulence as public personnel management. The concept of a merit system is really elitist, implying that citizens prefer that "the best and the brightest" individuals be employed in government. Although it has never enjoyed the public respect and appreciation accorded to British civil servants, the American civil service system has made important advances in this century. The determination of "spoils" or "where to draw the line" between political party patronage and the civil service is always difficult. Official contempt for the civil service and federal civil servants probably reached its height during the Nixon administration, when there was a conscious effort to subvert the federal civil service system.

The widespread utilization of merit systems does not mean, however, that there has not been considerable adaptation of public personnel systems in recent years. David Stanley opens this chapter by bringing the reader up to date on trends in public personnel management.

In the second article, E. S. Savas and Sigmund Ginsburg directly challenge some contemporary personnel practices. As Kaufman did with regard to administrative reorganization, Savas and Ginsburg question some of the conventional wisdom regarding civil service system operations.

Affirmative action, or the promotion of increased equality for groups that have suffered from discriminatory practices in the past, is one of the most controversial topics of our times. Many critics of affirmative action programs claim that civil service systems are moving from the concept of equality of opportunity to that of equality of result. In this, they also see a pattern of "reverse discrimination," but discrimination nonetheless (as in the recent Baake case before the U.S. Supreme Court). The opponents of affirmative action also feel that the ultimate risk in such practices is a downward leveling of excellence. Catherine Lovell disagrees and addresses the main issues in affirmative action programs in public personnel systems.

One of the most important issues in the study of personnel systems is that of professionalism. More and more specialists and experts, normally with advanced training, are being employed at all levels of public service. In addition, public administration is sometimes touted as a newly emerging profession. In the final article in this chapter, Richard Schott carefully examines the concept of public administration as a profession and its implications for government as well as for the education of public administrators.

What's Happening to the Civil Service?

DAVID T. STANLEY

The civil service in America—some 13 million people working for federal, state, and local agencies for some $9 billion in paychecks—is changing. It has become large, old, defensive, fragmented. It is attacked by critics, elbowed by competitors, confused by multiple objectives, yet it survives and performs—partly well, partly poorly.

What is the old model civil service? Essentially it is a defense against job-filling through politics—a merit system under which people compete for jobs according to their skills. Once appointed, employees are promoted on the basis of merit, trained to do their jobs efficiently, paid according to the difficulty of their duties and assured of tenure if they do their work satisfactorily and behave decently. This is the model system for which President Garfield unknowingly died, and for which the old civil service reformers turned around our system of public administration, such as it was.

PRESSURES FOR CHANGE

The civil service has always been under pressure from the very kinds of political job-dealing for which it was to be an antidote. Many state and city jobs are not covered by merit systems and are filled on the basis of party reliability or some form of "clearance."

The pressure is by no means all partisan or patronage-motivated. Public managers want flexibility to arrange their resources to get their jobs done, and they criticize the rigidity and complexity of civil service procedures. A nonpolitical executive may be just as pained as a highly political one if he is forced always to choose the top person on an eligible list, or if his freedom to select a branch chief is governed by examinations of dubious relevance to the work to be done, or if some other arbitrary numerical procedure infringes his freedom to make decisions. He finds too that it may be difficult to promote and transfer subordinate executives in accordance with the "best principles" of managerial development because the civil service system is trying so hard to make him be "fair."

Civil service and personnel officials have bent under these pressures and become more flexible. They have had to anyway because the public employment market no longer provides waiting lines for many public jobs. An alert civil service organization provides for same-day examining, immediate certification, selection from open lists, weekend screening of applicants, and many other desirable compromises in the interest of getting a share of the labor market and meeting the operating needs of the government organization.

Unionism

The most profound changes in the public service are being brought about by the enormous increase in unionism and in the extent to which collective bargaining has replaced unilateral decision-making by government officials. Something like a million and a half federal employees are unionized and an equal number of state and local employees. Unions have been growing in numbers and power regardless to the extent to which they are officially authorized and regardless of the scope they have been given. They are active and effective even in some states where there is no comprehensive state law governing their recognition, representation, scope of bargaining and other limits.

Unions have grown and become effective because they have three kinds of power: they are large blocs of voters; they lobby and exert pressure; and when a hopeless impasse is reached they have the power to shut down the government. Strikes of public employees are illegal in the federal government and in all but four states—and permitted there under strictly limited conditions. Nevertheless, unions do strike, generally with advantage and often with impunity. This issue is being debated at great length and not as yet conclusively. When strikes do occur they tend not to be prolonged and they are very often settled on favorable terms to the unions. Legislative and executive political leaders are most reluctant to be in the position of causing or prolonging a cessation of public services. The public may or may not be sympathetic with the strikers but seem to be opposed to harsh penalties for work stoppages. Several states are resorting to compulsory arbitration of impasses in lieu of strikes, and it is too early to tell whether this is a positive way to attack the problem. It would appear at this point an expensive way at any rate.

Looking at the unions' impact on various civil service functions, we find that they have not made significant inroads on the hiring process. They are beginning to exert a serious influence, however, on how long probationary periods shall be, on how promotions shall be made, and on how discipline shall be administered. They are having a profound effect on grievance procedures. A management-dominated grievance procedure with ultimate appeal to the chief executive or the civil service commission is more and more rare. It is being replaced by a bargained grievance procedure with ultimate resolution of controversies by outside arbitrators, as in private industry.

There has been an equally profound effect on pay-setting. Under the old model civil service system the personnel staff would make a survey of wages paid by private employers, recommend changes in pay rates if justified, and the legislative body would enact the changes. At those times government salaries tended to be lower than those in the private sector and fringe benefits higher. Now in more and more governments both pay and benefits are being set by collective bargaining. The bargaining process has helped raise government pay to levels that compete with and in some cases exceed those in private industry. Meanwhile pensions, leave, life and health insurance, and other fringe benefits have been rising too.

The unions are exerting growing influence too over how the work is actually managed. Trashmen are bargaining over routes, schedules and equipment. Policemen are resisting one man patrol cars; firemen are bargaining over how many city blocks a fire company has to cover and how many men will be used on given types of equipment; welfare case workers have struck over caseload. Overtime and the conditions under which it is required, assigned or permitted is also a bargainable issue in some places. So is the introduction of new technology, like garbage loading trucks that require fewer men, automated water and sewer plants, and so on. All the time the unions are bringing pressure on management to increase the scope of bargaining and limit the scope of management discretion, and management is resisting.

A related source of pressure on the old civil service model is the increased strength of professional employees and their organizations. Governments have to have professionals: engineers, lawyers, physicians, social workers, chemists, economists, many others. The professions demand and obtain high standards of work, but their interests do not always coincide with those of the public service. They may impose personnel requirements and work methods that are of more benefit to their membership than to the public at large. Thus, professional groups, no less than unions, are influencing the chain of political communications from the citizen to the legislative body to the executive to the staff which so profoundly affect public service. Indeed, some professional associations have actually acquired representation and bargaining rights as in the case of the American Nursing Association and the National Education Association. Unionized social workers are common, and even physicians have signed up in a few cities.

Hiring the Disadvantaged

Another challenge to the management of the public service as we have known it is the move toward equal employment opportunity, supported by law, regulations, and enforcement actions. It is ironic that this should be necessary; the public service is presumed to be anti-discriminatory. Every citizen has a right to compete for public employment on the basis of fitness for the job to be done. The problem has been, of course, that civil service processes operated by representatives of "the establishment" have tended to keep out people who really could do the work. Why, for instance, should a laborer have to take a written test? We are now belatedly facing the fact that we must not keep any groups out of public jobs by artificial, indefensible methods.

Rather, we must work them in, until, some say, they are up to a certain number or percentage of the government work force—possibly the same percentage as their proportion in the population. This is known as the "quota problem," a real source of controversy. Quotas have been rejected by the President of the United States, and the U.S. Civil Service Commission has found them inconsistent with merit principles. The antidote for quotas is goals, defined by the U.S. Civil Service Commission as a "realistic objective which an agency endeavors to achieve on a timely basis within the context of a merit system of employment." Goals are to be achieved, we infer, by "giving an edge" to women, blacks, Chicanos, others, in situations where the merit system permits some freedom of decision. In any particular system there are stressful problems in how to do this: change the rules to give added points? certify out of rank order from eligible lists? reduce the seniority factor in promotions? All have pluses and minuses. Some people are benefited; others are hurt.

Suppose in "giving an edge" we fudge just a little on qualifications, and a little more the next time. Soon we have a training problem or a work re-engineering problem or simply a problem of generally lowered standards. Public managers, who must unendingly keep on the pressure for high quality performance, are thus given a much more difficult task than they would otherwise have. Hence the goal of efficiency may come into conflict with the goals of evening up opportunities and achieving a more representative public service. Both purposes are valid, and their achievement is complicated by the state of the labor market—how many are available who can do the work?

This leads us to the problem of citizens who are available, who may *not* be able to do the work but who are going to be hired anyway. Here is another goal of public employment: to make work for people who don't have it. Accordingly, Congress passed the Emergency Employment Act of 1971. A billion dollars was authorized to support 140,000 jobs for the unemployed and underemployed. State and local governments were given a great deal of freedom to decide how to use this money, and considerable ingenuity was exercised to put people to work. This stimulus to public employment for lowly jobs (although aerospace engineering professionals and technicians were also underemployed and in some cases benefited) came at a time when the general movement of technology as always has been to replace persons with machines. Yet here, we have an effort to provide jobs for the sake of providing jobs in the public service and to spread them among the ages, sexes and races. This meant frequent exceptions to or relaxations of customary civil service employment provisions—another apparent assault on the public service, complained about and resisted by defenders of our old style model, commended and stimulated by others asking "what is the public service for, if not this?"

Contracting Out

Government provides work also by contracting with private industry. Public buildings are constructed by private industry; streets are generally paved by contractors; many a research and development laboratory or fabrication plant is a government contractor. There are other public service functions which are done sometimes publicly and sometimes privately, like trash collection, medical care, operation of public utilities, data processing and even in some cases education. Here again, as in the case of so many of these sources of tension and anxiety with respect to the public service, there are problems of objectives and politics. What are our purposes? To render the most service for the fewest dollars, to spread jobs, to support private industry, to keep political support? Probably some or all of these things depending on the law, customs, and attitudes of the areas of government that are involved. Contractors who do a great deal of government work acquire a stake in this game and become a political force. Witness the political horsepower that goes into matters related to the defense budget. The government employee unions tend to be a counterforce because they want the work to stay in the public service for themselves and their potential members. In some cities, unions have brought effective pressure against the contracting out of trash collection and building maintenance functions.

Many a government contract is either threatened or undertaken because government pay is too low or civil service red tape too difficult. So here we have government paying to circumvent its own procedures—an ironic twist.

And just to complicate things a little more, we have government agencies becoming public corporations so that they can better handle their labor relations and get a little more protection from political interference (the U.S. Postal Service). We also have new public corporations to perform functions no longer profitable in the private sector (AMTRAK). Are such corporations (both kinds) in the public service? Are they subject to merit principles more or less than an audit clerk in the U.S. Department of Agriculture? These questions are difficult and about the only thing we can hold onto is the need for quality service to the citizens. These are the alleged purposes of contracting out and of setting up the public corporations. The growing movement to evaluate public services may gradually begin to tell us how truly effective they are.

PAYING FOR CHANGE

All these changes are part of the reasons for rising government expenses. In a typical local government personnel costs may be anywhere from 50% to 75% of the operating budget. In the federal government personnel costs are only about 15%, but remember that a lot of the "nonpersonnel" money goes to state and local governments. Meanwhile citizens want public services maintained or even increased while they want taxes reduced.

The resulting fiscal strain is sharpening the conflict between management officials and organized employees. Management is trying to discourage salary increases, new fringe benefits, and expensive work rules. The employee unions say that they will not be exploited in order to help balance a government budget. They also oppose layoffs, object to staffing limitations, and complain about economies in equipment and supplies.

The Productivity Movement

Hence employees are wary of the major efforts now being made to improve productivity in government at all levels. The federal government has a joint project led by the General Accounting Office, the Office of Management and Budget, and the Civil Service Commission to explore methods of measuring and improving productivity. Foundations and universities are sponsoring conferences, and professional literature on the subject is starting to pile up. The City of New York is already using productivity as a factor in collective bargaining.

These efforts are much more difficult in government than in a manufacturing industry because government's end products are hard to identify, there are a greater number of variables, and the means of measurement are underdeveloped. Nevertheless, progress is being made and unit costs and measures are being refined. It should become more and more possible to identify the productivity of individual workers and particular groups as a basis for work assignments, pay setting, and employee rewards. All this is desirable from a management viewpoint, but there are elements in it that smack of unpopular time and motion studies and speed-up movements in industrial plants some 50 years ago. They will be opposed unless the human relations aspects are carefully considered. Job engineering deserves exhaustive attention. We read of the desperate boredom of production line workers, and this too is becoming a factor in collective bargaining. Also management literature is beginning to tell us that job enlargement may result in benefits to management as well as in gains in morale.

The Federal Presence

State and local officials struggle with all these problems we have mentioned with the federal government looking over their shoulders. Standards of merit system administration continue to be established and enforced as the basis for states receiving certain federal grants-in-aid. The Equal Employment Opportunity Program is now enforced in state and local governments. Public employment programs have put new workers into state and local governments under conditions monitored by federal officials. Grants are made under the Intergovernmental Personnel Act to upgrade personnel systems and to finance training assignments of employees from one level of government to another. Much of this is so new that it is difficult to evaluate the effectiveness of either the relationship or the output. Clearly there is a closer partnership that can be a cause of complexity and tension as well as of cooperation.

The federal government has done relatively little so far to move in on the state and local labor relations scene. The Department of Labor is showing restraint but is already beginning to serve as a trainer and clearinghouse and to make the assistance of the Federal Mediation and Conciliation Service available in the solution of impasses at other levels of government. If collective bargaining and unionism continue to grow at their present rate and if certain states are slow and conservative in passing legislation to provide a good foundation for public employment labor relations, then the federal government might possibly want to move in and mandate some standards for this field. This, of course, would raise a new crop of political questions.

THE FUTURE SUMMARIZED

These developments and problems that we have enumerated are all exercises in how people behave, how politicians operate, and how multiple tensions are resolved by our political system. We can predict with some confidence that:

- Public employees will be less ''neutral;'' rather they will be participants, co-managers through their organizations; political forces in their own right.

- The traditional civil service model as we have known it will continue to wither and be perforated but will probably retain some measure of identity particularly with respect to hiring new employees.

- Unionism will continue to grow and professional associations will act more and more like unions; this will give employees a growing sense of participation and responsibility.

- Costs of salaries and benefits will continue to rise, adding to the pressure of the never-ending fiscal crisis.

- There will be continuing pressures, but slow progress, to take in the discriminated-against and the underemployed groups in our society.

- There will be pressure both for and against contracting out public services with mixed results depending on the strength of political strengths in each situation.

- There will be an intensified effort to measure and increase the productivity of public employees along with efforts to limit staffing.

All this will take place in an atmosphere of contention, frustration and worry. This emotional overtone would have been less severe if over the years past we had faced up to political and theoretical realities. It is simply a confusing multifaceted situation with all kinds of groups and all kinds of purposes meeting on the scrimmage ground of public employment. There are many contenders for advantage, many purposes to be served.

None is more important than the goal of high quality service from able employees. To achieve this, management officials have to "hang tough," bargain hard, face political activity openly, and be zealous proponents of equal employment programs. How to reconcile all this is what makes the future anxious.

The Civil Service:
A Meritless System?

E. S. SAVAS
SIGMUND G. GINSBURG

The nation's basic civil service law was written in 1883, following the assassination of President Garfield by a disgruntled job seeker. The goal at the time was both noble and urgent: to assure that the merit principle, rather than the patronage principle, would be used for the selection and promotion of federal employees. Subsequently, in reaction to the excesses of the spoils system which had prevailed for the preceding half-century, a civil service reform movement swept the land, spreading through states, counties, cities, and school systems during the next few decades. Today, the so-called merit system—the name given to the elaborate web of civil service laws, rules, and regulations which embrace the merit principle—covers more than 95 per cent of all permanent federal (civilian) employees, all state and county employees paid by federal funds, most state employees, many county employees (particularly in the Northeastern states), most employees in more than three fourths of America's cities, and almost all full-time policemen and firemen.

However, vast changes in government and society have taken place in the last 50 years, and the rules and regulations appropriate for 1883 have now become rigid and regressive. After 90 years, the stage is set for a new era of civil service reform. Recent court decisions have ruled out several civil service examinations which had no demonstrable relation to the job to be performed; scholars and political leaders recognize the many shortcomings of today's civil service systems; and now the general public is stirring as well. The citizen sees that government—and tax collection—is a growth industry. (If we extrapolate the current rate of growth of the governmental work force, by the year 2049 every worker in America will be a government employee!) He sees that job security (tenure) exists for his "servants" but not for him. State and local governments spend as much as the federal government (excluding defense), and the citizen can see *their* work at close hand in his daily life. And what he sees is *not* a merit system—certainly not in the common usage of the word "merit." The low productivity of public employees and the malfunctioning of governmental bureaucracies are becoming apparent to an increasing number of frustrated and indignant taxpayers. The problem shows up all over the country in the form of uncivil servants going through pre-programmed motions while awaiting their pensions. Too often the result is mindless bureaucracies that appear to function for the convenience of their staffs rather than the public whom they are supposed to serve. It is the system itself, however, rather than the hapless politician who heads it or the minions toiling within it that is basically at fault.

COUNTERPRODUCTIVE POLICIES

Imagine a large, multi-divisional organization with an annual budget of 10 billion dollars. Imagine further that the organization has the following personnel policies and practices:

- Most entry positions are filled on the basis of written examinations scored to two or three decimal places.

- There is no scientifically supportable evidence that these examinations are related to subsequent on-the-job performance.

- Once a ranked list of examination scores is established, management must choose one of the top three names on the list regardless of special qualifications, knowledge, experience, aptitude, or training of other applicants on the list.

- After an employee has spent six months on the job, he is virtually guaranteed the job for life, unless his supervisor files a special report urging that the employee be discharged or at least that the granting of tenure be deferred; it is very unusual for a supervisor to take such action.

- An employee, after acquiring such tenure, can be fired only on grounds of dishonesty or incompetence of a truly gross nature, and cannot be shifted to a less demanding assignment.

- An employee is "milked" of his ability and dedication, while given little significant opportunity for advanced training, personal development, career counseling, mid-career job change, or an enriched job that fully engages his evolving interests; no manager cares about this situation.

- Promotions are generally limited to employees who occupy the next lower position within the same division; qualified employees in other divisions of the organization are discriminated against, as are applicants from outside the organization.

- Promotions are made primarily through written examinations, with no credit given for good performance.

- Salary increases are virtually automatic and, with rare exception, are completely unrelated to the employee's work performance.

- Supervisors belong to unions, sometimes to the same unions as the employees they supervise.

- All personnel practices are regulated by a three-man commission, whose powerful chairman is the Director of Personnel. Managers and supervisors must defer to his judgment on all personnel matters except those involving top-level executives.

- The employee unions have enough political power to influence the decision concerning whether or not the chief executive is permitted to stay on; furthermore, they also influence the appointment of top-level managers.

One does not have to be a management expert to be appalled at this array of counterproductive policies or to predict that the hypothetical organization employing such policies would be laughably ineffective.

Unfortunately, neither the policies nor the organization is hypothetical. The foregoing is an accurate description of the venerable civil service system under which New York City is forced to operate. In summary, the system prohibits good management, frustrates able employees, inhibits productivity, lacks the confidence of the city's taxpayers, and fails to respond to the needs of the citizens. While this bleak picture may not yet be fully representative of all civil service systems in the country, neither is it uncommon. Furthermore, considering that New York often serves as a leading indicator of societal problems, this pattern, if it has not already been reproduced elsewhere, may be soon—unless a groundswell of popular opinion leads to a new wave of reform.

More than half of New York's 9.4-billion-dollar budget is spent on the salaries and fringe benefits of its employees. In the last decade, personnel costs have risen by roughly 150 per cent, while the number of employees has increased by about 75 per cent—to 400,000. (Genghis Khan conquered Asia with an army less than half this size; however, he used certain managerial techniques of reward and punishment which are mercifully denied to today's more circumscribed and more humane chief executive.) Of this number, about a quarter of a million(!) constitute the "competitive class" of civil service—that is, employees who are hired and promoted on the basis of competitive examinations. This is the aspect of the civil service system dealt with here.

In order to understand fully the shortcomings of the current system in New York, it is useful to look in turn at each of its major elements: the jobs themselves, recruitment practices, examinations, selection procedures, promotions, and motivational rewards.

JOBS, RECRUITMENT, AND EXAMINATIONS

Jobs

Very narrow, specialized jobs have gradually emerged, in part because this makes it much easier to produce an examination specific enough to give an appearance of relevance and fairness. Credentialism runs rampant, and prerequisites are sometimes introduced with no discernible value except bureaucratic convenience in the subsequent selection process. As a result, artificial and nonsensical divisions have proliferated, and New York City now has Methods Analysts, Management Analysts, and Quantitative Analysts, as well as Office Appliance Operators, Photostat Operators, Audio-Visual Aid Technicians, Doorstop Maintainers, and Foremen of Thermostat Repairers. When the human cogs in the General Motors assembly line at Lordstown stopped working, it was a clear and obvious revolt against the dehumanizing nature of their activity. Could it be that the human cogs in the municipal machinery stopped functioning long ago, for the same reason, and we are just now indirectly noticing their sullen revolt?

Recruitment

The recruiting process for civil service jobs is similarly arbitrary. The law requires only that advertisements of openings appear in certain specified, obscure places and in formidable terminology: the formal descriptions, in "bureaucratese," of the narrow kinds of specialties mentioned above. The Personnel Department seldom goes far beyond this minimal legal requirement. This means that current employees (and their families) have an advantage over outsiders because they know where to look and how to decode the message. This fact, coupled with job qualifications of questionable value, serves to limit access into the service by other potential applicants.

In fact, this traditional process has been so ineffective that out of exasperation a competing recruiting organization was set up within the Mayor's office, not for dispensing patronage, but for recruiting the kind of professional and technical personnel without which modern government cannot really function. The most capable managers in the entire organization devote much of their effort and ingenuity to subverting and bypassing the regulations in order to hire such recruits from outside the system.

Examinations

About 400 civil service examinations are conducted each year in New York City, at great effort and expense, and about half of them consist primarily of written tests. *Yet not a single case could be found where the validity of a written test— with respect to predicting performance on the job—was ever proven.* That this problem transcends New York's borders is indicated by the following statement by the U.S. District Court in Massachusetts in regard to an examination for police officer:

> The categories of questions sound as though they had been drawn from "Alice in Wonderland." On their face the questions seem no better suited to testing ability to perform a policeman's job than would be crossword puzzles.

Heavy reliance on written examinations at least has the advantage of being "safe." No bureaucrat need be saddled with the difficult task of using his judgment somewhere in the selection process. Exclusive reliance on an "objective" test score creates a situation where no one can be accused of favoritism or overt bias, even though a test may demonstrate inherent discrimination against certain cultural minorities.

At present, candidates who pass an examination are ranked on an eligible list based on their adjusted final average, *carried to as many as three decimal places*. (Adjusted final average is derived from the candidate's scores on the individual tests which comprise an examination: written, practical, technical, oral, etc., plus veteran's preference credit, where applicable.) A manager must appoint one of the top three scorers. Now, no one seriously contends that a person who scores 92.463 on an examination of dubious validity is likely to perform better on the job than someone who scores 92.462, or even 91.462. This scientifically unsupportable custom is just another defense against accusations of bias and should be abandoned. Test scores should be rounded off, thereby creating more ties and giving managers more choice and flexibility in selecting their subordinates from among those candidates with the same score. The potential impact of this change, recently endorsed in New York City by Mayor Lindsay, can be indicated by noting that on the 1968 examination for Fire Lieutenant, 25 men scored between 86 and 87, and 203 scored between 81 and 82.

Another vexing problem with the existing system was described by one frustrated manager:

> The City's unimaginative recruitment mechanism, combined with generally unappetizing work surroundings, makes it virtually impossible to recruit stenographers at the entry level. Accordingly, we keep filling entry-level stenographer positions with candidates who make it through a relatively undemanding stenography test which has been watered down to qualify those with minimal skills. No attempt is ever made to differentiate between candidates on the basis of intelligence, work attitudes, motivation, reading comprehension. Thus, we start with an entry group whose competence has not really been tested—and may well be minimal—and proceed to lock ourselves in by demanding that all candidates for higher level positions be selected from this pool, even though the pool may be drained of some of its best talent over time.

An example of the straitjacket created by this rigid procedure can be found in the agency that needed a mechanical engineer for maintenance of heating, ventilating, and air-conditioning equipment. The experience of the six highest-ranking candidates on the "Mechanical Engineer List" was inappropriate, consisting of machine design, drafting, and the like; the seventh-ranked engineer, however, was ideally suited for the job. Nevertheless, the agency was constrained by civil service rules to hire one of the top three. Only by finally persuading four of the top six to waive their legal claims to the job, thereby elevating Number Seven to Number Three, was the agency able to hire the man with the needed experience.

If any one of the four who reluctantly withdrew had joined the other two of the top six in refusing to do so, the agency would have faced the choice of hiring either no one or someone with an inappropriate background, even though a suitable candidate was available only a few meaningless points further down the list.

SELECTION PROCEDURES: AN INVERSE MERIT SYSTEM

The most surprising finding is that the current legally mandated selection procedure, ostensibly designed to hire the most meritorious applicants into city service, appears to be a failure according to that very criterion: *It discriminates against those applicants who are most qualified according to its own standards.* Candidates with low passing grades are actually *more* likely to be hired than those with high passing grades! Furthermore, this perverse result seems to hold true for all skill levels.

This finding emerged from a careful study of three representative (written) examinations, which span a broad gamut of entry-level skills: Railroad Porter, a position which requires minimal education; Clerk, a position which requires some educational attainment; and Professional Trainee, a job which requires a college degree. Each examination showed the same general pattern—roughly speaking, the *lower* the percentile ranking, the *greater* the number of hires drawn from that percentile group! Conversely, the *higher* the percentile, the *fewer* the number of people hired from it.

Corroborating evidence was found by analyzing a 10 per cent sample of those 1970 and 1971 examinations which resulted in actual hiring: In almost half of the examinations analyzed (14 of 30), none of the four highest scorers was appointed; in a third of the examinations no one was appointed from the top 10 per cent; and in two of the 30 examinations, no one was appointed from the upper half of the eligible candidates.

These anomalous and unexpected results are presumably due to the long delay between the closing date for applications and the date of the first appointment. Delays are produced by a combination of administrative procedures and applicant-initiated protests, appeals, and law suits. The sample of examinations revealed that in 1970, the median delay was *seven months* and the maximum (of the sample) was *15 months.* If we assume that the "best" people score highest, then it seems reasonable to assume that many will find jobs elsewhere and that as time goes on a decreasing number of them will still be available when "their number is called." Analysis of the data showed that the greater the delay, the deeper into the lists one had to dig to find people still willing to accept appointment. When the delay was "only" three months, the openings were filled from the top 15 per cent of the list, but when the delay was six months, hires were drawn from the top 37 per cent, and when the delay was 15 months (for the Clerk examination), it was necessary to dip all the way down to 63 per cent in order to fill the vacancies.

One could argue that this finding is true but irrelevant, and that the 6,000th person on the Clerk list, for example, is really not significantly worse than the fifth, both of whom were hired. But if this assertion is accepted, then one is essentially admitting that the entire examination process is virtually useless.

In summary, as far as drawing new recruits into public employment via examination is concerned, the evidence strongly suggests that *New York City's civil serv-*

ice system functions as an inverse merit system (something the public at large has cynically assumed for years). Although additional verification is needed before this finding can be generalized, at the moment the burden of proof must fall on those who would maintain that New York's civil service really is a merit system in this respect. Indeed, to anyone familiar with both public and private personnel systems, it is quite obvious that large corporations today are much closer to a true merit system than are our governments.

PROMOTION AND MOTIVATION

With regard to promotions, the civil service can be described more accurately as a seniority system than as a merit system. The rules discourage "lateral entry" into upper-level positions by outsiders. This means that one usually starts at the bottom and works his way up, which sounds fine: All organizations find it beneficial as a general practice to promote from within, and their current employees have a natural and desirable advantage over outsiders. In New York's civil service, however, this practice is carried to an extreme and becomes an exclusionary device that limits competition. One frustrated high-level city official offered a striking example of the problem:

> In an occupational area like computer operations, applying the usual rigid procedures denies us the option of hiring experienced computer programmers, systems analysts, and data processing managers. It would force us to appoint only computer programming trainees and to wait for these to be trained and developed by years of experience. This is patently absurd.

The current promotion procedure is as follows: Vacancies in positions above the lowest level in an agency are generally filled by promotion on the basis of competitive examination from among persons holding tenured positions in the next lower grade *in the same agency*. If the Civil Service Commission concludes that there are not enough people available at the lower grade to fill all the vacancies via promotion examination, it may decide to conduct an open-competitive examination as well. An open-competitive examination is open to individuals in other city agencies, to individuals in other grades within the same agency, and to complete "outsiders."

But this openness is illusory. Assuming that the "outsider" has somehow ferreted out the fact that an open-competitive examination is being conducted, he is still at a significant disadvantage compared to the "insiders" who take the promotion examination. Any "insider" who passes the promotion examination will be offered the vacant position before it is offered to anyone who passes the open-competitive examination. Even if one accepted the validity of the examinations, one can seriously question whether it is always better for the public to promote an "insider" who scores 70 than to hire an "outsider" who scores 99.

A study was made of 10 pairs of written open-competitive and promotion examinations given for such positions as engineer, accountant, stenographer, planner, and so on. For each position the promotion and the open-competitive examinations were almost identical. Though the results are not conclusive, they are suggestive, to say the least: The lowest-ranked "insider" was selected over the highest-ranked "outsider" despite the fact that the latter scored higher than the former in all cases but one; "insiders" who averaged 14 points below "outsiders" were nevertheless chosen before the latter. One can legitimately ask how the public interest is served by this policy.

Damning though such findings may be, the worst feature of the promotion system is that an employee's chance of promotion bears no relation to his performance on the job. It is the promotion examination that counts and not performance, motivation, or special qualifications. Distressing examples of the unfairness that this system produces are legion. For instance, a man responsible for the successful completion of an important health program failed to pass the promotion test for Senior Public Health Sanitarian. To all who were familiar with his excellent work, this result was positive proof that the examination was completely invalid. At the top of the list on that examination was someone who has never been able to supervise people and has been mediocre on the job. The demonstrated inability of such tests to predict supervisory competence remains one of the major weaknesses of the examination system.

Given the nature of the promotion procedures, there are relatively few ways in which an agency head, manager, or supervisor can motivate, reward, or penalize his workers. Yearly salary increases are authorized under union contracts, while cost-of-living and comparability adjustments occur automatically for non-union employees. In principle, an outstanding employee can receive a special salary increase, but in fact the vast majority of employees are never really evaluated for such increases, as few agencies and few positions come under this policy. How long will a highly motivated and competent individual be willing to put forth extra effort when he receives no real reward compared with others who do much less? A sensible individual would conclude that instead of spending extra energy and effort on doing his job well, his time would be better spent studying for promotion examinations, or simply relaxing. Also demoralizing for supervisors is the knowledge that it is almost impossible to penalize or discharge the barely competent or even incompetent permanent employee. The administrative procedures involved, the time lags, the large amount of managerial effort needed "to make a case," all force the manager to live with the problem rather than to solve it.

COLLECTIVE BARGAINING VS. CIVIL SERVICE

The single most compelling reason for major reform of public personnel systems—even aside from the mounting evidence of their meritlessness—is the fact that a new system, collective bargaining, has grown up atop the old system, civil service. The enormous growth in membership, power, and militancy of unions of civil servants has resulted in increased protection, wages, and benefits for New York City employees—and in decreased productivity. The ultimate monopoly of power held by municipal unions raises fundamental and disquieting questions about public employee unionism that are not yet resolved.

It is an inescapable fact, however, that union power has produced a second personnel system overlapping and at times conflicting with and negating the civil service system. Job classifications and duties, recruitment, promotion paths, eligibility for advancement, and grievances all fall within the purview of the civil service system, yet all are in fact negotiated, albeit informally, with the municipal unions. Initial selection of employees had remained the one area under the exclusive regulatory authority of the Civil Service Commission, but this, too, is now becoming subject to joint policy determination with the unions.

A strong argument can therefore be made for acknowledging reality and abolishing the civil service system, relying instead on the collective bargaining system. In effect, this has already been done in one area, the municipal hospitals, which have been taken over by the independent Health and Hospitals Corporation. Its employees are no longer civil servants but continue to be represented by a union, and there has been no discernible harm to them or to the body politic. At the very least, a "Blue Ribbon Commission" should be appointed to consider long-term, fundamental reform of New York's civil service system, with particular focus on the overlap between collective bargaining and civil service.

WHAT SHOULD BE DONE?

In trying to prevent itself from doing the wrong things—nepotism, patronage, prejudice, favoritism, corruption—the civil service system has been warped and distorted to the point where it can do hardly anything at all. In an attempt to protect against past abuses, the "merit system" has been perverted and transformed into a closed and meritless seniority system. A true merit system must be constructed anew, one that provides the opportunity for any qualified citizen to gain access non-politically, to be recognized and rewarded for satisfactory performance, and even to be replaced for unsatisfactory service. The improvements that are needed are obvious:

- The principal determinant of promotions should be a performance appraisal and potential assessment system, based upon performance standards and established with union cooperation. Such a system should include an employee's right to review and appeal the appraisal report.

- An individual's salary increase should be a function of his performance. Salary Review Boards with union representation should be established in each agency to set annual guidelines for allocating salary increases in the agency out of a lump-sum annual budget for raises; for example, "standard" performers might get a five per cent raise, "superior" performers a larger one.

- Examinations should be for broad categories of related positions, with "selective certification" used to appoint specialists from within the pool of qualified candidates.

- Written examinations should be employed only where their validity can be demonstrated. Oral examinations should be used more extensively for both selection and promotion. (We are not referring to the kind of "oral examination" now sometimes given—namely, a stilted interview in which competent interviewers are asked to camouflage their reasonable but subjective impressions of the interviewees by asking the exact same questions in the same sequence and giving numerical ratings to the responses. These "oral examinations" are then graded by employees who conscientiously average the interview scores.)

- In selecting new employees, the emphasis should be on evaluation of qualifications, experience, assessment by prior employers, and an oral or practical examination.

- The custom of scoring examinations to several decimal places should be abandoned. Round off the test scores; this will create more ties and give the appointing authority more freedom to use his judgment.

- Positions should be evaluated regularly to weed out rampant credentialism.

- More upper-level positions should be filled at the discretion of management. A good model can be found in the New York Police Department, where the highest rank attainable by examination is captain, and the Commissioner has the authority to assign captains to higher ranks as long as he is satisfied with their performance.

- The system should stop discriminating against "outsiders." Open-competitive and promotion examination lists for a given title should be merged into a single ranked list; alternatively, "outstanding" outsiders should be selected before "good" insiders, and so on. Experience in New York City government should be one of the criteria used in evaluating individuals.

- A flexible system of probationary periods should be instituted, with the duration of the period bearing some logical relationship to the job. The granting of tenure should require a positive act, as it does in universities.

- To improve the performance and motivation of employees, training opportunities should be greatly increased. Job counseling and career planning should be introduced, and tuition-refund plans, evening courses, and released-time programs should all be utilized. Job responsibilities should be enlarged ("enriched") commensurate with employee acceptance. The constricted domain of the unfortunate doorstop maintainer might be expanded to include hinges and doorknobs, and in time even simple locks. So far Victor Gotbaum, the municipality's farsighted union leader, has done more for job training and enrichment than anyone on the management side.

The recommendations presented above would tend to make New York City's system more similar to the federal civil service. The federal system 1) makes far greater use of selective certification; 2) more readily accepts outside applicants for middle and upper positions, and evaluates them on the basis of their education and experience rather than by written examination; 3) bases promotions on performance rather than examination; 4) has a much shorter average time span for promotions; 5) identifies talented individuals early, at the time of the entrance examination; 6) encourages movement between government agencies; 7) is more concerned about training and identification of persons with higher potential; and 8) has a one-year probationary period for new appointees, with positive action by supervisors necessary for retention.

People who have served in both consider the federal system vastly superior to the one under which the city operates. However, some of the recommendations we have made would also apply to the federal government: 1) the need for evaluating duties and responsibilities of positions regularly to insure against demanding greater or different qualifications than the job requires; 2) strengthening the performance evaluation and potential assessment system; 3) doing away with automatic raises and tying them more closely to performance; and 4) making it easier to reward good performers and to demote or remove incompetent performers.

RACIAL AND ETHNIC PROBLEMS

The managerial virtues of such proposed changes are clear, but would they create an even worse problem of racial and ethnic patronage? In New York today, the civil service system is undergoing strain in part because of the widespread belief that to be successful in certain jobs one must possess traits that the system was designed to ignore: culture, class, neighborhood, and other such euphemisms for race and ethnicity. Hence the color-blind hiring practices which successfully staffed city agencies a half-century ago are not well suited for staffing the new municipal agencies that deal with problem families, drug addicts, and unemployed youths. Nor do they adequately provide the recruits needed by a police department whose job has changed significantly and now requires considerable community cooperation for effective crime control. Cultural rapport is vital for success in both the new agencies and old ones facing new challenges.

Ingenious job descriptions (with the adjective "community" frequently in the titles), public employment programs aimed at reducing unemployment in particular neighborhoods, and carefully targeted recruitment campaigns are being used to get around the color-blind system, but such policies have hardly gone unnoticed. Those groups that are already well represented within the civil service decry the "decline in standards," and attack such hiring programs in the courts and at the bargaining table. They may recognize the irrationality of the system, but they fear that civil service reform and greater managerial flexibility will be used to advance newcomers at their expense.

Those major groups that are not yet proportionally represented, black and Spanish-speaking New Yorkers, recognize the irrationality of the system; they are successfully challenging discriminatory examinations which exclude them, and thereby introducing greater flexibility into the system. At the same time, though, they fear that a reformed civil service will allow supervisors the flexibility to discriminate against them.

We conclude that the civil service system is already enmeshed in all the strains of racial and ethnic politics in the grand New York tradition, and that a reformed system would be embroiled in similar, but hardly worse, fashion. This endemic condition, therefore, offers no grounds for abandoning the civil service changes advocated here, changes that are likely in time to provide improved delivery of public services to all citizens and neighborhoods.

THE PROSPECTS FOR REFORM

How can civil service reform be brought about? At first glance, the picture is not very promising. Elected chief executives are understandably wary of the issue, on two counts. First, an attempt at reform might easily lead to demoralization of the work force, with employee resentment leading to a further drastic decline in government performance, to the chagrin of its head. Second, elected officials fear the voting power of the growing army of civil servants. In New York City, the conventional wisdom runs as follows: There are some 400,000 employees. Each one votes himself and influences several relatives and friends. Hence municipal employees represent a voting bloc of more than a million votes, more than enough to ensure victory or defeat. Therefore, the logic goes, don't do anything that might antagonize the work force—and be sure to treat it especially well in election years.

It is not at all clear, however, that this simplistic arithmetic really applies: At least one seventh of the work force lives out of town and is therefore ineligible to vote in New York's municipal elections; voter registration, turnout, and bloc voting may be no greater for civil servants than for other groups; many of those influenced by government employees are themselves in public service and should not be counted twice; and other friends who are not on the public payroll might resent the "good deal" that they attribute to the tenured civil servant, and hence would approve of reform.

Furthermore, candid discussions with many public employees reveal support for civil service reform; able and devoted civil servants—and there are many thousands of them—resent it when they see incompetent co-workers receive equal pay and pass promotion examinations, and they are tired of being vilified by the public for the lethargy of such colleagues. They would respond favorably to sensible improvements, for the overwhelming majority want to be effective in their work and to have pride in their organization. Therefore, the irreconcilable opposition to civil service reform probably numbers far, far less than one million, and political leaders should be able to deal with such opposition by mobilizing the many latent forces for reform.

But for too long there has been a mutually convenient conspiracy of silence among civil service employees, their unions, and public officials about the quantity and quality of work performed, the productivity of government agencies, and the level of service delivered to the public. Employees received security, generous fringe benefits and pensions, and constantly improving salaries. (The top civil service salary is now close to $40,000.) The unions acquired members and political power. The public officials' reward was the possibility of reelection or reappointment. However, that era is drawing to a close as taxpayers demand better performance and as alert political leaders sense the popular mood.

The time now seems right for a long-overdue reform of the civil service. The intent of reform should be to adapt the civil service system to changing times and changing needs in order to bring about more efficient and more effective government. Several of the steps recommended by us were accepted in New York and are being implemented. Although the procedures will generally vary from state to state, many of the changes needed in the nation's civil service system can be effected by the direct and indirect authority of the chief executives. Other changes may require enlightened rule-making by appointed civil service commissions. Still others will require action by state legislatures.

Inevitably, there will be oppositon to any changes, and the dread spectre of the 19th-century spoils system is already being exhumed and summoned to the battlements. Certainly, safeguards will be needed. But the surest safeguard of all is the fact that current political realities have greatly reduced the threat of the spoils system. Today an elected official can best secure his own reelection by creating and maintaining an efficient and effective organization to deliver governmental services to the public. He cannot do this without a competent work force. Trite though it may sound, the best protection against abuses is an enlightened citizenry, demanding performance and accountability of its government, and aided by a vigilant free press. These conditions exist today in New York, and in other places as well.

The argument for reform is overwhelming. The potential future imperfections of a revitalized personnel system are small and distant compared to the actual weaknesses, large and immediate, of today's illusory merit system. Undoubtedly, the prescription should be applied selectively. Some states and cities are still suffering under a corrupt spoils system and can benefit from the kinds of changes introduced long ago by the *first* wave of civil service reform. By far the most common affliction, however, is the rigor mortis of overdeveloped and regressive civil service systems. If these are reformed, no doubt the time will come again, in another 50 or 100 years, when the disadvantages of the system advocated here will outweigh its advantages. At such time, new reforms—reforms that meet the needs of those new conditions—will again be in order, for no system devised by man works well forever.

Three Key Issues in Affirmative Action

CATHERINE LOVELL

As we attempt to implement affirmative action policies, three key issues always arise. *First,* the distinction between affirmative action and "non-discrimination"; *second,* why preferential hiring and the setting of target quotas are necessary to the affirmative action process; and *third,* why traditional standards of "quality" must be reexamined.

Until these issues are resolved, successful affirmative action programs cannot be implemented and substantial progress toward eliminating job discrimination will not be made. Their resolution will require fundamental shifts in individual values as well as changes in some of our collective norms.

UNDERSTANDING THE DIFFERENCE BETWEEN AFFIRMATIVE ACTION AND NON-DISCRIMINATION

The distinction between affirmative action and non-discrimination is the difference between the *active* and the *passive* mode. It is illustrated by the difference between management by objectives and incrementalism. All of our public agencies have been "equal opportunity employers" operating under fair employment practices laws for nearly 30 years. What those laws require are policy statements against discrimination. The absence of overt discrimination has sufficed to meet this standard. Action is left to the individual applicant. Affirmative action, in contrast, requires more than passive non-discrimination by the organization—it demands active programs of broadly applied preferential hiring systems. It requires definition of objectives for redressing employment imbalances and implementation of plans for reaching those objectives.

Setting operational goals, and developing criteria for measurement of progress toward these goals, is much talked about these days in management theory. Administrators, however, still more often than not observe such decision rules more in theory than in the doing, particularly in situations of strongly conflicting objectives and values. Yet, goal setting, action programs, and evaluation are the *modus operandi* of affirmative action. Affirmative action demands more from organizational leaders than lack of prejudice and belief in equal opportunity; operationalizing affirmative action requires leaders to take action stances in which priorities are reordered and time and energy is allocated to affirmative action *above other goals.*

There are many reasons why such a shift is extremely difficult even if the administrator is basically unprejudiced. Many see affirmative action as a diversion from "real" organizational goals. How do we answer the director of a city public works department who says, "My job is to repair roads and keep the storm drains operating. I need the best engineers I can get for that. My job isn't to solve social problems"?

Questions of this variety must be satisfactorily answered if affirmative action is to go forward. Public managers must be convinced to broaden their perspectives and to redefine their standards of performance if the values inherent in affirmative action are to be upgraded to an operational level. This will require new standards for evaluating what is important in public organizations and strategic revisions of reward systems to support new standards.

WHY IS PREFERENTIAL HIRING AND THE SETTING OF TARGETS AND QUOTAS ABSOLUTELY NECESSARY TO THE PROCESS?

Affirmative action guidelines require specified objectives, usually translated into numerical quotas, as minimum goals for the employment of minority individuals and women. Numerical objectives have emerged for the present as the only feasible mechanism for defining with any clarity the targets of action and the criteria for evaluation of progress toward achieving them within a given period of time. Thus, the courts have upheld the validity of goals and quotas in civil rights enforcement efforts and have stated that color-consciousness and sex-consciousness are both appropriate and necessary remedial postures.[1]

Nevertheless, the issue of preferential hiring has assumed the proportions of a major national controversy. The issue is partly one of varying definitions of the situation. Preference and compensation can be seen as words of positive connotation or as words of condescension and disparagement. Preference can be defined as choosing the more highly valued candidate at a given point in time and circumstance, and compensation can be defined as redress for past failures to reach the actual market of human resources available to our organizations. From a very different perspective, these words in combination may be defined as "reverse discrimination."

The characterization of preferential hiring and quotas as reverse discrimination provides a crutch for those who would avoid the changes in organizational behavior required by management by objectives. Obviously, to the extent that quotas as targets for progress become job "slots" and maximums rather than minimums, they perpetuate race and sex discriminations. Otherwise, the argument is diversionary and should be treated as such.

Until we are ready to recognize that years of experience with passive non-discrimination in the public sector have not substantially changed its white, middle-class, male-dominated employment patterns and until we are ready to set objectives wherein results are what counts, it is unlikely that change will take place. Yet, when people with differing perspectives are asked to agree on concrete goals, and must attempt to reach collective agreement on priorities, conflict becomes inevitable.

However, we have learned to submerge conflict in organizations by avoiding explicit goal statements. We escape confrontations by letting statements of *intent* substitute for *action* plans in the most controversial areas. Conflict is also avoided by allowing sub-units to pursue their primary objectives with as little pressure as possible on them to agree on or produce on broader system goals. To the extent that affirmative action clashes with individual values or requires diversion of resources from each sub-unit's highly ranked goals it is met with avoidance or outright resistance. A serious affirmative action program, therefore, demands substantial departures from traditional policy-making practices and managerial styles.

WHY MUST OUR TRADITIONAL STANDARDS OF "QUALITY" BE REEXAMINED?

Most attacks on preferential hiring programs are grounded in the assumption that the quality of performance and work standards will be severely diminished as a result of the systematic employment of minorities and women. They are also grounded in the assumption that few "qualified" Blacks, Chicanos, other minority individuals, and women are available. Both assumptions stand on the third assumption that present criteria of merit and procedures for their application can be accepted uncritically and have yielded the excellence intended. We have not asked ourselves why the use of certain standards has resulted in the virtual exclusion of women and minorities from many professional positions and almost all high-level positions. To the extent that the use of our present standards has resulted in this exclusion (or inclusion in only token proportions), our organizations have been denied access to important sources of intellectual and physical vitality. Thus, the logic of affirmative action says that where a particular criterion of merit, even while not discriminatory on its face or in its intent, operates to the disproportionate elimination of women and minority group individuals, the burden on the organization to defend it as an appropriate criterion rises in direct proportion to its exclusionary effect.

The problems raised by the quality issue are probably the most difficult of those faced in affirmative action. Questioning our accepted standards of quality strikes at tradition and destroys some of the most important groups of our individual self-definitions. The less secure the institution, occupational group, or individual concerned, the more threatening such examination becomes. Degrees and other labels provide a much more comforting definition of quality than does a continuing evaluation of job performance. The more the occupational group is involved in processes of professionalizing itself or is striving for higher status, the greater the tension between those processes and inclusionary requirements. All of these changes increase exclusivity. Attempts at implementation of affirmative action in police departments, for example, are running head on into the federally financed drive to "professionalize" according to traditional measures—particularly degree attainment.[2]

The case of several state colleges in California which are undergoing a change of status from colleges to "universities" provides us with another example. In this instance one of the main criteria for change of status is the number of PhD degree holders on the faculty. Teachers with master's degrees who had been receiving excellent evaluations from deans, peers, and students are suddenly being reevaluated according to a more "professional" standard, i.e., the PhD. Job performance is the same, but some are now being dismissed or not advanced because external criteria have changed. Any attempt to implement affirmative action programs in this atmosphere of degree consciousness is difficult. Suggestions that alternative standards of faculty quality be considered (for example a bachelor's or master's degree plus experience, cultural knowledge, ability to relate to students, ability to serve as a minority role model, and warmth, energy, and decency) are met with fears about lowering standards and allusions to the importance of "quality." We see here two conflicting sets of standards about what is important and what quality means.

Organizational leaders dedicated to pursuing inclusionary policies must be prepared to meet the "quality" issue head on. The development of alternative measures of accomplishment is essential to the success of affirmative action programs at this period in time. A complex of social factors has combined to exclude minorities and women from the higher levels of formal educational attainment, and great numbers have pursued avenues of development other than that of formal education. Yet, their experience paths prepare them to bring new perspectives, different values, and perhaps even equal or higher capabilities to many public jobs. If, as we say, our objective is the best person for the job, we are *committed* to affirmative action.

Finally, in the broadest sense, a public employee group representative of the differing values and various perspectives in our total society is essential to public accountability. Any procedures which exclude multiple experience paths and disparate values from organizations *will* in these terms *lower standards* of public accountability as well as organizational effectiveness.

NOTES

1. For a summary of court decisions regarding quotas, see Herbert Hill, "Preferential Hiring, Correcting the Demerit System," *Social Policy.* July-August 1973, pp. 96–102.
2. For further discussion of this problem as it relates to an actively professionalizing sheriff's department, see Catherine Lovell, "Accountability Patterns of the Los Angeles County Sheriff's Department," *Institute on Law and Urban Studies,* manuscript, November 1973.

Public Administration as a Profession: Problems and Prospects

RICHARD L. SCHOTT

A strong-running current in the mainstream of contemporary public administration is the assumption that its practice is, or could become, a profession. The pages of the *Public Administration Review* and related journals are laced with references to the "profession" of public administration. The National Association of Schools of Public Affairs and Administration (NASPAA) has issued a clarion call for the adoption by member institutions of a "matrix of professional competencies" as a guideline for graduate education in the field and has established a committee on professional standards. As ennobling and attractive the aura produced by such references to professional public administration, they are misleading: public administration, as the practice of public management, is not now and has little chance of becoming a true profession.

Perhaps part of the confusion stems from popular misunderstanding of what "profession" and "professional" really mean. In the crudest sense, and the one common in everyday parlance, professional is simply the opposite of amateur—work for which one is paid. Thus we have "professional" life insurance salesmen, "professional" carpet cleaners, even "professional" pest exterminators. But in the scholarly literature of the professions, derived largely from sociology, the term profession refers to occupations which exhibit certain rather carefully specified characteristics. Two early students of the professions, and the first to examine them in detail, identified as their central elements a special technique acquired by extended training, a sense of collegial responsibility, and the existence of a professional organization which has the power to insure the competence of practitioners and to enforce ethical standards. It was basically specialized technique, "acquired as the result of prolonged training," they concluded, "which gives rise to professionalism and accounts for its peculiar features."[1]

Among sociologists who have studied the professions in depth, William Goode suggests that two characteristics are "sociologically causal." These are: (1) lengthy training in a body of specialized, abstract knowledge, and (2) a service ideal or orientation. From them flow such attributes as a profession's control over the curricular content and quality of its schools of training, a strong collegial relationship among its members, legal recognition of the profession and the licensing of its practitioners, and relative freedom both from lay control over the profession and from lay judgments as to the quality of the professional service performed. Especially important, he argues, is the sense of community: professionals share values and perceptions (and often an esoteric language) and exercise substantial peer control over their colleagues.[2] Although there is disagreement among scholars as to the essential or core characteristics of professionalism, there is substantial congruency in definition. Among attributes commonly cited by these and other observers are the possession of systematic or scientific knowledge, a service ethic, self-policing by fellow practitioners, extended formal training, and the existence of codes of ethics.[3]

The historical route by which an occupation becomes established as a profession, suggests Harold Wilensky, progresses through certain stages which are common to most professions. The process of professionalization begins with the emergence of a full-time occupation which develops a self-conscious concern for the development of schools for the training of practitioners. These schools of training, at first organized outside of the universities, gravitate toward association with them. Professional organizations then emerge, followed by a struggle over defining the central tasks of the practice between the old guard, who were trained largely through raw experience, and the new practitioners who emerge in increasing numbers from the professional schools. Next, the emergent profession struggles with neighboring occupations over the boundaries of professional activity; a drive for licensing and legal recognition proves successful; and finally, codes of ethics and mechanisms for their enforcement appear. Those occupational groups which have completed the transition to a full-fledged profession, Wilensky argues, are medicine, law, the clergy, university teaching, dentistry, architecture, accounting, and some fields of engineering.[4]

Scholars from fields other than sociology have also contributed to an understanding of the nature of professions. Especially relevant to an examination of the professions and public administration is the analysis offered by Don K. Price, whose study of the relationships between science and government led him to a consideration of the societal roles played by four basic groups or "estates"— science, the professions, administration, and politics. These estates can be arranged along a continuum from the search for truth (science) at the one end to the exercise of power (politics) at the other.

FIGURE 1   THE FOUR ESTATES (After Don K. Price)

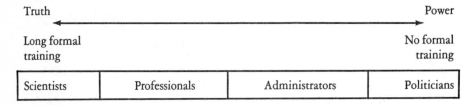

Science is concerned with the discovery of knowledge; the professions with the application of knowledge; politics with the selection of ends or values; administration with the translation of these ends and values into practice (thus setting the parameters for the activity of the professions where they intersect with government). Entry into the scientific estate requires the longest and most specialized training and is the most meritocratic and peer-oriented; entry into the political estate requires no formal training at all, access to it being granted by the electoral marketplace. In terms of career development, it is relatively easy to move from left to right along the continuum: a scientist may become a professional, a professional an administrator. But movement in the opposite direction is usually difficult, due largely to the time and effort required to gain the requisite knowledge for the adjacent, more "knowledge-intensive" estate on the left. Movement from left to right also involves a decrease in status: pure scientists look down on "applied" professionals, professionals on administrators, administrators on politicians. What is especially striking in Price's analysis is the hard distinction between the professional and the administrator. These for him are two separate activities, two worlds, two estates distinguished by their own norms and values.[5]

In light of current scholarly views of the nature of professionalism, the practice of public administration can hardly be ranked among the professions. It exhibits few if any of the attributes commonly associated with professional status. First of all, its stock of systematic, coherent knowledge is slim indeed. Despite attempts to establish the study of administration as a science, first by Luther Gulick and his colleagues in the 1930s[6] and after the failure of this attempt by Herbert Simon in the 1940s,[7] public administration as a field of intellectual inquiry has yet to develop a body of systematic, scientific theory or knowledge. The impediments to such a development described by Robert Dahl several decades ago—the inclusion of normative values, the unpredictability of human (administrative) behavior, and the problem of cross-cultural consistency—are still salient today.[8] The attempt to create a science of public administration has remained, however, a theme in the literature of the post-World War II period and is among the driving forces behind a behavioral approach to its study. A stronger (and, I would argue, more generally accepted) thrust, dating back at least to Paul Appleby's *Policy and Administration*,[9] has been an emphasis on the study of public administration as part of the political process and on its political environment—on administration as politics rather than on administration as science. This thrust has helped move the center of gravity of the field away from science and towards the "politics" end of Price's continuum.

PROFESSIONAL SCHOOLS

Another commonly accepted dimension of professionalism is an extended period of technical training in professional schools as a requisite for professional practice. Here again the weak position of public administration is evident. The employment of the generalist administrator in the public service is almost never contingent on the applicant's possessing a degree in public administration or public affairs, nor do schools of public affairs and administration control the entry of their graduates into practice. The vast bulk of officials at the middle and upper levels of the public service not only do not hold degrees in public affairs or administration, but have little if any formal training in the field. John Corson and Shale Paul, in their sample of federal executives at levels GS16-18 (including PL 313 appointees) found that only three per cent reported public administration as their field of study,[10] and John Honey has estimated that the number of public officials at "responsible levels" who come from a background of training in public administration is probably not more than four per cent.[11] The failure of schools of public affairs and administration to dominate (or even strongly influence) recruitment to the public service may be due in part to a lack of evidence that formal training is essential to superior performance on the job. As one student of the professions observes, neither public nor business administration, as fields of academic study, has demonstrated that the training they provide the practitioner is really superior to raw experience in business or public life.[12]

Whereas curricula in the professional schools are accredited by the relevant educational organizations, the parallel organization for public administration, NASPAA, has yet to develop and apply accreditation standards for its member schools (as have professional school associations in law, medicine, engineering, social work, etc.) Indeed, it appears that a majority of schools of public affairs and administration will fight any attempt at accreditation—which they view as a move toward stultifying conformity. Part of what has inhibited the growth of accreditation in public administration and public affairs education is disagreement over what an accredited curriculum should cover, a situation which reflects the lack both of systematic knowledge in the field and of consensus as to its "core."

Dispute as to what would constitute a core curriculum has led to wide diversity in course offerings and approaches of the various schools of public affairs and administration. Some emphasize administrative management, with a concentration on public personnel, budgeting, organization, and methods courses and the like—a curriculum built around the older POSDCORB approach. Others pay attention to public management, but at the same time require the student to pursue the study of a particular functional or policy area, such as urban affairs, criminal justice, higher education, or social services. Still others construct a curriculum around the study of policy making and policy processes, hoping to produce policy analysts and researchers as well as administrators. Further, there is great variation in the degree to which the various curricula are prescribed; the number of required courses varies from two or three to a completely prescribed program.

SENSE OF COMMUNITY

On a third measure of professionalism, a sense of community, public administration also ranks low. This may stem from the fact that the number of practicing generalist public administrators is so vast—probably several millions in all governmental jurisdictions—as to inhibit the development of shared values, cohesiveness, or community. And the variety of functional specialties in which public administrators move may exacerbate the problems caused by sheer size. There is, moreover, no one "professional" organization to which a majority of practicing public administrators belong. The membership of the American Society for Public Administration (ASPA), the closest thing to a broadly based professional organization in the field, is miniscule compared to the number of practitioners. Nor is ASPA representative of its practitioner membership in the way in which, for example, the American Medical Association speaks for physicians or the American Bar Association for lawyers.

Finally, it is obvious that public administration has yet to develop peer control over the quality of work performed by its practitioners. Public administration is practiced almost exclusively in large bureaucratic organizations, where the assessment of the individual's performance is made by his superior in the organizational hierarchy rather than by his peers. Hierarchical rather than collegial control of the quality of work is the rule. Nor has public administration gained legal recognition of its status. In such professions as law and medicine, for example, professional practice may, under state statute, be undertaken only by those who have completed training at an accredited school and passed a general, state-regulated examination—the medical boards, the bar, etc. Such, obviously, is not the case in public administration. And it is readily apparent that public administration lacks a code of ethics and the mechanisms for the enforcement of such a code.

In sum, on none of the more often-cited indices of professionalism does the practice of public administration rank very high. It may be an occupation, an activity, an applied art—but it is most certainly not a true profession. In terms of Wilensky's process model of the development of a profession, public administration would appear to be at the beginning of the stage where the new, school-trained practitioners are beginning to challenge the old guard. Whether this challenge will prove successful and whether the field will develop further along the lines Wilensky describes is doubtful.

"ADMINISTRATOR—PROFESSIONALS"

It is at least ironic that at the same time as generalist public administration, as a field of practice, has been struggling to become more professional (and thereby more respectable), the practice of public administration at the upper levels of government has become the province of scientists and the established professions. The public service *has* become professionalized, not because of the development of the field of public administration, but because governments have relied increasingly on scientists and professionals to do their work. Dependence of government on professional talent is especially striking at the federal level, where professionals make up nearly a quarter of federal white-collar workers. Accompanying the flow of scientists and professionals into the public service has been their movement into positions of executive and managerial leadership and the emergence of a breed of what could be called "administrator-professionals" (as opposed to professional administrators), persons hired originally for their professional and technical competence who have moved into administrative positions.

That the administrative and policy-making leadership of the federal Executive Branch has become the province of science and the professions is suggested by a number of studies. Corson and Paul found that a significant proportion of upper-level federal civil servants whom they studied were professionals, and that a majority of them hold supervisory positions.[13] Lloyd Warner and his associates have stressed the professional educational backgrounds of many of those at the upper reaches of the federal service.[14] An analysis of the occupational categories of federal executive positions (GS 16 to 18 and equivalent) provided by the U.S. Civil Service Commission demonstrates the rather startling fact that scientific and professional categories (physical and natural sciences, medicine, law, and mathematics and statistics) account for over two-thirds (68 per cent) of all federal executive positions and thus are accessible only to those with scientific or professional training. Occupational categories encompassing non-professional, generalist positions (those of "administration," "fiscal," and "personnel") account for less than one-third.[15] Even this one-third figure may overstate the number of federal executives from non-professional backgrounds, since at least some of these positions are held by persons originally trained in such professions as law and engineering. One could hazard the guess that the number of persons from scientific and professional backgrounds in the top three grades of the federal service is closer to

75 per cent. Not only do the scientific and professional estates dominate the upper reaches of the federal career service, but they are beginning to bulk large in the second tier of political appointees (formerly Schedule C, now "Non-career Executive Assignments") as well.

The executive-level professionals have for the most part left the practice of their profession for administration. They are much more likely to be involved in the administration of men, money, and programs than in the application of professional technique. Many have consciously chosen the administrative "track" as a route to career advancement and better remuneration. A recent study of the engineering profession in the federal service suggests that by the time the engineer reaches the upper-middle levels of the civil service (GS 14 and 15), his work is at least half if not predominantly administrative rather than technical in nature, and that as he moves up further in his organization, administration becomes his primary activity.[16]

The domination of the upper reaches of the federal Executive Branch by those trained in the professions rather than in public affairs and administration is among the most important issues facing the public service today. The implications of this dominance have been discussed in some detail and with great insight by Frederick Mosher, who warns that the pre-eminent position of a professional elite has a limiting effect on the breadth of analysis and quality of decisions made at the top levels of the federal service. Through its reliance on professionals, government has increased its ability to cope with complex, technical public problems, but it has at the same time given to professionals substantial influence over the administration of public programs and the definition of their content. Once ensconced in public agencies, professionals attempt to stake out organizational territory and reserve it for their peers, to protect their colleagues through self-governing career systems, and to remove their protected areas of decisions from outside or overhead political control. Due partly to their socialization and extended training in a particular technical area, professionals often bring a narrow perspective to bear on broad public policy issues, a perspective distorted by their professional lenses. The influence of professional cadres, Mosher warns, may be "gradually but profoundly moving the weight toward the partial, the corporate perspective and away from that of the general interest."[17]

Mosher's argument may somewhat overstate the problem. Socialization, it is generally recognized, is a process which takes place over the entire lifetime of an individual. Granted that the attention of the professional schools (through which the budding professional is socialized at a very impressionable time in his intellectual development) to public affairs, public policy, and the political environment is meagre indeed, one should not overlook the possibility that the professional may, during his tenure in a public agency, be socialized further to broader, more "public" norms. This, certainly, would appear to be an important and fruitful area for future research.

One development which offers at least a partial solution to the problems raised by Mosher is the growth, especially at the federal level, of training programs intended to educate the prospective administrator-professional to managerial techniques and responsibilities. A variety of continuing education courses have emerged, spurred in part by the requirement that all new supervisory personnel be given a prescribed minimum of appropriate training. Several of these are especially tailored to the needs of the professional. For attorneys, the U.S. Civil Service

Commission (CSC) offers a short course in management; for engineers, it conducts a week-long Management Institute for Supervisory Scientists and Engineers designed to provide, among other things, an appreciation of the tentativeness and ambiguity of the administrative environment and an insight into the psychological tensions which often accompany the professional's adjustment to it. The CSC has also encouraged federal agencies to develop similar programs; some agencies, among them the Department of Defense, the National Institutes of Health, and the National Bureau of Standards, have moved on their own to provide mid-career training in management and supervision for their professional and scientific cadres.

Also emerging are a scattering of programs beyond those at an introductory level. The CSC, for example, now offers a course for officials at GS-15 and above in the management of scientific and engineering organizations which emphasizes the political environment of administration, including an appreciation of an agency's relationships with Congress and with interest groups. And through its Executive Seminar Centers, the Commission offers scientists and engineers a two-week seminar in Science, Technology and Public Policy.

Open to question, however, is whether these and similar training courses address the more basic issues which the ascendancy of the administrator-professional raises for the quality of the public service, especially the biases which professional perspectives exert on these executives as they approach the broader issues of public policy formulation, execution, and evaluation. It is doubtful that such continuing education programs as those mentioned above go very far in counteracting the norms, attitudes, and views of the political process to which the professional was socialized during his professional education.

These observations as to the lack of professional status of those trained in public affairs and administration and the domination of the higher levels of (at least) the federal public service by science and the professions are not meant to disparage the attempts of schools of public affairs and public administration to educate their students, nor are they meant to suggest that public administration, because it is less than a profession, is therefore less desirable or less important a societal activity. On the contrary, the training of talented men and women for positions of responsibility in public life by schools of public affairs and administration remains of great importance. The training their graduates receive often provides them with a breadth of view, an understanding of the approaches, modes of analysis, and paradigms of other disciplines and professions—a socialization to more comprehensive, "public interest" norms which may lead eventually to a leavening of the professional, corporate perspective found at the middle and upper reaches of the public service.

What the threads of the argument do suggest is that these schools take an open and honest look at their aspirations, claims, and potential for education for the public service. One response may well be the continuation of the present diversity of curricular emphases and patterns, for there will continue to be a need for (and acceptance of) the young graduate trained at the master's degree level in public affairs and administration. The fact that schools of public affairs and public administration are not "professional" need not mitigate against their making a substantial contribution to the public service. Dwight Waldo, for example, has suggested that training in public administration may in some ways be similar to that in medicine—drawing on the contributions of a range of (social) sciences as its theoretical base. Public administration, he proposes, might "try to act as a profession without actually being one, or perhaps even without the hope or intention of becoming one in any strict sense."[18]

Another approach, and one which has great potential for making a contribution to the quality of the public service, is consciously to increase the interaction of schools of public affairs and administration with the professions—both with those of their practitioners already in governmental positions and with their schools of training. Such interaction might take the form of increased emphasis by schools of public affairs and administration on continuing education for those professionals who already hold responsible administrative positions or who are likely to attain such positions. It might also take the form of greater dialogue and liaison with existing professional schools, including the continued expansion of dual or joint degree programs between them and schools of public affairs and the development of public administration or public affairs options within the professional schools themselves. This approach is especially appropriate for schools of engineering and law, whose graduates provide a steady stream of talent for governmental agencies.[19] Public affairs education, in short, may complement, rather than compete with the education of those who are or will become administrator-professionals.

The implied caveat is that public administration become more modest in its claims to professionalism. Such modesty may enhance the quality of its contribution to the practice of public affairs and avoid a frustration of its scholars, educators, and practitioners due to impractical or impossible aspirations.

NOTES

1. A.M. Carr-Sunders and P.A. Wilson, *The Professions* (New York: Oxford University Press, 1933), pp. 284ff.
2. William J. Goode, "The Theoretical Limits of Professionalization," in Amitai Etzioni (ed.), *The Semi-Professions and Their Organization* (Free Press, 1969), p. 277; "Community Within a Community: The Professions," *American Sociological Review*, Vol. 22, No. 2 (April 1957), pp. 194–195; "Encroachment, Charlatanism and the Emerging Profession," *American Sociological Review*, Vol. 25, No. 6 (December 1960), pp. 902–914.
3. See, for example, Bernard Barber, "Some Problems in the Sociology of Professions," in Kenneth S. Lynn (ed.), *The Professions in America* (Boston: Houghton-Mifflin, 1965), pp. 18–19; Ernest Greenwood, "Attributes of a Profession," in Sigmund Nosow and William Form (eds.), *Man, Work and Society* (New York: Basic Books, 1962), pp. 214–215; and Wilbert E. Moore, *The Professions: Rules and Roles* (New York: Russell Sage, 1970), pp. 4–16.
4. Harold Wilensky, "The Professionalization of Everyone?" *American Journal of Sociology*, Vol. 70, No. 2 (September 1964), pp. 138–139.
5. Don K. Price, *The Scientific Estate* (Cambridge, Mass.: Harvard University Press, 1965), pp. 120–269.
6. Luther Gulick and L. Urwick (eds.), *Papers on the Science of Administration* (New York: Institute of Public Administration, 1937).
7. Herbert Simon, *Administrative Behavior* (New York: Macmillan Co., 1947).
8. Robert Dahl, "The Science of Public Administration," *Public Administration Review*, Vol. 7, No. 1 (Spring 1947).
9. Paul Appleby, *Policy and Administration* (University, Ala.: University of Alabama Press, 1949). The development of the study of public administration as a discipline in

its own right, Dwight Waldo observes, is "too ambitious in believing . . . that it is possible to identify and develop a coherent body of systematic theory which will be substantially independent of other social sciences and will concern itself only with *public* administration." See his "Scope of the Theory of Public Administration," in James C. Charlesworth (ed.), *Theory and Practice of Public Administration: Scope, Objectives and Method* (Philadelphia: American Academy of Political and Social Sciences, 1968, p. 9.

10. Those from the professions of law, medicine, engineering, forestry, engineering, and accounting, on the other hand, made up 49 per cent of the sample. John J. Corson and L. Shale Paul, *Men Near the Top* (Baltimore: Johns Hopkins Press, 1966), p. 167.

11. John C. Honey, "A Report: Higher Education for the Public Service," *Public Administration Review*, Vol. 27, No. 4 (November 1967), p. 301.

12. Wilbert Moore, *op. cit.*, p. 123. I know of no research which focuses directly on the relevance of education in public affairs and administration to the career progression of public officials. It would be most useful to trace the careers and performance of those, for example, who entered public service with backgrounds in public affairs and administration education compared to another group with similar characteristics who came from other fields. It is quite possible that the relationship between public affairs education and performance in the public service is much weaker than often assumed.

13. Corson and Paul, *op. cit.*, pp. 97–102.

14. Lloyd Warner, Paul van Riper, et al., *The American Federal Executive* (New Haven: Yale University Press, 1963), pp. 107–141.

15. U.S. Civil Service Commission, *Executive Manpower in the Federal Service: March 1973* (U.S. Government Printing Office, 1973), p. 8.

16. Richard L. Schott, *Professionals in Public Service: The Characteristics and Education of Engineer Federal Executives* (Beverly Hills, Calif.: Sage Publications, 1973), pp. 16, 20.

17. Frederick C. Mosher, *Democracy and the Public Service* (New York: Oxford University Press, 1968), pp. 132, 210–212.

18. Waldo, *op. cit.*, p. 10.

19. The growth of joint or dual degree programs between these schools and those of public affairs and administration has been substantial over the past decade. Roughly a dozen programs combining the study of law and public affairs/administration are currently approved by the American Bar Association, including those offered at Syracuse University, Ohio State University, Indiana University, and Harvard. There are also a number of programs which combine engineering of public works with public affairs/administration, including those at the University of Pittsburgh, Indiana University, the University of Cincinnati, the University of Michigan, and the University of Southern California. New programs in these two areas are currently under consideration or awaiting final approval at several institutions.

9

THE IMPACT OF PUBLIC EMPLOYEE UNIONISM

Collective bargaining in government in this country dates in many ways from 1954 in New York City, after which, in 1959, Wisconsin became the first state to authorize public employees' organizing and bargaining collectively. Although unionism has been declining in the private sector, it has been growing rapidly in government.

Labor-management relations in the federal government has been greatly altered since 1962, when President Kennedy fulfilled a campaign promise by allowing federal employees to organize. By late 1976, 1.2 million federal employees were organized into exclusive bargaining units in fifty-four departments and agencies. The Federal Labor Relations Council—consisting of the chairman of the U.S. Civil Service Commission, director of the Office of Management and Budget, and the secretary of labor—is responsible for the general supervision of the labor-management relations program.

However, it is principally at the state and local levels where this relatively new phenomenon has had its greatest impact. Public employees are highly organized and exert considerable political clout. Strikes or threats of strikes to suspend essential services can pressure public executives to submit to union demands. Moreover, public management's authority is frequently diffused. In government the negotiation of public employee contracts has often appeared to be unaffected by the kinds of economic restraints that are recognized by labor and management in the private sector. The actual impact of public employee unions is still far from clear.

In the first article in this chapter, union leader Jerry Wurf explains from his perspective how the merit system and unionism interrelate. In many states and localities, there is actually a "dual" personnel system, in which both the civil service and the contract influence public employees and government personnel practices. Sometimes these dual systems reinforce the worst aspects of both, limiting public executives' ability to manage.

Regarding the actual impact of employee unionism in local government, Raymond Horton and his associates studied the situation in Chicago, Los Angeles, and New York City; their findings appear as the second article in this chapter.

Merit: A Union View

JERRY WURF

The winds of change that blew Franklin D. Roosevelt into the White House and gave birth to the New Deal nationally were ominous winds for civil service employees in the State of Wisconsin. The first Democratic state administration in 40 years was carried into office with the FDR victory. With jobs a scarce commodity, Democrats in the executive and the legislature wasted little time before turning to the business at hand: finding work in state government for the faithful.

The state's civil service system, enacted in 1905 and one of the best in the country at the time, was to be chopped up at the expense of the cadre of career civil service employees assembled during the LaFollette Progressive Republican years. To fend off this assault, state employees, with support from LaFollette administrators who were genuinely opposed to the spoils system, banded together into what became the Wisconsin State Employees Association. Through lobbying and political activity they saved the civil service system. The association stayed together and prospered. Today it is the nation's largest public employee union—the American Federation of State, County, and Municipal Employees (AFSCME).

The phenomenal growth of the union in recent years and the ballyhooed "new militancy" of the public worker has shaded over those modest beginnings. There has been a common assumption among many students of public employee labor relations, including many who are actively involved, that the rising chant for full collective bargaining on wages, hours, and working conditions by public workers inevitably amounts to capital punishment for civil service as a personnel tool in public administration.

It isn't true. The emphasis that AFSCME and a few other unions have placed on collective bargaining should not be seen as an abandonment of the merit ideal. It merely reflects a firming-up into policy of a view which has been held for many of us who have been intimately involved with the civil service during the past 20 years: that the civil service or merit system is first, second, and finally, management's personnel tool.

WHAT IS MERIT?

Merit means different things to different people. What I mean by merit is a set of standards set up by management which permit a reasonable and objective judgment of an applicant's ability to perform a job. The criteria may include education standards, tests, or experience requirements. The criteria must vary to fit the job, must reasonably relate to the work to be performed, and must be insulated from politics, favoritism, and caprice on the part of management. Those who meet the criteria should qualify, but from among those who qualify, the senior employee should be chosen. Merit, as we see it, involves meeting a basic standard—not running a foot race with the world.

Merit plays an important role in civil service administration. It provides a point from which collective bargaining can begin. But however well-intentioned public management may be, it cannot unilaterally devise a merit system that will provide objective, third-party treatment for public employees.

To pose an "either—or" relationship between merit and collective bargaining is to ignore reality. Both have a legitimate place in government labor-management relationships. Both are here to stay. Our union's International Constitution, the document binding on every AFSCME local, lists among the union's seven central objectives this one: "To promote civil service legislation and career service in government."

When we speak of merit, we primarily are concerned with the procedure under which employees are recruited and, in some instances, promoted or awarded tenure. We do not, of course, believe that "civil service" or "merit" should pose a roadblock to bilateralism between public employees and their employer. From the founding days of the union, a constant source of irritation has been the tendency on the part of management to rationalize all sorts of rules and arbitrary procedures by calling them "civil service" procedures.

The distinction between principle and system posed by David Stanley is a useful one:

> What do we mean by merit systems? We should distinguish them from the merit principle under which public employees are recruited, selected and advanced under conditions of political neutrality, equal opportunity and competition on the basis of merit and competence. Public employee unions do not question this principle in general and have done little to weaken it. . . .
>
> When we say merit systems, however, this has come to mean a broad program of *personnel management* activities [emphasis supplied]. Some are essential to carrying out the merit principle: recruiting, selecting, policing of anti-political and anti-discrimination rules, and administering related appeals provisions. Others are closely related and desirable: position classification, pay administration, employee benefits and training. Unions are of course interested in both categories.[1]

We see merit as a personnel system defined and controlled by management in pursuit of reasonable recruitment, promotion, and classification policies for its work force. It's the bosses' system—one that they have substituted (voluntarily or otherwise) for the old political patronage selection process.

By removing the protections of merit and collective bargaining in public employment you might or might not get an increase in productivity from the work force. There should be no inclination for our national government to forego individual freedoms and to adopt totalitarian methods on the grounds that democracy may be less efficient than fascism. We feel the same way about employee protections.

FIGHTING POLITICS IN PERSONNEL

Far from seeking to move away from merit, public employee unions probably have been more faithful to the merit ideal than any of the other components in public service.

Political leaders who profess devotion to the merit principle, for example, undercut it all the time. Mayors from California to New Hampshire and governors from right to left have taken the whole of management and a good part of the upper echelon supervisory staff and sought to keep it outside of the civil service system. The key criteria for filling these vacancies becomes politics, and so men who could not successfully manage a candy counter (a disproportionate number of them lawyers) are put in charge of large and complex departments. Predictably, services deteriorate and the departments function chaotically, if at all. The civil service and the employees take the rap.

There is another manifestation of this political manipulation. Lincoln Steffens wrote at the turn of the century of the "boodle" system in which politicians looked upon payoffs and graft as appropriate cogs in the wheels of government.[2] This went beyond the filling of jobs through political hirings to the actual shaking down of contractors and the like.

These political shakedowns aren't so common any more. Still, a Vice President of the United States took a great fall recently when his misdeeds as a county executive and governor were brought out into the light of day. Like polio, spoils no longer is epidemic, but the germs are still around.

Much more commonplace in 1974 America is a new kind of patronage—a more subtle form of scratch-my-back government in which whole service delivery programs are doled out by contracts with private companies. Frequently those companies have executives who are friendly to the political leadership, but even when that isn't the case the potential for corruption runs high. Maybe it's not "boodle," but Steffens wouldn't like it, because its impact is the same: a deterioration of services in the absence of accountability by the private service agent to the taxpaying public.

If the politicians don't speak up for merit, then, should we not at least expect civil service commissioners and administrators to do so? Perhaps, but the reality is that the commissions lack jurisdiction when it comes to persuading legislators, and legislators often have their own agenda. Civil service associations proclaim a devotion to "merit," but by relying solely upon lobbying and suasion as subordinates they become supplicants in a process that is first of all political.

COLLECTIVE BARGAINING AND CIVIL SERVICE

The size and impersonality of government can be overwhelming to the individual worker. In the absence of an outlet for expression, public employees may perform their jobs in mechanical, uncommitted ways. The collective bargaining process and the input it affords is no panacea but it gives the employee a degree of involvement which strengthens his perception of his role and of the work he performs. It guarantees the worker a degree of consideration in the decisions that affect him.

We see the civil service and collective bargaining processes meshing in this way:

- Recruitment by management, on the basis of merit and fitness. The union's role is that of a watchdog in this instance, insisting that merit and fitness be uniformly defined and non-discriminatory, and that requirements bear some reasonable relationship to the work involved (e.g., does a trash collector really need a high school diploma?).

Merit procedures must be used to assure that a job applicant can do the job—not necessarily that he can do it better than anyone, anywhere. If one must, to qualify for a typist position, type 60 words per minute, that is well and good. But it does not follow that an applicant typing 70 or 80 words a minute is the better qualified.

Similarly, one need not be Charles Atlas to qualify for a strenuous job. It is enough that the merit criteria properly measure the health and fitness of the applicant to perform the job.

- Promotion on the basis of merit and fitness—but the rules must be negotiable. Seniority must be the key determination for distinguishing between qualified applicants.

Among professional employees there is perhaps a caveat to be made, and that is that seniority alone is not always enough for distinguishing between candidates for a job—although it remains an important consideration.

In these instances, it may be possible to devise a formula combining education, experience, and general seniority in such a way as to fairly protect the interests of the employees involved and still guarantee that the position is filled by a suitably equipped individual. But promotion mechanisms should be subject to bargaining. There should be employee input into every step in the promotion process, and there must be equal access to promotions through job vacancy postings and regular, conveniently scheduled testing procedures. Promotion decisions should always be subject to the grievance machinery, and, again, insulated from politics, favoritism, and capriciousness.

- Bilateral determination of wages, within a rational classification framework. The rules governing that framework must be negotiable.
- Bilateral determination of fringe benefits, and other conditions of employment.
- Job retention based on merit and fitness, subject to a bilaterally established grievance mechanism that ends with final, impartial, and binding arbitration.

A UNION VIEW OF AFFIRMATIVE ACTION

There is a sticky problem that has become a fact of life in both public and private personnel offices—and that is the certain conflict that comes from an official (if late-blooming) desire by management to open up new job opportunities for women, blacks, and other minorities, while maintaining a practice of last-hired, first-fired in case of layoffs and reductions-in-force.

It is a legitimate social dilemma—but a dilemma that is broader than the immediate personnel problem on a given day in a given agency. Our union, for one, has no quarrel with affirmative action and other efforts to open up job opportunities. We were advocating those policies long before Title VII of the Civil Rights Act made true believers out of public administrators.

But it is unfair and outrageous for administrators to hide behind affirmative action requirements as an excuse for circumventing seniority rules. If the City of Hartford suddenly discovers that it has an all-white police force, then let it devise a means of rectifying that shameful situation—but not at the expense of the incumbent work force.

Nor is there any legitimacy to the argument that public employees, once organized, will become "too powerful" and tilt the employee-employer relationship through the use of political power and pressure. Public employees, after all, tend to be rather conservative, conscientious people. While there have been and will be instances of confrontation between employees and management over economic questions and perhaps even on occasional questions of policy, anyone who believes that organized public workers are on the brink of reordering the social fabric simply misreads the desire of the men and women who work for government to be a part of a reasonable system.

A COUNTER-FORCE TO POLITICS

In the absence of organization, however, we have a long history of abuse and political manipulation which victimizes public employees, making them pawns in a rather cruel patronage game, but also victimizing taxpayers by robbing them of decent services. One need not harken back to Steffens and Ida Tarbell for examples. As recently as 1971, an otherwise decent new liberal governor in Pennsylvania sought to replace thousands of low-paid state highway workers with new employees who happened, like the governor, to be Democrats. It took a monumental effort by the union, newly certified to represent these workers, to convince the governor that a worker's political preferences were a private matter, and that the state had no right to intrude into them, nor to dilute the delivery of public services through political manipulation.[3]

There are still those, of course, who view collective bargaining as inimical to the well-being of taxpaying America, even as there still are those who will break the silence of a morning bus ride arguing that the decline of civilization as we know it can be measured from the advent of the New Deal. With widely varying degrees of enthusiasm, however, most of public management has accepted the arrival of public employee unionism and "bargaining" (although what passes for bargaining is a subject for another, longer article). The fact that in some jurisdictions unionization has not yet occurred and therefore bargaining is unheard of should not be viewed as a flag for a merit system that works. There is, after all, a tomorrow. Many public officials and employer groups have begun to see the advent of bargaining not as a death-struggle to preserve or upend the status quo but rather as a new approach to serving the public interest.[4] Why shouldn't government work more efficiently if there is a "partnership of equals," as Governor Dan Evans of Washington State has called it, between public management and public employees?[5]

There need be no confusion about the functions of management and the functions of labor in that partnership. They are separate and distinct, but with common objectives: to provide decent public services to a demanding public. There is a role for merit, but it mustn't be the only game in town. The fusing of merit with bargaining is essential to maintaining a dignified management-labor relationship and to assuring a working partnership in the achieving of excellence in the public service.

NOTES

1. David T. Stanley, "What are Unions Doing to Merit Systems?" *Public Personnel Review* (January 1970), as cited in Harry H. Wellington and Ralph K. Winter, Jr., *The Unions and the Cities,* (Washington, D.C.: The Brookings Institution, 1973).
2. *The Shame of the Cities,* 1904.
3. "Unionization Delivers Body Blow to Patronage Power," *The Philadelphia Evening Bulletin,* March 18, 1974, p. 2.
4. See, for example, David D. Rowlands, "Unions Enter City Hall," *Public Management,* Vol. XLVIII, No. 9 (September 1966), pp. 244–252.
5. Speech before a Symposium on Equity and the Public Employee, sponsored by the Coalition of American Public Employees and the American Arbitration Association, March 25, 1974, in Washington, D.C.

Some Impacts of Collective Bargaining on Local Government: A Diversity Thesis

RAYMOND D. HORTON
DAVID LEWIN
JAMES W. KUHN

In recent years, government has grown faster than any other sector of the American economy. This growth has been accompanied by a major expansion of public employee unionism and collective bargaining. Consequently, widespread scholarly interest has developed in public sector labor relations, particularly the structure of collective bargaining and the process by which bargaining decisions are reached. Relatively little attention, however, has been paid to the impacts of collective bargaining on governmental management.

Utilizing a diversity-of-impacts theory, this paper discusses some of the conceptual and methodological approaches useful in an impact analysis of labor relations decisions in the public sector.[1] Central to the theory is the notion that the impacts of public sector labor relations decisions on governmental management reflect sharp differences that exist among and even within governments with respect to structural, political, organizational, and union variables.

TRENDS IN GOVERNMENT EMPLOYMENT, PAY, AND UNIONISM

Between 1960 and 1973, public employment in the United States grew by more than 60% or approximately 25% faster than employment in the private nonfarm sector of the economy.[2] The increase was especially sharp in state and local government where employment rose almost 78% over this 13-year period. Employment advanced more rapidly in state than in local government (89 versus 74%), but more than two and one-half times as many persons, 8.3 million, were employed in the latter sector than in the former in 1973. Employment growth rates varied substantially among state and local government functions, with the largest increases recorded in public welfare (161%), health (120%), education (102%), corrections (91%),[3] general control (72%), hospitals (63%), and police (57%). However, growth rates were large in virtually all public categories compared to the overall growth rate in the private economy (35%).

While the number of government employees has grown rapidly since 1960, public payrolls have risen even faster. For example, average monthly earnings of full-time employees of state and local governments increased 112.3% during the 1960–1973 period. Average hourly earnings in the private nonfarm sector rose three-fourths as much, 86.1%, and manufacturing earnings increased but 79.6%. Government workers who enjoyed the largest earnings increases over this period were employed in hospitals (132%), fire protection (123%), general control (119%), police protection (119%), health (115%), and highways (115%). These increases were all greater than earnings changes in the high-wage private construction sector (110%). So rapid and large have been the earnings increases for public employees that many of them now are paid more than their private sector counterparts (Perloff, 1971; Fogel and Lewin, 1974). These rates of pay increase may help explain why payroll costs represent well over half of all state and local government expenditures, and also why state and local governments accounted for more than 61% of all government purchases of goods and services in 1973, compared to 49.6% just six years earlier (Joint Economic Committee, 1974: 2). Government compensation expenditures now are claimed by some (Kuhn, 1972) to be an important element of modern inflation in the United States.

Finally, government workers continue to join unions and employee associations in record numbers, and to push for collective bargaining rights in public employment. In the federal sector, 52% of all employees were members of labor organizations in 1970, although much of this membership was concentrated in the postal service (Goldberg, 1972). More important, by 1972, slightly more than half of the 8.3 million full-time state and local government employees had enrolled in unions and employee associations (Labor Management Relations Service, 1975:1; hereafter, LMRS).[4] The extent of employee organization in the public sector is particularly impressive when compared with private industry, where about 25% of all wage and salary workers belong to unions and employee associations, and 30% in the nonagricultural sector (U.S. Department of Labor, Bureau of Labor Statistics, 1972: 72).

In response to the heightened organizational activity of public employees, governments at all levels have attempted to formalize and treat labor relations as a functional specialty. In the federal government, the framework for labor relations was established in 1962 by President Kennedy's Executive Order 10988, and was subsequently modified by Executive Orders 11491 and 11616 in 1969 and 1973, respectively (see Taylor and Witney, 1975: 545–556). By 1973, two-thirds of American states had enacted legislation providing for some form of collective negotiations in their respective public sectors (U.S. Department of Labor, 1973), and in every one of the 50 states at least some governments engaged in such negotiations (LMRS, 1975: 1). In summary, government has been a major source of growth in the American economy since 1960 and an important arena of labor relations activity.

ASSUMPTIONS ABOUT THE PUBLIC AND PRIVATE SECTORS

The aforementioned developments raise major questions about the role of collective bargaining in the public sector and the impacts of unionism and collective bargaining on various dimensions of governmental management and operations. In addressing these issues, both scholars and policymakers generally have emphasized the peculiarities of the public sector; specifically, their analyses stress essential differences between the private and public sectors. Representative of this view are Wellington and Winter (1971: 8), who claim that "the public sector is *not* the private, and its labor problems *are* different, very different indeed." Differences indeed do exist, though to us some are not as pronounced as they appeared initially and others are more important than usually recognized.[5]

The difference identified earliest and to which the most attention has been paid concerns the legal position of government. Elected officials possess or are delegated rights that did not, at first glance, easily mesh with the concept and practice of collective bargaining. The problems of introducing collective bargaining and of adjusting legal perspectives to produce a tolerable fit with the "sovereignty" doctrine have been examined closely, and we have little to add to this literature. Suffice it to say that the sovereignty doctrine is withering away as the practice of collective bargaining continues to grow in government.

A second celebrated difference between the public and private sectors is the monopoly aspect of governmental services (Wellington and Winter, 1971).[6] Often, consumers have no, or few, alternatives; even if they choose not to avail themselves of a publicly provided service, they nevertheless must pay for it through taxes. However, not all state and local governmental services occupy a monopoly position. For example, alternative private services are typically available in sanitation and transportation. Some consumers have purchased protective services in the private market to supplement police protection. Given time for adjustment through relocation, some consumers can escape a government's high taxes. The costs and feasibility of alternatives to local government services cover a wider range than has been recognized and deserve further exploration, for they may be important determinants of manpower utilization and collective bargaining outcomes in the public sector. The diversity of government services needs to be emphasized, rather than being considered monolithic simply because they are publicly provided.

A third difference between public and private employment pertains to personnel administration. Civil service and the practices characteristic of it form a more common and broader personnel system than ever existed in private industry before, and probably even after, workers employed in that sector turned to collective bargaining. However, civil service systems vary markedly in operation from one government to another. The interaction of collective bargaining with civil service systems appears to produce a variety of outcomes that can be delineated, although much more work in this area is required.[7]

A fourth difference between the public and private sectors, only recently mentioned in the literature (see Fogel and Lewin, 1974; Lewin, 1974), but appearing to be one of signal importance, is governments' egalitarian pay structure: pay differentials between high and low positions are narrower in the public than in the private sector. Individuals in low positions—unskilled, blue-collar, and entry level white-collar jobs—enjoy higher pay in public than in private employment, while the opposite appears to be true for those in high positions—professionals, managers, and executives. Significantly, these pay patterns antedate the development of unions and collective bargaining in the government sector. The egalitarian pay structure in government also provides a set of constraints and opportunities for negotiators on both sides of the bargaining table not present for bargainers in the private sector. The effects of relatively well-paid public employees working in various capacities, directed by managers who are relatively poorly paid, deserve careful scrutiny by those concerned with collective bargaining in government.

A DIVERSITY MODEL

Certainly as a consequence of the four major differences mentioned above, labor relations and patterns of manpower utilization in the public service display some features not found in the private sector. To focus on these differences as a key to understanding governmental labor problems, however, may mislead both scholars and policy-makers. It implies that government officials face unique problems and can expect little or no help from examining the solutions devised in the private sector. Similarly, it is unwise to assume that collective bargaining processes and solutions to industrial relations problems developed in the private economy provide "the answer" for public managers. In fact, managers and union leaders in private employment have elaborated a wide variety of roles, styles, procedures, and approaches to labor and manpower problems. They respond in many different ways because the situations in which they find themselves and the purposes they pursue are widely different.

Too often, observers of the labor scene implicitly assume a model of private sector labor relations and manpower management that describes only the manufacturing sector—and, more precisely, a model descriptive of large production firms and large industrial unions. In it, managers retain the initiative in directing employees, while the union concentrates its activities through grievance procedures on deflecting or modifying the thrust of managerial decisions. Alternatively, in other models, such as those provided by organized musicians and workers in the building trades and garment industry, union leaders have assumed a number of functions in decision-making areas usually regarded as strictly managerial, such as hiring, layoffs, and discipline. In some of these industries as well as in others, workers' representatives play important roles in strategic decisions affecting plant location, investment, subcontracting policy, and accounting methods, as well as wages, hours, and working conditions. Grievance handling plays a far less important part in labor relations patterned after the second model than the first.

If differences in labor relations and patterns of manpower utilization *within* the private sector are as wide and significant as suggested here, imputed differences *between* the public and private sectors may well be exaggerated and even misleading. For example, public employees not only bargain for benefits over the negotiating table, but through voting and other political activities may also punish or reward their employing managers. In the private sector, some unions occupy an analogous position. The coal miners' union, as a large stockholder in several coal-producing and transportaion companies, has "sat" on both sides of the bargaining table; the garment unions and the Teamsters in local trucking are powerful enough in their respective industries to influence small employers directly as well as through collective bargaining.

Exaggeration of the differences between the public and private sectors arises not only from assuming more uniformity in private industry than actually exists, as noted above, but also from ignoring the diversity in the public sector with respect to control devices, organizational structures, services, and occupational and work groups. We believe this diversity, which is rooted in historical, legal, functional and political features of government, contains several implications for public sector labor relations. There may be no a priori reason to assume that labor relations in New York City ever will closely resemble those in Chicago or Los Angeles, even after formal collective bargaining has been introduced in Chicago and has matured in Los Angeles.[8]

The foregoing discussion suggests, then, that to conceive of governmental labor relations as sui generis and to hypothesize that only one pattern of union impact on public sector management will occur, overlooks the diversity of organizations, relationships, and impacts that may occur even within a single jurisdiction. Thus, a diversity model of public sector labor relations and collective bargaining impacts seems especially appropriate.

THE IMPACTS OF COLLECTIVE BARGAINING ON GOVERNMENTAL MANAGEMENT

All but the most inconsequential political decisions produce impacts, latent as well as manifest, that change some patterns of relationships in the political system. The most important evidence in analyzing the impact of political decisions concerns the exchange or redistribution of resources that usually (but not always) accompanies a political decision. The process leading up to a political decision and the decision itself may permit hypotheses about decisional impacts, but observation of actual resource exchanges is necessary to translate hypotheses into findings (see Horton, 1974).

As noted earlier, labor relations and collective bargaining decisions appear to be playing an increasingly important allocative or redistributive role in American government, especially at the local government level. While some evidence and much speculation has surfaced concerning the impact of public employee labor relations on government, little systematic, comparative research has been conducted.[9] Five impact areas warrant particular analytical concern: compensation, service production and delivery, personnel administration, formal governmental structure, and informal politics.

Compensation

The level of wages (or, more accurately, total compensation) which induces or maintains employment in a given organization represents perhaps the most important labor relations exchange. This is true in public or private organizations, and it is true whether or not employees are organized and bargain collectively with management to establish wages.[10]

Popular opinion is divided over the cause of the relatively rapid increase in public employee wages that has occurred in the United States during the last two decades. One school of thought emphasizes the emerging political strength of public workers, including their organization and, in some jurisdictions, the introduction of collective bargaining, while another branch of opinion interprets public sector wage developments as essentially economic phenomena whereby intersectoral wage differentials were erased or even reversed by exceedingly strong demand for public services (see Wellington and Winter, 1971; Hayes, 1972; and Ehrenberg, 1973).

Our inclination, at present, is to view both explanations, standing alone or in conjunction, as overly simplistic and incapable of explaining what appears to be an extremely diverse pattern of wages and wage development—not only within and between the aggregate private and public sectors, but within and between private and public industries.

There are, to be sure, considerable data which suggest that for certain occupations in the public sector wages are higher than for comparable positions in the private sector,[11] but this neither establishes the political explanation based on emerging public sector bargaining nor disproves the explanation centered around market considerations. That the causal scenario is more complex is indicated by the fact that some public workers were paid as much, if not more, than comparable private employees *before* public sector unionization and bargaining and *before* the strong demand for public services that emerged in the 1960s (see Smith, 1975).

Service Provision and Delivery

Here we refer to collective bargaining impacts on work rules and procedures (broadly defined), manning schedules, job assignments, and the like. According to some industrial relations theorists (Kuhn, 1968: 284–309), organized workers in the private sector of the American economy are concerned primarily with protecting their "property in work" as reflected in the detailed provisions of collective agreements and the informal working rules of the shop, office, and factory. While this claim may be accurate as a generalization, it covers a wide variety of practices and relationships—ranging from a situation in which bargaining occurs only over wages and fringe benefits to one in which the union plays a major role in production, marketing, and financial decisions.

It has been argued (Wellington and Winter, 1971: 137–153) that workers in the public sector seek to negotiate over a broad range of employment-related issues, and that the impact of bargaining upon governmental management policy and decision-making will be greater than in industry. (For a contrary view, see Gerhart, 1969). Alternatively, however, our diversity thesis suggests major differences among and within local governments in the extent to which unions endeavor to bargain over or "control" so-called management rights. For example, in Chicago's local government, where formal collective bargaining does not exist outside of the educational sector, some public employee unions—the building trades,

Teamsters, and Service Employees International Union (SEIU)—to a considerable degree control access to city jobs. None of the labor organizations in cities with more "developed" labor relations systems (for example, New York and Los Angeles) exercises similar control. In New York City, several important unions, including firemen, police, teachers, and municipally employed interns and residents, negotiate over hours of work and job assignments, but other unions limit their concerns to grievance procedures and/or compensation. In Los Angeles, public employee labor organizations are also differentially concerned with service production and delivery issues; however, in response to the bargaining efforts of these organizations, the city and county governments now are attempting to identify more accurately public managers, devise incentive systems appropriate to their functions, and hold them more closely accountable for the performance of their departments, bureaus, and agencies. Further empirical work is necessary, of course, to fully identify the impacts of collective bargaining on governmental service production and delivery, but preliminary evidence supports the view that these impacts will be diverse rather than singular.

Personnel Administration

Most students of the governmental labor relations-personnel interface see substantial conflict between the emergence of collective bargaining and traditional civil service (i.e., "merit") rules.[12] We neither see nor predict inherent pervasive conflict between collective bargaining decisions and merit rules, but, rather, diverse impacts on merit administration resulting in some instances in a strengthening and in other instances in a weakening of traditional merit rules.

Our central hypothesis is that labor relations conflict in this area is concerned not with merit rules per se, but with deep-seated divisions between labor and management regarding control over the rules by which employees are selected, promoted, and disciplined (see Lewin and Horton, 1975). Thus, where merit rules are supportive of control over the personnel process, management will assert and unions will attack traditional merit concepts in collective bargaining; but where management's personnel goals are inconsistent with merit rules, the positions of labor and management with respect to the validity or lack thereof of merit rules will be reversed.

This hypothesis appears to rationalize much of the seemingly contradictory discussion of union impacts on personnel administration recorded in the literature. Seniority, for example, clearly is not a merit rule, but it is gradually being implanted in personnel systems where unions possess substantial bargaining power. Many unions that have succeeded with respect to seniority also have succeeded in instituting the rule-of-one, an appointment procedure clearly more consistent with the merit concept than the rule-of-three, management's generally preferred position.

Adding additional validity to this diversity thesis is the fact that public managers and public unions appear to have differing degrees of allegiance to the merit principle.[13] Finally, we suspect that differences in the scope of bargaining and in bargaining power among and within jurisdictions further weaken the notion that collective bargaining and unionism in the public sector will lead to "zero-sum" impacts on merit rules.

Government Structure

In order to promote and administer the public policy of collective bargaining, most governments have instituted structural as well as legal changes in their institutional make-up. In some instances, existing agencies such as personnel boards have been charged with the responsibility for representing management in collective bargaining, but for the most part new labor relations departments have been created specifically for this purpose. Furthermore, many collective bargaining programs create independent or quasi-independent agencies responsible for administering labor relations and providing third-party assistance in conflict resolution.

In addition to structural additions, accretions of power and responsibility to new agencies from traditional overhead and line agencies are likely to occur when formal collective bargaining programs are instituted in government. Personnel commissions, budget bureaus, line agencies, and even legislative bodies quite often lose authority (sometimes not reluctantly) to new administrative agencies.

The structural impacts of unionism and collective bargaining on government have received relatively little scholarly attention. Most academics (for example, Burton, 1972) who have studied this phenomenon have concluded that the impact of new labor relations programs has tended to centralize previously fragmented personnel decision-making systems.[14]

While fragmentation of managerial structure and authority is, in our opinion, an impediment to the development of effective labor relations in the public sector, for a variety of reasons we are not as sanguine as others about the presumed centralizing effects of new labor relations programs and institutions. First, the formal dispersion of political power, particularly at the local governmental level in American cities, is so well-advanced that political "end-runs" around newly designated labor relations agencies and actors remain possible. Second, and closely related to the above point, one must distinguish between formal and informal power structures. The mere act of creating new labor relations institutions and delegating to them responsibilities to make decisions previously reached elsewhere in government does not mean, in fact, that the locus of control over decision-making also changes. Third, in certain cities where public employees are well-organized and politically strong, formal bargaining programs may result in a redistribution of power from public officials to municipal unions. This may represent a form of centralization, but not of the kind customarily anticipated by academics or public officials.

Again, we return to a more plausible hypothesis than the centralization thesis— namely, that diverse impacts on governmental structure will result from the promulgation of formal collective bargaining systems. In a sense, our focus here shifts from the concerns of industrial relations and economic analysis to those of political science and public administration.

Politics

One rationale for the introduction of formal collective bargaining programs into government has been to insulate labor relations from the unwholesome reach of "politics," but we are struck with the vigorous and often successful attempts of political actors, particularly mayors, to use emerging labor relations systems for their own political purposes. This has occurred despite the wide differences in politics and public employee labor relations among New York, Los Angeles, and Chicago.[15]

At first glance, it might be assumed that the rapid growth of public employment and public employee organizations virtually dictates that mayors pursue policies of accommodation rather than conflict over not only the introduction of formal bargaining into government but also over bargaining itself. Collective bargaining settlements would appear to be a rich source of "patronage" for mayors seeking wider political constituencies.

Closer examination of the politics of municipal labor relations, however, discloses a number of quite varied mayoral reactions to public employee unionism. In Chicago, where a centralized party apparatus works closely with powerful private sector unions, Mayor Daley has vigorously opposed the formalization of bargaining. He has sustained this position by pursuing a high-wage policy under that city's "prevailing rate" system. In New York, however, where party organizations are fragmented, Mayors Wagner and Lindsay were influential proponents of extending bargaining rights to municipal workers, though not entirely for the same reasons. Both mayors reaped important electoral benefits from civil service unions during critical election campaigns. The Los Angeles situation is more complex, in part because of the chief executive's more diffuse governing responsibilities in that city; but it appears that Mayor Bradley, unlike his predecessor, Samuel Yorty, realizes both the potential managerial problems and political opportunities posed by public employee unionism. Bradley is emerging as a key actor in that city's youthful labor relations program.

POLICY AND RESEARCH IMPLICATIONS

Public policies designed to regulate state and local government labor relations are in flux. To date, these policies largely have been constructed in the absence of impact analysis—a sequence which violates the policy scientist's admonition that policy-making should reflect, rather than precede, analysis of various policy options and their consequences.

While several policy implications ranging from the macro to the micro level are suggested by the aforementioned diversity thesis and discussion of collective bargaining impacts on government management, only two will briefly be considered here. The first is the issue of comprehensive labor relations. If, as the present analysis indicates, divergent labor relations processes and impacts reflect functional adaptations to the peculiarities of state and local governments, it is questionable whether a comprehensive federal law should be enacted to regulate labor relations at the state and local level. Instead, federal legislation based on the "minimum standards" concept may be preferable either to extending the National Labor Relations Act to the public sector or to instituting a "model" public sector labor relations law.[16]

A second important policy issue germane to this paper concerns public employee strikes. For various reasons, we are skeptical about the dominant (though not exclusive) view that favors blanket no-strike laws in the public sector. Once again, recognition of clearly disparate political and bargaining relationships within and among governments argues for a more sophisticated approach to the admittedly serious problem of public sector strikes than simply (and often unsuccessfully) prohibiting them. Similar difficulties are raised by the use of compulsory arbitration as a substitute for public sector strikes. The rationale for a no-strike/arbitration law may be far stronger in one jurisdiction than another, and applicable only to some, not all, employee groups within a single jurisdiction.

With respect to research implications of the present study, perhaps the key point is that collective bargaining impacts on governmental management must be examined longitudinally, if they are to be understood and properly evaluated. This is particularly true in those impact areas which are at best only partially amenable to quantitative analysis—for example, service production and delivery, personnel administration, and government structure. This is not to gainsay the importance of cross-sectional studies or survey data in the examination of public sector labor relations; indeed, these methodologies dominate the current literature on this subject. Rather, it is to emphasize the special value of the longitudinal method in analyzing the dynamics of a public sector labor relations system.

Finally, the diversity thesis and the accumulating evidence regarding public sector labor relations, especially the impacts of collective bargaining on governmental management, could well be used as a basis for reexamining labor relations in (and public policies governing) the private sector of the American economy. Much of what we presume to know about the latter sector has taken on connotations of the conventional wisdom and rests, in part, on old evidence. The aforementioned reexamination not only would challenge this conventional wisdom, it also would represent a "revised sequence" of research in this field—i.e., using the accumulating knowledge about *public sector labor relations* to better understand those in industry.

NOTES

1. This paper is based on an as yet uncompleted study of public sector labor relations in New York City, Chicago, and Los Angeles which is being supported by the Ford Foundation and U.S. Department of Labor and conducted under the auspices of the Conservation of Human Resources Project, Columbia University. The larger study relies on a variety of research methodologies and data sources to analyze the diversity-of-impacts thesis outlined in the paper. The central empirical concern, the impact of labor relations decisions on the five areas described in this paper, is being analyzed longitudinally through data collected in on-site research and cross-sectionally through a survey of 2,200 American cities. The survey questionnaire is designed by the authors and administered by the International City Management Association.
2. Unless otherwise indicated, all data presented in this section were obtained from U.S. Department of Commerce, Bureau of the Census (1961 and 1974).
3. For corrections, the change reported is for the 1961–1973 period; 1960 data for this function were not available.
4. Previous estimates had placed state and local membership at only about 33%. See Steiber (1973) and U.S. Department of Labor (1971).
5. Assumption of major differences between the public and private sectors leads to another familiar theme: prediction of dire outcomes resulting from collective bargaining in government. For a critique of these assumptions and additional insights into the approach followed in the present study, see Lewin (1973).
6. Wellington and Winter (1971) feel that the existence of such monopoly requires the imposition of restrictions on the bargaining activities of organized public employees.
7. A framework for analyzing these impacts is provided in Lewin and Horton (1975).

8. The development of collective bargaining in New York City government is reviewed in Horton (1973 and 1971). Chicago has received little analysis in terms of its municipal labor relations system, but see Derber (1968) and Jones (1972). The Los Angeles experience is analyzed in Lewin (1976).
9. For a general critique of the literature of public sector labor relations, see Lewin (1973).
10. It should be kept in mind, despite the heavy attention paid to the impact of collective bargaining on wages in both sectors, that wages of a substantial majority of private workers (75%) and more than half of public workers are not established by collective bargaining.
11. Publications of the regional offices of the Bureau of Labor Statistics comparing salaries and benefits of municipal workers with those of private sector counterparts show that in most metropolitan areas public workers are better compensated. These comparative surveys, unfortunately, were not begun until 1970.
12. For a thorough review of the literature, see U.S. Department of Labor, Labor Management Services Administration (1972). See also Morse (1973) and Stanley with Cooper (1971: 32–59).
13. For instance, the Lindsay administration in New York City for eight years attempted through a variety of administrative initiatives to circumvent certain strictures of the "civil service" system. One of Mayor Beame's first formal acts upon succeeding Lindsay in 1974 was to issue an executive order replacing the rule-of-three with the rule-of-one. Civil service unions also display divergent attitudes toward merit rules. Unions based on departmental rather than citywide units often favor closed rather than open promotional exams.
14. For a different viewpoint emphasizing the fragmentation theme, see Kochan (1971), Horton (1973), and Lewin (1976).
15. New York City represents a "mature" system—that is, one in which the institutional and legal structures surrounding formal collective bargaining are well-entrenched (see Horton, 1975). Los Angeles, including both the City and County, may be characterized as a "transitional" system moving from an informal to a formal labor relations system (see Lewin, 1976). Chicago's public sector labor relations system for the most part remains underdeveloped. For a description of the Chicago system, see Jones (1972: 195–226).
16. A discussion of the minimum standards concept and various types of federal labor legislation for public employees is contained in Bureau of National Affairs (1974: B12–19 and F1–9).

REFERENCES

Bureau of National Affairs (1974) Government Employees Relations Report 575 (October).
BURTON, J. F., JR. (1972) "Local government bargaining and management structure." Industrial Relations 11 (May): 133–139
DERBER, M. R. (1968) "Labor-management policy for public employees in Illinois: the experience of the Governor's Commission, 1966–67." Industrial & Labor Relations Rev. 21 (July): 541–558.
EHRENBERG, R. G. (1973) "The demand for state and local government employees." Amer. Econ. Rev. 3 (June): 366–379.
FOGEL, W. AND D. LEWIN (1974) "Wage determination in the public sector." Industrial & Labor Relations Rev. 27 (April): 410–431.
GERHART, P. F. (1969) "Scope of bargaining in local government labor negotiations." Labor Law J. 20 (August): 545–553.
GOLDBERG, J. P. (1972) "Public employee developments in 1971." Monthly Labor Rev. 95 (January): 56.

HAYES, F. O. (1972) "Collective bargaining and the budget director," pp. 89–100 in S. Zagoria (ed.) Public Workers and Public Unions. Englewood Cliffs, N.J.: Prentice-Hall.

HORTON, R. D. (1975) "Reforming the municipal labor relations process in New York City." Study prepared for the State Charter Revision Commission for New York City (January).

———— (1974) "Public employee labor relations under the Taylor Law," pp. 172–174 in R. H. Connery and G. Benjamin (eds.) Governing New York State: The Rockefeller Years. New York: Academy of Political Science.

———— (1973) Municipal Labor Relations in New York City: Lessons of the Lindsay-Wagner Years. New York: Praeger.

———— (1971) "Municipal labor relations: the New York City experience." Social Sci. Q. 52 (December): 680–696.

Joint Economic Committee, Council of Economic Advisers (1974) Economic Indicators, February 1975. Washington, D.C.: Government Printing Office.

JONES, R. T. (1972) "City employee unions in New York and Chicago," Ph.D. dissertation, Harvard University.

KOCHAN, T. A. (1971) City Employee Bargaining with a Divided Management. Madison: University of Wisconsin, Industrial Relations Institute.

KUHN, J. W. (1972) "The riddle of inflation: a new answer." Public Interest 27 (Spring): 63–77.

———— (1968) "Business unionism in a laboristic society," pp. 284–309 in I. Berg (ed.) The Business of America. New York: Harcourt, Brace & World.

Labor Management Relations Service (1975) Labor Management Relations Service Newsletter, Vol. 6, No. 3. Washington, D.C.: Labor Management Relations Service.

LEWIN, D. (1976) "Local government labor relations in transition: the case of Los Angeles." Labor History 16.

———— (1974) "Aspects of wage determination in local government employment." Public Administration Rev. 34 (March-April): 149–155.

———— (1973) "Public employment relations: confronting the issues." Industrial Relations 12 (October): 309–321.

———— and R. D. HORTON (1975) "Evaluating the impacts of collective bargaining on personnel administration in government." Arbitration J. 30 (September): 199–211.

MORSE, M. M. (1973) "Should we bargain away the merit principle?" Public Personnel Rev. (October): 233–243.

PERLOFF, S. H. (1971) "Comparing municipal salaries with industry and federal pay." Monthly Labor Rev. 94 (October): 46–50.

SMITH, S. P. (1975) "Wage differentials between federal government and private sector workers." (unpublished manuscript)

STANLEY, D. T. with the assistance of C. L. Cooper (1971) Managing Local Government Under Union Pressure. Washington, D.C.: Brookings.

STEIBER, J. (1973) Public Employee Unionism: Structure, Growth, Policy: Studies of Unionism in Government. Washington, D.C.: Brookings.

TAYLOR, B. J. and F. WITNEY (1975) Labor Relations Law (second ed.). Englewood Cliffs, N.J.: Prentice-Hall.

U.S. Department of Commerce, Bureau of the Census (1974) Public Employment in 1973. Washington, D.C.: Government Printing Office.

———— (1961) State Distribution of Public Employment in 1960. Washington, D.C.: Government Printing Office.

U.S. Department of Labor (1973) Summary of State Policy Regulations for Public Sector Labor Relations: Statutes, Attorney Generals' Opinions and Selected Court Decisions. Washington, D.C.: Government Printing Office.

———— (1972) Directory of National Unions and Employee Associations. Washington, D.C.: Government Printing Office.

_____ Bureau of Labor Statistics (1971) "Labor union and employee association membership." News Release (September 13).

U.S. Department of Labor, Labor Management Services Administration (1972) Collective Bargaining and the Merit System. Washington, D.C.: Government Printing Office.

WELLINGTON, H. H. and R. K. WINTER, JR. (1971) The Unions and the Cities, Studies of Unionism in Government, Washington, D.C.: Brookings.

10

GOVERNMENTAL BUDGETING

Budgeting is one of the most important games played in government. Key actors at the federal level include individual public agencies, the Office of Management and Budget, the president, and the appropriations committees in both houses of Congress. The scenario is not terribly different in many states and localities. Choices, rules, and timetables are invariably involved. Budgetary decisions are some of the most important in public administration.

Some of the key questions students should ask about governmental budgeting are

Who are the participants in the budgetary process?

What roles do these participants play?

How do these participants, interacting as a system, affect government spending?

Aaron Wildavsky addresses these questions in his classic analysis of the politics of federal budget making. Largely because of the nature of budgetary politics as it turns out, budgets do change, but incrementally, from year to year, they change only modestly.

One of the several attempts to reform or alter the budgeting process occurred during the Johnson presidency with PPBS—planning, programming, and budgeting systems—which sought to link annual budgeting with multiyear planning and careful analysis. It generally did not succeed.

The current reform proposal, called ZBB (zero-base budgeting), was used by President Carter when he was governor of Georgia and has since been instituted in a number of states and localities. In the next two articles, Peter Pyhrr explains ZBB and the reasons for it, then President Carter tells why he is committed to implementing ZBB throughout the federal government.

In a final article on ZBB, James Wilson, with tongue in cheek, suggests the possible result of trying to implement ZBB. As Wildavsky told us at the outset, it is very difficult to alter the politics of budgetary routines in Washington, in state capitals, and in city halls.

The Budgetary Process

AARON WILDAVSKY

For our purposes, we shall conceive of budgets as attempts to allocate financial resources through political processes. If politics is regarded as conflict over whose
preferences are to prevail in the determination of policy, then the budget records
the outcomes of this struggle. If one asks "who gets what the (public or private)
organization has to give?" then the answers for a moment in time are recorded in
the budget. If organizations are viewed as political coalitions,[1] budgets are
mechanisms through which sub-units bargain over conflicting goals, make side
payments, and try to motivate one another to accomplish their objectives. In a
study such as this, which stresses the appropriations process in Congress, the
political context of budgeting can hardly be overemphasized.

The making of decisions depends upon calculation of which alternatives to consider and to choose. Calculation involves determination of how problems are identified, get broken down into manageable dimensions, are related to one another,
and how choices are made as to what is relevant and who shall be taken into
account. A major clue toward understanding budgeting is the extraordinary complexity of the calculations involved. In any large organization, there are a huge
number of items to be considered, many of which are of considerable technical
difficulty. Yet there is little or no theory in most areas of policy which would
enable practitioners to predict the consequences of alternative moves and probability of their occurring.[2] Man's ability to calculate is severely limited; time is
always in short supply; and the number of matters which can be encompassed in
one mind at the same time is quite small.[3] Nor has anyone solved the imposing
problem of the interpersonal comparison of utilities. Outside of the political process, there is no agreed upon way of comparing and evaluating the merits of different programs for different people whose preferences vary in kind and in intensity.

Participants in budgeting deal with their overwhelming burdens by adopting
heuristic aids to calculation. They simplify in order to get by. They make small
moves, let experience accumulate, and use the feedback from their decisions to
gauge consequences. They use actions on simpler matters that they understand as
indices to complex concerns. They attempt to judge the capacity of the men in
charge of programs even if they cannot appraise the policies directly. They may institute across-the-board ("meat-axe") cuts to reduce expenditures, relying on outcries from affected agencies and interest groups to let them know if they have gone
too far.[4]

By far the most important aid to calculation is the incremental approach.
Budgets are almost never actively reviewed as a whole in the sense of considering at
one time the value of all existing programs compared to all possible alternatives.
Instead, this year's budget is based on last year's budget, with special attention
given to a narrow range of increases or decreases. The greatest part of any budget is
a product of previous decisions. Long-range commitments have been made. There
are mandatory programs whose expenses must be met. Powerful political support

makes the inclusion of other activities inevitable. Consequently, officials concerned with budgeting restrict their attention to items and programs they can do something about—a few new programs and possible cuts in old ones.

Incremental calculations, then, proceed from an existing base. By "base" we refer to commonly held expectations among participants in budgeting that programs will be carried out at close to the going level of expenditures. The base of a budget, therefore, refers to accepted parts of programs that will not normally be subjected to intensive scrutiny. Since many organizational units compete for funds, there is a tendency for the central authority to include all of them in the benefits or deprivations to be distributed. Participants in budgeting often refer to expectations regarding their fair share of increases and decreases. The widespread sharing of deeply held expectations concerning the organization's base and its fair share of funds provide a powerful (although informal) means of coordination and stability in budgetary systems that appear to lack comprehensive calculations proceeding from a hierarchical center.[5]

Roles (the expectations of behavior attached to institutional positions) are parts of the division of labor. They are calculating mechanisms. In American national government, the administrative agencies act as advocates of increased expenditure, the Bureau of the Budget acts as presidential servant with a cutting bias, the House Appropriations Committee functions as a guardian of the Treasury, and the Senate Appropriations Committee as an appeals court to which agencies carry their disagreement with House action.

Possessing great expertise and large numbers, working in close proximity to their policy problems and clientele groups, and desirous of expanding their horizons, administrative agencies generate action through advocacy. But how much shall they ask for? Life would be simple if they could just estimate the costs of their ever-expanding needs and submit the total as their request. But if they ask for amounts much larger than the appropriating bodies believe is reasonable, their credibility will suffer a drastic decline. In such circumstances, the reviewing organs are likely to apply a "measure of unrealism"[6] with the result that the agency gets much less than it might have with a more moderate request. So the first decision rule for agencies is: do not come in too high. Yet the agencies must also not come in too low, for the assumption is that if the agency advocates do not ask for funds they do not need them. Since the budgetary situation is always tight, terribly tight, or impossibly tight, reviewing bodies are likely to just accept a low request with thanks and not inquire too closely into its rationale. Given the distribution of roles, cuts must be expected and taken into account. Thus, the agency decision rule might read: come in a little high (padding), but not too high (loss of confidence). But how high is too high? What agency heads usually do is to evaluate signals from the environment—last year's experience, legislative votes, executive policy statements, actions of clientele groups, reports from the field—and come up with an asking price somewhat higher than they expect to get.[7]

Having decided how much to ask for, agencies engage in strategic planning to secure their budgetary goals. (Strategies are the links between the goals of the agencies and their perceptions of the kinds of actions which their political environment will make efficacious.) Budget officers in American national government uniformly act on the belief that being a good politician—cultivation of an active clientele, development of confidence by other officials (particularly the appropriations subcommittees), and skill in following strategies which exploit opportunities—is more important in obtaining funds than demonstration of efficiency. Top agency officials soon learn that the appropriations committees are very powerful; committee recommendations are accepted by Congress approximately 90 percent of the time.[8] Since budgetary calculations are so complex, the legislators must take a good deal on faith; thus, they require agency budget officers to demonstrate a high degree of integrity. If the appropriations committees believe that an agency officer has misled them, they can do grave damage to his career and to the prospects of the agency he represents. While doing a decent job may be a necessary condition for the agency's success in securing funds, the importance of having clientele and the confidence of legislators is so great that all agencies employ these strategies.[9]

In addition to these ubiquitous strategies, there are contingent strategies which depend upon time, circumstance, and place. In defending the base, for example, cuts may be made in the most popular programs so that a public outcry will result in restoration of the funds. The base may be increased within existing programs by shifting funds between categories. Substantial additions to the base may come about through proposing new programs to meet crises and through campaigns involving large doses of advertising and salesmanship.[10] The dependence of these strategies on the incremental, increase-decrease type of budgetary calculation is evident.

The Bureau of the Budget in the United States has the assigned role of helping the President realize his goals (when it can discover what they are supposed to be). This role is performed with a cutting bias, however, simply because the agencies normally push so hard in making requests for funds. The Bureau helps the President by making his preferences more widely known throughout the executive branch so that those who would like to go along have a chance to find out what is required of them. Since Congress usually cuts the President's budget, Bureau figures tend to be the most that agencies can get, especially when the items are not of such paramount importance as to justify intensive scrutiny by Congress. Yet the power of the purse remains actively with Congress. If the Budget Bureau continually recommended figures which were blatantly disregarded by Congress, the agencies would soon learn to pay less and less attention to the President's budget. As a result, the Bureau follows consistent congressional action.[11] It can be shown empirically that Bureau recommendations tend to follow congressional actions over a large number of cases.[12]

In deciding how much money to recommend for specific purposes, the House Appropriations Committee breaks down into largely autonomous subcommittees in which the norm of reciprocity is carefully followed.[13] Specialization is carried further as subcommittee members develop limited areas of competence and jurisdiction. Budgeting is both incremental and fragmented as the committees deal with adjustments to the historical base of each agency. Sequential decision making is the rule as problems are first attacked in the subcommittee jurisdiction in which they appear and then followed step-by-step as they manifest themselves elsewhere.[14] The subcommittee members treat budgeting as a process of making marginal monetary adjustments to existing programs rather than as a mechanism for reconsidering basic policy choices every year.[15] Fragmentation and specialization are further increased through the appeals functions of the Senate Appropriations Committee which deals with what has become (through House action) a fragment of a fragment. When the actions of subcommittees conflict, the difficulties are met by repeated attacks on the problem or through reference to the House and Senate as a whole.[16]

The members of the United States House Appropriations Committee consider themselves guardians of the Treasury who take pride in the frequency with which they reduce estimates.[17] They reconcile this role with their role as representatives of constituency interests by cutting estimates to satisfy one role and generally increasing amounts over the previous year to satisfy the other. As guardians of the public purse, committee members are expected to cast a skeptical eye on the blandishments of a bureaucracy ever anxious to increase its dominion by raising its appropriations. In order to provide an objective check on the effectiveness of the committee's orientation, Fenno[18] examined the appropriations histories of 37 bureaus concerned with domestic policies from 1947-59 and discovered that the committee reduced the estimates it received 77.2 percent of the time.

Tough as they may be in cutting the budgets of their agencies, appropriations committee members, once having made their decisions, generally defend the agencies against further cuts on the floor. This kind of action is in part self-interest. The power of the appropriations subcommittees would be diminished if their recommendations were successfully challenged very often. Members believe that the House would "run wild" if "orderly procedure"—that is, acceptance of committee recommendations—were not followed. The role of defender also has its roots in the respect for expertise and specialization in Congress, and the concomitant belief that members who have not studied the subject should not exercise a deciding voice without the presence of overriding consideration. An appeal to this norm usually is sufficient to block an attempt to reduce appropriations.[19]

A member of the Senate Appropriations Committee is likely to conceive of his proper role as the responsible legislator who sees to it that the irrepressible lower house does not do too much damage either to constituency or to national interests. The senators are rather painfully aware of the House committee's pre-eminence in the field of appropriations and they know that they cannot hope to match the time and thoroughness that the House body devotes to screening requests. For this reason, the Senate committee puts a high value on having agencies carry appeals to it. The senators value their right to disagree on disputed items as a means of maintaining their influence in crucial areas while putting the least possible strain on their time and energy. The Senate role of responsible appeals court is dependent, of course, upon agency advocacy and House committee guardianship.

The Budgetary Process Reconsidered

In describing the budgetary process, we have identified a number of basic characteristics that have called forth a great deal of criticism from many sources. For example, the aids to calculation have been described as arbitrary and irrational. It has been said that, instead of concentrating on grand policy alternatives, the appropriations committees interfere mischievously with the administrative process through excessive concern with small details. Some critics go so far as to state that this petty intervention takes place without adequate information so that administrators are harassed for all the wrong reasons by men who lack knowledge. The specialized, incremental, fragmented, and sequential budgetary procedures have been faulted as leading to a lack of coordination and a neglect of consequences of the actions that are taken. At the same time, Congress is said to be losing its control of appropriations because its meager efforts cannot keep pace with the superior information resources of the federal bureaucracy. Nor, the critics add, are the appropriations committees willing to make the vast increase in staff which would enable them to make their will felt through intelligent decisions on broad policies. Instead, they combine dependence on the executive for information with "irrational" practices such as across-the-board cuts. The participants in budgeting have been taken to task for serving local interests rather than the national public interest. Their roles are considered to be excessively narrow, and the strategies they follow are condemned as opportunistic if not immoral. Finally, the appropriations process is deemed much too slow and too late: actions are taken on material which is out of date, and administrators are left uncertain how much money they will have until long after the previous fiscal year has ended.

It is immediately evident that many of these criticisms are contradictory. Increasing the staff of the appropriations committees hardly seems like a good way to cut down on detailed oversight of administration. Concern with local interests is one way of dealing with the differential consequences of national policy. Congress can hardly interfere less with administrators by making all the basic policy decisions for the executive agencies. That the critics of Congress are confused is an old story; let us make the best sense we can out of the criticisms and deal with the serious concerns which they raise.

The alternative budgetary process envisioned by the critics is quite different from the one we now have. Instead of aids to calculation such as the incremental method, they prefer comprehensive and simultaneous evaluation of means and ends. In their view, coordination should be made the explicit concern of a central hierarchy that should consider a wide range of alternative expenditures and investigate rather fully the consequences of each and the probability of their occurring. Each participant should seek to protect the general interest rather than the particular interests directly within his jurisdiction. Strategies should be eschewed or, at least, based on the merits of the program rather than on making the best possible case. Congressmen should avoid interferences in the administrative process and concentrate on developing superior knowledge and greatly enlarged staff assistance in order to make the most general determinations of governmental policy. The following pages deal in detail with various critical approaches.

COMPREHENSIVENESS

One prescription offered by the critics for "rationally" solving problems of calculation is to engage in comprehensive and simultaneous means-ends analysis. But budget officials soon discover that ends are rarely agreed upon, that they keep changing, that possible consequences of a single policy are too numerous to describe, and that knowledge of the chain of consequences for other policies is but dimly perceived for most conceivable alternatives. The result, as Charles Lindblom has demonstrated, is that although this comprehensive approach can be described, it cannot be practiced because it puts too great a strain by far on man's limited ability to calculate.[20] What budget officials need are not injunctions to be rational but operational guides that will enable them to manage the requisite calculations. Commands like "decide according to the intrinsic merits," "consider everything relevant," "base your decision on complete understanding," are simply not help-ful. They do not exclude anything; unlike the aids to calculation, they do not point to operations that can be performed to arrive at a decision.

All that is accomplished by injunctions to follow a comprehensive approach is the inculcation of guilt among good men who find that they can never come close to fulfilling this unreasonable expectation. Worse still, acceptance of an unreason-able goal inhibits discussion of the methods actually used. Thus, responsible offi-cials may feel compelled to maintain the acceptable fiction that they review (almost) everything; and yet when they describe their actual behavior, it soon be-comes apparent that they do not. The vast gulf between the theories espoused by some budget officials and their practice stems, I believe, from their adherence to a norm deeply imbedded in our culture, which holds that the very definition of ra-tional decision is comprehensive and simultaneous examination of ends and means. In this case, however, the rational turns out to be the unreasonable. Sad experience warns me that even those who agree with the analysis thus far are prone to insist that governmental officials must "take a look at the budget as a whole," even though neither they nor anyone else has any idea of what that might mean or how it might be accomplished. Surely, considering "the budget as a whole" does not mean merely putting it between the covers of one volume, or letting one's eyes run over the pages, or merely pondering the relationship between income and expenditures. Yet, if (to take current examples) evaluating the most important re-lationships between the space program, the war on poverty, and aid to education appears to be extraordinarily difficult, what is the point of talking about reviewing "the budget as a whole" in the real sense of analyzing the interrelationsips among all the important programs. The perpetuation of myth is an old story. What is un-fortunate is that insistence on an impossible standard takes our attention away from real possibilities for change.

Failure to consider the contributions toward calculation of the existing budget-ary process distorts the magnitude of the problem. New programs and substantial increases and decreases in old programs do not receive close attention when inter-est groups, politicians, or bureaucrats, anxious to make an issue, demand an inves-tigation. What escapes intensive scrutiny is not the whole but only certain parts, which carry on as before. The fact that some activities do not receive intensive scru-tiny is hardly sufficient reason to do everything over every year. In my recommen-dations, I shall deal with the problem that remains.

COORDINATION

The fact that the budgetary process is not comprehensive has given rise to charges that it is uncoordinated. Indeed, the very terms that we have used to describe budgetary practices—specialized, incremental, fragmented, sequential, non-pro-grammatic—imply that at any one time the budget is not effectively considered as a whole so as to systematically relate its component parts to one another. As long as the lack of coordination is the result of ignorance of other people's activities or the complexity of organization, there is a good chance of overcoming it by dedi-cated staff work or some formal coordinating mechanism. But, in many cases, lack of coordination is a result of conflicting views about policy that are held by men and agencies that have independent bases of influence in society and in Congress.

The only way to secure coordination in these cases is for one side to convince or coerce or bargain with the other. When it is understood that "coordination" is often
just another word for "coercion," the full magnitude of the problem becomes apparent. For there is no one, the President and congressional leaders included, who
is charged with the task of dealing with the "budget as a whole" and who is capable of enforcing his preferences. Vesting of formal power to coordinate the budget
effectively would be tantamount to a radical change in the national political system, requiring the abolition of the separation of powers and a federally controlled
party system, among other things.

What may be said about coordination, then, if we take the existing political system as not subject to drastic change? By taking as our standard of coordination the
existence of a formal structure charged with the task and capable of executing it,
we come up with an obvious answer: there is very little coordination excepting
what the President can manage through the Budget Bureau. By accepting the possibility of informal coordination, of participants who take into account what
others are doing, we can say there is a great deal of coordination that has escaped
the notice of observers.

Let us pose the following question: how does an appropriations subcommittee
know when things are not working out in other areas affected by its actions? Are
its budgetary decisions coordinated with those decisions made by other subcommittees? Part of the answer is found in a comment by a committee member to the
effect that "people can't be too badly off if they don't complain." The subcommittees do not consider themselves to be the only participants in budgeting. They
expect, in accordance with sequential decision making, that committees and organizations in the affected areas will take corrective action. When an agency
shouts more loudly than usual, when an interest group mounts a campaign, when
other congressmen begin to complain, subcommittee members have a pretty good
idea that something is wrong. If their perceptions of the array of political forces
lead them astray, the appropriations subcommittees can be brought back into line
by a rebellion within the full committee or by an adverse vote on the floor. For, as
we noted earlier, unless members have an exceedingly intense preference, they
will try to come up with appropriations that will not be reversed on the floor; to do
otherwise would be to risk losing the great prestige the committee enjoys. The
subcommittee may be thought of as exercising discretion over a zone of indifference, within which others are not aware enough or not concerned enough to
challenge them, but beyond which others will begin to mobilize against them. In
this way, a semblance of coordination is maintained. And as time passes, the participants come to develop a tacit understanding as to the general level of most appropriations, a phenomenon we have previously designated by the notion of fair
shares. No one has to check up on everyone; it is sufficient that occasional marked
departures from commonly held notions of fair shares would generate opposition.

Widespread acceptance of this concept of fair shares may go a long way toward
accounting for the degree of coordination (the extent to which participants take
into account what others do) that does exist in calculating expenditures totals. The
total budget was rarely drastically out of line with expenditures before it was formalized in 1921, and even without control by a central authority today we do not
usually get extraordinary increases or decreases except during national emergen-
cies. There has been much more subtle and informal coordination by tacit
agreements and accepted limits than there has previously been thought to be.

To some critics the procedure by which the agencies (as well as the appropriations committees and the Budget Bureau to a lesser extent) try to gauge "what will go" may seem unfortunate. They feel that there must be a better justification for programs than the subjective interpretation of signals from the environment. Yet we live in a democracy in which a good part of the justification for programs is precisely that they are deemed desirable by others. What is overlooked is that these informal procedures are also powerful coordinating mechanisms: when one thinks of all the participants who are continuously engaged in interpreting the wishes of others, who try to feel the pulse of Congress, the President, interest groups, and special publics, it is clear that a great many adjustments are made in anticipation of what other participants are likely to do. This, it seems to me, is just another term for coordination, unless one insists that coordination be redefined to require conscious control by a single individual or group.

The interaction between appropriations committees and administrative agencies includes at least seven modes of coordination:

1. Laws commanding specific actions;
2. Committee reports demanding specific action on (implicit) pain of future penalties;
3. Exchange of indulgences;
4. Taking each other's preferences into account with direct contact;
5. Accommodations to prior actions of the other without consultation;
6 Argument in which one side convinces the other;
7. Granting of side payments by one participant in return for action by the other.

NEGLECT OF CONSEQUENCES

The budgetary process is sometimes attacked for its apparent neglect of consequences, and there can be no doubt that lack of comprehensiveness in budgeting means that a participant making a specific decision will often neglect important values affected by that decision. However, Lindblom has proposed that consequences neglected by one participant may be considered by another, or by the same participant working on another problem.[21] To the extent, therefore, that all significant interests tend to be represented in a fragmented political system, decision makers may reduce their information costs, by neglecting many alternatives, in the confidence that they will be picked up by others or by themselves at another time. Thus, the budgetary process as a whole may be considered rational even though the actions of individual participants may not seem to be because they omit from their calculations consequences important for others.

The political process in a democracy has a built-in feature that assures that some presently neglected values will be considered. This mechanism exists because politicians and interest-group leaders are motivated, by their hope of retaining or winning office, to find needs that have not been met and proposing to fulfill them in return for votes.

No doubt the neglect of some values (say those dear to Negroes) could be better avoided by increasing the weight of the appropriate interests in the political process. There is no point, it seems to me, in faulting the budgetary process for the lamentable failure of some groups to be properly represented in the political life of the nation. Political mobilization of Negroes will obviously do much more to protect their neglected interests than any change in the mechanism for considering budgets.

The most powerful coordinating mechanisms in budgeting undoubtedly are the various roles adopted by major participants in the budgetary process. Because the roles fit in with one another and set up a stable pattern of mutual expectations, they do a great deal to reduce the burden of calculations for the individual participants. The agencies need not consider in great detail how their requests will affect the President's overall program; they know that such criteria will be introduced in the Budget Bureau. The appropriations committees and the Budget Bureau know that the agencies are likely to put forth all the programs for which there is prospect of support and can concentrate on fitting them into the President's program or on paring them down. The Senate committee operates on the assumption that if important items are left out through House action the agency will carry an appeal. If the agencies suddenly reversed roles and sold themselves short, the entire pattern of mutual expectations might be upset, leaving the participants without a firm anchor in a sea of complexity. If the agency were to refuse the role of advocate, it would increase the burden on the congressmen; they would not only have to choose among desirable items placed before them with some fervor, but they would also have to discover what these items might be. This is a task ordinarily far beyond the limited time, energy, information, and competence of most congressmen.

The roles appear to be "natural" to the occupants of these institutional positions. A man who has spent many years working in, say, the natural resources area can be expected to believe that his programs are immensely worthy of support. (He may try to eliminate programs he deems unworthy, but there are always others to take their place.) Indeed, he would hardly be worth having as a governmental employee if he did not feel this way in his position. By serving as advocate in the real world, he sees to it that important values in his area are not neglected if he can help it.

The House Appropriations Committee's role of guarding the Treasury, with its emphasis on reducing requests, makes sense in the context of agency advocacy. If the congressmen can be reasonably certain that the agency has put its best foot forward, then their decisions may be viewed as choices along the margins of the top percentage of expenditures advocated by the agencies. The role of guardianship provides the congressmen with a stance that supplies reasonably clear instructions—cut the estimates—while keeping the area within which they must focus their attention (the largest increases) manageable in terms of their limited time and ability to calculate.

Some critics suggest that appropriations committee members should adopt a different role. In this "mixed" role, the congressman would be oriented toward neither cutting nor increasing but to doing both in about equal proportions. Each case would have to be considered on its own merits. To some extent, of course, this balance occurs under the present system. The difference is one of degree, but not less important for being so. For where they are in doubt or do not care to inquire in detail, the congressmen may now follow their prevailing orientation—usually to cut at the margin—expecting to receive feedback if something drastic happens. Under a "mixed" role, however, an exhaustive inquiry into all or most items would be called for. The resulting increase in amounts of calculation required would be immense. And to the extent that other participants adopted a mixed role, the pattern of role expectations upon which participants are now dependent as a calculating device would no longer prove stable. The calculation of preferences, essential in a democratic system, would become far more burdensome since inquiries would have to be instituted to find out what the various groups wanted in specific cases.

Furthermore, the adoption of a mixed role would be likely to lead to a greater neglect of values affected by decisions. Unless the ability of each participant to calculate the consequences of his actions is much more impressive than the evidence suggests, he is bound to neglect more if he attempts to do more. Yet this is precisely what a mixed role would force him to do. Instead of concentrating on a limited range of values within his jurisdiction, as his present role requires, he would have to consider the widest possible range of values in order to make a mixed role work. In place of the reasonable certainty that each participant does a good job of looking after the relatively narrow range of values entrusted to his care, there would be little certainty that any particular value would be protected because no one had been especially directed to look after it. Let us explore this question further as a fundamental problem in normative political theory.

INTERESTS

Why, it may be asked, should the various participants take a partial view? Why should they not simply decide in accordance with what the public interest requires? Actually, this is the principle that participants think they are following now; they all believe that their version of the public interest is correct. It is their differing institutional positions, professional training, and group values that lead to perspectives producing somewhat different interpretations of the public interterest. Let us, then, rephrase the question and ask whether it is better for each participant to put first the achievement of his own goals (including the goals entrusted to him by virtue of his position) when he considers what is meant by "public interest," or whether he should view the goals of others as of prime or at least equal importance to this consideration?

I am prepared to argue that the partial-view-of-the-public-interest approach is preferable to the total-view-of-the-public-interest approach, which is so often urged as being superior. First, it is much simpler for each participant to calculate how the interests he is protecting might best be served without requiring that he perform the same calculation for many others who might also be affected. The "partial" approach has the virtue of enabling others to accept as an input in their calculations the determination of each participant as to his preferences, which is not possible under the total approach. The danger of omitting important values is much greater when participants neglect the values in their immediate care in favor of what seem to them a broader view. How can anyone know what is being neglected if everyone speaks for someone else and no one for himself?

The partial approach is more efficient for resolving conflicts, a process that lies at the heart of democratic politics. Because the approach is partial, it does not require its practitioners to discover all or most possible conflicts and to work out answers to problems that may never materialize. It permits each participant to go his own way until he discovers that the activities of others interfere. Effort can then be devoted to overcoming the conflicts that arise. The formation of alliances in a political system requiring them is facilitated by the expression and pursuit of demands by those in closest touch with the social reality from which they issue. It is not, then, *noblesse oblige* but self-interest that assures that all demands insist on being heard and find the political resources to compel a hearing. A partial adversary system in which the various interests compete for control of policy (under agreed upon rules) seems more likely to result in reasonable decisions—that is, decisions that take account of the multiplicity of values involved—than one in which the best policy is assumed to be discoverable by a well-intentioned search for the public interest for all by everyone.

STRATEGIES

If it is granted that budgetary practices based on a partial view of the public interest are desirable, then it would appear necessary to accept the use of strategies designed to secure appropriation goals. It is not surprising, however, that critics find something basically underhanded, even undemocratic, in the maneuvering of "special interests" for strategic advantage. Would not a straightforward approach based on the "merits" of each program be preferable?

Requiring that an individual commit suicide for the public good may at times have an acceptable rationale; suggesting that it become a common practice can hardly claim as much. I shall take it as understood, then, that asking participants in budgeting consistently to follow practices extremely disadvantageous to themselves and their associates is not reasonable. The participants must be able to maintain themselves in the environment.

The notion that administrators go around telling each other (or believing in secret) that the purposes for which they request funds are not valid but that they want the money anyway in order to advance themselves and build empires is not worthy of consideration. It would be exceedingly difficult to keep people in an organization if they could not justify its purposes to themselves. Such an attitude would be bound to come to the attention of other participants, who would take appropriate action. It would be bad strategically as well as morally. Attempts to reduce a complex distributive process like budgeting to the terms of a western melodrama—the good men ride white horses and advance on their merits; the bad men wear black masks and rely on strategies—do away with the great problem of deciding upon expenditures advocated by officials who are sincere believers in their proposals, and who know that all demands can be satisfied.

Budgetary strategies may generally be characterized as attempts to make the best case for the agency at the best time and thus to get as large an appropriation as possible. This behavior follows from the role of the agency as advocate. As a practical matter, we would expect any agency head worth his keep to respond to opportunities for increasing appropriations and warding off cuts. The contrary position—making the worst case at the worst time—is not likely to be greeted with enthusiasm by either congressmen or agency staff.

Seizing on the opportune moment for advancing the agency's budgetary goals has much to commend it. The nation is served by initiative in meeting the needs of the time. An element of flexibility is generated that helps ensure that opportunities for action will be taken. "Crisis" strategies belong in this category. What is the difference, we may ask, between using a crisis to increase appropriations and acting to meet the nation's requirements in an hour of need? The desire to present the agency's requests in the best light can be used in a positive sense to improve the thinking of the operating units. The budget office can play an important mediating role because it must explain and justify agency actions to the outside world. By playing devil's advocate to agency personnel, by pointing out that justifications are not clear or persuasive, by saying that the program heads have to do better to convince the Budget Bureau or the appropriations committees, the budget office may compel or encourage thinking from diverse perspectives. In this way, a wider range of interests and values receive consideration.

Clientele and confidence strategies are desirable as well as inevitable in a democratic society. The feedback that clientele give to the participants is essential political information about who wants what programs, at what level, and with what degree of intensity. The establishment of confidence in an agency and its officers provides the trust necessary for congressmen who must live with complexity; the sanctions upon that agency that follow from lack of congressional confidence represent a great safeguard against duplicity. That morality is to some extent the handmaiden of necessity does not make it any less real or valuable.

A naked recital of strategies is bound to suggest that a certain amount of trickery is involved. Some strategies that appear to be deceitful represent amoral adjustments to an environment that does not give the participants much choice. Consider the kind of duplicity that appears to be involved in the game wherein agency people make believe that they are supporting the President's budget while actually encouraging congressmen to ask questions that will permit them to talk about what they would really like to have. Is this behavior immoral or does the immorality belong to the Executive Office directive that tries to compel agency personnel to say things that they do not believe in order to support the President? Congress has the power of the purse and it is difficult to argue that it should not have the kind of information about what the people in charge of the program think they ought to get that might help it to arrive at decisions. If one wants to get rid of Congress, then the problem solves itself. But if one accepts the separation of powers, then it may well be that it would be destructive to deny Congress information it would like to have, especially when for Congress to have it is manifestly in the interests of administrators. The Biblical injunction against excessive temptation is appropriate here.

MERITS

Despite all that has been said, the very idea that strategies are employed may still appear disturbing. Why cannot programs be presented on their merits and their merits alone? The most obvious answer is that the question presupposes popular, general agreement on what constitutes merit when the real problem is that people do not agree. That is why we have politics. To lay down and enforce criteria of merit in budgeting would be, in effect, to dispense with politics in favor of deciding what the government shall do in advance.

Much of what is meant by merit turns out to be "meets my preferences" or "serves my interests" or "the interests of those with whom I identify." It would be most peculiar for a nation calling itself a democracy to announce that only the most meritorious policies were carried out despite the fact that they were not preferred by any significant group in the population. The degree to which widespread preferences are met not only *is* but *ought* to be *part* of why policies are deemed meritorious.

We all know that people do not always realize what is good for them. They are occupied with many things and may not recognize the benefits flowing from certain policies. They may find it difficult to support policies that are meritorious but not directly related to their own immediate needs. Here is where strategies come in. Where support is lacking, it may be mobilized; where attention is unfocused, it may be directed by advertising; where merits are not obvious, they may be presented in striking form. Ability to devise strategies to advance the recognition of merit is immensely more helpful than cries of indignation that political artistry should be necessary.

Merit consists, in part, of the effectiveness with which programs are formulated and carried out. No one should doubt that this criterion is recognized in the budgetary process; estimates, justifications, and presentations are directed to this end. Though effectiveness is indispensable—confidence would be lacking without it, for one thing; clientele would be dissatisfied, for another—agencies find that it does not take them far enough. An agency may be wonderfully effective in formulating and carrying out its programs and yet see its fortunes suffer because of the need for Congress to cut that year or to shift funds to some other vital area. Defense appropriations are often a function of domestic concerns; stabilization policy may be constrained by military needs; the complexity of a project or the difficulty of demonstrating immediate results may militate against it. Consequently, the agency invariably finds that in some areas its good works and best efforts are not being rewarded. Prizes are simply not distributed for good deeds alone. The agency's mode of adapting to this circumstance is to use demonstration of good works as one among a number of strategies. Forbidding agencies to use strategies designed to   give its good requests a better chance, because bad requests can also be dressed up, seems inadvisable as well as unlikely to succeed.

MOTIVATION

Instead of bewailing the use of strategies, it would be immensely more fruitful to arrange incentives within the system so as to insure that good strategies and good programs will go together as often as possible. Budgeting would be conceived of in this sense as constituting a problem in human motivation. When the motivation is disregarded, it is no wonder that unsatisfactory results ensue. In order to demonstrate that this problem is by no means peculiar to the national budgetary process let us take a brief look at budgeting in Soviet and American industrial firms.

Rewards to managers in Soviet industrial firms depend on their meeting production quotas assigned in economic plans. But necessary supplies—skilled labor and financial resources—are often lacking. The first consequence of this is that the quota is not set from above but becomes the subject of bargaining as the managers seek to convince the ministries that quotas should be as low as possible. Yet the managers find it prudent not to hugely exceed their quota, for in that case next year's quota will be raised beyond attainment. The second consequence is that production is not rationalized to produce the greatest output at the lowest cost, but is geared instead to meeting specific incentives. Heavy nails are overproduced, for example, because quotas are figured by weight. Maintenance may be slighted in favor of huge effort for a short period in order to meet the quota. Funds are hidden in order to provide slack that can be used to pay "pushers" to expedite the arrival of supplies. The list of essentially deceitful practices to give the appearance of fulfilling the quota is seemingly endless: producing the wrong assortment of products, transferring current costs to capital accounts, shuffling accounts to pay for one item with funds designated for another, declaring unfinished goods finished, lowering the quality of goods, and so on.[22] The point is that the budgetary system arranges incentives in such a way that managers cannot succeed with lawful practices. When similar incentives are applied in American industrial firms, similar practices result, from running machines into the ground, to "bleeding the line," to meeting a monthly quota by doctoring the accounts.[23]

As in the Soviet Union, American firms often use budgets not to reflect or project reality but to drive managers and workers toward increased production. Budgets are conceived of as forms of pressure on inherently lazy people[24] so that (to paraphrase Mao Tse-tung) the greater the pressure the better the budget. Inevitably, managers and workers begin to perceive budgets as "perpetual needlers" or as "the hammer that's waiting to hit you on the head."[25] In some cases, this leads to discouragement because it is apparent that whatever the effort, the budget quota will be increased. Since accounting is separate for sub-units in the firm, it is not surprising that fierce negotiations take place to assign costs among them. As a result, top officials find it necessary to engage in campaigns to sell budgets to the units. Otherwise, sabotage is likely.[26] While some attention has been given to human relations in budgeting,[27] only Stedry[28] has attempted to explore the essential motivational problems of budgeting within an organizational framework. Yet, without an understanding of the impact of different goals and incentive systems on human activity, reliable statements about the likely consequences of different budgetary incentives can hardly be made. I shall attempt to deal with this problem in my recommendations.

POWER

The strategy which critics of the budgetary process find most objectionable is Congress's use of the appropriations power to alter policies of executive agencies. To say that congressmen interfere too much in the details of administration, however, is to consign them to impotence. Grand policy decisions come few and far between. Most policy is made through interpretation of statutes by administrators or through a succession of marginal adjustments in the form of legislative amendments. If by "administrative detail" one means "trivial," then it would seem that the administrators who are presumably being defended would have little to worry about. A basic analytic problem, preventing meaningful thought, is that "policy" is identified with "Congress" and "administration" with the executive branch. By definition, Congress should not tell administrators what to do, because administrators administrate and Congress is supposed only to make policy. I agree so completely with the position taken by Richard Fenno that I would like to quote his comments at some length:

To relegate Congress to the making of broad policy decisions and to oversight in terms of broad program management is to prescribe precisely those tasks which Congress is least capable of performing. To criticize Congress for intervening in a specific and detailed fashion is to attack it for doing the only thing it can do to effectively assert its influence. Specifics and details are the indispensable handles which Congressmen use to work inductively toward broader kinds of oversight judgments. Specifics and details are what concern the constitutents on whose behalf Congressmen must intervene with the bureaucracy. Specific and detailed requests from an interested Congressman to a bureau head or division chief do more to "galvanize the internal disciplines of administration" (Arthur Macmahon's phrase) than any broad statement of policy. The profusion of committees and subcommittees make possible a degree of specialization which gives to Congressmen the detailed and specific information they find most useful in influencing executive behavior.

Specific and detailed controls by individuals and small committees give Congressmen their maximum influence because these controls are best adapted to the realities of executive decision-making. If executive decision-making is basically piecemeal, incremental and marginal, then congressional control, if it is to be effective, must be basically piecemeal, incremental and marginal. What is or is not "appropriate" congressional control cannot be prescribed *a priori*. . . . Congressional control is or is not appropriate in the context of the realities of legislative and executive decision-making. The legislator ought not to be criticized for using those controls which are available to him and which his experience tells him bring the greatest influence over executive activity. If we do not recognize this, we will continue to prescribe impossible control tasks. . . .[29]

The power of Congress to control budgetary decisions depends on the power of its appropriations committees. For no large assembly of men can develop the expertise, self-direction, cohesiveness, and dispatch which are necessary to do the large volume of budgetary business. A good index of the power of any legislature is whether it develops and follows committees of experts in specific areas of decisions. Where such committees are absent, as in Great Britain, the power of Parliament becomes a fiction. (A common definition of a cabinet is a committee which permits no rivals.) The appropriations committees measure up exceedingly well when we consider that their recommendations are adopted by the houses of Congress approximately 90 percent of the time. Although one might contemplate with equanimity some reduction in this record of success, a drop below, say, 75 percent would seriously compromise the appropriations committees with the President and the agencies. For a great deal of the ability to have agencies follow congressional will is dependent on the knowledge that the appropriations committees are watching and that their actions will be upheld with a high degree of certainty. Once the power gets transferred to Congress as a whole, its exercise becomes so uncertain and diffuse that no one can count on it. Congressmen simply do not have the time and the knowledge to debate a very large number of appropriations with sense and then follow through. The general body of congressmen do well to keep the appropriations committees in line with an occasional defeat on the floor to remind them whom they are ultimately beholden to.

The great power of the appropriations committees consists in the extent to which agencies and the Bureau of the Budget systematically take account of their preferences. Anyone who has seen budget offices in operation knows that the unseen hand of Congress is never far from the surface. The agency practice of holding mock hearings in which some officials are assigned the role of appropriations committee members is a vivid illustration of how Congress makes its will felt indirectly.

The power of the appropriations committees depends on their ability to command regular support in Congress, support which in turn is dependent on the cohesiveness of the committees. Fenno[30] has shown that support for the House Appropriations Committee drops markedly when its subcommittees issue split recommendations. The internal norms and calculating mechanisms whereby the committee achieves a high degree of integration are therefore of extreme importance in the maintenance of congressional power. The incremental, fragmented, non-programmatic, and sequential procedures of the present budgetary process aid in securing agreement. It is much easier to agree on an addition or reduction of a few thousand or a million dollars than to agree on whether a program is good in the abstract. It is much easier to agree on a small addition or decrease than to compare the worth of one program to that of all others. Conflict is reduced by an incremental approach because the area open to dispute is reduced. Agreement comes much more readily when the items in dispute can be treated as differences in dollars instead of as basic differences in policy; calculating budgets in monetary increments facilitates bargaining and logrolling. It becomes possible to swap an increase here for a decrease there or for an increase elsewhere without always having to consider the ultimate desirability of programs blatantly in competition. Procedures that de-emphasize overt conflicts among competing programs also encourage secret deliberations, nonpartisanship, and the recruitment of personnel who feel comfortable in sidestepping policy decisions most of the time. The prospects for agreement within the House Appropriations Committee are enhanced by closed hearings and mark-up sessions, and by a tradition against publicity. Were deliberations to take place in public—"open covenants openly arrived at"—committee members might find themselves accused of "selling out" if they made concessions. Willingness to compromise, to be flexible, is a quality sought in choosing members to serve on the appropriations committees. Party ties might be disruptive of agreement if they focused attention on the policy differences between the two political persuasions. Instead, party differences are submerged during committee deliberations, and the usual process of taking something from a program here, adding to a program there, swapping this for that, can go on.

However the committee's practices are subject to attack precisely because of their de-emphasis of large policy considerations. Manifestly, the House Appropriations Committee does not normally consider its task to lie in rehashing every year the arguments over the fundamental desirability of the legislation already considered by the substantive committees and passed by Congress. Fortunately, Richard Fenno[31] has provided us with a splendid analysis of a committee whose members took fierce partisan and ideological positions on virtually all the issues that came before them. The norm of reciprocity—accepting the recommendations of other subcommittees if they accept yours—was unknown on the House Education and Labor Committee in the years after the Second World War. The members went after each other with abandon. They appeared to glory in differences and to stress the ultimate values which divided them. As a result, the committee was supremely ineffective in getting its recommendations accepted in the House. Internal committee warfare contributed to the long delay in producing any important legislation on education. Were these norms to prevail on the appropriations committees it is doubtful that a congressional budget could be produced at all. In the presence of delay and confusion and in the absence of party majorities to resolve these matters consistently on a strict partisan basis, Congress would be faced with the choice of abandoning its budgetary prerogatives or of indulging in the grossest forms of action leading to wild and unpredictable swings in the levels of appropriations. . . .

SUMMARY

In appraising the budgetary process, we must deal with real men who know that, in this real world, the best they can get is to be preferred to the perfection they cannot achieve. Unwilling or unable to alter the basic features of the political system, they seek to make it work for them rather than against them in budgeting. Participants in budgeting not only work within the specified constitutional rules, they also make active use of them. Problems of calculation are mitigated by the division of labor in the separation of powers; morality is enforced by substantial external checks as well as by inner motives; a wider range of preferences is taken into account by making the institutional participants responsible for somewhat different ones. A great deal of informal coordination takes place as participants adjust to their expectation of others' behavior. An incremental approach guards against radical departures most of the time, whereas agency advocacy and strategies designed to take advantage of emergent needs help ensure flexibility. A basic conclusion of this appraisal is that the existing budgetary process works much better than is commonly supposed.

There is, however, no special magic in the *status quo*. Inertia and ignorance as well as experience and wisdom may be responsible for whatever problems exist in the present state of affairs. Improvements of many kinds are undoubtedly possible and desirable. The heart of the problem of budgetary reform lies in the inevitable tension between the practice of incrementalism and the ideology of comprehensiveness. The assumption of all previous proposals for reform has been that incrementalism must be sacrificed to comprehensiveness. But as this section has suggested formal coordination and comprehensive calculation of budgets are unfeasible, undesirable, or both. If comprehensiveness is rejected, however, there turn out to be other significant directions for reform that have not yet been tried. My view is that the present budgetary process should be taken as far as it will go and then corrected for its worst deficiencies. Proposals for reform should advocate a more thoroughgoing incremental approach, not its opposite—a more comprehensive one. There should be greater use of aids to calculation rather than less. Agencies should not be told to give up advocacy, but should be motivated to make their best case even more persuasive. There should be even less formal unity and more conflict in budgeting than there is today.

NOTES

1. Richard Cyert and James March (eds.), *A Behavioral Theory of the Firm* (Englewood Cliffs, N.J.: Prentice-Hall, 1963).
2. David Braybrooke and Charles Lindblom, *A Strategy of Decision* (New York: Free Press of Glencoe, 1963).
3. Herbert A. Simon, *Administrative Behavior*, 2nd ed. (New York: Macmillan, 1957), pp. 172-97.
4. Aaron Wildavsky, *Politics of the Budgetary Process* (Boston: Little, Brown, 1964), pp. 1-13.

5. *Ibid.*, pp. 16-18.
6. J. S. Hines (Research Officer) and R. W. Edwards (Chairman), *Budgeting in Public Authorities* (New York: A Study Group of the Royal Institute of Public Administration, 1959), p. 245.
7. Wildavsky, pp. 21-32.
8. Richard F. Fenno, Jr., "The House Appropriations Committee as a Political System: The Problem of Integration," *American Political Science Review*, LVI, 1962, pp. 310-24.
9. Wildavsky, pp. 65-98.
10. *Ibid.*, pp. 101-23.
11. *Ibid.*, pp. 4-42.
12. Otto Davis and Aaron Wildavsky, "An Empirical Theory of Congressional Appropriations." (Mimeograph, 1965).
13. Fenno, pp. 310-24.
14. Wildavsky, pp. 56-64.
15. Fenno, pp. 310-24.
16. Wildavsky, pp. 1-13.
17. Fenno, pp. 310-24.
18. *Ibid.*, p. 312.
19. *Ibid.;* Wildavsky, pp. 1-13.
20. Charles Lindblom, "The Science of 'Muddling Through'," *Public Administration Review*, XIX, 1959, pp. 79-88.
21. See his *Decision-Making In Taxation and Expenditures, Public Finances, Needs, Sources and Utilization* (Princeton: National Bureau of Economic Research, 1961), pp. 295-336.
22. Joseph S. Berliner, *Factory and Manager in the USSR* (Cambridge: Harvard University Press, 1957).
23. Frank Jasinsky, "Use and Misuse of Efficiency Controls," *Harvard Business Review*, XXXIV, 1956, p. 107; Chris Argyris, *The Impact of Budgets on People* (New York: Controllership Foundation, Inc., 1952), pp. 12ff.
24. Argyris, *op. cit.*, pp. 6ff.
25. *Ibid.*, pp. 12-13.
26. *Ibid., inter alia;* Bernard H. Sord and Glenn A. Welsch, *Business Budgeting: A Survey of Management Planning and Control Practices* (New York: Controllership Foundation, Inc. 1958), pp. 140-50.
27. Arnold A. Bebling, "A Look at Budgets and People," *Business Budgeting*, X, 1961, p. 16.
28. Andrew C. Stedry, *Budget Control and Cost Behavior* (Englewood Cliffs, N.J.: Prentice-Hall, 1960).
29. Richard F. Fenno, Jr., review of Joseph P. Harris, "Congressional Control of Administration," in *American Political Science Review*, LVIII:3, 1964, p. 674.
30. Fenno, "The House Appropriations Committee as a Political System: The Problem of Integration," *op. cit.*
31. Frank Munger and Richard Fenno, Jr., *National Politics and Federal Aid to Education* (Syracuse, N.Y.: Syracuse University Press, 1962), pp.106-36.

The Zero-Base Approach to Government Budgeting

PETER A. PYHRR

MISDIRECTION BY TRADITIONAL BUDGET PROCEDURES

The traditional budget procedure is based on "incremental budgeting." Most organizations start with the current operating and expenditure levels as an established base. They then analyze, in detail, only those desired increases (i.e., increments) from this established base—thus looking at only a small fraction of the total dollars budgeted.

These traditional budget techniques reinforce, and are reinforced by, the psychology of governmental institution. This psychology was effectively explained by Peter F. Drucker in a recent article in *The Public Interest* on "Managing the Public Service Institution."[1] Mr. Drucker pointed out that service institutions were paid out of a budget allocation, whose revenues are normally allocated from a revenue base not directly tied to what the institution is doing. In addition, institutions usually have monopoly powers, and the intended beneficiary therefore has no choice in obtaining the desired services.

> "Being paid out of a budget allocation changes what is meant by 'performance' or 'results.' 'Results' in the budget-based institution means a larger budget. 'Performance' is the ability to maintain or to increase one's budget. The first test of a budget-based institution and the first requirement for its survival is to obtain the budget. And the budget is, by definition, related not to the achievement of any goals, but to the intention of achieving those goals.
>
> This means, first, that efficiency and cost control, however much they are being preached, are not really considered virtues in the budget-based institution. The importance of a budget-based institution is measured essentially by the size of its budget and the size of its staff. To achieve results with a smaller budget or a smaller staff is, therefore, not 'performance.' It might actually endanger the institution. Not to spend the budget to the hilt will only convince the budgetmaker—whether a legislature or a budget committee—that the budget for the next fiscal period can safely be cut."[2]

This psychology is often manifested in the fourth quarter rush to commit unspent funds. If all funds are not committed, not only is there the fear that others might consider the budget to be inflated, but the institution would lose these unspent funds from their "base" level of expenditure on which the next year's increase is predicated. (Industry, in contrast, must satisfy the customer in order to retain business and has profit as a readily identifiable measure or performance.)

This traditional approach has often been described as "creeping incrementalism." Unfortunately, spurred by inflation and changing situations, the "creep" has turned into a "gallop" in many organizations.

Traditional budgeting is a static tool, weighted down by masses of detailed numbers for every conceivable type of expenditure. It does not provide management with a viable decision making tool to react to changing situations since the budget procedure does not ask:

- Are the current activities efficient and effective?
- Should current activities be eliminated or reduced to fund higher priority new programs or to reduce the current budget?

THE ZERO-BASE APPROACH

On December 2, 1969, at the Plaza Hotel in New York City, Dr. Arthur F. Burns, then counselor to the President of the United States, addressed the annual dinner meeting of the Tax Foundation on the "Control of Government Expenditures." In this speech, Dr. Burns identified the basic need for zero-base budgeting; but he also expressed his concern that such a process would be difficult if not impossible to implement:

> "Customarily, the officials in charge of an established program have to justify only the increase which they seek above last year's appropriation. In other words, what they are already spending is usually accepted as necessary without examination. Substantial savings could undoubtedly be realized if (it were required that) every agency . . . make a case for its entire appropriation request each year, just as if its program or programs were entirely new. Such budgeting procedure may be difficult to achieve, partly because it will add heavily to the burdens of budget-making, and partly also because it will be resisted by those who fear that their pet programs would be jeopardized by a system that subjects every . . . activity to annual scrutiny of its costs and results."

Dr. Burns was advocating that government agencies re-evaluate all programs and present their requests for appropriation in such a fashion that all funds can be allocated on the basis of cost/benefit or some similar kind of evaluative analysis.

A methodolgy to implement zero-base budgeting was developed and implemented at Texas Instruments during 1969. The process was first adopted in Government at the direction of Governor Jimmy Carter of Georgia. The state of Georgia adopted zero-base budgeting for the development of its fiscal 1973 budget. The process was successful and is still being used. Zero-base budgeting is an emerging process which has been adopted by a variety of industrial and governmental organizations, and is a process which is being continually developed and modified to meet the needs of its users.

The fears of Dr. Burns that a zero-base approach "will add heavily to the burdens of budget-making" have not proven to be the case. None of the organizations that I am familiar with who have implemented the approach have added additional time onto their calendar for the preparation of a zero-base budget (other than design and training prior to the budget preparation process which is a normal start-up requirement of any new process). Although the zero-base process does not take more calendar time, it usually involves more managers and takes more management time than the traditional budget procedures. However, the zero-base approach includes objective setting, program evaluation, and operational decision making, as well as budget making. Traditional budgeting procedures often separate these management aspects. In the worst case, the traditional budget process is merely a way to obtain an appropriation with the operational decision making and operating budgets determined after the appropriation has been determined. If we added the time requirements of these additional management elements to the time requirements of the traditional budgeting process, then the time requirements of zero-base budgeting do not add to management's burdens. In fact, after the initial year's implementation, the zero-base approach can actually reduce management's burden as the zero-base thought process and methodology become ingrained into management's normal way of problem solving and decision making.

ZERO-BASE BUDGETING PROCEDURES

The zero-base approach requires each organization to evaluate and review all programs and activities (current as well as new) systematically, to review activities on a basis of output or performance as well as cost, to emphasize manager decision making first, number-oriented budgets second, and increase analysis. However, I should stress that zero-base is an approach, not a fixed procedure or set of forms to be applied uniformly from one organization to the next. The mechanics and management approach has differed significantly among the organizations that have adopted zero-base, and the process must be adapted to fit the specific needs of each user.

Although the specifics differ among organizations, there are four basic steps to the zero-base approach that must be addressed by each organization:

- Identify "decision units."

- Analyze each decision unit in a "decision package."

- Evaluate and rank all decision packages to develop the appropriations request.

- Prepare the detailed operating budgets reflecting those decision packages approved in the budget appropriation.

DEFINING DECISION UNITS

Zero-base budgeting attempts to focus management's attention on evaluating activities and making decisions. Therefore, the "meaningful elements" of each organization must be defined so that they can be isolated for analysis and decision making. For the sake of terminology, we have termed these meaningful elements "decision units." The definition of decision units in most organizations is straightforward, and the decision units may correspond to those budget units defined by traditional budget procedures.

For those organizations with a detailed budget unit or cost center structure, the decision unit may correspond to that budget unit. In some cases, the budget unit manager may wish to identify separately different functions or operations within his budget unit if they are significant in size and require separate analysis. He may therefore identify several "decision units" for a budget unit. If an organization has a well developed program structure, the decision unit may correspond to that lowest level of the program structure (program element, activity, function). Decision units may be defined at the sub-program level if there are separate organizational units within that program element. The resulting decision packages at the sub-program element level can then be grouped to evaluate the program element. In the same manner, decision packages for each program element (or sub-program element) can be grouped to evaluate each program.

The decision packages built around each decision unit are the building blocks of the budget and program analysis. These building blocks can be readily sorted either organizationally or programatically. For those organizations without a detailed program structure, the information and analysis provided by zero-base provides a readily usable data base from which a program structure can be developed.

Decision units can also be defined as major capital projects, special work assignments, or major projects. Each organization must determine for itself "what is meaningful." In practice, top management usually defines the organization or program level at which decision units must be defined, leaving it to the discretion of each manager to identify additional decision units if appropriate.

THE DECISION PACKAGE CONCEPT

The "decision package" is the building block of the zero-base concept. It is a document that identifies and describes each decision unit in such a manner that management can (a) evaluate it and rank it against other decision units competing for funding and (b) decide whether to approve it or disapprove it.

The content and format of the decision package must provide management with the information it needs to evaluate each decision unit. This information might include:

1. Purpose/objective
3. Description of actions (What are we going to do, and how are we going to do it?)
6. Costs and benefits
5. Workload and performance measures
2. Alternative means of accomplishing objectives
4. Various levels of effort (What benefits do we get for various levels of funding?)

The key to developing decision packages is the formulation of meaningful alternatives. The types of alternatives that should be considered in developing decision packages are:

1. Alternative methods of accomplishing the objective or performing the operation: Managers should identify and evaluate all meaningful alternatives and choose the alternative they consider best. If an alternative to the current method of doing business is chosen, the recommended way should be shown in the decision package with the current way shown as the alternative not recommended.
2. Different levels of effort of performing the operation: Once the best

method of accomplishing the operation has been chosen from among the various alternative methods evaluated, a manager must identify alternative levels of effort and funding to perform that operation. Managers must establish a minimum level of effort, which must be below the current level of operation, and then identify additional levels or increments as separate decision packages. These incremental levels above the minimum might bring the operation up to its current level and to several multiples of the current level of effort.

The identification and evaluation of different levels of effort is probably the most difficult aspect of the zero-base analysis, yet it is one of the key elements of the process. If only one level of effort were analyzed (probably reflecting the funding level desired by each manager), top management would be forced to make a yes or no decision on the funding request, thus funding at the requested level, eliminating the program, making arbitrary reductions, or recycling the budget process if requests exceeded funding availability.

A decision package is defined as one incremental level in a decision unit. Thus, there may be several decision packages for each decision unit. It is these incremental levels that get ranked. By identifying a minimum level of effort, plus additional increments as separate decision packages, each manager thus presents several alternatives for top management decision making:

Elimination:
Eliminate the operation if no decision packages are approved.

Reduced Level:
Reduce the level of funding if only the minimum level decision package is approved

Current Level:
Maintain the same level of effort if the minimum level, plus the one or two incremental levels (bringing the operation from the minimum level to the current level of effort) are approved
(NOTE): The current level of effort refers only to the level of output or performance sometimes referred to as a "maintenance level." However, even at the current level of effort, managers may have changed their method of operation and made operating improvements, so that the current level of effort may be accomplished at a reduced cost.)

Increased Levels:
Increased levels of funding and performance if one or more increments above the current level is approved

The minimum level of effort is the most difficult level to identify since there is no magic number (i.e., 75 per cent of the current level) that would be meaningful to all operations. The minimum level must be identified by each manager for his operations. The minimum level must be below the current level of effort. The minimum level should attempt to identify "that critical level of effort, below which the operation would be discontinued because it loses its viability or effectiveness." There are several considerations which can aid managers in defining the minimum level of effort:

1. The minimum level may not completely achieve the total objective of the operation (even the additional levels of effort recommended may not completely achieve the objective because of realistic budget and/or achievement levels).
2. The minimum level should address itself to the most critical population being served or attack the most serious problem areas.
3. The minimum level may merely reduce the amount of service (or number of services) provided.
4. The minimum level may reflect operating improvements, organizational changes, or improvements in efficiency that result in cost reductions.
5. Combinations of 1 through 4.

By identifying the minimum level, each manager is not necessarily recommending his operation be funded at the minimum level but is merely identifying that alternative to top management. If a manager identifies several levels of effort, he is recommending that all levels be funded.

EXAMPLE: AIR QUALITY LABORATORY

The following example of the Georgia Air Quality Laboratory (Air Quality Control) illustrates the type of analysis that each manager needs to make in order to prepare his decision packages. The Air Quality Laboratory tests air samples collected by field engineers throughout Georgia. It identifies and evaluates pollutants by type and volume, then provides reports and analyses to the field engineers. The manager involved made the typical two-part analysis; first, identifying different ways of performing the function; and secondly, identifying the different levels of effort.

1. Different ways of performing the same function:
   a. Recommended decision package: Use a centralized laboratory in Atlanta to conduct all tests (cost: $246,000). This expenditure would allow 75,000 tests and would determine the air quality for 90% of the population (leaving unsampled only rural areas with little or no pollution problem).
   b. Alternatives not recommended:
   (1) Contract testing to Georgia Tech (cost: $450,000). The $6 per test charged by the University exceeds the $246,000 cost for doing the same work in the Air Quality Laboratory, and the quality of the testing is equal.
   (2) Conduct all testing at regional locations (cost: $590,000). Cost $590,000 the first year due to setup cost and purchase of duplicate equipment, with a $425,000 running rate in subsequent years. Many labs would be staffed at a minimum level, with less than full utilization of people and equipment.
   (3) Conduct tests in Central Laboratory for special pollutants only, which require special qualifications for people and equipment, and conduct routine tests in regional centers (cost: $400,000). This higher cost is created because regional centers have less than full workloads for people and equipment.

The recommended way of performing this laboratory function was chosen because the alternatives did not offer any additional advantages and were more expensive. The manager therefore recommended the level of 75,000 tests, at $246,000. Each manager has complete freedom to recommend either *new way* or the current way of doing business.

Once he had defined the basic alternatives and selected the one he considered best, he completed his analysis by describing different levels of effort for his chosen alternative. For the recommended Central Laboratory in Atlanta, the Air Quality Laboratory manager described and evaluated decision packages that called for different levels of effort for air quality tests. In this case, the manager believed that he could reduce the level of testing to 37,300 samples and still satisfy the minimum requirements of the field engineers who used his services. Therefore, he completed his analysis by identifying the minimum level and additional levels of effort for his recommended way of performing the testing as follows:

2. Different levels of effort of performing the function:
    a. Air Quality Laboratory (1 of 3), cost $140,000. Minimum package: Test 37,300 samples, determining air quality for only five urban areas with the worst pollution (covering 70% of the population).
    b. Air Quality Laboratory (2 of 3), cost: $61,000. Test 17,700 additional samples (totaling 55,000, which is the current level), determining air quality for five additional problem urban areas plus eight counties chosen on the basis of worst pollution (covering 80% of the population).
    c. Air Quality Laboratory (3 of 3), cost: $45,000. Test 20,000 additional samples (totaling 75,000), determining air quality for 90% of the population, and leaving only rural areas with little or no pollution problems unsampled.

The Air Quality Laboratory manager thus prepared three decision packages (1 of 3, 2 of 3, and 3 of 3).

Development of different levels as separate decision packages indicates that the functional manager thinks all levels deserve serious consideration within realistic funding expectations. He identifies three possible levels and leaves it to higher management to make tradeoffs among functions and level of effort within each function.

THE RANKING PROCESS

The ranking process provides management with a technique to allocate its limited resources by making management concentrate on these questions: "How much should we spend?" and "Where should we spend it?" Management constructs its answer to these questions by listing all the decision packages identified in order of decreasing benefit to the organization. It then identifies the benefits to be gained at each level of expenditure and studies the consequences of not approving additional decision packages ranked below that expenditure level.

The ranking process establishes priorities among the incremental levels of each decision unit (i.e., decision packages). The rankings therefore display a marginal analysis. If the manager of the Air Quality Program in Georgia developed decision packages for the Air Quality Laboratory, Reviews and Permits, Source Evaluation, Registration, and Research, his ranking might appear as follows:

Rank	Decision Package	Incremental Cost	Cumulative Program Cost
1	Reviews and Permits (1 of 2)	$116,000	$116,000
2	Source Evaluation (1 of 4)	103,000	219,000
* 3	Air Quality Laboratory (1 of 3)	140,000	359,000
4	Registration (1 of 3)	273,000	632,000 .
5	Source Evaluation (2 of 3)	53,000	685,000
* 6	Air Quality Laboratory (2 of 3)	61,000	746,000
7	Source Evaluation (3 of 3)	45,000	791,000
* 8	Air Quality Laboratory (3 of 3)	45,000	836,000
9	Reviews and Permits (2 of 2)	50,000	886,000
10	Research (1 of 2)	85,000	971,000

From a practical standpoint, the rankings of the minimum levels for Reviews and Permits, Source Evaluation, Air Quality Laboratory, and Registration may be requirements, so that the absolute ranking of those decision packages (ranked 1–4) are not meaningful. However, the priority of the packages with a lower ranking becomes significant since management will ultimately make a decision on which packages will be funded. If packages one through eight are funded, management would approve a budget for Air Quality Control of $246,000. Management would have funded all three levels of the Air Quality Laboratory, thus increasing that budget; funded only the minimum level of Registration, thus decreasing that budget; and not funded any Research, thus eliminating that function. Discretionary programs may have the minimum level ranked at a medium or low priority, while increased levels for other programs may be given a high priority. Therefore, the rankings can produce dramatic shifts in resource allocations.

The key to an effective review and ranking process lies in focusing top management's attention on key policy issues and discretionary expenditures. In a small organization such as the city of Garland, Texas, all decision packages were reviewed by the City Manager. The City Manager took the lower priority packages from each organization that he thought were somewhat discretionary and concentrated his ranking efforts on developing a consolidated ranking across all city organizations for those discretionary decision packages.

In large organizations, top management may be forced to rely primarily on management summaries in lieu of concentrating on the decision packages. In the state of Georgia, decision packages are ranked to the program level in each agency. The Budget Office prepares executive summaries based on the decision packages and program rankings submitted by each agency for the Governor's review. It is also possible to prepare "activity decision packages" (an activity being the lowest element in the program structure). Activity decision packages would then be ranked for each program. "Program decision packages" could then be prepared based on the activity decision packages and the ranking at the program level. The program decision packages could have a similar format and content as the activity decision package, but provide a summary and program analysis for use by top agency management and the executive and legislative review process.

Regardless of organizational size and form of top management review, the decision packages and rankings form the backbone of analysis and decision making. The specific nature of each review process must be specifically designed to fit the size and personality of each organization.

PREPARING THE DETAILED OPERATING BUDGET

The budget or appropriation requests prepared by each organization are usually subject to some form of legislative review and modification. If the legislative appropriation differs markedly from the budget request, many organizations who have used traditional budgeting techniques are forced to recycle their entire budgeting effort to determine where the reductions should be made. Under the zero-base budgeting approach, the decision packages and rankings determine specifically the actions required to achieve any budget reductions. If the legislature defines reductions in specific program areas, we can readily identify the corresponding decision packages and reduce the appropriate program and organizational budgets. If the legislature identifies an arbitrary reduction (e.g., reduce budgets 5 per cent), each agency can use its rankings and eliminate those decision packages that it considers to be the lowest priority.

In the final analysis, each organization will have a number of approved decision packages which define the budget of each program and organizational unit. The decision packages also define the specific activities and performance anticipated from each program and organizational unit. This information can provide the basis for both budget and operational reviews during the year.

PRACTICES AND PROBLEMS

The term "zero-base' has many different connotations. To those who have merely heard the term, it tends to mean "the process of throwing everything out and starting all over again from scratch" or "reinventing the wheel." These connotations are incorrect and imply an effort of impractical magnitude and chaos.

In a more practical vein, "zero-base" means the evaluation of all programs. The evaluation of alternatives and program performance may occasionally lead us to completely rethink and redirect a program, in which case we do "throw everything out and start all over again." However, in the great majority of cases, programs will continue, incorporating modifications and improvement. For the majority of programs, we will concentrate our analysis on evaluating program efficiency and effectiveness and the evaluation and prioritization of different levels of effort.

This pragmatic approach offers us an extremely flexible tool. Managers can "reinvent the wheel" in those situations where preliminary investigation indicates the need and potential benefits of such an approach and can concentrate their effort on improving programs that appear to be headed in the right direction.

The zero-base approach has led to major reallocation of resources. For example:

The state of Georgia experienced a $57 million (5 per cent of general funds) revenue shortfall. Governor Jimmy Carter used the zero-base analysis to reduce budgets across 65 agencies, with reductions ranging from 1 per cent to 15 per cent. Program reductions within each agency ranged from no change to elimination.

In a political environment, the expectations for major shifts in resource allocations must be qualified. The major reallocations of resources will normally take place within major agencies such as shifting administrative and maintenance cost savings into direct program delivery. However, it is unrealistic to expect a 20 percent decrease in the Department of Education to fund a 40 per cent increase in Mental Health. The political realities do not usually allow such shifts. It is also unrealistic to expect an automatic tax reduction due to zero-base budgeting. When cost reductions are achieved, the overriding political tendency is to plow the money back into increased services in other programs.

"If we can't realistically expect major funding reallocations among major agencies, and if we can't expect a tax decrease, then why do zero-base budgeting?" I believe that there are four overriding reasons that make the zero-base approach worthwhile:

1. Low priority programs can be eliminated or reduced. How the savings are used is a completely separate question.
2. Program effectiveness can be dramatically improved. Such improvements may or may not have a budgetary impact.
3. High impact programs can obtain increased funding by shifting resources within an agency, whereas the increased funding might not have been made available had the agency merely requested an increase in total funding.
4. Tax increases can be retarded. The first three benefits can significantly reduce the necessity for increased taxes by allowing agencies to do a more effective job with existing revenues. For the hard nosed executive or Legislature budgets can be reduced with a minimum of reduced services.

The zero-base approach is not without its problems. The major problem is the threat that many bureaucrats feel towards a process which evaluates the effectiveness of their programs. The zero-base process also requires a great deal of effective administration, communications, and training of managers who will be involved in the analysis. Managers may also have problems in identifying appropriate decision units, developing adequate data to produce an effective analysis, determining the minimum level of effort, ranking dissimilar programs, and handling large volumes of packages. For many programs, workload and performance measures may be lacking or the cause/effect and program impact may not be well defined so that the analysis will be less than perfect. Therefore, zero-base budgeting should be looked upon as a longer term management development process rather than a one year cure-all.

Fortunately, the zero-base approach is not subject to the gamesmanship one might anticipate. The traditional budget approach offers maximum opportunity for gamesmanship because current operations are seldom evaluated and many discreet decisions are never explicitly identified and get "buried in the numbers." However, the zero-base approach removes the umbrella from covering current operations and requires managers to clearly identify operating decisions. In zero-base, most obvious forms of gamesmanship would be to avoid identifying reasonable alternatives, to include the pet projects within the minimum level package, and to rank high priority progams low in the ranking in order to obtain additional funding. If the decision packages are formatted adequately to display the alternatives considered, workload and performance data, descriptions of actions, and enough cost data so that discretionary items cannot be built into the cost estimate, it becomes very obvious when such gamesmanship is attempted. Also, because the entire ranking of decision packages must be displayed, it is very easy to challenge a high priority item that received a low ranking or a low priority item which received a high ranking.

The problems in implementing zero-base budgeting are not to be minimized. The specific needs, problems, and capabilities of each organization must be considered in adapting the zero-base approach. Although most of the basic concepts of the zero-base approach have been maintained, the specifics of administration, formats, and procedures have been different for each organization that has adopted the approach. Zero-base can be applied on an intensive basis throughout all levels of an organization, applied only to selected programs, or applied only at major program levels rather than involving all operating managers. The strategy of implementing the zero-base approach must be developed for each organization depending on its specific needs and capabilities. It should be considered a management and budgetary improvement effort that may require several years to reach full utilization and effectiveness.

Zero-base budgeting challenges the security blanket and misdirection of traditional budget procedures. It is certainly not a cure-all to improve services and reduce taxes, but it offers a more rational approach to managing government.

NOTES

1. Peter F. Drucker, "Managing the Public Sector Institution," *The Public Interest*, No. 33, fall 1973, pp. 43-60.
2. *Ibid.*, p. 50.

Jimmy Carter Tells Why He Will Use Zero-Base Budgeting

JIMMY CARTER

When I became governor of Georgia in 1970, one of my first jobs was to finalize the budget for the coming year. The departmental funding requests amounted to more than half again as much money as would be available. No one had made any attempt to arrange the requests in any sort of priority.

I saw the need for a budgeting technique in Georgia which I now see as needed for the federal government.

That technique is zero-base budgeting.

Immediately after my inauguration, I will require zero-base budgeting for all federal departments, bureaus, and boards by executive order.

Zero-base budgeting is well-known to many business people [see "One Way to Erase Needless Government Programs," *Nation's Business*, November, 1976]. Some 300 businesses and a dozen state governments are now utilizing the concept. However, allow me to define it for you.

BACK TO THE BEGINNING

In contrast to the traditional budgeting approach of incrementing the new on the old, zero-base budgeting demands a total rejustification of everything from zero. It means chopping up the organization into individual functions and analyzing each annually, regardless of whether it is 50 years old or a brand-new proposal for a future program.

The budget is broken into units called decision packages, prepared by managers at each level. These packages cover every existing or proposed activity of each department. They include analyses of purposes, costs, measures of performance and benefits, alternative courses of action, and consequences of disapproval.

Packages are also ranked in order of priority. After several discussions between department heads and the chief executive, the rankings are finalized, and packages up to the level of affordability are approved and funded. In the case of the federal government, of course, final approval would be up to Congress.

Zero-base budgeting has had a rather long gestation period and a brief infancy. It draws on a number of innovative techniques developed in the early 1960's in systems analysis, problem-solving, cost-benefit analysis, and program management. Budgeting applications of these disciplines were being developed and employed in various staff functions at several major companies.

Since then, dozens of public and private organizations have applied the technique, and the roster of its disciples has continued to grow. Each has shared a need to plan and allocate resources more rationally.

As the new governor of Georgia, I quickly moved to implement zero-base budgeting by executive order. Major benefits for the taxpayer resulted. For example:

- Previously, every major department had its own computer system. Through zero-base budgeting, we created one central computer system.

- We merged 43 print shops into one.

- Georgia patrolmen—expensively trained, uniformed, and provided individually with automobiles—often were assigned to administrative chores or radio dispatching. Through zero-base budgeting, we moved almost 100 of these troopers out to patrol the highways and replaced them with handicapped Georgians trained by vocational rehabilitiation. The many benefits are obvious.

BIG REDUCTION IN COSTS

These and other achievements resulted in a 50 percent reduction in administrative costs. I see no reason why benefits of the same magnitude can't be captured in the federal government.

There was, of course, intense opposition to zero-base budgeting from bureaucrats who thrived on confusion, from special interests that preferred to work in the dark, and from a few legislative leaders who did not want to see their fiefdoms endangered. But with forceful leadership and persuasiveness by our key men, the new approach was widely accepted. That acceptance was accompanied by gratitude that the state's resources were being allocated openly, decently, and free of political intrigue.

NO INSTANT MIRACLES

I don't want to mislead you and leave the impression that implementing zero-base budgeting will create instant miracles in the federal government. In Georgia, its impact during my incumbency was quite subtle, but nevertheless real, in making basic changes in our government's operation. No doubt it will continue to generate improvements in the years ahead.

Many seasoned executives have raised specific and sometimes well-intentioned concerns about zero-base budgeting. Here are some of the most frequent ones and how I and others have handled them.

1. *Zero-base budgeting is threatening. Therefore, budget submissions will be less than candid.* This challenge is not unique to zero-base budgeting. I know of few managers who enjoy completely open and frank discussions during the budget cycle. Reluctant participants should be approached with a dialogue that focuses on what the process can do for them rather than to them. For unlike traditional approaches, zero-base budgeting offers them a genuine opportunity to increase their resources where they can demonstrate greater effectiveness or need.

2. *Administration and communications become more complicated as more people become involved.* In its formative years, this concern was probably valid. It is less so now that procedures and forms have been refined and tested, and a substantial number of planning executives have gained experience in the technique. But in a more fundamental sense, I have found that the best ideas for improvement have often come from the rank and file who know their operations intimately and are seriously committed to improving them. Zero-base budgeting can provide these people a channel of communications for their day in court, nothwithstanding administrative difficulties. The trade-off is worth it.

3. *Zero-base budgeting requires more time.* That may be true during the learning process, but my own experience suggests that, after a year or so, the time required for budgeting is substantially lessened, often by as much as a third. More importantly, the quality of budget requests improves dramatically.

4. *Zero-base budgeting forces decision-making.* Forcing decision-making is one of zero-base budgeting's greatest strengths and an obviously healthy one for a government or other organization that uses the technique. But since forced decision-making can be a bitter pill at times, a carefully devised implementation plan, worked out well in advance and rigorously adhered to, can minimize this risk. In Georgia, we further minimized this

risk by amending the state constitution to permit payment of incentive awards amounting to up to ten percent of first-year savings. These payments were to reward those employees who made cost-saving suggestions.

5. *Large volumes of decision packages place an unmanageable burden on the budget staff.* In Georgia, we managed this problem with a computer routine. Each decision package was assigned a code number to describe the kind of service being delivered, thus enabling us to detect duplication automatically. Among other things, this allowed us to identify seven agencies responsible for the education of deaf children and 22 responsible for the utilization of water resources. Even if we could claim no benefits from zero-base budgeting in the first year (which we could), the technique provided us with a massive data base that was a critical information source for a major reorganization.

From my experience in government as well as the experiences of corporations in the business world, a number of clear-cut benefits from an effective zero-base budgeting effort can be cited. These benefits include:

- Focusing the management process on analysis and decision-making rather than simply on numbers—in other words, the what, why, and how issues as well as how much.

- Combining planning, budgeting, and operational decision-making into one process.

- Forcing managers to evaluate in detail the cost-effectiveness of their operations. This includes specific programs—both new and old—all of which are clearly identified rather than functionally buried.

- Providing a system to trade off between long-term and short-term needs during the budgeting period, as well as a follow-up tool on cost and performance during the year.

- Allowing for quick budget adjustment or resource shifts during the year, if necessary when revenue falls short. In so doing, zero-base budgeting offers the capability to quickly and rationally modify goals and expectations to correspond to a realistic and affordable plan of operation.

- Identifying similar functions among different departments for comparison and evaluation.

- And most important to me, broadly expanding management participation and training in the planning, budgeting, and decision-making process.

A NEED AT THE TOP

Zero-base budgeting procedures are one of the best tools for ensuring constant reassessment of staff programs, new as well as old. But no system will work unless those at the top understand the workings of a large bureaucracy, are willing to work long hours to find out what is really going on, and have the political courage to make tough decisions.

The best creative energies are needed to work out a zero-base budget. Nothing is sacred; new and innovative techniques must be conceived, assessed, and compared to traditional approaches.

However, zero-base budgeting has proved its value.

In the private sector, misdirected or redundant staff efforts never paid a dividend; provided a meaningful, rewarding job for a competent employee; launched a successful product to specification on time; or satisfied a demanding customer.

Similarly, in the public sector, there is no inherent conflict between careful planning, tight budgeting, and constant management reassessment on the one hand, and compassionate concern for the deprived and afflicted on the other. Waste and inefficiency never fed a hungry child, provided a job for a willing worker, or educated a deserving student.

Zero-Based Budgeting Comes to Washington

JAMES Q. WILSON

You remember ZBB—that government reform candidate
Jimmy Carter promised. Here's how it will work.

Charles Pettypoint, the newly-installed efficiency expert in the White House, was eager to see at firsthand how Zero-Based Budgeting was working. He decided to drop in on an agency getting ready to use it, and selected the National Park Service in the Department of the Interior.

He arrived to find the entire senior staff of the Park Service seated around a big table. The Director seemed pleased to have so distinguished a visitor, and asked Mr. Pettypoint to explain ZBB to his aides.

"Well, the idea is to get the most out of the taxpayer's dollar by making sure that every cent we spend is justified."

Everybody around the table nodded. "Hear, hear," one said.

"What we do," Pettypoint continued, "is to assume that the agency—in this case, the Park Service—has no money at all and then. . . ."

Murmurs of outraged disbelief erupted, but the Director silenced the room with a firm glare.

"As I was saying," Pettypoint went on, somewhat stiffly, "we then ask the Park Service to justify each dollar of its budget and every activity it carries out. You will have to show us how much of your product or service you can produce for a given amount of money."

Only after a pin dropped noisily to the floor did everyone realize how quiet the room had become. Two older Park officials had turned pale, and the hands of another began to shake uncontrollably.

"Justify *everything?*" the Director asked.

"Everything," Pettypoint replied.

"This year?"

"This year: In fact, within the next three months."

A long pause.

"Men," the Director finally said, "I think we ought to cooperate 100 percent with this splendid idea."

"Sir, you can't be serious. . . ." An aide started to rise, but was waved back to his seat by the Director.

"Of course I am serious. Mr. Pettypoint is serious. The President of the United States is serious. We will all be serious."

"Here is what we will do," the Director continued. "Smith, you tell Senator Henry Jackson, the chairman of the Interior Committee, that we are considering what would happen if we closed all the national parks."

"Even those in the state of Washington?" Smith asked incredulously.

"Especially those in Washington," the Director replied. "But stress to the Senator that it is just a mental experiment, a planning exercise. We probably won't *really* close any of the parks in his state."

Suddenly, a beatific expression of sudden enlightenment spread across Smith's face. "Gotcha, chief."

"Gorstwinkle, I want you to get right to work on making up a list of national parks in the order of their importance, so we will know which ones to leave open if we can't reopen all of them," the Director said.

Gorstwinkle started to giggle uncontrollably: "Right away. Of course, I won't be able to keep the list secret, chief. You know, Freedom of Information and all that . . . . " He broke up in laughter.

"I understand," the Director replied, allowing a thin smile to crease his stern features. "Nothing's ever secret any more. I suppose the Sierra Club is bound to find out that we are thinking of closing Yellowstone."

"The Audubon Society will suspect that we might be cutting back on bird sanctuaries," someone remarked.

"Wait until the Daughters of the American Revolution finds out that we are . . . ." the speaker gasped for breath, as he shook convulsively with laughter, "that we are analyzing whether it makes sense to leave Independence Hall open!"

Howls rang through the room. One man staggered to the drinking fountain, and another had to loosen his tie to avoid choking.

Pettypoint bristled. "You are not looking at this constructively."

"Oh, but we are, Mr. Pettypoint," the Director replied. "I firmly believe that, as a result of this ZBB exercise, the public will realize that we need more money for more parks."

"But that isn't the purpose," Pettypoint rejoined.

"Isn't it?" the Director asked innocently.

Smith, wiping his eyes, shouted: "Hey, Pettypoint, did you know that some of those women in the Garden Club can hit a moving White House staffer at twenty paces with a potted geranium?" He collapsed back in his chair, overcome with hilarity.

Crestfallen, Pettypoint said plaintively, "Well, maybe the Park Service is not the place to begin. I suppose ZBB would work best applied to a program that didn't have this kind of organized public support."

The Director stared at him for a long moment.

"Name one."

11

ANALYTICAL APPROACHES TO GOVERNMENTAL DECISIONS

For many students of public administrative behavior, decision making is the key activity, the goal being to make decisions in a rational way by weighing the benefits and costs of various programs and program options. This, it is hoped, will improve the quality of government decision making.

Herbert Simon begins this chapter with a discussion of the basic decision-making concept and its significance. This is followed by Alice Rivlin's recommendations for more analysis, more experimentation, and more performance management in government.

Although the commentary of James Schlesinger included here is over ten years old, he fully understood the conflict between the systems approach and the standard political approach. His perceptive observations suggest that the two approaches can be made to fit together.

Public administrators are increasingly called on to evaluate the effectiveness of their programs. In the concluding article in this chapter, Joseph Wholey defines program evaluation and explains its uses. Wholey provides examples of program evaluation at work and points out the difficulties that decision makers face in obtaining useful evaluations.

Decision Making

HERBERT A. SIMON

There is no need, at this late date, to justify the study of organization and administration in terms of the decision-making process, for decision-making concepts and language have become highly popular in writing about administrations.[1] This paper will describe some of the progress that has been made over the past quarter century, employing this approach, toward deepening our scientific knowledge— what new facts have been learned about human behavior in organizations, what new scientific procedures for ascertaining facts, what new concepts for describing them, and what new generalizations for explaining them. This progress extends both to descriptive and normative matters: to the pure science of administration, and its application to the practical business of managing.

To satisfy limits on this journal's space, your patience and my time, the account will be highly selective. Only a few notable and significant advances have been selected; others for which equally plausible claims might be made are ignored. A frequent practice in the social sciences is to bemoan our present ignorance while making optimistic predictions about future knowledge. It is a pleasure to survey an area of social science where, by contrast, we can speak without blushing about our present knowledge—indeed, where only a small sample of the gains in knowledge that have been achieved in the past quarter century can be presented.

OPERATIONS RESEARCH AND MANAGEMENT SCIENCE

One obvious answer to the question "What's new?" is the spectacular development in the normative theory of decision making that goes under the labels of "operations research" and "management science." Through these activities, many classes of administrative decisions have been formalized, mathematics has been applied to determine the characteristics of the "best" or "good" decisions, and myriads of arithmetic calculations are carried out routinely in many business and governmental organizations to reach the actual decisions from day to day. A number of sophisticated mathematical tools—linear programming, queuing theory, dynamic programming, combinatorial mathematics, and others—have been invented or developed to this end.

Like all scientific developments, this one has a long intellectual history, and did not spring, full-grown, from the brow of Zeus. Nevertheless, the state of the art today is so remarkably advanced beyond its position before World War II that the difference of degree becomes one of kind.[2]

The quantitative decision-making tools of operations research have perhaps had more extensive application in business than in governmental organizations. It is worth recalling, however, that many of these tools underwent their early development in the American and British military services during and just after the Second World War (where the terms "operations research" and "operations analysis" were coined). Among the inventors of linear programming, for example, were Tjalling Koopmans, seeking, as statistician with the Combined Shipping Adjustment Board, a means for scheduling tanker operations efficiently; and George B. Dantzig and Marshall K. Wood, in the Office of the Air Force Controller, who used as one of their first (hypothetical) programming problems the scheduling of the Berlin Airlift.

Operations research, particularly in its governmental applications, has retained close intellectual ties with classical economic theory, and has sought to find effective ways of applying that theory to public budgeting and expenditure decisions. This has been a central preoccupation of the RAND Corporation effort, as exemplified by such works as Charles J. Hitch and Roland N. McKean, *The Economics of Defense in the Nuclear Age*.[3] In the past several years, Hitch, as Controller of the Department of Defense, and a number of his former RAND associates have played major roles in bringing the new tools to bear on Defense Department budget decisions. Thus, while the quarter century begins with V. O. Key's plaint about "The Lack of a Budgetary Theory,"[4] it ends with a distinct revitalization of the whole field of public expenditure theory, and with a burgeoning of new analytic tools to assist in allocating public resources.

OPTIMALITY AND ALL THAT

In many ways the contributions of operations research and management science to decision-making theory have been very pragmatic in flavor. The goal, after all, is to devise tools that will help management make better decisions. One example of a pragmatic technique that has proved itself very useful, and has been rapidly and widely adopted over the past five years, is the scheduling procedure variously called PERT, or critical path scheduling. This technique does not use any very deep or sophisticated mathematics (which may account partly for the speed of its adoption), but is mainly an improvement of the common sense underlying the traditional Gantt Chart.

Contrasting with this pragmatic flavor, advances in operations research have been paralleled by developments in the pure theory of rational choice—a theory that has reached a very high level of mathematical and logical elegance and rigor. Among these developments perhaps the most important are: (1) rigorous, formal axiom systems for defining the concept of utility in operational terms, (2) extension of the theory of rational choice to encompass the maximization of expected utility under conditions of uncertainty, (3) extension of the theory to repeated choices over time—dynamic optimization, and (4) extension of the theory to competitive "gaming" situations. These formal advances have had an important influence, in turn, on directions of work in theoretical statistics (statistical decision theory, Bayesian statistics), and on the kinds of models that are preferred by operations researchers—or at least by the theorists among their number.[5]

An evaluation of these contributions on the pure theory of rational choice would return a mixed verdict. On the positive side, they have provided enormous conceptual clarification for discussions of "rationality." For example, it has always been unclear what rationality meant in a pure outwitting or bargaining situation, where each party is trying to outguess, and perhaps bluff, the other. If the theory of games, due to von Neumann and Morgenstern, did not solve this problem for all situations, it at least made painfully clear exactly what the problem is.

On the negative side, fascination with the pure theory of rational choice has sometimes distracted attention from the problems of decision makers who possess modest calculating powers in the face of a world of enormous complexity. (In the real world, the calculating powers of electronic computers as well as men must be described as "modest.") A normative theory, to be useful, must call only for information that can be obtained and only for calculations that can be performed. The classical theory of rational choice has generally ignored these information-processing limitations. It has assumed that rationality was concerned with choice among alternatives that were already specified, and whose consequences were known or were readily calculable. It has assumed, also, comparability of consequences—that is, a practically measurable utility index.

Since these conditions, on which the classical theory rests, are so seldom satisfied in the real world, great interest attaches to procedures that make less heroic assumptions about the "givens" and the knowns; and there is considerable progress in devising less-than-optimal decision procedures for situations where the optimum is unknown and practically undiscoverable. These procedures, often called heuristic methods, are distinguishable from optimizing techniques in three respects: they grapple, as most optimizing techniques do not, with the problems of designing and discovering alternatives, as well as with choosing among given alternatives; they frequently "satisfice," or settle for good-enough answers in despair at finding best answers; they commonly do not guarantee the qualities of the solutions they provide, and often do not even guarantee they will find a solution. The second and third of these characteristics are, of course, not virtues, but are the price that must be paid for extending our theory and tools for decision making to the wide range of real-world situations not encompassed by the classical models.

By way of illustration, a common problem of business and governmental management involves locating a system of warehouses over a country so that products can be distributed from production points to ultimate users as economically as possible. Attempts to formulate the warehousing problem so that the optimizing methods known as linear programming can be used have failed because the computations become too lengthy. However, heuristic techniques have been applied successfully to find "good" solutions to the problem where "best" solutions are unattainable.[6]

It is traditional to observe, in any discussion of the modern decision-making tools, that knowledge of these tools runs far in advance of application, and that the domain of application has been limited largely to decisions that are well-structured or "programmed," and quantitative in character. The warehousing problem described above has both of these characteristics. Whether this limitation on applications is inherent or temporary is a more controversial question. One of the important tasks before us now is to see how far we can go in extending the applicability of the new decision-making tools to areas that are ill-structured, and qualitative, calling for "judgment," "experience," and even "creativity." To do this, we shall presumably have to understand what "judgment," "experience," and "creativity" are, a topic discussed later.

EXPERIMENTS ON DECISION MAKING

A second area of significant advance has been in applying the experimental method to the investigation of decision making. This has been done both by arranging for experiments on live real-world organizations—on the model of the Hawthorne experiments—and/or by bringing organizations, or organizationoid systems into the laboratory. For obvious reasons, the latter has been done more often than the former.

The first volume of the *Public Administration Review* contained a report of a large-scale field experiment on the decision-making processes of social workers,[7] but similar experiments have been exceedingly rare in the succeeding twenty-five years. One of the few other examples to which I can refer is the study done in the Prudential Life Insurance Company by the Survey Research Center of the University of Michigan.[8] Either researchers on organizations decided that the information attainable from field experiments was not worth the trouble and cost of carrying out such experiments, or they found it difficult to secure the cooperation of business and governmental organizations in arranging such experiments—or both. Whatever the reason, field experiments have not been an important procedure for learning about organizational decision making.

In a few cases researchers have tried to import relatively sizeable organizations into the laboratory—hence, their studies lie on the boundary line between field and laboratory experiments. The Systems Research Laboratory of the RAND Corporation, for example, studied decision making by simulating, under controlled conditions, an entire air defense control center and associated early warning stations, manned on a full-time basis over a period of several months by a staff of some thirty subjects. While the studies conducted by the Systems Research Laboratory had as their direct outgrowth a major Air Force training program, the laboratory proved less tractable as a setting for obtaining data for testing theories of the decision-making process, and there has been no subsequent rash of studies of this kind.[9]

In contrast to the dearth of field experiments and large-scale laboratory experiments, laboratory experimentation with relatively small groups has been a thriving enterprise. Several examples of methodological advances in the art of small-group experimentation can be mentioned. Fred Bales, with his interaction process analysis, developed a scheme of data processing useful for studying the interaction of task-oriented and social-system oriented behavior in small problem-solving groups. Alex Bavelas devised a small-group task that permitted the experimenter to alter the decision-making process by opening or closing particular channels of communication between members of the group. In succeeding years, the Bales coding scheme and the Bavelas small-group task have both been used in a substantial number of studies, manipulating a great many different independent variables. Both have proved exceedingly valuable in permitting the cumulation of comparable knowledge from a whole series of experiments carried out by different investigators in different laboratories.

It is impossible to summarize here, or even to reference, the numerous contributions to the substantive knowledge of decision making that have been contributed by the small-group experiments. A single example will convey the flavor of such work. Cyert and March were able to produce bias in the estimates of members of a simulated organization by creating partial conflict of interest among them, but showed that under certain circumstances this bias did not affect organizational performance.[10]

New knowledge about organizational decision making can be obtained from appropriately planned experiments on individuals as well as from small-group experiments. Andrew Stedry, for example, has tested in this way theories about how budget controls affect behavior in organizations.[11] The series of studies of influence processes carried out at Yale by the late Carl Hovland and his associates belong in the same category.[12]

PERSUASION AND EVOCATION

Mention of the Yale research on influence processes marks a good point in our discussion to turn to several substantive developments in the theory of decision making. The notion that a decision is like a conclusion derived from a set of premises has been a useful metaphor for analyzing the decision-making process. Following the metaphor a step further, we can view each member of an organization as "inputting" certain premises, and "outputting" certain conclusions, or decisions. But each member's conclusions become, in turn, the inputs, that is to say, the premises, for other members. For one person to influence another involves inducing him to use appropriate premises in his decision making.

What happens in an organization, or in any kind of social system, when there are conflicting premises pushing a particular decision in different directions? Much of the research on influence processes has been aimed at answering this question. In much of this research, influence has been conceived as a kind of "force," so that when several influences are brought to bear simultaneously, the outcome is interpreted as a "resultant" of the impinging forces. Persuasion is then a process of exerting such a force.

An important advance in understanding decision making has been to complement the notion of persuasion with the notion of evocation. When we want someone to carry out a particular action, we may think of our task as one of inducing him to *accept* latent decision premises favorable to the action that he already possesses. Thus, writing about food will often make a reader hungry, but we would hardly say that we had "persuaded" him that he was hungry; it would be better to say that we had "reminded" him.

Processes of persuasion play their largest role in decision making in conflict situations—where the issue is already posed, and the alternatives present. This is the framework within which most of the Yale studies on attitude change were carried out. It is also the framework for the important and well-known study of *Voting* by Berelson, Lazarsfeld, and McPhee.[13]

On the other hand, in studies of decision making where the focus of attention of the participants is one of the main independent variables, the evoking processes take on larger importance. The recent study of the Trade Agreements Act renewal, by Raymond Bauer, Ithiel Pool, and Lewis Dexter indicates that these processes played a major role in deciding the issue.[14] The authors describe the setting of their study thus (p. 5): "We are interested in the sources of information for each of these populations, the bases of its attitudes on the trade issues, *and the circumstances which lead some individuals to take active roles in the making of policy.*" (Emphasis supplied.) They demonstrate convincingly that the behavior of particular Congressmen on the trade issue depended as much on the alternative claims on their time and attention as on the distribution of interests of their constituents.

To the extent that the mechanism of evocation is important for decision making, many new ways arise in which organizational arrangements may affect behavior. As example, one of the findings of the study just mentioned (p. 229) can be cited:

> In summary, we would suggest that most significant of all to an understanding of what communication went out from business on foreign trade was neither self-interest nor ideology, but the institutional structure which facilitated or blocked the production of messages. Whether a letter to a congressman would get written depended on whether organization facilitated it, whether the writer's round of daily conversations would lead up to it, whether a staff was set up to produce it, and whether the writer conceived writing this letter to be part of his job.

Evoking mechanisms take on special prominence wherever dynamic change is occurring. Studies of the diffusion of innovations show that the timing of adoption of an innovation depends critically on the means for getting people to attend to it.[15] From every point of view, the new knowledge gained about evoking and attention-directing processes is a major substantive advance in our understanding of organizational decision making.

THE STRUCTURE OF DECISIONS

A decision is not a simple, unitary event, but the product of a complex social process generally extending over a considerable period of time. As noted, decision making includes attention-directing or intelligence processes that determine the occasions of decision, processes for discovering and designing possible courses of action, and processes for evaluating alternatives and choosing among them. The complexity of decision making has posed grave difficulties in its study and description, difficulties only now being overcome by recent methodological innovations.

Traditionally, a decision-making process was captured and recorded by the common sense tools of the historian using everyday language. The notion that a decision might be viewed as a conclusion drawn from premises—a notion mentioned earlier—introduced a modicum of system into the description of decision making. According to this view, in order to record a decision-making process it was necessary to discover the sources of the decision premises, and the channels of communication they followed through the organization to the point where they became the raw materials of decision.

Studies that adopted this general approach to the description of decisions, while remaining within the traditional case-study framework, became increasingly frequent during the period under discussion. One example is Herbert Kaufman's excellent study of *The Forest Ranger*, aimed at analyzing "the way their decisions and behavior are influenced within and by the Service."[16] Another is the study by the Carnegie Tech group of the influence of accounting information on operating decisions in large companies.[17]

The method of these studies is best described as "systematized common sense." The decision premise concept provides an ordering and organizing principle; it reduces somewhat the subjectivity of the description and the dangers of observer bias; but it falls far short of allowing complete formalization of the description. And it cannot, of course, solve the problem of how to validate generalizations with data from single cases.

The invention of the modern digital computer radically changed the situation. As gradually became apparent to those who came into contact with computers, the computer is a device that is capable of making decisions. (One demonstration of this is its use to implement the analytic decision-making schemes introduced by operations research.) Hence, a language suitable for describing the processes going on in computers might well be appropriate for describing decision making in organizations. At least the notion appeared to be worth a trial: to equate "decision premise" with the concepts of data input and program of instructions in a computer, and to equate the concept of a conclusion with the concept of the output of a computer program.

An early, and rather primitive, attempt to describe an organization decision-making process in computer programming terms appeared in 1956.[18] In this study the authors recounted the steps taken by a business firm to reach a decision about the installation of an electronic computer. They then showed how this sequence of events could be explained by a program composed of an organized system of relatively simple and general information-gathering, searching, problem-solving, and evaluating processes. Of particular interest was the fact that the decision examined in this study was not a highly structured, quantitative one, but one that called for large amounts of professional and administrative judgment.

Encouraging results from early studies of this kind raised hopes that it might be possible to use computer programming languages formally as well as informally to construct theories of organizational decision making, and to test those theories by simulating the decision process on the computer. Computer programs seeking to explain several kinds of organizational decision-making situations have, in fact, been constructed, and have shown themselves adequate to simulate important aspects of the human behavior in these situations. The decisions that have been simulated in this way to date are still relatively simple ones, but they encompass behavior that would generally be regarded as professional, and as involving judgment. Two of the best-developed examples are a simulation of a department store buyer and simulation of a bank trust investment officer.[19]

I am not aware that any single comparable simulation of a decision-making process in the area of public administration has yet been carried out, but it appears that several are under way in current research. Perhaps the most likely target for initial attempts is public budgeting. If we examine the strategies described in recent empirical studies, like those of Wildavsky,[20] we will see that they can be rather directly translated into components of computer programs.

Parallel with these simulations of administrative decision making there has been a considerable exploration of individual thinking and problem solving processes, also using computer simulation as the tool of theory formulation and theory testing.[21] Today, we have a considerable specific knowledge on how human beings accomplish complex cognitive tasks. We have reasons for optimism, too, that this body of knowledge will increase rapidly, for in the digital computer language we have an analytic tool and a means for accurate expression whose powers are commensurate with the complexity of the phenomena we wish to describe and understand.

LANDMARKS AND NEW ROADS

These, then, are some of the more prominent landmarks along the road of decision-making research over the past twenty-five years. On the normative side, the analytic tools of modern operations research have secured an important place in the practical work of management. Their role in everyday decision making promises to be much enlarged as present techniques are supplemented by new heuristic approaches.

On the side of the pure science of administration, there have been equally fruitful developments. The experimental method, in the small-group laboratory, can now be used to study a wide range of decision-making behaviors that are relevant to organizations. We have introduced the concept of evocation into our theories of influence, and have used it to gain new understanding of the decision-making process in changing environments. Finally, the modern digital computer, a powerful new tool, has provided both a language for expressing our theories of decision making and an engine for calculating their empirical implications. Theories can now be compared with data of the real world of organizations.

The attention-directing mechanisms so important in decision making also have played their part in determining the particular developments sampled in this paper. Another scientist, with a different set of research concerns, would choose a different sample. The fact that even one such sample exists shows how far we have come during the past twenty-five years toward understanding human behavior in organizations.

NOTES

1. The term "decision-making" occurred three times in the titles of articles in the first fifteen volumes of the *Public Administration Review*—that is, through 1955; it occurred ten times in the next eight volumes, or about six times as often per annum as in the earlier period.
2. Some notion of the state of proto-operations-research just before World War II, as it applied to municipal administration, can be obtained from Ridley and Simon, *Measuring Municipal Activities,* (Chicago: International City Managers' Association, first edition, 1938).
3. Cambridge: Harvard University Press, 1960.
4. *American Political Science Review*, December 1940, p. 1142. Labels have an unfortunate tendency to compartmentalize knowledge. Thus, the literature of "budgeting" has been only partly informed by the literature on "decision making," and vice versa, and both of these have sometimes been isolated from the economics literature on resources allocation and public expenditure theory. Variants on the same basic sets of ideas are rediscovered each generation: "measurement of public services," "program budgeting," "performance budgeting," "engineering economy," "cost-benefit analysis," "operations analysis." What is genuinely new in this area in the past decade is the power and sophistication of the analytic and computational tools. Some impression of these tools may be gained from the Hitch and McKean book previously mentioned; from Roland N. McKean, *Efficiency in Government Through Systems Analysis* (Wiley, 1958); Arthur Maass, *et al.*, *Design of Water Resource Systems* (Harvard U. Press, 1962); or Allen V. Kneese, *The Economics of Regional Water Quality Management* (Johns Hopkins U. Press, 1964), and the references cited therein.
5. Since I have discoursed at length on these matters elsewhere, I shall be brief here. See "Theories of Decision Making in Economics and Behavioral Science," 49 *American Economic Review* 253–283. (June 1959), and Part IV of *Models of Man* (Wiley, 1957).
6. Alfred A. Kuehn and Michael J. Hamberger, "A Heuristic Program for Locating Warehouses," *Management Science*, July 1963.
7. Herbert A. Simon and William R. Divine, "Human Factors in an Administrative Experiment," 1 *Public Administration Review* 485-492 (Autumn 1941).

8. N. C. Morse and E. Reimer, "Experimental Change of a Major Organizational Variable," 52 *Journal of Abnormal and Social Psychology* 120-129 (1955).
9. Robert L. Chapman, *et al.*, "The System Research Laboratory's Air Defense Experiments," 5 *Management Science* 250-269 (April 1959).
10. Richard M. Cyert and James G. March, *The Behavioral Theory of the Firm* (Prentice-Hall, 1963), pp. 67-77.
11. *Budget Control and Cost Behavior* (Prentice-Hall, 1960), Chapter 4.
12. See the Yale Studies in Attitude and Communication, edited by Hovland and Rosenberg, and published by the Yale University Press.
13. University of Chicago Press, 1954.
14. *American Business and Public Policy: The Politics of Foreign Trade* (Atherton Press, 1963).
15. See J. Coleman, E. Katz, and H. Menzel, "Diffusion of an Innovation Among Physicians," 20 *Sociometry*, 253-270 (1957); also, H. A. Simon and J. G. March, *Organizations* (Wiley, 1957), Chapter 7.
16. Johns Hopkins U. Press, 1960, p. 4.
17. *Centralization versus Decentralization in Organizing the Controller's Department* (New York: The Controllership Foundation, 1954). The study is summarized in John M. Pfiffner and Frank P. Sherwood, *Administrative Organization* (Prentice-Hall, 1960), Chapter 21.
18. R. M. Cyert, H. A. Simon, and D. B. Trow, "Observation of a Business Decision," 29 *Journal of Business*, 237-248 (1956).
19. Descriptions of these two simulations may be found in Chapters 7 and 10, respectively, of Cyert and March, *Behavioral Theory of the Firm, op cit.*
20. Aaron Wildavsky, *The Politics of the Budgetary Process* (Little, Brown and Company, 1964).
21. For a survey, and numerous examples, see Edward Feigenbaum and Julian Feldman, *Computers and Thought* (McGraw-Hill, 1963).

Making Federal Programs Work Better

ALICE M. RIVLIN

As statisticians and analysts have become increasingly engaged in the federal government's social action programs in the last few years, their studies have broadened our knowledge of American social problems—of who is poor or sick or inadequately educated. Two important technical developments have assisted the analysts in accumulating new data. One is the improvement and wider use of sample survey techniques; the other is the astonishing increase in the data processing capacity of computers.

Better statistics on poverty have influenced the way people think about the problem and have dispelled some myths and false impressions. For example, the widespread belief that most of the poor are black mothers with lots of children living in big cities dissolves when the numbers are examined. Most of the poor are white and more than half of all poor families have male heads. Another myth that will not stand up to the statistics is that poverty is largely a problem of people who cannot or will not work. About 55 percent of all poor families in 1969 had members who worked full- or part-time and almost a third were headed by males who worked full-time. The statistics dramatize the plight of the working poor and show the inadequacy of an income transfer system that would aid only persons who cannot work.

Although survey methods and computer technology have improved our understanding of the distribution of social problems and their interrelations, there is still a need for more information, particularly about what happens to the same individuals as the years pass—about what happens to children as they move through a school system, or the extent to which people move into and out of poverty. The technical capacity to answer such questions now exists, but a critical problem of organization remains: Can information useful to policymakers be collected and applied without undue inconvenience or danger to privacy?

ESTIMATING COSTS AND BENEFITS

To know what the social problems are is to make only a start toward solving them. In choosing a course of action, decision makers need to know the costs of a program, whom it would help, and how much. Analysts have in part succeeded in estimating the initial benefits and costs of social programs, especially when the benefits are financial. The usefulness of the techniques for estimating costs and benefits of social programs is illustrated in the development of government policies for income maintenance.

By the mid-1960s, concern about income maintenance was already high in the United States, for the existing patchwork of programs—most of which had been designed in the 1930s to protect certain groups against specific kinds of income loss clearly was not solving the problem of poverty. In the last three years of the Johnson administration, a heated debate arose over income maintenance and welfare reform. Fairly wide agreement had been reached on what was wrong with the existing welfare system, as well as on general objectives to be sought in improving income maintenance, but no legislation was enacted before the administration ended. The new Republican administration came in with a conviction that "something had to be done about welfare," but without a clear commitment to a particular course of action. After reviewing the arguments that had occupied its predecessors, the new team eventually reached consensus on a form of negative income tax—the Family Assistance Plan— with the income guarantee set at a level consistent with federal budget constraints. A proposed federal floor under welfare payments was aimed at reducing disparities between richer and poorer states, while the inclusion of the working poor would equalize the treatment of families with male and female heads and reduce incentives to break up families.

Once the basic decisions were made, the analysts were called on to estimate the costs of numerous variations, and to determine what kinds of families would benefit from each and how they would affect individual states. Aided by the Survey of Economic Opportunity, the analysts were able to provide prompt, detailed answers to these questions. Dozens of computer runs were made before a version of the plan was chosen to submit to the Congress in October 1969. Dozens more were performed at the request of Congress as both houses considered changes in the bill.

Although it is too soon to predict the outcome, substantial welfare reform along the lines proposed by President Nixon seems likely to be adopted eventually. Social analysis has played two important roles toward that end. First, as policymakers and analysts pored over the numbers, they gained new insight into what was wrong with the existing welfare system and arrived at new solutions to propose. Second, the analysts were asked at all stages to estimate the distribution of costs and benefits—who would win and who would lose—under alternative plans, and to compare their cost, effectiveness in reducing poverty, and effect on incentives so that informed choices could be made.

Analysts so far have been most successful in helping policymakers understand the implications of particular options within a given social action program. But what can they contribute to decisions on the comparative value of social programs that are competing for priority? The orthodox answer of economists would be to add up the costs and benefits of each course of action and choose the program with the highest excess of benefits over costs. How helpful are cost-benefit analyses in the real world of decisions? Analysts would probably be wasting time and effort if they gave high priority to making dollar estimates of the benefits of social action programs. Such estimates involve a great deal of guesswork, and politicians and decision makers are unlikely to pay much attention to them anyway. On the other hand, these analyses contribute to precision in knowing what is being bought and for whom, and they increase the accountability of managers of social action programs to their clients.

PRODUCING EFFECTIVE SERVICES

The analysts of social service programs cannot say what the goals of society ought to be, nor should they; but there is hope that they can at least distinguish effective from less effective approaches to goals that are already defined. At present, however, little is known about how to produce more effective health, education, and other social services, partly because social service programs—governmental and private—are not organized to produce information about their performance. Moreover, new techniques or combinations of resources are not tried out systematically. Until programs are organized so that analysts can learn from them and systematic experimentation is undertaken on a significant scale, the prospects are dim for learning how to produce better social services.

Education provides a good example of the problems involved. For many years, policymakers were concerned with building and staffing more schools to keep pace with the population, with keeping children in school more years, with eliminating double shifts, with adding kindergarten or preschool facilities—in short, with how to provide more education, not how to make it better. To the extent that they were concerned with quality, they concentrated on giving children access to schools that met minimum standards by getting rid of the one-room schoolhouse and the uncertified teacher. But access is not enough. Children go to school but do not learn. Ways must be found to make education more effective.

In seeking how to do this, the analyst depends on two premises. The first is that at least some of the important outcomes of education are identifiable and measurable. Reading skills, mathematical proficiency, and acquired knowledge of certain subjects can be approximated by test scores, even if they are imperfect measures and even if such skills are not the sole goals of education. The second premise is that there is some stable relationship between the resources expended on education and the results—that different kinds of teachers, facilities, equipment, curricula, and methods affect the outcome. This is a reasonable assumption, but difficult to prove.

One difficulty lies with the data. Most studies have been based on measurements showing the relation between school variables and the performance of children in a single year. Since a longer time period might reveal outcomes that could not be expected to occur in just one year, an intensive longitudinal analysis of education should be attempted on a large scale. In view of the potential usefulness of the results, it is surprising that more school systems are not collecting and analyzing such data. Most are still using test information mainly for individual diagnostic purposes, not for program evaluation.

Even intensive longitudinal analysis, however, might prove to be little more conclusive than superficial cross-sectional studies. Perhaps the real world is not organized to generate information about "production functions"—the relation between efforts expended and results—no matter how skillfully the statistics are collected. Perhaps the schools are too uniform, with too few important differences that are not correlated with the socioeconomic status of students. It may be necessary deliberately to experiment with radically different curricula, resources, or approaches before any significant differences emerge. Experimentation is so expensive, however, that a major effort should be made to learn from the variety of existing programs throughout the country wherever possible.

If it is so hard to analyze usefully the education systems themselves, what can one learn from the federal programs designed to increase the effectiveness of education, such as Headstart or Title I of the Elementary and Secondary Education Act of 1965? Unfortunately, not much, for the programs were not designed with evaluation in mind. They have neither an experimental design nor control groups, nor do they attempt to define promising methods and try them out in enough places to determine their value under different conditions. Moreover, in most places, the additional resources devoted to "compensatory" education have been too limited to support hope of finding effects that would stand out clearly over those of other school and nonschool factors.

THE NEED FOR SYSTEMATIC EXPERIMENTATION

Greater efforts to learn from the "random innovation" encouraged by government programs are certainly called for, but an additional strategy is needed in the form of systematic experimentation under conditions resembling those of the scientific laboratory. The strategy includes three steps, the first of which is to identify new teaching methods, new ways of organizing or paying for health services, or new types of income transfer systems that show promise of increasing effectiveness. The second step calls for *systematically* trying out new methods in various places and under various conditions on a large enough scale and with sufficient controls to permit valid conclusions. The final step is the evaluation of new methods and their comparison with each other and with methods already in use.

The federal government must take the lead in organizing, financing, and evaluating systematic experimentation with various ways of delivering education, health, and other social services. Enormous problems of organization and execution will arise, for this kind of experimentation involves different people in different places working within a carefully drawn overall plan. Complicating the undertaking is the fragmented way in which social services are provided in the United States.

Some attempts at systematic experimentation using federal funds are now under way. Perhaps the best-known example is the New Jersey Graduated Work Incentive Experiment financed by the Office of Economic Opportunity (OEO). Begun in 1968, this project is an attempt to see how a negative income tax would affect work incentives. Opponents of a negative income tax claimed that it would induce men in low-income families to quit working or reduce their hours of work. Would this be so? Would there be a significant exodus from the labor force? Would the level of the guarantee or the steepness of the marginal tax rate make a difference in working behavior? Since even rough answers seemed impossible to extract from available statistics, the OEO decided to experiment with several variants of a negative income tax on a sample of families in several communities. Altogether, eight different combinations of guarantee levels and tax rates were established for the experiment; a control sample was observed but received no payment except a modest inducement to provide information.

The experiment was planned to run for three years, with attention centered mainly on the administrative feasibility of the program and the effects of alternative guarantees and tax rates on labor force behavior. When President Nixon proposed the Family Assistance Plan in 1969, an upsurge of interest in the negative income tax idea stimulated demands for early release of information on the results of the experiment. The preliminary findings were notable chiefly for what they did not show. The first year's experience revealed no significant differences in labor force behavior between negative income tax recipients and control families, and the expectation that a negative tax would induce low-income families to work less was not substantiated. Of course some questions remain to be answered before extrapolating from any income maintenance experiment to a national income maintenance system. Would participants in the experiment behave differently than they would if all their neighbors were also participants? Would they keep more accurate records than they would if they were not being observed? Would their buying habits change? Since we lack the experience needed to answer these questions, in a sense these experiments test not only substantive issues but the validity of social experimentation itself.

Other kinds of experiments in the field of education are currently of special interest. *Performance contracting* is an attempt to harness the profit motive to improvement of the effectiveness of teaching. In it, school systems contract with private firms to increase the measured performance of children in, say, reading or mathematics, and pay the contractors according to their success. Despite an unpromising beginning, with evidence that in one case the contractor influenced the results by giving the children a chance to practice the test questions during their regular instruction, the government considers the concept of performance contracting worth pursuing if adequate safeguards are built in.

The *voucher system* would enable parents to buy education with public funds at whatever private or public school they found best for their children. Some school reformers believe that the only way to get effective education is to break the monopoly of the public school and allow the consumer to have a choice. While the voucher system has attracted many proponents, it has also aroused criticism. One serious objection is that it might accentuate existing problems of income inequality: Schools offering more expensive education to those willing to pay a premium in addition to the voucher are likely to spring up. The other major problem is consumer ignorance. Unless he knows what he is buying, a consumer cannot choose rationally. Nor can parents move a child from one school to another in search of one they like without endangering the child's educational and social progress. If a voucher system, or any other method, is to increase the effectiveness of education, performance measures will have to be devised to enable parents to judge how much progress their children are making in school and how much they might make if they went to a different school.

Despite the persuasiveness of the arguments for systematic experimentation, many thoughtful people have doubts about it. Is it ethical to experiment with people? Is it politically feasible? Can experimental results have validity in the social action area?

The courts are only beginning to come to grips with the problems raised by unequal distribution of publicly provided services. They have yet to give any real guidance on the equity of inequalities deliberately created for experimental purposes. Whichever way the courts move, organizers of experiments clearly have a public responsibility to be sure that the knowledge to be gained will justify the denial of a new service to some groups that a carefully designed experiment requires. Aside from legal and moral issues, it will be politically difficult to provide services to some people and not to others. Concern for fairness may inhibit good experimental design. A government official may find it far more difficult to explain to the public that he is allocating a scarce resource on the basis of chance, necessary for a valid experiment, than to defend some other selection criterion, such as need or merit or "first come, first served."

Another reservation about the desirability of social experiments concerns the honesty with which experimental results will be reported. Will government officials be willing to release results showing the failure of a program to which the agency is already committed? Might there be a tendency to emphasize and publicize the positive results while deemphasizing, if not actually suppressing, the negative ones? While the possibility of less than honest use of experimental results exists, it does not seem a valid reason to forgo the potential benefits of an experimental strategy. One would hope that, as social experimentation becomes more widespread, high standards of ethics would be maintained and that public officials would respect them and find it impolitic to be caught transgressing them.

PROVIDING INCENTIVES

Finding more effective methods of producing education, health, and other social services is not enough. They must be put to use. At present the system provides few rewards for those who produce better services and few penalties for those who fail to produce. As the public sector of the economy grows larger, the problem of building incentives to effective performance into public programs becomes more and more crucial. The voucher system in education, discussed above, is a proposed method for establishing incentives *through the market* to provide higher quality services. Two other proposals—*decentralization* and *community control*—have been put forward. Each holds some promise, but neither is a cure-all.

Decentralization of decision-making has always been popular with conservatives, but in the last several years liberals have come increasingly to favor it as well. Its advocates hold that the federal government is efficient in collecting taxes and writing checks but inept in administering service programs. They contend that its role should be restricted to collection and disbursement, leaving the detailed administration of social action programs to smaller units of government. This view implies that universal rules are likely to do more harm than good, spawning red tape and rigidity. For example, there are more than 25,000 school districts, and their needs, problems, and capacities differ widely. Recipients of federal grants should be free to vary the way they spend the money, so long as they accomplish specified results.

The push for community control, especially in the black ghetto, reflects the feeling that schools, hospitals, and welfare centers are alien institutions run by hostile members of another culture. If these institutions were controlled by and accountable to the community, the belief runs, they would be more effectively, or at least more sensitively, managed.

At the moment, the movement for community control is concentrated on gaining power. Its advocates have not yet focused on new methods or organization, nor do they support experimentation or systematic testing. If community control in the big-city school systems becomes a reality, the community and its representatives will have to face up to the question: Now that we have control, what shall we do? They will begin to search for proved models of more effective education, to demand the results of systematic experimentation. And they will need improved measures of school performance, for the general city taxpayer will have little enthusiasm for turning over funds to community boards without some assurance that he will get his money's worth.

DEVELOPING PERFORMANCE MEASURES

All the proposals for improving the effectiveness of education, health, and other social services dramatize the need for better performance measures, no matter who makes the decisions. Therefore, analysts who want to improve the delivery of social services should give high priority to developing and refining measures of performance. Relatively little effort has gone into this task thus far, despite its importance and intellectual challenge. In education, it will be necessary to move beyond standardized tests to more sensitive and less culturally biased measures that reflect not only the intellectual skills of children, but also their creativity and faith in themselves and enthusiasm for learning. In health, it will be necessary to move beyond the conventional disease and hospitalization statistics to more refined measures of health and vigor. In antipoverty programs, job satisfaction should be measured as well as income.

Two general rules can be suggested. First, single measures of social service performance should be avoided, for they always lead to distortion, stultification, or cheating to "beat the system." Multiple measures are necessary to reflect multiple objectives and to avoid distorting performance. Second, the measures must reflect the difficulty of the problem. If absolute levels of performance are rewarded, then schools will select the brightest students, training programs will admit only the workers who will be easiest to place in jobs, health centers will turn away or neglect the hopelessly ill. To avoid these distortions, social service effectiveness must always be measured in relation to the difficulty of the task.

None of this will be easy to accomplish. But we are unlikely to get improved social services (or to know if we have them) until we make a sustained effort to develop performance measures suitable for judging and rewarding effectiveness. Measurement is not, of course, an end in itself; but all the strategies for finding better methods—especially social experimentation—depend for their success on improving performance measures. So do all the models for improved incentives. Put more simply, to do better, we must have a way of distinguishing better from worse.

Systems Analysis and the Political Process

JAMES R. SCHLESINGER*

My purpose in this paper is to evaluate the role for systems analysis—particularly as it functions in a highly politicized environment. I shall not devote any attention to discussing whether cost effectiveness procedures are hypothetically desirable. Far too much attention—in Congress and elsewhere—has been wasted in this strange dialectical tilting ground. Viewed abstractly, systems analysis implies rigorous thinking, hopefully quantitative, regarding the gains and the resource expenditures involved in a particular course of action—to insure that scarce resources are employed productively rather than wastefully. It is almost tautological therefore to state that systems analysis effectively employed will be beneficial. The real questions arise when we descend from a high level of abstraction and begin to grapple with the practical issues. Attention must be given to such questions as (1) the quality of information bases and analyses, (2) methodology, (3) bias, (4) the impact of politicized environments on analytical efforts and analytical results.

These issues cannot be treated wholly in isolation. The quality of information, for example, is very much influenced (and biased) by the structure of and alliances within the bureaucracy. The methodology chosen for analytical efforts will in itself introduce a specific form of bias. These in turn, reinforced by the specific interests

*Any views expressed in this paper are those of the author. They should not be interpreted as reflecting the views of The RAND Corporation or the official opinion or policy of any of its governmental or private research sponsors. Papers are reproduced by The RAND Corporation as a courtesy to members of its staff.

and functions of separate sections of the bureaucracy, will increase tensions within the Government and make more costly the introduction of changes which might objectively be regarded as desirable. Nonetheless, the effort to sort out different classes of issues must be made. One may categorize issues (1) and (2) as "mechanical" and issues (3) and (4) as "organizational." Without implying a judgment regarding the relative importance of these problems, it is plain that a paper directed to political scientists should concentrate on the latter class of problems. After a few words on the way in which the data base and methodology may influence the quality of analysis, the balance of the paper will be devoted to the implications of these broader organizational issues.

Where gross wastage and irrationality have flourished it is relatively easy (in principle) to indicate very improved patterns of resource allocation even in the face of rather skimpy data. In all other cases the quality of the underlying data will determine the quality of analysis. The fact must be recognized that the data presently available to the Government for analytical work are not in good shape. One of the reasons for the success of systems analysis in the DoD under McNamara is that considerable prior effort had been invested in the development and study of the data relevant to defense problems. For most of its other functions the Government faces an uphill fight simply in developing useful data.

In part, this problem will yield to steady effort especially as more trained personnel become available. However, it would be utopian to expect agencies automatically to provide data useful for analytical purposes. Knowledge is a form of power, and most institutions exhibit an understandable reluctance to dissipate this power in the absence of compensating advantages. While newer or favored agencies, which anticipate expanded budgets, are likely to prove cooperative, the old-line agencies, especially those that have established a degree of independence, are likely to prove obdurate. In many cases data of appropriate quality can only be obtained through the wholehearted cooperation of the relevant agencies. Since the indicated tactic for many agencies will be to hide some information and to release much of the balance in warped form, many decisions will continue to be based on deficient information with only limited confidence being placed in the results.

The problems that established methodology can create ought not be ignored, even though a sense of proportion suggests that in relation to the enormous potential payoff of systems analysis the errors attributable to methodological bias should be relatively small. While at its best systems analysis insists only on "rigorous thinking," the background of systems analysis in lower-order operations research problems has resulted in a lingering preference for formal models, preferably mathematical. In numerous cases this leads to the neglect of important variables which are not readily subject to manipulation of the existing methods. The normal association of model-building and simplification cannot be avoided in analytical work in the social sciences, but there is cause for concern if such analytical work becomes the sole basis for decision-making. The stress on quantifiable elements is particularly risky in cost-benefit work where objectives are hard to define or subject to change. In most cases the cost elements can be reduced to money terms. By contrast, objectives may be numerous, mutually incommensurable, and reducible to money terms only on the basis of rather arbitrary and subjective judgments by the analyst.[1] The result is that what started as a cost-benefit analysis becomes primarily a crude cost comparison—with inadequate attention either to a number of the potential benefits or to the adaptability of the preferred alternative to a number of unforeseen contingencies. Countervailing tendencies toward prodigality in pursuit of misconceived or ill-defined objectives may bulk larger overall, yet there is no assurance that such tendencies will serve as direct offsets to the biasing of specific analyses toward the choice of the low-cost alternative. When and if systems-analytical work becomes routinized, the risks implicit in methodological bias will rise.

As distinct from methodological bias, the more general forms of bias reflect the pressures of a large and variegated organizational structure. Among the causes of bias are: asymmetry in the sources of information, disproportionate attention by the analyst to preferred information sources, prior intellectual commitment on the part of the analyst, selectivity in organizational recruitment, and other bureaucratic pressures. From these sources a great deal of bias, reinforced by slipshod and mechanical work, inevitably slips in, even on those occasions that it is not deliberately introduced. It scarcely needs saying that in so complex an organization as the United States Government, viewed from its highest levels, that deliberate introduction of misinformation and distortion is no insignificant problem in itself, as will be seen below. The point being made here is that a very large proportion of total bias springs from honest conviction rather than the attempt to deceive, and it is particularly difficult to compensate for bias in this form. Contrary to a widespread hope the solution does not lie in the training and upgrading of personnel —in getting more honest (or more intelligent and capable) personnel. The most damaging forms of bias spring from an honest, if misguided, conviction of the correctness of one's own views. Where biases clash they may be viewed with less apprehension under the classification of the "competition of ideas." But all too frequently biases are mutually reinforcing. And, in any event, the introduction of bias (inevitable in all save the lowest-order decisions) contaminates the detached and quantitative analysis which a widespread myth holds to be attainable.

The final question bearing on the effectiveness of systems analysis for governmental decision-making is the impact of politicized environments on analytical efforts and analytical results. The deliberate introduction of distortion and fuzziness to improve the competitive position of one's own agency or division is an unavoidable and dominant feature of the bureaucratic landscape. At lower levels the tendency to pick and choose those data which support one's position results in analyses which may be uncritically accepted at higher levels, if the conclusions are palatable. Only if the conclusions are unpalatable, will searching questions be raised regarding the underlying data. Not infrequently, the very agencies whose premises are most questionable, are the very ones which are most adept in handling the new quantitative tools, and in developing a superficially convincing presentation that may beguile those charged with responsibility for review.

The techniques of deception are legion; the effectiveness of intelligence operations and the available sanctions frequently low. In the variegated structure of the Government (with innumerable agencies and sub-agencies), deliberate distortion is reinforced by honest conviction, bias, recruitment, limited information, and the structure of power. It becomes impossible to separate one such element from another. In a perpetual rutting season, these mutually-reinforcing tendencies coagulate in their separate sectors of the lattice structure of the Government. How much systems analysis can do to counteract the pernicious results of such coagulative tendencies remains an open question. Certainly it can accomplish something—hopefully a great deal. Nonetheless, the resistences to the application of systematic and rigorous analysis in a highly politicized environment are sufficient to make even the stoutest heart grow faint. Our purpose is to examine how analytical techniques will fare in this political environment. Let us consider four aspects of the problem: (1) the general limitations, (2) the relevancy of experience in the Department of Defense, (3) bureaucratic problems in a wider compass, and (4) what systems analysis can accomplish.

GENERAL LIMITATIONS

With perhaps a tinge of self-satisfaction on the part of its practitioners, systems analysis has been advertised as the application of logical thinking to broad policy issues. The implication is that logic comes in only one guise. Yet, whatever the doubts of those who seek to rationalize politics, the political process is dominated by a species of logic of its own, one that diverges from the brand germane to systems analysis. The domain of politics is a far broader system than that to which systems analysis is typically applied. Systems analysis applies to substantive issues susceptible to definition, where linkages exist among costs, technologies, and closely-related payoffs. The criterion is some substantive (and presumably measurable) utility which is more or less directly relevant to the enhancing of national security or citizen well-being. The pride of systems analysis is its ability to take a long-run view and to disregard prior commitments, if they are too costly or nonproductive.

By contrast, in politics one is concerned with more than the substantive costs and benefits involved in a specific decision area. One is engaged in mobilizing support by words and by actions over a wide range of ill-defined issues. The ultimate criterion will remain the psychological and voting responses of the general electorate and of important pressure groups. Positive responses in this realm are only irregularly correlated with those actions preferred on the basis of cost-benefit criteria. The focus of political action tends to be short run. The wariness with which the approaching election is watched is tempered only by the precept that the half life of the public's memory is approximately three months.

Put quite briefly, political decision operates under the normal constraint to avoid serious risk of the loss of power. The tool of politics (which frequently becomes its objective) is to extract resources from the general taxpayer with minimum offense and to distribute the proceeds among innumerable claimants in such a way as to maximize support at the polls. Politics, so far as mobilizing support is concerned, represents the art of calculated cheating—or more precisely how to cheat without being *really* caught. Slogans and catch phrases, even when unbacked by the commitment of resources, remain effective instruments of political gain. One needs a steady flow of attention-grabbing cues, and it is of lesser moment whether the indicated castles in Spain ever materialize. The contrast to the systems-analytic approach with its emphasis on careful calculation of resources required to implement real alternatives could not be greater. In political decision, the *appearance* of effort, however inadequate, may be overwhelmingly more remunerative than the costly (and thereby unpleasant) implementation of complete programs.

Consider two of the guiding principles of systems analysis: (1) the avoidance of foot-in-the-door techniques leading to an unintended commitment to large expenditures and (2) the orientation of analysis and allocation decisions toward output rather than input categories. These go to the heart of systems analysis with respect to the quest for the proper relating of resources provided and goals adopted. Output-orientation is designed to measure the extent to which adopted goals are actually achieved. Avoidance of foot-in-the-door is designed to prevent the preliminary wastage of resources on purposes for which one is unwilling to pay full costs. These are laudable principles, but they conform poorly to the realities of political decision.

Politics, it was hinted above, requires the systematic exploitation of foot-in-the-door techniques. One wishes to attract current support from various voting groups by indications or symbolic representations that the government will satisfy their aspirations. One wishes to attract the support of many groups, but there are limits to the size of the budget. Consequently, resources are applied thinly over a wide array of programs. The symbolism of concern is enough and the last thing that is desired is the totting up of the full costs of a program with the implication that one should not go ahead unless willing to incur the costs involved.

Similarly, in the real world of political decision it is immensely difficult to concentrate on outputs rather than inputs. A very large proportion of political pressure is concerned with the sale of preservation of specific types of socio-economic inputs. The preservation or expansion of vested interests implies that political decision will be much concerned by and may be overwhelmed by inputs rather than outputs. No doubt, the behavior of politicians reflects a total disregard of Kant's categorical imperative, but that viewed realistically is the name of the game. Classical liberals may stress the desirability of advancing one's component of the general interests rather than one's special interests, but it requires no great amount of shrewdness on the part of politicians to see that such behavior will not lead to political success. The systems analyst may search for new and more efficient means for achieving objectives, but these new means are by definition likely to have little political support both within and without government, depending on the affected groups. Both within and without the government (depending on the locus of affected interests) the opposition to new methods will be powerful. Consequently political leaders who are interested in maintaining a consensus (as all political leaders must be) must continue to pay close attention to input-oriented interest groups.

As a result, there is an inevitable note of paradox when systems-analytic techniqes are endorsed at the highest political level. For such an endorsement implies, in principle, the partial renunciation of the most effective tools of the politician. That systems-analytic techniques are being diffused throughout the Federal bureaucracy in response to a directive[2] of President Johnson is both understandable and ironical. It is understandable in that the pressures for sensible use of resources will be most keenly felt during an administration with high aspirations and expanding programs (much more so than, for instance, in the Eisenhower administration). Yet, it is also ironical in that no recent administration has been more alert to the direct political implications of domestic programs. Lyndon Johnson prides himself on the widespread recognition of his superb political instincts—and on his understanding of what makes the electorate tick. Repeatedly he has extracted political gain through the announcement (during the low-cost initial stages) of new programs—before the costs have been thought through or the bills presented for payment. Though this be the political replica of what the analyst decries as foot-in-the-door techniques, few political leaders will be restrained by such an observation. Politics is geared to the hopes of the voters rather than to the calculation of the cost accountant. In politics one is almost driven to overstate the benefits and understate the costs of controversial programs.

The keynote of the Great Society has been the launching of new programs associated with substantial increases in government expenditures. Goals have been announced (like the elimination of poverty) before the means of achieving them have been developed. Neither alternative policies nor the costs have been studied until *after a decision has been reached.* No one would suggest that such programs as "demonstration cities"[3] or rent subsidies have been carefully analyzed with respect to benefits in cost, especially in relation to the alternative employment of the same resources. My point here is neither to ascribe praise or blame to what is effective politics, nor is it to raise questions regarding the merits of the programs themselves. Rather it is to suggest the inherent difficulties of reconciling such procedures with the precepts of systems analysis.

These problems are not new ones. For generations men have sought methods for introducing more "rationality" into the government allocations. Systems analysis is a powerful technique, but like all techniques, it will be germane only when there is a willingness to employ it systematically in dealing with issues of public policy. In fact, systems analysis is only the latest in a series of attempts to achieve more rational allocation. Moreover, prior attempts bear at least a family resemblance to what we now propose to do with systems analysis. For example, Public Law 801, passed in 1956, required the presentation of five-year cost estimates when new programs were adopted. The five-year cost estimates have a familiar ring, but the law is a dead letter. It has been ignored, not because it is undesirable, but because it expresses a pious hope but disregards the underlying realities of political life. Once again it suggests the barriers of imposing upon political decision a method for efficiently using resources to provide direct, substantive benefits.

There is an old yarn which concerns a farmer who was approached by an enthusiastic extension agent pushing a new technique which allegedly would raise the farmer's output by 10 percent. The farmer is supposed to have replied: "I'm only farming half as well as I know how to, right now." It was just too much bother to take advantage of opportunities for improvement. There is a moral in the story for the improvement of the operation of the Government. In many, perhaps most, lines of activity, we already know—even without systems analysis—how to improve efficiency and shave costs by eliminating obsolescent activities. In principle, we could easily do far better. The problem is not absence of knowledge; it is rather that appropriate actions are constrained by political factors reflecting the anticipated reactions of various interest groups. In such lines of activity, if analysis is to be useful, it will not be by contributing to knowledge, but rather by serving as a political instrument through which the relevant political constraints can be relaxed. This is both a more modest and a more ambitious objective for systems analysis than is generally stated, but it is suggestive of the true role that analysis can play once we recognize the serious limitations imposed upon it by the political process.

THE RELEVANCY OF DOD EXPERIENCE

The application of cost-effectiveness techniques in the Department of Defense since 1961 is regarded as a model for reform. While unspoken, there exists an underlying premise that "what's good for the DoD, is good for the rest of the government bureaucracy." While this is, of course, true with regard to the *role* of analytical probing, it is not necessarily the case with regard to the *implementation* of analytical results. It is necessary, therefore, to explore certain differences between the Department of Defense and other elements of the bureaucracy. Moreover, we should examine the actual workings of the new procedures in the DoD, for a somewhat idealized picture has been disseminated which diverges in part from the reality. In so doing we shall be stressing the structural and political aspects of decision-making rather than the substantive issues that have been a controversy since 1961. In a sense, this represents an injustice to Secretary McNamara and his aides for omitting reference to the substantive issues ignores the truly remarkable way in which the new team took hold with respect to the main strategic and postural issues in 1961.

Controversies regarding budgetary allocations in defense are fought out *within* a single Department. Outsiders, even the Congress itself, have only a nominal influence on allocation. Since the Defense Reorganization Act of 1958, the Secretary of Defense has had sufficient authority to impose his will on the Services. Moreover, the DoD does not supply final goods and services highly valued by influential portions of the electorate, nor is its use of specific inputs such that affected interest groups are normally in a position to block specific allocative decisions. In the United States the military has a relatively weak political position. In the absence of influential public support the traditional tactic of cultivating Congress is inadequate. When the Executive Branch stands firm behind its budgetary decisions (whether based on sound analysis or not), the military has no real alternative to accepting the decision.[4] The means of direct resistance, available to other components of the bureaucracy, are largely denied to the military.

Consequently the Department of Defense, relative to other components of the bureaucracy, has provided an abnormally easy place to apply program budgeting and systems analysis. Only in the case of the closing of the obsolete or redundant bases were vested interests sufficiently involved requiring major political courage to override. With the support of the President the Department of Defense can follow *internally-generated* guidelines, rational or otherwise, with only ineffectual resistance from below or outside. Moreover, the bulk of Defense's allocative decisions are internal to the Department. The linkages to allocative decisions by other Departments or Agencies are relatively weak, by contrast to the major civilian programs.

For those civilian programs in which improved-performance-through-analysis is hoped for, the situation is far less favorable. A number of the newer Departments represent a gathering-in of pre-existing entities with the tradition of independence and outside sources of support serving to sustain that independence. The Secretary is in a weak position to impose decisions; he is rather like a weak feudal overlord attempting to control some ill-governed baronies. The equivalent of the Defense Reorganization Act of 1958 does not exist to establish the authority of the Secretary. This condition applies, moreover, to some of the older Departments in which nominally subordinate units are in reality independent baronies.

The services provided by the various bureaus and agencies regularly create clienteles within the electorate, whose interests it is politically risky for the President to override in preparing his Budget. These interests are strongly represented in Congress, and even a bold President could not afford to take on too many of them within a brief span of time.

The weakness of the Departments, relative to the DoD, implies that allocative decisions cannot be based upon *internally-generated* guidelines. Consequently guidelines must be imposed from above, which is both difficult and politically risky for the President and his principal aides. More important, the appropriate analytical and decisionmaking domain is much broader than the individual bureaus and agencies in question. There are important linkages and spillovers in costs, in technologies, and particularly in payoffs across agency lines. The improvements to be obtained by intra-organizational changes are small relative to those obtainable by inter-organizational adjustment. This is particularly dramatic, for example, in the natural resources area. Here the Bureau of Reclamation, the Corps of Engineers, the National Park Service, the Forestry Service, the Bureau of Land Management, and the Bureau of Mines are only the more prominent among the *Federal* Agencies involved (whose activities must be reconciled with such State entities as the Texas Railway Commission). Each has a position to maintain and a "suboptimizing" mission to perform, and as we shall see later, the concept of that mission is frequently based upon obsolescent views and obsolescent professional functions. Each, moreover, is involved in a symbiotic relationship with a clientele, which it partially supports and from which it gains significant political backing. The "systems" to which "analysis" should be applied are far broader than the ones which are the concern of the existing entities. Yet, the existing organizational structure makes it virtually impossible to implement the recommendations which would come from good analyses. Thus, the underlying question remains: how strong is the will and ability to achieve a modernization of the structure of the Federal Government?[5]

To this must be added one final point. Both intensive and extensive research had been done on the problems of defense before 1961. This body of research was available to Secretary McNamara when he began to introduce his reforms in 1961, and the reforms underlay many of the decisions regarding allocations. For most of the civilian programs, very little policy-oriented research bearing on allocative decisions has been done. In some areas the problems have not even been formulated. Consequently, there is no capital of pre-existing research to be milked. It may be years before adequate analyses have been performed. While in no way does this suggest that analytical effort should not be pushed, it does suggest that our expectations should not be pitched too high with respect to immediate benefits.

Let us turn briefly to consider the other relevant aspect of DoD experience: the actual workings of the evaluative procedures as opposed to the idealized model. In understanding the results we must bear in mind that analytical work is performed and decisions are reached, not by disinterested machines, but by individuals with specific views, commitments, and ambitions. The normal bureaucratic tendencies may be weakened, but will not disappear. We might anticipate the following.

- Where centralized evaluative procedures are applied, certain proposals, towards which the reviewers are predisposed, will be subject to less rigorous scrutiny than will other proposals.

- An administrator will have powerful incentives to preserve his own options by vigorously suppressing foot-in-the-door attempts by *his* subordinates; he may have a strong desire to commit his superiors or his successors to those policies that he personally favors. Moreover, there may be a weak impulse to preserve options favored by subordinates, but which he opposes.

- Finally, while the impulse to justify the commitments or disguise the errors in judgment of subordinates may be weak, the impulse to justify policies and programs to which one's own name has become attached may be correspondingly strong. Consequently, the hope that prior commitments can be disregarded appears utopian. Over time current decision making may increasingly be influenced by prior decisions.

Manifestation of such tendencies has not disappeared in the DoD since 1961. The Department's leaders have been capable men—and their preferences quite defensible. Yet, one must examine how such bureaucratic tendencies might influence the results, not only if the DoD's decisions were in the hands of men of lesser caliber, but also when the tendencies are exhibited in the more politicized environment affecting the civilian programs. For example, under the first heading above, contract definition procedures require the judgment that the relevant technology is in hand before signing. It is rumored that DDR & E takes a far more tolerant view of "technology in hand" when it wants a contract than when it does not. While I cannot confirm this assertion from direct observation, I would not find it surprising.[6]

On the second point, it is plainly desirable to suppress the attempts of subordinates to commit a Department or the Government to certain courses of action, even when this does not preclude such attempts at higher levels. The point we must keep in mind is that outside the DoD there may be a closer identification of senior officials with the proposals made by subordinate units in their Departments. There may be less ability to control and suppress attempts to gain Departmental support. In that case the willingness of senior administrators to push for commitments at higher levels would not imply a willingness to suppress such pressures from below. Consequently, the Departments could become transmission belts to move the pressure for commitments from lower units to higher political levels.

Enough has been said to suggest that there is some discrepancy between the theory and the practice of systems analysis. While the theory is unexceptionable, the practice is subject to the temptations and distractions that characterize the real world. Actual experience in the DoD ought not be treated as synonymous with the idealized theoretical statement of the procedures. Perfection and elegance exist but rarely in the real world. When the natural impediments to implementation, which were encountered in DoD experience, are extended to the more raucous and politicized environment of the civilian programs, we should not be too surprised if the DoD experience proves to be a rather inexact model for what will actually take place.

THE ENCOUNTER WITH THE BUREAUCRACY

In predicting how systems analysis will fare as it encouters the passive resistance of the bureaucracy, one might start with E. L. Katzenbach's observation in his classic study of the Horse Cavalry that "history . . . is studded with institutions which have managed to dodge the challenge of the obvious."[7] The reference is to military history, but observers as diverse as Thomas Jefferson and C. Northcote Parkinson suggest that the dictum may also be relevant to the civilian bureaucracy. For the military, as Katzenbach indicates, the difficulty of serious inter-war testing of the effectiveness of forces partially accounts for the longevity of obsolescent institutions. But Katzenbach wrote prior to the impact of systems analysis, and it is arguable that the new techniques have eased the problem of testing and have made it more difficult for obsolescent institutions to withstand the challenge of the obvious. In civilian activities, however, the problem is less one of devising suitable instruments for testing than of overcoming inertia and the political strength of supporting constituencies. It is rare that the obsolescence of civilian functions becomes *obvious*. The dramatic evidence of an opponent's military capability is absent. The civilian agencies make contributions to the well-being of portions of the electorate, and it is difficult to make a persuasive case that the functions or technologies in question have been superseded. Perhaps only dramatic, interest-arousing events are sufficient to persuade the public that the productive period of an institution's life is near its end.[8]

The barriers to the effective utilization of analysis are formidable. The older agencies, anxious to preserve their traditional orientations and functions, will be reluctant to view problems in terms of "broader systems." Given the narrow perspective of most agencies, the spillovers are already large and growing. Yet, if the spillover problem is seriously attacked, it would certainly imply radical change in the well-established ways of doing business and could imply a shrinkage of budgets. By contrast, the DoD has energetically dealt with the issues of spillovers between the Services. Spillovers from the DoD to the outside are perhaps another matter, but these are relatively small—in comparison to those existing at the relevant decision-making level in the civilian agencies.

Collectively the programs of the Government are like an iceberg with only a small portion appearing above the surface. Most of the existing arrangements continue from year to year; in a brief period only relatively minor perturbations are feasible, whereas to implement analytical conclusions may require radical modernization. Thus, the difficulties are substantial. The older agencies will resist either the imparting of information or the development of analyses which would cut into their treasure troves. Unhappily, the new agencies, from which better things might be hoped, are put under unremitting pressure to produce glamorous new programs—before the necessary analysis has been performed.

These are the "obvious" obstacles, but there are others more subtle and less obvious.

First, there is the ease with which all parties may fall into describing as "end use" or as outputs what are essentially inputs. The temptation is strong to continue to describe as an output what it has always been the agency's purpose to produce. The organization of the Government for providing "outputs" has normally been on an "input" basis.[9] The Forestry Service produces forests; the Bureau of Reclamation builds dams; the Corps of Engineers creates canals and flood control projects; the Atomic Energy Commission is charged with the responsibility aggressively to push the development of nuclear power. What is needed is a broader view of power developments or water resources developments or land use—with the evaluation of the relative benefits that component programs could provide on an integrated basis. But the existing organizations are in no position, either structurally or temperamentally, to provide such an evaluation. Even where an agency is organizationally charged with a broader responsibility, confusion may remain regarding just what the "output" is. The Forestry Service is charged not only to manage the forests efficiently for production purposes, but to provide recreation for the public. However, the Forestry Service is dominated or strongly influenced by professional foresters, sometimes known as "timber beasts." Foresters certainly love trees and productive forests as such, and may view the town-dwellers who invade their forests as a nuisance to be tolerated. Consequently, the suggestion is hardly surprising that the Forest Service has overinvested in timber production and underinvested in recreation. Moreover, the Forest Service is interested in *timber* rather than in *lumber*. Yet, from the national standpoint, it is arguable that small sums invested in research and development on sawmill operations would have a much higher payoff than much larger sums invested in expanded tree production.

This leads into the second difficulty, which may be the most baffling and intractable of all. This is the orientation of research personnel in the agencies to prevailing notions of professional standards and scientific integrity. This orientation tends to overshadow a concern for the broader policy objectives of the agency. Reduced payoffs in this case reflect the highest rather than the lowest motives, but the impact on government efficiency may be the same. Researchers who respond mainly to the interests of their professional peers in universities and elsewhere may keep the research shop so pure that it is of little use to the agency in developing improved techniques or policies. This is the opposite extreme from use of research as an unimaginative and low-level tool for management, but it can occur within the same organization. A portion of the Forestry Service's research personnel are primarily concerned with maintenance of professional status among foresters located in large measure outside the Service. Perhaps a more interesting example is the Geological Survey, which played so large a role in stimulating hydrological research in this country. In any attempt to achieve a coordinated water research program in the Government, the Geological Survey would be a key element. However, Survey personnel have been reluctant to be included in any such plan for fear that the Survey would become embroiled in policy issues and lose its identification with pure science. One is not without sympathy for such an attitude. Yet, effective policy research—at an intermediate level high science and prosaic managerial research—must be carried out somewhere in the Government, if the new analytical techniques are to be exploited. The reorientation and broadening of professional attitudes is an essential ingredient for the more effective performance of many governmental functions. Yet, it is a problem that is easier to indicate than to solve. At best, many years will be required before the professional bodies are appropriately reoriented.

Third, there exist certain fundamental issues of choice, which even complete modernization of the governmental structure cannot resolve. Analysis cannot bridge the gap between irreconcilable objectives. At its best, analysis can shed some light on the costs of accepting one objective at the expense of others. But there is a danger that analysis may help to disguise fundamental choice problems as efficiency problems. Analytical techniques have been most successful in obtaining efficient mixes through the compromising of several objectives. But some objectives are not susceptible to compromise, and such objectives could easily be ignored in the simple-minded quest for efficient solutions. Consider one important form of land use, that of wilderness preservation. The now dominant approach to land use analysis is that of multiple use with utilities balanced at the margin. But, by definition, a wilderness cannot be "improved" for other purposes. The preservationist impulse is one of exclusionary use of unique ecological or geological settings. One must face the fundamental choice issue *before* one seeks efficiency, or the issue of choice will be prejudged. The difficulty in the extended discussions of improved managerial or analytical tools is that it distracts attention from these more fundamental questions which deserve study in depth. By establishing efficiency as a goal one is deflected from examining those positions in which the question is: how much "efficiency" should we sacrifice in order to preserve a particular style of life or physical environment?

These are examples of the less obvious obstacles in the path of improved-government-service-at-lowered-unit-cost through analysis. But enumeration of these problems should not be taken to imply that we should be deterred from pushing ahead with the development and the exploitation of analytical techniques. These problems will yield to persevering effort. In the long run, they may prove to be less of a barrier than the more obvious one embodied in the formidable powers of resistance represented by the existing organizational structure and division of labor within the government.

Without modernization of the bureaucratic structure, a large portion of the potential gains of the broad application of systems analysis will be foregone. The existing structure, organized in large measure around inputs and supported by clienteles with sizable political influence, may become adept at presenting drastically-suboptimized (input-oriented) or misleading analyses, which it is more convenient to accept than reject. To accept the spirit of systems analysis is exceedingly hard, but to learn the language is rather easy. There is a danger that the same old programs will be presented in new costumes. In this regard our little experience is not altogether encouraging. A number of the agencies which were early users of cost-benefit techniques have demonstrated a proficiency in presenting questionable cost-benefit analyses for questionable programs. Quantitative documentation is presented in full, but with a willing audience it appears subject to easy manipulation.

One glaring example is in water resources, for there Congress early required responsible agencies to justify proposals in terms of cost-benefit calculations. But Congress displays a willingness to be persuaded, even when the calculations are only *pro forma*. In developing the case for the Marble Canyon dam, the Bureau of Reclamation calculated costs on the assumption that the load factor would be 80 percent. More recently, in response to certain criticism, the Bureau has indicated that the dam would be used for firming power—and the estimated load factor has slipped to 50 percent. No one has insisted that the Bureau go back and recalculate its estimates of costs on the basis of the adjusted figure. When there is a willingness to be persuaded, fundamental changes in the data may be treated as minor perturbations.

Another example, happily more straightforward, is the case presented by the Atomic Energy Commission to keep in operation the three gaseous diffusion plants at Oak Ridge, Paducah, and Portsmouth—which are no longer required for military production. The Commission's argument is that there will be a strain on production facilities around 1980, and there should be "pre-production"[10] of slightly enriched uranium to provide for power reactors some 15 years in the future. Given any reasonable rate of discount, 5 percent for purposes of discussion, the Commission's argument says, in effect, that it will be unable 15 years hence to perform separative work at less than double the present cost. Since work is going forward on improving gaseous diffusion and other technologies; since it may be more efficient (given the pattern of demand) to scrap the present plants and build new ones at a later date; and since a main cost item in the gaseous diffusion process is the cost of electric power (which the Commission repeatedly has insisted will be reduced), it would seem that one might reasonably forecast a fall in the cost of separative work rather than an increase. Nonetheless, it would not be wise to assume that the Commission will be unsuccessful in pressing its case or that the diffusion plants will, in fact, be closed down when the existing power contracts have been terminated.

These cases may indicate the shape of things to come in the future. It should come as no great surprise that Government agencies, like other entrenched interests, will fight vigorously to preserve their activities.

WHAT CAN SYSTEMS ANALYSIS ACCOMPLISH?

The number of apprehensions that have been expressed might make it appear that I am indifferent, or even opposed, to the attempt to introduce systems analysis throughout the Government. On the contrary, I am hopeful and even, within moderation, enthusiastic. This is a case of two and a half cheers for systems analysis. But before we begin to cheer we should be fully aware of what systems analysis cannot accomplish as well as what it can.

In the first place, systems analysis cannot achieve wonders: it cannot transmute the dross of politics into the fine gold of Platonic decision making, which exists in the world of ideas rather than the world of reality. Political decisions in a democratic society can hardly be more "rational" than the public, the ultimate sovereign, is willing to tolerate. All of the old elements remain: the myths and ideologies, the pressure groups, the need for accommodation and compromise, the decision made under duress. Systems analysis may modify, but it cannot extirpate these elements. Analysis is not a substitute for any form of decision making, but for political decision making it will be an even less effective guide than in narrower decision contexts.

As long as the public displays an insatiable appetite for "constructive new ideas" (whether or not they have been systematically designed), democratic politics will inevitably revolve around the foot-in-the-door techniques that the analysts criticize. As long as interested clienteles will support inefficient or counter-productive government activities, obsolescent functions will be preserved. Democratic politics will remain unchanged: a combination of pie in the sky and a bird in the hand. Tokenism, catch phrases, and cultivation of various interests will remain the guideposts.

What then can systems analysis accomplish? The question is perhaps most relevant for the long run, since we must recognize the problem of transition. The qualities that make for good analysis—detachment, breadth, interdisciplinary sympathies—do not appear like manna from heaven. It will take time to train an adequate supply of personnel and to produce good analysis. One cannot put new wine into old bottles. Even though the language of cost-effectiveness analysis is adopted by the agencies, one cannot expect a miraculous change of attitudes. At best, it will be years before analysis begins to have a significant influence in many agencies.

Nonetheless, even in the shorter run analysis will serve an educative function. In ways that may go unrecognized, analysis will begin to reshape the way that agencies view their own problems. While the desire to preserve empires will not disappear, the concept of the agency's functions will undergo change. Perhaps this is the major accomplishment of analysis: it sharpens and educates the judgments and intuitions of those making decisions. Even when analytical drapings are employed consciously or unconsciously as a camouflage for prejudged issues, the intuitions will have become sharper.

In the early stages, this educative function may be reinforced by the shock effect. The need to respond to probing questions will shake up many a stale mill pond. An advantage of all new techniques of managerial decision making is that it forces management to think through its problems anew. In an environment so readily dominated by routine, this cannot help but have a favorable impact.

The other major function of analysis is to smoke out the ideologies and the hidden interests. By introducing numbers, systems analysis serves to move arguments from the level of ideology or syllogism to the level of quantitative calculation. Of course, numbers alone are not necessarily persuasive. The ideologies and the established interests may not be rooted out, but the whole character of the discussion is changed. There will be a far greater awareness of how much it costs to support programs revolving about particular interests or resources. The public may be willing to pay the price—at least temporarily—but such a program is put on the defensive. Ideology alone will no longer suffice. In the longer run less resources are likely to be committed to the program and less will be wasted than if the cost-effectiveness calculations had not been done.

Finally, we must remember that there is a certain amount of gross wastage in the Government, which serves nobody's purpose. These situations reflect not differences of opinion, not interests, not ideologies, but simply the failure to perceive dominant solutions. It is in this realm that McNamara achieved his great savings within the Pentagon. With the elimination of these obvious sources of waste, analyses have had to become more subtle and recondite, but they are not necessarily as productive. Sources of gross waste may have been more common and certainly easier to get at in the Services than in the civilian programs. But within the civilian programs there remains a margin which can be squeezed out—even without the modernization of the Government's administrative structure.

NOTES

1. It is infeasible to go into the criterion problem at any length. Suffice it to say that for most higher-order problems adequate measures of merit have yet to be devised. Even if some improvement may be hoped for, the irreducibly subjective element in such measures will remain substantial.
2. For details see Bulletin No. 66-3, issued by the Bureau of the Budget on October 12, 1965.
3. "Doing more for the cities" has become the latest arena for political competition. The new programs are to be superimposed on the old without too much study. Indicative

of the pre-existing casualness in the attitude toward costing (one of the two legs of cost-benefit analysis) are two recent items bearing on the Federal Government's urban programs. First, in testifying on New York City's budgetary problems, Mayor Lindsay was unable to indicate "what is the total Federal figure?" (Senator Kennedy's words) —in assistance to the City. No one was able to establish whether Federal contributions were closer to the half billion dollar mark or the billion dollar mark. Second, Senator Abraham Ribicoff, whose subcommittee is investigating the problem, stated in an interview: "No one really knows how much we are spending on the program to help cities. . . . What are these programs doing? What should they be doing? Have the cities the men to spend this money properly? What have they duplicated, what have they wasted?"

4. While this judgment conflicts sharply with the interpretation represented by General Eisenhower's "military-industrial complex" or C. Wright Mill's "power elite"—to say nothing of the standard Leninist view, I believe that the evidence will bear out that only in periods of national hysteria does the "complex" have much influence on broad defense allocations. One need inquire only into what has happened to the Strategic Air Command under McNamara, and compare the results with the many long-lived and obsolete civilian programs.

5. The recent refusal of the Congress to sanction the transfer of the Maritime Administration from the Department of Commerce to the new Department of Transportation is symptomatic of the broader problem of achieving a more coherent structure for Federal Government activities.

6. Such an attitude of easy tolerance could be disastrous in the civilian programs. As we shall see later, certain civilian agencies take quite readily to the language of systems analysis and are able to construct superficially plausible, but basically misleading analyses. Where strong political pressures are involved, there may be no inclination to scrutinize and challenge superficially plausible analyses, and consequently costly and ineffective programs may win easy acceptance.

7. E. L. Katzenbach, Jr., "The Horse Cavalry in the Twentieth Century: A Study in Policy Response," *Public Policy*, 1958, Graduate School of Public Administration, Harvard University, p. 121.

8. Conceivably the Bureau of Reclamation's invasion of the Grand Canyon may be such an event, bringing to the attention of the public that (a) the supply of suitable dam sites in the U.S. is nearing exhaustion and (b) hydropower has in large measure been superseded in its economics by both coal-fired and nuclear plants.

9. The establishment of single-function agencies is both a reflection of and a promoter of what may be called "resource ideologies"—in which "water," "nuclear energy," "timber," and the like become valued for their own sake and become the measure of value.

10. The term "stockpiling" has acquired some unfortunate connotations, and is going out of favor.

What Can We Actually Get From Program Evaluation?

JOSEPH S. WHOLEY

INTRODUCTION

As an analyst and as a public official, I have been interested for some time in the role that quantitative analysis can play in assisting decisions on public programs—in particular, in the role that evaluation of program results can play.

The essence of *program evaluation*, as I use the term today, is the assessment of program *outcome*—what happened that would not have happened in the absence of the program?—and *relative effectiveness* within national programs—what individual local projects or types of projects work best? The purpose of evaluation is to provide objective feedback to program managers and policymakers on the cost and effects of national programs and local projects, to assist effective management and efficient allocation of limited resources.

Evaluation has come into its own over the past few years. There has been rather wide acknowledgement by public officials of the need to evaluate social programs. Federal legislation has called for it, money has been provided, evaluation staffs have been created or strengthened, and some major evaluation studies have been undertaken.

During this time, we have all learned that evaluation is difficult, takes a lot of time to carry out, and can be very expensive. We have discovered that the information generated by evaluation studies is often incomplete, suspect, and unrelated to the problems at hand. We have found bureaucratic and organizational constraints so formidable that today, after investment of significant resources and effort, *not one* federal agency has an overall evaluation system and few programs are able to make any use of the evaluations produced. On the whole, *federal evaluation efforts have not been cost-effective* in terms of impact on policy or program development.

In this paper, I consider the points of view of decisionmakers at two levels—*policymakers* concerned with legislative changes and budget levels—and *program managers* at various levels. What can policymakers and what can program managers actually *get* from program evaluation?

EVALUATION FOR POLICYMAKERS: NATIONAL PROGRAM IMPACT EVALUATION

First, what can policymakers get from evaluation? Two major types of evaluation are of interest to policymakers: national program impact evaluation, which may throw light on the effects of a national program, and evaluation of field experiments and demonstration projects, which may throw light on the desirability of new operating programs while there is still time to learn from experience.

Head Start

The Westinghouse-Ohio University evaluation of the national Head Start program is a leading example of program impact evaluation.[1] The Westinghouse study design was not perfect, but the results of the study probably furnished a correct assessment of the impact of the national Head Start program. It revealed that one, two, and three years after children from low-income families had gone through the Head Start program, there was little or no improvement in their cognitive achievement or motivational attitudes (when compared with similar children in the same communities).

The Westinghouse evaluation of the Head Start program therefore produced generally negative findings. The negative findings, however, did not significantly reduce the budget level of Head Start. Powerful constituencies would have fought any reduction in funding for Head Start. Results that seem to have come from the Westinghouse Head Start evaluation are (1) the "hold" placed on the program—increased funding levels would not be sought; (2) the diversion of some Head Start program funds into experimental child development programs, "planned variations," designed to test whether there are better approaches than those that were being used in the national Head Start program; and (3) the reduction of the proportion of Head Start funds now going into *summer* Head Start (the Head Start component with the *least* apparent value).

Manpower Training

Perhaps a more typical outcome of national program impact studies can be seen in the manpower area. The Department of Labor spends $4 million per year on evaluation of manpower programs. Yet a recent Urban Institute study for the Joint Economic Committee concluded that: "Differences in research design and wide natural variations within programs have led to unreliable cost and effectiveness findings for manpower training programs. . . . The manpower training benefit/cost studies reviewed had methodological limitations which made it impossible to be sure that the true average results of the manpower programs were measured."[2]

Cost-benefit studies of national impact programs consume a large share of the Labor Department's evaluation resources. But the results of these studies play almost no part in the administration of Labor Department programs. *Even if* reliable and valid data *were* being generated in the national program impact studies being done, such studies are not appropriate support for the types of decisions actually made within the Labor Department. National program impact evaluation studies circulate from office to office in the Labor Department without being acted upon or in most cases even read, because Labor Department administrators do not make the types of decisions which these studies are designed to support. There is room for well-designed cost-benefit studies, but not to the exclusion of other more relevant types of evaluation.

Title I, ESEA

Another area in which we have examined the feasibility and desirability of national program impact evaluations is that of compensatory education. The federal government spends $1.5 billion per year on education of disadvantaged children, under Title I of the Elementary and Secondary Education Act. It might seem important to evaluate the national impact of these large expenditures. Yet, a year ago, the Urban Institute urged the Office of Education not to put $800,000 of its scarce evaluation funds into a national impact evaluation of Title I. The argument concluded:

> "While Title I program impact evaluation is feasible, it faces severe methodological problems in sample selection, in defining the treatments provided, in designation of comparison groups, and in dealing with student mobility. . . . As a result of both our inability to distinguish Title I services from other services provided to program participants (by local funds) and the fact that Title I accounts for a relatively small proportion of total per pupil expenditures, it will be very difficult to attribute observed changes in student achievement to Title I. . . .
>
> "A national program impact evaluation of Title I, even if methodologically feasible, seems undesirable in comparison with more constructive uses of the evaluation funds available. . . . The Office of Education can and should work with those states that are interested to develop better monitoring systems, to improve local evaluation, to locate and document successful compensatory education projects, to distinguish better from worse Title I projects. . . . The Office of Education can also work through State Educational Agencies to improve the usefulness of local project evaluation efforts by subsidizing cooperative local evaluations which utilize at least some common output measures. . . ."[3]

We are not saying that national program impact studies are never appropriate. What we *do* suggest is that this type of evaluation is too often done for people who need other types of information to help them select among the options in their decision space. Evaluations have been too willing to accept neat, over-simplified decision-making models. While evaluators have always recognized the need to understand thoroughly the programs being evaluated, rarely if ever is evaluation preceded by an analysis of the decision-making process and the constraints on the options open to the decision makers for whom the evaluation is being done. If evaluation results are expected to affect policy or program management decisions, then an analysis of the *planning-management-control* process to be affected and the development of realistic models of this process must become integral parts of evaluation planning and design.

EVALUATION FOR POLICYMAKERS: EXPERIMENTATION

A second type of evaluation important to the policymaker, but less often carried out, is evaluation of demonstration projects and field experiments—areas in which evaluation is politically and technically more feasible—and may have more chance to influence decisions. The typical demonstration projects demonstrate only that it is possible to spend public funds in a particular way. The results of the "demonstration" usually go unevaluated.

Police Fleet Plan

The Urban Institute's study of the Indianapolis Police Fleet Plan is an interesting example of an evaluation of a demonstration program.[4] In the Indianapolis Police Fleet Plan, police patrolmen are allowed to take their police cars home with them for their private use in off-duty hours—thus putting a lot more police cars on the city streets. The Urban Institute worked with the city of Fort Worth, which had some interest in possibly adopting the Police Fleet Plan. While the evaluation results were quite positive in favor of the Police Fleet Plan (auto thefts went down, auto accidents went down, outdoor crime, purse snatching, and robbery went down),[5] the study's sponsor (the Fort Worth City Manager) chose not to implement the findings of the study. After the study was published, however, at least one other local government did decide to implement a police fleet plan based on the results of the evaluation study.

Experiments

In the past few years, there has been a new trend in the development of federal programs. Instead of beginning major new programs or demonstration projects designed to be entering wedges for such programs, the federal government has turned toward using *field experiments* in an attempt to find out what is effective and what is not, *before* a program is implemented nationally. True experiments differ from typical demonstration projects in that those responsible exercise control over inputs and process variables—and carefully measure outputs to determine the extent to which the project reaches its objectives. Five years ago, the idea of conducting large-scale social experiments was neither practical nor realistic, for political reasons. The fact that income maintenance experiments are successfully underway and that money has been earmarked for a housing allowance experiment indicates that federal administrators are increasingly willing to take the political risks involved in running a carefully controlled set of experiments.

Outstanding examples of field experiments are OEO's negative income tax experiment now under way in New Jersey; HEW's income maintenence experiments in Gary, Seattle, and Denver; and OEO's experiments with performance contracting in elementary school education. OEO's experiments in performance contracting and the proposed experiments with education vouchers are beginning to break some new ground which may prove important in a number of ways. Private sector agencies will be tested and given a chance to develop new educational program models.

There are two ways to introduce the experimental approach into public programs — or two times at which experiments can be introduced: (1) before a major operating program is undertaken; (2) simultaneously with a major operating program. An experimental program may be started as a possible forerunner of a larger social program; or it may be set up to run alongside a large operating program, to learn things that might improve the operating program. (See, for example, the Office of Education's Follow Through program, in which a dozen or more approaches to the education of disadvantaged children are simultaneously being tested—each in several communities.) There is growing support in Washington for both of these approaches.

EVALUATION FOR PROGRAM MANAGERS

Let's turn our attention now to evaluation for program managers, those at federal, state, or local level who have responsibility for operating major programs. Over the past two years, members of the evaluation group at the Urban Institute have become more and more convinced that the primary evaluation pay-off (in terms of decisions actually influenced) may be in evaluation that is done in enough detail to get at the effects of operational changes within operating programs. Many program managers really want to know *what works best, under what conditions.* There is a market, a use, for this type of detailed evaluation information.

Following are three examples (or two-and-one-half examples) of evaluation systems designed to help program managers.

Solid Waste Collection

The Urban Institute recently developed a monitoring system for the District of Columbia Sanitation Department.[6] Inspectors, supplied with reference photographs, drive along city streets and alleyways with a tape recorder microphone in hand. For each block covered, they rate the cleanliness of the block as 1, 2, 3, or 4 (by comparing the street or alleyway with the reference photographs). This system therefore produces data on the *outputs* of services, not simply inputs or estimates of outputs.[7] One can imagine this system being used to assess the results of operational changes in Sanitation Department activities (as is now being done in the District of Columbia) or to justify budget requests [once it is determined that particular additional inputs in the way of increased services can in fact produce differences in outputs, for example, moving a neighborhood's streets and alleys from an average condition 3 or 4 (dirty) to a condition 2 (relatively clean)].

Public Schools

Urban public school systems have increasingly been called upon to address and correct major inequities in our society while providing quality education to large, heterogeneous school populations. School personnel are bombarded with numbers, which are supposed to be useful in making decisions affecting the operations of the school system. Rarely, however, are the data which pour out of large school systems relevant to the needs of school system decision makers. If, in the future, school systems are to respond to the challenges they face, then the objectives of education must be clarified and information about the performance of the school system in meeting those objectives must be improved and used effectively.

At present, most local educational evaluation focuses on analysis of special projects that occupy only a small fraction of the input to a particular school, while opportunities are ignored to make comparisons of input and output across the entire school system. Experience has shown that these local project evaluations, usually carried out to fulfill federal requirements, are of little use to local decision makers because their results are neither timely nor comparable. Project evaluations also operate under severe methodological constraints, which often make their results inconclusive.

The Urban Institute is now working with the Atlanta Public School System trying to develop a system for estimating the relative effectiveness of different public schools in the city.[8] In this project, Atlanta schools are being classified by the economic level of the students (currently measured by proportions of children receiving free lunches or reduced-price lunches) and by the amount of pupil turnover in the school during the year. The Institute is testing the notion that information on the relative effectiveness of schools serving comparable student populations could be useful to the superintendent and his staff. This work is still in the research and development phase.

Legal Services

Some federal agencies are giving attention to improved systems for program monitoring, where evaluation feedback is used directly to assist management decisions (for example, decisions on the refunding of individual projects and decisions on provision of technical assistance or training to projects performing below expectations). The Urban Institute designed, for the OEO Office of Legal Services, a systematic monitoring system that classifies local Legal Services projects into groups according to the kinds of communities in which they are operating, so that projects operating in similar circumstances can be compared with one another.[9] (Projects are classified by budget size, type of population served, and type of community in which the projects operate). When feasible, the same evaluators visit the projects within the same class, to enhance the prospects of making valid comparative judgments among projects that are in fact comparable.

The Office of Legal Services monitoring system rates the quality and quantity of the work being done by local Legal Services staff attorneys and provides Office of Legal Services management with estimates of the results achieved by every one of these projects toward Legal Services program goals (to promote economic development, to reform laws and administrative regulations bearing unfairly on the poor, and to provide individual legal services).

Hard work is required to get evaluative information in enough detail and with enough reliability to help program managers—but that's where real pay-offs for evaluation can occur. And this kind of evaluation is also more acceptable to program managers, who after all are the people who have to provide much of the data required for evaluation studies.

The Legal Services monitoring system and the D. C. Sanitation monitoring system are alike in their emphasis on outputs. For the Legal Services program, all that could be obtained through the on-site evaluations were relatively soft data on *estimated* outputs. The D. C. solid waste collection monitoring system adds the collection of hard output data on the effectiveness of solid waste collection activities—new data not available in any city records.[10]

PROBLEMS WITH EVALUATION

Let's turn now to some of the real problems in getting useful evaluation. From the point of view of decision makers, evaluation is a dangerous weapon. They don't want evaluation if it will yield the "wrong" answers about programs in which they are interested.[11] On the other hand, decision makers are more advanced in their ability to ask pertinent questions than evaluators are in their ability to provide timely answers at reasonable cost. Valid, reliable evaluation is very hard to perform and can cost a lot of money.[12] Evaluators have real problems in detecting causal connections between inputs and outputs—and in doing so in timely enough fashion to be useful to decision-makers. The structure of a program can have an important influence on the technical feasibility of separating the effects of the program from the effects of other, often more powerful, forces *not* under control of the program. To the extent that a program is run as a controlled experiment, for example, the evaluator's chances of separating out causal connections may be greater.

Our reviews have found typical federal program evaluation studies marked by certain design characteristics which severely restrict their reliability and usefulness:

1. They have been one-shot, one-time efforts, when we need *continuous* evaluation of programs.
2. They have been carried out in terms of national programs and are very weak on process data.
3. They have been small sample studies working with gross averages, when we need studies large enough to allow analysis of the wide variations we know exist in costs and performance among projects within programs.

These studies have often been accompanied by conclusions and recommendations based on unsupportable or unmeasured assumptions and weak, and often confusing data. In these cases, the evaluation results *should* be ignored by policymakers. Other evaluation studies, while competently conceived, are so severely constrained by time, money, and an inadequate data base that the results at best have only limited significance for policy changes or program improvement.

Experimentation presents new opportunities for the evaluator—and a new set of problems. There are important tensions between the evaluator and the program official, tensions which arise out of the very notion of experimentation. The criteria for selection of sites, the carefully controlled design of the experiments, and the random assignment of participants (or communities) to treatments are basic to experimental design. The program administrator may not see the utility of such ideas, however. What is so wrong, he may wonder, about calling an existing exemplary program an "experiment"? Or why not choose the people most in need of housing to participate in a housing allowance experiment? The evaluator must woo and win the administrator to the need for preserving the experimental character of the experiment.

Time also presents an enormous problem for the evaluator of experimental programs. As soon as there is sufficient legislative support to fund a series of experiments, there may be enough support to enact such a program nationwide. The concern that legislation will be enacted before the experiments have had time to produce reliable results may lead to pressures for the release of early, less reliable findings. The New Jersey Income Maintenance experiments experienced this pressure. Some early tentative results from the study were released with reluctance and heavy qualifications. If experimentation is to become a major vehicle in policy research, then ways must be found to anticipate and deal with these types of pressures.

Despite the differences, evaluation of experiments has a great deal in common with the evaluation of on-going programs. In both cases, the evaluator must resist the temptation to search for answers to questions that interest *him*, but which may not be high on the list of questions the *decision maker* wants answered. Decision makers will be convinced of the worth of evaluation only if evaluation meets the needs of the decision maker and provides information useful to him.

Conclusion

What can we actually get from program evaluation? From the point of view of a skeptical, but interested policymaker or program manager, evaluation has a mixed record. From the point of view of the analyst, the problems in doing useful evaluation are formidable. Over the past few years, however, there has been some progress, enough to indicate that certain directions in evaluation have promise.

NOTES

1. Westinghouse Learning Corporation—Ohio University (1969), "The Impact of Head Start: Evaluation of the Effects of Head Start on Children's Cognitive and Affective Development."
2. Nay, Joe *et al.* (1971), *Benefits and Costs of Manpower Training Programs: A Synthesis of Previous Studies with Reservations and Recommendations,* Washington, D.C.: The Urban Institute.
3. Joseph S. Wholey and Bayla F. White, letter to Dr. John W. Evans, Assistant Commissioner of Education, November 18, 1970. See Wholey, Joseph S. *et al.* (1971), *Title I Evaluation and Technical Assistance: Assessment and Prospects,* Washington, D.C.: The Urban Institute.
4. See Fisk, Donald M. (1970), *The Indianapolis Police Fleet Plan: An Example of Program Evaluation for Local Government,* Washington, D.C.: The Urban Institute.
5. It's worth noting that the Police Fleet Plan study was done primarily using existing effectiveness data on crime rates, accidents, etc., together with development of cost data from city records. It took only a month or two of an analyst's time to put this study together.
6. See Blair, Louis and Schwartz, Alfred (1971), *Improving the Measurement of the Effectiveness of D. C. Solid Waste Collection Activities,* Washington, D.C.: The Urban Institute.
7. It turned out that the ratings for streets and alleyways were relatively stable within a census tract and over time. Therefore, it was possible to develop an efficient monitoring system using sampling techniques.
8. See White, Bayla F. (1970), *Design for a School Rating or Classification System,* Washington, D.C.: The Urban Institute; and White, Bayla F. *et al.* (1971), *The Atlanta Urban Institute School Classification Project,* Washington, D.C.: The Urban Institute.
9. See Duffy, Hugh G. *et al.* (1971), *Design of an On-Site Evaluation System for the Office of Legal Services,* Washington, D.C.: The Urban Institute.
10. The Legal Services monitoring system was developed for less than $50,000 and is now being used by the OEO Legal Services program to keep track of their 260-odd local projects. The D. C. solid waste collection monitoring system was developed for approximately $70,000 and is now being implemented in the District of Columbia.
11. In some cases, political pressures will simply override the empirical evidence without the formality of a methodological argument. Here, the only recourse open to the evaluator is to publish the results and hope that some other more enlightened or less pressured decision maker with similar problems will make use of the results.
12. The Stanford Research Institue evaluation of the Office of Education Follow Through program, for example, has already cost approximately $7 million.

12

AGENCY ADMINISTRATION AND PROGRAM IMPLEMENTATION

In many ways, the core of public administrative practice is the line management of public agencies and programs. In this chapter Peter Drucker explains the components of effective public management, his principal focus being on the problem of performance—productivity and effectiveness—in public agencies.

One of the most difficult tasks of a public executive is to take over the management of an agency. Elliot Richardson had a unique administrative career in moving from one federal cabinet post to another. Charles Peters explains what Richardson and his top aides learned in their series of moves.

Promoting maximum individual performance in public organizations is another important theme in agency administration. One approach to reconciling the needs and performance of an individual with those of the agency is called management by objectives. George Odiorne explains what this approach is and how it works, using an example from state government.

Getting more for the same amount of dollars or getting the same results for fewer dollars is the essence of productivity. New pressures are on public agencies to become increasingly productive (or efficient, an older term with approximately the same meaning). Nancy Hayward outlines the need for and various approaches to increased productivity in public administration.

Brian Rapp concludes this part by returning the discussion to the importance of performance in the delivery of governmental services. Rapp's particular concern is understanding the nature of municipal management.

Managing the Public Service Institution

PETER F. DRUCKER

Service institutions are an increasingly important part of our society. Schools and universities; research laboratories; public utilities; hospitals and other health-care institutions; professional, industry, and trade associations; and many others—all these are as much "institutions" as is the business firm, and, therefore, are equally in need of management.[1] They all have people who are designated to exercise the management function and who are paid for doing the management job—even though they may not be called "managers," but "administrators," "directors," "executives," or some other such title.

These "public service" institutions—to give them a generic name—are the real growth sector of a modern society. Indeed, what we have now is a "multi-institutional" society rather than a "business" society. The traditional title of the American college course still tends to read "Business and Government." But this is an anachronism. It should read "Business, Government, and Many Others."

All public service institutions are being paid for out of the economic surplus produced by economic activity. The growth of the service institutions in this century is thus the best testimonial to the success of business in discharging its economic task. Yet unlike, say, the early 19th-century university, the service institutions are not mere "luxury" or "ornament." They are, so to speak, main pillars of a modern society, load-bearing members of the main structure. They *have* to perform if society and economy are to function. It is not only that these service institutions are a major expense of a modern society; half of the personal income of the United States (and of most of the other developed countries) is spent on public service institutions (including those operated by the government). Compared to these "public service" institutions, both the "private sector" (i.e., the economy of goods) and the traditional government functions of law, defense, and public order, account for a smaller share of the total income flow of today's developed societies than they did around 1900—despite the cancerous growth of military spending.

Every citizen in the developed, industrialized, urbanized societies depends for his very survival on the performance of the public service institutions. These institutions also embody the values of developed societies. For it is in the form of education and health care, knowledge and mobility—rather than primarily in the form of more "food, clothing, and shelter"—that our society obtains the fruits of its increased economic capacities and productivity.

Yet the evidence for performance in the service institutions is not impressive, let alone overwhelming. Schools, hospitals, universities are all big today beyond the imagination of an earlier generation. They all dispose of astronomical budgets. Yet everywhere they are "in crisis." A generation or two ago, their performance was taken for granted. Today, they are being attacked on all sides for lack of performance. Services which the 19th century managed with aplomb and apparently with little effort—the postal service, for instance—are deeply in the red, require enormous and ever-growing subsidies, and yet give poorer service everywhere. In every country the citizen complains ever more loudly of "bureaucracy" and mismanagement in the institutions that are supposed to serve him.

ARE SERVICE INSTITUTIONS MANAGEABLE?

The response of the service institutions to this criticism has been to become "management conscious." They increasingly turn to business to learn "management." In all service institutions, "manager development," "management by objectives," and many other concepts and tools of business management are becoming increasingly popular. This is a healthy sign—but no more than that. It does not mean that the service institutions understand the problems of managing themselves. It only means that they have begun to realize that, at present, they are not being managed.

Yet, though "performance" in the public service institutions is the exception rather than the rule, the exceptions do prove that service institutions can perform. Among American public service agencies of the last 40 years, for instance, there is the Tennessee Valley Authority (TVA), the big regional electric-power and irrigation project in the Southeastern United States. (TVA's performance was especially notable during its early years, in the 1930's and 1940's, when it was headed by David Lilienthal.) While a great many—perhaps most—schools in the inner-city, black ghettos of America deserve all the strictures of the "deschooling" movement, a few schools in the very worst ghettos (e.g., in New York's South Bronx) have shown high capacity to make the most "disadvantaged" children acquire the basic skills of literacy.

What is it that the few successful service institutions do (or eschew) that makes them capable of performance? This is the question to ask. And it is a *management* question—of a special kind. In most respects, the service institution is not very different from a business enterprise. It faces similar—if not precisely the same—challenges in seeking to make work productive. It does not differ significantly from a business in its "social responsibility." Nor does the service institution differ very much from business enterprise in respect to the manager's work and job, in respect to organizational design and structure, or even in respect to the job and structure of top management. *Internally,* the differences tend to be differences in terminology rather than in substance.

But the service institution is in a fundamentally different "business" from business. It is different in its purpose. It has different values. It needs different objectives. And it makes a different contribution to society. "Performance and results" are quite different in a service institution from what they are in a business. "Managing for performance" is the one area in which the service institution differs significantly from a business.

WHY SERVICE INSTITUTIONS DO NOT PERFORM

There are three popular explanations for the common failure of service institutions to perform:

1. Their managers aren't "businesslike";
2. They need "better men";
3. Their objectives and results are "intangible."

All three are alibis rather than explanations.

1) The service institution will perform, it is said again and again, if only it is managed in a "businesslike" manner. Colbert, the great minister of Louis XIV, was the first to blame the performance difficulties of the non-business, the service institution, on this lack of "businesslike" management. Colbert, who created the first "modern" public service in the West, never ceased to exhort his officials to be "businesslike." The cry is still being repeated every day—by chambers of commerce, by presidential and royal commissions, by ministers in the Communist countries, and so on. If only, they all say, their administrators were to behave in a "businesslike" way, service institutions would perform. And of course, this belief also underlies, in large measure, today's "management boom" in the service institutions.

But it is the wrong diagnosis; and being "businesslike" is the wrong prescription for the ills of the service institution. The service institution has performance trouble precisely because it is *not* a business. What being "businesslike" usually means in a service institution is little more than control of cost. What characterizes a business, however, is focus on results—return on capital, share of market, and so on.

To be sure, there is a need for efficiency in all institutions. Because there is usually no competition in the service field, there is no outward and imposed cost control on service institutions as there is on business in a competitive (and even an oligopolistic) market. But the basic problem of service institutions is not high cost but lack of effectiveness. They may be very efficient—some are. But they then tend not to do the right things.

The belief that the public service institution will perform if only it is put on a "businesslike" basis underlies the numerous attempts to set up many government services as separate "public corporations"—again an attempt that dates back to Colbert and his establishment of "Crown monopolies." There may be beneficial side effects, such as freedom from petty civil service regulation. But the intended main effect, performance, is seldom achieved. Costs may go down (though not always; setting up London Transport and the British Post Office as separate "businesslike" corporations, and thereby making them defenseless against labor union pressures, has led to skyrocketing costs). But services essential to the fulfillment of the institution's purpose may be slighted or lopped off in the name of "efficiency."

The best and worst example of the "businesslike" approach in the public service institution may well be the Port of New York Authority, set up in the 1920's to manage automobile and truck traffic throughout the two-state area (New York and New Jersey) of the Port of New York. The Port Authority has, from the beginning, been "businesslike" with a vengeance. The engineering of its bridges, tunnels, docks, silos, and airports has been outstanding. Its construction costs have been low and under control. Its financial standing has been extremely high, so that it could always borrow at most advantageous rates of interest. It made being "businesslike"—as measured, above all, by its standing with the banks—its goal and purpose. As a result, it did not concern itself with transportation policy in the New York metropolitan area, even though its bridges, tunnels, and airports generate much of the traffic in New York's streets. It did not ask: "Who are our constituents?" Instead it resisted any such question as "political" and "unbusinesslike." Consequently, it has come to be seen as the villain of the New York traffic and transportation problem. And when it needed support (e.g., in finding a place to put New York's badly needed fourth airport), it found itself without a single backer, except the bankers. As a result the Port Authority may well become "politicized"; that is, denuded of its efficiency without gaining anything in effectiveness.

"BETTER PEOPLE"

The cry for "better people" is even older than Colbert. In fact, it can be found in the earliest Chinese texts on government. In particular, it has been the constant demand of all American "reformers," from Henry Adams shortly after the Civil War, to Ralph Nader today. They all have believed that the one thing lacking in the government agency is "better people."

But service institutions cannot, any more than businesses, depend on "supermen" to staff their managerial and executive positions. There are far too many institutions to be staffed. If service institutions cannot be run and managed by men of normal—or even fairly low—endowment, if, in other words, we cannot organize the task so that it will be done on a satisfactory level by men who only try hard, it cannot be done at all. Moreover, there is no reason to believe that the people who staff the managerial and professional positions in our "service" institutions are any less qualified, any less competent or honest, or any less hard-working than the men who manage businesses. By the same token, there is no reason to believe that business managers, put in control of service institutions, would do better than the "bureaucrats." Indeed, we know that they immediately become "bureaucrats" themselves.

One example of this was the American experience during World War II, when large numbers of business executives who had performed very well in their own companies moved into government positions. Many rapidly became "bureaucrats." The men did not change. But whereas in business they had been capable of obtaining performance and results, in government they found themselves producing primarily procedures and red tape—and deeply frustrated by the experience.

Similarly, effective businessmen who are promoted to head a "service staff" within a business (e.g., the hard-hitting sales manager who gets to be "Vice President—marketing services") tend to become "bureaucrats" almost overnight. Indeed, the "service institutions" within business—R&D departments, personnel staffs, marketing or manufacturing service staffs, and the like—apparently find it just as hard to perform as the public service institutions of society at large, which businessmen often criticize as being "unbusinesslike" and run by "bureaucrats."

"INTANGIBLE" OBJECTIVES

The most sophisticated and, at first glance, the most plausible explanation for the non-performance of service institutions is the last one: The objectives of service institutions are "intangible," and so are their results. This is at best a half-truth.

[handwritten margin notes: "Comment on their vulgarization", "SONY, IBM, etc do not live with # of customers"]

The definition of what "our business is" is always "intangible," in a business as well as in a service institution. Surely, to say, as Sears Roebuck does, "Our business is to be the informed buyer for the American family," is "intangible." And to say, as Bell Telephone does, "Our business is service to the customers," may sound like a pious and empty platitude. At first glance, these statements would seem to defy any attempt at translation into operational, let alone quantitative, terms. To say, "Our business is electronic entertainment," as Sony of Japan does, is equally "intangible," as is IBM's definition of its business as "data processing." Yet, as these businesses have clearly demonstrated it is not exceedingly difficult to derive concrete and measurable goals and targets from "intangible" definitions like those cited above.

"Saving souls," as the definition of the objectives of a church is, indeed, "intangible." At least the bookkeeping is not of this world. But church attendance is measurable. And so is "getting the young people back into the church."

"The development of the whole personality" as the objective of the school is, indeed, "intangible." But "teaching a child to read by the time he has finished third grade" is by no means intangible; it can be measured easily and with considerable precision.

"Abolishing racial discrimination" is equally unamenable to clear operational definition, let alone measurement. But to increase the number of black apprentices in the building trades is a quantifiable goal, the attainment of which can be measured.

Achievement is never possible except against specific, limited, clearly defined targets, in business as well as in a service institution. Only if targets are defined can resources be allocated to their attainment, priorities and deadlines be set, and somebody be held accountable for results. But the starting point for effective work is a definition of the purpose and mission of the institution—which is almost always "intangible," but nevertheless need not be vacuous.

It is often said that service institutions differ from businesses in that they have a plurality of constituencies. And it is indeed the case that service institutions have a great many "constitutents." The school is of vital concern not only to children and their parents, but also to teachers, to taxpayers, and to the community at large. Similarly, the hospital has to satisfy the patient, but also the doctors, the nurses, the technicians, the patient's family—as well as taxpayers or, as in the United States, employers and labor unions who through their insurance contributions provide the bulk of the support of most hospitals. But business also has a plurality of constituencies. Every business has at least two different customers, and often a good many more. And employees, investors, and the community at large—and even management itself—are also "constituencies."

MISDIRECTION BY BUDGET

The one basic difference between a service institution and a business is the way the service institution is paid. Businesses (other than monopolies) are paid for satisfying the customer. They are only paid when they produce what the customer wants and what he is willing to exchange his purchasing power for. Satisfaction of the customer is, therefore, the basis for performance and results in a business.

Service institutions, by contrast, are typically paid out of a budget allocation.

Their revenues are allocated from a general revenue stream that is not tied to what they are doing, but is obtained by tax, levy, or tribute. Furthermore, the typical service institution is endowed with monopoly powers; the intended beneficiary usually has no choice.

Being paid out of a budget allocation changes what is meant by "performance" or "results." *"Results" in the budget-based institution means a larger budget. "Performance" is the ability to maintain or to increase one's budget.* The first test of a budget-based institution and the first requirement for its survival is to obtain the budget. And the budget is, by definition, related not to the achievement of any goals, but to the *intention* of achieving those goals.

This means, first, that efficiency and cost control, however much they are being preached, are not really considered virtues in the budget-based institution. The importance of a budget-based institution is measured essentially by the size of its budget and the size of its staff. To achieve results with a smaller budget or a smaller staff is, therefore, not "performance." It might actually endanger the institution. Not to spend the budget to the hilt will only convince the budget-maker—whether a legislature or a budget committee—that the budget for the next fiscal period can safely be cut.

Thirty or 40 years ago, it was considered characteristic of Russian planning, and one of its major weaknesses, that Soviet managers, toward the end of the plan period, engaged in a frantic effort to spend all the money allocated to them, which usually resulted in total waste. Today, the disease has become universal, as budget-based institutions have become dominant everywhere. And "buying-in"—that is, getting approval for a new program or project by grossly underestimating its total cost—is also built into the budget-based institution.

"Parkinson's Law" lampooned the British Admiralty and the British Colonial Office for increasing their staffs and their budgets as fast as the British Navy and the British Empire went down. "Parkinson's Law" attributed this to inborn human perversity. But it is perfectly rational behavior for someone on a budget, since it is the budget, after all, that measures "performance" and "importance."

It is obviously not compatible with *efficiency* that the acid test of performance should be to obtain the budget. But *effectiveness* is even more endangered by reliance on the budget allocation. It makes it risky to raise the question of what the "business" of the institution should be. That question is always "controversial"; such controversy is likely to alienate support and will therefore be shunned by the budget-based institution. As a result, it is likely to wind up deceiving both the public and itself.

Take an instance from government: The U.S. Department of Agriculture has never been willing to ask whether its goal should be "farm productivity" or "support of the small family farm." It has known for decades that these two objectives are not identical as had originally been assumed, and that they are, indeed, becoming increasingly incompatible. To admit this, however, would have created controversy that might have endangered the Department's budget. As a result, American farm policy has frittered away an enormous amount of money and human resources on what can only (and charitably) be called a public relations campaign, that is, on a show of support for the small family farmer. The effective activities, however—and they have been very effective indeed—have been directed toward eliminating the small family farmer and replacing him by the far more productive "agribusinesses," that is, highly capitalized and highly mechanized farms, run as a business and not as a "way of life." This may well have been the right thing to do. But it certainly was not what the Department was founded to do, nor what the Congress, in approving the Department's budget, expected it to do.

Take a non-governmental example, the American community hospital, which is "private" though "non-profit." Everywhere it suffers from a growing confusion of missions and objectives, and the resulting impairment of its effectiveness and performance. Should a hospital be, in effect, a "physician's facility"—as most older American physicians still maintain? Should it focus on the major health needs of a community? Or should it try to do everything and be "abreast of every medical advance," no matter what the cost and no matter how rarely certain facilities will be used? Should it devote resources to preventive medicine and health education? Or should it, like the hospital under the British health service, confine itself strictly to repair of major health damage after it has occurred?

Every one of these definitions of the "business" of the hospital can be defended. Every one deserves a hearing. The effective American hospital will be a multi-purpose institution and strike a balance between various objectives. What most hospitals do, however, is pretend that there are no basic questions to be decided. The result, predictably, is confusion and impairment of the hospital's capacity to serve any function and to carry out any mission.

PLEASING EVERYONE AND ACHIEVING NOTHING

Dependence on a budget allocation militates against setting priorities and concentrating efforts. Yet nothing is ever accomplished unless scarce resources are concentrated on a small number of priorities. A shoe manufacturer who has 22 per cent of the market for work shoes may have a profitable business. If he succeeds in raising his market share to 30 per cent, especially if the market for his kind of footwear is expanding, he is doing very well indeed. He need not concern himself too much with the 78 per cent of the users of work shoes who buy from somebody else. And the customers for ladies' fashion shoes are of no concern to him at all.

Contrast this with the situation of an institution on a budget. To obtain its budget, it needs the approval, or at least the acquiescence, of practically everybody who remotely could be considered a "constituent." Where a market share of 22 per cent might be perfectly satisfactory to a business, a "rejection" by 78 per cent of its "constituents"—or even by a much smaller proportion—would be fatal to a budget-based institution. And this means that the service institution finds it difficult to set priorities; it must instead try to placate everyone by doing a little bit of everything—which, in effect, means achieving nothing.

Finally, being budget-based makes it even more difficult to abandon the wrong things, the old, the obsolete. As a result, service institutions are even more encrusted than businesses with the barnacles of inherently unproductive efforts.

No institution likes to abandon anything it does. Business is no exception. But in an institution that is being paid for its performance and results, the unproductive, the obsolete, will sooner or later be killed off by the customers. In a budget-based institution no such discipline is being enforced. The temptation is great, therefore, to respond to lack of results by redoubling efforts. The temptation is great to double the budget, precisely *because* there is no performance.

Human beings will behave as they are rewarded for behaving—whether the reward be money and promotion, a medal, an autographed picture of the boss, or a pat on the back. This is one lesson the behavioral psychologist has taught us during the last 50 years (not that it was unknown before). A business, or any institution that is paid for its results and performance in such a way that the dissatisfied or disinterested customer need not pay, has to "earn" its income. An institution that is financed by a budget—or that enjoys a monopoly which the customer cannot escape—is rewarded for what it "deserves" rather than for what it "earns." It is paid for good intentions and for "programs." It is paid for not alienating important constituents rather than for satisfying any one group. It is misdirected, by the way it is paid, into defining "performance" and "results" as what will maintain or increase its budget.

WHAT WORKS

The exception, the comparatively rare service institution that achieves effectiveness, is more instructive than the great majority that achieves only "programs." It shows that effectiveness in the service institution is achievable—though by no means easy. It shows what different kinds of service institutions can do and need to do. It shows limitations and pitfalls. But it also shows that the service institution manager can do unpopular and highly "controversial" things if only he makes the risk-taking decision to set priorities and allocate resources.

The first and perhaps simplest example is that of the Bell Telephone System. A telephone system is a "natural" monopoly. Within a given area, one supplier of telephone service must have exclusive rights. The one thing any subscriber to a public telephone service requires is access to all other subscribers, which means territorial exclusivity for one monopolistic service. And as a whole country or continent becomes, in effect, one telephone system, this monopoly has to be extended over larger and larger areas.

An individual may be able to do without a telephone—though in today's society only at prohibitive inconvenience. But a professional man, a tradesman, an office, or a business *must* have a telephone. Residential phone service may still be an "option." Business phone service is compulsory. Theodore Vail, the first head of the organization, saw this in the early years of this century. He also saw clearly that the American telephone system, like the telephone systems in all other industrially developed nations, could easily be taken over by government. To prevent this, Vail thought through what the telephone company's business was and should be, and came up with his famous definition: "Our business is service."[2] This totally "intangible" statement of the telephone company's "business" then enabled Vail to set specific goals and objectives and to develop measurements of performance and results. His "customer satisfaction" standards and "service satisfaction" standards created nationwide competition between telephone managers in various areas, and became the criteria by which the managers were judged and rewarded. These standards measured performance as defined by the customer, e.g., waiting time before an operator came on the line, or time between application for telephone service and its installation. They were meant to direct managers' attention to results.

Vail also thought through who his "constituents" were. This led to his conclusion—even more shocking to the conventional wisdom of 1900 than his "service" objectives—that it was the telephone company's task to make the public utility commissions of the individual states capable of effective rate regulation. Vail argued that a national monopoly in a crucial area could expect to escape nationalization only by being regulated. Helping to convert the wretchedly ineffectual, corrupt, and bumbling public utility commissions of late 19th-century populism into effective, respected, and informed adversaries was in the telephone company's own survival interest.

Finally, Vail realized that a telephone system depends on its ability to obtain capital. Each dollar of telephone revenue requires a prior investment of three to four dollars. Therefore, the investor too had to be considered a "constituent," and the telephone company had to design financial instruments and a financial policy that focused on the needs and expectations of the investor, and that made telephone company securities, whether bonds or shares, a distinct and preferred financial "product."

The American University

The building of the American university from 1860 to World War I also illustrates how service institutions can be made to perform. The American university as it emerged during that era was primarily the work of a small number of men: Andrew D. White (President of Cornell, 1868–1885); Charles W. Eliot (President of Harvard, 1869–1909); Daniel Coit Gilman (President of Johns Hopkins, 1876–1901); David Starr Jordan (President of Stanford, 1891–1913); William Rainey Harper (President of Chicago, 1892–1904); and Nicholas Murray Butler (President of Columbia, 1902–1945).

These men all had in common one basic insight: The traditional "college"—essentially an 18th-century seminary to train preachers—had become totally obsolete, sterile, and unproductive. Indeed, it was dying fast; America in 1860 had far fewer college students than it had had 40 years earlier with a much smaller population. The men who built the new universities shared a common objective: to create a new institution, a true "university." And they all realized that while European examples, especially Oxford and Cambridge and the German university, had much to offer, these new universities had to be distinctively American institutions.

Beyond these shared beliefs, however, they differed sharply on what a university should be and what its purpose and mission were. Eliot, at Harvard, saw the purpose of the university as that of educating a leadership group with a distinct "style." His Harvard was to be a "national" institution rather than the parochial preserve of the "proper Bostonian" that Harvard College had been. But it also was to restore to Boston—and to New England generally—the dominant position of a moral elite, such as in earlier times had been held by the "Elect," the Puritan divines, and their successors, the Federalist leaders in the early days of the Republic. Butler, at Columbia—and, to a lesser degree, Harper at Chicago—saw the function of the university as the systematic application of rational thought and analysis to the basic problems of a modern society, from education to economics, and from domestic government to foreign affairs. Gilman, at Johns Hopkins, saw the university as the producer of advanced knowledge; indeed, originally Johns Hopkins was to confine itself to advanced research and was to give no undergraduate instruction. White, at Cornell, aimed at producing an "educated public."

Each of these men knew that he had to make compromises. Each knew that he had to satisfy a number of "constituencies" and "publics," each of whom looked at the university quite differently. Both Eliot and Butler, for instance, had to build their new university on an old foundation (the others could build from the ground up) and had to satisfy—or at least to placate—existing alumni and faculty. They all had to be exceedingly conscious of the need to attract and hold financial support. It was Eliot, for instance, with all his insistence on "moral leadership," who invented the first "placement office" and set out to find well-paying jobs for Harvard graduates, especially in business. It was Butler, conscious that Columbia was a late-comer and that the millionaire philanthropists of his day had already been snared by his competitors (e.g., Rockefeller by Chicago), who invented the first "public relations" office in a university, designed—and most successfully— to reach the merely well-to-do and get their money.

These founders' definitions did not outlive them. Even during the lifetime of Eliot and Butler, for instance, their institutions escaped their control, began to diffuse objectives and to confuse priorities. In the course of this century, all these universities—and many others, like the University of California and other major state universities—have converged toward a common type. Today, it is hard to tell one "multiversity" from another. Yet the imprint of the founders has still not been totally erased. It is hardly an accident that the New Deal picked faculty members primarily from Columbia and Chicago to be high-level advisors and policy makers; for the New Deal was, of course, committed to the application of rational thought and analysis to public policies and problems. And 30 years later, when the Kennedy Administration came in with an underlying belief in the "style" of an "elite," it naturally turned to Harvard. For while each of the founding fathers of the modern American university made compromises and adapted to a multitude of constituencies, each had an objective and a definition of the university to which he gave priority and against which he measured performance. Clearly, the job the founders did almost a century ago will have to be done again for today's "multiversity," if it is not to choke on its own services.

SCHOOLS, HOSPITALS, AND THE TVA

The English "open classroom" is another example of a successful service institution. It is being promoted in this country as the "child-centered" approach to schooling, but its origin was in the concern with performance, and that is also the secret of its success. The English "open classroom" demands that each child—or at least each normal child—acquire the same measurable proficiency in the basic skills of literacy at roughly the same time. It is then the teacher's task to think through the learning path best suited to lead each child to a common and pre-set goal. The objectives are perfectly clear: the learning of specific skills, especially reading, writing, and figuring. They are identical for all children, measurable, and measured. Everything else is, in effect, considered irrelevant. Such elementary schools as have performed in the urban slums of this country—and there are more of them than the current "crisis in the classroom" syndrome acknowledges—have done exactly the same thing. The performing schools in black or Puerto Rican neighborhoods in New York, for instance, are those that have defined one clear objective—usually to teach reading—have eliminated or subordinated everything else, and then have measured themselves against a standard of clearly set performance goals.

The solution to the problem of the hospital, as is becoming increasingly clear, will similarly lie in thinking through objectives and priorities. The most promising approach may well be one worked out by the Hospital Consulting Group at Westinghouse Electric Corporation, which recognizes that the American hospital has a multiplicity of functions, but organizes each as an autonomous "decentralized" division with its own facilities, its own staff, and its own objectives. There would thus be a traditional care hospital for the fairly small number of truly sick people who require what today's "full-time" hospital offers; an "ambulatory" medical hospital for diagnosis and out-patient work; an "ambulatory" surgical hospital for the large number of surgical patients—actually the majority—who, like patients after cataract surgery, a tonsilectomy, or most orthopedic surgery, are not "sick" and need no medical and little nursing care, but need a bed (and a bedpan) till the stitches are firm or the cast dries; a psychiatric unit—mostly for out-patient or overnight care; and a convalescent unit that would hardly differ from a good motel (e.g., for the healthy mother of a healthy baby). All these would have common services. But each would be a separate health care facility with different objectives, different priorities, and different standards of performance.

But the most instructive example of an effective service institution may be that of the early Tennessee Valley Authority. Built mainly during the New Deal, the TVA today is no longer "controversial." It is just another large power company, except for being owned by the government rather than by private investors. But in its early days, 40 years ago, the TVA was a slogan, a battle cry, a symbol. Some, friends and enemies alike, saw in it the opening wedge of the nationalization of electric energy in the United States. Others saw in it the vehicle for a return to Jeffersonian agrarianism, based on cheap power, government paternalism, and free fertilizer. Still others were primarily interested in flood control and navigation. Indeed, there was such a wealth of conflicting expectations that TVA's first head, Arthur Morgan, a distinguished engineer and economist, completely floundered. Unable to think through what the business of the TVA should be and how varying objectives might be balanced, Morgan accomplished nothing. Finally, President Roosevelt replaced him with an almost totally unknown young lawyer, David Lilienthal, who had little previous experience as an administrator.

Lilienthal faced up to the need to define the TVA's business. He concluded that the first objective was to build truly efficient electric plants and to supply an energy-starved region with plentiful and cheap power. All the rest, he decided, hinged on the attainment of this first need, which then became his operational priority. The TVA of today has accomplished a good many other objectives as well, from flood control and navigation to fertilizer production and, indeed, even balanced community development. But it was Lilienthal's insistence on a clear definition of the TVA's business and on setting priorities that explains why today's TVA is taken for granted, even by the very same people who, 40 years ago, were among its implacable enemies.

THE REQUIREMENTS FOR SUCCESS

Service institutions are a most diverse lot. The one and only thing they all have in common is that, for one reason or another, they cannot be organized under a competitive market test.³ But however diverse the various kinds of "service institutions" may be, all of them need first to impose on themselves the discipline practiced by the managers and leaders of the institutions in the examples presented above.

1. They need to answer the question, *"What is our business and what should it be?"* They need to bring out into the open alternative definitions and to think them through carefully, perhaps even to work out (as did the presidents of the emerging American universities) the balance of different and sometimes conflicting definitions. What service institutions need is not to be more "business-like." They need to be more "hospital-like," "university-like," "government-like," and so on. They need to be subjected to a performance test—if only to that of "socialist competition"—as much as possible. In other words, they need to think through their own specific function, purpose, and mission.

2. Service institutions need to derive *clear objectives and goals* from their definition of function and mission. What they need is not "better people," but people who do the management job systematically and who focus themselves and their institutions purposefully on performance and results. They do need efficiency—that is, control of costs. But, above all, they need effectiveness—that is, emphasis on the right results.

3. They then have to think through *priorities* of concentration which enable them to select targets; to set standards of accomplishment and performance (that is, to define the minimum acceptable results); to set deadlines; to go to work on results; and to make someone accountable for results.

4. They need to define *measurements of performance*—the "customer satisfaction" measurements of the telephone company, or the figures on reading performance by which the English "open classroom" measures its accomplishments.

5. They need to use these measurements to *"feed back"* on their efforts—that is, *they must build self-control from results into their system.*

6. Finally, they need an organized audit of *objectives and results,* so as to identify those objectives that no longer serve a useful purpose or have proven unattainable. They need to identify unsatisfactory performance, and activities which are obsolete, unproductive, or both. And they need a mechanism for *sloughing off* such activities rather than wasting their money and their energies where the results are not.

This last requirement may be the most important one. The absence of a market test removes from the service institution the discipline that forces a business eventually to abandon yesterday's products—or else go bankrupt. Yet this requirement is the least understood.

No success lasts "forever." Yet it is even more difficult to abandon yesterday's success than it is to reappraise failure. Success breeds its own *hubris.* It creates emotional attachments, habits of thought and action, and, above all, false self-confidence. A success that has outlived its usefulness may, in the end, be more damaging than failure. Especially in a service institution, yesterday's success becomes "policy," "virtue," "conviction," if not indeed "Holy Writ," unless the institution imposes on itself the discipline of thinking through its mission, its objectives, and its priorities, and of building in feedback control from results over policies, priorities, and action. We are in such a "welfare mess" today in the United States largely because the welfare program of the New Deal had been such a success in the 1930's that we could not abandon it, and instead misapplied it to the radically different problem of the black migrants to the cities in the 1950's and 1960's.

To make service institutions perform, it should by now be clear, does not require "great men." It requires instead a system. The essentials of this system may not be too different from the essentials of performance in a business enterprise, as the present "management boom" in the service institutions assumes. But the application will be quite different. For the service institutions are not businesses; "performance" means something quite different for them.

Few service institutions today suffer from having too few administrators; most of them are over-administered, and suffer from a surplus of procedures, organization charts, and "management techniques." What now has to be learned—it is still largely lacking—is to manage service institutions for performance. This may well be the biggest and most important management task for the remainder of this century.

NOTES

1. Government agencies and bureaus are also "service institutions," of course, and have management problems which are comparable to those of the institutions I have mentioned. But because they also partake of a general "governmental" purpose, not usefully defined in management terms, I shall not be dealing with them in this article. I shall feel free, however, to include such quasi-governmental organizations as the TVA or the post office in my discussion.
2. This was so heretical that the directors of the telephone company fired Vail when he first propounded his thesis in 1897—only to rehire him 10 years later when the absence of clear performance objectives had created widespread public demand for telephone nationalization even among such non-radicals as the Progressive wing of the Republican Party.
3. This may no longer be necessarily true for the postal service. At last an independent postal company in the U.S. is trying to organize a business in competition to the government's postal monopoly. Should this work out, it might do more to restore performance to the mails than the recent setting up of a postal monopoly as a separate "public corporation" which is on a "businesslike" basis.

How to Take Over the Government

CHARLES PETERS

What might be called the lesson of Albert Speer—that sound principles of management can be put to evil uses—has been much commented on as a result of the experience of the Kennedy-Johnson-Nixon years. This has produced a tendency, at least on the Left, to scorn the study of process, a scorn that also derives inspiration from the sterility of much of the literature of public administration.

However, while it's true that a mastery of process can lead to evil, it is also true that from time to time good men with good policies will come to office and be confronted with the problem of how they will go about doing their good deeds. It is with this thought in mind that I have looked for instruction at the unique experience of Elliot Richardson as he proceeded to take over major responsibility in four different departments of the executive branch. Richardson became Under Secretary of State in January, 1969, then Secretary of Health, Education and Welfare in June, 1970, then Secretary of Defense in January, 1973, and finally, Attorney General in June, 1973. What he and his close associates learned about managing the people, processes, and policies of government is the subject of this article, as is how the lesson of Albert Speer might require refinement in light of our experience watching the Richardson team in action.

Richardson relied on a triumvirate of top assistants: Jonathan Moore, who is now Director of the Institute of Politics at Harvard, J.T. Smith, who is now associated with the Washington law firm, Covington and Burling, and Richard Darman, who has joined Richardson as a fellow at the Woodrow Wilson Institute in Washington. Moore ranked first and functioned in the areas of politics and people. He was, for example, the clearance point for all contacts between the White House and Department of Justice personnel. Smith was the guardian of the gate, controlling access to Richardson. Darman organized substantive staff work and prepared policy papers. I talked extensively with each of these men. In addition, I interviewed Richardson and two others who played important roles in Richardson transitions: Wilmot Hastings, now a Boston lawyer, who participated in the transition into State and was in charge of the transition into HEW (some say he was the most liberal of Richardson's top assistants), and Richard Mastrangelo, who now schedules Richardson's political appearances and was in charge of the logistics of the last two transitions.

Some interesting differences emerged from their accounts. One assistant described Larry Lynn, Assistant Secretary for Planning and Evaluation at HEW, as the most brilliant and innovative man he had ever known, while another said he was the worst son-of-a-bitch he'd ever met. Richardson told me he thought he had accomplished more at HEW than at any of the other departments; two of his assistants thought the least had been done there.

Another area of disagreement was over how much they had even a chance of accomplishing at the Defense Department. Jonathan Moore felt pessimistic. He pointed out that the President and his chief man, Kissinger, were in very strong assertive control of State-Defense policies. "They had lots of momentum and we were going to have a hell of a time trying to make an impact of our own." Moore also complained that there was too much direct connection between the Joint Chiefs and the White House, leaving the Secretary of Defense out.

J.T. Smith agreed: "The military really runs Defense." But he added an important distinction for those who have a "Seven Days in May" view of the services: "Anytime you can find out enough to give the military a sensible order, the military will follow it. They aren't indifferent to the Constitution. But figuring out what order to give is the trick. It's like trying to give an order to a tank while running along beside it not knowing what is going on inside."

Smith had one other reason for thinking the Richardson group would have had little impact on the Pentagon: "So much policy is already made, so many programs are already in the pipeline. What other agency has Trident submarines in the works for 1983?''

Darman was more hopeful: ''At Defense we had almost everyone in the country in agreement on reducing the defense budget.'' Darman may have been wrong about that, but I think he was right in his next observation, which was that a limited budget would have given the Secretary power to say ''no'' to different services. ''Power to compel reform is greatest when you have a limited amount of dough to pass around. It's easier to persuade the boys to reform when they need to increase their public support than when they already have it.''

But there were large areas of agreement, especially on one subject about which the Richardson team became unusually expert—the process of transition. Their comments amounted to a convenient guidebook for taking over a part of the government.

PASSING THE BATON

Everyone said the first thing that must be done is for the incoming official to designate his transition chief and to get his predecessor to do the same. For example, John Kennedy named Clark Clifford and Eisenhower named Major General Wilton Perkins. Jonathan Moore headed both the Richardson transition into Defense and the one into Justice. Melvin Laird named Carl Wallace as his man and Richard Kleindienst designated Sol Lindenbaum.

The purpose of publicly designating one man is to avoid bureaucratic end runs, a great temptation to the Indians in the new department who are seeking to establish their own lines to the new chief.

The next step is the formation of a transition team. Here one should look for a combination of people who know the new boss and people who know the new department.[1] Sometimes a special problem will dictate a member of the team. John Duffner's selection for the Justice team probably owed something to the fact that he was close to Senator James Eastland, chairman of the Senate Judiciary Committee, and so could help with another key element in transition—the confirmation process. This was particularly important in the Justice transition, where Richardson had a tough time dealing with Senate demands for assurances that the Watergate special prosecutor would be independent. In that transition, confirmation was so time-consuming that during the first month Darman and Smith worked on nothing else.

FRIENDS ON THE HILL

Getting to know your congressional committees is an important part of the transition process, whether you have a confirmation problem or not. Key members of both your authorizing and appropriating committees in both houses must be cultivated. You also have to get to know the White House people—Domestic Council or National Security Council—who oversee your operations, as well as your Office of Management and Budget men. Each department has reporters who are regularly assigned to cover it, and they, too, must be met and charmed. Most departments have an immediate constituency—doctors, educators, defense contractors, etc.—with a large, practical interest in the way the department is run, and the team must learn about them, too. The importance of these groups is illustrated by the fact that at HEW they were the main obstacle to most of the reforms attempted by the Richardson team, at least in the view of most of its members.

Once the transition team is organized, its primary priority should be personnel. Jonathan Moore puts it this way, "Who are the key people, are they for you or against you? Who do we get rid of, keep, transfer, promote?"

A publication called "the plum book" has been the constant study of the Richardson transition teams. Its full title is *Policy and Supporting Positions in the U.S. Government.* These are the non-career jobs that the new department head can fill with relative ease. As he develops bureaucratic skill, he can also fill many Civil Service jobs with people of his choice and, if not fire people, learn to get rid of the ones he doesn't want by transferring them or abolishing their jobs.

In the beginning he looks for people in the new agency whom he can trust to give an objective, insightful picture of what's going on and to assess the capabilities of their colleagues. Thus at HEW Richardson turned to Jim Kelly, a friend from the days of Richardson's service in HEW under Eisenhower,[2] and Undersecretary Robert Veneman, whom Richardson had gotten to know at the monthly undersecretaries meeting while Richardson was at State.

Once these contacts are made, the new boss must win over the people he needs. Wilmot Hastings says of the transition into HEW, "What we tried to do was seek out and form bonds of mutual confidence with people who were the key to the operation of the agency." The method for doing this was to involve Richardson in decision-making meetings from the start so that the division and bureau chiefs could see him in action, be impressed with the openness with which decisions were arrived at and, as Hastings put it, "have their negative preconceptions dispelled and the positive ones reinforced."

Richardson had a number of ways of strengthening bonds with his subordinates. One was to write comments on, say, page 36 of a 52-page memorandum. As often as conscience permitted, he would make the comments strongly favorable. He thus filled two human needs that often go unsatisfied in government, the need to know that the boss knows what you are doing and the need to know that he values what you are doing. Although one can't help suspecting that occasionally he turned to page 36 right away, Richardson's capacity for wading through written material was prodigious.[3] He told subordinates to err on the side of giving him more rather than fewer briefing papers, memoranda, etc. Richardson also sought to give recognition to those lower-level assistants who actually wrote the memoranda by insisting that they be identified as the authors rather than their chiefs, as is usually the custom in the government.

WHY SAXBE WON'T READ

In personnel matters, Richardson, like most bureaucrats, found it easier to resist Administration efforts to get him to fire people than to get approval to hire the people he wanted. Thus at HEW, during the height of Nixon's power, he was able to fight off White House attempts to make him fire Robert Ball as head of social security. On the other hand, even when Nixon was weak, after Richardson had taken over Justice, Richardson was unable to overcome White House resistance to his appointing Robert Freidman, then HEW regional director in Chicago, as Assistant Attorney General for Administration. Jonathan Moore says, "We could never figure out whether it was because Freidman was a political opponent of Daley, whose support Nixon was courting, or because he was a friend of Charles Percy, whom Nixon couldn't stand, or maybe it was because they wanted to show who was running things. Whatever it was, Haig told us we couldn't hire him."

Moore was one success—or at least partial success—that Richardson had against the White House. When Richardson was going to Defense, he planned to make Moore Assistant Secretary for Internal Security Affairs. Kissinger's office leaked hostile material to the press accusing Moore of being a dove, and for a while it appeared Moore would stay at HEW. But Richardson appealed to Nixon personally, and Moore was permitted to go to Defense, not in the prestigious ISA job, but as a special assistant to Richardson.

As the transition team and the new department head proceed to interview the people working in the department, they should seek to kill two birds with one stone by not only getting to know the veteran employees but also learning what the veterans know about the department. As Wilmot Hastings put it, "Find out what happened before, who had responsibility for what and why? The participants' perception of what went well and what went badly." Darman said, "The important thing is to really have the inclination to find out the experience." William Saxbe, for instance, did not have the inclination. According to both Richardson and Moore, Saxbe was the least interested of Richardson's successors in finding out what Richardson and his associates had learned and were trying to accomplish.

In mastering a new department, Richardson and his assistants all emphasize the importance of learning about its process and structure, or as Richardson says, "What are its structural arrangements for doing what it is supposed to do and for getting information about what it is doing."

The worst organized of the departments Richardson took over turned out to be the Department of Justice. Richardson observed, "What an irony—through the LEAA, the Department of Justice is supposed to guide states and local governments in the administration of law enforcement, while the Department itself is the scene of the greatest administrative chaos in the American government."

TAKING A LEAF FROM GOGOL

The Richardson team was fascinated by two administrative reforms. One was an executive secretariat, geared to produce an orderly flow of paper, to involve all interested parties in the formulation of policy, to present to cabinet officers a concise statement of all the options and supporting arguments, to follow up to see that action is taken on the decision. "Each of the bureaucracies we entered was byzantine," according to Darman, "and one of our main objectives was to set up a decision-making process that would exclude ex parte special pleading and give everyone a fair opportunity to be heard." At HEW, the Richardson team succeeded in expanding an executive secretariat that had been established by Finch. The other reform was an Office of Inspector General which they were proposing to institute at Justice at the time of the Saturday Night Massacre.

I strongly share their interest in the inspector general, and in fact some years back wrote with Russell Baker one explanation of why such an office is needed:

"In any reasonably large government organization, there exists an elaborate system of information cutoffs, comparable to that by which city water systems shut off large watermain breaks by closing down, first small feeder pipes, then larger and larger valves. The object is to prevent information, particularly of an unpleasant character, from rising to the top of the agency where it may produce results unpleasant to the lower ranks.

"Thus the executive at or near the top lives in constant danger of not knowing, until he reads it on Page One some morning, that his department is hip-deep in disaster. . . ."

The other reason for having an inspector general is to deny the executive "deniability." In other words, some leaders want to avoid official knowledge of the horrors their workers are perpetrating in the field. Once they have received the inspector general's report, they can no longer plead ignorance as a defense.

The main reason inspector general offices don't work is that they are usually staffed by people whose primary loyalty is to the organization they are evaluating and who are strongly tempted to cover up truly embarrassing material. The ideal staffing for such an office would be journalists and lawyers with nonrenewable appointments not to exceed three or four years.

SECRETARIAT'S TRACK RECORD

In the article in which Baker and I discussed the need for an inspector general, we also explored one of the problems that an executive secretariat can solve:

"Chronic paranoia is the common affliction of government executives. They live in constant fear that the man down the hall or over in the next agency has plots afoot to steal their programs or their jobs, or to make them look incompetent before their superiors. There is good reason for this suspicion; it frequently turns out to be founded in fact.

"The reason the man down the hall or over in the next agency has plots afoot is that he has been persuaded that other men down other halls and over in other agencies have plots afoot against him."

With an executive secretariat, your bureaucratic enemy can no longer sneak in the boss' side door with a proposal to abolish your office. Instead, he has to send the proposal through the executive secretariat, which would send it to you for comment and then forward the proposal with your comment to the boss.

The wisdom of having an executive secretariat seems most compelling when you're the victim of the proposal. It is less obvious when you're the man with the bright idea—one that you know the time is right for and that you want to serve to the boss while it's piping hot. Suppose that the executive secretariat decides that there are 15 of your colleagues whose views should be sought. You know they range from bureaucrats with a gift for obscuring any bright idea they touch to those who are dedicated to shooting down absolutely anything that might possibly reflect credit on you. Your proposal, which you had envisioned reaching your boss as one snappy paragraph, now goes in weighed down with all the attached comments, and if your boss does not share Richardson's zeal for perusal of the written word, its doom is already sealed.

The place where the executive secretariat is most firmly established, the Department of State, was described by the late John Franklin Campbell as "the foreign affairs fudge factory.'' This suggests that the executive secretariat idea requires care in its implementation to avoid the fudge effect. Still, despite their pompous names, both the executive secretariat and the inspector general are reforms in the direction of openness, and I think the Richardson team was on the right track in being concerned about them.

Along with figuring out how each department works comes another central consideration—issues. ''What are the key issues that are pressing on you as you come in?'' asks Jonathan Moore. What are the key signals you want to give about those issues—both to the country and to your new department? Then come the beginnings of long-range thinking. What do you want to accomplish, what do you want to leave behind when you go?

An example of a pressing problem requiring immediate signals was the collapsed morale at the Department of Justice in the spring of 1973, after there had been enough Watergate revelations to make clear that a number of leading figures at the Department were involved. Richardson immediately set out to give the necessary signals. One was the appointment of William Ruckelshaus, who was widely admired in the Department (he had been an assistant attorney general before his appointment as head of the Environmental Protection Agency) as Deputy Attorney General. Another signal was Richardson's first message to the employees, which in its opening sentence spoke of his ''respect for the integrity and competence with which you do your jobs.'' But most important was his first press conference, in which he expressed with these statements the independence which should characterize an Attorney General:

1. the Plumbers were not justified,
2. he was not the President's lawyer,
3. he couldn't say whether the President was implicated and had told Cox to follow the evidence wherever it led.

An issue on the table at the time of transition that the Richardson team could do nothing with was the Family Assistance Program, or ''welfare reform'' (words had to be found to disguise what it really was—a guaranteed annual income). Richardson and his staff recognized its tremendous importance and fought hard for it but were undercut by the President's desertion from the cause. Darman calls this failure his greatest disappointment in government.

HAPPY TO SURVIVE

Base closing at Defense was an issue on the table that the Richardson team took over and dealt with successfully. By late December, 1972, the base closing had been negotiated between Laird and the Office of Management and Budget, but the President felt that announcing it would not be the right signal to give Hanoi during the final phase of the Vietnam peace talks. It was decided to have Richardson do it, which left Richardson and his staff with the nasty job of implementing the closings. A Secretary of Defense from New England had the dubious honor of shutting down the Boston Navy Yard and the Newport Navy Base. Richardson's other accomplishments at Defense were reducing the enlisted aide—or free servants for the brass—program and telling the Navy it had to stop shelling the Puerto

Rican island of Culebra, where a practice firing range had been shattering the eardrums of the local citizenry for years.

However modest, these accomplishments exceeded the substantive actions taken at HEW and Justice, both of which were left awash in a sea of un-carried-out Richardson proposals. Richardson's assertion that his MEGA proposal[4] at HEW represented his greatest accomplishment illustrates a psychological pitfall of working with superiors such as Nixon, Haldeman, and Ehrlichman. You become grateful for survival, for the fact that even though they don't support your ideas, they don't fire you. Gratitude for the right to speak one's mind without penalty creates a state of mind in which it is easy to confuse proposal with accomplishment. This confusion is made even easier when one reflects that many public servants don't even have the courage to propose. And in Richardson's case it is at least arguable that formulating proposals was all he could do because he never had the genuine support of the White House in any of his cabinet jobs. Maybe he was just windowdressing all the time.

It is clear, however, that Richardson made a real contribution to employee morale at State, HEW, and Justice. (At Defense this was not so clear because he succeeded Laird, a reasonably popular figure, and he sufficiently resembled McNamara to arouse suspicion that another round of whiz kids with slide rules was at hand.) At Justice, his effect on morale was spectacularly demonstrated when the week after the Saturday Night Massacre he appeared before a packed audience of employees in the Department's Great Hall to receive an ovation that went on and on and on. It sounded like a march to the Bastille was next. But the audience was soon quieted by Richardson's soporific rhetoric. Some critics of Richardson's platform ability contend that recordings of his speeches should be played at prisons and other points of smoldering discontent as a riot control measure. One of his assistants speaks of Richardson's instinct for the capillaries. And another, in describing the kind of memorandum that impressed Richardson, said that "Richardson preferred prose like his own, not overly succinct." This is probably the reason there is such mutual admiration between Richardson and the civil servants. They are very much alike.

Richardson and his men are fond of technocratic usages such as this statement of a Justice Department objective: "Develop post-adjudication strategies which are cost-effective and which work." An air of laudable practicality accompanies the vaguest possible suggestion of what they are really talking about, which could be anything from closing down the federal prisons to imposing mandatory life sentences on all two-time losers.

The good side of the approach is that it gets discussion off to a non-inflammatory start. Richardson doesn't want to lead charges on the Bastille. He wants to take the sharp edges off words and issues so that men can talk together with civility. Like the Chinese, who, instead of saying Chou En-lai is a goddam liar, refer vaguely to possible prevarications by a minor courtier to the Emperor Tsu in the early years of the third century, the professional civil servants have learned that one can live to fight tomorrow's battle if one fights with indirection today. Their weakness is that they put too much emphasis on survival. There are hardly any who would not have gone along, as Richardson did, with the Stennis compromise, or with Nixon's inflammatory use of the busing issue or—and this was the one that hurt the reputation of the professionals the most—with Vietnam.

But if you want a professional civil service, you have to accept men in it who

place a strong value upon survival, for the continuity that is an essential characteristic of such a service can come only from those who manage to survive.

A BUREAUCRACY THAT CAN SAY 'NO'

Still, nobody wants a civil service whose only standard is survival. What else can
you ask for—and reasonably hope to find in the men you select to work for you
when you take over the government? Richardson and his men are good examples.
They have high competence. They are men of their word. They resigned rather
than betray Richardson's pledge to the Judiciary Committee.

There was something else good that used to live in the hearts of civil servants—
and that was a scrupulous regard for legality. It was at once their most infuriating
and their most reassuring characteristic. Those guys at the Internal Revenue Service may have driven you crazy with their nit-picking forms and regulations, but
you knew they were doing exactly the same thing to your neighbor across the
street, applying the law equally to every man, not doing anything that was not
strictly in accord with the letter of the law. A few yielded to the Nixon gang—but
every professional is proud of the majority in the IRS who said "no" to the White
House just as they are troubled by Helms, who wavered too long before saying
"no," and shamed by the Petersens and Pat Grays, who said "yes."

Finally, we can ask for a concern with the substance of their work. One test of
this concern is their attitude toward briefing their successors. The Richardson team
passes this test nobly. In the transition between HEW and Defense, for example,
Jonathan Moore spent even more time on HEW than on Defense business, and
Richardson, even after he had left the Administration last November, wrote Robert Bork a long letter explaining 15 reforms he had been seeking to make at Justice
and trying to persuade Bork to pursue them.

Distinguishing between good and bad professionals is going to be an important
activity during the next few years. The Nixon gang infiltrated more of its people
into the middle-managerial levels of government than any administration since
the New Deal. We need to know who are the Elliot Richardsons and who are the
H.R. (Bob) Haldemans.

NOTES

1. In staffing the Defense transition team, Moore enlisted Darman and Mastrangelo, who
   had worked with Richardson, J.T. Smith (he had served with the CIA), and Morton
   Abramovitz (he had been on Richardson's staff at State), who were experienced both
   with Richardson and the national security bureaucracy, and Robert Murray, who was
   expert in the inner workings of the Defense Department, and was a friend of Moore's,
   himself an alumnus of Defense who thus combined knowledge of the boss with knowledge of the department. When they went to Justice, Moore again included Smith,
   Darman, and Mastrangelo on the team. Wilmot Hastings was borrowed from HEW to
   help with the search for a Watergate special prosecutor, and from inside Justice,
   Patrick McSweeney and John Duffner were selected.
2. Prior service that equipped him with the knowledge of people and problems of his
   new department helped Richardson in three of his transitions. In addition to his early
   experience at HEW, he was the only Attorney General to have also served as both a
   United States Attorney and Attorney General for a state. His national security ex-

perience at State helped prepare him for Defense. Only at State was he new to the game. He left his family in Boston and worked until midnight for the first six months to fill himself in. He also added—or retained on the undersecretary's staff—people who had the foreign office experience he lacked: Jonathan Moore, Morton Abramovitz, Arthur Hartman and Richard Moorstein.

3. The usefulness of his unusual capacity is illustrated by this account of the amount of material briefers can throw at you (from *Changing Administrations* by David Stanley): "The Army gave its new appointees a 150-page book on its philosophy, organization and activities—a booklet of personnel information for presidential appointees (tenure, benefits, conflict-of-interest roles, etc.), a three and a half inch book full of directives and statutory references; a booklet summarizing the backgrounds of key personnel; a survey of current major problems—including priority decisions facing the new Secretary, a history of the Army. . . and a set of organization charts."

4. A sensible new federalism that combines an incomes strategy (giving people money directly to buy the things government had been buying for them) with a program of decentralization that provides incentives for local governments to deliver services more efficiently.

MBO in State Government

GEORGE S. ODIORNE

A constructed case study probably provides the best object lessons on managing public affairs by objectives. This is a composite of experience with MBO in three different states compiled into a single illustrative case example.

Recently the State of Old West opted in the direction of MBO and decentralized management of the state tied to MBO. It broke itself into a half dozen or more "mini-states." Each area was headed by a professional public administrator, quite similar in education and experience. Most had MPA degrees; most were old enough to have had some solid experience, but young enough to be energetic and ambitious. All were males. All were informed that they would be in charge of their own area of the state in all respects except higher education and one or two other areas. All were solemnly informed that they would be managed "by objectives" and that they were admonished to do likewise with their own responsibilities. Extensive training in MBO accompanied the program. The basic pattern of MBO as it was defined consisted of a five-part program:

1. *Goal Setting:* Each administrator would strike agreements with his or her superior about what was expected in terms of results, and such statements would be made in advance of the period.
2. *Budgeting:* The objectives would be related to resources which would be released to achieve the job. That is, the budgets would be forthcoming for

the tasks to be achieved, or the results would be amended if resources were for some reason not forthcoming.

3. *Autonomy:* Each person would be left alone to make decisions affecting his or her territory or responsibility, except that reporting periods and forms were agreed upon in advance. It was also agreed that each would obey the law and the policies affecting the various responsibility areas.

4. *Feedback:* Since the managers would know how well they were doing in their work while it was going on, they were expected to know when their results were faulty, to initiate corrective action upon learning of such shortcomings, and to *notify or ask for help* if things went clearly beyond permitted exceptions in a serious fashion.

5. *Payoffs:* There would be rewards in proportion to achievement. For one thing, the merit system would reflect achievements rather than personality or political affiliation. Furthermore, performance reviews would be related to achievements against goals. A proposed incentive plan for managers was not strong enough to survive the political buffeting encountered, and was abandoned before birth.

As a theoretical example Old West's MBO had much to commend it. Yet it was not without its troubles, most of which comprise a cautionary tale to those in public administration wishing to use this most useful and stimulating method of management. In each of the five basic precepts which comprised the system, problems, and lessons, emerged.

"TELL ME WHAT'S EXPECTED IN ADVANCE"

From the beginning when the area managers sat down with their boss to discuss objectives, it was apparent that the superiors and cabinet ranks didn't really have a clear fix on what they expected from such line managers. "When I find out what we are here for, I'll try to let you know" was one kind of response. This of course was not a defect in MBO, but in the existing state of management, for it described what had been going on for some time. In areas like conservation the results sought were clearer than in the prison system, where nobody could agree on what prisons were supposed to produce. In environment the law was reasonably clear, but the development of strategies for getting to compliance wasn't all that lucidly defined. A major corporation and large employer in one region stated baldly that to live within the state air quality laws would put the organization out of business. It was agreed that more thought would have to be given to this case, since unemployment in that sector was already over the national average. The state unemployment service, the welfare chief, and the director of economic development of the state broke into a rather noisy argument over what the environmental objectives should be.

This led to the conclusion that each mini-state must have a person responsible for shaping and recommending objectives in each functional area for its own geographical area. The bureaucracy in the state office building resisted this flowing away of their power and personnel out to the field. This battle came to a head when the state chief of mental health services went to the press over an unfortunate death of a mentally retarded child in a program initiated at the mini-state level. MBO had killed this child, he charged. The governor backed the decentralization system in this case, and the MBO program survived.

Object lesson: Decentralization, or the moving of important decisions to lower levels in the organization is not a natural phenomenon in political organizations, and when it occurs will meet resistance from those in the bureaucracy whose power flows away from them.

There are other important lessons which were learned about goal setting in this case. First, while operational objectives must be measurable, many of the best strategic goals were not reduced to measurement, but to verbal statements of conditions which would exist if the goal were attained. Strategic objectives require criteria, but not all criteria will be measureable. . . . This distinction between strategic and operational goals is an important one in government.

The patent and staple argument against MBO in public administration that "my most important responsibilities can't be measured" is of course true, not only in government but in business. The similarities between strategic staff work in corporations and government are startling. Neither relates to the production of things. Neither in fact directly and immediately relates to profits. Neither is free of unexpected changes in the world. Both work in multi-year time frames. Both produce software rather than hardware. Both entail judgments of small groups of experts and professionals rather than short-term leadership of large corps of workers.

Yet all of these conditions have not prevented the best-run organizations from using staff MBO superbly well. Service organizations, it was discovered in the mini-state's case at hand, can state their goals if they abide with some guidelines which have evolved in practice.

1. Anticipate strategic missions as much as is possible, in defining objectives, but adjust as often as necessary.
2. Developing indicators to be watched is a means to improving output and should not become an end in itself. The indicators themselves should be changed if needed, and no manager should have more than a dozen key indicators to be watching, and probably less than that. If there are more, there should be somebody helping watch and respond to them.
3. It is important to answer the question "are we doing the right things" prior to answering the more explicit questions of measurement, and "doing things right."
4. Timing is of the essence in goal setting. Those objectives which are multi-year in character (to clean up the pollution in the Cupcake River to federal standards by June 1978) need to be stated before the budget allocations are decided, not after. Those of an operational character can be stated at the beginning of an operating period after the budget allocation and not before (to buy a new patrol boat for the Cupcake River by June 1, 1976).

The best MBO programs in government will probably have two sets of objectives, one long-range set stated prior to budgeting or resource movement, and the second or short-range set after the budget is decided.

5. Any operational indicators should be related to some kind of important output and should contain some element of time (such as park visitors per month).

6. It is a mistake to expect too much precision in operating objectives. The most exact science consists of approximations, and goal setting is far from an exact science. This need for reasonableness in goals can be achieved by stating them in *ranges* ("between 22,000 and 23,000 violations processed during the coming six months"). If some precision-obsessed soul insists upon a single number, pick the middle of the range and state it as the target.

7. Despite the special character of government objectives which often makes them difficult to measure, a *rule of rigor* can be applied: "measure that which is measurable, describe that which is describable, and eliminate that which is neither."

8. There is a division of labor in goal setting and management. A final lesson is that higher-level people who constantly are interfering in operational management will cause the MBO program to abort. The proper function of cabinet or policy-level positions is to define strategic goals. The function of operating heads is to be responsible for operations and commit to short-term (one year) goals. The case of the cabinet person who insists upon knowing every operational detail is commonplace in government. In addition to being a serious handicap to management by objectives, it is also easily recognized as bad management in general.

GIVE ME THE RESOURCES TO DO THE JOB

Precept two of the case study at hand was the provision of resources to do the job. This meant that the manager at the lower level was given budgetary resources. But it meant more than simply getting *more* resources, it also meant some latitude in moving resources. Many state and local governmental accounting systems are labyrinths of regulations which prevent such movement ("01 funds can be spent for 01 purposes only, but 03 funds may be spent for personnel or for any other purpose exclusive of travel and entertainment").

A strategic planning system within the MBO system provided much flexibility in moving resources, for it required that for each program four questions be answered:

1. Where is this program now? Statistically, factually, and in judgments about strengths and weaknesses?

2. What trends are apparent? If we didn't do anything differently where would we be in five years?

3. What mission statements could be shaped for this program?

4. What would be the financial consequences of each mission?

These budgetary-mission statements were prepared about January of each year and forwarded upward to the state level where they comprised working papers for the compilation of the immediate budget requests and for multi-year budget planning.

The most successful application of this plan was executed by one mini-state area manager who moved personally and individually with each of the key subordinates through an interview using these four questions as an agenda. Each manager prepared some notes, but the process was operated basically on a face-to-face basis. The superior then dictated the results of the interview with the subordinate and the resulting memorandum became the strategic goals position paper for the two to make their budgetary-allocation decisions upon. The questions are not simple. For example, in one discussion these kinds of questions came about:

Superior: "Let's look at the first topic: Where is your program now? What statistics are generated for your program? Who creates them? Are we well enough informed about the present situation? Do you have enough information to know what your strengths, weaknesses, and problems are? Do there seem to be any impending threats? What risks are we exposed to in your area? What are some opportunities which you see that might be pursued in the coming year or five years?"

Note that these are probing questions which force the subordinate to dig deeply into his or her own business before sitting down with the superior. It requires judgments about threats, risks, and opportunities. It also requires that people begin to think about new and original things as well as thinking about unthinkable possibilities.

Among the more interesting questions overheard in one such discussion were the following:

- Imagine that your budget were suddenly cut 20 per cent. What would you be forced to stop doing? Then imagine after that move were completed that budget was restored again. What would you then add? Is it the same as the thing you dropped? If not, why not? Why can't you just do the new things within the existing resources?

- Are there skills in your organization, or even that you yourself possess, that aren't being fully used? Is there any way you could use them more fully, given the existing resources?

- What resources could be used well in your job that you don't now have? For example, what could I do, do differently, or stop doing to help you succeed?

The most important single reason for failure of MBO in government is the tendency to treat it as a paperwork system, rather than a face-to-face management system.

Memoranda are essential to verify and follow up on agreement made face-to-face. When used in the absence of such face-to-face dialog, they can be poisonous. The MBO system becomes bogged down in a morass of forms, memoranda, and unintelligible evasions. The logic of MBO alone won't carry it off if the system is depersonalized and mechanistic. This is especially true in the movement of resources, for such shifts often require human ingenuity, managerial support, and some confidence which comes with personal assurances that risks are worth taking.

This is even more valid when the manager in state government must interface with local and county officials. For them, there is no compulsion which requires that they cooperate, and only personalized and face-to-face discussions have any hope for getting mutual information, cooperation, and commitment. A random sample of the relationships which system people call "interfaces" shows that in most government agencies they are not interfaces at all, but a crossing of memorandum.

Object lesson: The allocation of resources and their movement should always be done on a face-to-face basis.

LEAVE ME ALONE AS MUCH AS POSSIBLE TO DO MY JOB

Because steps one and two are necessary, step three is not possible until one and two have been completed. If subordinate managers know what is expected, and what resources and help are available, they can then be relied upon to show self-control, and govern their actions to achieve the commitments they have made. People who make commitments to somebody else whose opinion is important to them are practically obliged to do something about those commitments. This is especially true if those commitments have been made in face-to-face discussion, and have been confirmed in writing.

The power of commitment is what makes MBO work, and the absence of such commitment can cause it to fail.

The objectives and constraints are known in advance. Thus the subordinate knows that he is to "achieve my commitments, and stay within my constraints," and thus can operate freely within these boundaries. This is significantly different from "doing what you are told to do." Under such a constraining rule, innovation and variations in methods require lengthy requests for permission, funneled through the hierarchy, and producing three effects:

1. Decision making is slowed down.
2. Innovation is dampened and ultimately dies.
3. There can be no excellence at lower levels.

The problem of managerial control remains, however. The higher level official is always responsible for the actions of subordinates, and it would be unrealistic not to expect that higher level persons will be concerned about lower level performance. Yet, through the completion of explicit goals, stated in far more detail than ever was thought necessary or possible, managerial control through subordinate self-control is possible. The tightest form of control is self-control.

The exception principle requires four major rules for subordinates if it is to function as a tool of managerial control in an MBO system:

1. The subordinate must be clear on the goals and know when they are not being met, and know earlier than anybody else.
2. The subordinate should know the reasons those goals are not being achieved.
3. The subordinate should be able to initiate corrective action as soon as a deviation appears and he or she knows its reason, even before the boss learns of the problem.
4. The subordinate should be able to call for help, and thereby notify the superior early enough. Most bosses do not favor unpleasant surprises, and should be protected against them.

In the case study at Old West State, one manager described his rules for deciding whether to call the boss for help for notification purposes:

> If the boss could hear about it from some third party, I make sure I get there first. That third party could be a peer, a higher up, or simply an indignant client.

In one instance a highway patrol team ran into a dispute with the Air Police from an Air Force base in the area. On the supposition that the commanding colonel might call the state capital, the regional manager called his boss and explained the situation. When the complaint arrived in due course, no adrenalin flowed at the higher levels.

The boss, on the other hand, must show some restraint when receiving a single isolated report from a citizen. Such letters to the governor or a legislator should be bucked down through the channels for more grass-roots information, and not become a basis for tearing down the management system and recentralizing all decision making.

In one highly publicized incident the entire decentralization MBO process was nearly scuttled because a state truck ran over a cow. The owner wrote an indignant letter to the legislature, and the state office bureaucracy attempted to use the incident as proof that MBO produced reckless and irresponsible behavior at lower levels, implying that every cow in the state was endangered by MBO. Fortunately the director of administration for the state was able to resolve the question quickly. One of the major influences was the fact that a speedy response was forthcoming. Within an hour of the report's reaching the state capital, a responsible official from the region was on the scene, viewing the bovine's remains, and making specific arrangements with the farmer for fair reimbursement from local funds. Under a more centralized system the payment would have been years in coming, for the state capital was more than a hundred miles from the cow.

MBO should produce a more personalized responsive system of government for citizens, by placing decision making over small matters affecting citizens in the hands of lower level organizations.

Delegation, and leaving lower level subordinates alone once their objectives are established clearly and resources defined accordingly, produces a more localized decision system to allow for local variances.

LET ME KNOW HOW WELL I AM DOING IN MY WORK

Objectives, properly defined, should comprise an instrument panel of vital signs of the organization. These vital signs are analogous to the pulse, body temperature, blood pressure, and other vital signs of the human organism. Such a vital sign as body temperature could be "normal" within a range as follows:

normal at rest   98.6

after exercise   99.9

in cool climate   98.0

The physician doesn't demand that every temperature be identical with the at-rest norm. Nor should managers expect precision in measuring their own performance, nor should their superiors demand such uniformity. Take the case of the park system in Old West. Records of parks use by summer months for the past four years showed the following:

1968 - 7,601

1969 - 7,950

1970 - 8,310

1971 - 8,734

For planning purposes it was noted that a secular trend upward in excess of 300 to 400 a year was observed. Thus it could be anticipated, "other things being equal," that a rise of another 400 to 500 could be expected in 1972. This became the *normal* objective. This meant that the preparation of staff assignments, preparation of park sites, tons of refuse disposal planned, and similar demands upon the park management and staff could be anticipated.

Yet, the purpose is *not to forecast nor to predict.* The prediction is that park use in 1972 will be at a rate of about 9,200 persons per month, and the *prediction itself is a means to better management.* It affords the management a vital sign. If it goes above 9,500, then some kind of response is indicated. If it goes below 8,700, then some kind of investigation and possible response should be made by management.

The idea of measurement is not to punish the people for being poor forecasters. The forecast is created to provide vital signs for management to make managerial responses.

Thus, when the energy crisis came along and cut sharply into the park use, for motorists could not obtain gasoline, the use of the park went down to 3,165 per month. The park manager used this opportunity to move personnel from planned services to other approved projects within the park, and to other projects which had not been thought feasible outside the park.

REWARD MY ACCOMPLISHMENTS

Perhaps the major distinction between government and business applications of MBO is not in the profit motive for the firm, but in the willingness of industry to relate achievement to pay. This is achieved in several ways, and the experience of those municipalities who have developed and installed performance payment systems has been sufficiently good that it proves such incentive compensation is viable for government.

Clearly managerial or professional compensation in government cannot be related to *profit.* But it can be related to *performance* if these performance objectives exist.

1. There must be a norm or standard of performance which is related to the public purposes of the organization and the specific performance objectives of the job.
2. Such standards must be related to *output* for a period of time, usually a year.

3. The standard should be written as a form of performance contract for that year, which require objectives to be carefully negotiated.
4. There should be statements of special conditions under which the incentive pay will not apply. If the job holder is penalized for hard luck, or rewarded for windfalls not of his own doing, the system can fail.
5. Provision for review at the highest levels must be made, both of the goals used as standards, and of the results actually achieved. This assures uniformity of treatment among equals, and prudent use of public funds.
6. Selective application of incentive payments is possible without destroying the system. For example, in one city the incentive pay principle was applied to revenue producing positions. Where the revenues went beyond historic normal standards, an ascending scale of compensation was awarded, provided certain other kinds of objectives were also met.
7. Incentives for innovative objectives can be managed through suggestion award plans. Under current systems, it would seem to be more prudent to relate the award to the achievement by rewarding only proved savings, or demonstrated innovations which increase yield from resources.
8. Relating rewards to achievement requires a change in many performance reviews or appraisal forms and procedures. The old form of adjective-rating of performance against a list of personality traits, if related to pay increases or merit ratings, will compete and perhaps extinguish achievement-centered behavior.

In an MBO management system, performance review and merit rating must be directly related to goals and results statements, and adjective rating systems abandoned.

SUMMARY

MBO in government is confronted with the same kinds of bureaucratic and political traps which every new program runs into. Strong administrative overtures are met with equal and opposite countermoves. When power flows from one place to another, people from whom it is flowing will resist that flow away from themselves. The political leader tends to seek ever-increasing amounts of power, in contrast with the economic sector where leaders operate on a principle of acquisition. It is difficult to say which is loftier. Procedures which were once important, perhaps even noble, persist long after their useful life has ended. Activity for its own sake becomes a false goal, becomes firmly embedded, and ultimately becomes a religion. Changing behavior of bureaucrats is not done easily, for their security lies in doing what has worked in the past. There is a general reluctance to invest heavily in training which is innovative in character, for it promises to produce an unwanted change, and perhaps new centers of power. Finally the culture of government, especially state government, is more *affiliation centered* than achievement centered. Ideology seldom dominates state government, nor is there a strong culture of performance on behalf of the constituency, with some notable exceptions.

These are the lessons of MBO in Old West state's program of applying MBO. It does not prove that MBO has procedural nor logical flaws, nor that government is evil. It does demonstrate, however, that some special efforts are required to make it work. Turning a government into an achieving organization is never easy.

The Productivity Challenge

NANCY S. HAYWARD

For every public official who strives to meet the needs of the public within available revenues, improved governmental productivity is a necessity. For every citizen who expects more public services without increased taxation, productivity improvement must become a priority concern. For every public employee whose job depends upon the continuation of public services despite the pressures of inflation and tax reductions, governmental productivity increases must be realized. For every business which must minimize costs to remain competitive, governmental productivity growth is a significant factor.

The extent to which the public sector has heretofore recognized and addressed the importance of productivity improvement cannot be documented. We lack, in the aggregate, adequate data to determine at what rate productivity is changing—up or down—relative to government's historical pattern, to other sectors of the economy, or to other countries. However we do know from studies of certain public functions that differences of up to 500 per cent exist in productivity rates between jurisdictions with similar demographic characteristics, service variables, and wage levels. Therefore it is evident to us that, within the constraints of current knowledge, technology, and legislation, the productivity of public service delivery can be increased. Even those skeptical of this conclusion will agree that, under the demands for more public services, higher wages, and lower taxes, methods for improving governmental productivity must be identified and implemented.

Despite the benefits of increased productivity—higher standards of living, increased real wages, less costly goods and services—the governmental process inherently neither provokes nor supports productivity improvement. The challenge of increasing governmental productivity is not limited to the most progressive public officials and students of government. The targets of opportunity are different in each community as are the barriers to implementation and the alternative methods of resolution. Yet while the parameters of the challenge are unique to each jurisdiction, productivity improvement is for every public official not merely an opportunity but a necessity.

WHAT IS PUBLIC SECTOR PRODUCTIVITY?

Governmental productivity is the efficiency with which resources are consumed in the effective delivery of public services. The definition implies not only quantity, but also quality. It negates the value of efficiency, if the product or service itself lacks value. It relates the value of all resources consumed—human, capital, and technological—to the output of public services or results achieved. Improved productivity results in:

- More and/or better services for the same unit cost.
- The same quantity and quality of services at less unit cost.

The inadequacy of the industrial definition (productivity = output/input) to account for effectiveness and quality in the absence of a competitive market is reflected in the breadth of the public sector definition. Parenthetically it is important to note that private industry feels the traditional output per manhour measure of productivity used by the Bureau of Labor Statistics is also inadequate in that it excludes the cost of other such resources as energy, which are gaining relative value. To this end, the private sector is developing indicators of total factor productivity which would, as does the public sector definition, reflect the contribution of capital and technology in addition to manpower.

Governmental productivity increases most frequently result from:

- Optimum utilization of manpower, equipment, and capital

- Better trained, equipped, and motivated employees

- Higher quality raw materials

- Improved technology

- Substitution of capital and technology for manpower

- Elimination of ineffective laws, regulations, and standards

- More precise identification of needs and users

- Better design of services to meet constituent needs.

Measurement is the yardstick by which the value of productivity improvements can be quantified and assessed. Productivity measures at a single point in time can be used to compare the efficiency and effectiveness of similar operations in different jurisdictions or among sectors of the economy. Productivity data collected over time can be used to monitor performance, identify problem areas, establish standards for improved performance, evaluate the benefits of alternative improvement strategies, and refine resources needed relative to estimated demands. For the citizens, productivity data provides a means for holding governmental officials accountable for public resources.

Productivity measures are only one source of information. They must be reviewed in conjunction with organizational objectives and other existing sources of management data. Although the mere existence of a measurement system may temporarily motivate performance improvements, meaningful productivity increases will not be achieved without analysis of the data and implementation of policy or operational changes.

WASHINGTON STATE'S EXPERIENCE

The variety of techniques and approaches through which governmental productivity can be improved is exemplified by efforts in the State of Washington. Individually each improvement project addresses the need for increased productivity, and in most cases the benefits can be at least partially quantified. What cannot be fully accounted for is the value of the added benefits derived from a broad-based approach of simultaneously addressing different types of productivity problems. Subjectively, it appears that the full benefits of each individual effort would not have been attained had the Washington program not tried to address related and contributory problems as well. Psychologically, it makes all levels and functions of the government feel a part of the process and avoids creating the impression that any one area has been singled out for poor performance.

Advisory Council

Building on the resources available within the state, and in recognition of the importance of developing a broad-based consensus for choosing among difficult alternatives, a 28-member Advisory Council was established. Members include business executives, state management and employees, union officials, legislators, local government officials, and representatives of higher education and civic organizations. The Council designed and conducted some of the individual improvement efforts; others have been identified and implemented by state staff under the Council's guidance. The Council has brought to the state government the best ideas, experiences, and resources of the organizations which its members represent; the members have also effectively communicated back to their colleagues the needs and accomplishments of the state.

Organizational Restructuring

The Council identified as primary to institutionalizing the productivity concern a need to establish clear lines of accountability and eliminate organizational redundancy. They have concluded that the state's organizational structure adversely affects productivity and are currently reviewing alternative mechanisms for reorganization.

Human Resources

As a result of a survey of state employees, deficiencies in communications between management and employees have been identified which, according to the employees, directly affects their productivity and job satisfaction. Through analysis of the responses the Committee will prepare recommendations on how communications can be improved for the purpose of enhancing employee and organizational productivity.

An analysis of the Employee Suggestion Award System indicated that neither the process for making awards nor the value of the award functioned as an incentive for generating employee recommendations. The system has been strengthened by legislation which increases the maximum award from $300 to $1,000; expanding coverage to all state employees including those working in higher education; and providing for post-auditing of suggestions. This project is an example of the benefits which can be achieved through executive and legislative branch cooperation in improving productivity.

In recognition of the need to emphasize employee understanding and cooperation in productivity improvement efforts, a state labor relations assistant in the Office of the Governor is working with agencies and employee organizations on labor relations issues. As a result of a practice by which each agency bargains independently with either of the two employee unions, significant disparities in labor relations policy have developed among bargaining units. To increase communications between agencies and to enhance the state's labor-management environment, an interagency Labor Relations Task Force has been created. The Task Force is reviewing problems of consistency in interpreting and implementing executive labor relations policy, adequacy of negotiating data, and deficiencies in managerial labor relations training. In addition to facilitating better communication between agencies, the Task Force is expected to identify legislative and executive policy needs in this area.

Since the productivity of all organizations reflects to a large extent the capabilities of an organization's employees, the Advisory Council encouraged the creation of a comprehensive training and career development program. Legislation creating this program is expected to be passed during the 1977 legislative session. It will expand programs for developing skill levels of employees and establish a special system for the selection, advancement, and promotion of managers on the basis of proven managerial ability.

At the same time, the Department of Personnel is proposing a new "General Manager" category within the merit system which would consolidate numerous managerial classifications into meaningful management groups. The proposal also calls for the establishment of a Management Assessment Center to identify and develop managerial skills.

Technology

A Technology Transfer Center has been established in the Office of the Governor to increase the use of technology in the state government. The Center is concerned with both "hard" (such as computers or work processing) and "soft" (such as parole guidelines) technology. Washington is also considering the creation of a "technology bank" to identify resources in the public and private sectors which can assist state government to implement technological advances.

Tools and Measurement

A number of analytical tools are being introduced into all levels of government, including operational auditing, value engineering, and quality assurance. In addition the state is working from several different perspectives to improve their productivity measurement capability, including with the help of the National Science Foundation, a study of techniques and indicators in two of the less tangible service areas, foster care and nursing homes.

The need for more precise knowledge of the time and resource requirements of specific tasks has resulted in the establishment of a work measurement program. Orientation for all agency managers on the meaning and importance of work measurement has been conducted. By December 1976, 20 per cent (11,000) of the employment force including higher education will be covered by engineered work standards.

To increase the usefulness to managers of existing measurement data, there has been introduced, on a pilot basis, a Total Performance Measurement System in the Department of General Administration. This integrates efficiency measures with employee and customer attitude surveys, to relate not only efficiency and effectiveness but also point out specific causes of problems reflected in performance variations.

The Washington state program endeavors to realize potential improvements through technology, labor, management, and structure. The effort has the governor's full commitment. It has the support of management, labor, and the citizenry. It depends on the ingenuity of all state employees.

IMPROVEMENT STRATEGY

No one model exists, nor if it did, would it be applicable to every state or local government which wanted to establish a broad-based productivity improvement program. Few governments have been able to muster the executive and legislative commitment, along with the internal staff and financial resources, to initiate an organization-wide productivity improvement program. While the highly publicized problems of some prominent American cities have drawn attention to the need for efficiency and effectiveness, public pressures for increased services have forced allocation of all available resources to service products instead of improved service administration. At the same time every governmental unit *does* improve the productivity of certain functions in the course of its daily "firefighting," for the solution to many public administration problems usually results, as a side benefit, in some percentage increase in efficiency and effectiveness. However, a broad-based continuing program provides additional benefits. These include:

- Avoidance of potential problems.

- Increased benefits as a result of better designed improvement strategies.

- Better reallocation of savings achieved.

- Increased support by all employees as a result of incorporating employee ideas and accommodating employee needs in designing and implementing improvements.

- Increased transfer of improvement strategies among functions.

- Departmentally shared responsibilities and costs for mutually beneficial improvements.

Jurisdictions face a number of problems when trying to increase productivity. In overcoming these constraints the most successful efforts have pointed out key elements of productivity improvement programs. These are:

- To insure implementation of improvement recommendations, full commitment of the chief executive officer and senior management is necessary.

- To minimize politically motivated rejections of improvement recommendations and to encourage appropriate statutory revisions, support by the legislative body is desirable.

- To sustain the program's momentum despite limited staff resources, designate a dedicated analytic capability resident in the chief executive's office, or the budget office, or, increasingly, within the departments themselves.

- To avoid reinventing the wheel at great cost and to minimize risk, insure cognizance of methods used by other jurisdictions or other departments within a jurisdiction to effect improvements.

- To gain agreement on areas of deficiency and to justify results, establish or incorporate in existing mechanisms a measurement system to monitor ongoing governmental performance and supply base-line data for assessing improvements.

- To instill managerial accountability and motivation, link improvement projects to the budget process for reallocating cost savings, but not to be used automatically to justify budget cutting when improvements are achieved.

- To dispell the myth that productivity means harder work and to gain labor support for changes, involve all employees by considering employee suggestions, retraining where necessary, and explaining all changes in advance of and during transition.

- To maintain job security to the extent possible, effect necessary employment reductions through attrition.

- To anticipate citizen reactions toward service changes, use techniques to identify more precisely citizen needs, desired service levels, and satisfaction with service quality.

- To minimize union opposition and insure a smooth transition, communicate with labor unions on proposed changes, methods of labor force reduction, training, safety, quality of work environment.

In essence, the most successful efforts require not only the involvement of all segments of the community, but also an understanding that all government employees have a responsibility for improving productivity.

SOURCES OF PRODUCTIVITY GAINS

A sampling of the types of improvements being effected will illustrate typical targets of opportunity:[1]

Technology

While the federal government and private suppliers account for most of the development of new or improved technology, some jurisdictions are designing their own improvements or working closely with equipment manufacturers. Examples, all of which have been well publicized, include automated garbage collection equipment, mini fire pumpers, automated fire nozzles, longer lasting road patching materials, and multi-use chassis for heavy equipment.

While new technology offers great potential for future productivity gains, many jurisdictions are attempting to make better use of the equipment on hand. Greater value from investments previously incurred is being realized by increasing the availability of equipment through more efficient repair, more extensive preventive maintenance, and cost-effective replacement policies. By sharing expensive, low-demand equipment among departments or jurisdictions, high initial investments are prevented and flexibility is provided in adapting to new technologies. Further advances in technological innovation and adoption will require both a better articulation of needs and revised financing practices to minimize the single-year impact of large investments which provide multi-year benefits.

Human Resources[2]

Since human resources represent the largest and most valuable resource available to government, the utilization, development and motivation of employees may be our greatest target of opportunity. Improved employee utilization is being achieved through demand-oriented deployment plans, better equipped and supplied employees, reassignment of personnel to back-logged functions, redesign of inefficient tasks, reduced non-work time, especially in functions which include travel time, and reclassification of underutilized positions.

The most deficient area of governmental management is in the development of human resources. Only a few jurisdictions provide adequate career development paths for skilled and unskilled employees or management. Programs in existence are usually limited to job rotation at the managerial level, although one jurisdiction does provide career development opportunities for unskilled employees. Similarly, training—internal or external—for all employees is very limited, especially managerial training for supervisory personnel.

Increased attention is being given to motivating employees. Where financial incentives are precluded, innovative methods are being developed. These include greater public recognition, competition, support of professional dues, and increased employee autonomy including flextime and floating holidays. Where financial rewards are permissible, innovations include sharing cost savings with employees, piece work incentive programs, and improved suggestion systems. Despite these innovations the most powerful motivation for improved employee performance appears to be a meaningful, well-designed job with fair and competent supervision, performance feedback, equitable compensation, and recognition. These are a management responsibility which must be given higher priority if productivity is to be increased.

Financial Resources

Many opportunities for improvement exist through better use of financial resources. Some of those being pursued include better cash and debt management, consolidated purchasing, streamlined payment practices to gain purchase discounts, and development of capital operating plans.

Alternative Delivery Options

When considering alternatives for achieving improved productivity, some jurisdictions have included options for service delivery by organizations outside the governmental unit directly responsible for rendering a service. In some cases, contracting with private organizations occurs; this can allow for reduced investments in expensive equipment, access to new technology, greater flexibility in employee utilization, service redesign, and program elimination.

In other cases, service delivery can be contracted with government—either with other jurisdictions or higher levels of government. This usually permits greater economies of scale and better utilization of equipment; it also often provides improved service coverage for the citizens. However, contracts with either private industry or other governments must incorporate performance standards. Furthermore, consideration must be given to the employees affected by the transfer of responsibility.

THE NATIONAL PERSPECTIVE

While specific improvement opportunities vary from jurisdiction to jurisdiction, certain targets of opportunity are felt to be common across the nation. To identify these opportunities, the National Center for Productivity and Quality of Working Life established a committee of appointed and elected local, state, and federal officials, which also includes representatives of labor, citizens, industry, and higher education. From deliberations over the past year this committee has concluded that individually and as a nation we must improve the management of state and local government and strengthen the financing of governmental operations.

The committee is persuaded that improved management of the delivery of services in state and local government is vital to improving productivity. The committee's research has demonstrated that while important, the traditional approaches to improving management—training, technology transfer, imposition of management and budgetary techniques—are not sufficient to develop strong and lasting productive management in state and local governments. Rather, good government performance results from a strong local commitment to manage services better with lines of accountability drawn more clearly. Encouraging a greater commitment to manage is derived from a clear understanding by public officials of:

- What services are being delivered at what cost.

- The manner in which public services meet citizen needs and expectations.

- Recognition of the importance of employee participation.

- Comparison of performance with similar jurisdictions.

In order for elected officials, citizens, and higher levels of government to hold public managers accountable for the delivery of services, a better definition of what government produces is required, as well as performance indicators to measure progress toward clearly stated objectives. In the opinion of the Committee, emphasis should be placed on broader utilization of existing management tools and techniques for the purpose of raising all governmental performance to the level of the best known. Increased sharing of information and expertise among governmental units could facilitate the adoption of these practices.

The Committee has identified two areas which may require further development of managerial tools—citizen involvement and finance. The perceived and actual effectiveness of public programs would be increased by more precise identification of citizen needs and methods of designing public services in response to these needs. This can be achieved by wider application of marketing and citizen involvement tools in the design and implementation of public services. In emphasizing the need for better financial management tools the Committee cited opportunities in both cash management and cost accounting procedures.

The Committee especially underlined the importance of improved labor relations practices and capabilities. In the opinion of the members, the problem lies not with the worker per se, but in the employee-management relationship. Research and experimentation is necessary in the areas, at the very least, of work force planning; employee development and training; pension funding, design, and portability; lateral entry positions; performance evaluation; data on employment; and compensation at national and regional levels. In addition, both labor and management negotiators require additional skills and information. It is suggested that labor-management committees may offer potential for addressing a number of employee and productivity concerns.

Within the intergovernmental system burdensome administrative regulations and reporting requirements significantly increase the cost of public service delivery. In some cases regulatory requirements actually force resources to be used inefficiently. In many cases they thwart the more efficient use of resources to achieve the same end. Regulations which prescribe methods of delivery to insure maintenance of service quality should be replaced by standards of performance developed between governmental units. Transfer of funds programs between levels of government which provide for administrative reimbursements should comprehend incentives for productivity improvement. Such incentives include support of costs for analysis and new equipment that will result in savings to the funding and administering governments as well as a shared savings mechanism.

Despite myths that suggest productivity improvement is motivated by economic declines, real productivity growth stems from a healthy economy. It is crucial to the success of productivity improvement that state and local governments function from a sound financial base. To the extent that recent indicators of financial insolvency are proved accurate, corrections in our tax policy and pension funds must be made.

In addition, governmental units must have access to sufficient capital for support of productivity-enhancing improvements. Public use of capital to improve productivity must be accorded higher priority by public administrators, the citizenry, and investors. It is felt that undercapitalization in the public sector may be leading to higher operating costs. In addition "capital improvement" decisions must be based on better estimates of resulting increases in operating costs in the event that design modifications can be made in advance.

In order to address this broad agenda, the Committee is working to gain consensus among all affected parties on the importance of these topics. From the Committee's perspective, many improvements are directly under the control of state and local officials. In some cases support and assistance is required from the federal government, the research community, and private industry. To achieve any improvements constituent support is essential.

CONCLUSION

As has been previously suggested by others, productivity improvement in government represents a need whose time has come. Drawing upon the capabilities of their own organizations, many are already responding to this challenge. Every public interest organization has addressed the topic during its annual conference. Some federal agencies have initiated governmental productivity studies within their research and demonstration programs. The League of Women Voters has been engaged in a productivity project during the past year. Several public employee unions have participated in either national or local productivity improvement projects. An increasing number of governmental units are incorporating productivity data into the budget or institutionalizing the consideration of productivity implications in the regular policy-making process. The research community is turning its resources toward issues of governmental productivity improvement. Graduate degree programs are revising curricula to equip the new generation of public administrators with the necessary tools and techniques for effecting productivity improvements.

Continued pursuit of these efforts will enable practitioners to build on the experiences of their peers and to develop, as quickly as possible, the capabilities and techniques necessary for increased productivity growth. The real bottom line is, however, the commitment of every public official—federal, state, and local—to better manage public resources. While improved management of capital and technological resources offers significant promise, the greatest untapped potential lies in the management of human resources.

NOTES

1. Descriptions of current projects in state and local governments are available from several sources: (a) newsletters and reports of the Public Interest Groups, Public Technology Inc., Labor-Management Relations Service, National Training and Development Service; (b) *Guide to Productivity Improvement Projects,* National Center for Productivity and Quality of Working Life; and (c) *Public Productivity Review,* published by Center for Productive Public Management, John Jay College of Criminal Justice, City University of New York, which published a bibliography in the August 1976 edition.
2. For a broader discussion of this area, see *Employee Incentives to Improve State and Local Government Productivity,* National Center for Productivity and Quality of Working Life, Washington, D.C.

You Can't Manage City Hall the Way You Manage General Motors

BRIAN W. RAPP

As the jaws of financial crisis tighten their grip on cities throughout the country, the anguished cry of public officials grows louder: "we need more money!" Repeatedly, we read or hear statements by mayors, county executives, and city managers that despite the addition of revenue sharing they can no longer finance their operating budgets from available revenues and therefore must choose between two undesirable alternatives: increasing taxes or decreasing services.

There is, however, a third alternative that is rarely mentioned: improving the performance of local government—providing the same level of service at reduced cost or increasing levels of service at the same cost. A city government is a public business that consumes resources (tax dollars), provides measurable levels of service, and is managed by identifiable elected and appointed officials. As a business, the performance of city government can be significantly increased through better management. The question is how to manage the business of city government better.

In answering this question it is tempting to advance the time-honored proposition that the performance of city government can be improved if the city were managed just like a private business. How often have we heard the lament, "if only they could run City Hall the way they run General Motors," or its corollary, "if only someone who has successfully run a private business were running city government, think how much better off we would be?"

It is easy to be seduced by the simplicity of this approach. To be sure, many management tools and techniques used in private business are transferrable to the management of a public business. And, these tools and techniques should be transferred more rapidly than they have been in the past. But, the "business" of city government has certain characteristics that are not found in a private business. These characteristics in combination result in major differences between the management of a public and a private business. In developing a strategy to improve the performance of city government, it is imperative that we understand and take into account these differences.

EXISTENCE NOT DEPENDENT ON PERFORMANCE

In private business success in the marketplace determines the viability of an enterprise. Consumers, through their decisions to select one product over another, collectively determine whether a given private business can earn sufficient revenue to cover the costs and the risks of being in that business. If not, the business ceases to exist.

The existence of city government, unlike a private business, is not solely dependent on satisfying its customers (city residents and users). The revenue collected by city government is not based on the value of a product or a service to a consumer. Rather, it is based on the level of taxation that is politically feasible at the time tax rates are established. The criteria for determining revenue are political, not economic. Peter Drucker, in his recent book, *Management,* points out that:

> "Businesses, other than monopolies, are paid by satisfying the customer. They are paid only when they produce what the customer wants and what he is willing to exchange his purchasing power for. Satisfaction of the customer is, therefore, the basis for assuring performance and results in the business.
>
> Service institutions (city government), by contrast, are typically paid out of a budget allocation. This means that they are not paid for by what the taxpayer and the customer mean by results and performance. Their revenues are allocated from a general revenue stream which is not tied to what they are doing but obtained by tax levy or tribute."

Freedom from performance imperatives is explained, in part, by the fact that city government is a monopoly, responsible for the provision of public services that are essential to the well-being of city residents. Citizens cannot in the short-run postpone the consumption of certain city services (fire and police protection) nor can they substitute for others (water supply, garbage disposal and sewage removal). Moreover, the city is responsible for producing certain "public goods" which can only be provided on a collective basis (street construction and repair, public transportation, park development). These public goods, unlike the products of a private business, satisfy a collective *need* that the political process has determined should be collectively satisfied independent of the economic value of the service to the individual consumer.

Freedom from performance imperatives has important implications for the conduct of the public management process. Most importantly, there is no externally imposed discipline or incentive to produce more and better services with fewer dollars or less people. In the absence of competition, there is no incentive to curtail non-productive, high cost activities. There is no incentive to reallocate scarce resources from marginally-valuable services to services that represent greater value to city residents and users. City governments often decide to begin new things, but they rarely decide to terminate old things.

The fact that revenue is received regardless of the quality or the quantity of results produced eliminates a critical check or penalty for poor performance. External groups (the media, major private interest groups, citizen groups, and even the judiciary) are therefore substituted for the marketplace as a constraint on negative governmental performance.

LACK OF PERFORMANCE MEASURES

In private business there are generally accepted measures of performance. In addition to the time-honored, "bottom-line" measure of profit, there are measures such as sales, sales growth, earnings per share, stock price, and return on investment. Different people (stockholders, managers, division heads) may use different measures at different times for different purposes. Also, there may not always be complete agreement on any one measure. In general, however, the language of private-sector decision-making is quantitative and relatively clear so that groups of investors or managers can usually decide on which performance measures will be used to determine success or failure.

In city government this is not the case. There is less agreement about which, if any, measures of performance tell political leaders, managers, or citizens whether the public business is succeeding or failing. Even though city government may be viewed as a business, its decision-making environment, in contrast to a private business, is political, not economic. In private business, economic measures provide a common denominator for making management decisions; for a public business, there is no such common denominator.

The absence of accepted performance measures in city government results from three principal factors: first, the overall purpose of city government—improving the quality of life of its citizens—is intangible. Second, political leaders are resistant to the establishment of measures that can be used by their constituents to hold them accountable for their own performance. Finally, there is less incentive to develop performance measures where there is no competition or marketplace in which the value of services is tested.

The implications of managing a business where there is little ability to measure success or failure is considerable. The absence of accepted performance measures makes it impossible to establish achievable objectives which, in turn, are the basis for setting priorities, allocating scarce resources, organizing personnel, and evaluating program implementation. For example, without accepted performance measures it is difficult to determine which investment—more police, more street cleaners, or more garbage collectors—will provide citizens with the highest level of satisfaction and the greatest return on their tax dollars. In addition, anyone who has attended a City Council meeting or worked in a governmental agency will understand that when objectives are not clear and no measures exist to evaluate them, means tend to become more important than ends, style replaces substance, and preoccupation with procedure replaces a willingness to make tough decisions.

Moreover, an inability to measure performance makes it impossible to objectively evaluate the performance of city government personnel. Therefore, it is impossible to translate organizational objectives into personal objectives. This often results in a situation where personal objectives are in conflict with organizational objectives. If, for example, a Mayor believes that citizens cannot really measure how well city government is performing, she or he may place a higher priority on personal ends (running for Congress) than on community ends. The inability to measure adequately the performance of city operations has also led to the creation of personnel systems in which promotion and compensation decisions are based on the size of a manager's budget, the number of people supervised or the length of government service, rather than on the quality of results produced. This makes the task of managing people for improved performance significantly more difficult.

In addition, the absence of performance measures also makes it difficult for citizens to recognize the gap between what a city government could produce (optimum performance) and what it does produce (actual performance), or to compare the results of one city government with the results of another.

CONSTRAINTS ON THE ACHIEVEMENT OF OBJECTIVES

The stockholders of a private enterprise are more concerned with the results achieved by the organization than they are with the means used to achieve these results. Most private businesses establish policies that govern the actions of managers and employees. But, such policies generally place far fewer limitations on the actions of managers and employees than is the case in a public business. In city government *how* things are done often has greater impact on public confidence than *what* is done. Political leaders are inclined to take a short-term view that places greater emphasis on means than on ends. The selection of means may be dictated by prospects of political return, regardless of the impact on city government performance. For example, political leaders may find it in their interest to adopt a policy of investing city money in local banks rather than earning greater revenue through the investment of funds in external banks. Or, political leaders may determine that it is in their interest to do business with local contractors rather than to obtain the same services elsewhere at less cost to the taxpayer.

The implication of this difference on the conduct of the management process is primarily reflected in higher costs of doing business. When employees are rewarded for how they do things rather than what they do, it is exceedingly difficult to motivate them to be productive.

CONFLICTING INCENTIVES AMONG PARTICIPANTS IN THE MANAGEMENT PROCESS

A private business involves four different groups of participants in the management process. These include: (1) stockholders, (2) directors, (3) managers, and (4) labor. The basic division of incentives is between the first three groups, loosely termed "management," and labor. In a private concern, the interest of stockholders, directors and managers are generally the same; that is, they want to maximize profit—the difference between revenue and costs. Labor is a cost element in the production process and therefore is an element which management tries to control in the interest of both directors and stockholders. Labor groups, on the other hand, want to ensure that employees are properly rewarded for the service they provide. However in private business, labor also benefits from good economic performance. Poor performance may mean fewer jobs and tougher contract negotiations. Therefore, to some extent, *all* participants involved in the process of managing a private business have a common incentive to improve the performance of that business.

City government also has four groups of participants. These include: (1) citizens, (2) political representatives (City Council, Mayor), (3) managers and (4) labor. In this model, there is little or no reason for alliances among participants based on common incentives that are related to performance. We find that any combination of the four can share similar incentives at any given time. For example, labor has the same basic incentive it has in private business—to ensure proper compensation for its members. Managers, however, do not necessarily have the same incentive as political representatives (the elected Board of Directors). In fact, managers may have incentives that are more like those of labor; that is, they may be more interested in continuing their jobs and protecting themselves from exploitation by politicians than they are in maximizing the performance of city government. Citizens may not necessarily have the same motivation as their political representatives. A politician may be more interested in retaining his office, or aspiring to higher office, than in finding ways to deliver better quality services to his constituency.

Conflicting incentives among major participants in city government (citizens, political leaders, and municipal managers) may be attributable to the following factors. First, as we stated earlier, the absence of performance imperatives makes it more difficult to establish a basis for relating personal compensation to business performance. Second, when the revenue received by a city government is independent of the quality of results produced, there is no reason for citizens, political leaders, municipal managers—or even labor—to be concerned about how their actions (or inactions) will affect performance. Finally, within city government there is a significantly greater confusion of roles than is the case in a private business. Every employee is a stockholder, and may be a member of labor. Political leaders may well owe their election to, and be dependent on, public employee labor unions—a condition that significantly enhances labor's influence in the management process.

The primary implication of this difference for the management of city government is that there is less willingness to delegate to managers the necessary authority required to maximize performance. Also when there are no consistent incentives that link the interests of political leaders, citizens and municipal managers there is a greater hesitancy on the part of managers to take risks and explore innovations. Moreover, shifting incentives and alliances among participants in the management process make it harder to attract and retain competent managers. When the responsibilities of municipal managers are unclear and requisite political support is uncertain, few competent managers will take the job.

Finally, in private business the power of organized labor is offset by the common incentives of management. In city government, labor is often the *only* participant with consistent incentives. This significantly enhances its ability to pursue narrow interests, which, at times, may be at the expense of governmental performance.

ABSENCE OF ACCOUNTABILITY

In private business a chief executive officer is responsible for the conduct of the management process and the performance of the organization. Some decisions in a private business do require the approval or consent of the Board of Directors or of a management committee. The chief executive, therefore, does share some management responsibility. But, the Board of Directors' involvement in administrative decision-making is generally minimal.

In city government this is not the case. In addition to the separation of powers between the executive and the legislative branch, there is usually an additional, and less desirable fragmentation of authority and responsibility within the executive branch. Most city governments by Charter and by law have created numerous decision-making authorities which are independent or semi-independent of the chief executive, (or in some cases, of the legislature). These bodies (including planning commissions, elected city department heads, park and recreation boards, transportation authorities, and the like) play an active role in the conduct of the management process. This fragmentation of executive responsibility has an adverse affect on the ability of cities to get things done. Not only does it lengthen the decision-making process and create a duplication of effort, both of which can be very costly, it also leaves citizens with no clear basis for determining where the "buck" stops. As city government becomes less responsive and less accountable for its performance there is a greater tendency for citizens to become alienated and apathetic.

INCREASED ROLE OF NON-PROFESSIONALS

In many cities we find a number of important functions performed by non-professionals. For example, we find Civil Service Commissions that make significant personnel decisions, Planning Commissions that make major land-use decisions, Park Commissions that make recreation decisions, and so on. Such commissions may be comprised of citizens who have no special expertise with which to make these decisions. By contrast, non-professionals do *not* play a significant role in the decision-making process of most private businesses.

The continuing involvement of non-professionals in city government can, in part, be explained by three historical legacies: the town meeting ethos in which citizens could meet and confer on important municipal decisions; a fear of concentrated political power and the abuses it may foster; and a democratic belief that public decision-making is within the competence of "Everyman." Non-professional involvement continues today due to a lack of appreciation of the complexity of city management and of the need to bring professional skills to bear on the process of solving municipal problems.

The role of non-professionals in the governmental decision-making process often results in major delays in making routine decisions and, more importantly, in uninformed decisions. Moreover, non-professionals are inclined to place total reliance on special interest groups whom they feel obligated to represent.

The fact that you cannot manage a public business exactly the way you manage a private business should *not* lead to the conclusion that there is no basis for evaluating and improving the performance of city government. Rather, we should conclude that there is a need to develop an analytical framework, tailored to the specific characteristics of city government, that will enable all those who are interested in improving governmental performance to identify where the management process within city government can be strengthened.

It is interesting, and a bit surprising, to find that volumes of material have been written and numerous analytic tools have been developed to evaluate and to improve our understanding of what affects the process of management within a private business. Yet, very little has been written about what affects the same process in a public business like city government. Consequently, we must fashion new tools that will help us evaluate a public business that performs important economic functions within a decision-making environment that is non-economic. This effort must begin with the realization that you cannot manage City Hall exactly the way you manage General Motors.

PART FOUR

The Public
Service
of the Future

13

THE ROLE OF GOVERNMENT AND PUBLIC BUREAUCRACY IN AMERICAN SOCIETY

Many Americans believe that government does too much, whereas others contend that government does too little. Businessmen complain about too much regulation, and citizens of all kinds complain about the red tape and paperwork they encounter in dealing with government.

American society appears to be in the midst of a fundamental rethinking about the scope of government activity. Much of this discussion centers on the role and functions of large public bureaucracies.

Both former President Ford and President Carter, representatives of the country's two major political parties, have talked about "deregulation." Both have wanted to simplify and improve federal regulation. But the issue goes far beyond regulatory administration. Public opinion seems to be moving toward the reconsideration of the government's ability to solve societal problems that has not been seriously challenged since the presidency of Franklin D. Roosevelt.

In this chapter, Caspar Weinberger and then Robert Nisbet suggest that big government and big bureaucracy unnecessarily interfere with the lives and livelihoods of individuals. Charles Reich and Burke Marshall, on the other hand, ask whether the federal government has as yet actually confronted the many problems of postindustrial America.

Those who agree with Weinberger and Nisbet point to affirmative action quotas, lengthy environmental impact statements, and the debate over saccharine (a low-calorie sugar substitute). Although state and local governments present a significantly different context for this debate, a new conservativism is also noticeable there. The approaches of Democratic governors Michael Dukakis of Massachusetts and Edmund G. (Jerry) Brown, Jr., of California are good examples of this. Keeping New York City's flirtation with bankruptcy in mind, cost-conscious local government executives are also concerned with restricting the scope of activity in their jurisdictions.

At the same time, Reich and Marshall also have a long list of followers. Governmental action is needed to deal with the crisis in health care delivery, energy, and environmental pollution. Senator Hubert H. Humphrey of Minnesota and Congressman Augustus F. Hawkins of California have proposed legislation (the Humphrey–Hawkins bill) for the national government to promote full employment. The Initiative Committee for National Economic Planning, headed by Harvard economist Wassily Leontief and former United Auto Workers President Leonard Woodcock, has called for increased national economic planning. Ralph Nader, Mark Green, and others seek federal rather than state chartering of big corporations, and still others seek a federal consumer protection agency. All these measures, if implemented, would expand the scope of the federal government.

Also in this chapter, we have Colorado Senator Gary Hart's illumination of the debate over the size of government. He concludes his commentary with a discussion of citizen expectations about the future of the public service. It is very well to talk about restricting the role of the public sector, he says, but individuals often find it difficult to decide precisely which existing governmental program should be cut.

The real problem in the debate, according to George Cabot Lodge, is the need for many citizens, especially those active in the private sector, to modernize their attitudes about the role and scope of government in a complex society. He challenges the long-held belief that the least government is invariably the best government.

Taking a pragmatic approach, Charles Schultze tries to find a constructive direction for some of this debate. He suggests that a free market approach to regulatory policy holds great potential. In this, government would provide incentives to obtain cooperation from regulated enterprises.

Finally, Anthony Downs returns to some of the original issues brought up by Weinberger and Nisbet. Downs analyzes the long-term implications of increased bureaucratization for American society.

Do More Public Programs Equal Less Private Freedom?

CASPAR W. WEINBERGER

When I came to Washington in 1970, the federal budget outlay stood at $196.6-billion. It is now $358.9-billion—an increase of 83 per cent. Lest you think there is a causal connection between that increase and my residence in Washington, I ask you to read a bit further.

Apart from its sheer magnitude, the most noteworthy thing about this trend is that federal spending has shifted away from traditional federal functions such as defense and toward programs that reduce the remaining freedom of individuals and lessen the power of other levels of government.

This shift in federal spending has transformed the task of aiding life's victims from a private concern to a public obligation.

There are benefits and burdens in this. One is that the care of the less fortunate is guaranteed under law. The sweep of our social-program commitments has brought secure incomes for the elderly, the ill, those who are alone, and those who are disabled. They have provided health care for millions and opened the doors of college to young people whose families could not otherwise have given their sons and daughters this opportunity.

But in the process of pouring out all of these compassionate and humanitarian blessings and institutionalizing our social obligations, we have built an edifice of law and regulation that is clumsy, inefficient, and inequitable. Worst, the unplanned, uncoordinated, and spasmodic nature of our responses to these needs—some very real, some only perceived—is quite literally threatening to bring us to national insolvency.

We are also creating a massive welfare state that has intruded into the lives and personal affairs of our citizens. This intrusion affects both those it seeks to help and those who do the helping. The entire human-resources field is under the lash of federal law—doctor, hospital, teacher, college president, student, voluntary agency, city hall, and state capital. All of these are subject to the steadily increasing intrusion of the Congress—which requires that drastic and often unnecessary regulations be adopted by the executive branch.

There is an overriding danger inherent in the growth of an American welfare state. The danger simply is that we may undermine our whole economy. If social programs continue growing for the next two decades at the same pace they have in the last two, we will spend more than half of our whole gross national product for domestic social programs alone by the year 2000.

Should that day ever come, half of the American people would be working to support the other half. At that point, government would be like a gigantic sponge, sopping up all the nation's surplus capital needed for industrial growth and modernization. Lacking funds for these vital purposes, we would no longer have enough surplus capital left to invest in job-producing activities in the private sector—and it is that kind of investment which has always pulled us out of recessions and depressions in the past. In all likelihood, we could not maintain our free-enterprise, incentive-capitalistic economy if 50 per cent of the whole G.N.P. had to be used to pay for domestic social programs alone. And if we lose our free-enterprise incentive system, we will have destroyed, by inaction, the system that has brought more benefits to more people at home and throughout the world than any other system since recorded history began.

Those who urge still more social programs view the problem upside down. It is not more social programs that will solve our nation's ills, but more economic growth. Growth alone provides the jobs that reduce social ills. Growth alone provides the revenues that finance our social-program commitments, yet one of the most iniquitous of the new philosophies we hear today is the smug assertion that "less is better and more is worse."

What we do have to limit is the growth of the welfare state in America. We must summon up a common determination as a people to change drastically our present approach because not only is it not working—but it can ruin all of us. Only a wave of public sentiment in this direction can give Congress the nerve to say No to more social programs. As it is, Congress quite evidently believes that the road to popularity and re-election is to say Yes to every demand for every increase in all existing programs and to agree to most demands for new ones. Above all, we must recognize that personal freedoms diminish as the welfare state grows. The price of more and more public programs is less and less private freedom. . . .

Leviathan and Laissez-Faire

ROBERT NISBET

There is another side to the current disaffection with political government, party and the whole political habit of mind that has been so widely noted.

I refer to the burgeoning of the social impulse among disparate groups in the population: a social impulse manifest in the spreading interest at all levels in voluntary association, ingenious forms of autonomous mutual aid, and what for want of a better term can be called social inventions.

Liberation of the social from the political may yet prove to be the single greatest contribution to stability and freedom alike in this century.

It is impossible to miss the degree to which the idea of social initiative appeals to all age levels and social-economic strata in the population, and, far from least in importance, to the left as well as the right.

Behind political disenchantment and renewal of interest in voluntary association lies a common enemy: the leviathan that was first conceived for the American political order during Woodrow Wilson's war years, that was resuscitated by the New Deal, that somehow managed to develop and enlarge even during the years of affluence following World War II, and that finally turned into a virtual burlesque of itself during the Kennedy-Johnson years of endless political promises and endless political failures.

To what end, it began to be asked, by youth as well as other segments of the population, were the "wars" against poverty, illiteracy, urban blight and other social ills when the price was not only failure but often reverse consequences and invariably the spread of inquisitorial and repressive bureaucracy?

The combination of evil and ineptitude that marked the Nixon years seemed to many a logical, if extreme, emergent of the very leviathan mentality that had become the stock-in-trade of American liberals and progressives and the unvarying platform of first the Democratic, then increasingly the Republican party.

By itself political alienation spread widely could be dangerous, with consequences to be seen in a kind of social anemia matched by political apoplexy.

In such consequences, quite often in history, popular-rooted militarized dictatorship takes root. But disenchantment with the political state that is accompanied by the spirit of authentic social renewal, by search for non-political, autonomous, cooperative alternatives to bureaucratic paternalism is, it would certainly seem, very different. We could, if present signs are reliable, be on the way to exactly this kind of social renewal.

Self-help is illusory as long as the referent is the individual alone. "Multiply your associations and be free," Proudhon is said to have exhorted. He might have added: "and also secure."

Tocqueville thought the urge to voluntary association one of the most distinctive characteristics of the America he visited, and declared it the supreme guarantor of freedom in democracy where, as he realized, the tendency to enlarge government in the name of humanitarianism becomes almost irresistible. Such association, diversely constituted, is at once refuge of the individual and buffer against political power.

Historical ages vary in the fertility of their voluntary associations and their social inventions. The 19th century was remarkably fertile in this respect, its vaunted individualism notwithstanding. One thinks of the innumerable social utopias in the wilderness, the rise of labor unions, cooperatives, assurance societies and mutual-aid groups of every kind.

I am inclined to think it was the combination of politically rooted "progressivism" and the impact of World War I that killed a good deal of the spirit of social inventiveness that had existed in all parts of America.

Increasingly the political liberal could see no farther than the kind of agency or bureau that became a byword of the New Deal and its successors down through the Presidencies of Kennedy, Johnson and Nixon.

But things are changing and the conventional wisdom of our spokesmen of power looks less and less attractive to those who have too often seen so-called liberalism take on the trappings of bureaucracy that shows itself to be uncontrollable by Cabinet heads, even Presidents.

The appeal of the nonpolitical, the genuinely social, the voluntary and the cooperative at the grass roots becomes steadily greater. The youth communes, now in their thousands, are certainly, for all their occasional gaminess, reflections of this appeal. But there are many other kinds of voluntary association forming, and the social sciences would do well to uncover and study these.

Is there anything a wise government might do to further the social impulse? There is.

First, decentralize, diffuse, and divest itself. Government has a crowding-out effect on social inventiveness when it seeks, as ours does, to move into even the most intimate recesses of society.

Second, create the conditions of a new *laissez-faire;* not the kind that in the 19th century was directed to the lone individual, to economic man, but instead to the social group, the voluntary, mutual-aid association.

Needed: A Government That Governs

CHARLES A. REICH
BURKE MARSHALL

The most important thing about the energy crisis is what it tells us about how inadequately we have been governed. Our Government has permitted this whole society to be built upon the assumption of an unlimited supply of gasoline and other fuel. The pattern of suburban living, second homes, shopping centers and industrial parks assumes this. The travel, transportation and recreation industries assume it.

Yet in the last decade our Government has never really taken the responsibility for making us question whether the assumption was valid. We have never effectively been asked to learn the facts, we have never been given the opportunity to make serious choices. Suddenly, out of the blue, the energy shortage is discovered. Can any society afford such folly, such shortsightedness, such lack of planning?

Watergate is a far less serious disaster than the fact that we have a Government that has so utterly failed to govern. Watergate has, of course, contributed to that failure by occupying the center stage. And to the extent that Watergate means more than mere personal corruption on the part of officials, its abuses very likely stem from an effort to retain political power in spite of the underlying failure to govern. But our present approach to national politics shows we have not yet really seen our predicament. On all sides, it seems to be assumed that if President Nixon is replaced by a man who is personally honest and willing to obey the Constitution, that will mean a resumption of responsible national government. It will not, if we do not face our problems more squarely.

- We can no longer afford a government that does not engage in long-range planning and have the courage openly to persuade, through law or otherwise, the necessary sectors of our society to follow its plans.

- We can no longer afford a government that does not assume fundamental responsibility for income distribution effects, for the equality or inequality with which economic events burden different individuals in our society. The very idea that the fuel shortage, which no one knew about, will arbitrarily make some people richer and other people poorer strikes at the heart of any concept of social justice.

- We can no longer afford a democratic system in which basic choices that have to be made—such as how to allocate our limited resources—are not presented to the people for their ultimate decision, a decision that should be based upon facts which even at this late date are still unknown to most of us and appear to be dribbled out in a deliberately misleading fashion.

- We can no longer afford an economic system in which giant units obey only their own internal needs to expand or develop and are not subject to external restraints representing the needs of society as a whole.

- We can no longer afford the irresponsibility of tax-deductible advertising that recklessly goes along creating needs which either cannot be satisfied at all or cannot be satisfied without a socially disastrous misallocation of resources.

The problem, in short, is not that we are governed by bad men and women. What we really have to confront is the fact that we are governed by people who do not know what they are doing, who lack the knowledge and time to understand how a society works, what it needs, what means might be taken to insure its survival. We are governed in the first instance by people who necessarily spend most of their energies getting themselves elected, selling themselves like merchandise, and who are apt to devote their time that is not expended in that effort to exercising power for its own value or simply because they possess it. And below that level, we are governed by bureaucracies organized and devoted to perpetuating their own power niche in tasks that are often outdated by the time the bureaucracies get to them.

The end of the last decade saw the election of many candidates for office whose main appeal was to fear. There were appeals to fear of crime, fear of racial violence, fear of youth and the antiwar movement. What we got for our fears was government, at the national, state, and local levels, that promised repression under the name of law and order, but had no real idea of the nation's needs except to let the powerful grow yet more powerful and uncontrolled. Watergate and the energy crisis are only the first fruits of this flight from responsibility. The domestic ills that brought forth the discontent of the sixties are with us still, more urgent than ever. It is these problems of an advanced industrial society—and no government will be able to face them until we do ourselves.

Big Government: Real or Imaginary?

GARY HART

It is time to come to grips with what is popularly called "Big Government." It is certainly no secret that public officials have detected rising public disillusionment with big government. Big government, the "mess" in Washington, and the "Washington establishment" have become major themes of presidential candidates. I decided to start at ground zero and appraise just what has happened to big government over the last 10 or 20 years.

The Federal bureaucracy is the element of big government most frequently the topic of cocktail party abuse and campaign rhetoric. It is widely assumed to grow at an alarming rate and expand to control every aspect of our lives. I have seen figures, as you probably have, showing agencies of government being constantly created, but virtually never being abolished. So I decided to begin my inquiry into big government with a close look at the size and shape of the Federal bureaucracy.

The bureaucracy is, of course, people—Federal employees. In 1974, the Federal Government employed about 5 million persons. But, surprisingly to me, that was almost exactly the same number of Federal employees on the payroll 13 years earlier, back in the year 1961.

Not only has a huge expansion in Federal employment not occurred, a significant number of important Government agencies are noticeably smaller. For example, three major agencies are smaller now than they were in 1961—the Department of Defense, the Department of State, and the Agency for International Development.

Another three important agencies were smaller in 1975 than they were in 1970. These are the Department of the Interior, the Department of Agriculture, and the Postal Service.

Thus, the critics point out that new agencies are created and others grow. But they omit the important fact that agencies are also cut back.

One statistically sound way to measure the size of the bureaucracy is to compare it, year by year, with the population. This tells how many of each 1,000 citizens are now working for the Government. In 1950—that is 26 years ago—13 out of every 1,000 persons were civilian Government employees. In 1955, 14 out of every 1,000 citizens were Federal employees. Jumping 20 years later—to 1975—we discover that the statistic is exactly the same: 14 out of every 1,000 citizens are civilian employees.

Even though the size of the bureaucracy has not grown out of control, it seems possible that pay for Federal employees was eating up the budget. In short, they are being paid too m.h. That idea, unfortunately, is no more valid than the myth of the constantly growing bureaucracy. In 1950, the payroll amounted to 16 percent of the Federal budget. In 1960 it was 14 percent of the Federal spending. Last year it amounted to 13 percent of Federal spending.

But even if it is not growing, the idea of a "Federal bureaucracy" is still a vague term. It doesn't have real and precise meaning. So let's look at what our Federal employees actually do.

As I mentioned, last year about 5 million persons worked for the Federal Government on a full-time basis. What did they do? First, the overwhelming majority—64 percent to be exact—worked in just one huge agency: the Department of Defense. So most of the famous "big government bureaucracy" turns out in reality to be our national security forces. About two-thirds of these bureaucrats are in uniform and one-third are civilians. So that takes care of 3.2 million of our 5 million Federal employees. What about the rest?

The next largest agency—and the only other real giant of the bureaucracy—is the U.S. Postal Service with about 700,000 employees. This is no real surprise either, since we know that delivering the mail is a labor-intensive business.

The Postal Service is three times larger than any other agency except Defense. So all other agencies seem small by comparison. HEW—the welfare giant—has 139,000 employees and Treasury, a total of 126,000.

Some agencies with a big job are remarkably small. The Arms Control and Disarmament Agency, for example, has just 179 employees. It is outnumbered nearly three-to-one by the American Battle Monuments Commission.

Perhaps that cuts the bureaucracy down to size and gives us a little feel for what Federal employees really do. Most are involved in defense. A large number deliver the mail. And just over 1 million perform all the other functions of the Federal Government for 220 million fellow citizens.

I'm sure some of you are trying to remember those figures that showed that if things kept up, soon we all would be working for the government. There have been areas where government employment has grown rapidly and substantially. But not at the Federal level.

The startling growth in government has been at the State and local level. Let me give you some examples. In 1960, there were about 5.5 million State and local government employees. By 1975, the figure had more than doubled to 11.7 million employees. That is where the growth has occurred—not in distant Washington, but in the governments closest to the people. Let me give you another example.

In 1960, the Federal Government employed 3.3 percent of the work force. In 1975, that figure declined to 3.1 percent of the work force. State and local government, on the other hand, presented a vastly different picture. In 1960, 7.7 percent of all workers were employed by State and local government. By 1975, this grew to 12.6 percent of the work force.

This should clearly illustrate the trend: the so-called bureaucracy has grown at the State and local level—and not at the Federal level. Again, bureaucracy is a vague concept, so we ought to take a quick look at what these State and local employees are actually doing.

Most of the growth has occurred, and most of the people actually work, in a single area: our local schools. Of the 11.7 million State and local employees, nearly half of them work as teachers or in other support roles in our educational system.

This makes sense. Since 1960, this country has made an enormous commitment to expand and improve our educational system. Elementary schools, junior colleges, and colleges sprang up all over this country, responding to the baby boom and the importance we placed on education in an increasingly technological society.

The remaining State and local employees perform a wide variety of tasks that defy neat categorization. However, just about 1 million are police and about the same number are firemen. A much smaller number are employed in the delivery of welfare and similar social services.

So slicing through all the rhetoric about bureaucracy, we find some simple and down-to-earth facts that reflect a clear national consensus. At the Federal level the largest so-called ''bureaucracy'' is our national defense effort, reflecting both the importance and the labor-intensive nature of national security. On the State and local level, our educational system—expanding rapidly for about 15 years—accounts for much of the higher public employment.

Bureaucracy, however, is only one popular villain in the attack on big government. Government spending is an equally frequent target of criticism. And you all have heard how it's getting out of hand. So it seems only reasonable to take a hard look at Government spending.

But before we delve into government spending, a few notes of caution. Government spending figures are the most difficult to interpret and the most frequently distorted. This happens for three reasons: First, the numbers are so large they tend to lose all meaning. Second, inflation, a worldwide phenomenon, alters the value of a dollar, so that the same Government purchase made 10 years ago will appear smaller than an identical purchase made today. Because of inflation, for example, a $170 million Government program in 1975 is exactly the same size as a $100 million program in 1967. Third, both our economy and our population are growing.

So in making an honest examination of Government spending, we have to keep all these factors in proportion or we will end up with false comparisons that sound good in speeches but do not reflect reality.

With those conditions in mind, let's address the question: How much has Government spending really grown? The answer is again surprising: "A little but certainly not a lot."

To compensate for both inflation and economic growth, one valid measure of Government spending is a comparison between public expenditures and the gross national product.

For example, in 1952, the Federal budget amounted to 19 percent of the gross national product. That means that Government accounted for nearly one-fifth of all goods and services in the country. In 1973, the percentage remained just about the same: the Government budget amounted to 20.9 percent of the gross national product. In other words, in that 21-year period the portion of the gross national product accounted for by the Federal Government changed little.

Let me make another contrast to show how inflation and a growing economy can distort the statistics. In 1961, the Federal budget amounted to 19.6 percent of the gross national product. Ten years later it amounted to virtually the exact same proportion: 20.9 percent of the gross national product. That means that compared to the *size* of our economy, Government spending did not change.

But if you want to distort the figures, you don't adjust for inflation or economic growth. You would then point out that in 1961, the Federal budget amounted to a paltry $149 billion. In 10 years it leaped to an astounding $220 billion. That sounds impressive but creates a false impression, for in fact Government spending has moved along, in lock step, with inflation and economic growth. It has not taken a significantly larger share, not a notably smaller share either.

A final note on Government spending. If you compare the percentages year by year, you will discover quite a lot of fluctuation. The Government's share of the GNP rises to 20 percent or a little higher during wars and during recessions. It drops off to about 16 or 17 percent when the economy is booming in peacetime.

But the important point is this: there has been no major change in the *proportion* of our economic output consumed or distributed by the Federal Government. That is contrary to those who would like to use Federal spending as a whipping boy.

Like numbers of employees, these gross Federal budget figures don't have much meaning by themselves, because the billion dollar figures are so mind boggling. But we can bring the Federal budget down to earth, too, just as we did the Federal bureaucracy.

In Fiscal Year 1976, the Federal budget totals about $374 billion, a figure so large as to lack real meaning. So let's slice up the Federal pie to see who gets what.

Although the Department of Defense employs 64 percent of the Federal work force, it accounts for only about one-quarter of the Federal budget. Again inflation and economic growth can be deceiving. Because while the dollar totals for defense have climbed steadily year by year, these numbers conceal the fact that defense has gotten a progressively smaller slice of the Federal pie—largely due to the so-called "entitlement" programs.

A package of two major social programs directed at a single constituency accounts for by far the biggest share of the Federal budget. The constituency is the elderly, and the programs—social security and medicare—will equal more than $108 billion.

The nation's financial commitment to the elderly does dwarf all other Federal social welfare programs. The assistance provided to the elderly is five times that provided other welfare programs added together.

Painting with a broad brush, the Federal share of the nation's production has remained about the same. But Federal spending priorities have shifted, from defense into income security and medical assistance for the elderly.

We have now examined two of the villains of big government—bureaucracy and Federal spending—let us now turn from the bark of big government to the bite: Federal tax collections.

Is there a person alive who does not believe that the Federal Government is taking a bigger chunk each year of his paycheck? That leads us to a close look at the Federal tax burden, and once again we will find some surprising answers.

In 1951, the Federal Government collected in taxes about 20 cents of every dollar on goods and services produced in the United States. One decade later the Federal Government was still collecting 20 cents for every dollar of goods and services. Two decades later—in 1971—the Federal Government took the same 20 cents and not until 1973 did the Federal share increase to just over 21 cents. Thus, in broad terms, the Federal tax burden has not changed significantly in 25 years. These figures count all Federal tax collections including social security, income taxes, and corporate taxes. But lumping these taxes together blurs the fact that significant changes have occurred in the tax burden.

Two taxes paid by individuals have indeed increased, both in absolute and relative terms. These are income taxes and social security or payroll taxes. Despite wailing by some in business, the corporate tax burden has declined steadily since 1969. Even though the legal corporate tax rate has remained constant at 48 percent, so many tax "incentives," credits, and other tax breaks have been enacted that the "real" or effective corporate tax rate is now down to about 35 percent. On the other hand, inflation has pushed individuals into higher tax brackets, even though their purchasing power has remained the same.

At this point let me stop and sum up. So far I have been describing the trends in the Federal Government that can be statistically verified. These facts show that the three popular villains of big government are largely mythical. The Federal bureaucracy is not an expanding octopus. On the contrary, it has remained about the same size. Federal spending has grown in proportion with the economy and inflation—maintaining a roughly constant share of our output of goods and services. The overall Federal tax burden also has not grown, but it has shifted from business to individuals.

I have dwelled so long on these statistics for two purposes: First, to try to give you a more direct feel for the dimensions of that vague entity called the Federal Government; second, I believe we have a problem with big government. But, it is *not* just the size of the Government bureaucracy. It is *not* uncontrolled increases in Government spending. It is *not* enormous increases in the Federal tax burden.

Once the erroneous charges against big government are put in perspective, we can begin to zero in on what is left. We definitely have a problem with big government, but it is not simply a problem of size or spending or taxes.

The problem of big government is less tangible but much more important. And it extends from Washington into every community and home in this nation.

The central problem of big government springs from our attitudes and expectations. The problem of big government is big promises that cannot be backed up by performance. The problem of big government is inflated expectations that generate disillusionment rather than hope and progress. The problem of big government is the myth that it can solve every problem and meet every challenge. The problem of big government, frankly, is the demand placed upon it by every interest group in our society.

There are two corrosive results of a generation of false promises, increased demands, and inflated expectations. The first cost is the growing disillusionment and loss of confidence in our government. It results from performance falling short of expectations. But let me emphasize, the *expectations* are as faulty as the performance—and performance is the customary scapegoat. The second cost affects every citizen. When problems are shipped wholesale to Washington for intended solution, it strips all of us not only of the responsibility of problemsolving but also the rewards.

When problems are exiled to Washington for solution, people become clients of government programs rather than sovereign citizens to whom government must be accountable. The result of this process over the years is that people are stereotyped and stripped of humanity to fit into cold definitions of program categories. Real people become "recipients," consumers, clients of health care delivery systems. What we need are citizens and human beings.

Let me offer some illustrations of how we can begin to bring inflated expectations down to earth:

- This government was established to *promote* prosperity. No government can *guarantee* prosperity.

- This government can encourage the creation of jobs. It cannot guarantee everyone a job of his choice.

- Government can and must try to minimize inflation. But no government can terminate a worldwide problem by act of law.

- The Federal Government must insure and promote the legal rights of minorities. But in the long haul, subtle human discrimination will be ended by citizens of understanding and compassion who grow beyond narrow prejudice.

This nation must grow beyond the arrogant and ill-considered promises that government could "whip" inflation, immediately win a "war on poverty," or guarantee world peace.

Does that mean that we give up on these problems and goals? Absolutely not. I am saying that this country and particularly the Federal Government must learn to live within limits. The days of the unlimited frontier are over. We are up against the last frontier and it is ourselves.

Learning to live within limits is the essential lesson for a strong nation growing up. We have discovered that our natural resources are finite. Finite resources mean that we must begin to develop an economic program that is no longer premised on unlimited growth or endless consumption. For the three-fourths of us who are wasteful consumers, sacrifices, self-denial, and restraint will be necessary.

Learning to live within limits means beginning the long job of reshaping our economy to emphasize the quality of life over the quantity of consumption.

Learning to live within limits means seeking a new balance of shared responsibility between the citizen and his government. We need to share not only revenue but responsibility. We have to begin to ask: If I don't have what I want, is something wrong with our economic policy in Washington or are my expectations and values simply excessive? Too often a little of both is true.

Learning to live within limits means admitting that some kinds of problems will probably be solved most effectively by citizens and groups of citizens. A neighborhood working together without a dime of Federal money might be more effective in preventing crime than another billion dollar program.

Let us raise our spirits but limit our expectations to a reasonable level. There is much work to be done for a nation with the strength and patience to understand that to learn to live within limits is not to give up. The price of progress has not increased for those who sustain their commitment to our nation's goals.

Top Priority: Renovating Our Ideology

GEORGE CABOT LODGE

We are living in a time of growing suspicion about the purposes and effectiveness of the major institutions of the United States—business, government, the universities, and the churches, among others. We are also living in a time when great things must be done quickly. We are confronted with social problems on an unprecedented scale—so large a scale, in fact, that we now use the all-embracing term "environmental crisis" to describe them as a group.

To many people, it seems that it is business's job to meet this crisis—to bring to bear its particular skills, its huge resources, and its unique talent for getting the job done. The social responsibility of business is assumed today, not merely discussed or suggested; and few seem to doubt that if U.S. business were to concentrate its power on the body of the problems of U.S. society, those problems would yield to its assault.

> By "ideology" I mean a collection of ideas, a dynamic vision, that makes explicit the nature of a good community. Rooted in philosophy and science, it is an action-oriented formulation of objectives, priorities, and criteria for measuring progress.[1] It is distinguishable from pragmatism, which holds that no such explicit formulation of ideas is necessary for good and right action. Pragmatism simply holds that that which works is good and true.

Can business make such a unified assault? As matters stand today, I do not believe it can do so directly. Disunity and alienation abound. The ideological bridgework that related the timeless values of our Western civilization to the real world and guided the activities of our institutions has become palsied and obscure.

This is not new. As a nation we have tended to be unmindful of our ideology and we have allowed it to degenerate. Some social commentators, most notably

Daniel Bell, have even said it is dead.[2] In spite of the profound effect of this degeneration on the U.S. community, we have deferred the renovation of our ideology. We have been able to do this, in part, because its function has been filled, on a temporary basis, by a continuous series of national crises—the great depression, World War II, the threat of communism, and so on—each of which evoked in its turn a degree of unity in the community.

Today, surely, we are in a crisis, but its exact nature is more controversial than earlier ones; its challenge is less clear; it is hardly unifying. To bring the community together so it can work on our problems in concert, we need a unifying vision. We need to examine and renovate our ideology.

Thus there is something business must do before it can make a broad attack on our social problems; it must press for a renovated ideology in the United States—a new, dynamic vision of the community and how it ought to operate. Without such guiding principles, any actions business can take to benefit the society at large are likely to lead to confusion and anarchy, an overall fragmentation of our efforts.

Before discussing this challenge to business in more detail, let me offer an example of a company that, by virtue of the business it is in, is under heavy pressure to take radical action, while its ideological context and foundation constrict or prohibit it from taking any radical action at all.

CON EDISON POWERLESS?

Consolidated Edison Company of New York is a privately owned utility that provides electricity, gas, and steam to some 9 million people in metropolitan New York and Westchester County. This company is an integral part of that vast community:

- It sells $70 million worth of electricity a year to the City of New York alone.
- It pays the City roughly $140 million a year in taxes.
- It spends an average of $250 million a year on construction in the City, providing 20% of all the employment in the building trades in New York.
- It is the second largest employer in the metropolitan area.

With the lowest rate of return of any private utility in the country, it has been plagued with myriad difficulties: power shortages causing blackouts and brownouts, high rates, customer complaints, and continued wrangling with government officials. At this writing, Charles Luce, Chairman of the Board of Con Edison, says that the company may well be unable to supply sufficient power to meet the demand it expects during the summer. It faces the need to ration power, to decide who will get it and who will not. To say that it is difficult to find a politically acceptable formula for rationing electricity in New York is to understate the case.

This shortage is hardly the result of mismanagement—the company is headed by exceptionally intelligent and competent managers. Instead, this problem and the other pressing problems of the company derive from the political structures that surround it and the tension, confusion, and competition of interests they embody. The ideological underpinning of these structures—the whole community and the company within it—is the real villain of the piece.

For example, the company is squeezed between its expenses and income. Company costs and services are determined by the City, directly or indirectly, while its rates—i.e., income—are subject to approval by a board at the state level.

Again, it badly needs a very large, new plant to keep pace with the demand, but completion of a 2-million kilowatt plant at Cornwall-on-the-Hudson has been blocked since 1965 by the court action of the Scenic Hudson Preservation Conference. It also needs additional nuclear-power facilities badly, but these are subject to the sometimes erratic determination of the AEC, which is concerned, among other things, with the public safety.

The matter of new power plants reduces to this: the area needs and wants more power, but it does not want, and perhaps cannot safely tolerate, any more plants. Years of debate in the courts have done nothing to erode this impasse.

When one looks at this situation in the context of the power needs of the northeastern United States over the next 50 years, and from the point of view of Con Edison's customers (not to mention its stockholders), one cannot help asking whether the company is properly constituted, in political terms. Would it not make more sense for the New York State Power Authority or a new northeast regional public power authority to be charged with the task of power production, leaving to private companies the distribution of power on a decentralized basis to meet local consumer needs?

The problems are too complex to do more than raise the question here. But if the answer to this question is *yes,* as it seems it might well be, then we must confront the task of forcing this change through the enormous tangle of political jurisdictions and interests which must be consolidated and rationalized for such a change to take place. Robert Wood, the noted urbanologist, for example, tells us that from the top of the Empire State Building on a clear day, one can see 1,400 political jurisdictions.

There is also the formidable ideological obstacle which any notion of "public power" causes in the mind of Con Edison itself. Formed in 1936 by a group of powerful New York financiers, the company has religiously opposed any and all suggestions that any of its operations be governmentally controlled. In earlier times, it had sufficient political clout to make its will felt. Today the old religion survives, but the clout is fast disappearing. Not only is efficient service to the community involved, but also return to Con Edison shareholders. It may well be that by turning power production over to a public authority the company would be more profitable. We face an odd irony: the company may be willing to sacrifice profits for a noble ideology of privacy.

Hence, it is in the interest of Con Edison and of business in general to press and assist government to come to this confrontation. Any lingering delay out of affection for the status quo would seem to be unprofitable folly.

ORIGINS OF IMPOTENCE

How has it happened that a dynamic utility, whose services are necessary to the very continuance of life in New York City, has been shackled into impotence? Its problems, which are also its community's problems, it apparently cannot solve.

We ought to ask why this situation exists, how it could have come about. The answer will help explain what business can do, and *must do*, before it can cope effectively in today's environment.

Finding the answer to this question entails some discussion of "official" American political and social theory—ideology—and of our practical way of life, which has, especially for the businessman, usually been at variance with the theory. This kind of discussion is ordinarily distasteful to the businessman, who prefers to leave ideology strictly alone and to concentrate on the practical question of how to get something done. His implicit pragmatism leads him away from theories in general. Interestingly, it is in large part exactly this pragmatic approach that has undercut our ideology to the point where business lacks an exact idea of what its social responsibility is; and this has deprived business, even if it *did* have such an idea, of knowing how to fulfill it.

LOCKE, PROPERTY AND 1776

Our Protestant beginnings, the challenges and opportunities of our national geography, indeed our entire national experience, have made us what we are: "primarily a people for whom the deed to be done strikes us first, and the theory for doing it comes along afterward, if at all."[3] This national predilection has been a great strength, but also a weakness. We have moved fast and far, relatively unencumbered by fear of inconsistency with political doctrine or theory, but in the process we have become increasingly confused about what we have done and where we are going.

Often, when an American is "up against it" ideologically—when he is abroad, say, and must describe the United States to a foreigner—this confusion becomes dramatically evident. The man will lapse into a quasi-official, ideological jargon that seriously misrepresents reality. He will speak of "capitalism" and "private enterprise," of "individualism" and "initiative," to people for whom these words may well mean abusive exploitation, selfishness, monopoly, imperialism, and worse.

Rarely does one hear an American abroad speak of his country as a social unit or hear him mention the vast array of restrictions, curbs, supports, subsidies, controls, bargains, and pressures—both governmental and nongovernmental—which we have installed to ensure that our "private enterprise system" maintains harmony with the public consensus concerning the nation's good. These measures, we feel, are vaguely un-American; they seem inconsistent with our image of ourselves; we see them as unavoidable, but somehow not entirely legitimate, necessities.

This formalistic jargon has its source in an ideology that lies deep within the U.S. community, an ideology which we have regularly and consistently ignored in working out the practical mechanics of our political, social, and economic order, but which we have never explicitly rejected or replaced, and which therefore retains a moral and political force. It is time that we identified and examined this ideology and its effect on us.

It comes to us from European political thought of the seventeenth century, via the Declaration of Independence of July 4, 1776. It is there that we find set down the inalienable rights of man which we believe it is the function of our government to safeguard. This Declaration asserts the primacy of *individual* rights and the equality of *individuals,* and limits the role of government to just those functions necessary to protect the individual and his property.

The utopian ideal our Declaration and Constitution thus represent had been formulated a century earlier by European philosophers, the most important of whom was John Locke. F.S.C. Northrop, Yale professor of law and philosophy, writes: ''The traditional culture of the United States is an applied utopia in which the philosophy of John Locke defines the idea of the good.''[4] Harvard's Louis Hartz says: ''Locke dominates American political thought as no thinker anywhere dominates the political thought of a nation. He is a massive national cliche.''[5]

The influence of Locke's thought on American life has been various and profound. Indeed, more fertile soil for his philosophy could scarcely have been cultivated. The American had left the organic society of Europe for the atomistic one of America. Liberated from the feudal tradition and structures of Europe, he lived in the free air of a vast new frontier. He was indeed an individual, equal to all other individuals and able to feel his equality. There was property enough for all. As Jefferson wrote to John Adams: ''Here everyone owns property or has a sufficient interest in it to guarantee its protection.''[6]

Our national preoccupation with this strain of political thought has had three important consequences that relate to our present dilemma.

1. *Government should exist, we believe, solely to protect the individual and his property.*

Locke, significantly, said nothing about the relations between individuals; he therefore prescribed no social laws, either of God or of nature. The laws of civil and ecclesiastical government were for Locke mere conventions deriving their entire authority from the private opinions of the independent individuals in a society and their joint majority consent.[7] In Locke there are none of the organic social principles of Plato and Aristotle, for whom man was, in his essential nature, a ''political animal.'' There is none of the idealism of Kant. Indeed, he sets out no criteria for communitarian existence.

Thus the two basic premises of Locke's theory of government and the Declaration of Independence arose in their familiar form: all men are born free and equal, and the origin and basis of government is ''the consent of the governed.''

Where the individual is his own concern and government's chief business is to protect him and his property, it is difficult for government to place the rights of society at large—human rights, if you will—above property rights. This is a consequence that we must hold in serious question today.

Do we really intend that any vote, no matter how democratic or consonant with the public needs, shall be unconstitutional if it violates the principles of private property? In our official tradition, we have intended exactly this. ''The justification for the doctrine of private property is not democratic processes,'' writes Northrop. ''Instead the preservation of private property is the justification for the existence of any government whatever, even a democratic one.''[8]

The transcendent importance of property was appropriate and natural in the American ideology in 1776. But is it still effective today? What, for example, will be the sense of our political philosophy when most Americans are renters?

And again, how shall we define ''property''? Surely Locke and the founding fathers did not have in mind the large publicly held corporations and conglomerates when they used the word. There is little private about such companies in the

Lockean sense. Indeed, Adam Smith, following the spirit of Locke directly, had profound distrust for the British joint-stock companies, which he conceived as essentially public bodies; "being the managers of other people's money than their own, [they] cannot well be expected to watch over it" with the "same anxious vigilance" as an individual over his property. "Negligence and profusion, therefore, must always prevail, more or less, in the management of the affairs of such a company."[9]

2. Hence, we believe, the least government is the best government.

The assumption, implicit in Locke, that the least (and weakest) government is the best, is at the root of Americans' suspicion and disrespect for government, particularly central government. Although this suspicion is apt to be submerged in times of crisis, as it was in World War II, for example, it quickly surfaces in normal times. But the pattern of practical action we have built up for dealing with crises is extremely important in this connection, especially since we seem to live and act today in an atmosphere of "total" crisis.

Originally, we had only a small, weak government. Lockean influence in the United States impeded the establishment of a strong federal principle in the Constitution and strengthened the notion of states' rights. In the early days of the Republic, Hamilton and Jay were forced to bring forth new arguments, different from those of Jefferson and his Lockean followers, for the establishment of a federal system. These included the cultural unity of the colonies, the geographic unity of the country, and the aristocratic, elitist, thoroughly non-Lockean conception of government as planner and developer of the resources of an underdeveloped nation.

It is significant that Hamilton and Jay, like those who followed them, supported their position with *pragmatic*—not ideological—arguments. Neither they nor any of their successors challenged the rightness of Locke directly.

In the crisis of the Civil War the great test came, when Hamilton's admirer, Lincoln, took up the cause of the Union against the Lockean notion that the consent of the governed gave the South the right to secede. Lincoln victoriously pressed a pragmatic federalism that weakened forever the Lockean principle of "the less government, the better." The phrase lost none of its currency, but it did lose a large measure of its applicability.

Lincoln introduced another anti-Lockean concept which was to be carried forward and developed by Theodore Roosevelt, Woodrow Wilson, and Franklin D. Roosevelt; namely, the idea of the good state having a responsibility for the human and social welfare of the people and for planning the allocation of power and resources accordingly.

Again, however, it is significant how gingerly these men proceeded with their radical view, even in the midst of the crises of war and depression. They did not hesitate to take strong executive action, but they were very careful to justify it on the basis of public exigency; they avoided constitutional—*ideological*—questions as much as possible.

Even F.D.R. did not confront Locke and the Constitution directly. Hartz refers to "the experimental mood of Roosevelt, in which Locke goes underground, while problems are solved often in a non-Lockean way."[10] He goes on to say that "what makes the New Deal 'radical' is the smothering by the American Lockean faith of the socialist challenge to it." Roosevelt did not need and did not want a new ideology. Indeed, the last thing he would like to have been called was an ideologist, a socialist, or whatever.

Thus the traditional ideology, as a concept, has repeatedly survived the on-slaughts of pragmatic wisdom, although its practical force was continually diminished as the country grew through its crises and strengthened the federal principle.

3. *This Lockean ideology has been thoroughly subverted by our pragmatic approach to both government and business.*

When a problem presents itself, the typical American response is to improvise a workable solution pragmatically.

Considered in a body, a batch of solutions of this kind may lack ideological consistency, but, the pragmatist argues, no ideological bridgework is necessary for right action. Indeed, he says it is downright harmful; it tends to be rigid, artificial, authoritarian, confusing, and quickly outdated. He believes that the individual (or a group) can at any one time apply values to the world almost intuitively—experimenting, testing, and modifying until he achieves a proper fit. To oversimplify, the pragmatist believes: that which works is good and true. Or, to put it in more specialized form, what works for one individual is good, presumably, for all.

But pragmatism slowly and steadily destroys Lockean thinking. As Hartz puts it, "Pragmatism . . . feeds on the Lockean settlement."[11] Locke's laissez-faire, individualistic doctrine can be very easily adjusted to the notion that what works for the individual in experience and experiment is useful and good.

If we combine this vulnerability with (a) the Darwinian lesson that only the fit survive and (b) the Protestant premise that success in the marketplace is a sign of God's blessing, we have the energetic ideology underlying traditional American business practice. That it is a gross perversion of Locke is obvious, since it has frequently entailed serious curtailment of the freedom and equality of individuals, which he held paramount.

The inequities of this perversion as well as the interests of business itself caused the emergence of interest groups as a vital part of the American political process. Seeking to press government to provide whatever supports served their cause at the moment—be it subsidies, protection, or regulation and control—interest groups have further compounded the break between American political practice and the Lockean view of government and democratic individualism. That our times ring with the charge of hypocrisy is not surprising.

Interest group pluralism: While pragmatism has strengthened the federal principle, it has also contributed heavily to our tradition of interest group pluralism. America's central political problem has been the classical liberal dilemma of majority rule versus minority rights. Interest group pluralism partially resolves this dilemma by playing on the power consoles of government to bring about balanced change. The well-known pendulum effect produced by the interests of business and labor is a good example.

In spite of the undoubted practicality—the essential *pragmatism*—of interest group pluralism, however, it has today left us with profound distortions. Two of these distortions seem particularly relevant here:

First, and most important, it has brought us into conflict with our basic ideology, the freedom and equality of the individual—particularly the black American, the Mexican-American, the American Indian, and other such groups, which have been denied not only the opportunity to form effective interest groups but also the right of access to the political process itself.

The power, force, and necessity of radical black organizations, for example, are perfectly consistent with the demands of interest group pluralism. The American system invites the crises which such movements evoke—crises which, in turn, it has hitherto resolved by its pragmatic improvisations, which, in *their* turn, laid the foundations for the additional splintering of the society. "Today's solution to today's problem" is not a prescription that conduces to farsighted statesmanship.

Second, interest group pluralism has also seriously warped the activities of government, directing them toward whatever interest group has the most compelling force. Theodore J. Lowi persuasively documents the effects, for example, of farmers on the Agriculture Department and its programs, of business on the Commerce Department, of labor on the Labor Department, and of other interests on specialized agencies of the government.[12] He argues that during the last 40 years government has taken onto itself virtually unlimited scope of power, but at the same time has reaffirmed and expanded the notion of interest group pluralism. Thus government has become powerful but formless, a victim of the "pulling and hauling among competing interest groups."[13]

The liberal state, he contends, has a weakened thrust and has become essentially amoral. It has diminished the power and meaning of law by leaving the power to make public policy to private interests. For the requirements of standards it has substituted the requirement of participation. It has solidified bureaucratic conservatism and all in all created a "crisis of public authority . . . [and] the crisis deepens because its nature has not yet been discovered. . . . The zeal of pluralism for the group and its belief in a natural harmony of group competition has tended to break down the very ethic of government by reducing the essential conception of government to nothing more than another set of mere interest groups."[14]

The failure is particularly notable when important segments of society—blacks, militant youth, or whatever—are excluded from prevailing interest groups or when public problems, such as environmental pollution and the complex of urban difficulties, are not solvable through interest group activity.

Consolidated Edison, to return to my opening example, is a company hedged in by many interest groups in a free-for-all in which the only winner can be the principle that a society divided against itself cannot stand. This is no time to assume that "something can be worked out" by all the competing groups. It is a time to think seriously about the shape we want the solution to take.

THE VESTIGE OF IDEOLOGY . . .

Our ideology has always remained largely inexplicit. Our pragmatic preference has caused us to avoid any rigorous or continuing formulation of ideology. We have preferred to remain flexible.

Equally, the pragmatic enlargement and extension of the role and function of government by every powerful President has been profoundly discordant with the Lockean ideology with which we were founded as a nation—that government is a necessary evil, an unfortunate infringement on individual freedom, and best when it governs least.

The vestige of this ideal, as it exists today, is still surrounded with and bolstered by a body of myths—of the frontiersman, who tames the wilderness and is a law unto himself; of Horatio Alger, who can rise from rags to riches by virtue of his own effort; of the founding fathers, as "men of superhuman wisdom and courage whose deeds correspond to the work of Theseus in founding Athens";[15] of nationalism, which so often has manifested itself in the notion that the American people have a mission or destiny that the nation as a whole has an obligation to fulfill; and, among all these others, of the near omnipotence of American business.

Although these myths have been profoundly useful in uniting our social and political order, they have also been profoundly misleading in some ways. Notably, they have retarded and restrained sober and realistic thought about the need to reform our ideology. Today American ideology and the myths surrounding it are under attack.

. . . AND THE DEMAND FOR CHANGE

This attack is aimed primarily at the two most significant embodiments of American ideology, government and business. It is ill-formed and contradictory, like the interest groups from which it emanates. Individualistic assertions are mixed with broad demands of the community; complaints about the power, size, and bureaucracy of government are interspersed with calls for more powerful and far-reaching government; and, most relevant for my purposes here, in many instances the assault on business raises issues which business itself is powerless to resolve.

The attack takes the form of a demand for change—rapid, radical, revolutionary change. In presupposing that the direction which the change is to follow is clear or determined, the attackers confuse themselves. The direction is unclear, as are the priorities of change, the speed with which it should be made, and the means to be used. Further, we can no longer attempt to deal with radical change pragmatically because the distinction between what is "desirable" change and what is "undesirable" change is *fundamentally an ideological distinction*. For example:

- We hold abolition of or infringement on private property to be undesirable change, and yet pressures grow to control and regulate the uses of property ever more stringently in accordance with certain public goals, such as clean air and water, urban development, and improved transportation systems.

- Full employment is desirable, according to the Employment Act of 1946, but its achievement will conflict with several components of traditional ideology, particularly the notions of the limited role of government in planning the allocation of resources and of manpower and the freedom of individuals and of enterprises to locate where they choose and produce what the market will buy at any point in time.

- Competition is held to be ideologically desirable, and yet increasingly it appears that consumers are better served in many instances by economies of scale that restrain competition.

- The concept of profit, which is profoundly ideological, raises other conflicts. In the abstract, profitability is the best measure we have of effective economic employment of economic resources. It objectively tests business's performance; it provides business with its singular strength as an economic institution, namely, its capacity to go out of business.

On the other hand, profit is really a somewhat ineffective measure of business's social and political effectiveness. If profit, therefore, is taken as the sole or major aim of business, other social and political relationships between business and the surrounding environment may be neglected, and business may ultimately be denied even its objective of profit.

It is these "other relationships," concerning business's purpose, function, and role in the community, that rest on and are derived from ideology. They evolve out of the social and political order through the priorities it sets and the rules it adopts for fulfilling its fundamental values. Unless we explicitly describe the comprehensive vision of a functioning ideology, we cannot see these relationships clearly as they affect each other in their combinations in the real world.

Therefore, it is no longer realistic to suppose that the old ideology can remain part of the substratum of American life while pragmatic adjustments are made on the surface. The speed and profundity of change required are too great to allow for the short-term experimentation of the pragmatist; we need some new and more explicit framework to bring basic values to bear directly on the world around us.

NOTES

1. See Carl J. Friedrich, *Man and His Government* (New York, McGraw-Hill Book Company, Inc., 1963), pp. 91–92.
2. Daniel Bell, *The End of Ideology: On the Exhaustion of Political Ideas in the Fifties* (New York, The Free Press of Glencoe, Inc., 1959).
3. F.S.C. Northrop, *The Meeting of East and West* (New York, The Macmillan Company, 1960), p. 67.
4. Ibid., p. 71.
5. Louis Hartz, *The Liberal Tradition in America* (New York, Harcourt, Brace and World, Inc., 1955), p. 140.
6. Ibid., p. 130.
7. Northrop, op. cit., p. 87.
8. Ibid., p. 97.
9. Adam Smith, *Wealth of Nations*, Book V, Chapter 1, Part III, Article 1st, 2nd Section.
10. Hartz, op. cit., p. 260.
11. Ibid., p. 10.
12. Theodore J. Lowi, *The End of Liberalism: Ideology, Policy and the Crisis of Public Authority* (New York, W.W. Norton and Company, Inc., 1969).
13. Ibid., Preface, p. x.
14. Ibid., Preface, p. xiii; see also Arthur Schlesinger, Jr., *Washington Monthly*, January 1970, pp. 59–61.
15. Carl J. Friedrich, *Man and His Government* (New York, McGraw-Hill Book Company, Inc., 1963), p. 96.

The Public Use of Private Interest

CHARLES L. SCHULTZE

In 1929, some 9 percent of the gross national income was spent by federal, state, and local governments for purposes other than national defense and foreign affairs. Between 1929 and 1960, however, the proportion of gross national income spent for domestic programs rose to 17.5 percent. Today, only sixteen years later, that figure is 28 percent.

The growth of federal regulatory activities has been even more striking. There is no good way to quantify regulatory growth, but a few figures will illustrate its speed. Even as late as the middle 1950s, the federal government had a major regulatory responsibility in only four areas: antitrust, financial institutions, transportation, and communications. In 1976 eighty-three federal agencies were engaged in regulating some aspect of private activity.

Even more relevant to my theme is the changing nature of government intervention. Addressed to much more intricate and difficult objectives, the newer programs are different; and the older ones have taken on more ambitious goals. In the field of energy and the environment the generally accepted objectives of national policy imply a staggeringly complex and interlocking set of actions, directly affecting the production and consumption decisions of every citizen and every business firm.

In a society that relies on private enterprise and market incentives to carry out most productive activity, the problem of intervention is a real one. After the decision to intervene has been taken, there remains a critical choice to be made: should intervention be carried out by grafting a specific command-and-control module—a regulatory apparatus—onto the system of private enterprise, or by modifying the informational flow, institutional structure, or incentive pattern of that private system? Neither approach is appropriate to every situation. But our political system almost always chooses the command-and-control response, regardless of whether that response fits the problem.

Once a political battle to intervene has been won in some broad area—environmental control, reduction of industrial accidents, or standards for nursing homes and day-care centers—the extent and scope of the resulting social controls are seldom grounded in an analysis of where and to what extent the private market has failed to meet acceptable standards. Similarly, there is seldom any attempt to design techniques of intervention that preserve some of the virtues of the free market.

VIRTUES OF THE MARKET

We acknowledge the power of economic incentives to foster steadily improving efficiency, and we employ it to bring us whitewall tires, cosmetics, and television sets. But for something really important like education, we eschew incentives. We would laugh if someone suggested that the best way to reduce labor input per unit of production was to set up a government agency to specify labor input in detail for each industry. But that is precisely how we go about trying to reduce environmental damage and industrial accidents.

The buyer-seller relationships of the marketplace have substantial advantages as a form of social organization. In the first place, relationships in the market are a form of unanimous-consent arrangement. When dealing with each other in a buy-sell transaction, individuals can act voluntarily on the basis of mutual advantage. Organizing large-scale social activity through the alternative open to a free society—democratic majoritarian politics—necessarily implies some minority that disapproves of each particular decision. To urge that the principle of voluntary decision should be given weight is not to make it the sole criterion. But precisely because the legitimate occasions for social intervention will increase as time goes on, preserving and expanding the role of choice take on added importance.

A second advantage of the market as an organizing principle for social activity is that it reduces the need for hard-to-get information. The more complicated and extensive the social intervention, and the more it seeks to alter individual behavior, the more difficult it becomes to accumulate the necessary information at a central level. Obviously, one does not rush out, on the basis of informational economies alone, and recommend, for example, that simple effluent charges displace all pollution-control regulations. But, where feasible, building some freedom of choice into social programs does offer advantages, either in generating explicit information for policy-makers about the desirability of alternative outcomes or in bypassing the need for certain types of information altogether.

A third advantage of the market is its "devil take the hindmost" approach to questions of individual equity. At first blush this is an outrageous statement and, obviously, I have stated the point in a way designed more to catch the eye than to be precise. To elaborate, in any except a completely stagnant society, an efficient use of resources means constant change. From the standpoint of static efficiency, the more completely and rapidly the economy shifts to meet changes in consumer tastes, production technologies, resource availability, and locational advantages, the greater the efficiency. From a dynamic standpoint, the greater the advances in technology and the faster they are adopted, the greater the efficiency. While these changes on balance generate gains for society in the form of higher living standards, almost every one of them deprives some firms and individuals of income. Under the social arrangements of the private market, those who may suffer losses are not usually able to stand in the way of change.

Dealing with the problem of losses is one of the stickiest social issues. There is absolutely nothing in either economic or political theory to argue that efficiency considerations should always take precedence. And sometimes there is no way to avoid unconscionably large losses to some group except by avoiding or at least moderating changes otherwise called for by efficiency considerations. Nevertheless, in designing instruments for collective intervention that will avoid loss, we place far too much stress on eschewing efficient solutions, and far too little on compensation and general income-redistribution measures. Over time, the cumulative consequences are likely to be a much smaller pie for everyone.

The final virtue of market-like arrangements that I wish to stress is their potential ability to direct innovation into socially desirable directions. While the formal economic theory of the market emphasizes its ability to get the most out of existing resources and technology, what is far more important is its apparent capacity to stimulate and take advantage of advancing technology. Living standards in modern Western countries are, by orders of magnitude, superior to those of the early seventeenth century. Had the triumph of the market meant only a more efficient use of the technologies and resources then available, the gains in living standards would have been minuscule by comparison. What made the difference was the stimulation and harnessing of new technologies and resources.

From a long-range standpoint, the effectiveness of social intervention in a number of important areas depends critically on heeding this lesson. Much of the economic literature on pollution control, for example, stresses the role of economic incentives to achieve static efficiency in control measures—that is, the use of existing technology in a way that reaches environmental goals at least cost. In the long run, however, the future of society is going to hinge on the discovery and adoption of ever-improving technologies to reduce the environmental consequences of expanding production. If, for example, we assume that per capita living standards in the United States improve from now on at only one-half the rate of the past century, the gross national product a hundred years from now will still have risen more than threefold. Median family income, now about $14,000, will equal about $55,000. Only if the amount of pollution per unit of output is cut by two-thirds can we maintain current environmental performance, let alone improve it—even on the assumption that the rate of economic growth is halved. There is simply no way such reductions can be achieved unless the direction of technological change is shifted to minimize pollution.

The point is not that the unfettered market can deal with the problem of environmental quality—or other problems for which some form of regulation already exists. Indeed, the problems arise precisely because the market as it is now structured does not work well. But the historically demonstrated power of market-like incentives warrants every effort to install such incentives in our programs of social intervention.

THE CAUSES OF MARKET FAILURE

Within the sphere of activities not excluded from the market by considerations of liberty and dignity, there remain many situations in which private enterprise operating in a free market as we now know it does not produce efficient results. Where the deviations are serious, a prima facie case arises for collective intervention on grounds of efficiency alone.

Every modern society is based upon a set of property and contract laws that specify a highly complex set of does and don'ts with respect to owning, using, buying, and selling property. The structure of the private enterprise system and the efficiency with which it operates depend on the content of this system of laws. How efficiently that system works at any point in time is strongly conditioned by how well it matches the underlying technological and economic realities.

A second basic proposition underlies an identification and analysis of market failure: to be an efficient instrument for society a private market must be so organized that buyers and sellers realize *all* the benefits and pay *all* the costs of each transaction. In other words, the price paid by the buyer and the costs incurred by the seller in each private transaction must reflect the full value and the full cost of that transaction not only to them, but to society as a whole.

As a rough-and-ready generalization, the body of laws governing property rights and liabilities is likely to yield inefficient results principally when dealing with the side effects of private market transactions. The problem is not that side effects exist, but that the benefits they confer or the costs they impose are often not reflected in the prices and costs that guide private decisions.

Where side effects are confined to the parties to a transaction, proper specification of the laws governing private property can sometimes ensure that they are properly reflected in the private accounting of costs and benefits. Under these circumstances, establishing some continuing mechanism of social intervention is unnecessary. Individual buy-and-sell arrangements can efficiently reflect social values. In many cases, however, the very nature of the situation is such that merely redefining property rights will not resolve the problem; markets can be organized by purely private efforts only at great costs, if at all.

There are essentially four sets of factors that lead to market failure: high transaction costs, large uncertainty, high information costs, and, finally, what economists call the "free rider" problem.

Transaction costs

Markets are not costless. There are expenses of money, time, and effort in setting and collecting prices. Sometimes transaction costs are virtually infinite: there is no conceivable way that a market can be formed to deal with side effects. Sometimes transaction costs, while not infinite, exceed the benefits that a market could otherwise confer, and so it does not pay to set one up. Very often the scope and nature of the transaction costs strongly limit the range of effective social intervention and force society to organize markets in less than an ideal way.

Uncertainty and Information Costs

It is easier to treat the problems of uncertainty and information costs together since it is through information that we can, at least sometimes, reduce uncertainty. Market transactions cannot be an efficient method of organizing human activity unless both the buyer and the seller understand the full costs and benefits to them of the transactions they undertake, including any side effects that impinge on their own welfare.

However, in the case of hazards that are highly complicated, the provision of technically complete but neutral information may not be very helpful. Evaluating the significance of such hazards may itself require more technical ability and judgment and more time than it is reasonable to expect from most consumers. Where the potential harms from a product feature are serious and where the technical difficulty of evaluating information is very great, regulation may be the best alternative despite its inefficiencies—and in some cases a ban on certain types of products may be required. But in all cases the comparison should be between an imperfect market and an imperfect regulatory scheme, not some ideal abstraction.

The "Free Rider" Problem

Where the side effects of private transactions have a common impact on many people—for example, in the discharge of sulfur into the atmosphere from coal-burning utilities—the possibility of purely private action is severely limited. In theory, if the rights to the use of the clean air were assigned by law to the polluter, those affected might band together and pay the polluter to reduce the emissions. But any one individual would enjoy the benefits of the improvement whether he paid his share of the cost or not. He could be a "free rider" on the efforts of everyone else. How could cost shares be decided and enforced? Without the coercive power of government, purely voluntary arrangements could not be successful.

CHANGING ATTITUDES

Relying on regulations rather than economic incentives to deal with highly complex areas of behavior, as we do for control of air and water pollution and industrial health and safety, has a built-in dynamic that inevitably broadens the scope of the regulations. Under an incentive-oriented approach—effluent charges, injury-rate taxes, or improved workmen's compensation—the administering agency does not itself have to keep abreast of every new development. The incentives provide a general penalty against unwanted actions. But if specific regulations are the only bar to prevent social damages, the regulating agency must provide a regulation for every possible occasion and circumstance. First it will take twenty-one pages to deal with ladders and then even more as time goes on. Social intervention becomes a race between the ingenuity of the regulatee and the loophole closing of the regulator, with a continuing expansion in the volume of regulations as the outcome.

We try to specify in minute detail the particular actions that generate social efficiency and then command their performance. But in certain complex areas of human behavior, neither our imagination nor our commands are up to the task. Consistently, where social problems arise because of distorted private incentives, we try to impose a solution without remedying the incentive structure. And equally consistently, the power of that structure defeats us.

Market-like instruments can supplant current command-and-control techniques only gradually. But not much thought has been devoted to dynamic strategies that, step by step, mesh a dwindling reliance on regulations with a cautiously expanding use of market instruments.

When social intervention into new areas is considered, we start with a more or less clean blackboard. We do not have to erase an existing maze of command-and-control laws. But a different kind of problem then confronts us—impatience. Major political initiatives come only after the public has been persuaded that an important problem exists. A sense of urgency has developed. How can politicians then put before the public a ten-year plan for gradually developing a new market structure? Instead, the inevitable strategy is to enact ambitious legislation stipulating sharp and immediate results, and then to erode the regulations piecemeal with postponements and loopholes as problems develop. The very rhetoric and political process that moves us finally to get something done often puts us in a position where that something is done poorly.

The American political system has been a marvelously effective tool for providing both freedom and governance. Its institutions have been well suited for generating the compromises and accommodations about national issues needed in a large and heterogeneous society. But those institutions were especially designed to settle conflicts of value. As society has intervened in ever more complicated areas, however, and particularly as it aims to influence the decisions of millions of individuals and business firms, the critical choices have a much lower ideological and ethical content. For economic or social reasons, we may still want to move some area of decision-making completely out of the market and into the sphere of specified rights and duties. And the necessity will remain to form political battle lines around the very real question of whether to intervene at all. We cannot abandon the standard techniques and institutions for forming consensus and negotiating compromises among groups with widely different values.

But how does an ingrained political process which stresses value adjustments come to grips with the critical choices among technically complicated alternatives when some of the very political techniques that move society toward a decision themselves make it difficult to pursue workable methods of intervention? Identifying heroes and villains, imputing values to technical choices, stressing the urgency of every problem, promising speedy results, and offering easily understandable solutions which specify outputs and rights—these are the common techniques of the political process whereby consensus is formed and action taken.

There is no obvious resolution to this dilemma. The suggestion that the political debate be confined to ends, while technicians and experts design the means once the ends have been decided, is facile and naive. Ends and means cannot and should not be separated. In the real world they are inextricably joined: we formulate our ends only as we debate the means of satisfying them. No electorate or politician can afford to turn over the crucial question of how social intervention is to be designed to supposedly apolitical experts.

The only available course is a steady maturing of both the electorate and political leaders. How to intervene, when we choose to do so, is ultimately a political issue. I am convinced that the economic and social forces that flow from growth and affluence will continue to throw up problems and attitudes that call for intervention of a very complex order. How we handle those questions not only will determine our success in meeting particular problems, but cumulatively will strongly influence the political and social fabric of our society. Even if it were politically possible—which it is not—we cannot handle the dilemma by abjuring any further extension of interventionist policies. But, equally, we cannot afford to go on imposing command-and-control solutions over an ever-widening sphere of social and economic activity.

I believe—I have no choice but to believe—that the American people can deal intelligently with issues painted in hues more subtle than black and white. Indeed, the political winds of the last few years can be read as a sign that the electorate is somewhat ahead of many of its political leaders. Voters are not disillusioned with government per se. But they are fed up with simple answers to complicated problems. They are ready, I think, for a more realistic political dialogue. Almost two centuries ago the arguments for the ratification of the Constitution were laid out in *The Federalist* papers—perhaps the most sophisticated effort at political pamphleteering in history. I have good reason to hope—and to believe—that voters can accept the same high level of political argument as the farmers, mechanics, and politicians of the eighteenth-century colonies.

Increasing Bureaucratization, Social Efficiency, and Individual Freedom

ANTHONY DOWNS

INTRODUCTION

There is a widespread belief that U.S. society is becoming more and more "bureaucratized" because of the rising prominence of large organizations in American life. This trend is universally regarded as undesirable. Its stronger critics think that the average individual will become enmeshed in a tightening net of rules and regulations formulated by huge, "faceless" organizations. They also fear that society will become dominated by empire building, wasteful spending, egregious blunders, miles of red tape, frustrating delays, "buck-passing," and other horrors they attribute to bureaucracy.

This chapter will discuss whether or not bureaucratization is really increasing, what might be causing its prevailing trends, and what their likely impact will be upon individual freedom and the efficiency of social action.

IS SOCIETY BECOMING MORE BUREAUCRATIC?

The following phenomena could be interpreted as evidence that a given society is becoming more bureaucratic:

- A rising proportion of the labor force employed by large, nonmarket organizations (such as government agencies).

- Increasing regulation of political, economic, social, and cultural life by such organizations.

- A rising proportion of the labor force consisting of persons who work for large, market-oriented firms but who produce outputs that cannot be evaluated in markets. This could occur in one or both of the following ways:

    1. A rising proportion of the labor force employed in large firms, but without any accompanying change in the proportion of employees within those firms who produce no directly marketable products.
    2. A shift of employment distribution within large firms that increases the proportion of workers therein who produce no directly marketable products.

Since this is primarily a theoretical study, we will not try to make a thorough examination of the facts concerning these potential indicators. Rather, we will merely cite a few relevant statistics.

First, the proportion of the total labor force in the United States employed by all governments is rising at an impressive rate. This is shown in the accompanying table.

Total Government Employment Including Military

Year	Number (thousands)	Percentage of Total Employed Labor Force
1900	1,110	4.1%
1910	1,736	4.9
1920	2,529	6.3
1930	3,310	7.3
1940	3,762	8.3
1950	7,245	12.3
1960	10,867	15.7
1965	12,534	16.8

Sources: U.S. Bureau of the Census, *Statistical Abstract of the United States: 1965*, 86th Edition (Washington, D.C., 1965), pp. 216, 440; Council of Economic Advisers, *Economic Indicators: November 1965*, (Washington, D.C., 1965), pp. 10–13; Solomon Fabricant, *The Trend of Government Activity in the United States Since 1900* (New York: National Bureau of Economic Research, 1952).

Since most government employees work in bureaus, this is significant evidence that the government bureaucracy of the United States is growing both absolutely and relatively. Moreover, it has grown considerably faster since World War II than it did before.

Second, we cannot formulate any measures that would reliably indicate whether the degree of regulation by bureaus is rising or falling. However, there is a widespread informal consensus that the absolute level of government regulation over a wide spectrum of activities has markedly increased since World War II. This conclusion is supported by the fact that governments employ a higher proportion of the labor force and absorb a higher proportion of the total national output than ever before in peacetime.

Third, there is some evidence that large firms in the private sector of the U.S. economy have recently grown faster than small ones. From 1947 to 1961, the number of corporations rose 115.6 per cent, whereas the total number of firms rose only 41.0 per cent.[1] Although not all corporations are large, average total receipts per corporation in 1961 were $692,389. This is 37 times greater than the analogous average for sole proprietorships ($18,500), and almost nine times greater than the average for active partnerships ($78,182). Moreover, although corporations comprised only 10.5 per cent of all private firms in 1961, they took in 77.1 per cent of all private business receipts. These data also indicate that corporations have grown in relative importance, since in 1947 they comprised 6.8 per cent of all firms and took in 68.8 per cent of all private business receipts.

These figures do not prove that large private firms employ a higher proportion of the total labor force than they did right after World War II. However, the data do indicate that they account for a growing proportion of total employment by all private firms, thereby increasing the possibility that a person working for a private firm will be a bureaucrat since bureaucrats can exist only in large organizations.

Finally, within large private firms there has been a significant shift from production jobs to administrative jobs.[2] By 1964 this percentage had risen to 26.0. Production jobs are much easier to relate to market prices through cost accounting methods than administrative jobs. Hence this rise in the relative significance of administration in manufacturing firms indicates at least a strong possibility that bureaucracy in such firms has increased.

Admittedly, the above evidence is hardly conclusive. Nevertheless, it tends to provide some confirmation for the impression that bureaucratization in the United States is on the increase.

SOME POSSIBLE CAUSES OF INCREASING BUREAUCRATIZATION

Four possible causes of such increasing bureaucratization are all connected with the tendencies of modern societies to grow larger in total population, more complex in specialization, more sophisticated in technology, more urbanized, and wealthier per capita as time passes.

First, as societies become more complex, they generate more conflicts requiring settlement through nonmarket action, particularly government action. The economic growth of modern societies has occurred through more intensive division of labor, as well as greater extension of given techniques and organization. Intensive specialization generates an extremely complicated web of relationships among individuals. Many of these relationships involve externalities, that is, actions of one individual that directly affect the welfare of others without passing through a market. Moreover, because urbanization groups people close together, increasing urbanization plus more intensive specialization are likely to cause a continuous rise in the proportion of all relationships that have such external effects. These effects frequently lead to regulation by nonmarket organizations, as pointed out in Chapter IV.

Second, the growing population and wealth of modern societies tend to increase the average size of many organizations therein, and large size is a necessary characteristic of bureaucracy. Private firms become larger because the possibilities of mass producing specialized goods create economies of scale, making big firms more efficient. Governmental agencies become larger because they must deal with bigger constituencies, or handle more complex interdependencies with other agencies (including other bureaus). The larger an organization becomes, the higher the probability that jobs therein will meet our four criteria for bureaucratic positions.

Third, technological change has encouraged mechanization of market-oriented jobs. These jobs have two characteristics conducive to mechanization. The processes they involve and the outputs they produce are more clearly definable, and any operation must be precisely defined before it can be mechanized. It is also easier to make economic calculations involving such jobs, since the costs and revenues involved can also be clearly identified. This makes it simpler to decide whether substitution of machinery for labor will pay off. Faster mechanization of nonbureaucratic jobs tends to increase the proportion of bureaucrats in the employed labor force (though not necessarily the proportion of their outputs in the total output volume).

Fourth, as societies grow wealthier, their members prefer more of those goods best furnished by nonmarket-oriented organizations. Economists have long noted systematic shifts in the composition of a nation's labor force as its per capita income rises. At first the proportion of workers in the primary occupations (mining, fishing, agriculture) declines, and that in secondary occupations (manufacturing and material processing) rises. Then secondary employment begins to decline relative to that in tertiary occupations (distribution and services), perhaps even in absolute terms. The latter shift may include an increased emphasis on certain services that must be (or have traditionally been) furnished by nonmarket-oriented organizations. One example is education; another is public subsidization of non-self-supporting aesthetic or recreational facilities, such as art museums, music centers, sports stadia, and large parks.

HAS THERE BEEN AN EXCESSIVE EXPANSION OF BUREAUS?

These reasons for expecting increased bureaucratization do not provide any indication of whether the actual expansion of bureaus is likely to correspond to their theoretically optimal growth. This problem can be restated as follows:

1. Is there any inherent tendency for an excessive number of bureaus to exist, either because too many are created or because obsolete bureaus fail to disappear?
2. Is there any inherent tendency for each individual bureau to expand excessively in total output, in units of input per unit of output, or in total scope of activities?
3. Is there any inherent tendency for all bureaus considered as a whole to expand excessively in total output, in units of input per unit of output, or in total scope of activities?

Clearly, the concept of "excessiveness" must be defined unequivocally before these questions can be answered. Yet this is impossible. Since the value of a bureau's output cannot be determined in a free market, it must be determined some other way, often through political choice mechanisms. With different values existing in society, bureau outputs worthless to some people may be extremely beneficial to others. This makes it almost impossible to determine their true value. The above questions then are essentially ethical or political in nature, and cannot be answered scientifically.

This does not mean that no scientific measures of efficiency can ever be applied to the operations of individual bureaus. In many cases, certain ways of doing things can definitely be proved superior to others. Also, scientific analysis can be an extremely valuable aid to bureau decisionmaking even when the ultimate choices depend upon values or opinions. Furthermore, we can intuitively postulate that the total amount of waste and inefficiency in society is likely to rise as bureaucracy becomes more prominent. This seems probable because true waste is so much harder to define and detect in bureaus than in private firms. Also, there are no automatic mechanisms for limiting it in the former as there are in the latter. This admittedly untestable conclusion implies that society should arrange to have services produced by market-oriented firms rather than bureaus when possible, other things being equal. However, it does not imply that recent trends toward bureaucratization of society are excessive or will become so in the future.

Even though our theory does not enable us to judge whether bureaucratization has become excessive, it does provide an important conclusion relevant to this issue. Critics of bureaus often claim that their growth has been excessive because it results from inherent tendencies to expand rather than from any true social needs for the service. However, bureaus cannot expand without additional resources, which they must obtain either through voluntary contributions or from some government allocation agency. But, as we have seen, in a democratic society these external agents will not give a bureau such resources unless it produces outputs of commensurate value to them (assuming the bureau is not a military organization willing to coerce them). Hence, in a gross sense, bureaus do engage in voluntary *quid pro quo* transactions with the agents that support them. Therefore, the recent expansion of bureaus in democracies has occurred largely in accordance with the desires of major nonbureaucratic institutions therein. Consequently, we may presume that these institutions do not believe the overall bureaucratization of society has been excessive, or they would not continue to support them.

This conclusion is valid even if every citizen believes that a majority of all government bureaucratic effort is wasteful. Each citizen can easily identify many government bureaus whose costs to him outweigh the benefits they provide him. But certain other bureaus provide a surplus of benefits to a minority of citizens, including him. These beneficiaries must form coalitions with the supporters of other minority-serving bureaus in order to obtain such large benefits. As long as the total utility received by most citizens in this logrolling process exceeds the total cost they pay, they tacitly support the resulting expansion of bureaucracy, even though they may overtly complain loudly about waste in those bureaus that do not benefit them directly.

If the bureaucracy as a whole were really excessive in size, some political party would advocate drastic reductions affecting a whole spectrum of minority-serving bureaus. This party would receive the vote of every citizen who believed he was paying more to support wasteful bureaus than he was receiving from those minority-serving bureaus that benefited him directly. If such citizens were in the majority, the bureau-wrecking party would be elected, and would presumably slash the size of the bureaucracy as a whole. Until this occurs, we are forced to conclude that the overall size of the bureaucracy is not excessive in relation to the services it is providing for society.[3]

This conclusion does not apply in nondemocratic societies. Since genuine opposition parties are not allowed to exist, the citizenry is never given a chance to vote on whether to accept the *status quo* or to engage in wholesale bureau reduction. Moreover, the reigning group controls the government, and probably indulges in the inherent tendency of government bureaus to expand. Hence it is likely that the government bureaucracy is actually excessive in all nondemocratic societies.

INDIVIDUAL FREEDOM AND THE GROWTH OF BUREAUCRACY

Comparing present life in the United States with that of past decades, we can hardly doubt that bureaus exert a growing absolute level of control over individuals. Everyone finds himself forced to fill out more forms, pay more taxes to support bureaus, obey more bureaucratic rules, and otherwise interact with more officials than ever before. Nevertheless, it would be a gross error to conclude from this

rich men more free than poor, because he has more choice open to him

that bureaus have reduced individual freedom of choice. The word *freedom* has two very different meanings: power of choice, and absence of restraint. It is true that bureaus place far more restraints on the average man today than they did formerly. However, today's citizen also enjoys a much greater range in choice of possible behavior than his predecessors did. Moreover, the number of behavioral options open to him is growing every year through such changes as supersonic aircraft, new medicines, rising real income, increased foreign trade, better highways, longer vacations, higher retirement pensions, and a host of others.

This analysis suggests four significant conclusions. First, the average individual's overall freedom is actually expanding rapidly. Even though the regulations imposed upon him by bureaus continue to multiply, his action alternatives multiply even faster.

Second, increased bureaucratic regulations are actually one of the causes of his greater freedom. The forces generating ever wider options are the same ones that generate the need for more bureaucratic rules. Without increased bureaucratic regulation, such forces as technological change, urbanization, and more intensive division of labor would either be impossible, or would lead to greater social disorganization and a narrower range of choice for the individual. Thus, greater bureaucratization is one of the inherent costs of greater freedom of choice, and could not be abolished without reducing that freedom.

Third, it is true that bureaus often place more restraints upon individuals than are necessary to accomplish their social functions. Thus, even though the total effect of increased bureaucratization is an expansion of individual choice, the marginal effect of some regulations is an unnecessary restriction of choice designed mainly to benefit the bureau's members.

Fourth, it is conceivable that bureaucratization might someday become so extensive as to result in an overall reduction of freedom of choice. This could happen if bureaus took over nearly all economic production and operated it without any market orientation. They might reduce total output significantly below what it would be under private market-oriented management. Or they might alter the composition of final output so that it did not correspond very closely to what consumers really desired (as has happened in the Soviet Union). Government bureaus might also control most of the country's activity and use a centralized personnel control system. Then occupational choices might be severely restricted for individuals considered undesirable by any one bureau. Even if no such system existed, persons with certain technical specialties might find their job choices limited if a single government bureau controlled all positions requiring their skills. This is true now regarding customs inspectors and supersonic bomber pilots. Whenever men know their livelihood is permanently dependent on a single employer, their willingness to voice opinions or undertake acts disapproved by that employer drops sharply. Hence the myriad-firm private economic sector plays a crucial political role as a source of market-oriented production jobs.

These freedom-reducing results of over-bureaucratization already exist in some nations. However, we do not believe they are very probable in the United States in the near future, except in a few occupations monopolized by individual bureaus. In the foreseeable future, then, the growth of bureaus in the United States will continue to represent the interaction of a long-run trend toward increasing individual choice, and short-run maneuvers by individual bureaucrats producing unnecessary restraints and inefficiencies.

NOTES

1. U.S. Bureau of Census, *Statistical Abstract of the United States: 1965* (86th Edition) Washington, D.C., pp. 489–508.
2. *Ibid.*, p. 221.
3. Further analysis of this problem is presented in A. Downs, *An Economic Theory of Democracy;* "Why the Government Budget Is Too Small in a Democracy," pp. 563; and "In Defense of Majority Voting," *Journal of Political Economy,* Vol. LXIX, No. 2 (April 1961), pp. 192–199.

14

CONTROLLING
THE BUREAUCRACY

Related to the issues of size and role of public bureaucracy, discussed in the preceding chapter, are the issues associated with the political control of bureaucratic power. In post-Watergate America, the problems of accountability and responsibility seem especially important.

Students of public administration have long realized that a *system* of restraints, always undergoing change, in effect controls the power of public bureaucracies. These restraints may be broadly divided into two types—*intra*governmental and *extra*governmental.

Regarding intragovernmental vehicles for control, most notable in the American context is the separation of powers. Through hearings and investigations, review of the budget, audits, confirmation of appointments, staff assistance, and individual monitoring of constituency complaints, legislative control of bureaucratic power has been especially important. The courts are increasingly active, and judicial review is also important. These were discussed at length in Chapter 4.

Hierarchical administration, sometimes referred to as "overhead democracy," is also an important vehicle. Chief political executives are frequently elected in our republican form of government, and citizens expect them to hold the bureaucracy accountable. This was discussed in the federal and state contexts in chapter 3. Increasingly, chief executives at all levels of American government have increased the size of their staffs to assist them in this function. Consolidation and centralization of agency structures is one common device. Increasingly, chief executives also use modern management techniques and information systems to supervise public agencies under their control.

The final intragovernmental factor that merits attention but is often neglected in the literature is internal control within the bureaucracy. Included here is administrative self-restraint, because—as many believe—total outside control is probably impossible. Increasing the sense of personal responsibility among public employees at all levels of government is one of the critical issues of our time. Ombudsmen and inspector generals seem to be increasing. There is also increasing discussion of using the market model—or competition—within public agencies as well as increased privatization of public services.

Extragovernmental forces are represented primarily by a variety of competing interest groups, political parties, the press, public opinion, and increasingly direct citizen participation. Scholarly research can also be included here.

Trends in the political control of bureaucratic power and the effectiveness of this system are the principal topics of discussion in this chapter. With recent revelations about the activities of the CIA, FBI, and IRS—not to mention former President Nixon's "enemies list"—controlling the bureaucracy is a topic of permanent importance as well as contemporary controversy.

This discussion begins with Herbert Kaufman's examination of the historic conflict among three contending factors in local government—the strength of the political executive, the demand for representativeness, and the need for politically neutral competence, embodied in the permanent bureaucracy. Issues of control, then, need to be understood in a broader context.

James Sundquist reiterates the essential importance of separation of powers and the need to make legislative bodies full partners in contemporary policy making. He also has some suggestions for changing the national patterns of checks and balances.

An important issue at all levels of government is the reduction of government secrecy and the increase in freedom of information. Open-meeting laws and open government files for the media and individual citizens are two areas in which there has been much recent legislation. Allen Schick examines the federal experience with the Freedom of Information act.

Direct citizen participation in agency decision making that affects their lives has been advocated by many contemporary observers. Governor Edmund G. (Jerry) Brown, Jr., of California outlines his reasons for promoting this practice as follows: "A Society *of* the People. And *by*. And *for*." Orion White provides a conceptual framework for understanding the potential role of clients as decision makers in public agencies.

Rufus Miles next speaks up for the public employee. Miles argues that the public worker must have a higher loyalty, a commitment to a public service ethic.

In an effort to place these various perspectives in a single context, Amitai Etzioni looks at accountability as a political process, as a system of checks and balances, as a symbolic process, and still more. He adds to this an active role for the individual public administrator. Etzioni's examples are drawn from the area of health care administration.

Administrative Decentralization and Political Power

HERBERT KAUFMAN

Curious as it may seem today, bureaucrats in the '30's were regarded by many as heroes in the struggles for a better social order. As late as 1945, Paul Appleby, a prominent New Deal official, felt impelled to dedicate a book to "Bill Bureaucrat,"[1] and much of the literature of professional and academic public administration had a confident, approving, consensual tone.

By mid-'50's it was possible to discern emerging conflicts of doctrine and practice among those who previously applauded and defended bureaucrats. A major shift of outlook and values in governmental design seemed to be taking place.

It was not the first such shift to occur in our history. On the contrary, the administrative history of our governmental machinery can be construed as a succession of shifts of this kind, each brought about by a change in emphasis among three values: representativeness, politically neutral competence, and executive leadership.[2] None of these values was ever totally neglected in any of our past modifications of governmental design, but each enjoyed greater emphasis than the others in different periods.

Thus, for example, our earliest political institutions at all levels can be interpreted as reactions against executive dominance in the colonial era. Later on, extreme reliance was placed on representative mechanisms, which made the post-Revolutionary years an interval of great power for legislatures and elective officials and of comparative weakness for executives in most jurisdictions. By the middle of the 19th century, however, legislative supremacy, the long ballot, and the spoils system resulted in widespread disillusionment with our political institutions, which in turn gave impetus to efforts to take administration out of politics by lodging it in independent boards and commissions and by introducing the merit system to break the hold of parties on the bureaucracies. But the fragmentation of government reduced both efficiency and representativeness, and the search for unification led to the popularly elected chief executives; the 20th century was marked by a rapid growth in their powers.

This is not to say the values are pursued abstractly, as ends in themselves, or that there is universal agreement on which should be emphasized at any given time. On the contrary, different segments of the population feel differentially disadvantaged by the governmental machinery in operation at any given moment, and agitate for structural changes to improve their position—i.e., to increase their influence—in the system. Discontent on the part of various groups is thus the dynamic force that motivates the quest for new forms. Some groups feel resentful because they consider themselves inadequately represented; some feel frustrated because, though they are influential in forming policy, the policy decisions seem to be dissipated by the political biases or the technical incompetence of the public bureaucracies; some feel thwarted by lack of leadership to weld the numerous parts of government into a coherent, unified team that can get things done. At different points in time, enough people (not necessarily a numerical majority) will be persuaded by one or another of these discontents to support remedial action—increased representativeness, better and politically neutral bureaucracies, or stronger chief executives as the case may be. But emphasis on one remedy over a prolonged period merely accumulates the other discontents until new remedies gain enough support to be put into effect, and no totally stable solution has yet been devised. So the constant shift in emphasis goes on.

No matter how vigorous the pursuit of any one value at any given time, the other two are never obliterated. And no matter how determined the quest for any one value, it is never realized as fully as its most extreme advocates would like. Even after a century of efforts to strengthen neutral competence and executive leadership, partisan influence still retains great vitality and executive institutions at all levels of government are still remarkably fragmented. And after a century of denigration of "politics," politicans, and "special interests," representativeness is still a powerful force in American government. But in that century of building professional bureacracies and executive capacities for leadership, the need for new modes of representation designed to keep pace with new economic, social, and political developments did not arouse equal concern. Partly for this reason, and partly because the burgeoning of large-scale organizations in every area of life contributes to the sensation of individual helplessness, recent years have witnessed an upsurge of a sense of alienation on the part of many people, to a feeling that they as individuals cannot effectively register their own preferences on the decisions emanating from the organs of government. These people have begun to demand redress of the balance among the three values, with special attention to the deficiencies in representativeness.

CURRENT DISSATISFACTION

America is not wanting in arrangements for representation. More than half a million public offices are still elective.[3] Legislatures and individual legislators retain immense powers, and do not hesitate to wield them liberally. Parties are still strong and attentive to the claims of many constituencies. Interest groups are numerous and press their demands through myriad channels. The mass media serve as watchdogs of governmental operations. Administrative agencies incorporate manifold procedures for representation into their decision-making processes, including quasi-judicial and quasi-legislative hearings, representative or bipartisan administrative boards, and advisory bodies.[4] Opportunities for participation in political decisions are plentiful. Why, then, is there dissatisfaction with these arrangements?

Fundamentally, because substantial (though minority) segments of the population apparently believe the political, economic, and social systems have not delivered to them fair—even minimally fair—shares of the system's benefits and rewards, and because they think they cannot win their appropriate shares in those benefits and rewards through the political institutions of the country as these are now constituted. These people are not mollified by assurances that the characteristics of the system thwarting them also thwart selfish and extremist interests; it appears to them that only the powerful get attention, and that the already powerful are helped by the system to deny influence to all who now lack it. Thus, the system itself, and not just evil men who abuse it, is discredited.

At least three characteristics of the system contribute heavily to this impression on the part of the deprived: first, existing representative organs are capable of giving only quite general mandates to administrative agencies, yet it is in the day-to-day decisions and actions of officials and employees in the lower levels that individual citizens perceive the policies. There are often gross discrepancies between the promise of the programs (as construed by the populace to be served) and performance—sometimes because programs are impeded by difficulties that could not be foreseen, and sometimes because bureaucracies are too bound by habit or timidity to alter their customary behavior in any but the most modest ways.[5]

Second, the pluralistic nature of the political system provides abundant opportunities for vetoes by opponents of change. Each proposed innovation must run a gamut of obstacles, and ends as a product of bargains and compromises. So change usually comes slowly, by small advances, in bits and pieces. Those who regard particular problems as requiring urgent, immediate action are prone to condemn a system that behaves so "sluggishly."

Third, the scale of organization in our society has grown so large that only through large-scale organization does it seem possible to have a significant impact. This impression alone is enough to make individual people feel helplessly overwhelmed by huge, impersonal machines indifferent to their uniqueness and their humanity. In addition, however, some interests—notably those of Negroes and of youth—have recently begun to develop the organizational skills to mobilize their political resources only to find that it takes time to build channels of access to political structures. Rather than wait for admission to these structures—where, incidentally, they are likely to encounter larger, more experienced, well-entrenched organizations opposed to them—these groups, while continuing to strive for recognition in the older institutions, have adopted a strategy of deriding those institutions and seeking to build new ones in which they can have greater, perhaps dominant, influence.

Thus, the plenitude of traditional modes of representation no longer suffices; the existing methods do not adequately accomodate many of the demands upon them. Just as the adaptation of governmental design during the past century has gravitated toward furnishing expertise and leadership, so it is now under pressure from several quarters to accord a greater role to representativeness.

INCREASING REPRESENTATIVENESS THROUGH ADMINISTRATIVE CHANGE

The quest for representativeness in this generation centers primarily on administrative agencies. Since administrative agencies have grown dramatically in size, function, and authority in the middle third of this century, this is hardly surprising. Chief executives, legislatures, and courts make more decisions of *sweeping* effect, but the agencies make a far greater number of decisions affecting individual citizens in *intimate* ways. In them lies the source of much present unrest; in them, therefore, the remedies are sought.

One type of proposal for making administrative agencies more representative is traditional in character; situating spokesmen for the interests affected in strategic positions within the organizations. Often, this means nothing more than filling vacancies on existing boards and commissions with appointees enjoying the confidence of, or perhaps even chosen by, those interests.[6] In the case of the controversial police review boards, it involves injecting into administrative structures new bodies, dominated by ethnic minority groups or their friends, to survey and constrain bureaucratic behavior. Architecturally, such plans do not require drastic modifications of existing organizations, and their objectives could probably be met by changes in personnel at high organizational levels.

More unorthodox, but swiftly gaining acceptance, is the concept of a centralized governmental complaint bureau, clothed with legal powers of investigation, to look into citizen complaints against administrative agencies and to correct inequities and abuses—the office of "ombudsman."[7] Once, it was chiefly through his representative in the appropriate legislative body, or through the local unit of his political party, that a citizen of modest status and means petitioned for a remedy of a grievance. But professionalization of administration and the insulation of bureaucrats from party politics have reduced the ability of the parties to be of real help, and the constituencies of legislators have grown so large that they rarely intervene in more than a *pro forma* fashion on behalf of most individual constituents. Today, some observers contend that only a specialized, full-time official, wise in the ways of bureaucracy, having a vested interest in correcting its errors, and supported by adequate staff and authority, can perform this function effectively; apparently, it takes a bureaucrat to control a bureaucrat. Advocates of this proposed new agency defend it on the grounds that it would constitute a channel of representation for people who now have no satisfactory alternative.

The most sweeping expression of the unrest over lack of representativeness is the growing demand for extreme administrative decentralization, frequently coupled with insistence on local clientele domination of the decentralized organizations. Dramatic manifestations of this movement occurred in the antipoverty program and in education.

In the antipoverty program the original legislation included a provision that community action be "developed, conducted, and administered with maximum feasible participation of residents of the areas and members of the groups served." Initially by interpretation of the Office of Economic Opportunity, and later by statute, the provision was construed to mean that community action boards should try to allot some of their chairs to the poor, so that the poor would have a voice in the highest policy councils of the community programs. Whatever the original intent of the drafters of the phrase (about which there is some disagreement), it has come to mean the program is to be run in substantial degree *by* the poor, not merely *for* the poor.[8]

In public education the new trend is exemplified by recent events in New York City. During 1967, demands for decentralization of the municipal school system gathered force swiftly: Leaders in the state legislature urged it. Three separate public reports recommended it in the strongest possible terms. The mayor endorsed the principle unequivocally. When concrete proposals were introduced into the legislature the following year, however, vehement opposition from the teacher's union, the school administrators' association, and the City Board of Education resulted in modification of many of the provisions the objectors found unacceptable. The measure ultimately enacted emerged weaker than the plans favored by the advocates of decentralization, but it was a major step in their direction; the thrust toward decentralization and neighborhood control of schools was slowed but not stopped, and resistance, however determined and forceful, seemed destined to give way over a broad front.

The outcry has not been limited to the war on poverty and to education. It was taken up in public housing when the Secretary of Housing and Urban Development unveiled a program to modernize low-rent projects that included an augmented role for tenants in their operation.[9] At a meeting of the American Institute of Planners, a dissenting group, calling itself Planners for Equal Opportunity, demanded a larger place for the poor in city planning, and exhorted its members to engage in "advocate planning," which is to say expert counsel for neighborhood associations unhappy with official plans for renewal in their areas. New York City recently began experimenting with a process of "affiliating" its public hospitals with voluntary hospitals that would be responsible for their administration, a plan that would presumably include lay boards representing the community served by each institution, and its Police Department is cooperating with experimental community security patrols of locally recruited young people. Similarly, a neighborhood council in Washington, D.C., "asked for more citizen control over police, either in the form of local police aides or resurrection of the auxiliary police force used here in World War II." The American Assembly, assessing the role of law in a changing society, called for development of "rapid procedures at the neighborhood level . . . to adjudicate disputes over simple transactions."[10] In response to the Poor People's Campaign in Washington, "Five agencies—Health, Education and Welfare, Agriculture, Labor, Housing and Urban Development and the Office of Economic Opportunity—said they would review their plans to involve poor people themselves in local decisions affecting welfare, food, employment, housing and other antipoverty programs."[11]

The movement is not confined to public agencies; it reaches into colleges and universities, where students, often by direct action, have been asserting a claim to participation in the policies of these institutions—one activist reportedly going so far as to predict that American universities will soon resemble Latin American institutions, in which students hire and fire professors and determine the curricula. A sociologist recently suggested establishment of closed-circuit television stations in which the neighborhood listeners might control programming.[12] In the Roman Catholic Archdiocese of New York, a committee of priests presented a petition to the archbishop-designate requesting, among other things, a voice in the selection of auxiliary bishops and other high officials, and establishment of a Pastoral Council of priests, nuns, and laymen to be consulted in advance on projected programs and budgets, a request to which he partially acceded on taking office. Later, priests formed a national organization, the National Federation of Priests Councils, to seek a stronger voice in church affairs. In Washington, D.C., classes at a high school were suspended in the face of a boycott by students demanding "a real say on what goes on inside the school."

But it is in the government sphere that the tendency has been winning widest endorsement. Indeed, some of our general forms of government, as well as specific agencies, have come under attack. The president of the American Political Science Association, for example, in his 1967 presidential address,[13] raised questions about the compatibility of large units of government—national, state, and urban—with the principles of democracy. Searching for a unit large enough to avoid triviality yet "small enough so that citizens can participate extensively," he suggested 50,000 to 200,000 as the optimum size range for democratic city governments. Moreover, he concluded that even in polities of this size, "participation is reduced for most people to nothing more than voting in elections," and he therefore commended experimentation to decentralize power and authority still further in order to discover viable "smaller units within which citizens can from time to time formulate and express their desires, consult with officials, and in some cases participate even more fully in decisions."

Similarly, the Advisory Commission on Intergovernmental Relations in Washington, at almost the same time, was recommending that "Neighborhood initiative and self-respect be fostered by authorizing counties and large cities to establish, and at their discretion to abolish, neighborhood subunits endowed with limited powers of taxation and local self-government."[14] At Ithaca, N.Y., the Office of Regional Resources and Development concluded that larger metropolitan centers should be decentralized because they have reached a point at which "it is almost impossible to deal with human problems on a human scale," and called for investigation of strategies for more effective use of cities with 50,000 to 500,000 residents—proposals that won the editorial plaudits of *The Washington Post*.[15]

A meeting of Americans for Democratic Action was warned by Daniel P. Moynihan, an outspoken liberal, that "Liberals must divest themselves of the notion that the nation, especially the cities of the nation, can be run from agencies in Washington.[16] Senator Robert F. Kennedy, campaigning for the Democratic presidential nomination in Los Angeles, promised audiences a revolution in the distribution of political power that would, among other things, reduce the authority of the federal bureaucracy in Washington. "I want," he said, "the control over your destinies to be decided by the people in Watts, not by those of us who are in Washington."[17] Richard M. Nixon similarly urged the federal government to relinquish some of its powers to state and local governments, voluntary associations, and individuals, saying, "One reason people are shouting so loudly today is that it's far from where they are to where the power is," and that power should be brought closer to them rather than exercised from remote centers. In important respects, the Heller-Pechman plan rests partly on the premise that federal surpluses should be shared with states and cities in time of peace because they can be more effectively spent by the smaller units of government than by Washington directly.[18]

In short, "decentralization" of administration is in the air everywhere.[19] While it is sometimes defended on grounds of efficiency, it is more frequently justified in terms of effective popular particpation in government. Reformers of earlier generations succeeded in raising the level of expertise and professionalism in the bureaucracies, and to a lesser extent, in improving capacity of chief executives to control the administrative arms of government. Now, people are once again turning their attention to representativeness, and are trying to elevate it to a more prominent place in the governmental scheme of things.

THE CONTINUING SEARCH FOR LEADERSHIP

Public bureaucracies are under fire not only from critics outside the machinery of government, but also from inside. Chief executives who once championed measures to insulate the bureaucracies from partisan politics as steps toward enlarging their own control over administrative agencies discovered that these measures did not make the agencies more responsive to executive direction; rather, they increased agency independence. This independence, in turn, makes it difficult for the executives to secure enthusiastic adoption of new approaches to social problems; money pumped into new programs administered by established agencies tends to be used more for intensification of traditional ways of operating than for inventive departures from familiar patterns. Furthermore, it results in massive problems of coordination of effort, and even in dissipation of energies in inter-bureau rivalries. Consequently, just as segments of the public are upset by the alleged unresponsiveness of administration to their demands, so chief executives have been increasingly concerned about the unresponsiveness of agencies to their leadership.

We may therefore look forward to new waves of administrative reorganization proposals. One principal thrust of the movement will, as in the past, be toward rationalizing, enlarging, and strengthening the executive-office staffs of the heads of governmental units at all levels, and toward building up the staffs of the administrators who report directly to the heads. More and more, chief executives will reach out for new devices to coordinate policy decisions, to work up fresh programs to deal with emergent problems, and to maintain the momentum of innovations adopted.[20] Executive offices will be redesigned; the U.S. Bureau of the Budget, for example, has only recently undergone a major reorganization.[21] New vigor will be applied to the exploration of "superdepartments," with the Department of Defense as a prototype; Mayor Lindsay, for instance, has expended much political capital on introducing this concept into the government of New York City. Programming-planning-budgeting systems, in many variants, will continue to spread.[22] There will be a new burst of literature calling attention to the relative powerlessness of our highest public executives.[23]

Another stream of recommendations will urge strengthening executive leadership through what its advocates will call "decentralization," but which, in fact, is better characterized as organization by area as opposed to the present almost exclusive organization by functional departments and bureaus.[24] The justification for it will be couched in terms of efficiency—the need to speed decisions in the field without referral to headquarters and without loss of coordination among field personnel in different bureaus. The consequences will extend further, however, because areal officers in the field would give top executives lines of communication and control alternative to existing functional channels, thus actually strengthening central authority. At the federal level, this will mean renewed attempts to set up much stronger regional representatives of the heads of cabinet departments than any we have had in the past. It will also mean intensified efforts to establish regional presidential representatives in the field.[25] Similarly, we may anticipate governors and their department heads will follow the same strategies with respect to regions within the states. At the local level, Mayor Lindsay has already sought—with very limited success—to win approval for "little city halls" throughout New York. Distinctively American versions of the European prefect may yet make an appearance.

In short, dissatisfaction with public bureaucracies will furnish ammunition for the defenders of executive leadership as well as for the proponents of increased representation of the consumers of public services. The bureaucracies will be pressed from both above and below.

CONFLICT AND COALITION

Sources of Conflict

It has long been recognized that much public policy is shaped largely by clusters of bureaus, their organized clienteles, and legislative committees and legislators specializing in each public function [26]—health, education, welfare, etc. The arguments for strengthening chief executives and their department heads *vis-à-vis* the clusters are based chiefly on the need to offset the resulting fragmentation of government by introducing sufficient central direction to unify the policies and administration of these separate centers of power. The arguments for new modes of participation by the public in these centers rest on the conviction that hitherto excluded and unorganized interests have little to say about decisions that affect them profoundly. But it is most unlikely that the arguments of either kind will be warmly received by those already in key positions in each decision center.

They will resist not simply out of abstract jealousy of their own power or stubborn unwillingness to share their influence with each other, though these motives will doubtless not be absent. They will oppose because, in addition, the proposed reforms threaten those values which present arrangements protect. Bureau chiefs and the organized bureaucracies perceive intervention by political executives as the intrusion of partisan politics into fields from which doctrine has for many years held that politics should be excluded; they see jeopardy for the competence nurtured so carefully and painfully against political distortion or extinction. Similarly, opening the system to lay members of local communities looks like a negation of the expertise built up by the specialist. Legislators regard strong regional officials responsive to chief executives and their cabinets as executive attempts to invade legislative districts and usurp the representative function of legislative bodies. In like fashion, local control of administrative programs could conceivably weaken the representative basis of legislative institutions, a development that men of goodwill may fear for quite public-spirited reasons.

So the champions of executive leadership and the evangelists of expanded representativeness have many obstacles to overcome before they have their respective ways. For example, Congress has been cautious about presidential recommendations of added funds and personnel for the heads of cabinet departments, and has always looked with suspicion on so relatively innocuous an innovation as field offices for the Bureau of the Budget. [27] The Office of Economic Opportunity in the Executive Office of the President always operated chiefly through established bureaus and engaged in independent administration only in limited ways; gradually, through delegation, it has been relinquishing its control over programs to the bureaus and the future of even those few programs it manages directly is uncertain. Moreover, its community-action program aroused resentment among both congressmen and local executives, to whom the action agencies appeared as springboards for political rivals; consequently, legislation in 1967 authorized greater control of the agencies by local governments. In New York City, the mayor's "little city halls," which he presented as a device for bringing the people and their government closer together, were soundly defeated by a City Council (dominated by the opposite party) denouncing the plan as a strategy for establishing political clubhouses throughout the city at public expense. [28] And, when the plan for school decentralization appeared, the largest teachers' union and the Board of Education—which not long before had been at each other's throats in labor disputes—each took a similar firm stand against it. In Board-sponsored experiments with community control of schools in Harlem and in Brooklyn, the community leaders and the head of the same teachers' union engaged in acrimonious battles with each other. The reformers are not having an easy time of it.

A Coalition of Executives

To advance their cause, troubled chief executives at all levels, all suffering similar frustrations, could conceivably make common cause with one another. Thus, the President may well find it strategically advantageous to build closer ties with governors and big-city mayors than was ever the case before. Congress would find it more uncomfortable to resist presidential demands for creation of strong field representatives with jurisdiction over bureau field personnel if state and local officials in their own home areas support the demands than if the President alone advances them. And these state and local officials may be receptive to such an association because the fragmentation of the system is as vexing to them as it is to the President himself.

Gubernatorial and big-city mayoral vexations spring from three sources. First, procedures in many intergovernmental programs are irritatingly slow; it often takes months—sometimes more than a year, in fact—to get decisions on projects and financing from federal agencies, partly because so much business is referred to Washington for approval.[29] To be sure, state and municipal executives have no wish to speed negative decisions on their requests, but hanging decisions are even worse; they can neither plan programs nor try to get the decisions reversed. They can only wait while dangerous pressures build up in their jurisdictions, and whole networks of interrelated programs are slowed or brought to a halt.

Second, procedures are often labyrinthine and uncoordinated,[30] so that it takes specialists to keep track of terminal dates, filing of applications for renewal of grants, compliance with accounting requirements, meshing of separate grants in individual projects, and explanations of variations in allowances (such as differences in relocation allowances for businesses and individual tenants moved for highway construction on the one hand and urban renewal on the other), that bewilder and annoy the public. These intricacies almost paralyze action at the grassroots, and divert needed manpower from substantive program operations to administrative routine.

Third, federal grants for very specific purposes encourage a tendency toward what the 1955 Commission on Intergovernmental Relations referred to as "a more or less independent government of their own" on the part of functional specialists at all levels of government who are only nominally under the control of their respective chief executives.[31] In point of fact, the chief executives are apparently reduced in many instances to virtually ceremonial ratification of the intergovernmental arrangements worked out by such specialists, and to the most superficial oversight of the administration of the arrangements.

So governors and big-city mayors have reason to applaud the introduction of federal regional officers with authority to rationalize the actions of federal field personnel in the bureaus. For reasons of their own, they may well find the "prefectoral'' pattern of organization, which, as we have seen, will suggest itself ever more insistently to the President, coincides with their own preferences.

This congruence of presidential, gubernatorial, and mayoral interests is not entirely speculative; indications of it have already appeared. Late in 1966, for example, President Johnson sent to a number of his top officials a memorandum[32] directing that federal assistance programs ''be worked out and planned in a cooperative spirit with those chief officials of State, county and local governments who are answerable to the citizens. To the fullest practical extent, I want you to take steps to afford representatives of the Chief Executives of State and local governments the opportunity to advise and consult in the development and execution of programs which directly affect the conduct of State and local affairs.'' A few months later, to implement the President's memorandum, the Bureau of the Budget issued a circular[33] spelling out procedures for consultation, and identifying as one of its central policies the requirement that ''The central coordinating role of heads of State and local governments, including their role of initiating and developing State and local programs, will be supported and strengthened.'' Meanwhile, former Florida Governor Farris Bryant, director of the Office of Emergency Planning in the Executive Office of the President, was leading teams of federal officials to 40 state capitals for discussions with governors and other state administrators;[34] Vice President Humphrey was conducting a program of visits and discussions with mayors, county officers, and other local executives;[35] and the President was formulating and announcing a plan to assign each member of his cabinet responsibility for liaison with four or five states, ''with instructions to maintain personal contact between the Governors and the White House.''[36] And in early 1968, the Advisory Commission on Intergovernmental Relations recommended that:

1. Coordination of Federal grant programs being administered by a variety of Federal departments and agencies be strengthened through the Executive Office of the President;
2. The authority to review and approve plans developed as a condition of Federal formula-type grants to State and local governments be decentralized to Federal regional offices and wide variations in boundaries of Federal administrative regions be reduced.[37]

An alliance of public chief executives is already taking shape.

The Confluence of Representativeness and Leadership

At the same time, groups clamoring for local control of administrative programs, confronted with the suspicion and resentment of bureaucracies and their legislative and interest-group allies, will probably discover that they get their most sympathetic hearings from chief executives, especially from big-city mayors. For such groups can provide the executive with the counterweights to the bureaucracies: they constitute an alternative channel of information about administrative performance, reducing executive dependence on the bureaucracies on the one hand and on the mass media (with their bias toward the sensational) on the other. The groups are a constituency that can be mobilized to help exert leverage on bureaucracies resistant to executive leadership. They furnish a direct conduit to localities from the executive mansions. They can serve as the nuclei of discrete, executive-oriented campaign organizations. Chief executives probably could not create the groups if they set out deliberately to do so, but it would be surprising if they did not eventually perceive the advantages of collaborating with them now that a variety of complaints has brought the groups spontaneously into being.

It will be an uneasy, mutually wary relationship. To neighborhood and community associations, the paradox of turning to remote chief executives in a quest for local control will be disturbing. To chief executives, the risk of opening a Pandora's box and releasing uncontrollable disintegrative forces will give pause. Yet each can gain so much from an alliance with the other that it is hard to avoid the feeling the attractions will overcome the anxieties. I do not mean to imply the alliance will be formal or structured. I mean only to suggest each side will turn to the other as appropriate occasions arise, and that the occasions will arise with increasing frequency in the years ahead. In this way, the new voices of representatives and the more familiar voices of executive leadership will be joined in a common challenge to those who speak for neutral competence and for older institutions of representation.

THE SUBSEQUENT PHASE OF THE CYCLE

So it seems reasonable to anticipate that "decentralization" of two types will indeed occur: concessions will be made to the demands for greater local influence on public programs, and there will be some headway toward establishing territorial officers with at least limited authority over field personnel of the functional bureaus.

It will not take long for the price of these changes to make itself felt. Decentralization will soon be followed by disparities in practice among the numerous small units, brought on by differences in human and financial resources, that will engender demands for central intervention to restore equality and balance and concerted action; the factors underlying the movement toward metropolitan units of government and toward conditional federal grants-in-aid will, in other words, reassert themselves. Decentralization will stand in the way of other goals, such as school integration (as did "states' rights" doctrines in other times). It will give rise to competition among the units that will be disastrous for many of them, which will find it more difficult to attract talent and money than others that start from a more advantageous position. In some units, strong factions may well succeed in reviving a new spoils system, thus lowering the quality of some vital services. Decentralization of public administration will not necessarily be accompanied by decentralization of the other institutions with which public units deal, such as unions of public employees, so that the local units may find themselves at a serious disadvantage in negotiations and unable to resist the pressures of special interests. Economies of scale, which are admittedly overstated very frequently, nevertheless do exist, and the multiplication of overhead costs in local units will divert some resources from substantive programs to administrative housekeeping. Initially, all these costs will be regarded by those concerned with representativeness as well worth paying, but the accumulation of such grievances over time will inspire a clamor for unification and consolidation.[38]

Similarly, area officials reporting directly to chief executives will soon develop autonomous bases of political power in the regions to which they are assigned. Rapid rotation from area to area will help to reduce their independence, but the rate of rotation will decline because each new assignment will necessitate a period of familiarization with the new territory during which actions and decisions are held in abeyance, and because local interests, having established comparatively stable relationships with their regional officers, will protest and resist frequent transfers. As the regional officers get more and more involved in regional complexes, they will become more and more ambassadors from the regions to the chief executives instead of the executives' men in the regions.[39] Regional differences and competition will become sources of irritation and controversy. Moreover, regional posts may become convenient and effective springboards to elective office. At first these dangers will seem remote and therefore less important than the immediate gains, but time is likely to reverse the balance.

So the wave of reform after the one now in progress will rally under a banner of earlier days: Take administration out of politics and politics out of administration. Disappointed partisans of the current movement on behalf of representativeness, having won some of their points, will acquiesce in the efforts of a new generation of idealists to elevate the quality, the consistency, the impartiality, the morale, and the devotion to duty of bureaucrats by strengthening and broadening central control and supervision. Chief executives anxious to regain command of the administrative field forces in each of their regions will rediscover the virtues of strong central direction of those forces by functional administrative agencies whose chiefs identify with the executives,[40] and whose standards can be applied even-handedly everywhere. From above and below, to escape the distortions of purpose inflicted by the vigorous factional politics of localities and regions (as they once sought to free themselves from the toils of self-seeking factions in state and congressional district politics), the apostles of good government will turn back to insulating the bureaucracies against such political heat. The neutrality and independence of the civil service will again be extolled.

It should not be inferred that the process is fruitless because the succession of values is repetitive. Wheels turning on their own axles do advance. Each time the balance among the values is redressed, only to require redress again, some new accommodation among the myriad interests in the society is reached.

Precisely what shape the subsequent resurgence of neutral competence will take in the years beyond, it is impossible to prophesy now. But if the hypothesized cycle of values is at all valid, then strange as it may seem to this generation of reformers, innovators of tomorrow will defend many of the very institutions (as transformed in the course of current controversies) under attack today. And many a forgotten tome and obscure article on public administration, long gathering dust on unpatronized shelves and in unopened files, will be resurrected and praised for its prescience, only to subside again into temporary limbo when another turn of the wheel ends its brief moment of revived relevance.

NOTES

1. Paul H. Appleby, *Big Democracy* (New York: Knopf, 1945). Actually, the dedication was "To John Citizen and Bill Bureaucrat."
2. Herbert Kaufman, "Emerging Conflicts in the Doctrines of Public Administration," *American Political Science Review,* Vol. 50, No. 4 (December 1956), p. 1073.

3. U.S. Bureau of the Census, *1967 Census of Governments,* Volume 6, *Popularly Elected Officials of State and Local Governments,* pp. 1 ff.
4. Avery Leiserson, *Administrative Regulation: A Study in Representation of Group Interests* (Chicago: The University of Chicago Press, 1942).
5. See, for instance, the criticism of professional bureaucracy and the demand for "public participation" in resource management decisions by Yale Law School Professor Charles A. Reich in his *Bureaucracy and the Forests* (Santa Barbara, Calif.: Center for the Study of Democratic Institutions, 1962).
6. For example, *The New York Times* reported on November 29, 1967, that "A [New York City] citizen group demanded yesterday that a Negro and a Puerto Rican be named to the city's nine-man Community Mental Health Board." And a high-ranking city antipoverty administrator (suspended for failing to file tax returns) went on a hunger strike to dramatize his demand that Puerto Ricans be named to the Board of Education, the State Board of Regents, the citywide Model Cities Advisory Committee, the Civil Service Commission, and the City Housing Authority (*The New York Times,* June 29, 1968).
7. Walter Gellhorn, *When Americans Complain* (Cambridge: Harvard University Press, 1966), and *Ombudsmen and Others* (Cambridge: Harvard University Press, 1966); Stanley Anderson (ed.), *Ombudsmen for American Government* (Englewood Cliffs, N.J.: Prentice-Hall, 1968).
8. See the article by S. M. Miller this symposium.
9. *The New York Times,* November 18, 1967. John W. Gardner, former Secretary of Health, Education, and Welfare, and currently chairman of the Urban Coalition, went even further and urged a larger role for Negroes in helping solve the urban crisis generally (*The New York Times,* May 6, 1968).
10. *Report of the American Assembly on Law and the Changing Society* (Chicago: Center for Continuing Education, University of Chicago, March 14–17, 1968).
11. *The New York Times,* June 30, 1968.
12. Seymour J. Mandelbaum, "Spatial and Temporal Perspectives in the U.S. City," mimeo., (University of Pennsylvania, 1968).
13. Robert A. Dahl, "The City in the Future of Democracy," *American Political Science Review,* Vol. 61, No. 4 (December 1967), pp. 967, 969.
14. Advisory Commission on Intergovernmental Relations, *Ninth Annual Report* (Washington, D.C.: the Commission, 1968), p. 21.
15. *The Washington Post,* October 10, 1967.
16. *The New York Times,* September 24, 1967. But he criticized school decentralization a short time later (*The New York Times,* June 5, 1968).
17. *The Washington Post,* March 26, 1968. See also the arguments of a former foreign service officer for "dismantling the present overgrown bureaucratic apparatus" in Washington. Gordon Tullock, *The Politics of Bureaucracy* (Washington, D.C.: Public Affairs Press, 1965), chapter 25. That liberals have thus adopted a position taken by conservatives in New Deal days is an irony to which attention has been drawn by James Q. Wilson, "The Bureaucracy Problem," *The Public Interest,* Vol. 2, No. 6 (Winter 1967), pp. 3–4. Note the similarities between the new liberal language and the position of former Governor George C. Wallace of Alabama: "I would," he said, "bring all those briefcase-toting bureaucrats in the Department of Health, Education, and Welfare to Washington and throw their briefcases in the Potomac River. . . ." *The New York Times,* February 9, 1968. His attack on bureaucrats is, of course, based on their zeal in defense of civil rights; the liberals' indictment is constructed on a diametrically opposite appraisal. The impulse toward decentralization thus comes from both the political right and the political left for entirely different reasons—but with combined force.
18. "Revenue sharing expresses the traditional faith most of us have in pluralism and decentralization. . . ." Walter W. Heller and Joseph A. Pechman, *Questions and An-*

swers in Revenue Sharing (Washington, D.C.: The Brookings Institution, 1967), p. 12.

19. Like all slogans, it means different things to different people, however. It is a much more complex and ambiguous concept than it seems; see note 24, below.

20. The Executive Office of the President was created in 1939, when the federal budget was under $9 billion. It has grown since, but not nearly as much as the budget, now 15 times larger and many hundreds of times more complex. Some reordering seems almost inevitable.

21. U.S. Bureau of the Budget, "Work of the Steering Group on Evaluation of the Bureau of the Budget: A Staff Study," July 1967. The reorganization took effect shortly afterwards.

22. The origins of PPBS are many and varied; see Allen Schick, "The Road to PPB," PUBLIC ADMINISTRATION REVIEW, Vol. 26, No. 4 (December 1966), pp. 243–258. But it was the system's utility to the Secretary of Defense from 1961 on in gaining control of his own department that gave widespread currency to the idea and induced the President to make it governmentwide in 1965; see U.S. Senate, 90th Congress, 1st Session (1967), Committee on Government Operations, Subcommittee on National Security and International Operations, *Program-Planning-Budgeting: Official Documents*, pp. 1–6, and *Program-Planning-Budgeting: Hearings, Part 1* (August 23, 1967). This new impetus will doubtless lead to adaptive imitation in other governments.

23. Arthur M. Schlesinger, Jr., *A Thousand Days* (Boston: Houghton Mifflin, 1965), pp. 679–680, reports, "he]President Kennedy] had to get the government moving. He came to the White House at a time when the ability of the President to do this had suffered steady constriction. The cliches about the 'most powerful office on earth' had concealed the extent to which the mid-century Presidents had much less freedom of action than, say, Jackson or Lincoln or even Franklin Roosevelt. No doubt the mid-century Presidents could blow up the world, but at the same time they were increasingly hemmed in by the growing power of the bureaucracy and of Congress. The President understood this." Similarly, President Johnson's assistant for domestic programs, Joseph A. Califano, Jr., recently complained publicly of the limitations of presidential power, observing that the powers of the office have not kept pace with its growing responsibilities: *The Washington Post*, May 6, 1968.

24. James W. Fesler, *Area and Administration* (University, Ala.: University of Alabama Press, 1949), especially pp. 8–18, and "Approaches to the Understanding of Decentralization," *Journal of Politics*, Vol. 27, No. 3 (August 1965), pp. 557–561. See also the essay by John D. Millett, "Field Organization and Staff Supervision," in *New Horizons in Public Administration: A Symposium* (University, Ala.: University of Alabama Press, 1945), pp. 98–118.

25. Fesler, *op. cit.*, pp. 88–89. Fesler's writing on this subject anticipated long in advance the problems that were to engender a more general awareness when programs of the New Frontier and the Great Society overwhelmed the administrative machinery.

26. See J. Leiper Freeman, *The Political Process: Executive Bureau-Legislative Committee Relations* (New York: Random House, revised edition, 1965), and the works therein cited in chapter one.

27. Bureau of the Budget field offices were set up in mid-1943 but were eliminated in the early years of the Eisenhower Administration. Recent efforts to revive them, even on a limited basis, ran into stiff opposition; see U.S. Senate, 90th Congress, 1st Session, Subcommittee of the Committee on Appropriations, *Hearings on H.R. 7501: Treasury, Post Office and Executive Office Appropriations for Fiscal Year 1968* (Washington, D.C.: U.S. Government Printing Office, 1967), pp. 973–990. Note especially the comments of Senator Monroney at p. 981: "The reason the committee cut your request for additional personnel last year was because it did not wish to have field offices established. . . . My impression was that we were afraid they would grow into a 50-state bureaucracy with state and regional offices."

28. The mayor proposed 35 local mayor's offices soon after his inauguration; encountering opposition in the Board of Estimate, he tried to set up five by executive order, but the City Council refused to support him, and the comptroller refused to approve payment of their bills. The mayor tried again in May 1967, but was again rebuffed by the Council and the Board of Estimate. Evenutally, four local offices were opened, but they were much weaker than was originally anticipated. For the time being, at least, the plan seems emasculated.
29. Stephen K. Bailey, "Co-ordinating the Great Society," *The Reporter*, Vol. 34, No. 6 (March 24, 1966), p. 39.
30. *Ibid.*
31. *The Final Report* of the Commission on Intergovernmental Relations (Washington, D.C.: U.S. Government Printing Office, 1955), p. 44. See also Coleman B. Ransone, Jr., *The Office of the Governor of the United States* (University, Ala.: The University of Alabama Press, 1956), p. 249.
32. "The President's Memorandum to Heads of Certain Federal Agencies. November 11, 1966. Subject: Advice and Consultation with State and local officials."
33. Bureau of the Budget Circular No. A-85, June 28, 1967.
34. Advisory Commission on Intergovernmental Relations, *Ninth Annual Report* (Washington, D.C.: the Commission, 1968), p. 12.
35. *Ibid.*, pp. 12–13.
36. The plan grew out of "Mr. Johnson's continuing determination to build domestic as well as foreign bridges by working to sort out the tangled Federal-state relations that have been increasingly complicated by the administration of the Great Society Programs." *The New York Times*, June 8, 1967. See also Terry Sanford, *Storm Over the States* (New York: McGraw-Hill, 1967), pp. 164–166; here a former governor calls on the White House to help state and local governments and quotes James Reston's comment that "He [the President] is reaching out to the governors and mayors of America for a new political, social, and economic partnership."
37. Advisory Commission on Intergovernmental Relations, *op. cit.*, p. 22.
38. Some anxieties about the costs of decentralization have already been voiced in Irving Kristol, "Decentralization for What?" *The Public Interest*, No. 11, Spring 1968, p. 17, and echoed by Daniel P. Moynihan as he assailed school decentralization as likely to lead to segregated bureaucracies, *The New York Times*, June 5, 1968. Note also the dissents by Governors Rhodes and Rockefeller from a hearty endorsement of neighborhood subunits with limited powers of taxation and local self-government. Advisory Commission on Intergovernmental Relations, *op. cit.*, p. 21.
39. Herbert Kaufman, *The Forest Ranger* (Baltimore: The Johns Hopkins Press, 1960), pp. 75–80.
40. A hint of what lies ahead is suggested by the experience with regional development commissions. Encouraged by the federal government, their establishment was hailed as a step toward decentralization. But their plans began to conflict and compete with each other, and with the work of other federal and state agencies; moreover, powerful political blocs began to aggregate around them. The President had to direct the Secretary of Commerce to coordinate them, giving strong powers of review over their proposals and the aid of a council of assistant secretaries from ten federal agencies, a measure greeted as a partial recentralization. *The Washington Post*, December 30, 1967. This dilemma was explicity foreseen by James W. Fesler, *op. cit.*, especially pp. 100–102.

Reflections On Watergate: Lessons for Public Administration

JAMES L. SUNDQUIST

If a great epidemic swept the land, the public health profession would look in upon itself, I suppose, and ask, "Where did we go wrong?" And if they didn't, someone else would look to them and ask, "Where did *you* go wrong?" It is now just as incumbent upon those in public administration to look upon themselves and ask that question, "Where did *we* go wrong?" For Watergate—whatever else one may call it—*was* public administration. It was the breakdown of public administration, to be sure, as an epidemic is a breakdown of public health. But it is the business of both professions to prevent pathology. The question, "Where did we go wrong?" needs to be asked very seriously—and answered.

It might not be so significant if Watergate, and all that that term conveys, were an isolated episode. But it followed right on the heels of another breakdown, which is called Vietnam. What follows is the product of reflection on not just one of those but both. Together, they have created a crisis of confidence in the entire system. Never—at least never during the period that polls have been taken on the subject—has the public respect for government, and the people in it, been so low.

So, what *did* go wrong? We start from the fact that what has brought the country to this low state is the way in which presidential power has been used—or abused, or misused, whichever one prefers. In the one case a President got the nation deeply mired in a war that the people did not know they were getting into, that the Congress did not consciously authorize, that turned out to be a ghastly mistake in almost everybody's view—and then kept the country there long after it wanted only to get out. And in the other case, those who exercised presidential authority did all manner of things—that need not to be recited here—to misuse the agencies of government for partisan ends and bring disgrace upon a President, and a party, and a whole governmental system.

PUBLIC ADMINISTRATION HAS GLORIFIED THE PRESIDENCY

And what did the profession of public administration have to do with that? Quite a bit, I think. The profession has devoted 40 years to aggrandizing presidential power. It has consistently sought—and contributed in no small measure to the consequence—to strengthen the President at the expense of all the other elements that make up the governmental system. Or, to put it in a more invidious way, to undermine the checks and balances that have existed in the American system— put there partly by accident and partly by design for the specific purpose of keeping the President from gaining too much power.

Sometimes we in public administration repeated Lord Acton's phrase, "Power tends to corrupt, and absolute power corrupts absolutely,'' but we didn't really believe it. Instead, we believed Louis Brownlow when he said, ''during the whole history of the thrity-two Presidents, not one has been recreant to his high trust—none has used his power to aggrandize himself at the expense of our settled institutions.''[1] And that may have been true enough when it was said—in 1947.

The literature of public administration is shot through with the doctrine of the strong executive (influenced, no doubt, by the literature from business administration, from which so many of its early theses were taken). Indeed, until very recently, there was not even any rival doctrine. One can reread the works written before the late 1960s by the men who have represented the mainstream of thinking in the profession—the men who, for example, like Brownlow, have been presidents of the American Society for Public Administration—and find not so much as one dissenting word. Every writer was for a strong presidency. Absolutely nobody was for a weak one.

In his pioneering article of the 1930s, ''Notes on the Theory of Organization,'' for instance, Luther Gulick put forward the doctrine of the strong executive categorically and confidently. ''Coordination,'' said Gulick, is ''mandatory,'' and one of the two ways coordination is achieved is ''by orders of superiors to subordinates, reaching from the top to the bottom of the entire enterprise.'' ''Organization requires . . . a system of authority,'' he goes on, and that ''requires . . . a single directing executive authority.''[2]

The Brownlow Committee on Administrative Management, of which Gulick was a member, applied that doctrine to the Executive Branch of the United States government. Its object was to make the President the ''single directing executive authority'' by giving him in an Executive Office of the President the staff assistance he needed for that purpose. The plan was adopted, the office created, and then those who sought to aggrandize the President could pursue their mission from the inside. William Carey, a member of the Executive Office staff almost from its beginning, wrote of that mission a generation later in words Gulick would have approved: the object of a presidential staff was to help the President attain ''command and control.''[3]

It did this in many ways, through protection and development of the functions assigned the office, particularly those of budgeting, legislative clearance, and the preparation of government reorganization plans. The presidential staff constantly asserted the President's prerogatives in his struggles with the Congress, on matters that the Nixon Administration has now carried to the ultimate, like impoundment of funds and the doctrine of executive privilege. Not least important were the reorganization plans. Power was systematically taken from bureau chiefs and placed in department heads, for the latter were the President's men, and whatever strengthened the President's men enhanced the President's own control. One of the two criteria by which any reorganization plan should be judged, wrote Herbert Emmerich, was whether ''the ability of the President to see that the laws are faithfully executed'' was ''strengthened.''[4]

I do not suggest that this was any kind of sinister conspiracy. Of course, in aggrandizing the President, public administration did aggrandize itself. But there is nothing reprehensible about that. To be a good member of the public administration profession, one must love and respect administration—just as a good lawyer reveres the law or a good doctor venerates the practice of medicine. One has to believe in one's own calling; otherwise, who in the world would believe in it? But administration is what the executive does. So our reverence—our veneration—

went to the Executive Branch, and particularly to the President as the chief of that branch, and it was our purpose in life, bred into us from our earliest days in graduate school, to advance our professional ideals by aggrandizing him.

And all the while we forgot Lord Acton. We forgot that the power to do great good is also the power to do great harm. If we strengthen the presidency for *our* purposes—all of them noble, of course—we will strengthen it also for the purposes of *others* whose ends may turn out, in our eyes if not in theirs, to be less than noble.

AND SO HAS POLITICAL SCIENCE

If the public administration fraternity was bound by its very nature to exalt presidential power, could one look to the political scientists to take a broader view? The answer is no: they, too, were part of the cult of the executive. Most leading political scientists since the 1930s, after all, have been liberals, believers in strong government—if they weren't, they probably wouldn't have been drawn into political science in the first place. But, more, they were Franklin Roosevelt, New Deal liberals. They had lived through the 1930s, and so they could have no doubt whatever—it was a strong and activist President, and no one else, who had rescued the country from despair and set it right again. The other branches of government, at best, fell in behind the presidential leadership or, at worst, obstructed. Roosevelt took an honored place in the galaxy of national heroes, so many of whom, as it happens, were also strong Presidents—from Washington and Jackson and Lincoln in the last century to Theodore Roosevelt and Woodrow Wilson in this one. After the war, Harry Truman saved Europe from communism. The liberals chafed during the Eisenhower hiatus; but then came Kennedy and Johnson, and the country was back in the pattern of activist Presidents carrying the banner for liberal causes—that is, until things went sour in Vietnam.

Thomas Cronin has drawn a composite picture of the presidency as it is presented in standard political science textbooks. Here are some phrases that Cronin lifted from those works: The presidency is "the great engine of democracy," the "American people's one authentic trumpet," "The central instrument of democracy," a "glittering mountain peak," "the chief architect of the nation's public policy," "he symbolizes the people [and] also runs their government," "Presidential government is a superb planning institution," "He is . . . a kind of magnificent lion who can roam widely and do great deeds."[5]

The cult of the executive reached its zenith, perhaps, with publication of Richard Neustadt's influential book, *Presidential Power.* Neustadt wrote that book with the explicit purpose, he explains in the preface, of teaching activist Presidents about "personal power . . . how to get it, how to keep it, how to use it." A President seeking to "maximize his power" energized the government, said Neustadt. What is good for the President, he concluded, is therefore good for the country.[6]

OVERLOOKED: THE POTENTIAL FOR ABUSE

In all of this, there is surprisingly little concern about the potential for abuse of all that power. The public administration literature all but ignores the possibility. Paul Appleby, after praising the President as "the symbol of all the government's executive power,'' simply assures us that "through Congress, and through elections, it is a power popularly controlled."[7] Emmerich strikes a similar note: "The centrifugal forces in our society are so strong and the checks and balances in our governmental system so powerful that we are in danger not of giving too much power to the President but of having many conflicting, mutually-cancelling centers of power that will defeat the general interest."[8] The political scientists had sounded no warnings either. Neustadt worries only about the non-use, not about the use, of presidential power. Cronin summarizes the theme of all the textbooks as one of simple faith: "whoever is in the White House [will turn out to be] the right man."

But the two Presidents last elected to that office were subsequently adjudged by overwhelming popular majorities to have been the wrong men, the public opinion polls make clear. Now, as one looks back on history, one can reach the same verdict on other Presidents as well. The New Deal years bring to mind not just Franklin Roosevelt but also Herbert Hoover—honorable, well-motivated, unlucky, but surely the wrong man to have in the White House for those long years between October 1929 and March 1933.

"CHECKS AND BALANCES" TURN OUT NOT TO BE THERE AFTER ALL

What of Paul Appleby's assurance that through the Congress and elections presidential power is controlled? And Emmerich's similar reliance upon the checks and balances of our governmental system?

We can dispose of elections simply: Yes, they are a control, but only when they happen. Unlike many other democratic countries, the United States votes only by the calendar. The Johnson adventure in Vietnam ran for more than three years before the people could call him to account. Now, assuming that impeachment fails, the country will be constrained to limp along with a government discredited by scandal for almost four full years. Hoover was useless as a national leader for longer than three years. Elections as an ultimate check, yes. As a timely check when desperately needed to restore presidential leadership, no.

And the Congress? We learn now that the checks and balances are really not there, after all. Their existence has been mostly a myth. All it took was a couple of Presidents back to back, with the temperament of monarchs, determined to press their powers to the full, with a penchant for secrecy, to demonstrate that.

We get the idea that the checks are checking and the balances balancing because almost every day's newspaper tells us how the President and the Congress are in one conflict or another, each branch of government blocking and stalemating the other. But the effective stalemating is primarily in one field of governmental action—legislation. There Emmerich is quite right in talking about "mutually-cancelling centers of power." The legislative power *is* divided, with each branch given a veto over the other.

But not so the executive power. The Constitution gives the Congress no role in the execution of laws once they are enacted—save for the power in the Senate to ratify treaties (and Presidents have learned that if agreements with other nations are embodied in documents other than treaties this senatorial check can be evaded). Beyond that, executive power is assigned wholly to a single branch of government—the Executive Branch. The Congress has no right to share in the executive power, or even any right to be consulted.

That does not mean that the Congress does not find ways of "horning in," but it does so with very blunt and indirect instruments. Sometimes, if the Congress does not like the way the President is executing the laws, it can deal directly with the matter, by passing new legislation to make its intent clear. But the President can veto that kind of legislation and, if upheld by one-third plus one of either house—and normally he can expect to have at least that much support from members of his own party alone—he can go on doing as he pleases. Moreover, this recourse is of no avail at all if the intent of the Congress was clear all along—which seems to be the case most of the time—and the President is just choosing to ignore it. Take, for instance, the President's recent attempt to liquidate the Office of Economic Opportunity in open defiance of the law and of the clear intent of Congress. There would not have been much point for the Congress to pass still another law reiterating that intent.

The vaunted power of the purse is similarly limited. It can be used directly only to prevent, but not to compel, executive action. It might have been used to force an earlier end to the war in Vietnam, for instance; but if the problem is, say, the use of the FBI or the Internal Revenue Service by a President against his political enemies, the Congress cannot get at that matter by cutting the budgets for those agencies. That would only mean that more criminals would run loose and more tax evaders would go undiscovered.

The power of the Senate to confirm presidential appointees is even more ineffectual. At the time an appointee comes up for confirmation, the Senate rarely knows what kind of an administrator he is going to be and what commitment it needs to extract from him. One need only point to the number of Watergate figures who had been confirmed easily by senators who could not know how the appointees were going to behave in circumstances that had not arisen and could not be foreseen.

Finally, there is the general right of the Congress to inquire and to expose—the congressional investigation. Here the Congress can be frustrated, initially, by the exercise of executive privilege to withhold information, even if that turns out to be a not unlimited right. But when the Congress does obtain the information it wants about what the executive is doing, it cannot order him to change his ways. It can heckle, entreat, bulldoze, and threaten, but it cannot tell him what to do. A congressional investigation is essentially an appeal to public opinion, which a determined or obsessive President can ignore. In the end, the President's responsibility under the Constitution for the execution of the laws remains exclusive.

So if the Congress wants to restrain the President, what it is compelled to do most of the time is resort to a kind of blackmail: The members who are aggrieved threaten to use against the President the powers they *do* share with him—the legislative powers, including the power of the purse. Sometimes this works, but more often it does not, because the President's position is much the stronger one. In the first place, threats run both ways: The President can bring senators and congressmen into line by using *his* powers against *them*—by granting or withholding all kinds of favors, in appointments, projects, legislative bargaining, and all the rest. In the second place, the Congress is not organized to bargain effectively with the President. The 535 members are divided into two houses, two parties, and a multiplicity of committees and subcommittees; they have no way of arriving at a common strategy to combat a monolithic Executive Branch, and they have not delegated to their leaders the responsibility to strike deals on their behalf.

That leaves the courts. True, the judiciary provides a check of sorts, if a case can be brought (Vietnam, for instance, was not litigable), if executive secrecy can be breached—which, as has been demonstrated, is not easy—and if retribution is the only object. But if the basic need is institutional mechanisms that will *prevent* the damage from occurring in the first place—that will forestall the abuses of power that cause the loss of confidence of the people in their government—then putting people in jail long after the damage has been done is not quite good enough. Moreover, the legal processes only cover outright violations of the law. There is a wide range of circumstances where presidential power can be used legally enough but unwisely, from simple mistakes to egregious folly. The courts are useless here. And the same limitations apply also to that ultimate remedy—impeachment— which is a judicial-type process based upon a concept of the illegal use of power.

The checks and balances, such as they are, operate either long *before* the fact, in the case of the confirmation power, or else *after* the fact—after the damage has been done. None of them operate *during* the fact, while the executive power is being used—and abused—which is the crucial time if the damage is to be prevented. They can be marginally improved here and there within our present constitutional system—the War Powers Act was one such improvement—but basically they are barriers to presidential power made of very thin stuff.

THE INTERNAL CHECKS: CABINET AND BUREAUCRACY

What of checks and balances provided internally within the Executive Branch? Time was that the cabinet meant something. During the first century of the Republic, the United States had cabinets patterned on the British model. Presidents chose as department heads men who represented a broad spectrum of the party's top leadership—prominent members of the Congress, party leaders from the largest states, major rivals for the presidential nomination, all with independent political strength and power bases. So men of the stature of Hamilton and Webster, Clay and Calhoun, Seward and Sherman and Bryan, sat in presidential cabinets. And they were used as a consultative body. Presidents made decisions in cabinet, rather like kings-in-council.

But Presidents have now discovered, in these days of direct communication between them and the people, that their political strength is highly personal. It is not compounded from the strength of other party leaders assembled in a cabinet. That being the case, they can avoid the pain of surrounding themselves with department heads who have independent sources of political strength. Such men or women can be defiant, and cause trouble; they have to be conciliated, because if they resign they can do so with a splash. Far better, Presidents have learned to appoint nameless and faceless men, who are wholly dependent upon the President who gave them what stature they can claim. They can be counted on not to defy the President—or, if by any chance they do and he is forced to fire them, their departure will go unnoticed and unregretted. John Ehrlichman described the modern version of the ideal cabinet member shortly after the Miami convention in 1972; "The Cabinet officers must be tied closely to the chief executive, or to put it in extreme terms, when he says jump, they only ask how high."[9] A cabinet so composed would hardly be worth much as a collective consultative body to check the presidential judgment—which may be one reason that no President since Eisenhower has even tried to use his cabinet that way.

Finally, these days, public administrators are taking some considerable pride that the bureaucracy has acted as a check upon the President. Career civil servants have been tarnished very little by Watergate, and in the FBI and the Criminal Division, the IRS, and the CIA, they did act as a restraint upon the President—which is why the "plumbers" were forced to operate directly out of the White House. But those who talk about encouraging bureaucratic restraints upon Presidents as a kind of general principle are surely grasping at the wrong straw. Bureaucratic footdragging may save the Republic from unwise or illegal conduct, now and then, but in the normal course the bureaucracy simply has to be effectively subordinated. A few questions should settle any doubts: Should the military establish its own war policies and conduct its own operations, outside of civilian control? Should the FBI make its own policies about wiretapping and privacy? Should the foreign service have its own foreign policy, whether or not that is in accord with the policy of the President and the Secretary of State? The answers are obvious. If a career civil servant objects to presidential policies, he may argue his case as forcefully as he wishes, but if the decision goes against him he has the choice to either accept it or resign. If he resigns, he can take his case to the public to get the decision changed, but if he stays he has no right to obstruct, or countermand by indirection, his superiors' policy. The object must not be to encourage the defiance of political decisions by those whose job it is to execute them, but rather to take steps to get better political decisions made in the first place.

THE SAFEGUARD OF PLURAL DECISION MAKING

Here is where public administration as a profession, as a branch of the social sciences, should take a careful look at other institutions. That examination would at once reveal a basic principle of institutional design that has been applied all but universally in the English-speaking world: the principle that major decisions shall be made not by one man acting alone but by a collective body of some kind. I say "all but" because of that great and glaring exception, the Executive Branch of the United States government (as well as the executive branches of the state governments and some city governments that are patterned after it). Legislatures are all plural bodies. So are the higher courts, and juries. So are regulatory commissions. In corporations and labor unions and voluntary service organizations the ultimate authority is in plural boards of directors, who select and supervise the managers. Likewise the universities and the public schools, as well as most local governments—particularly those whose form of government is the one that reformers and public administrators designed and most admire, the council-manager form. In political parties the authority is in conventions and committees. That is true of most churches that took form in the English-speaking world. Indeed, in the entire institutional structure, public and private, it is difficult to find an organization of any size or consequence that is not subject to the direct control of a plural body—except, to repeat, the executive branches of the national and state governments and some cities.

In other English-speaking countries, even those exceptions do not exist. Executive authority there rests not in lone individuals but in plural cabinets. That is largely true in non-English-speaking democracies as well.

The principle is often violated, of course. In many organizations where authority is formally vested in a plural body—notable in private organizations, such as corporations and labor unions—the executive is able to dominate the organization, even to the point of controlling the selection of members of the governing body. But this is a corruption, commonly recognized as such when it occurs. The *form* of organization is designed to protect against such executive bossism, and the basic right of the governing body to impose its will on the executive remains unimpaired—and is even enforceable in the courts. It is the model, not necessarily its application in every instance, that embodies the folk wisdom evolved over centuries of experience with human organization.

To put power in one man, societies have learned over and over again, is inherently dangerous. A single man may be erratic or impulsive or obsessive in his judgments. He may be arbitrary and unfair. He may be incompetent, a bungler. He may be lazy, or negligent, or corrupt. He may pervert the ends of the organization for his own benefit, whether that be to gain money or punish enemies or reward friends or simply to perpetuate himself and his followers in office.

And so, in almost every organization, a restraint of collective decision making has been forced upon the leader. He is made subordinate to, or required to act as a member of, a plural body of some kind. It may be called by many names—commission, council, board, committee, Senate, House, cabinet—but the important thing is that its members have a degree of independence from the leader. Then if the leader is impulsive, cooler heads can prevail. If he is unfair or arbitrary, his colleagues can refuse to go along. If his policies are unwise, they can be corrected. If he is negligent, he can be goaded. If his tendency is to corrupt the system, he can be watched and checked. If he tries to pervert its purposes for his own ends, he can be overruled.

Plural decision making has its own drawbacks, obviously. It can mean delay and caution and conservatism. But the folk wisdom, over the centuries, has weighed the disadvantages against the merits and given its verdict: the plural body, not the single leader, is better to be trusted.

Yet in the case of this one great office—the presidency—the office with the greatest consequences for good or ill in all our lives—the folk wisdom has been violated. Enormous power is in a single man, unrestrained by any requirement of collective decision making. The Founding Fathers, interestingly enough, were not unanimous on that. A significant minority in the Constitutional Convention desired a plural executive, a three-man presidency, but they were outvoted, seven states to three, by those who argued that, in Luther Gulick's later words, a hierarchical organization requires "a single directing executive authority." So now the people are left to worry about what Arthur Schlesinger, Jr., calls "the imperial presidency" or "the runaway presidency" or "the revolutionary presidency," like so many Frankensteins wondering what this monster they have created—with all the same innocent enthusiasm of Baron Frankenstein—will do next. So what can be done?

One school of thought says nothing much has to be done. The nation will have learned great lessons from Vietnam and Watergate. No President for a long time will dare to embark on any such headstrong foreign adventures as Lyndon Johnson did. No President will be so careless in choosing subordinates as Richard Nixon was, or so lax in supervising them. The elements of the bureaucracy that stood up well against the presidency will stand up even better next time. Besides, any remedy might make things a good deal worse, because—to put the shoe on the other foot—any measure that restrains the President's power to do bad things will also restrain his power to do good things. In other words, those who sought to aggrandize the power of the President were right all along. The nation does need a strong President, for all of the reasons given by public administrators and political scientists for 40 years. Those who believe in liberal causes should not let themselves be led by the clamor of the moment to impair the instrument that they correctly and wisely saw was necessary for their purposes. Clean the system up a bit around the edges, but don't attempt any fundamental constitutional change.

This seems to me to leave entirely too much to luck. There is so much risk—given our selection system—of putting the wrong man in the White House that I would like to find some means of forcing upon our chief executive some of the restraints of collective decision making that in this country we routinely insist upon in lesser organizations. There is something about the White House, as George Reedy has suggested, that can bring out latent traits of megalomania in any human being who finds himself there. And let's face it: it is not inconceivable that a President could become mentally or emotionally unstable while in office—as has happened to the heads of other governments—yet not be removable for disability nor guilty of impeachable crime.

DISMANTLE PRESIDENTIAL POWER?

Another school of thought looks at all that concentrated power and sees the answer in taking some of it away. All kinds of proposals are heard: Give power back to the Congress, elect the key members of the cabinet, take certain sensitive agencies such as the Department of Justice out of the Executive Branch, limit by law the size of the White House staff, and so on. A few of these proposals—a permanent independent prosecutor, for instance—may have merit but, generally speaking, most of these proposals seem to move in the wrong direction. For, no matter how doubtful it may seem at the moment, the public administration fraternity *has* been right all along in its arguments for a powerful presidency. Governmental functions do need to be directed and coordinated from a single point of leadership. There does need to be "command and control," in Carey's words, so that within limits set by law there can be worked out a coordinated economic policy, a military policy and a foreign policy and a food policy consistent with one another, a coordinated system of intergovernmental relations, and all the rest. If the functions of the Executive Branch were to be scattered among persons of independent authority, any chance of the government's making sense with what it tried to do would be lost, and the cry would immediately arise: Give the President the authority to make order out of this shambles. Indeed, a strong case can be made for giving some additional powers to the President—for instance, clear control over the personnel management functions of the Civil Service Commission (as distinct from its inspection and policing functions) and over the activities of the Federal Reserve Board, which now has the authority to pursue a monetary policy that can cancel the President's fiscal policy and thus prevent the government from having any effective economic policy at all, and the power to raise and lower tax rates, within limits, for fiscal policy purposes. In short, there is no substitute for a powerful presidency in the complex modern world, for all the reasons public administrators have given from Gulick and Brownlow to the present time.

OR TRY TO PLURALIZE THE EXERCISE OF POWER?

But—and this is all-important—a powerful presidency under equally powerful control. That suggests looking for the answer in a third direction. Instead of trying to reduce the presidential power, can a way be found to heed the folk wisdom of the ages by pluralizing that power in its exercise? In other words, by establishing institutions that would force the President into some kind of collective process in making major national decisions.

Where are the people of independent stature with whom the President could be forced to consult? Not the cabinet, obviously, or any other group of Executive Branch subordinates; a President cannot be required to appoint strong men to the Executive Branch, or permit them to restrain him. The only people around, apart from the President and Vice President, who are elected, and hence who have any independent power base at all, are the members of Congress. But to force the President into a closer relationship with the Congress—which, as a practical matter, would have to mean the leaders of the Congress—would clearly require some additional sanctions in the hands of the Legislative Branch, so that he could not just ignore its leaders or defy them, as he does now

I think that sanction has to take the form of a simpler way of removing Presidents. That object would serve a double purpose.

First, it is a necessary end in itself, in view of the limitations of the courts and of the impeachment process. It does not take high crimes or misdemeanors to destroy the capacity of a President to lead and inspire and unify the country, as he must. If one starts from the proposition that the United States needs at all times an effective government, that it cannot afford to wait for as long as three years or more if its President loses his ability to lead and govern, then one has to conclude that the present removal process is too limited.

Second, it would tend to impose upon the President, to some degree, the restraint of collective decision making. If the Congress had a greater discretion in removing Presidents, he would have to keep its confidence. And to keep its confidence, he would have to take its leaders into his. He could not hide from them essential information. He could not abuse his powers and then defy them to do anything about it. He would have to make sure, through consultation in advance, that major decisions met with their concurrence.

The problem is to strike exactly the right balance in making presidential removal easier. The presidency obviously should not be destabilized too much. If the opposition party has a majority in the Congress, which is so often the case, it should not be able to turn out a President for trivial or partisan reasons. Perhaps the British system comes closest to the model: there, prime ministers normally serve their full five-year term (assuming that the governing party has a clear parliamentary majority, which it usually has), but when a prime minister botches his job and so loses the confidence of the country—and hence of the House of Commons and its governing majority—the majority does have means to force him out and get the country off to a fresh start under a leader who can lead and a government that can govern. So when prime ministers can no longer govern, they step—or are pushed—aside, as Neville Chamberlain gave way to Winston Churchill after Narvik, and Anthony Eden to Harold Macmillan after Suez. In the American system, a Neville Chamberlain would hold onto his office as a kind of property right even if, in the judgment of the country, he had no capacity to lead the people in time of peril.

ALTERNATIVE CONSTITUTIONAL AMENDMENTS

Several types of constitutional amendments to ease the removal process have been suggested. One idea is just to broaden the impeachment clause—by adding after the phrase "high crimes and misdemeanors" five little words, "Or for any other reason." Removal would then become a political rather than a juridical type of action, taken through a "no confidence" vote, as in the parliamentary countries. But under this amendment two-thirds of the Senate would still be required to remove the chief executive, and that seems to embody the wrong principle. To govern effectively, a President needs to sustain the confidence of the majority of the country and of the legislature, not just a one-third-plus-one minority.

A proposal by Congressman Bingham runs into the same objection. He would empower the Congress by law to call a new presidential election at any time. This is somewhat like the recall provisions of some state constitutions, except there the recall is initiated by petition of a specified number of voters. But the Bingham proposal to act by statute would require a two-thirds vote of both houses, in order to override the inevitable presidential veto.

Congressman Reuss has tried to meet the objection to the two-thirds requirement by providing for a "no confidence" removal by 60 per cent of both houses. But that still violates the majority principle while at the same time probably making removal too easy. Sometimes the opposition party in the Congress by itself has a 60 per cent majority.

My favorite approach, therefore, is this: Empower Congress to act by a simple majority to remove the President and call a new election. But, to deter the Congress from acting from trivial or fractious causes, require that the Congress upon removing the President itself be dissolved and all its members forced to face a new election. They would have to take their decision, in effect, to a referendum. That would surely be a very great restraint upon the exercise of the congressional prerogative. Those who know the Senate have difficulty visualizing any circumstance in which its members would voluntarily subject themselves to an election when they did not have to. But perhaps that strikes the right balance. A procedure for removing incompetent or unstable or discredited Presidents would be available to a national majority as expressed through its representatives—which is not now the case, at grave risk to the nation—but the process would be sufficiently unattractive to assure that it would be used only when absolutely, and incontrovertibly, necessary, and when public support was overwhelming.

Perhaps better ideas will be heard as this whole problem is considered. The important thing is that the country begin talking seriously about what should be done about the presidency—about how that awesome concentration of power can somehow be hedged in with the kind of restraints that our society tries to make sure exist in every other lesser organization.

NOTES

1. *The President and the Presidency* (Chicago: Public Administration Service, 1949), a compilation of lectures given in 1947.
2. Luther Gulick and L. Urwick (eds.), *Papers on the Science of Administration* (New York: Institute of Public Administration, 1937), pp. 6–7.
3. William D. Carey, "Presidential Staffing in the Sixties and Seventies," *Public Administration Review*, Vol. 29, No. 5 (September/October 1969).

4. *Essays on Federal Reorganization* (University, Ala.: University of Alabama Press, 1950), p. 8.
5. "The Textbook Presidency and Political Science," paper prepared for delivery at the annual meeting of the American Political Science Association, 1970.
6. *Presidential Power* (New York: John Wiley and Sons, 1960), pp. vii, 181–185.
7. *Big Democracy* (New York: Knopf, 1945), p. 124.
8. *Essays on Federal Reorganization, op. cit.,* p. 147.
9. Quoted by Harold Seidman in National Academy of Public Administration, Preliminary Papers, Conference on the Institutional Presidency, March 1974, p. 40.

Let the Sun Shine In

ALLEN SCHICK

Information is one of the perennial battlegrounds of American politics. The issue cannot be settled by words or sentiments, for divergent interests and values are at stake. The same revolutionary generation which gave America the First Amendment closed the doors of its Constitutional Convention. The same President who on July 4, 1966, told us "a democracy works best when the people have all the information that the security of the Nation permits," made "credibility gap" a household phrase. It is now five years since the Freedom of Information Act (FOI) took effect, yet the Pentagon Papers, the Anderson columns, and hundreds of lesser-known episodes attest to the closure of vital public acts from public view.

THE FREEDOM OF INFORMATION ACT

Under the Act which went into effect in 1967, all persons are entitled to access to the records of federal agencies. Exempting nine categories of information to protect national security, confidentiality, personnel files, and certain other specified interests, the Act strives for a "formula which encompasses, balances, and protects all interests, yet places emphasis on the fullest possible disclosure." The Act also requires each federal agency to publish regulations governing access to its records, and provides judicial remedies in case a request for information is turned down. But the Act is not self-enforcing; it takes an attempt to obtain information to activate the law, and willingness to go through a costly and time-consuming litigative process to make use of the judicial remedies. Thus, the actual effects of FOI depend on how it is used by the public and how it is interpreted by administrators and the courts. Because many of its provisions—in particular the nine exemptions—are worded ambiguously, FOI furnishes ample room for political controversy, administrative maneuvering, and judicial activity.

Most requests for information have been granted routinely, even before FOI, and most have been handled on an informal basis. Each day, thousands of exchanges are processed over the phone, through office visits, etc. What is important about FOI is the fraction of instances in which access is denied, for these are likely to be the cases in which public policies are contested; there is a need to balance conflicting rights and interests, and agencies are unwilling to open themselves to public scrutiny.

The difference between routine and difficult explains one of the anomalies of the FOI field. For years there has been controversy over the openness of government operations, and this has not been abated by passage of the legislation. One organization that spends full time tracking FOI conditions has written of the law's first years: "it has been hailed as a triumph for freedom of information and condemned as a poor substitute for a viable open records law." Generally, those who argue that FOI is ineffective point to difficult cases in which access was refused. The Freedom of Information Act has operated under political conditions and with effects that were not foreseen by its sponsors, who waged a decade-long campaign to establish the "right to know" as federal information policy in place of the "need to know" test that had been promulgated under the Administrative Procedures Act of 1946. The political climate of the late 1960's and early 1970's has been quite different from what it was in the years preceding the enactment of FOI. In particular, the rise and activism of public interest groups dealing with consumer and environmental protection have turned FOI from a declaration of the public's right to be informed into a potent and much-used instrument of political pressure. Moreover, the implementation of FOI has coincided with growing concern over the right to privacy and the confidentiality of government-held data.

INFORMATION AS A POLITICAL RIGHT

The coalition which led the protracted campaign for FOI was drawn primarily from the news media (especially newspapers) and certain congressional committees. Both groups were irked by the proclivity of federal agencies to conceal their actions and records from public view—the media, because secrecy interferes with their news-gathering functions; congressmen, because it bars effective legislative oversight of administrative agencies. The "people's right to know" (the title of an influential book by an early FOI crusader) was the guiding principle of the movement, and it dominated the many congressional hearings and investigations that preceded enactment of the law. The original FOI'ers wanted "to establish a general philosophy of full agency disclosure" that would make impossible attainment of important democratic values: an informed and responsible electorate; a government accountable to the public; an independent and vigilant press; and an Executive Branch that is responsive to the people's representatives in Congress. Thus they conceived of FOI in terms of the political processes of democracy (informed voters, free competition of ideas, and separation of powers) and personal liberty (freedom of expression and communication).

But in the several years since FOI was passed, a new political force with a substantially different conception of the political use of information has moved to the forefront, while the original FOI sponsors have been relatively quiescent. The media have made little discernible use of FOI; very few of the more than 100 lawsuits challenging agency refusal to grant access have been brought by newsmen.

Yet, the significance of FOI has grown, for it has been activated by public interest groups for whom the right to know is not an end in itself but an instrument of anti-bureaucratic political action. As one of Ralph Nader's associates has explained:

> Some who urged the adoption of new legislation simply believed that unclassified information should be available to private persons. Others. . .also sought an instrument to expose some of the internal workings of government agencies. . .the ultimate goal was substantial administrative reform, achieved in part through heightened public awareness of administrative deficiencies.

By prying information loose from recalcitrant administrators and by focusing public attention on controversial administrative policies, the public interest crusaders aim to challenge both the ways government agencies decide and the decisions themselves, and in addition to break what they regard as the unwarranted bonds between government agencies and their regulated clients. To accomplish this, the convergence of FOI and public interest law has been very crucial. Before FOI, public records were available to "persons properly and directly concerned," a standard which could easily be satisfied by business firms and trade associations, but not by consumers or environmentalists. The emergence of public interest law has brought political organization and resources to these previously under-represented areas; FOI has given these groups administrative and judicial standing which they previously lacked. Many of the FOI suits, and some of the most far-reaching ones, have been brought by public interest groups, and many have involved consumer and environmental interests.

FOI AS A POLITICAL PROBLEM

FOI has become enmeshed with the separable but often conjoined issues of privacy and confidentiality. Through FOI, government can become the vehicle for informing citizens of the activities of others. This danger has been heightened by the role of government as the leading collector of private data, by the prospect of what the Ervin Subcommittee on Constitutional Protection recently termed "dossier dictatorship," and by the pressures to open government records to public scrutiny. Although several of the exemptions in FOI pertain to confidential or private matters, the fact is that agencies are buffeted by powerful pressures to disclose and, as Alan Westin has pointed out in *Privacy and Freedom*, "the difficulty with the Freedom of Information Act . . . is that it seems to appoint the government the necessary champion of the citizen's right to privacy." The person whose private affairs are to be unveiled is not a party to the FOI process.

PUBLIC AND PRIVATE INFORMATION

As the growth of government has turned information from a political right into a political resource, the struggle for access has entered new ground. No longer is it a matter of an informed citizenry alone, information is now sought to bolster the private roles of consumers, investors, and all partners in the ecological drama of our times. This broadened concept has its antecedents in the first consumer protection laws enacted early in this century which cast the federal government as the agent of private citizens. Through governmental intervention, foods and drugs had to be accurately labeled, and stock underwriters were required to disclose basic financial data. The case for full disclosure of private information was put in a Nicholas Von Hoffmann column of May 12, 1972:

> From every standpoint, the public's need to know how immense corporations like RCA are run is as important as its need to know how the government is run. All sorts of laws and public policies in everything from foreign trade to tax allowances are predicated on the assumption of optimally efficient managers chosen by merit and not by their taste in tailors. If management productivity is slacking off, we needs must know it.

The struggle thus boils down to the issue of whether there exists any longer a meaningful and clear distinction between public and private. At the present time, a unit of the American Institute of Certified Public Accountants is at work trying to redefine the principles of the profession. It must decide between those who demand that social impacts should be incorporated into corporate financial statements (led by Ralph Nader's Corporation Accountability Research Group) and those who believe that corporate reporting should concern itself primarily with the interests of shareholders and creditors.

The issue carries one step further because the federal government accumulates vast amounts of information by virtue of being a buyer and seller in private markets. What about the test data gathered by federal agencies when they evaluate products offered by private vendors? One of the early freedom of information suits was brought by the Consumers Union to obtain VA data on hearing aids. Following a partial defeat in the courts, the Veterans' Administration (along with other federal agencies such as GSA) reversed its policies and decided to make public much product information.

Those who insist on full disclosure are fearful that any breach in their access to governmental files would enable the government to withhold information which is of incontestable public value. They do not trust government with the role of arbiter of the conflicting interests which must be balanced. Under the Freedom of Information Act this task now is within the jurisdiction of the courts which, in effect, weigh the equities in much the manner that bureaucracies once did. The advantage of a judicial remedy is not only that it affords a review of agency actions, but also that it breaks the bonds between regulating agencies and their regulated clients.

This does not mean, however, that private data always will be stripped of confidential protection. Coexisting on the books with the Freedom of Information Act are dozens of statutes which authorize or require confidentiality, including the blanket provision of 18 USC 1905, which puts under lock and key all information pertaining "to the trade secrets, processes, operations, style of work" of any firm. Exemption three of the FOI preserves these statutory prohibitions. Nevertheless, there is a broad grey area covering instances where confidentiality is not tendered but expected, and where the public is denied access even when no specific statute can be cited. Concerning these, the President's Commission on Federal Statistics recommended in September 1971 that "a promise to hold data in confidence should not be made unless the agency has authority to uphold such a promise."

CONFIDENTIALITY VS. PRIVACY

The Freedom of Information Act recognizes that a difference must be made between business confidentiality and personal privacy. Thus, one of the exemptions covers trade secrets and financial information, while another deals with personnel and medical files. In practice, however, it is not always easy to maintain the distinction. An interesting case arose out of a newsman's request to the Internal Revenue Service to inspect the lists of persons and firms registered under the Gun Control Act of 1968. Insisting that confidentiality and privacy must be treated differently, IRS granted access to lists of gun dealers, but refused permission for the lists of gun collectors.

A claim of privacy has dubious validity when it is used to withhold information from the person whose privacy presumably is being protected. From time to time the House Subcommittee on Foreign Operations and Government Information (now chaired by Representative William Moorhead), which acts as an unofficial ombudsman on informational policies, receives complaints from federal employees that they were denied access to their own personnel files. Proposals are pending in Congress to establish a new writ of *habeas data*, under which a citizen would have the right to inspect private credit files. No less a right ought to be available to citizens in their dealing with government.

When privacy involves someone else's desire to inspect the files, consideration might be given to a reinstatement of the discredited ''need to know'' test that was operative under the Administrative Procedure Act of 1946. In fact, the U.S. Court of Appeals recently applied a version of that test in allowing university professors to examine certain NLRB records. The Court felt assured that the data drawn by academic researchers would not be misused, but it suggested that a different outcome might be appropriate if the same data were requested for a different use or by a different user. In deciding on the basis of the quality of the user, the Court cast aside the FOI standard which entitles all persons to equality of access, but it was weighing the conflicting equities as courts have done for many centuries.

THE CONTINUING STRUGGLE

Public versus private is only one version of the never-ending battle over freedom of information. Over the past year, attention has been fixed on the issue of national security classification, a problem which will not now disappear because President Nixon issued Executive Order 11652 on March 8, 1972. That order tightened the rules for classification, cut in half the number of agencies authorized to classify and by two-thirds the number of classifiers, and established a timetable for the automatic declassification of most documents. In addition, a committee has been appointed to monitor the classification system. Yet, these moves, desirable as they are, will not keep the Pentagon from overclassifying, for the incentives built into the national security apparatus of the United States are overwhelmingly on the side of secrecy and hidden files.

Nor will the warring end between those interdependent adversaries—the news media and government agencies. Nothing less than full disclosure will satisfy the media, except perhaps when truly national security matters such as troop movements are involved. For its part, government will want to maneuver news reporting to ensure favorable coverage, and news leaks will coexist with secrecy as two of the main ploys. A 1972 survey by the American Society of Newspaper Editors asked 28 top Washington correspondents whether, in their opinion, governmental secrecy has increased or decreased. Only one replied that more information is

EDMUND G. BROWN, JR.

available today, while 19 said that secrecy has increased, and 8 detect no substantial change in governmental practices.

Another battleground will be the relationship between Congress and the President. While Congress has been ambivalent about the openness of its own operations, it has no doubt that it is entitled to just about everything in the possession of federal agencies, including files developed by the White House bureaucracy. In his article for this forum, Professor Arther Miller suggests that the issue be given to the courts for resolution. However laudable and effective the recourse to judiciary, I suspect that the matter cannot be put to rest in a courtroom. The Constitution and American political processes cast the President and Congress in adversary roles, and they will continue to battle over scraps of paper whenever their divergent political interests are involved.

If the informational wars ever end, it will not be because government is an open book, but because the public and its agents no longer care or fight. In urging a continuing struggle, it is worth bearing in mind what Mr. Justice Brandeis wrote nearly 60 years ago: "Sunlight is said to be the best of disinfectants; electric light the most efficient policeman." Let the battle go on and let the sun shine in.

A Society of the People. And by. And for.

EDMUND G. BROWN, JR.

People sit back and wonder why their taxes keep going up, why it is that government keeps getting bigger. And it has gotten bigger. It has taken a dramatic jump forward under the leadership of individuals whose entire philosophy and public utterances are to the exact opposite. I refer not only to my predecessor, but to President Carter's predecessor.

So I think we have to ask ourselves, and I'm not raising this as a political question, but as just a way to understand the nature of reality that we all face. Why is it that despite the public philosophy of those in key positions, government gets bigger and bigger, more complex, more involved, and your taxes keep going up?

The very simple reason is that it takes more than words to put some limit on that growth. There are certain needs and obligations in the community that just have to be taken care of, and if you don't do it, through some volunteer movement, some other arrangement outside of the public sector, then inevitably government will take the task and assume those obligations.

If you take, let it be the mentally ill, the narcotic-abuse program, the alcohol programs, child-care, nursing homes, hospitals, training activities, and you meet every need that can be identified, you would have to double and possibly even triple the existing government activity that we now have at the state, local, and Federal level.

Something as straightforward as police activity—how many police can you hire and how many are patrolling the streets? The ratio will never be high enough unless people assume a greater degree of responsibility for their own defense and protection. That's not to say that we don't need police—sure we have to have them—but unless the public sector in its manifestation of security by police activity will link itself with the citizens, then all the money in the world will not make the streets safe.

In Santa Ana, there is a police chief who has inaugurated a community-oriented police program and has involved the community through neighborhood meetings, through block captains, in their own security along with the activities of the police.

There is no substitute for neighborhoods, for mutual-support systems in the private sector. Whether it be neighbors who know each other, who have some responsibility for someone other than themselves and their family—you can't get away from it. The idea that you can put it on government, if you want to, is going to triple your taxes because then you have to hire a full-time person who doesn't have the commitment involved in it that you would to do that kind of work.

That's my simple message: that voluntarism is not a luxury, it is a necessity for a civilized society that wants to truly meet its human needs. And we have to expand it in a dramatic way across a broad front of government and human activity. We have to find some way to re-create the spirit of neighborliness and mutual self-support that existed before the mobility and the anonymity and increasing information flow that has been the product of this very prosperous society.

When the historians write the pages of California and the United States of America in the 20th and 21st centuries, what are they going to find? I don't want to see just one big government because everything in government at one point or another tends to get politicized; it's an adversary relationship.

When we take these basic human needs, give them to a professional class, everyone else sits back and pays their taxes and gets more and more irritated because they want to know why they're going up. That's because you can't just have rights to things, because for every right you have to have a correlative duty or obligation. There is no escaping that.

You may think you have more mobility and freedom and liberty—a "do-your-own-thing" kind of ethic—but in reality it comes back in the form of government, taxation, crime and mental confusion.

That's what we have in this culture today, and unless you who have been in the forefront accelerate your efforts even further, and all of us who have some degree of responsibility magnify and expand what we're doing, then we really face a civilization that is not what I think anybody wants. And that's why voluntarism is so important.

When I went back to Williams, Calif., where my great-grandparents came from Germany in the 1850's, I walked into a nursing home. It was a very nice place, people were working hard cleaning and making sure the residents were attended, but I thought to myself, here's a place where elderly people are sent when they reach a certain age, and are paying $600-$700 a month for strangers to take care of people that not too many years before would have been upstairs in the bedroom, or in rocking chairs sitting in the living room. It would have been a part of the context of normal life.

But in order to expand the productivity, the freedom, the mobility, the prosperity, we have segregated, we have specialized, so we have nursing homes for the old, child-care for the young, mental hospitals for those who act in a rather strange way or are different from the rest of us. And schools that start early and keep going till one's mid-20's, longer if possible.

We're institutionalizing everybody. And I'd like to de-institutionalize everybody, I'd like to have a community that has a more human spirit to it. I think people are ready for that. I think they are ready to do something more than what they are doing now, because they can understand the needs, they're not going to go away, people are living longer, they are going to need more care, and it isn't all the work of specialists—that is a myth.

Dying for people is not a sickness, it's not something we necessarily have to go to a hospital for, it's part of the cycle. And as there is joy at the beginning, there is sorrow at the end, but let us at least make it human. There are hospices for the dying now, started by Elisabeth Kubler-Ross, where people actually help those people who are going through this necessary human transition. It helps them; they are support and take people out of hospitals. This woman told me that 70 percent of the terminally ill people do not need to be hospitalized. They want to be among friends. They ought to be going out with some dignity and joy and laughter. The same thing is true about lots of things in life. We have got to pull together and try to bear one another's burdens in some human, compassionate way. And this is something I've been thinking about for a long time: How do we bring that about?

One strategy is to get a bill, a tax, and more people on the public payroll. And the problem with that is that the power in the cities is moving out of this community, up to Sacramento, over to Washington, and those who make the decisions don't get that face-to-face contact so they understand the real nature of the problem.

What we do is deal with paper, and we deal with money and we keep shuffling it around. A lot of good things happen out of that, but it's not the same as people in a local community, who recognize their problems—whether they be low-income people, the elderly, whether they be different cultures from Anglos, Chicanos, blacks—and try to face up and deal with the implications of them; and own a society and a culture that we ought to be proud of.

It's not all by government; it's not all by professionals. A lot of these decisions, whether they be in medicine or law, welfare or schools, are not just the prerogative of the specialists, or a licensed person with that little seal under the diploma hanging on the wall. That's the myth of specialization and division of labor.

What that is creating is a solitary society of dependent people who have to go to a paid professional to tell them how to make basic human decisions. Yes, you need a lot of these professions: I'm not saying you don't. But a lot of what goes on is something you, your friends, your neighbors, those in coalitions—whether they be religious, political, labor, or voluntary—can do to look after yourselves.

The Dialectical Organization: An Alternative to Bureaucracy

ORION F. WHITE, JR.

One of the more interesting aspects of the early development of public administration in the United States was the extent to which sociological factors apparently affected the prescriptions and principles of which its literature was composed. Faced with the task of making a secure role for themselves in the American academic, governmental, and societal structure, writers of the early public administration literature hardly felt impelled to notice or to dwell in their work on the less attractive aspects of administration in the governmental process. As a consequence of this shading in the early perspective, however, a literature was produced which explicitly disavowed but nonetheless contained significant ideological premises.[1] This ideological bent was characterized by the tendency to see administration as the solution—a remedy which is only technically problematical and without side effects—to most problems of government.

This picture of administration—through the early teachings, the successes of the reform movement, and the widespread adoption of the city-manager form of government—has been widely distributed both through academia and the general public.[2]

This strain of thinking probably is still the dominant one in the established centers of public administrative study in the United States. However, there is quite definitely a tangent of thought which is moving out from the established core. Political scientists and sociologists have begun to raise questions about the operation of administrative structures in and on government and society.[3] It seems odd that the field of public administration itself has not evidenced a general awareness of the rumblings of change that are being heard in the public and from some intellectuals—especially in light of the fact that in its early days as a discipline it prompted a radical governmental reform movement. There does appear to be some cognizance of the increasing criticism of government administration, but there is little orientation toward change in the sense of reaction to broader problems.

What is the problem of administration which is creating the public and intellectual reaction alluded to above? In a general sense, it is the way in which *people* are being treated by administrative systems: it is the problem of "clientele bureaucracies." The other aspects of the problem of formal bureaucratic organization— the problems of effective operation, capacity to plan effectively, and that of making job roles compatible with the healthy human personality—have been and are being given extensive attention by scholars in the general areas of administration, organization theory, and management, but little attention has been turned to the problem of understanding and improving the relations between organizations and their clients. It is not surprising that this is the case, however, since traditionally the client was viewed as demanding only "efficiency" defined in the same sense that administrators defined it. Hence the problem of effective clientele relations was seen as essentially a problem in effective "management."

TWO MODELS OF CLIENT RELATIONS: ADULTS AND CHILDREN

In order to understand fully the nature of the complaints about the treatment of clients in current administrative institutions, and in turn what can be done to meet these complaints, it is helpful to examine the question of what forms clientele relations can take.

The client-organization relation has not been a major theoretical concern of those interested in bureaucratic organizations and administration. However, one particularly relevant analysis does exist and it can be employed as an outline of a framework.[4] Basing an analysis on some suggestive data gathered by Alvin Gouldner, Victor Thompson conceptualized client-organization relations in terms of the maturity of personality brought to the relationship by the client. While he is definitely aware of the pathology of bureaucratic personality and structure, Thompson depicts much of the concern about "red tape" and other problems as stemming from excessive "childishness" in some clients. Thompson's perspective provides a useful basis for a dichotomous analysis of the problematic aspects of organization-client relations. Viewed at the one extreme, the client's posture *vis-à-vis* the organization with which he is interacting could be seen as essentially "childlike," while at the other extreme, essentially "adult."

The Client as Child

Though admittedly a somewhat artificial schema, the child's psychological makeup can be viewed in terms of five closely related aspects: (1) a feeling of powerlessness, (2) inability to abstract well and consequent tendency to personalize all relationships, (3) inability to cathect energy in future goals—i.e., to delay gratification of wants he seeks to satisfy, (4) inability to take the role of the other and hence to see the point in explaining or accounting for his behavior, and (5) an expectation that his needs will be met without his having to pay a price for the gratifications.

When confronted with the demands of a formal organization, the childlike client will find much that clashes with his personality. Because he feels powerless, he is somewhat afraid and suspicious of authoritative administrative institutions; his propensity to personalize all his relationships prevents him from understanding, much less accepting, the impersonal operation of formal organizations; his inability to tolerate delayed gratification causes him to become irritated at time-consuming formalities; and his expectation of reward without price leads him to resent the demands which organizations inevitably make on recipients of their services or goods. It is such clients—ones who carry childlike orientations to their organizational relations—who in large part define the "problem of bureaucracy."

The Client as Adult

In contrast, for the segment of clients which could be termed "adult," no such problem exists. The "adult client" finds that his basic personality inclinations coincide with the patterns of operation of formal organization. As an adult, he feels no relative power deprivation and hence no fear of powerful institutions. He is able to assume an impersonal attitude toward others when the occasion demands (probably most often in his own job role) and is thereby able to "understand" when organizations treat him in an impersonal fashion. The adult, since he understands the instrumental nature of the economic relationship and is able to distinguish it from the love relation, realizes both that he must by necessity pay for what he gets and most likely will have to wait for it in addition. As an adult he is probably able to achieve self-insight by assuming an "objective" posture toward his own personality structure. He sees that important segments of his self are obscure even to him. Hence he finds little offense in even somewhat personal organizational probing.

The current criticism of the way administrative bureaucracies are operating on clients in general fits the pattern of objections outlined in the client-as-child model, indicating that the Gouldner-Thompson analysis is still accurate. The charges against administrative structures as they are popularly framed are that they are too powerful, inhumanly impersonal, rather slow in acting (or, more often, simply do not help people at all), pry too far and too often into individuals' lives, and exact too heavy a price from individuals through the use of rules. Viewed from this perspective, the problem of bureaucracy can be viewed as a form of clash between generations, in that demands are being made that clients be treated in a more personal, childlike fashion by formal organizations.

TWO COMMENTS ON THE ADULT WORLD OF ORGANIZATIONS

In regard to the question of what justification there is for a serious response to demands from "childlike" clients, it is enlightening to examine two central tenets of traditional administrative structure: the concept of "policy rationality" and the "efficiency criterion." These mainly are the principles which define and justify the "adult" nature of administrative organizations, hence weaknesses in these tenets must be considered as rightful openings for arguments that the nature of such organizations be altered or transformed.

Regardless of whether or not the concept of rationality, to begin with, can adequately comprehend the reality of the process by which public goals are transformed into administrative action, it serves a useful purpose if it can be shown that it provides a basis for organizational coherence through systemization of policy.

However, Gideon Sjoberg, Richard Brymer, and Buford Farris have recently drawn attention to the striking and undeniable point that bureaucracies do not hold to truly systemized, rational policy.[5] Rather, they enforce policy differentially in response to pressures by clients and in accord with the clients' social class position. Just as is the case of children and adults in actuality, where parents enforce rules of behavior on their children which they violate themselves, "childlike" lower-class clients are forced to conform to rules and to patterns of treatment which "adult" middle-class clients are able to avoid.

Hence, the "rational" policy or rule is in many cases the "best way to do it" (or, as is often claimed, "the only way") mainly for those who lack the resources required to pressure the organization into using another and less onerous "best way" in their particular case. This inconsistency in rational policy application, when coupled with the related fact that rational policy is not "rational," but is actually based in large part on a less than comprehensive survey of possibilities thought out through only a political logic, should serve as substantial grounds for challenge of this concept as a basis of defense for traditional organizational structure.[6]

Just as with the rationality principle, so can the "efficiency" criterion be critically examined in light of its ideological aspect. What has tended to be obscured in discussions of organizational efficiency—because the dominant concern has been with how to measure and maximize it—is the fact that the criterion of efficiency itself is but a technical version of the classic and fundamental political question of order versus freedom. The degree of efficiency with which an organization works its way on a client is simply a lower-level framing of the question of how much freedom the client wishes or may have to yield in the name of the general order. Efficiency as an idea and operational standard is subject to political definition.

It thus appears that two basic tenets of traditional administration cannot serve as effective defenses for it. A helpful method for moving away from the traditional conceptualization might be to view the problem "dialectically." Rather than aim toward "balance," the dialectically formulated objective would be reversal of past patterns. By so doing, a picture could perhaps be drawn of an organization which could meet even the most extreme shift in its client environment.

DIMENSIONS OF A DIALECTICAL ANALYSIS OF BUREAUCRATIC ORGANIZATIONAL STRUCTURE

In order to carry out this type of analysis most effectively here, observational data from a case study of a small clientele-centered organization will be presented.[7] These data are directly relevant in that the organization is attempting to operate with a structure that is antithetical to the traditional bureaucratic type. Hence its experience provides both a concrete example of what a counter-bureaucratic model of organization would be like and what problems might be encountered in attempting to implement such a model in practice.

The agency to be analyzed is a private, church-related social service agency which operates in a low-income area of San Antonio, Texas. It has roots going back to 1909, but was officially constituted in its present form in 1958. While the agency is church related, it is definitely ecumenical in its approach to social service work. Policy control over the agency is carried out through a board of directors, which has authority to make policy and develop procedures for the agency consistent with the general guidelines of the national division in the church which governs such agencies. The great bulk of its sizable annual funds comes from church sources and the United Fund, but some money is received from membership and service fees, and from agency projects. With a staff of approximately 32 (at the beginning of the study), the agency maintains three separate neighborhood centers, which during fiscal years 1965-66 served 3,000 individuals (or approximately 1,200 families) through groups, special services, clinic programs, and home visiting.

In addition to carrying out such programs as building neighborhood organization, and maintaining a clinic and kindergarten, the agency has been carrying out a delinquency control program, and is involved officially in the "war on poverty." It supervises a day-care center financed with poverty funds, is involved in a Neighborhood Youth Corps program, and supervises a VISTA program. While the agency is firmly implanted in its environment and enjoys close ties to the neighborhoods it serves (some agency workers were involved in agency programs as children), it is by no means stagnant or fixed in its outlook or its actual operation. It is attempting a basic innovation in social work style, and along with this change in style have gone fundamental alterations in organization structure. The unorthodox patterns can be catalogued as in the areas of clientele interactions, administrative structure, organizational ideology, and the staff's "organizational mentality."

Dimension I: Client Relations

The nature of the interaction of client and organization is for the most part defined by the particular structural arrangements characteristic of the organization, since these not only impose formal constraints on the interaction, but also tend to shape its more subtle, informal aspects, as Merton showed when he detailed the structural sources of the bureaucratic personality and how this affects interactions with clients.[8] With the traditional bureaucratic organizational structure, relations to clients are quite definitely circumscribed in several ways.

The whole tenor of the interaction is set, in the first place, by the fact that the client is viewed as a subordinate to the bureaucrat.[9] The hierarchical pattern of authority in which the bureaucrat functions is simply extended into the client relation. This means, in addition, that the same process by which responsibility, or as Victor Thompson put it, "blamability," is transmitted from the powerful top to the weaker bottom levels of the hierarchy works on the client.[10] This means that the client is blamed or held responsible for the failure of the bureaucracy to treat or remedy his problems.

Second, just as the bureaucrat's role is specialized, so is his interaction with the client segmental—he relates to the client not as a total person, but as a specific type of problem or in terms of one part of a general problem.

Third, because bureaucratic structures are legitimate or authoritative, they usually represent and advocate the status quo to the client. Most social service organizations have traditionally stressed helping the client "adjust" to his life situation, rather than working for rearrangement of the social structure which is causing the client's problem.

Fourth, even though the client-oriented bureaucrat's task is the quite intimate one of helping effect a personal adjustment, he must carry out his interaction with the client in an impersonal fashion because he operates from a fixed role definition, the purpose of which is to insure "objectivity" and "impartiality" in his treatment of clients.

Fifth, because the bureaucrat operates under the norm of efficiency, he can invest his and his organization's resources in the client in only a qualified fashion. That is, if the client appears to require more resources or "input" for treatment than the solution of his case represents as a unit of organizational "output," he simply will not be treated. To treat him would be "inefficient."

The type of client relation which is dialectically opposite to the bureaucratic type is obvious and easily describable in terms of the five characteristics mentioned above. The opposite of the client-as-subordinate framework of bureaucratic organizations is the client-as-peer as the basic posture of the professional-client interaction. Instead of viewing the client segmentally as a "problem" or part of a problem, he would be viewed in terms of a "gestalt" type perspective as a total person. Rather than advocating the current social order to the client, the nonbureaucrat professional would, at least, be *willing* to solve the client's problem by removing its more general causes in society if this were the course of action indicated. A personal involvement rather than an objective-instrumental type relation would be characteristic of the nonbureaucratic client relation—perhaps at the expense of impartiality or bureaucratic "fairness." There would be a willingness, last, to keep on attempting to help clients—even supposedly helpless cases. The commitment to client service would be unequivocal.

Client Interaction

These conditions of client interaction are being realized in the Wesley agency. Instead of allowing the consideration of the structural integrity of the agency to dictate the mode of client interaction, the agency's conceptualization of the proper client-organization interaction prevails and the administrative structure is fitted to this. This conceptualization is based upon or derives primarily from two sources: a theologically founded service orientation and the new theory of social work practice which has been developed in the agency. The agency sees definite implications in its theological base for service to clients. As it is stated in personnel orientation materials discussing the service orientation, these implications are:

1. Service is not at a distance—it means personal involvement with people.
2. No person or problem is beyond our concern or attention. In fact, we are obligated to seek out the "outcasts."
3. Our motivation for service cannot be the possibility of success or any other condition that might be associated with the receiver of the service. We can never really give up on a person.
4. Our own interests or personal feelings are not of any importance as we serve. We may not personally like the person.
5. We must individually assume that we are responsible when others do not live up to their responsibility, and thus try our best to make a difference.

This explicitly stated orientation supports in obvious ways the dialectically defined client relation sketched earlier: in particular the personal involvement and disregard for "efficiency" (traditionally defined) in the helping relation are clearly supported by the agency's theological base. Also, the personal involvement with the client means that he will be viewed as a total person rather than segmentally. The other major source of the unorthodox client orientation, as noted above, is the theory of social work style developed in the agency. In broad terms, the Wesley agency theory of social work stresses mutual conciliation of all parts of a social problem situation. Hence it differs from the classical clinical style, which stresses a therapeutic role for the social worker through which a psychic rearrangement or restructuring of the individual client is effected. These excerpts from one document stating the Wesley agency theory summarize the points relevant to the present discussion:

> [Our] outlook involves a responsiveness to all of the perspectives of all participants involved in the social work process. It is assumed that all social processes involve the interaction of participants having similar and dissimilar perspectives. The social worker . . . is responsible for transcending these perspectives, and this transcendent ideology becomes the perspective to which he is accountable. However . . . the social worker may have to be more partisan in favor of the perspective of those having an unequal power position such as the poor. The goal of the social worker is a consensus or a "concord" of equals rather than a peaceful arrangement based on inequality. . . . [The] worker would help equalize the power positions of the participants before working on an agreement between different or conflicting perspectives.

The ultimate objective of this type of social work is to enable the client to represent himself as an equal in the process of working out a concord between himself and community institutions. Hence the goal is not to subordinate the client, but to elevate him to a position of equal power and negotiational effectiveness. On the other hand, workers must interact with representatives of community institutions in an effort to build good will or "credit" with them which can then be used to the benefit of the client. Also, an effort is made to alter the institutions' view of their lower-class clients.

Orienting professional workers toward clients in this fashion has created some problems for the agency, however. As has often been noted, a great deal of strain is introduced into the service role when a person who has undergone long and arduous professional education and training must relate to his client as a peer and thereby allow him, for example, to judge the success of the professional's effort to help him. A much more comfortable position for the professional is to utilize his organizational position, social status, and educational superiority to hold the client in a subordinate posture. Group work in the agency, where the social worker plays the role of leader adorned with obvious physical and symbolic status indicators, tends to be favored over individual work with problem cases "out in the neighborhood," where clients are confronted more on a peer basis and where the worker is responsible to the client, and not to his "profession," its organizations, nor to "professional knowledge."

Further, it is highly frustrating to work on really tough cases, with little hope of success and no possibility of simply "giving up." In addition, there is a tendency to avoid necessary efforts at building "credit" with the representatives of community institutions. These people often hold a higher status position than the workers, and sometimes regard them as nuisances. The agency must keep reinfusing its professionals with its conceptualization of clientele relations, so as to combat the inevitable tendency to slip back into the more secure bureaucratic posture.

Since the objective of the agency's style is to enable clients to fend for themselves before community institutions, its successes often turn out to have the quality of a double-edged sword. Since the agency is itself a community institution which is highly visible, it is often confronted with effective criticism from its own, successfully helped clients. While these attacks are problems for the agency, however, what they mean is that the agency is constantly forced to reevaluate its operations and change itself in the direction dictated by client needs as these become apparent. This is in effect a "dialectical administrative process," in that the agency is held constantly responsive to contradictions between itself and client needs.

A further problem is the one of resources. This difficulty has two essential aspects. On the one hand, given the unqualified commitment to all clients, a shortage of worker resources is virtually inevitable. One reaction to this is overwork on the part of the personnel—a problem which the organization must take explicit action against. The other aspect of this problem is maintaining a sufficient input of resources from the agency's supporting environment. Since the agency is committed to active social change where it seems necessary—especially in raising the power position of the lower class—it lives in danger of criticism from representatives of the status quo in the community. This criticism can result in threats or actual sanctioning of the agency. It possesses a major defense in this regard, however, in its theologically based operating philosophy. It can employ powerful and widely shared symbols from this philosophy in rationalizing its actions to its environment.

In spite of these problems, the agency's relations with its clients must be considered effective at least as far as current observations indicate. It has scored some striking successes with extremely hard cases—such as with an individual who at one point committed violent physical aggression against an agency social worker, but who through persistent personal involvement by the worker was developed into a stable, highly effective personality. In one other case, a young male was successfully reinstated in school after having been expelled from five different schools and dropped as a "case" by other welfare agencies. He was considered "hopeless" and public school officials stated flatly that they would never readmit him.

The religious base of the agency no doubt plays a part in its success in having its social workers relate to clients in the problematical, unorthodox fashion described. However, not all the staff have the same religious affiliation as the agency and not all are religious in the conventional sense. The conceptualization of the client relationship probably is generally a workable one, if the other aspects of an organization are such that the unorthodox client relationship is supported, and can yield distinctive success in some hard cases.

Dimension II: Administrative Structure

The traditional bureaucratic administrative structure possesses two central characteristics which are most relevant to the analysis here. The more basic of these two is the principle of hierarchy, which entails strictly defined roles articulated in terms of layers of authority. Policy is set at the top of the hierarchy and transmitted down through rules and close authoritative supervision which insures that the rules are followed. Categories of decisions, decision points, and decision criteria are all closely defined, and the most rule-bound of roles are those at the bottom of the hierarchy—where the client is met. In addition, bureaucratic structures promote a cohesive (*vis-à-vis* the environment) and homogeneous social structure. Conformity to a comprehensive and rather strictly defined set of norms is a primary characteristic of bureaucracies. (Because these norms are primarily middle class, bureaucratic organizations often find that they can neither understand nor communicate with lower-class clients.)[11]

In direct contrast to this type of administrative structure would be one where the basic principle of organization would be nonhierarchical—where roles are allocated authority functionally and equally, and where authority relations are thereby lateral instead of vertical. Hence at all levels roles would not be strictly defined, but would be fluid according to functional necessity. Also, policy would be set in a "balance of power" fashion by laterally related groups instead of "at the top." Instead of homogeneity, heterogeneity would prevail and be supported administratively in the organization. Conformity, in fact, would not be possible because there would be no predominant personnel "style" such as there is in a bureaucratic organization.

These are the administrative conditions which exist at the Wesley agency. Policy within the agency is fluid and is set, as an agency document notes, by "several bodies [executive staff, area staff, total program staff, and total staff] to insure flexibility and some balance of power within the staff." The two areas of policy not subject to change by the staff are those regarding alcoholic beverages and games of chance. Staff relations are explicitly designed on a principle of "non-dominance"—i.e., of not allowing individuals to possess or develop truly authoritative positions in the agency. Supervisory or management positions are periodically assigned by total staff decision, and in addition, the agency operates with overlapping administrative roles, so that one person may be over another in one functional area but under him in another area. While there are job descriptions, these are general in nature. No specific constraints except those relating to housekeeping activities (reports, records, etc.) are defined for the various roles. Also, except for such guidance as can be obtained from the agency's social work theory, few criteria for defining duties and effective role performance exist.

Heterogeneity is markedly evident in the organization, since it is only by maintaining a direct organizational cognizance of various perspectives and individual styles that the agency feels it can truly be responsive to its clients. Variety of three types is evident in the agency personnel: social class, personality, and service skill and style. Whereas bureaucratic agencies would not easily tolerate personnel who exhibited lower social class behavior patterns, such persons are valued staff people at the Wesley agency. By maintaining some lower social class personnel on the staff, the agency cannot readily develop a monolithic, class-based orientation. Heterogeneity in personality type and in service skills and style also help in this regard, in that a broad range of individuals and social service situations can be effectively communicated about and reacted to by the agency, and it is hence not forced by organizational necessity to define some persons or situations as "impossible" for it to handle.

The primary problem arising from use of this type of administrative structure is its "expense." Because of the rather unstructured, heterogeneous, and egalitarian nature of the agency, much flexibility and freedom of communication is obtained. At the same time, the efficient conflict-dampening and ambiguity-relieving effects of hierarchy are absent, and other more costly administrative techniques must be employed by the agency director as a substitute. A continuing socialization effort must be carried on in the agency. Through this process it is hoped that the staff will introject new norms which will supplant the culturally dominant norms of bureaucratic job structure which they had internalized.

This helps ease anxieties in a situation where duties, decision criteria, evaluation criteria, and a means for measuring output per unit of time are absent. Also, administrative supports for this same purpose must be provided. Salary is allocated by need and is not used as a technique of reward and punishment. The evaluation process is highly private and two-way and sanctions are not brought into play. Job tenure in the agency as far as possible is insured. Further difficulties are created by the regular conflicts and dissensions in the staff which arise out of its heterogeneous compositon. Personality frictions, disputes over priorities of skills, and social class-based conflicts in viewpoint occur and must be combatted through a resocialization effort and through administrative support for whichever perspective in dispute appears to be in the weaker position. These conflicts, it should be noted, are "valued" in the agency for the constant stimulus to evaluate which they provide. Hence the point of the administrative effort to contain them is not to smooth them out through human relations techniques, but rather to structure them so that they will be productive rather than destructive.[12]

In spite of the fact the agency employs an administrative structure which fosters diversity and dissent, and which creates anxieties among its personnel, it functions rather well administratively. It is quite organized in its internal procedures and so far even rather intense conflicts among the staff have been effectively mediated. Further, the problem appears to be lessening as the resocialization efforts led by the agency director continue.

Dimension III: Organizational Ideology

One way of conceptualizing organizational ideologies is in terms of an Apollonian-Dionysian continuum.[13] Norman O. Brown has characterized the human ego in such terms in order to denote the contrast between individuals who are unable to confront the reality of death and hence are oriented toward moderation and longevity—these he calls Apollonians after the Greek god of moderation, Apollo—rather than toward using themselves up in the process of life, as those people do who through a stronger ego are able to confront death without fear—these he calls "Dionysians" after the Greek god of the full life, Dionysius.[14]

There is a counterpart to this analogy at the organizational level. The traditional bureaucratic form of organization is clearly Apollonian in nature, in that it stresses first and above all self-preservation as an organizational structure—even at the complete expense of its goals. The numerous studies which document the phenomenon of goal succession in bureaucratic organizations bear this point out.[15] In contrast would be the nonbureaucratic organization form, which stresses first in a Dionysian fashion, the attainment of its purposes or goal.

It is possible to see from evidence already presented that Wesley agency's ideology at least approximates the nonbureaucratic Dionysian type. The heavy commitment to client service—even to the extent of actively working for changes in currently dominant community institutions—is one indicator of this, since activity of this sort could result in serious attack on the agency. More directly to the point, however, is the agency's position in regard to the involvement of staff or its neighborhood organizations in controversial issues or political issues. Each individual's or organization's civil right to participate in a controversial issue is supported explicitly in the agency. The decision of whether or not to participate is left up to the worker, and the agency will support him, even though his own differentiation of his agency and individual roles in the controversy is not accepted by the public. One such instance has occurred and it very nearly resulted in the effective destruction of the agency as it is presently constituted.

The only problem that exists because of the agency's Dionysian organizational ideology exists as a matter of definition. From the agency's own point of view, its willingness to spend itself in the service of its goal is natural and proper. It is only from a more Apollonian perspective that such a disposition could be faulted.

Dimension IV: Organizational Mentality

Herbert A. Shepard has effectively characterized the "mentality" of traditional bureaucratic structures as "primary" in nature.[16] At the individual level, the primary mentality, as Shepard puts it:

> . . . sees himself as separated from the rest of the world by his skin. . . . To provide what his internal environment needs . . . he must compete with other individuals for the scarce resources available in the external environment. Other individuals are at best instrumental to him in the satisfaction of his needs.[17]

This is, obviously, the mentality of the classical "economic man" and, indeed, of human nature itself as it has been defined by the most of psychology and our dominant socializing institutions.

The primary mentality is reflected in traditional organization structure in that it is built on the assumption that relations between people are threatful, competitive, and mutually exploitative. Cooperation and order must therefore be effected by coercion and compromise through a pyramidal structure of formal power. Individuals bargain across the levels of this pyramid as best they can and "win-and-lose" (go up, down, or stay put in the hierarchy) according to their skill in this competition. Organizational life in this situation has been aptly called "antagonistic cooperation," and the dysfunctional consequences it produces are many and serious.[18] The structure of most organizations, however, affirms the view of reality represented in the primary mentality, and thereby gives it the nature of a self fulfilling prophecy. Hence it appears that the only way to exact an organizational effort from people is through coercion and compromise.

In contrast to this type of mentality is the "secondary" type. Briefly, in Shepard's words:

> [The] secondary mentality assumes that individuals can have more than instrumental meaning for one another. . . . [It] assumes that personal development, well-being, self actualization are the products of authentic, non-exploitive interpersonal relations. . . . [This] means that the provision of the consumables needed for physical well-being can be accomplished through collaboration, and their distribution determined on a consensual basis. . . . The commitment of members of collaboration—consensus systems is to one another's growth, and to superordinate goals on which their growth in part depends.[19]

It should be clear from what has been said already about the Wesley agency that it must at least approximate the secondary mentality among its staff. The heavy emphasis on consensual decision in policy formulation and resource allocation and the nonhierarchial staff relationships indicates this. Further, while there is conflict, it is carried out for the most part through open, genuine confrontation about problems.

Most indicative, however, of the "secondary" nature of the organizational mentality of the agency is its intense commitment to the superordinate goal of service and the principle of existential responsibility which it espouses. Instead of attempting to avoid or shunt away responsibility in the way a primary mentality would in its attempt to win the organizational game of dominance he constantly plays, Wesley agency staff assumes a generalized existential responsibility for what happens in the agency. Each individual must be committed to the principle of shouldering whatever burden he sees must be shouldered in order to make the agency effective in its goal attainment effort without regard for the question of whether or not he is directly to "blame" for creating or for solving the problem.

It is probably by virtue of the fact that the staff is rather theologically oriented that they evidence secondary mentality traits to the extent that they do. At any rate, it is no doubt through a secondary mentality perspective and behavior patterns that the unorthodox structure of the agency functions so well. This apparent fact makes the organization type represented in the agency seem all the more feasible; since, as Shepard describes, people can be trained into the secondary mentality.

WESLEY AGENCY AS A DIALECTICAL ORGANIZATION

It is possible to see from the above description of a nonbureaucratic client organization that a central difference between the bureaucratic and nonbureaucratic types is the process by which client needs are defined. Every aspect of the bureaucratic type dictates that clients will be analyzed as subordinates by the organization and their problems will be organizationally diagnosed. It is largely because of this fact alone that bureaucratic organizations become unresponsive to their clients. Traditional definitions of problems and solutions to these become crystallized in rigid policies and rules which inevitably lose their relevance over time. Because of the highly fluid nature of Wesley agency's organizational stucture, however, and in addition its commitment to clients, this does not occur. Instead, as client demands change and inconsistencies between these and the agency develop, a new synthesis of agency operations and client demands is achieved through the fluxional internal decision process of the agency. Because this is a dialectical process, the nonbureaucratic organization type described here could be called the "dialectical organization."

TOWARD A DIALECTICAL POLITICAL SYSTEM

Transferring the experience of this small, private, and church-related agency into the arena of large-scale government and politics raises many large and complicated questions, but making the effort to answer these questions may become of critical importance to the effective continued functioning of our political system. It is interesting and instructive in this regard to view the United States Supreme Court in its recent history as performing a dialectical role. What it has done recently is react to inconsistencies in the structure of the American legal system by altering it in ways which reflect a personal, immediate, and human concern with the clients of the legal system and other institutions. Because it has worked out a contemporary synthesis of individual and system needs, it probably has saved the system from some mighty strains that would have originated from the unresolved inconsistencies.

The reverse of this trend appears to be occurring, however, in our public administrative institutions—probably in large part because of the ongoing influence of traditional patterns of administrative thinking. Instead of moving toward responsive, flexible, and human modes of operation, they are becoming more and more mechanical. There seems to be little possibility that the Court can take cognizance of the problem, hence it seems imperative that students of the administrative process set themselves at the task. The opportunity seems to be at hand to recall the heritage of radical reform out of which the study of administration grew. Certainly, the relevance and immediacy of the administrative process to effective democratic government is as great now as it was then.

NOTES

1. See Dwight Waldo, *The Study of Public Administration* (New York: Random House, 1955), and his *The Administrative State: A Study of the Political Theory of American Public Administration* (New York: The Ronald Press, 1948).
2. For a discussion which suggests the nature of this impact in regard to city-manager government for cities, see "Leadership and Decision-making in Manager Cities, a Symposium," *Public Administration Review*, Summer 1958, pp. 208–230.
3. The classic traditional work on this line of argument is Charles S. Hynemans' *Bureaucracy and Democracy* (New York: Harper and Brothers, 1950). More recent statements include James Q. Wilson, "The Bureaucracy Problem," *The Public Interest*, Winter 1967, pp. 3–9; Robert Presthus, "University Bosses: The Executive Conquest of Academia," *The New Republic*, February 20, 1965, pp. 20–24; Sheldon S. Wolin, *Politics and Vision* (Boston: Little, Brown and Company, 1960), pp. 352–434; William W. Boyer, *Bureaucracy on Trial* (Indianapolis: Bobbs-Merrill Company, 1964). Also, see Gabriel Almond and Sidney Verba, *The Civic Culture* (Boston: Little, Brown and Company, 1963), for data relating to the American attitude toward bureaucracy. Also, the work of Warren Bennis is relevant in this regard. See Warren Bennis, "Beyond Bureaucracy," *Trans-action*, July–August 1965, pp. 31–35. Recent widespread discussion of the possibility of establishing an "ombudsman" system in the United States also indicates the type of concern described here.
4. Victor A. Thompson, *Modern Organization* (New York: Alfred A. Knopf, 1965), pp. 170–177; Alvin W. Gouldner, "Red Tape as a Social Problem," in Robert K. Merton (ed.), *Reader in Bureaucracy* (New York: The Free Press, 1952), pp. 410–418.
5. Gideon Sjoberg, Richard A. Brymer, and Buford Farris, "Bureaucracy and the Lower Class," *Sociology and Social Research*, April 1966, pp. 325–337. It should be noted, also, that Weber himself made only a qualified claim for the rationality of bureaucratic structure, saying that it possesses a "formal" as opposed to "substantive" rationality. See Bertram M. Gross, *The Managing of Organizations: The Administrative Struggle* (New York: The Free Press of Glencoe, 1964), p. 142.
6. A major critique of the idea of a synoptic rationality is Charles Lindblom's *The Intelligence of Democracy: Decision-Making Through Mutual Adjustment* (New York: The Free Press, 1965).
7. The author entered the agency as a "research consultant" and maintained access for 16 months. Data were obtained from agency documents, lengthy unstructured interviews with the director and other personnel, and through direct observation.
8. Robert K. Merton, "Bureaucratic Structure and Personality," in Robert K. Merton (ed.), *op. cit.*, pp. 361–371.
9. Gideon Sjoberg, Richard A. Brymer, and Buford Farris, *op. cit.*
10. Victor A. Thompson, *op. cit.*, pp. 129–137.
11. Gideon Sjoberg, Richard A. Brymer, and Buford Farris, *op cit.*
12. The "power equalization" which has been effected in this agency is therefore unlike the commonly discussed pattern. See George Strauss, "Some Notes on Power-Equalization," in Harold J. Leavitt (ed.), *The Social Science of Organizations* (Englewood Cliffs, N.J.: Prentice-Hall, Inc., 1963), pp. 39-84.
13. This typology is developed fully in another paper: "Organization Structure and Political Process—From an Apollonian to a Dionysian Politics," forthcoming in a book of original papers edited by J. W. Dyson.

14. Norman O. Brown, *Life Against Death: The Psychoanalytic Meaning of History* (New York: Vintage Books, 1959).
15. David L. Sills, "The Succession of Goals," in Amitai Etzioni (ed.), *Complex Organizations* (New York: Holt, Rinehart, and Winston, Inc., 1961), pp. 146–159.
16. Herbert A. Shepard, "Changing Interpersonal and Intergroup Relationships in Organizations," in James G. March (ed.), *Handbook of Organizations* (Chicago: Rand McNally and Company, 1965), pp. 1115–1143.
17. *Ibid.*, p. 1118.
18. *Ibid.*, pp. 1122–1124.
19. *Ibid.*, pp. 1127–1128.

Non-Subservient Civil Servants

RUFUS E. MILES, JR.

Time was when public policy was made on high and civil servants carried it out. Once in a while it still happens. But the general practice is quite different and cannot help but be so. Policy is made by people with knowledge, ideas, analytical capability, beliefs, and persuasiveness, tempered by the realities of politics. Some such people within the Executive Branch are in appointive positions and some are in civil service positions. The interaction of the two groups produces the best policy.

Time was when civil servants were subservient. Some still are. The best ones develop not only a loyalty to their superiors, as they come and go, but to the special ethic of public service. No one who follows that special ethic could be called subservient, nor could he properly be called disloyal. But he may frequently be involved in the torment of conflicting loyalties.

The special ethic to which the best civil servants develop a loyalty is the ethic which allies them with the central purpose of government in a democratic society. It says that government should intervene to protect the interest of the general public against powerful and privileged private interests. It says that government should intervene to protect the weak and underprivileged against the tyranny of the majority, both intended and thoughtless. And it says that government should protect the interest of the taxpayer by fighting constantly against the inherent tendency to treat anything over $1 million as stage money. Oversimplified though it is, that is the heart of the ethic of the dedicated public servant.

What happens when a career civil servant, pursuing such an ethic as he sees it, finds himself in conflict with his superior who may or may not be a presidential appointee? Does he submit, meekly? He does not. He argues as effectively as he knows how for his conviction. He may lose the argument, but it is an absolute obligation on his part to present his point of view with clarity and vigor. If and when he is overruled, he carries out his superior's instructions to the full extent of his ability. He knows that you win some and you lose some, and as long as your percentage of wins is a tolerable average, you hang in there and feel that the ball game is worth the playing.

A career civil servant who behaves in this manner must operate from a set of well-thought-out ideas—a philosophy, if you please—as to what the nature of the public interest is in the field within which he is operating. He cannot argue persuasively and effectively on behalf of the public interest if he has vague, unformulated, unarticulated ideas as to what contributes to the public interest. He talks with others in and out of the public service, and uses them as testing grounds for his evolving philosophy, shaping and reshaping it as his experience grows and as he matures.

The antiestablishment youth who thinks government career civil-service jobs are a sell-out to the opposition should take another look. The leverage which can be exerted by a career civil servant who chooses to follow this kind of ethic can be greater than he has any realization of—probably greater than in most other lines of endeavor to which he may turn. When pursued in this manner, government service can be an exciting business, and sometimes hazardous. But security is, after all, a secondary and elusive value in life.

Alternative Conceptions of Accountability

AMITAI ETZIONI

The alternative conceptions of accountability are the focus of this article. While this is an issue of increasing importance to administrators in all sorts of institutions, for clarity and unity, the example of health administration will be relied upon to illustrate these alternative formulations.

THE SYMBOLIC USES OF ACCOUNTABILITY

Speakers and writers calling for greater accountability typically employ the term in three concrete contexts: to refer to greater responsibility and responsiveness; to allude to greater attention to the "community" (generally a euphemism for blacks, Mexican-Americans, American Indians, or other minorities); or the greater commitment to "values" (e.g., as in the phrase "higher standards of morality"). The unifying thread is the symbolic use of the term accountability. Though it may not necessarily be—indeed perhaps rarely is—the consciously intended meaning, the chief definition of this term which in fact emerges is that of "accountability as gesture." The hallmark of accountability as gesture is that it is pure norm with little or no instrumentality attached. That is, the speaker or writer advocating accountability fails to follow up the use of the term by outlining specific arrangements, e.g., that patients be made the controlling force on hospital boards; or, if such suggestions are made at all, the virtue held out for them is fully matched by their vagueness (e.g., making "more information" available to the public).

The sociological significance of such expressions, gestures, utterances, however, is more varied than one might immediately think. The point can be readily illustrated by reflecting on the differential significance of the word "integration" as used in the early '60s, in each case symbolically, by the following types of persons: a white legislator endorsing integration to black constituents, but failing to introduce or support bills enforcing specific aspects of integration; a black civil rights leader such as Martin Luther King or Roy Wilkins building a social movement; a white minister exhorting his white congregation in Scarsdale against racism.

The first use is inauthentic and manipulative. When divorced from any systematic efforts to promote actual attainment of the desired values, "accountability" becomes a thin cover for inaction, a "Sunday only" value mechanically acknowledged in a secular form of lip service. This kind of "accountability" can be easily and vociferously endorsed by boards of trustees, insurance lobbyists, and others in positions of power whose recitations of the phrase serve as a substitute for actual accountability. It becomes then only a verbal concession, like the rhetoric of the *Kerner Commission Report,* with little provision for follow-through, as a direct drain of the pressures to "do something" about the situation.

Murray Edelman, in his book *The Symbolic Uses of Politics,* devoted a good deal of space to a discussion of such hortatory uses of political slogans. According to Edelman, there is the solemn ritual incantation of political slogans by those in charge of formulating or carrying out policy that is unaccompanied by any effective attempts to achieve the goals incanted. This is particularly likely to occur in a situation where a large but politically unorganizaed group which feels itself threatened, desires certain resources or the substantive power claimed.[1] Under such circumstances, it is tempting for the politicians or administrators to satisfy the desires of those in the first groups through symbolic reassurance (that they are not being ignored or that their interests will be protected).

Often, symbolic reassurance from power wielders will provoke quiescence in an unorganized group—at the very least because it takes the edge off dissatisfaction and makes the difficulties of mobilization greater.[2] This quiescence may be quite temporary, soon yielding to a reawakening of demand and a resentment over being manipulated. But those who merely mouth "accountability" do not concern themselves with the longer run.

Following the analogy made to the word "integration" earlier, political and social movement leaders also use slogans and cue words in their attempts to mobilize followers. Perhaps they even use the same word that is being used by the power wielders in an attempt to provide symbolic reassurance to potential followers. In this context, however, though the use is still symbolic, the meaning is quite different. While group leaders may still be dealing largely with gestures rather than mechanisms, "accountability" in this instance serves as a rallying point around which mobilization can be affected and a movement built. In such a situation the demand for "accountability" becomes a shared symbol of all those individuals galvanized into a political force which aims at seeking and gaining specific concessions.[3] Once there is such an organized force, the question of how accountability can be actualized may be: confronted immediately, only a step away, or deliberately deferred as a bargaining technique.

Somewhere in between the "co-opting" inauthentic use of slogans as a political tranquilizer unresponsive to basic needs and its issue-flagging, group-rallying use by leaders seeking to mobilize a constituency is the use of "accountability" as the banner of a campaign for moral education. Typically such a campaign is undertaken by one professional *vis-à-vis* colleagues or by a concerned but unself-interested outsider. The moral educator views those proselytized in a manner very much akin to the way a socially conscious minister views his congregation: as persons who are basically anxious to do right by their values but whose behavior is not what it should be because of lack of knowledge and having been improperly taught, or because they have not been reminded of their duties, or because insufficiently "good" models suitable for emulation have been set before them. Thus, exhortation, moral suasion, lay preaching, and example setting are relied upon instead of introducing new accountability mechanisms—not to be inauthentic, but because these approaches are sincerely believed to be effective.

Dr. Avedis Donabidian attributes the tendency in health administration to emphasize moral education over regulation to the norm of colleaguality among physicians and the weakness of the formal and informal controls administrators have *vis-à-vis* physicians. He writes,

> The administrator must . . . determine the proper balance between the educational objectives of quality assessment and the need to deter and detect careless or incompetent practice. . . .
> In real life, the answer appears to depend in part on the role and influence of the practicing physicians on the program. Wherever this influence is small, as in some health insurance programs, there is either no responsibility for quality or, at best, emphasis is placed on the identification and correction of abuse that borders on the criminal. Wherever the role of the practicing physician is significantly large or dominant, the emphasis may fall so predominantly on the educational objective that the disciplinary objective is in danger of being ignored or explicitly excluded.[4]

As different as the different uses of the term "accountability" that have been discussed so far are, however, they all rely upon it as a symbol rather than as a social force and, unfortunately, tend to "run into" one another. As a result, on many occasions, when administrators talk favorably about accountability, one has a difficult time discerning whether their gestures are inauthentic, rallying, or educationalistic. Moreover, their social consequences will depend in part on the other accountability processes, which are explored next.

ACCOUNTABILITY AS REALPOLITIK

A contrasting view of accountability is that of an existing pattern of administration and government which reflects at any particular point in time the sum total of the forces working on the system, those working to maintain the status quo, and those seeking to reshape it. Such an outlook adapts the interest group theories of politics espoused by such political analysts as Robert Dahl, David Truman, V. O. Key, and Earl Latham.[5] From this perspective, the hospital, for example, is viewed as a polity, affected by its members and by outside forces, in the continual act of restructuring. Apart from its bookkeeping and managerial functions in the narrow sense, hospital administration is seen as a political process through which various groupings negotiate, confront, or adjust their claims. Thus, "accountability" becomes the actual degree to which the hospital administration is responsive to the claims and demands of the particular interests of doctors, nurses, union activists, patients, etc.

The hospital administrator is seen as being locked at the center of this process—the focal point of the pressure—not at the top, in charge. The hospital administrator's position in this theory in fact is analagous to that of a billiard ball in a physics diagram upon which various forces impinge. Typically, the administrator's actions are seen as almost totally determined by various partisan interest group pressures; predicting the behavior of the administrator then is a matter of knowing the coefficients of strength of the various groups.

Even when administrators are seen as having views of their own and a modicum of autonomy, they are not seen as representing the interests of the polity as a whole—but of having their own "vested interests," which are similarly parochial to those of the other pressure groups. In general, the interests imputed to administrators are those of the bureaucrat seeking either to expand his domain and, most especially, to defend his own incumbency in authority.[6] Such a view of administration and "accountability" we label as "Realpolitik" because it is characterized by the fact that power is viewed as the only significant variable.

The rules of Realpolitik are fairly well known. To list them here, briefly, is, of course, to report and not to bless their existence. By and large, groups with more status, income, and education have more power and hence make the system relatively more "accountable" to them. That is, they have more leverage. Accordingly one would expect a typical American voluntary hospital (and its administration and administrator) to be most "accountable" to the physicians and/or trustees, less so to the nurses and aides, least so to the patients, and especially inattentive to the poor, uneducated, non-paying customers. In terms of the typical American community, one would expect the hospital to be most responsive to the local business community, and less so to other groups. As a rule, following Realpolitik we would expect more responsiveness to government agencies of various levels, less to "consumer" groups and advocates.

Different types of hospitals—municipal, proprietary, voluntary, etc.—are expected to vary in the groups they respond to most readily and in the kinds of power base which has the greatest leverage. For instance, we might expect voluntary hospitals to be rather more insulated from the pressures of city politics than the municipal hospitals, but rather more dependent upon the good will and continued munificence of the cities' "first families."[7]

According to a Realpolitik analysis, groups will also differ in their leverage over time, depending on the extent to which they are organized and mobilized to affect the particular polity under consideration. Thus, if the physicians act chiefly as individuals, they will obtain fewer resources than if they set up hospitalwide committees, aiming to insure that their collective preferences will carry the day. And, as a rule, unionized hospital workers will be more "accounted to" than unorganized ones. Even patients, represented by patients' advocates, ombudsmen, lawyers, or consumer representatives—being weak and easy to deflect—will, according to this view, gain in more ways than they would without any of these organizations and mobilizing devices.

Thus, Reapolitik, a "hard-headed" view, suggests that the phrase "more accountable" is meaningless; the question is: to whom? The implication is that accountability to one group means almost by definition less accountability to another. Implicit in the Realpolitik position is that values per se—e.g., as represented by the moral education of the administrator—count for almost nil. A change in the relative power of the various groups is the only factor which could be expected to produce a significant change in accountability.

THE FORMAL, LEGAL APPROACH

Many subscribe to a view of accountability which defines it in legal or formal terms. The emphasis is on instituting "checks and balances." In the academic world, such an approach was once current in political science. While it has lost in following over the past 20 years, it is still quite popular in the field of public administration. Game theory and cybernetics are chiefly in this vein of thinking.

In hospital administration, this approach sees the administrators as having to be made "accountable" to one or more authorities—the board, his superior, the law, etc., and much ink is shed to clarify these legalities. A case in point is the following question: if a doctor misbehaves in a hospital, who is legally accountable: the doctor alone, the hospital and its administrator alone, or both?

Thus, there have been attempts to make hospitals more accountable to the public-at-large by requiring them to file detailed financial statements, and various mechanisms have been proposed to make such financial statements easily accessible to interested parties. In addition, laws have been put through requiring the participation of consumers on Hill-Burton advisory councils and on state and regional Comprehensive Health Planning organizations.[8]

Recent changes in hospital accreditation procedures are permitting consumers and consumer organizations to participate in the accreditation process. Citizens do this by learning when the biannual accreditations surveys of hospitals in their areas are to be held and by being present at an information interview to state complaints as they relate to the standards of the Joint Commission of Accreditation of Hospitals.[9]

And in an effort to make doctors and hospitals more accountable to the government in the spending of Medicare and Medicaid monies, Congress recently enacted the PSRO legislation designed to subject old and poor patients' admission to a hospital to pre-admission review in all but emergency cases by local committees of doctors. A tougher proposal requiring an in-hospital committee review of Medicare admissions to crack down on needless hospitalization or protracted stays was dropped by the Social Security Administration after drawing heavy fire from the AMA.[10]

Structural changes *within* the hospital are similar measures, because they work on the basis of changes in formal definitions. Thus, requiring that hospitals have a consumer representative on the board is a case in point; it is said to make the hospital more accessible. Following this logic, the OEO guidelines dictated that OEO and other neighborhood health centers funded by the Public Health Service had to form either governing boards or advisory committees composed of at least one-third "democratically selected representatives of the poor."[11]

Many social scientists are skeptical of such formal and legal accountability mechanisms. According to the most popular introductory textbook in sociology:

> The rules of the formal system account for much but by no means all of the patterned behavior in associations. The phrase "informal structure" is used to denote those patterns that emerge from the spontaneous interaction of personalities and groups within

the organization. . . . An organization's informal structure is made up of the patterns that develop when the participants face persistent problems that are not provided for by the formal system.[12]

In the health care system the consumer representative often turns out to be not "the people's" representative, but a businessman rather similar to the other board members in background and outlook. In addition, consumers on hospital boards often learn that formal entitlements do not necessarily confer real power just as stockholders long ago discovered in business corporations. The power wielders may hold their own meeting in a backroom prior to the formal meeting which then becomes a mere ceremony. Or, the doctors and administrators may have their way via the phenomenon of "partisan analysis"—if the consumers have no independent source of information they may have no way of arriving at and documenting a point of view opposing the administrative one. Similarly, the aura of expertise surrounding doctors and administrators vs. the low social status of the consumer representatives can be expected to contribute to the likelihood that the consumer representatives defer to the hospital officials. In addition, while the doctors and administrators have a continuing personal vested interest in the affairs of the hospital, the motivations of consumer representatives are more likely to be altruistic. Unless the position of consumer representative is one which confers great prestige in the person's social circle, or there is some other reward, there seems little incentive to attend meetings often and regularly and to engage in the necessary self-education. It seems almost inevitable for enthusiasm to decline over time.[13]

At first glance, the social science caveat, "not all that glitters with accountability truly enhances it," seems to be revalidated from data on the health system. Nevertheless, on balance, formal mechanisms do have an effect—especially when coupled with efforts to build consensus around values and to mobilize power through coalition building as discussed below. Thus, a study of the accomplishments of 37 Massachusetts Mental Health and Retardation Area Boards on which citizen participation had been required by legislation revealed four separate types of board accomplishment. Each one resulted from a different strategy pursued by the board: service creation of improvement, mobilization of outside resources (from state and federal government), achievement of local autonomy (mobilization of resources from the private sector or the local government), and coordination (integration of the efforts of a variety of social agencies).[14]

Although consumer representation on decision-making and advisory bodies overseeing health units has received the most attention as the solution to the problems of instituting accountability to the public-at-large, it is by no means the only mechanism available. Another promising approach is that of the regularly scheduled Comprehensive Health Audit (CHA). The principle behind the notion of the Comprehensive Health Audit is essentially the same as that behind the annual financial audit in the corporate world. In the case of the corporate financial audit, the law requires that an outside expert licensed by the government (a CPA) review the books of the joint stock company on a yearly basis so as to insure "accountability" of the firm and its managers to the stockholders or legal owners of the corporation.

The Comprehensive Health Audit would entail a regular assessment of cost-consciousness *and* quality of care delivered in each hospital by an outside team of health auditors licensed by the government. The chief advantages of the Comprehensive Health Audit are that: (a) it accords well with the American philosophy of harnessing the profit motive in the service of the public interest; (2) it avoids the necessity of setting up a costly and cumbersome governmental regulatory apparatus (which as we know from historical experience has typically ended by serving the purposes of those it was intended to watchdog); and (3) it relies upon a tried and true mechanism, known to be efficient in one area, and transfers it to a closely related field. The chief disadvantage of the Comprehensive Health Audit is that "input" measurements are so much more refined than "output" measures. Until more accurate output indices are developed, CHAs will have to employ fairly crude measures and their evaluations will not be nearly so reliable as the traditional financial audit.[15]

A "GUIDANCE" APPROACH

The following view of accountability—the "guidance" approach—is, I should hasten to admit, the view closest to my heart. It took me six hundred-odd pages to spell it out elsewhere.[16] Here, I will simply suggest its chief points relevant to the issue at hand.

As I see it, accountability is based on a variety of interacting forces, not one lone attribute or mechanism. The direction administrators take, in accountability as in other matters, is affected by *all* the factors already listed and some others still to be mentioned. In part, they respond to articulations of "rights" on the part of "the community," its leaders, the press, etc., that is, to *claims* of accountability. In part, their accountability is circumscribed and delineated by the legalities and *formalities* of the state, and so on. Hence, changes in any and all of these factors are effective ways to change the level and scope of accountability; none of them is all inclusive.

Moreover, several missing elements must still be added to complete the analysis: for example, in contrast to those who see power as the core explanatory factor, I see accountability as having both a power *and* a moral base, in the sense that the values which administrators "internalize" (as well as those of other participants, both in the health unit under consideration and persons acting on it from the outside) do both affect the direction the health unit takes. Thus, in a recent study by the Center for Policy Research, Dr. Steven Beaver and Dr. Rosita Albert found (in a study of which I am the principal investigator, supported by NIMH) that the administrators of several hospitals studied were more progressive on several counts than either the people in the area served by the hospital, or their patient-advocate, activist leaders.

This study but illustrates what we all know from personal experience: administrators are not neutral beings. They have sentiments, preferences, and above all, values—although, of course, they differ greatly among themselves as to what they value, how clearly they perceive their values, and how far they are willing to go in promoting their values against those of others, if a difference should become evident. The content and intensity of these value commitments are in part affected by the administrator's education.

The administrator need not be merely a broker of power, a meeting point of various internal and external pressures which he adapts the way a vectorgram would; adapting to the strongest pressure at the moment—although in reality quite a few administrators act in this way. Aside from his personal values and position of authority in the structure, which give him a separate backbone, i.e., a measure of direction other than the Realpolitik of give and take, there is, in addition, an opportunity for creative leadership.

I do *not* see the capacity for leadership as consisting of abstract, moralistic character traits; I see these as specific skills. The object is *not* to fly in the face of reality or power groups, nor to wildly pursue Utopian notions of social justice or accountability—such an administrator is all too likely to be quickly expelled—but to help shape, mobilize, and combine the vectors which determine the unit's direction and accountability model so as to bring them closer to the desired system. To shape *these* forces requires educating the various groups to definitions and demands which are closer to what is legal and ethical and just. This is probably the most difficult part of the creative administrator's job.

Also, for the administrator to *mobilize* one or more of the relevant groups is to bring about a change in the balance of vectors to which the administrator must later respond. Thus, if physicians are putting undue pressure on an administrator to take a course of action he considers undesirable, he may instigate a greater activization of the board or of consumer representatives to serve as countervailing forces, somewhat changing the vectorgram. This course can often not be followed because it leads to a measure of countermobilization by the other group, in this case the MDs, realizing next to no net change but creating a higher level of conflict all around.[17]

Somewhat better opportunities for creative leadership are open to the administrator in the area of coalition forming. Coalitions arise, not necessarily explicitly, when two or more groups favor the same or a similar course of action. They may be composed of insiders only, outsiders only, or varying combinations. For example, Dr. Lowell Bellin, when first deputy commissioner of the New York Department of Public Health, succeeded in forming a coalition between his hospitals into giving more resources and attention to ambulatory care.[18] In speaking about the accomplishments that have emerged from this active collaboration between consumers and professionals in private voluntary hospitals, Bellin listed the number of advances:

1. Instituting a unit record system.
2. Hiring an interpreter.
3. Establishing a primary physician system.
4. Developing a list of services for distribution.
5. Hiring a full-time director of ambulatory care.
6. Holding two open public hearings.
7. Adding preventive medicine services.
8. Assigning additional physicians, nurses, and clerks to the outpatient department.
9. Eliminating underutilized clinics.
10. Starting a community outreach program.
11. Starting a new clinic or other services.
12. Remodeling clinic and/or emergency room areas.
13. Running patient attitude surveys.
14. Providing music and snack machines.
15. Establishing a communication link between the medical board, administrators, and the consumers.

16. Changing the referral system.
17. Changing x-ray and laboratory follow-up.
18. Extending clinical hours.[19]

The reason coalition building is often effective is that while in isolation each vector is relatively given and unchangeable, on the other hand, the ways in which they may be combined to neutralize, to partially reinforce, or to fully back up one another is less fixed. The ultimate success lies in building a coalition in favor of greater accountability which is either very wide—or all-inclusive. Then the desired changes are introduced almost as if by themselves.

Closely related, but even more productive, is the formulation of new alternatives. Groups rarely have fully developed positions and almost always can find alternative ways toward their goals.[20] If ways can be found to allow them to advance their goals which at the same time lessen their opposition to other groups and to higher levels of accountability, then the program's success will be particularly pronounced. For example, the strength of the HMO pattern is said to be that it is both responsive to the doctors' legitimate needs *and* more responsive to the patients than solo practice; if this is the case, it is such a creative alternative.[21]

To advance any and all of these strategies, the administrator needs a considerable understanding of how social systems work, how polities function, what the various groups' values and needs are, and what alternatives are practical and acceptable. In part, he can get the needed knowledge from proper training; in part, from continual interaction with the various groups inside and outside his unit, which impinge on it. Experience suggests that without fixed "institutionalized" opportunities for communication, such regularized interaction is unlikely to occur with sufficient frequency. The explanation of the mechanisms of institutional communication cannot be undertaken here, but they constitute a vital element of any effective accountability system.[22]

NOTES

1. Murray Edelman, *The Symbolic Uses of Politics* (Urbana, Chicago, and London: University of Illinois Press, 1964), ch. 2.
2. *Ibid.*
3. For a concrete example of "accountability" as a rallying slogan in an attempt to build a social movement, see *The Consumer and Corporate Accountability,* Ralph Nader (ed.), Center for the Study of Responsive Law, Washington, D.C. (New York: Harcourt Brace, 1973).
4. Avedis Donabidian, *A Guide to Medical Care Administration*, Volume II: *Medical Care Appraisal,* American Public Health Association, 1969, pp. 100–101.
5. Hans J. Morgenthau's work is another example of this approach. See Morgenthau, *Politics Among Nations* (New York: Knopf, 1954), and his *Scientific Man vs. Power Politics* (Chicago: University of Chicago Press, Phoenix Edition, 1965).
6. See, for example, Ray Elling, "The Hospital Support Game in Urban Center," in Eliot Freidson (ed.), *The Hospital in Modern Society* (Glencoe, Ill: Free Press, 1963), pp. 73–111.
7. See Duncan Neuhauser and Fernand Turiotte, "Costs and Quality of Care in Different Types of Hospitals," *The Annals of the American Academy of Political and Social Science, The Nation's Health: Some Issues* (January 1972), pp. 50–61.
8. For more information on this, see the chapter entitled "Consumer Influence on the Federal Role" in *Heal Yourself,* Report of the Citizens Board of Inquiry into Health Services for Americans.

9. "The Public Gets Voice in Accreditation of Hospitals," Consumer Notes by Gerald Gold, *The New York Times*, December 20, 1973.

10. "HEW Drops Tough Peer Review Plan," *Medical World News,* October 5, 1973, p. 50.

11. For more on this, see "The Health Rights Defenders: All Power to the Patients," *Health-Pac Bulletin* (October 1969).

12. Leonard Broom and Philip Selznick, *Sociology* (New York: Harper and Row, 1963), third edition, pp. 227–229.

13. For examples and evaluations of more and less successful consumer participation schemes, see Jeoffrey B. Gordon, "The Politics of Community Medicine Projects: A Conflict Analysis," *Medical Care*, Vol. VII, No. 6 (November-December 1969), pp. 419–428; Roger G. Larson, "Reactions to Social Pressure," *Annual Administrative Reviews of Hospitals*, Vol. 46 (April 1, 1972), pp. 181–186; Donna Manderson and Markay Kerr, "Citizen Influence in Health Services Programs," *American Journal of Public Health,* Vol. 61, No. 8, pp. 1518–1523; Frank M. Shepard, MD.D., and Beulah Wiley, "A Community-University Cooperative Venture," *Hospitals J.A.H.A.,* Vol. 46 (September 16, 1972), pp. 64–70; Wilfred E. Holton, Peter K. New, and Richard M. Messler, "Citizen Participation and Conflict," *Administration in Mental Health* (Fall 1973), pp. 96–103.

14. William R. Meyers, Jane Grisell, et al., "Methods of Measuring Citizen Board Accomplishment in Mental Health and Retardation," *Community Mental Health Journal*, Vol. 8, No. 4 (1972).

15. For an example of a prototype Comprehensive Health Audit, see Carol Brierly, "Hospital Costs: What the Figures Really Say," *Prism* (February 1974), pp. 12–17, 62–64.

16. Amitai Etzioni, *The Active Society* (New York: Free Press, 1968)

17. *Ibid.*, ch. 15, 18.

18. Lowell Eliezer Bellin, Florence Kavaler, and Al Schwartz, "Phase One of Consumer Participation in Policies of 22 Voluntary Hospitals in New York City," *American Journal of Public Health*, Vol. 62 (October 1972), pp. 1370–1378.

19. Lowell Eliezer Bellin, "How to Make Ambulatory Care Start Ambulating," presented at the Joint Workshop sponsored by the AHA and ADAC, Cherry Hill, Pennsylvania, November 1971, p. 11.

20. For more on this, see Gabriel A. Almond and G. Bingham Powell, Jr. *Comparative Politics: A Developmental Approach* (Boston: Little, Brown and Co., 1966).

21. For an examination of some of the pros and cons of existing prepaid programs such as Kaiser-Permanente and HIP, see Merwyn R. Grunlick, "The Impact of Prepaid Group Practice on American Medical Care: A Critical Evaluation," *The Annals of the American Academy of Political and Social Science, The Nation's Health: Some Issues* (January 1972), pp. 100–113.

22. For additional discussion, see Etzioni, *The Active Society, op. cit.*, ch. 20.

15

THE CHANGING NATURE
OF PUBLIC ADMINISTRATION

No "real world" activity or academic field can stand still. Events—actual and intellectual—continue, and if public administration and public administrators are to retain their vitality, they must constantly be in the process of adaptation. As Alvin Toffler popularized in his book *Future Shock*, change is increasingly rapid in our society, promoted in large part by technological innovation.

Frederick C. Mosher has attempted to analyze these changes and their implications for the practice of public administration. Mosher is especially concerned with the likely, or at least desirable, impact of rapid change on public personnel systems.

Next Dwight Waldo reviews current issues in public administration with a future orientation. Waldo discovers five sets of contesting forces in society that have important implications for public administration in the future. Waldo also looks at recent issues of concern to government as they affect public agencies—poverty, equality, participation, and consumerism among others. He finally addresses the future of the academic field of public administration and the forces that seem to be shaping it.

As a conclusion for this section and for the volume as a whole, Warren Bennis calls for commitment, purpose, risk taking, and experimentation in the ongoing process in which public administrators are daily engaged—trying to improve the society in which we human beings live.

The Public Service In the Temporary Society

FREDERICK C. MOSHER

This essay is addressed to two related questions:

With respect to the public administrative services in the United States, where are we and where are we going?

and

How can and should we prepare our public services to meet probable future demands in our systems of higher education and public service management?

But there is a question prior to these which requires attention. It concerns the changing nature and probable future directions of the society from which the public services are drawn, within which they operate, and which they are presumed to serve. This essay therefore begins with some observations about the society and its demands upon government, including some of the underlying dilemmas which seem to me most salient to the public service of the near future. Its second part is a discussion of the probable implications of these social directions and dilemmas for public administrative organizations, the public service, public personnel systems, and the universities.

I pretend no expertise in that increasingly popular field of study and speculation known as futuristics. No predictions are offered about the public services and the society of the United States in the year 2000. My ambition is more modest. It is to cull from our experience of the last few years—the decade of the '60s—some probabilities about the next few—the decade of the '70s; and to deduce from these what we (in public administration) should be doing about it. The didactic tenor of many of the sentences which follow, the frequent use of the unqualified verb "will," conveys falsely a sense of confidence and even omniscience on the part of the author. All should be qualified by the adverb "probably"; and I would hesitate to give a numerical value to the margins of error. The prognostications are tentative and hopefully provocative, not definitive.

THE SOCIETY AND ITS GOVERNMENTS: THE TEMPORARY SOCIETY

"The Temporary Society" is an expression cribbed from the book of that title by Warren G. Bennis and Philip E. Slater[1] and is used here in two senses, only the second of which is theirs. In the first sense, the society is temporary in that it is widely known and appreciated that it is changing rapidly and will, in effect, be transformed into another society within a relatively short span of years, say 10 or 15. Societies of the past have of course changed, particularly in the West, but none with such speed and few with such awareness. Basic social changes of long ago can, by historians, be described in terms of eras; later, in terms of centuries; more recently in terms of generations. But the "social generation" of today is con-

siderably shorter than the "human generation." The parent of the '70's is preparing his infant offspring for a society not the same as his own and not even once
removed from his own. It is more nearly twice removed.

The second sense in which our society may be described as temporary concerns
the institutions and organizations within it and the attachments, the moorings of
those individuals who compose it. Bennis, in his chapters of the earlier-cited work,
connotes the term with the allegedly changing nature of productive organizations
and the evolving patterns of individual roles and associations within them.

> The social structure of organizations of the future will have some unique characteris-
> tics. The key word will be "temporary." There will be adaptive, rapidly changing *tem-*
> *porary* systems . . . of diverse specialists, linked together by coordinating and task-
> evaluating executive specialists in an organic flux—this is the organization form that will
> gradually replace bureaucracy as we know it.[2]

Although he acknowledges that "the future I describe is not necessarily a 'happy one.'"[3] Bennis is basically optimistic about the prospect as releasing the individual, encouraging his revitalization, and legitimizing fantasy, imagination,
and creativity. Slater, in his discussion of the social consequences of temporary
systems and particularly of the effects upon the family, is less reassuring.

In both of the senses here described, the term "temporary society" may exag-
gerate and overdramatize. As any student of anthropolgy or reader of Arnold
Toynbee knows, no society is permanent, although some manage to survive with
little change for some centuries. And clearly there are still many stable organizations in the United States and a good many people who do have firm organizational and institutional mooring—probably a solid majority in fact. But in both
senses the trend toward temporariness seems likely; and both have significance for
the American public service of the future.

OTHER OBSERVATIONS AND ASSUMPTIONS

First among the other assumptions that seem to me most significant for purposes
of this discussion is one that is negative, though, from my point of view at least,
optimistic: that, in the next several years, there will be no nuclear holocaust, no
civil war between races or other groups, no revolution which suddenly overthrows
governments or other established institutions, or which reverses existing systems of
values and beliefs. In other words, while social change and changes in institutions
and behavior will continue with a rapidity at least equal to that of the present,
steps in the future will be made from footprints marked today and in the recent
past.

A second assumption has to do with the extent, the depth, and the application
of human knowledge. The era since World War II has been variously labeled: the
post-industrial revolution, the scientific revolution, the professional revolution,
the information revolution, the cybernetic revolution, the knowledge explosion,
the technological era. The emphases among these various pseudonyms have differed, but the central themes are compatible: that knowledge, particularly in the
hard sciences and in technology, is growing at a rapid rate, and, as it is applied to
the affairs of people, is bringing about rapid and tremendous changes in the nature of society and the capabilities, the values, and the behavior of human beings.
Furthermore, in the words of Paul T. David,". . . the oncoming world of the fu-

ture, however described, will evidently be a world of increasing potential for human intervention and control both good and bad.''[4] As a correlate, knowledge itself, its procreation and its application, have assumed greater and greater importance in the eyes of men, as have the institutions which develop, apply, and transmit it. Wealth, or income-producing ability, is increasingly perceived as knowledge, and its application, decreasingly as property. It is here assumed that this emphasis will continue.

A third assumption concerns the role of government in determining the strategies, the courses and means of action, for the future. Government has ceased to be merely the keeper of the peace, the arbiter of disputes, and the provider of common and mundane services. For better or worse, government has directly and indirectly become a principal innovator, a major determiner of social and economic priorities, the guide as well as the guardian of social values, the capitalist and entrepreneur or subsidizer and guarantor of most new enterprises of great scale. This development has added to American politics and public administration dimensions both of scope and range and of centrality and importance for which the only precedents occurred in the conduct of the World Wars and during the depth of the Great Depression of the '30's. On virtually every major problem and every major challenge and opportunity we turn to government—whether it be the cultivation of the ocean bottom, control of the weather, exploration of outer space, training the disadvantaged for jobs, providing day-care centers for working mothers, controlling population growth, eliminating discrimination on the basis of race or sex, juggling the interest rate, reducing the impact of schizophrenia, rescuing a bankrupt railroad, safeguarding children from dangerous toys, or cleaning the air. True, government can turn its back on problems, but if the problems continue to fester and grow, it will eventually have to confront them. True, too, government relies heavily upon organizations and individuals in the private sector to carry out many of its programs, but it cannot escape responsibility for guidance, regulation, often financial support, and results.

Finally the variety and range of governmental responsibilities, coupled with the continuing development of new knowledge and new techniques with which to deal with them, have added enormously to the reliance of the whole society upon the people who man governmental posts, who collectively make its decisions. This is true of officials in all three branches of government, but it is most conspicuous and probably also most significant of the elective and appointive officers in the executive agencies. As the range of public problems and programs broadens, and as knowledge relevant to each grows and deepens, it becomes less and less possible for politically elected representatives to get a handle on more than a few of the significant issues. Even on these, they must rely heavily upon the information, analysis, and judgment of the appointive public servants. This reliance upon administrative personnel will, I assume, continue to grow.

ANOMALIES

But there are other areas relevant to the public service of tomorrow where the signals are less clear, where we seem to be moving in two or more directions at once. One of these concerns *rationality* and *objectivity* in reaching public decisions. It is epitomized by the system known as planning-programming-budgeting (PPBS), which future historians may consider the most significant administrative innovation of the 1960's. PPBS in some form and to some degree is now installed in most federal agencies—all the large ones—in the majority of states, and in many of the largest cities and counties. It is doubtful that any definition would satisfy all students and practitioners of PPBS, but most would agree that a central feature is the objective analysis of the probable costs and effectiveness of alternative courses of action to achieve goals, independent of political considerations (in the narrow sense of "political"), bureaucratic considerations, and personal wishes or hunches. In the words of one federal official: "PPBS is simply a means to make public decision making more rational."

Yet, during this same decade of PPBS rationality, there were at least three waves of thought or practice which were distinctively "unrational," if not "antirational." The first was the realist school which argued that public decisions, particularly budgetary decisions, are incremental in nature, based on last year's experience, seldom responsive to overall, comprehensive analysis. Year-to-year changes are relatively small in amount and reflect estimates of what the political market will bear rather than optimization in allocation of resources. Outcomes are the products of bargaining within fairly narrow ranges of political feasibility. Finally, policy decisions should give at least as much weight to political as to economic costs and benefits.

A second nonrational school of thought of the '60's is that now widely known as organizational development, an outgrowth of the earlier human relations movement. Its focus is upon the affective rather than the cognitive or analytical aspects of organizational behavior, and its premise is that organizational effectiveness (or health) will be improved if each member understands himself as a personality, is sensitive to the feelings of his associates, and is given a significant discretionary role in the shaping and carrying out of organizational goals. Among its by-words are openness, sensitivity, confrontation, democratic leadership, participation, flat hierarchy (if any at all), organization by objective.

The third movement of the 1960's is more clearly antirational than these other two, at least in the sense that term is used here. It is the politics of confrontation, which must by this time be familiar to most Americans. Its premises are moral categorical imperatives. Certain conditions or actions or decisions are wrong, in the sense not of being incorrect but of being evil. Such wickedness—whether it be war or racial discrimination or police brutality or alleged repression or the college grading system—is immediately apparent and should be instantly corrected. There is neither need nor time to analyze costs and consequences before taking action against things that are, on their face, evil. It is understandable but paradoxical that the politics of confrontation was born on the campuses of universities which one might have expected would be the seats of rationality and tolerance. But clearly it is a phenomenon of our times which must be reckoned with in the public service. Already, it is being practiced within some governmental agencies and is supported by a growing literature including some writings in the field of public administration.

Though their premises are different, it appears entirely possible that the incremental approach to decision making and the approach of organizational development can be reconciled with the rationality approach of PPBS. In fact, some students and practitioners have argued that policy analysis can be used effectively to enrich, rather than undermine, the bargaining process behind public decisions.

There has been less dialogue between the PPBS proponents and the disciples of organizational development. Yet, in one agency, the Department of State, the same group of officers endeavored to introduce both types of approaches at about the same time during the mid-'60's. Neither effort succeeded, but it was the conclusion of many participants that the systems approach failed because organizational development had begun too late. Reconciliation between the rationality emphasis and the politics of confrontation appears less likely because the two are so diametrically opposed in their central premises.

Emphases on Systems and Processes

A second area in which the crystal ball seems cloudy concerns the conflicting emphases upon *systems* and *processes*. The charge has been leveled by more than one critic that the study and the practice of government have overemphasized the processes through which decisions are reached and executed with too little consideration of the effects or outcomes of those decisions and actions.[5] They question—I think correctly—the assumption that if the democratic and administrative processes are legal and proper, the consequences will be optimal, or at least the best that is feasible in the American polity. They contest the line of thought growing from Bentley, that given appropriate access to decision channels, interest groups will conflict, balance each other out, and force proper decisions. Finally, they feel that too much faith has been lodged in the procedures governing nominations, elections, interest group access, the merit system, the budget system, and other related processes in the confidence that they will result in the best policies; in short, in a political/administrative "invisible hand" quite comparable to the market system so long relied upon by economists. Manifestly, the "invisible hand" has been less than optimally successful in both the political and economic realms. Yet, while the systems approach, which would analytically seek the best solutions to our public problems, is gaining in both administrative and academic circles, the emphasis upon process continues. In fact, the thrust of behavioralism in political and administrative sciences, with its undertones of determinism, tends to give it added support.

Participation

The current and increasing popularity of *participation* in decision making and in administration generally is a third source of confusion. It appears in at least three quite different forms. One is participation by those citizens most directly affected by given programs in decisions about those programs and their operations. Epitomized in the Economic Opportunity Act by the expression "maximum feasible participation," variations on the theme are found in a good many other federal programs, and some of them, like the draft, price control, and agricultural allotments, have a long history. It has been prominent at the local level in the drives to return the control of schools to local district boards and to govern the police through citizen review boards. A second manifestation of the participation drive has been the rapid growth of unionism, collective bargaining, and strikes of public servants. A third is the movement, mentioned earlier, toward organizational development, which includes among its central tenets participation, individually and in groups, in decision making.

Participation in decisions affecting public policy by any group of citizens (including employees) not politically representative of the whole or responsible to such political representation may, in theory and sometimes in practice, collide with that central premise of American governance which Redford has described as "overhead democracy."[6] The expression describes a polity resting ultimately on majority control through political representatives, wherein administrative officers are primarily responsible and loyal to their superiors for carrying out the directions of the elective representatives. Of course, legislatures may, and frequently have, delegated to citizen and employee participants policy areas over which they have discretion. But the proper and feasible limits of such delegation remain hazy.

All three types of participation mentioned here offer potential opposition to the ideal of rationality, and all three may lead—and sometimes have led—to the politics of confrontation. Participation by private citizens runs a collison course with the drive toward professionalization, which is discussed later.

Decentralization Trends

Associated and sometimes identified with the participation thesis is the recent push toward *decentralization* of governmental policy and action to lower levels—from Washington to regional offices or to states, cities, or school districts; from states to local jurisdictions; from cities and counties to community organizaions and districts. The paradox is that the decade of the 1960's was one of the most vigorously centralizing eras in our history except in wartime. And there is no sign that the trend is slackening, despite the pleas for decentralization. Growth, technology, population mobility are forcing geographic interdependence; and interdependence forces centralization in public (as well as private) policy. The people of California have a stake in the educational standards of Mississippi, as do those of Buffalo in the waste disposal practices of Cleveland, those of New York in the economic and manpower situation in Puerto Rico, and all of us in the antipollution devices put on new cars in Detroit. The advantage of the federal government and some of the states in access to revenues encourages centralization, as does the failure of many states and local units to realize their own revenue potential in response to public needs.

Continuing centralization seems inevitable; yet decentralization is a plain necessity. Only a small share, in number if not in importance, of public decisions should or can be made in Washington. The federal structure is so functionally specialized as to make broad developmental decisions on a geographic basis extremely difficult—whether for a federal region, a state, a city, or a community. A challenge for administrators of the present and future is to devise, test, effect, and operate mechanisms whereby we can move in both directions at the same time.[7] That is: devices for communities to initiate and make community decisions within regional and/or state guidelines, standards, and policies, and within nationwide objectives and standards. Already there are experiments with such mechanisms, as in the poverty program, model cities, and education. The recent proposal by CED for a two-tier, federated system for metropolitan government with a powerful metropolitan unit and semiautonomous community units is a move in the same two directions.

Specialization and Professionalization

Another anomaly arises from the narrowing and deepening of *specialization* and *professionalization* among organizations, fields of knowledge, and individuals. This phenomenon, which has been remarked by a great many writers before this one, is particularly significant in governmental enterprises, partly because professionalism has become so prevalent in so many public fields; partly because so many important public organizations are dominated by a single professional elite. As the focus of specialisms has narrowed, the boundaries around social problems have broadened and fuzzed. A consequence is that few professions can now claim total competence to handle basic problems even within those functional areas in which they once were recognized as exclusive monopolists. This is a product of growing *functional interdependence*, which is entirely comparable to the growing geographic interdependence mentioned earlier, and of the external effects—both costs and benefits—of actions taken in one field upon others. It would probably be more accurate to say that the growth has been less in the actual interdependence of different fields and more in the recognition of such interdependence. Crime is no longer a problem for the police alone nor health for doctors alone nor highways for engineers alone nor justice for lawyers alone. Progressive practitioners and educators are articulating and deploring the limitations of their own fields with increasing shrillness. As will be discussed later, this dilemma is bringing about a rethinking of professional—and interprofessional—education and practice.

Growth

A final anomaly for our future public administration is the impending desanctification of *growth*, particularly economic growth, as the ultimate goal of society and its rate as the measure of social progress. The process of defrocking has begun. Already it is clear: that overall population growth must ultimately be reduced to zero—and "ultimately" may not be very many decades away; that our largest, "greatest" cities are near-disaster areas for many of their inhabitants; that the biggest organizations are among the most dangerous threats to resources, environment, culture, and even people.

John Kenneth Galbraith, after emphasizing growth as a dominant and pervasive goal of the "technostructure," notes that it is supported by its consistency with the more general goal of economic growth. "No other social goal is more strongly avowed than economic growth. No other test of social success has such nearly unanimous acceptance as the annual increase in the Gross National Product."[8] But faith in GNP growth as an indicator of social betterment must soon decline in the face of its increasingly apparent clumsiness and flimsiness. Expenditures for war and defense are of course part of GNP, and indeed the surest way to increase it rapidly would be a major (non-nuclear) war. The social costs incident to productive enterprise and urbanization are nowhere deducted from GNP: despoliation of resources, pollution of all kinds, crime and other costs related to population density, and many others. Further, whatever dollar expenditures are made to counteract these real costs are *added into,* not *deducted from,* GNP.[9] The costs of producing and merchandising goods that are trivial, worthless, or actually damaging (like tobacco, liquor, guns, and DDT) are part of GNP. And GNP of course takes no account whatever of the distribution of income and wealth among the population.

Of course, much work has already been done toward the development of more sensitive and meaningful measures of social betterment than GNP. The harder and probably slower job will be to modify the underlying faith in growth per se that has served us reasonably well for many decades: the faith that equates "more" with "better" and "growth" with "progress." Administrators cannot much longer rely upon crude measures of growth—whether or not economic—to provide their goals or to appraise their effectiveness. They must help to find, and must learn and apply subtler and more qualitative goals and indices; and they must play some part in communicating these to the public.

To recapitulate: The emerging public administration, the truly "new" public administration, will bear responsibilities of a range and an importance that are hardly suggested in any current textbook. It will have to anticipate and deal with changes in a society that is changing more rapidly than any in human history. It, too, will have to be rapidly changeable and flexible. It will have to press for greater rationality and develop and utilize ever more sophisticated tools for rational decisions, at the same time accommodating to forces that seem unrational. It must concern itself more than in the past with human goals "life, liberty, and the pursuit of happiness"—but without damage to the processes which make democracy viable. And these goals must be more sophisticated than simple quantitative growth. It must recognize the functional and geographic interdependence of all sectors of the society without too much sacrifice to the values of professional specialism and local interest. It must develop collaborative workways whereby centralization and decentralization proceed simultaneously, and assure high competence at every level of government.

These are tall orders for public administration. Their implications are described more specifically in the balance of this article.

IMPLICATIONS FOR PUBLIC ORGANIZATIONS

The statements about public organizations which follow are not purely predictive. All have some basis in observations of current developments. And all are responsive to the societal trends and problems described earlier.

First are the increasing emphasis in and among organizations upon problems and problem solving, and the growing distrust of established and traditional routines which have failed to provide solutions.

There will be increasing dependence upon, and increasing acceptance of, analytical techniques in planning and evaluating public programs, centering upon specialized units near the top of agencies, but spreading downwards to lower and operating echelons seeking rationalized defenses of their programs. One might anticipate, too, a broadened and more sophisticated approach to analytic techniques which takes into account elements beyond purely economic and quantitative considerations. But there will be increasing concern about long-term objectives, alternative measures for reaching such objectives, social—as distinguished from purely economic—indicators, and improved information systems concerning both costs and effects of programs. There will also be more efforts toward experimentation in undertakings whose prospects are untried and unproven.

As the interconnection and interdependence of social problems is increasingly perceived, there will be growing reliance upon ad hoc problem-solving machinery—task forces, commissions, special staffs to executives, inter-agency committees, and institutionalized though ad hoc mechanisms within agencies.

Both the second and third developments cited above will force increased attention on the inherently obstinate problems of translating new or changed program decisions into effective action through—or in spite of—existing and traditional agencies and operations. In fact, one of the weakest links in public administration today is that of giving operational meaning to planning decisions, however sophisticated may be the analysis behind the plans and however effective the collaboration in reaching agreement on the plans.

Political executives, under unrelenting pressure from elements in the society and dissatisfied with the answers available from the established bureaucracy, tend to develop and utilize machinery directly responsible to them for developing new programs and changing old ones. At the national level, this is manifest in the emergence of the National Security Council, the new Domestic Council, and a number of presidential program initiatives. Governors like Rockefeller and mayors like Lindsay have responded in substantially comparable ways. So have strong department heads, dissatisfied with recommendations, or lack thereof, from established line bureaus.

There will continue to be vigorous attacks against "entrenched" bureaucracies within departments and agencies. They may be expressed through reorganizing a bureau out of business or scattering its functions or taking over key activities such as planning, personnel, and budget or politicizing its top positions.

Partly in self-defense, bureaus and comparable agencies will undertake to broaden their bases and broaden their capabilities through the engagement of people in relevant specializations but not typical of the elite profession of the bureau. They will also increasingly seek and welcome collaborative relationships with other bureaus and agencies and with other levels of government. And they, too, will become more problem oriented.

As these characteristics of problem orientation and collaboration develop at one level of government, particularly the federal, they will encourage and sometimes enforce comparable approaches at other levels with which it deals.

As local constituencies become more vociferous and more vigorous, and as the capabilities of personnel in federal regional offices, the states, and local governments are upgraded, there will be growing demand for decentralizing decision-making power. My guess is that this kind of decentralization will proceed but a little more slowly than the centralization process implied above.

Finally, there will be a growing premium on responsiveness to social problems and speed in planning and taking action on them. This will be forced, in part, by the politics of confrontation, mentioned earlier.

In short, administrative organizations will be more political, especially at the leadership levels, in the broader, Aristotelian sense of politics. But not with any loss of brain power and specialized knowledge. The movements toward the latter and the need for them will continue to grow. Agencies, though continuing to reflect a heavy functional emphasis in their structure, will necessarily look beyond their specific functions to related functions and agencies. And they will be more flexible.

These developments will not occur equally in all public agencies any more than they have to date. Indeed, there are a good many public activities for which they will not occur at all. They will be most evident in those problem areas of articulate public concern and in connection with new or radically changed programs; that is, in controversial fields. There will be an abundance of President Truman's "kitchens" around Washington and in other capitals in the United States. One can foresee no diminution of intra- and interorganizational conflict.

Partly as a result of the developments suggested above, there will probably be profound changes within administrative organizations in their patterns and behavioral styles. The old Weberian description of bureaucracy, with its emphasis upon formal structure, hierarchy, routinization, and efficiency in its narrow sense, is rapidly becoming obsolete in many organizations. It is inadequate particularly for "thought" organizations, agencies which operate within a particularly turbulent political environment, agencies facing increasing complexity in their programs, and agencies staffed heavily with highly professional or scientific personnel. Such organizations must, if they are to survive, be responsive, adaptive, flexible, creative, and innovative. This means, among other things, that they will increasingly be structured around projects or problems to be solved rather than as permanent, impervious hierarchies of offices, divisions, and sections. Permanent hierarchical structures will remain for a variety of administrative purposes and for the affixing of final responsibility. But work itself will be organized more collegially on a team basis. Generalist decisions will be reached through the pooling of the perspectives and techniques of a variety of specialists. Leadership will be increasingly stimulative and collaborative rather than directive.

This "new" style of bureaucracy is not wholly wishful nor simply the paraphrasing of the writings of social psychologists about what an organization ought to be. The movement toward it is evident in many public and private enterprises and dominant in a few, particularly those involved in research and development, such as units of NASA, NIH, and the scientific laboratories. It is more and more prevalent in the social fields as illustrated by their growing reliance upon intra- and inter-agency task forces, work groups, and committees. It is reflected also in the nature and assignments of a large portion of the so-called "political" appointees who are not politicians and whose party regularity is incidental, if not, in some instances, totally irrelevant. Many of these appointments appear to be predicated upon professional competence in an appropriate field, ability to apply their skills to a variety of problems, and competence in working with and through (rather than over) others.

IMPLICATIONS FOR THE PUBLIC SERVICE

More than half of the products of the nation's universities and colleges, graduate and undergraduate, are educated in specializations that are intended to prepare them for one or another professional or scientific occupation. Not including housewives, the majority of the other college graduates will later return for professional graduate training or will enter upon some line of work, like the Foreign Service, wherein they will acquire the accoutrements of professionalism on the job. Ours is increasingly a professional society or, more accurately, a professionally led society.

And American governments are principal employers of professionals. Very probably within a few years as many as two-fifths of all professionals in this country will be employed directly or indirectly by governments. I perceive no signals that this trend toward professionalism in government will decline. The programs now developing to help the underprivileged find satisfying careers in government and elsewhere may involve lowering educational requisites for some kinds of jobs. But the extent that such programs are successful will be measured by the numbers of their participants who rise to professional or at least paraprofessional levels. What is challenged is not professionalism but the orthodoxy of the traditional routes to attain it.

Books can and should be written about the impact of professionalism upon the public service. I would like to mention very briefly only a few implications that seem salient to this discussion.

- Professionals generally, though not universally, have an orientation to problems or cases; they are prepared to move from one problem to another, somewhat different, one, or to keep several balls in the air at the same time. The problem orientation described above in connection with public organizations is entirely in keeping with the professional way of life.

- All professions (with the possible exception of the ministry) view themselves as rational, but their ways of viewing and defining rationality vary widely. Rationality is no monopoly of administrators, economists, or lawyers. Probably the nearest approach to "pure" rationality, with respect to any given problem, must be the product of a mix of differing professional perspectives on that problem.

- Professional study and practice has tended to foster increasing specialism and increasing depth, decreasing breadth of both student and practitioner, in the professions. This has been further encouraged by the explosion of knowledge in most fields. Until quite recently it has tended to crowd out the consideration of general social consequences of professional behavior and the philosophical consideration of social values from both education and practice. In most fields it has also minimized education or practice in politics, administration, or organization.

- Insofar as professionalism requires many years of training and experience (varying in different fields) in specialized subjects, it has an inhibiting effect upon movement from one occupation to another. But it encourages mobility from place to place and from organization to organization (or self-employment) especially when the move promises new and greater challenges. This is probably truest among the best qualified, most innovative, and most problem-oriented individuals.

- Professional behavior tends to be conditioned more by the norms, standards, and workways of the profession than by those that may be imposed by an employing organization. Within those standards professionals seek a considerable degree of autonomy and discretion in the application of their particular skills. They resist working under close supervision of others, especially when the others are not members of the same profession.

- When professionals work on problems requiring a number of different occupational skills—and these include almost all problems in the social arena—they prefer to work with others on an equal or team basis, founded in mutual respect.

- Most of the professions are increasingly grounded in some branches of science. Science is in turn grounded in the search for truth and, for any given problem, the finding of the correct answer. Scientists—and many professionals—are intolerant of ambiguity, of politics, and all too often of other ways of looking at problems.

These alleged attributes of professionalism of course do not apply equally to all professions nor equally to all members of any given profession. Where and to the extent that they do apply, it may be noted that some of them are entirely congruent and encouraging to the kind of organizational behavior suggested in the preceding section. These include:

- orientation to problems, projects, and cases;

- mobility or willingness to move from place to place and from job to job;

- collegial relationships in working with others on common problems.

But in certain other respects, the education and practice of typical professions is a good deal less than optimal for the public service of tomorrow. First, there is insufficient stress upon and concern about human and social values. All professions allege their dedication to the service of society, and most take for granted that activities their members perform within professional standards are useful and beneficial to the public. There has been rather little reexamination of these assumptions in the face of a rapidly changing society and rapidly expanding governmental responsibilities. And individual practitioners are provided little motivation or intellectual grounding to stimulate concern about general social values in relation to their day-to-day problems. This is only incidentally a matter of codes of ethics, most of which are essentially negative and very few of which even mention any special ethical problems arising from public service, even when substantial portions of the profession are employed by governments. The kind of need I perceive is more of the order, for example, that:

- engineers who plan highways or airports or sewage plants take into consideration the secondary and tertiary effects of these undertakings on the quality of life in America and in the places for which they are planning;

- lawyers look beyond due process, *stare decisis*, the adversary system, etc., to the roots of our social difficulties;

- economists look beyond primary and quantitative costs and benefits, the market analogy, and the GNP growth rate to where we as a society and as individuals are going—both as a whole and in relation to individual economic decisions; etc.

Second and closely related to the values question is the need of a great many more professionals who have a sophisticated understanding of social, economic, and political elements and problems of our times, including an understanding of the relation of their own work to that setting. Third is the need for humility and for tolerance of others, their ideas and perspectives, whether or not professionals; and an ability to communicate with others on shared problems.

Fourth is an ability to work in situations which are uncertain and on problems for which there is no correct solution—in short, a tolerance for ambiguity.

Fifth is an understanding of organizations and how they work, particularly in the context of American politics and government; skill in managing in the larger sense of getting things done with and through other people.

Sixth, there should be greater incentive for—and much less discouragement of—creativity, experimentation, innovation, and initiative.

Seventh is the need for a much higher degree of mobility—within agencies, between agencies, between governments, and in and out of government. Despite the observation made earlier that professionalism encourages such mobility, public employment by and large has inhibited it, even for its professionals. One result is that the majority of those who rise to the near top have had effective experience in only one agency, often only one division of that agency. This is a disservice to the man—the absence of challenge and of different and broadening kinds of experiences. It is a misfortune for the government because it tends to solidify bureaucratic parochialism and, in some degree, discourages the problem approach which was stressed earlier. Ten years of experience in one job may be merely one year of experience repeated ten times. The idea of temporariness should extend much further than it has in the civil services of governments.

Finally, there should be greater opportunities for challenge and for rapid advancement for the able young, for the underprivileged, and for women. In government, this means opportunities for professionalizing the nonprofessionals and for rapid advancement through a variety of challenging assignments for those who prove effective.

IMPLICATIONS FOR PERSONNEL SYSTEMS

Obviously, the strengths and weaknesses of the public service can be attributed only partially to personnel systems—the systems whereby people are employed and deployed, advanced, and retired. And changes in the systems have only a partial and usually rather slow influence in changing the nature and calibre of the public service. Yet I doubt that there is any other manipulable element with as much potential impact. The system and its popular image condition the kinds and capabilities of people who seek entrance and their expectations. It also influences the expectations of those already on the job, their motivation, the rewards and penalties of differing kinds of behavior, their movement from job to job, and the way they work together.

Personnel administration has since World War II, but particularly in the decade of the '60's, been undergoing a radical transition in the national government and, in varying degrees, in the states and the cities. It has been marked by:

- decentralization and delegation from central civil service agencies in the direction of line managers;

- growing emphasis upon personnel as a management service rather than as a control or police activity;

- growth of employee and executive development programs, particularly through institutionalized training;

- growth and recognition of employee organizations and collective bargaining;

- concern about and programs for equal opportunity for the handicapped, underprivileged, minority groups, and women;

- relaxation of rules and requirements for standardized personnel actions, particularly as they apply to professionals;

- "positive" recruitment in the educational institutions and elsewhere.

The extent and significance of these and other changes are not, I think, sufficiently appreciated. If one were to compare an annual report of the U.S. Civil Service Commission of a pre-War year such as 1939 or even of 1955 with *Blueprint for the Seventies*, its report for 1969, he could hardly believe that they were produced by the same agency. (Though a glance at the appendices might make the identity of the three more recognizable.) Most of these changes have been consonant with the changing nature and needs of the society.

Yet there linger some tenets of civil service administration—and the image of them perceived by both bureaucrats and the general public—which seem inconsistent with the directions of the society and dysfunctional in terms of its demands upon the public service. I should like to focus upon two of them, both born of reform movements and both with a distinguished history of about half a century or longer. The first is here referred to as *careerism*. It is that feature built upon the expectation that individuals will be recruited soon after completion of their education; that they will spend the bulk of their working lives in the same organization; that they will be advanced periodically as they gain experience and seniority, such advancement made on the basis of competition with their peers; and that they will be protected in such advancement against competition with outsiders. The second is *position classification* or, more particularly, the thesis that the content of a given position or class of positions be the hub around which other personnel actions and indeed management generally should revolve.

Careerism has historically been associated with such commissioned corps systems as the Army, Navy, and Foreign Service, but it is now clear that it is equally or more virile in many of the well-established agencies under civil service in the federal and all other levels of government. Typically in the United States—and most other industrialized nations of the world—careers are associated with individual agencies—departments, bureaus, services, divisions—rather than with the government as a whole. And typically they are identified with a particular type of professional specialization, dominant or subordinate, within the given agency. Careerism may contribute to managerial flexibility in the provision of a corps of qualified people within the organization who are available for different kinds of assignments. At the same time, it inhibits overall elasticity in terms of quick changes in total manpower resources or the provision of persons with different kinds of skill and perspectives. It discourages lateral entry or the ingestion of new blood above the bottom of entering level, and some agencies have absolutely banned it. More often than not, careerism provides built-in, though usually unwritten, incentives for individuals to pursue orthodox careers within the agency and to avoid unusual assignments which might sidetrack or delay advancement. Overall, careerism probably is an important discourager of creativity, innovation, and risk taking because of the perceived or imagined dangers of stepping out of line. And insofar as it assures that the older officers within the system will hold the top positions of the agency, it assures continuity, stability, and conservatism in agency policy.[10] It is probably the principal ingredient of the cement which binds an agency into a strong, autonomous, and perhaps impervious entity against outsiders—whether above in the Executive Branch or outside in the legislature or the public.

It is apparent that many aspects of careerism run counter to effective government responsiveness to the needs of the temporary society. Among the items it discourages are: collaborative relationships with other agencies and specializations toward the solution of common problems; interchange of personnel among agencies, among jurisdictions of government, and between government and the private sector; ad hoc but temporary assignments that are unorthodox in terms of career advancement; responsiveness and rapid change to meet rapidly changing problems. Insofar as the gates of entry upon a government career are based upon orthodox educational credentials—and most of them are—it inhibits employment programs for aspiring potential professionals of minority groups. The bar against lateral entry effectively shuts out mature and qualified women after they have raised their families. And the whole image of government as life-long career systems in single agencies discourages some of the most alert, idealistic, and action-oriented of American youth.

Like careerism, position classification is not necessarily a dysfunctional process. Indeed, it is hard to imagine any sizable organization operating without at least a skeleton of a classification plan, even if it is unwritten. The problem arises from the centrality and dominance which positions and their classification came to assume in personnel administration, in management generally, and in the psychology of officers and employees. Thirty years ago classification had become the jumping-off point for most activities in the field of personnel: pay, recruitment and selection, placement, promotions, transfers, efficiency ratings, even training. It provided the blocks for what some have called the building-block theory of organization—an essentially static and mechanistic concept. It was the restraining leash around the necks of aggressive public managers, and the more successful of them were often the ones who could successfully slip or unfasten it. It has subtler though perhaps more important negative effects upon such matters as status, motivation, willingness to work with others on common problems, communications, flexibility, and adaptability; in short, pervasive impairment to what Argyris has labled "organizational health."

The whole concept of position classification runs somewhat counter, or restraining, to the concept of organization as a fluid, adaptive, rapidly changing entity, oriented to problems and motivated by organizational objectives. To the extent that it is coercive and binding, detailed and specific, and difficult to change, classification has the effects of:

- retarding organizational change and adaptation;

- discouraging initiative and imagination beyond the definition of the position class;

- inhibiting special, ad hoc assignments or otherwise working "out of class";

- discouraging recognition of unusual contributions and competence through rapid advancement.

Bennis confidently predicted that: "People will be differentiated not vertically according to rank and role but flexibly according to skill and professional training."[11] His forecast is not totally reassuring, since "skill and professional training" sound suspiciously like credentialism, and differentiation by credentials can certainly be vertical. But it is clear that the dominance of classification in government has declined a great deal and nearly vanished in some sectors except as a convenience to management. In the federal government the flexibility of the management intern and FSEE programs at the lower rungs of the ladder and, to a slight degree, of the Executive Manpower System at the upper rungs are examples. But clearly in many federal agencies and state and local governments we need to go much further and faster.[12]

I have not intended in this section to suggest that governments cease assuring careers to prospective and incumbent employees, nor that position classification be abandoned. Both seem to me essential. But some of the unintended consequences of both could and should be alleviated in terms consonant with the trends of the society and its demands on government. What is really needed is a PPBS-type analysis of public personnel practices in terms of their long-range costs and benefits towards governmental objectives. My prediction is that such analyses would indicate that there should be:

- a deemphasis of careerism and tenurism;

- more lateral entry, exit, and reentry;

- more mobility and flexibility in assignment and reassignments;

- rewards rather than implicit penalties for broadening experience in other agencies, other governments, and the private sector;

- more emphasis in rank, status, and rewards upon the man and his performance, less upon his position description;

- declining reliance upon examinations and rank-order lists in entrance and advancement, and more reliance upon performance and references;

- more opportunities for reeducation and retraining, and for broadening education and training, especially for professional personnel;

- more emphasis upon rewards and recognition for initiative and work well done, with less concern about discipline and penalties for nonconformity;

- broadening of the subjects of negotiation in collective bargaining and, with some exceptions, recognition of the right to strike.

. . .

NOTES

1. Warren G. Bennis and Philip E. Slater, *The Temporary Society* (New York: Harper and Row, 1968).
2. *Ibid.*, pp. 73–74, 76.

3. *Ibid.*, p. 75.
4. Paul T. David, "The Study of the Future," *Public Administration Review*, Vol. XXVIII, No. 2 (March/April 1968), p. 193.
5. Among the most forceful of these critics have been Theodore S. Lowi in his book, *The End of Liberalism: Ideology, Policy and the Crisis of Public Authority* (New York: W. W. Norton & Co., 1969), and Allen Schick in his article, "Systems Politics and Systems Budgeting," *Public Administration Review*, Vol. XXIX, No. 2 (March/April 1969), pp. 135–151. Comparable points of view are implicit or explicit in much of the writing of those who are identified with the "new left" in the fields of political science, public administration, other social sciences, and indeed intellectuals in general.
6. Emmette Redford, *Democracy in the Administrative State* (Fairlawn, N.J.: Oxford University Press, 1969), p. 70.
7. John W. Gardner, whose experience as head of the Department of Health, Education, and Welfare and then of the Urban Coalition would seem to qualify him uniquely on this subject, recently stated the problem succinctly: "I do not believe that major institutional change will be initiated at the local level. Local groups can do a lot of important things—significant, useful things. . . . If you want effective social change, you've got to know what's bothering people and you've got to have leadership at the local level. But grass roots leadership without national links just becomes sentimental." Quoted by the Associated Press in *The Daily Progress,* Charlottesville, Virginia, August 2, 1970, p. 3-A.
8. John Kenneth Galbraith, *The New Industrial State* (Boston: Houghton Mifflin, 1967), p. 173.
9. For a devastating and frightening analysis along this line, see the work by an unusual economist, Ezra J. Mishan, *The Cost of Economic Growth* (New York: Frederick A. Praeger, 1967).
10. Some of the dysfunctional effects of careerism in the upper levels of the U.S. civil service provoked the recent proposal of the Bureau of Executive Manpower, U.S. Civil Service Commission, for changes in the management of super grades. Among many other things, it recommended that super-grade employees be engaged on contracts of five-year duration. Upon completion of the contracts, they could be separated or returned to grade 15 levels or have their contracts renewed on a one-year basis.
11. Bennis and Slater, *op. cit.*, p. 74.
12. It is noteworthy that a congressional committee recently asked the U.S. Civil Service Commission to conduct a thorough two-year study, now under way, of federal classification and its effects.

Developments in Public Administration

DWIGHT WALDO

This report on recent and contemporary developments is centrally concerned with self-conscious Public Administration, that is, the academically centered area of inquiry and teaching that knows itself by this name.[1] It is concerned with the institutions and activities of public administration chiefly as these relate to Public Administration.

A vexing terminological problem has already presented itself. Economics is little likely to be mistaken for the economy, political science for politics, sociology for society. But "public administration" can mean, (1) the institutions and activity of public agencies; (2) self-conscious inquiry and teaching focused upon such public agencies: or (3) both (1) and (2) as a total field of institutions, activities, inquiry, and teaching. In this discussion the style Public Administration will be used in referring to self-conscious inquiry and teaching. The style public administration will refer sometimes to the public institutions and activities, sometimes to the total field of institutions, activities, inquiry and teaching. The reader will have to do his best to decide, from contextual clues, which of the two is meant.

Public Administration is in a period of stress and change. It is responding to many and often conflicting forces in a complex, sometimes turbulent environment. In the attempt to understand what is happening to and in Public Administration, attention is directed first to some aspects of the total field of societal forces to which it is responding. Then, narrowing the scope, I shall discuss interaction with its immediate "external" environment of public administration and with its "internal" environment of academically centered institutions and ideas. Finally, I shall try to decide what further observations are needed to complete the review and what speculations appear reasonable.

THE SOCIETAL CONTEXT OF CONFLICT AND TURBULENCE: ANTINOMIES AND PARADOXES

The plethora of problems with which public administration seeks to cope and the extraordinary level of societal conflict and turbulence which presently constitute its environment can hardly be ignored in any attempt to report on recent and contemporary Public Administration. These matters have of course been noted, analyzed, discussed, and debated at great length: and no brief treatment can pretend to add important new information. Perhaps, however, the relevance for public administration of some of the antinomies and paradoxes in the situation can be more clearly delineated. In any event that is the object of what follows.

Public-Private

Conflicting ideas on the proper division between the public and the private realms are hardly new. Neither is a measure of overlapping and intermixture. However, in the present period the conflict between the two principles has not only great intensity, but new aspects: and the growth of a "gray" area of public-private admixture, in its size and complexity, is creating a new situation in societal organization and administration.

Reaction against governmental institutions and solutions is massive, varied, and intricate. Manifestations abound: taxpayers' revolts, anti-busing movements, draft evasion, militancy of public employee unions, citizen vigilante organizations, withdrawn communal groups, and so forth. As well observed, the liberal consensus that formed about the New Deal has been greatly weakened: no longer is it easily presumed that a national problem can be solved by creating a national program with a matching bureaucracy. Much evidence indicates that belief in the intelligence, the justice, the honesty, and the efficiency of public officials and employees has declined during recent years. The reaction against government spans the socio-economic spectrum. Right, Center, and Left, with different motives and for different objectives, speak in concert in this regard.

Yet for all the crying of the "sickness of government," government grows, and it grows because society asks it to grow. It remains by the logic of circumstances society's "chosen instrument" to deal with problems of large scope and great complexity. It could hardly be otherwise short of societal disintegration, or reconstruction in some very different form. The area of *public* problems, that is, the area in which the actions of one or a few affect many, steadily expands: and government, for all its faults, was created to deal with public problems—and there is no obvious and accepted alternative. Except for those whose alienation has led to a "drop out" status, there is no other important "game."

The result of conflicting sentiments is conflicting actions: toward government and away from government. Simultaneously there is movement toward the publicization of the private and the privatization—"reprivatization," as some would have it—of the public. The result, when combined with important technological and social changes, is the expansion of an area in which public and private, as these have been conventionally conceived, are intermingled in new and often exceedingly intricate ways.

To be sure, the line of division between public and private was never clear and simple, as even a cursory view of American history indicates (as with respect to such areas as defense, transportation, and banking, but also including farming and—even—general "business"). But with the first measures—even pre-New Deal—to deal with the economic collapse of 1929, an upward curve in the size and intricacy of a "gray" area began. Every important program to raise income, employment, and productivity, ameliorate social distress, correct abuses, and protect rights has entailed the creation of new and complex arrangements in which the distinction between public and private has become more blurred.

The curve is upward: the movement accelerates. COMSAT (Communications Satellite Corporation), Amtrak, the U.S. Postal Service, and the Public Broadcasting Corporation are important in themselves and symbolic. The massive and intricate complexes of the public and private presented in urban renewal and housing, defense procurement, space exploration, as well as in other fields, are indicative of the future rather than reflections of the past. It is almost wholly predictable, for example, that when further legislation is passed seeking to improve national health care delivery, the prescription will be for a more complete and complex mixing of the public and the private. Some commentators now speak of the Third Sector, a major new realm on the socio-economic map.

Rising Expectations–Lowering Expectations

In the 1950s, the idea of a worldwide "revolution of rising expectations" was widely publicized. Around the world, we were told, peoples by the hundreds of millions who had accepted poverty as a part of the natural order had now come to realize that poverty is man-made and unnecessary. Now they had come not only to expect a rising standard of living, they looked forward—with varying degrees of confidence and differing time scales—to a standard of living essentially comparable to that of advanced industrial countries.

It is not necessary to agree with all that was said about the revolution of rising expectations—some of which was exaggerated or in error—to recognize that it concerns something true and important: A new, volatile element has been added to the world and national situations. "Development" has, since World War II, become something of a worldwide ideology and movement: "to develop" is to do something eminently desirable, and while development is susceptible to differing interpretations, its customary meaning is given by such concepts as productivity, industrialization, and standard of living. Undoubtedly, the fervor with which development was embraced—having some religious qualities, however secular its core objectives—has affected our domestic politics as well as our international role: We have had our own revolution of rising expectations, among and concerning the poor and disadvantaged generally, but centering upon racial-ethnic minorities.

Meanwhile, a revolution of quite different characteristics has come upon us, one which appears to dictate in many ways and for many people a lowering of expectations. This second revolution is centered in the concept of ecology. It concerns such matters as: environmental pollution, exhaustion of non-renewable resources, limiting population, de-emphasizing productivity as a goal, "quality of life" as against "standard of living." Ultimately, it concerns preservation of the biosphere itself.

To picture two monolithic forces in direct conflict would, of course, be oversimplification. But that the two streams of ideas and activities do already conflict and that the potential for much greater conflict exists is beyond cavil. One can, in his optimistic moments, hope for a world in which zero population growth has been achieved, essential human equality in enjoyment of goods is a fact, and a simple life-style obtains—a world that respects and cooperates with nature. But before anything of such kind comes to pass—if it ever does—it is wholly predictable that the collision of ideas and desires will bring confusion and conflict. Nothing less is involved than massive change in present living patterns and in expectations for the future, in *both* developed and developing countries—West and East, non-communist and communist.

Industrialism–Post-Industrialism

Closely related is another antinomy. Obviously, industrialization has been so far the heart of development; and a de-emphasis of the production of material goods is viewed by many as essential to adjusting man to a supportable environment. Yet however intertwined, the two antinomies are neither equivalents nor opposites. Many now argue that the development with which disadvantaged peoples are concerned, or *ought* to be concerned, can be conceived in nonindustrial terms; and post-industrialism can be conceived as a condition in which production of goods is decreased relatively and perhaps even absolutely.

A long shelf could now be filled with the works discussing the movement of modern man from an industrial period into a post-industrial period. In general they argue: that scientific and technical advances make possible and perhaps inevitable a new socio-economic condition of man; that organized and codified knowledge is becoming increasingly important as against the conventional factors of production, land, labor, and capital; that new knowledge and new technologies enable us to produce goods with such efficiency and in such abundance that the archetypical industrial institution, the "factory," is being transformed, evolving into new techno-social patterns: that the new efficiencies in production of goods (the solution of the ancient problem of scarcity) make it possible—and in some ways necessary—for society to emphasize the rendering of services and the enjoyment of leisure as against production of material goods: that these changes, at base technical and economic, have profound implications for total societal organization and style of life, as evidenced by the fact that as the economy of the United States becomes increasingly a service-rendering economy, we experience institutional and psycho-social crises.

To the extent such analyses and projections are correct, they are of course highly relevant to the several other antinomies here sketched. Can other societies—can parts of our society—move directly from pre-industrialism to post-industrialism? Is it realistic or humane to decry productivity while hundreds of millions are in dire need? If productivity as a goal and measure is inappropriate for a post-industrial, service-rendering economy, what—if anything—takes its place? What are the implications of the new modes of production and life-styles for the inter-mixture of public and private, and beyond that for the functions and organization of government?

Nationalism–Post-Nationalism

Nationalism–post-nationalism may not be the proper choice of terms. Though some of the phenomena to which attention is called undoubtedly can be so designated, others probably deserve another designation. Be that as it may, the purpose is to note the conflicting forces bearing on the establishment, the permeability, and the disappearance of political boundaries.

The thesis developed by Hans Kohn and others that nationalism is not a universal phenomenon, but one peculiar to the modern period, has a corollary; namely, that it may wither and disappear. Reasonable evidence suggests that nationalism has suffered a decline in some of the older nation-states: a growing disinterest in patriotic observances, a neglect of the duties of citizenship, growing estrangement from or hostility toward governmental institutions. Taken by themselves these signs would seem to be a trend toward the emergence of a—what to call it?—human homogenization or universalism. More, this trend would seem in concert with trends based upon and emerging from various economic, functional and technical considerations. The growth of transnational and sometimes world-encircling organizations, associated organizations, and complex systems of associated organizations, clearly is one of the important trends of the century.

But at the same time it seems indisputable that there are contrary trends in the direction of greater group self-consciousness and discreteness. This is manifest in the rise in the number of "new nations," of political entities that are nominally independent in terms of international law, a quadrupling in the fairly recent past. It is evidenced also in the rise of new, or renewed, racial-ethnic identities, often strident and militant: older nationalisms may become moribund; some countries may—from the evidence one may guess *will*—disappear, that is, lose their present identity; but the result may well be a progressive fractionalization of mankind instead of movement toward a common world culture and order.

Violence–Nonviolence

The mid- and latter-twentieth century presents a new condition of man with respect to the interaction of violence and nonviolence.

As to violence, The Bomb is not only an instrument beyond all past imaginings, it serves as symbol for a vast array of instruments either created afresh or reshaped and sharpened by modern science and technology. Paradoxically, both our successes and our failures in social organization act, according to circumstances, either to create violence or to enlarge its threat. Actual violence between nations, and within nations, as represented by crime, civil disorder, and repression, is high and probably trending higher: and the possibility of vastly accentuated violence, perhaps even holocaust, seems ever near.

In counteraction, sentiments and movements for nonviolence are high and also perhaps trending higher. To be sure paradoxes and ironies abound. Some movements for peace and brotherhood take violence as a means: Right and Left, conservative, centrist, and radical find themselves in varying stances, either by their own recognition or in the perception of their opponents; vast confusion and much controversy concern means and ends, instruments and objectives. For violence—nonviolence are seldom pure issues, but come entwined with issues of right and equity. In any case, the fear of dire consequences is high, and the longing for some state of relative nonviolence is strong across the wide social-ideological spectrum and around the world.

It is a truism to say the present situation is unique: of course it is. But this is also a profoundly important truth. The present moment cannot be understood without appreciation of the strength and the potential on both sides of the complex violence–nonviolence equation. The deepest springs of human action are tapped by the issues: in the shaping and reshaping of human culture and institutions this is a crucial period.

Implications for Public Administration

The five fields of contesting forces noted may not have been skillfully delineated: perhaps they were not even well chosen. But they represent an attempt to probe beneath the surface of the rapid change and frequent turbulence of the day—war, social dislocation, civil strife, generational conflict, drug abuse, and so on, through a long and somber list—with the object in view of understanding the context of public administration, and thus understanding public administration itself.

Fortunately the moral that is about to be drawn will stand whether or not the best choice of force-fields has been made or whether their explication has been skillful. The moral is that since public administration, by lack of alternatives if not by enthusiastic choice, is government's central instrument for dealing with general social problems, it is located in or between whatever force-fields exist. It is affected by whatever forces and turbulence there are: and it attempts also to *act*, to restrain or to increase the direction or the degree of change.

Given that the instruments of public administration must make choices and act—and on this there is no dispute whatever the contrary wishes and hopes—they are confronted by a range of difficult decisions. Within the constraints of the law, and these constraints are often broad, they must decide upon the ends to be sought in the name of a public interest. Again within constraints, but characteristically with a considerable range of choice, they must decide upon means to realize the objectives, and then take action based on choices made. They cannot refrain, even if they wish to, from making decisions that—singly or in combination—involve policy judgments, instrumental judgments, legal judgments, moral judgments.

THE EXTERNAL ENVIRONMENT OF PUBLIC ADMINISTRATION

I now narrow the focus, to note some of the events and developments of the recent past and present which "impact" public administration: to which it responds and with which it interacts. I shall then observe how some central and predurable aspects of public administration are affected by the larger societal forces noted above and by particular developments.

While for brevity this review of some prominent areas of activity must for the most part proceed as though each area is discrete, this is of course not the case. Typically, one is closely intermingled with another, and all are part of and suffused by the extraordinary social ferment and activism of recent years.

Anti-Poverty

As noted, the revolution of rising expectations has been a domestic as well as a foreign phenomenon. In the sixties poverty was rediscovered in the United States. Notable works exposed the depth and breadth of domestic poverty, low-income groups became more politically active, and a "war against poverty" became an official national cause.[2]

Much legislation and administration from the beginning of the Republic has been in some sense anti-poverty, and major programmatic additions, especially dealing with income maintenance for agriculture and labor, were made in the New Deal period. No great changes have been made in historically given programs: nor has much debate concerning the establishment of a national income floor yet resulted in legislation. The result of the so-called war against poverty has been rather a variety of special programs designed to improve living conditions, raise incomes, foster employability, and increase employment opportunitites. The recently formed Department of Health, Education and Welfare and the newly created Office of Economic Opportunity have been centrally involved. The administrative problems encountered have often been novel and always extremely difficult: by and large only limited successes in reaching objectives and solving the administrative problems can be claimed.[3]

Racial-Ethnic Equality

The movement of the early sixties to effect the civil rights of blacks in the South of course broadened in many directions. Equality for blacks in all respects quickly became an ardently sought goal. Chicanos, Puerto Ricans, and Indians, stimulated more or less by the black example, began to assert their identity and to press for more equality in education, housing, employment, and income.[4] There have been many reactive results, including something of a resurgence of ethnic self-identity among European populations that had seemed all but assimilated. To what extent the equality that is sought by all will, in the long run, entail separateness of racial-ethnic identity and culture is at this point quite unforeseeable.[5]

Historically, much governmental action in the United States has been not simply discriminatory, but massively and harshly so. Much governmental action has also, however, been directed toward achieving equality; paradoxically, action to secure assimilation and uniformity also has sometimes been insensitive and coercive. This is not the place to analyze a complex national experience. What needs to be noted is that in recent years the goal of equality has been taken with more seriousness, however contentious it remains and however ineffective the results. In large part, the story involves legislatures and courts; no large government agencies have been established of which the *primary* mission is achievement of racial-ethnic equality. But the issue of equality of treatment, especially for blacks, is nevertheless centrally and intimately involved in programs in such areas as education, housing, and employment; smaller agencies are created that do have equality of treatment as their central mission; and in the administration of government personnel programs, the issue of equal treatment is, as such, an increasingly important issue.[6]

Altogether, the matter of racial-ethnic equality is central to the understanding of much of recent and contemporary public administration.

Urban Problems

The shift from an agricultural economy to an industrial economy, with accompanying growth of the city, was reflected in American public administration well before the end of the nineteenth century, as in the civil service reform movement and the shaping of formulas for structural rationalization. After World War I the generations-old migration to the city was accentuated by technological developments and by agricultural policies: rapid population growth helped to increase city size; various policies, particularly with respect to housing, contributed to an expansion of suburban growth at the expense of the central city. For these and for many other reasons, by the sixties the city had become a problem center of a new order of magnitude for public policy and public administration.[7]

In a formal sense one can distinguish between city problems and problems that find their chief location and severest manifestations in the city. The former concern the location and specifications of urban artifacts; they pertain to such matters as physical planning, industrial and commerical location, housing, street layout, and public transportation. The latter concern the problems of an industrial society in transition to a new condition designated (negatively, because its defining characteristics are only emergent) as post-industrial—in any event, the worrisome problems of *this* society at this time: racial inequality, increasing crime, drug abuse, and so forth. In some measure these have a city focus simply because our national life now has a city focus. But such a formal distinction has only a limited relevance. In the city, problems meet, mingle, and meld; physical problems have human dimensions, and human problems are inseparable from physical problems, as of course only a superficial knowledge of any typical urban problem, such as educational inequality or central-city renewal makes clear. The incredibly complex mixture of differing problems and different kinds of problems is the essence of the matter. Few public problems are not now city problems.[8]

The implications for public administration are most visible in the creation of a new federal department, the Department of Housing and Urban Development.[9] But the implications run far beyond the easily visible, into the problems of the organization and administration of all recent or emerging national programs, and to every level and type of governmental jurisdiction.

Ferment and Change

Space does not permit extended discussion of many other themes and events relevant to recent and contemporary public administration. Brief notice of some of the more important must suffice. Again, it should be understood that separate notice does not imply separate existence. On the contrary, a complex pattern of overlapping and interaction—which would be beyond tracing even in book-length treatment—obtains.

Participation. A prominent theme and movement of the late sixties and early seventies has been participation. The participation movement has manifested itself in public administration in two ways: (1) internally, in actions directed both toward greater personnel involvement in decisions affecting the conditions of employment and toward rank and file involvement in decisions on agency programs:[10] and (2) externally, in actions aimed at greater community or clientele participation in both decisions on agency programs and the implementation of these programs.[11]

Devolution. In some measure related to the participation movement, but in some respects quite different, has been a movement aimed at bringing public programs more under control of the states and of local governmental jurisdictions. Typically, but not always, participation is associated with liberal or even radical sentiments; typically, but not always, devolution is associated with conservative or even reactionary sentiments. Both are responses to a feeling of powerlessness, even alienation; both manifest a distrust of bigness, and distance; both represent an attempt to gain control of decisions affecting vital personal concerns. Both movements, alone or in combination, have resulted in various types of action with the avowed objective of returning power to the people—or at least keeping it from further concentrating in the federal government.[12]

New Levels and Jurisdictions. Related both to participation and to devolution, but also to the programs mounted against poverty—and to other matters—has been the creation of more or less experimental jurisdictions operating in unconventional ways. These include regional organizations created as a part of a national program to raise the economic and social level of backward or depressed regions of the country;[13] and community action organizations, particularly in the central-city areas, created as a part of the war against poverty.[14] The participation motives as well as those ascribed to devolution have been operative in the creation of new levels and jurisdictions, in addition to administrative and economic considerations.

Management Techniques and Instrumentalities. Recent years have witnessed the growth and spread of various more or less new management techniques and instrumentalities in public administration. Characteristically, the techniques and instrumentalities involved are shared with business administration, and in some cases were invented or first developed there. But some of these have been, in the public administration context, refined, adapted, and expanded.

The techniques and instrumentalities involved cannot here be catalogued and explained, or their usage examined. The term "management science" would comprehend many of the specific techniques, especially those that make use of quantitative methods and have a relation to the newer means of data gathering, storage, and manipulation which center on the computer. The related term, "operations research," also denotes a perspective and a cluster of techniques of considerable importance. Some techniques, especially perhaps project management, have been notably expanded and refined in the public sector.[15]

It is characteristic of some of the techniques that they involve a joining or blending of public and private in the development and effecting of public policy. In this connection "contracting out" or "government by contract" warrants a special word. The legal-administrative device of contracting out to achieve public objectives has a long and complicated history. But the use of the contract device has greatly expanded in recent years at all levels of government. It has a new significance as a means of relating public jurisdictions one to another: and it has an especially important role in large-scale public programs in the areas of defense, economic development, and space exploration.[16]

Unionization and Collective Bargaining. The growth of public employee unionization and collective bargaining, at all levels of government, has been a major development in public administration during the past decade—this at a time in which unionization in some private sectors has been stationary or even declining. Public employee unions are hardly new, but their memberships have been comparatively small, and they have not been, characteristically, bargaining units. The growth of public sector unionism has various types of causes. These would include causes related to the national shift from a predominately goods-producing to a predominately service-rendering economy and an accompanying growth in the proportion of the working population in public employment: a relaxation of laws and regulations which have restrained public sector unionization: and the social-ideological ferment and economic recession of recent years.[17]

Increasing unionization, together with a new assertiveness—in some cases, even militancy—poses knotty new problems and has implications for much of traditional public administration. The traditional area of personnel administration obviously is most immediately affected: but the implications run to all of public organization and management. Indeed, they run to the role of the government in the country's economic and social affairs, and ultimately to the status and nature of government as a sovereign power.[18]

Productivity and evaluation. An issue that is rapidly coming to the fore is productivity in the public sector. Productivity is always an issue with respect to a modern economy, and the transition to a predominately service-rendering economy has changed and sharpened productivity problems: What is the nature and what are the indices of productivity when there is no tangible product? (Sometimes, even, the object of a program is to prevent something from occurring.) With the public sector of the economy steadily enlarging, the problems become more complicated and controversial. Various factors will operate to bring contesting forces into controversy and confrontation: the demands of unions not only for greater economic benefits, but for shorter hours and control of the conditions of labor—perhaps also some policy role; increases in taxes coupled with widespread sentiment that the public services are unresponsive, inefficient, unproductive, and wasteful; still further demands on government, such as subsidization of corporate enterprises that have become closely government-related—"Lockheed issues"; the rationalization and further public funding of medical care delivery; and programs that make government the employer of last resort.

A sharpening of controversy over productivity issues will increase the importance of what is already an important problem of current public administration:

evaluation. Evaluation is hardly a new problem in public administration. It is, in many respects, but a new term for many of the issues that have been involved in dealing with the perennial and often central issues of economy and efficiency. But now the nonmarket area grows in absolute and relative terms, and the mixture of economic rationality, political rationality, and social equity which must be addressed becomes more intricate and tangled.[19]

Two somewhat linked developments in public administration have a close relationship to productivity-evaluation issues and illustrate their importance. One is the attempt to install Planning, Programming, Budgeting Systems (PPBS). Cost-benefit and input-output studies are at the heart of this enterprise. Such studies essentially attempt to deal with productivity-evaluation problems: and so intractable are the problems, that PPBS has faltered and, often, been turned back.[20] The other is the burgeoning of evaluation studies. (These take many forms: Some are in-house, some are inter-agency, some are contracted out to consulting firms, think tanks and research institutes, universities, and even individuals.) The increase in number and complexity of socio-economic programs that came with the sixties has greatly intensified problems of judging effectiveness. Typically, the immediate outputs of the programs involved—as in education—are intangible, immeasurable, and controversial: and typically the difficulties in trying to assess effectiveness and comparative worth are complicated by the intricate administrative means: complex interrelations between public organizations and/or public-private organizations.[21]

Environmentalism and Consumerism. The greatly increased concern for pollution of the environment and an increasing, more generalized interest in the quality of life have significantly affected public administration and may be expected to affect it more with passing time.[22] The most obvious results to date have been the establishment of the Environmental Protection Agency, together with programs of action aimed at pollution control directed both externally—for example, automobile exhaust emissions—and internally—the requirement of the environmental impact studies for new federal programs. But the new currents affect many areas where public administration intersects an aspect of national life, including resource extraction, public works, transportation, recreation, and even the arts.

Governmental concern for the consumer, it is often observed, tends to be minuscule or half-hearted in comparison with concern for economic growth and productivity. Nevertheless, a sizable apparatus of regulation and control has been built up during the past several generations, some parts of which have at least significant consumer obligations in their mandates and some parts of which, as the Food and Drug Administration, have as their primary mission the protection of the consumer from fraud and direct harm.

To evoke the name Ralph Nader suffices to indicate that consumerism is presently in a period of increased interest and activity. In part the upwelling is an aspect of the social-ideological ferment and reformism of recent years; in part it may stand upon its own base. But it is reinforced by, and in a sense is, an aspect of the awakened environmentalism: both emphasize the citizen as consumer as against the citizen as producer.

The impact of the heightened interest in citizen-as-consumer on public administration is difficult to estimate, but it already has had various direct effects. It may bring renewed attention to one of Public Administration's perennial—but recently slighted—interests, regulatory administration; it may lead to a new interest in the administration of consumer protection; and it will reinforce—and be rein-forced by—environmental concerns.[23]

Other Vectors. The events, situations, movements, and so forth, with which pub-lic administration is presently concerned and to which it is more or less responsive are beyond even brief explication. But some of the other matters of import should at least be noted. One of these is the rising tide of domestic violence, with its im-plications for such matters as police and correctional administration, socio-eco-nomic policies, and judicial administration.[24] Another is the economic-financial difficulties which came to the fore in the late sixties; while no major new economy management devices have resulted, still the repercussions in public administration have been far from insignificant. Another is the Women's Liberation movement, which has been taken seriously in personnel administration—how seriously de-pending on jurisdiction and point of view.[25] Another is continued movement toward specialization and professionalization in American life and the public serv-ices;[26] a simultaneous, complicated, recently accentuated counter-movement, which attacks credentialism, seeks to broaden decision-making, to decrease rigidi-ties, to increase lateral communication—generally, to debureaucratize.[27] Still another is President Nixon's proposals with respect to the restructuring of federal administration and his proposals concerning, directly or indirectly, the allocation of responsibilities and functions as between the federal government, the states, and the cities.[28]

Finally, it may be noted that some of the important currents of recent years have slowed or reversed. It has been widely noted that a mood, if not a movement, of neo-isolationism has followed the international experiments and global activism of the post-World War II decades. It is thus not surprising that no report is neces-sary on new creativity in international organization; nor that aid to developing countries does not present recent administrative developments worthy of note. The Planning, Programming, Budgeting System, which may have been the major event in public administration in the sixties—and certainly was the central new item in the literature of Public Administration in that decade—has recently suf-fered a severe decline: given wide publicity for its putative successes in the Depart-ment of Defense in the early sixties, ordered broadly applied in federal agencies in the mid-sixties, it has been recently "non-required" in federal budgeting. This is not, however, to say that PPBS has suddenly disappeared. It continues, as such, in many state and local jurisdictions. It leaves, even where it is formally disestab-lished, a residue of techniques and altered perspectives; its impact will prove to have been permanent.[29] Above all, the problems to which it was addressed re-main.

THE INTERNAL ENVIRONMENT OF PUBLIC ADMINISTRATION

A distinction between the external and the internal environments of Public Ad-ministration may be more literary convenience than reflection of reality. Certainly the matters I now address are inextricably related to events and trends in the out-side world. But in any case, Public Administration interacts not only with the world of public affairs, but with the shifting currents of ideas and the changing in-stitutional arrangements of academia. Attention is now directed to some of these.

A Change in Mood

Paradoxically, though academia is the fount of much societal change, the university is in many ways remarkably conservative. It yields only slowly to demands for change in its own values, procedures, and organization. Revolutionary ideas become tenacious traditions; reforms tend to fade and be supplanted by older ways. So one generalizes at considerable risk.

Nevertheless, it may be noted at the outset that the recent period has been one of extraordinary ferment in the university. Society's turmoil has been reflected in the university: in fact, some of it has centered in the university, as the words Berkeley, Columbia, and Kent State signify. The result has been to weaken the hold of some dominant ideas, to further a search for and heighten receptivity to new ideas, to strengthen forces for change.[30] Much of what is relevant for Public Administration is to be understood as an interaction between old and new, inertia and change, tradition and experiment. The interaction is extremely complex, however, and interpretation is difficult, since one man's progressive perspective is frequently another's philosophical-methodological sterility—or menace.

Two related matters deserve brief attention. One is the cry for relevance. The sentiment that the university is, at best, indifferent toward society's urgent problems has found wide and sometimes ardent expression within the university; and from outside the university has come a variety of pressures—social, political, and economic—for altered perspectives and shifts in emphasis in research and instruction. The result is a heightened malleability, a quickening of change. Public-oriented programs and curricula are of course affected above all.

The other matter concerns changing intellectual-emotional orientations. These are difficult to cover in brief compass, but several generalizations can be made. While there has been no wholesale abandonment of the view that it is the fundamental objective of the social sciences to achieve a true and thorough scientific status, nevertheless a significant softening has occurred. To some extent belief in accepted theories has been shaken by the seeming inadequacies of the theories: thus doubts about Keynesian economic theories created by its putative failures in treating recent economic problems. To a notable extent social scientists—for various reasons from crassly economic to the moral and ideological—are more inclined toward addressing applied problems as against abstract theoretical problems: and since social problems typically ignore disciplinary lines, there is a corresponding rise in interdisciplinary interaction. Some movement is discernible toward more widespread acceptance of radical perspectives and ideologies. Philosophical orientations are shifting to some extent: logical positivism is no longer as widely and firmly espoused; neo-Marxism, existentialism, and phenomenology are frequently argued as bases or guides.[31]

It is within the context of an altered academic-intellectual environment that the following matters are to be construed.

Movement Away from Political Science

It is hardly too much to say that self-conscious Public Administration was the creation of professors of political science, so prominent were the roles of men such as Woodrow Wilson, L. D. White, and W. F. Willoughby. Beginning in the twenties it was customary to regard Public Administration as one of the fields or sub-fields of political science, and in fact probably most persons, both in and out of political science, still so regard it. But at the present time it would appear that significant changes are under way. These changes move in different directions, and the outcome is far from clear. Some forces in motion suggest the outcome will be a closer, but different, relationship with political science; some suggest the achievement of independent status in department and school; some suggest the disappearance of Public Administration as such, its absorption in general management synthesis.

On logical grounds the case for regarding Public Administration as a part of political science is a strong one. Political science concerns the state, government, and the public realm. Public administration would thus seem by definition a part of the total concern of political science. Most professors of Public Administration have regarded themselves as first of all political scientists. Many have found departments of political science congenial environments: some still do.

But in many, many ways the relation has not been a satisfactory one. Two reasons seem pre-eminent. One concerns the customary liberal arts location and orientation of political science. To the extent Public Administration has perceived itself and been perceived as training for a career of government service, and not with scholarship and the values of a liberal education, it has been accorded a type of second-class citizenship in its customary academic home. The fact that much of what has constituted its curriculum has been drawn from outside sources, such as psychology, business administration, and management science, has accentuated the lack of rapport. The second reason concerns the rise and increasing predominance of behavioralism in the post-World War II period. Public Administration was one of the parts of political science that lagged in the behavioral movement. (The reasons for this are varied: probably some of them reflect favorably, some unfavorably, on Public Administration.) Thus to the disdain of the traditionalists was added the reproach, if not contempt, of the new men of political science.

For whatever reasons, Public Administrationists have become increasingly restive with an environment regarded as, at best, merely tolerant. But the problem of an effective remedy is not easy to solve. To muster the resources in money, manpower, and political support to achieve the status of an independent program, department, or school is usually difficult to the point of impossibility. To move, individually or collectively, to a school of business or management may or may not be feasible according to circumstances; but regardless, this solution may appear as merely exchanging one type of second-class citizenship for another.

Movements in ideas, the growth and spread of various management-related technologies with little relation to political science, and increasing interdisciplinary penetration in Public Administration accentuate feelings that political science is no longer an adequate base. Increasingly, it is felt that political science neglects the intellectual-professional needs of public administration. Contrariwise, it is felt that other disciplines and intellectual clusterings, such as economics, sociology, and management science, provide the appropriate ideas and techniques. Some feel that Public Administration, while not a profession in a strict sense, represents a focus of interests and occupations not unlike that represented by medicine or the health services: and that it deserves, somehow, an organizational status which will enable it to represent the realities and muster and combine the needed resources.[32]

While the wish to escape from political science is widespread and growing, nevertheless it needs to be recognized that certain present and potential developments in political science might lead to changes which would make political science a more congenial and supportive environment. One of these concerns the emergence of a "post-behavioral" political science. The ferment of recent years has led, especially among younger political scientists, to something of a revolt against the behaviorally oriented establishment. Political science, and especially behaviorally oriented political science, it is charged, has been too much concerned with technique, too little with goals and values; too much concerned with science and too little concerned with society, with urgent public problems. Proper scientific concerns need not be abandoned—it is generally argued—but they need to be put to service in addressing real and urgent problems.[33]

It is too early to assess the strength and effect of these new currents. But they at least suggest the possibility of a substantial reordering of interests and resources in political science, making it more relevant to public problems, more policy-oriented, and more concerned with delivery. A political science concerned deeply with public policy and not disdainful of the means by which policy is effectuated would be much more attractive to Public Administrationists than has been the political science of recent decades.

Movement Toward Political Economy

Another development in political science that holds the possibility of making it more attractive is the movement toward political economy. Two decades ago Robert A. Dahl and Charles E. Lindblom, in their *Politics, Economics and Welfare* (New York: Harper & Brothers, 1953), argued for the establishment of a new political economy, a joining of political science and economics in the interest of greater theoretical coherence and better policy guidance. No rush and certainly no concerted effort to establish a new political economy followed. But slowly at first, and lately with increasing speed and mass, movement in this direction has taken place. Economists, such as Anthony Downs and Gordon Tullock, crossed the boundary into political science, experimenting with the application of economic methods and models to political problems. Political scientists, including—perhaps especially including—those making Public Administration their specialty, have familiarized themselves with economics, seeking theories and techniques applicable to their interests. The movement toward a new political economy now has considerable force, its supporters include prominent political scientists such as William Mitchell. Economists, for their part, evidence a "have tools, will travel" policy. Their willingness, even eagerness, to help a putatively weaker discipline with its problems has been reinforced by various recent events, including—ironically—the embarrassments arising from the weakness of strictly economic policies in dealing with national economic problems.[34]

Public administration, both as a part of political science and on its own, so to speak, has moved in the direction of liaison with economics. Of course the budgeting-fiscal-accounting complex of interests has always been an area of joint interest. But the wave of interest in Program Budgeting in the fifties, and especially the enthusiasm for Planning, Programming, Budgeting System in the sixties, did much to further interpenetration and foster mutual learning. Two books now in press argue—albeit in very different ways—that the way forward for Public Administration is the route of political economy.[35] At this time perhaps the majority of persons identifying themselves with Public Administration regard economics as a more relevant and useful discipline than political science.[36]

To the extent that political science moves toward political economy, this might, as suggested, increase its attractiveness to a Public Administration moving in a like manner in the same general direction. But the implications with respect to the future are not clear. If Public Administration were to find itself allied with—conceivably a part of—a vigorous political economy, this might move it in quite different directions.

Public Programs in Schools of Business and Managment

Two interrelated developments have great potential importance for the future of Public Administration. One is the growth of programs in Public Administration—designated by such terms as "public sector management"—in schools of business administration. The other is the increase in "schools of management," which characteristically have special curricula designed to prepare some of their graduates for management in the public sector.

Of course it is not new for schools of business to give some attention to public administration. Some have long designated themselves as schools of "Business and Public Administration," even "Government and Business." But even equal treatment in a title has not guaranteed equal status and resources; indeed, gross inequality in resources and emphasis has been the rule. Two factors, however, now bring the business schools to take their "public" programs with increasing seriousness.

One of these is the social ferment of recent years, particularly as reflected in the aims and interests of students. Increasingly it has become evident that many of the students in—or who might be brought into—the business schools hold different values and have other career interests than their fathers. They contemplate a regular business career with indifference or distaste; they wish to do something about society's problems and are seeking knowledge and skills to this end. The other factor has been noted above, namely, the related growth in the public sector of the national economy and the increasing—and increasingly complex—admixture of the traditional "public" and "private." It is now widely recognized in the business schools not only that greater knowledge of governmental affairs is useful in business, but that many business school graduates, whether by accident, choice, or necessity, will be employed in government agencies or mixed enterprises.

The business schools, some of the leading ones vigorously, are responding to these factors. Typically the response is not to import faculty or programs identified with Public Administration—or political science—though there is a certain amount of this. It is rather to draw upon indigenous resources, such as management science, augmented by further recruitment from sociology, social psychology and, especially, economics.[37]

The idea that administration or management is generic, a function common to all organized enterprise of significant scale, is, to be sure, now generations old. Only comparatively recently, however, did the idea find expression in schools of management per se. The number of such schools is still comparatively small, but is increasing, not so much through the establishment of new schools, but through a renaming of schools of business administration. The renaming, to be sure, is typically accompanied by an attempt to broaden the spectrum of institutional or sectoral concern and to expand and update curricula. Programs for areas such as public administration, educational administration, and health administration, are frequently established alongside the business administration curriculum.

What is evidenced in this development is not simply the abstract appeal of an idea whose time has come. (The future will instruct us on the degree to which this is true.) Certainly a degree of necessity and opportunism accompany the appeal of the idea—or ideal. Some of the factors involved here have been suggested and others are apparent: a fading lustre for the "business" label, new opportunities and demands, calculations of institutional survival or competitive advantage.

Whatever the reasons or causes, the important fact for the present purposes is that the generic schools as well as—perhaps more than—the business schools assert an interest in preparing for careers in public administration. The implications are indeterminate, the results unpredictable. At this point there is no way of knowing the extent to which the various curricula may come to have more of a public cast, through the introduction of new influences—whether or not from Public Administration or political science; or contrariwise, that public administration may be affected more than it has been to date by business concepts and techniques. Nor is there any way of knowing what will be the outcome of competition between varying types of schools seeking to prepare for public service.

Schools, Programs, Institutes, and So Forth

The current roster of the National Association of Schools of Public Affairs and Administration, an affiliate of the American Society for Public Administration, lists seventy-seven member institutions. The heterogeneity of titles and styles is arresting: There are schools, institutes, divisions, departments, programs, and centers. While of course Public Administration is often the identifying phrase, public affairs, public policy, government, public service, management science, as well as other labels, appear in the roster. Represented are schools of business, schools of business and public administration and schools of management. In a number of titles Public Administration or public affairs is combined with international affairs, urban affairs, or state and local government.

What conclusions can be drawn—or at least what speculations can be entertained—from a study of this roster?

First, the heterogeneity of titles and styles must be recognized as in itself an important datum, indicating a lack of consensus, but also reflecting flexibility and a wide range of experimentation. Second, as Public Administration is used as an identifying label more in the institutions established earlier, less in those established recently, it may not be regarded as being as strategic or fashionable as some alternatives; at least, recently appearing terms such as "public policy," "management," and "management science" indicate newly desired emphases. Third, obviously the movement of business and generic schools into public administration training is reflected. Fourth, nearly all titles and styles indicate attention primarily if not exclusively to the graduate level, suggesting that training for public administration is regarded as professional at least in the sense that it follows a general education. Fifth, in very few cases is a connection indicated with a department or program of political science, emphasizing the estrangement noted above.

Other conclusions emerge when the list is studied against a background of history and with some knowledge of recent events back of the titles. One is that there is a movement toward an interdisciplinary emphasis, with economics, sociology, social psychology, and management science playing large roles. Another is an emphasis upon some sort of research component and/or special functional-problem focus. Another (related) conclusion is that there is a growing interest in public policy—in all dimensions, so to speak: substantive, analytical, evaluative, and so forth.

What may be indicated above all is that Public Administration—at least education for public administration—is expanding. Not only has there been a recent increase in the number of educational institutions, but student bodies are enlarging, and markets are comparatively lively.

The "New" Public Administration

A significant development of recent years has been the emergence of a "new" Public Administration. The term that comes most readily to mind in describing the new Public Administration is "movement." But whether it now is, or indeed ever was, a movement is not clear: the appropriateness of the term is denied by some of the participants or exemplars. Also, the extent to which the positions taken and ideas espoused are in fact new is a matter of argument.

But in any case, events and writings usually referred to as "the new Public Administration" have been a part of the recent Public Administration scene. In general, new Public Administration is a reflection within the Public Administration community of the events and ideas of the recent period. Its participants—if this is the proper word—have been mainly the younger Public Administrationists. While none of them, by generally accepted usage of the term, could be called revolutionary—after all, as the most ardent point out, they want to change the system, not destroy it—in general they reflect in some degree the rebellion of youth, and certain ideas associated with the counter-culture and the non-Marxian Left.

In broad brush, the charges made against the old public administration are that it lacks a respectable and consistent ideological-philosophical frame and a sophisticated methodology; that in accepting an instrumentalist role it becomes a tool of a system or establishment that itself is in need of serious reform; that it is inefficient—or efficient in the wrong ways—unresponsive, and unimaginative. On one side the new Public Administration is linked to the forces in political science that have been responsible for the emergence of a post-behavioral mood; the acceptance of the critique of pluralism is, for example, prominent. On the other side the new Public Administration is linked, but only weakly, with certain radical movements within the public services.

On the positive side, new Public Administration urges a concern for social equity, a sensitivity to human suffering and social needs. It argues that public administration should be more activist: "proactive" and not simply "reactive." It professes not to be anti-scientific, but wishes advanced methodologies and procedures to be used in a context of concern and reform, not for their own sakes and certainly not as instruments of repression. It professes not to be anti-rational, but wishes the calculations of public administration to be more sensitive, subtle, and humane: the domain of public administration to be enlarged by recognition of the importance of affect. It has a special concern for the problems of the central city: racial inequality, poverty, violence, physical blight, and the like. It has a keen interest in and a receptivity toward organizational humanism and advanced techniques of organizational development. It reacts against logical positivism—it largely ignores pragmatism—and seeks philosophic guidance from such schools as existentialism and, especially, phenomenology.

As a movement—if it ever was one—new Public Administration has, within a few years of its attainment of self-consciousness, lost much of its coherence and identity. But this is not to deny it importance and impact. Its adherents were centrally involved in changes in the American Society for Public Administration designed to democratize its organization and procedures and to give it a more forward stance. The literature it has produced is widely read; its ideas and sentiments circulate in the public administration community, particularly in academia. As its adherents, both original and converts, are largely on the young side and still to reach positions of maximum influence, it is likely to exert a continuing, if unpredictable, influence. In brief, it is unlikely to transform radically Public Administration short run, but long run this is a possibility; and in any case it now is and will continue to be a yeasty addition to the entire complex of theories, techniques, and aspirations.[38]

Organizational Humanism and Organizational Development

Even a brief survey of the academic-intellectual vectors affecting public administration should include some note of the complexes of interests and ideas represented by the terms "organizational humanism" and "organizational development."

Organizational humanism—not surprisingly—denotes the continuing movement to humanize—and democratize—organizations. What is sought is more knowledge about and sensitivity toward the human components. The aims are dual: greater organizational productivity or effectiveness; and greater human happiness and increased self-realization. In a sense, organizational humanism is but a continuation of the human relations movement rooted in the Hawthorne studies; and the issue of manipulation, which troubled human relations, remains. But organizational humanism is more subtle and sophisticated, and addresses itself with great seriousness and sympathy to the manipulation issue. The saint of organizational humanism is Abraham Maslow, and the "needs hierarchy," topped by self-actualization, is a paradigm-ideal for much of what takes place. Prominent and influential writers include Douglas McGregor, Rensis Likert, Warren Bennis, and Chris Argyris.[39]

More than with any other academic discipline, organizational humanism is associated with social psychology. Its most influential writers are associated in the main with business or general administration rather than public administration. But organizational humanism as a complex of ideas and techniques exerts a significant influence on public administration through various channels.

Organization development (OD) refers to conscious attempts to improve organizational output, performance, or health through study of and change in the organization, especially change in organizational members. Broadly construed, organization development consists of a rather wide spectrum of outlooks and techniques. One author lists seven currently popular approaches: (1) direct consultation, (2) survey feedback, (3) process consultation, (4) team building, (5) human relations training, (6) packaged programs, and (7) socio-technical systems. At one end of a spectrum, OD may be mostly concerned with hardware and systems, have no direct concern with interpersonal relations, and not be inclined to concern itself normatively with organization goals. But at the other end of the spectrum, the emphasis is strongly on the human components of the organization; interpersonal relations are of central concern; and there is a normative concern for organizational goals.[40]

In its later and more popular forms, OD tends toward the second end of such a spectrum. It is closely related to organizational humanism, draws upon humanist psychologies as well as social psychology, and takes some variety of the training group as its characteristic methodology.

Organization development has many proponents and practitioners in and out of academia. While the great mass of all organizations remains unaffected by the movement, nevertheless its ideas and techniques now reach into many public as well as private organizations; and it appears at this point in time to be an incoming, not an outgoing, wave.[41]

SOME SUMMARY OBSERVATIONS AND SPECULATIONS: TWO PERSPECTIVES

Patently, if the foregoing account is reasonably perceptive and accurate, what is happening to and in Public Administration hardly presents a clear and simple picture. Here is no discipline with a neat paradigm, no curriculum with agreed boundaries and stable subject matter. Rather, Public Administration appears as a loose cluster of research and teaching interests, focusing primary—but by no means exclusive—attention upon organizations defined—by law and convention—as public, drawing ideas and techniques from a wide range of sources, and interacting with changing, sometimes turbulent environments of several kinds.

With the object of better understanding the complex of action and interaction, two perspectives are suggested. The first is the familiar one presented by the original, framing, and orienting ideas of Public Administration. The second views Public Administration as matrixed in and interacting with fundamental societal transformations. These are, in fact, related perspectives.

The Framework of Orienting Ideas

In the latter nineteenth century and early twentieth century, Public Administration was given definition by a cluster of beliefs. In brief, and to simplify, the main ones were as follows: Politics and administration—to decide and to execute—are the two basic aspects of the governmental process. In general, these two should be separated: politics should not meddle in administration. The objective of administration is to execute, with economy and efficiency, decisions reached in the political process. Free of politics, administration should be, and in important ways can be, scientific. The study of administration, approached in the proper scientific way, will yield principles that can be used to guide administration in becoming economical and efficient. In general the science of administration, and the principles it yields are the same for all governments, democratic or autocratic; the difference between democratic and autocratic governments, that is, pertains chiefly to the way policies are made—decisions are reached—rather than to the way they are executed.

Much of this outlook is expressed in the definition at the opening of the first, and highly influential, textbook [L. D. White's *Introduction to the Study of Public Administration* (New York: Macmillan, 1926)]: "Public administration is the management of men and materials in the accomplishment of the purposes of the state." This definition indicates at least two other important facts. One is a concept of authority: men, no less than materials, are to be managed. The other is a concept of state: early conceptualizing, rooted in the political science of the day—much affected by Continental writings—regarded the state as unquestioned possessor of sovereignty. It should be added, however, that there was a firm belief in republican-democratic ideals. The emphasis on efficiency, science, and authority was not—as it was viewed—at the expense of democracy. On the contrary, the problem was seen as how to fulfill democratic ideals by insuring that decisions reached through the means of democratic politics would be effectively realized, not thwarted.

As is well known, these orienting and motivating ideas were seriously eroded in the mid-century decades. Sometimes they were directly challenged and disproved. Sometimes they were updated and revised. Sometimes the march of events seemed to refute them, or simply made them seem irrelevant. (The "state" all but disappeared in post-World War II political science.)

The result has been an indeterminate, even confusing, situation. The original, orienting beliefs remain, not exactly like the smile of the Cheshire cat after the disappearance of the cat, if for no other reason that the fact that some of the "cat" remains. The original, orienting ideas were an intelligent response to a new historical situation: a large polity trying to combine republican-democratic ideals with the situation created by industrialism, urbanism, science, and so forth; and that situation has not disappeared, it only further evolves. The original ideas thus continue to have a certain force and persuasiveness: It is difficult to be for political meddling and against efficiency and science in public administration. On the other hand, the original ideas are seen by all—or nearly all—as simplistic if not mischievous when addressed to many present realities. The challenge to them on empirical grounds and on moral-ideological grounds has been so thorough and effective, and the historical circumstances to which they were addressed have so altered, that they can no longer serve—it is judged—without serious modification.

A great deal of Public Administration since World War II has been concerned, one way or another, with attempting to work our way forward from the first firm framework of beliefs to a situation in which there might again be general agreement on a set of guiding beliefs. Up to this point no consensus approaching the original one has developed. What has united the Public Administration community has been, rather, the continuing force of the original ideas even in the presence of altered perspectives and problems; plus the fact that public administration *is*: its massive institutions are there, and the problems to which they are addressed are seen as real and crucial, whatever the differences concerning philosophy and methods.

If one views the attainment of a consensus in Public Administration similar to the original one as a desirable state of affairs—a problem to be solved—what conclusion is warranted in view of the above review of the societal-problem context, the external and the internal environments of Public Administration? Again assuming the above review to be reasonably perceptive and accurate, the necessary conclusion would appear to be that no consensus comparable to the old is in view. It seems highly unlikely that there will soon emerge any general agreement on what democracy means for and in administration; on what efficiency "is" and whether, how and to what extent, it is a proper goal or criteria in public administration; on what science dictates—or makes possible—in the study or practice of administration. No single school of philosophy, academic discipline, or type of methodology—or combination of these—would appear likely to persuade Public Administration to march under its banner.

This is not, of course, necessarily an unhappy conclusion. An untidy, swiftly changing world may be better addressed by an enterprise which contains many facets, perspectives, interests, and methodologies: one which is eclectic, experimental, open-ended.

Public Administration and Societal Transformation

A voluminous interpretative and speculative literature concerns our disturbed and anxious time. One current essay develops the thesis that civilization is undergoing its most fundamental change since cities arose in the fertile valleys of the Near East, a challenge to and transformation of the basic institutions of family, religion, education, law, and government. Whether this is true we will not know, only our descendants. A now large body of writings deals with our transition from industrialism to post-industrialism. The meaning of this transition, the extent to which it is in fact taking place and its implications, is something we already know something about—not much, but something. It seems clear that more than public mood and literary-intellectual vogue are involved, that the rate of societal change is accelerating, and that the breadth and depth of change are increasing.

Accepting an increasing rate of change as a fact, and premising that the changes, cumulatively, will greatly transform historically received institutions, what are the implications for public administration? A large book could only begin to draw these out at any length, but this essay can appropriately end with some suggestions. To some extent this involves only restating what has already been said or implied.

First, public administration will be centrally involved in change and transformation. Administration is "the core of modern government"—in Carl Friedrich's oft-quoted phrase—and government itself is one of the basic societal institutions subject to change. But government is not merely acted upon, it acts; and public administration as its chief instrument is and will be a focal area for change and transformation in society generally. Much of the above review of recent and contemporary developments is, of course, commentary on this theme.

Second, what is patently implied is that public administration will itself be an area of stress, ferment, and accelerated change. Negatively, this means it is unlikely that any clear and generally accepted framework of orienting beliefs, comparable to that of the first generations, will soon evolve. The parameters are too indistinct, the variables too many—and too variable. Positively, this means philosophical, disciplinary, and methodological pluralism: continued proliferation of and competition between ideas and approaches in a continuing attempt to survive, adapt, and control change. What will hold Public Administration together—assuming it remains together as a self-conscious enterprise—will not be agreement on some one kit of tools or some one route into the future. Rather, it will be general agreement on the importance of the institutional area of public administration in making a societal transformation, a general interest in organizational phenomena, a comparatively high degree of "public regardingness" in outlook, and a wish to address—whether scientifically, professionally, "valuationally," or however—problems seen as problems in public administration.

Third, Public Administration, as represented by its curricula, its literature, and its organizations, will continue to change rapidly. For example, the old staples of personnel administration and budgetary-fiscal administration, now hardly recognizable as against their configuration of thirty years ago, will continue to enlarge their boundaries and respond to the many influences playing upon them. Fads, such as PPBS, will come and go—but in their coming they will be important, and even in their going they will have lasting effects. The writing of general textbooks will become an increasingly arduous, hazardous occupation. (Some argue that it is now an obsolete occupation. I think not: To the extent the textbooks provide perspective and synthesis they are invaluable.)

Fourth, public administration now is, and increasingly will be, concerned with administrative problems much different from those which it confronted even a generation ago. The administration of an organization is scarcely the center of the problem in many areas of activity. The continued increase in the demands—particularly with regard to "people" programs—placed upon public administration, the changes wrought by continued transition from a predominately goods-producing to a predominately service-rendering economy, the accelerating graying of the area between public and private and between governmental levels and jurisdictions: such phenomena have enlarged and transformed the nature of the administrative problem. The task now is the administration of systems—or at least complexes—of organizations, not single organizations; the establishment and monitoring of long, complicated chains as against single, bureaucratic pyramids; the creation and coordination of complex networks of subtle, shifting horizontal and/or diagonal interrelations as against neat, vertical command-obedience structures. In the words of the cliche, "It's a whole new ball game" for crucial areas of public administration.

Finally, the implications for public administration of its intimate involvement in societal transformation are beyond knowing, even beyond imagining. Beliefs and institutions that have given Western civilization its defining characteristics are under attack. The much discussed crisis of authority is real: traditional sources and loci, including family, religion, and law, exert diminishing influence. Ideas and institutions of modern vintage fare little better: industrialism and technology are under attack. Even science is now challenged as simply a "school of consciousness," not *the* approach to reality; only one way, and a limited or even dangerous way, of viewing and acting.

For one acquainted with the rise of the modern state out of feudalism, it sometimes appears that the film is now being run backwards: the sovereign state is being dissolved; its clear vertical authority structure is being replaced by complicated, contractual and informal, horizontal relationships—a new feudalism. Of course, the context is not medieval, and the comparison has but a limited value. It serves to remind us, however, that the modern state system is not necessarily the end of political evolution. In fact, it is now being transformed, and public administration is a part of the transformation process.[42]

NOTES

1. Those unfamiliar with the development of Public Administration and wishing more background information are referred to: Dwight Waldo, *The Administrative State; A Study of the Political Theory of American Public Administration* (New York: Ronald Press, 1948); Dwight Waldo, *The Study of Public Administration* (New York: Random House, 1955); Dwight Waldo, "The Administrative State Revisited," *Public Administration Review* 25, no. 1 (March 1965); Dwight Waldo, "Public Administration," *International Encyclopedia of the Social Sciences* 13 (New York: Macmillan and Free Press, 1968); Dwight Waldo, "Public Administration," *Journal of Politics* 30, no. 2 (May 1968)—printed also in Marian D. Irish, ed., *Political Science; Advance of the Discipline* (Englewood Cliffs, N.J.: Prentice-Hall, 1968); Keith M. Henderson, *Emerging Synthesis in American Public Administration* (New York: Asia Publishing House, 1966).

2. The poverty literature of the past decade is voluminous. Early, and highly influential, was Michael Harrington's *The Other America: Poverty in the United States* (New York: Penguin Books, 1963). The following are useful sources for present purposes: Margaret Gordon, ed., *Poverty in America* (San Francisco: Chandler Press, 1965); Oscar Onati, *Poverty Amid Affluence* (New York: Twentieth Century Fund, 1966); Thomas Gladwin, *Poverty U.S.A.* (Boston: Little, Brown, 1967); Burton Weisbrod, *The Economics of Poverty: An American Paradox* (Englewood Cliffs, N.J.: Prentice-Hall, 1966); Gilbert Y. Steiner, *Social Insecurity; The Politics of Welfare* (Chicago: Rand McNally, 1966); John C. Donovan, *The Politics of Poverty* (New York: Pegasus, 1967); Warner Bloomberg, Jr., and Henry J. Schmandt, eds., *Power, Poverty and Urban Policy* (Beverly Hills, Calif.: Sage Publications, 1968); Eleanor Burke Leacock, ed., *The Culture of Poverty: A Critique* (New York: Simon and Schuster, 1971).

3. In addition to the latter works just cited, various aspects of policy development and administrative experience are treated in the following: Sar A. Levitan, *The Great Society's Poor Law* (Baltimore: Johns Hopkins, 1969); Peter Maris and Martin Rein, *Dilemmas of Social Reform: Poverty and Community Action in the United States* (New York: Atherton, 1967); Advisory Commission on Intergovernmental Relations, *Intergovernmental Relations in the Poverty Program* (Washington, D.C., 1966); Daniel F. Halloran, "Progress Against Poverty: The Governmental Approach," *Public Administration Review* 28, no. 3 (May-June 1968); S. M. Miller and Martin Rein, "Participation, Poverty, and Administration," *Public Administration Review* 29, no. 1 (January-February 1969); James L. Sundquist, "Co-ordinating the War on Poverty," THE ANNALS 385 (September 1969). See also citations below on community action and intergovernmental relations.

4. On various aspects of civil rights, race, and related matters, the following are sources: *Report of the National Advisory Committee on Civil Disorders* (New York: Bantam Books, 1968); Carolyn Shaw Bell, *The Economics of the Ghetto* (New York: Pegasus, 1970); Lee Rainwater and William L. Yancey, *The Moynihan Report and the Politics of Controversy* (Cambridge, Mass.: M.I.T. Press, 1967); Martin Kilson, "Black Power: Anatomy of a Paradox," *Harvard Journal of Negro Affairs* 2 (1968).

5. In this connection see: Michael Novak, *The Rise of the Unmeltable Ethnics* (New York: Macmillan, 1972).

6. For an introduction to some of these matters see: Mark A. Haskell, *The New Careers Concept; Potential for Public Employment of the Poor* (New York: Praeger, 1969); Warren I. Cikins, "Graduate Education, Public Service, and the Negro," *Public Administration Review* 26, no. 3 (September 1966); Earl J. Reeves, "Making Equality of Employment a Reality in the Federal Service," *Public Administration Review* 30, no. 1 (January-February 1970).

7. Consult: James Q. Wilson, ed., *The Metropolitan Enigma: Inquiries in the Nature and Dimension of America's "Urban Crisis"* (Cambridge, Mass.: Harvard University

Press, 1968); John C. Bollens and Henry J. Schmandt, *The Metropolis; Its People, Politics, and Economic Life*, 2nd ed. (New York: Harper and Row, 1970); Simon R. Miles, ed., *Metropolitan Problems* (Agincourt, Ont.: Methuen Publications, 1970).

8. Suggested sources on these matters are: Alan K. Campbell, ed., *The States and the Urban Crisis* (Englewood Cliffs, N.J.: Prentice-Hall, 1970); Keith F. Mulrooney, ed., symposium on "The American City Manager; An Urban Administrator in a Complex and Evolving Situation," *Public Administration Review* 31, no. 1 (January-February 1971); Henry Reining, Jr., ed., symposium on "Governing Megacentropolis," *Public Administration Review* 30, no. 4 (September-October 1970).

9. See: Dwight A. Ink, "Establishing the New Department of Housing and Urban Development," *Public Administration Review* 27, no. 3 (September 1967); Robert C. Wood, "Federal Role in the Urban Environment," *Public Administration Review* 27, no. 3 (September 1967).

10. Joseph A. Alutto and James A. Belasco, "A Typology for Participation in Organization Decision-Making," *Administrative Science Quarterly* 17, no. 1 (March 1972); William G. Scott, "Organization Government: The Prospects for a Truly Participative System," *Public Administration Review* 29, no. 1 (January-February 1969); Mauk Mulder, "Power Equalization Through Participation?" *Administrative Science Quarterly* 16, no. 1 (March 1971); Robert B. Denhardt, "Organizational Citizenship and Personal Freedom," *Public Administration Review* 28, no. 1 (January-February 1968); Marvin Meade, "Participative Administration: Emerging Reality or Wishful Thinking?" in Dwight Waldo, ed., *Public Administration in a Time of Turbulence* (Scranton, Penna.: Chandler Publishing Company, 1971).

11. Jones C. Davies, *Neighborhood Groups and Urban Renewal* (New York: Columbia University Press, 1966); C. George Benello and Dimitrios Roussoupoulos, eds., *The Case for Participatory Democracy* (New York: Viking Press, 1971); Hans B. Spiegel, ed., (vol. 1) *Citizen Participation in Urban Development: Concepts and Issues* (Washington, D.C.: N.T.L. Institute for Applied Behavioral Science, 1968); Michael P. Smith, "Alienation and Bureaucracy: The Role of Participatory Administration," *Public Administration Review* 31, no. 6 (November-December 1971); S. M. Miller and Martin Rein, "Participation, Poverty, and Administration," *Public Administration Review* 29, no. 1 (January-February 1969). See also citations below on community control.

12. The "devolution" literature is not as focused as that on participation. Consult: Morton Grodzins, *The American System: A New View of Government in the United States* (Chicago: Rand McNally, 1966); Joseph Boskin, *Opposition Politics; The Anti-New Deal Tradition* (Beverly Hills: Glencoe Press, 1968); Herbert Kaufman, "Administrative Decentralization and Political Power," *Public Administration Review* 29, no. 1 (January-February 1969); James Q. Wilson, "The Bureaucracy Problem," *The Public Interest* 6 (Winter 1967); Donald Haider, "The Political Economy of Decentralization," *American Behavioral Scientist* 15, no. 1 (September-October 1971); M. Melrood, ed., *A Bibliography on Decentralization* (Milwaukee: Institute of Governmental Affairs, University of Wisconsin, 1970).

13. Gordon C. Cameron, *Regional Economic Development; The Federal Role* (Baltimore: Johns Hopkins Press, 1971); Edward F. R. Hearle, "Regional Commissions: Approach to Economic Development," *Public Administration Review* 28, no. 1 (January-February 1968); Randy Hamilton, "The Regional Commissions; A Restrained View," *Public Administration Review* 28, no. 1 (January-February 1968); Niles M. Hansen, *Rural Poverty and the Urban Crisis; A Strategy for Regional Development* (Bloomington, Ind.: Indiana University Press, 1971).

14. Alan A. Altshuler, *Community Control* (New York: Pegasus, 1970); Warner Bloomberg, Jr., and Henry J. Schmandt, eds., *Power, Poverty and Urban Policy* (Beverly Hills, Calif.: Sage Publications, 1968); Thomas D. Lynch, ed., symposium on "Neighborhoods and Citizen Involvement," *Public Administration Review* 32, no. 3

(May-June 1972); Dale Rogers Marshall, *The Politics of Participation in Poverty* (Berkeley: University of California Press, 1971); Ralph M. Kramer, *Participation of the Poor; Comparative Community Case Studies in the War Against Poverty* (Englewood Cliffs, N.J.: Prentice-Hall, 1969).

15. The literature of business administration and general management should be consulted on these matters. For some reflection on public administration see: Ida R. Hoos, "Automation, Systems Engineering, and Public Administration: Observations and Reflections on the California Experience," *Public Administration Review* 26, no. 4 (December 1966); Edward F. R. Hearle, ed., symposium on "Computers in Public Administration," *Public Administration Review* 28, no. 6 (November-December 1968); Anthony J. Catanese and Alan W. Steiss, "Programming for Governmental Operations: The Critical Path Approach," *Public Administration Review* 28, no. 2 (March-April 1968); John P. Crecine, "Computer Simulations in Urban Research," *Public Administration Review* 28, no. 2 (March-April 1968); Fremont J. Lyden, "Project Management: Beyond Bureaucracy," *Public Administration Review* 30, no. 4 (July-August 1970).

16. Andrew Shonfield, *Modern Capitalism: The Changing Balance of Public and Private Power* (New York: Oxford University Press, 1965); Murray Weidenbaum, *The Modern Public Sector; New Ways of Doing the Government's Business* (New York: Basic Books, 1969). These works are also commentaries on the increasing "gray" area. See also: Walter Adams, "The Military-Industrial Complex and the New Industrial State," *American Economic Review* 58, no. 2 (May 1968); C. H. Danhof, *Government Contracting and Technological Change* (Washington, D.C.: Brookings Institution, 1968).

17. On public sector unionism consult: Advisory Commission on Intergovernmental Relations, *Labor-Management Policies for State and Local Government* (Washington D.C., 1969); Hugh O'Neill, "The Growth of Municipal Employee Unions," *Academy of Political Science Proceedings* 30, no. 2 (New York: Columbia University, 1970); David T. Stanley, "The Effects of Unions on Local Governments," *Academy of Political Science* 30, no. 2 (New York: Columbia University, 1970); Robert H. Connery and William V. Farr, eds., *Unionization of Municipal Employees* (New York: Academy of Political Science, Columbia University, 1971); Felix A. Nigro, ed., symposium on "Collective Negotiations in the Public Service," *Public Administration Review* 30, no. 4 (July-August 1969); Felix Nigro, ed., "Collective Bargaining in the Public Service: A Reappraisal," *Public Administration Review* 32, no. 1 (March-April 1972): K. O. Warner and M. L. Henessy, *Public Management at the Bargaining Table* (Chicago: Public Personnel Association, 1967).

18. Here, in addition to the immediately preceding citations, see: Morris Sackman, *The Crisis in Public Employee Relations in the Decade of the Seventies* (Washington, D.C.: Bureau of National Affairs, 1970); David H. Rosenbloom, "Some Political Implications of the Drift Toward a Liberation of Federal Employees," *Public Administration Review* 31, no. 4 (July-August 1971); Robert E. Catlin, "Should Public Employees Have the Right to Strike?" *Public Personnel Review* 29, no. 1 (January 1968). A work which puts much of unionism, as well as professionalism, in the public sector into perspective is: Frederick C. Mosher, *Democracy and the Public Service* (New York: Oxford University Press, 1968).

19. On productivity see: Orville F. Poland, "Why Does Public Administration Ignore Evaluation?" *Public Administration Review* 31, no. 2 (March-April 1971); Joseph S. Wholey, John W. Scanlon, Hugh G. Duffy, James S. Fukomoto, and Leona M. Vogt, *Federal Evaluation Policy: Analyzing the Effects of Public Programs* (Washington, D. C.: Urban Institute, 1970). Evaluation broadens into economic analysis and technology assessment, and the literature is extensive. The final issue of *Public Administration Review* for 1972 will contain a lengthy symposium on "Productivity in the Public Sector." Charles L. Schultze, *The Politics and Economics of Public*

Spending (Washington, D.C.: Brookings Institution, 1968) provides useful context for this subject as well as some of the preceding and following.

20. On the PPBS see: Dwight Waldo, ed., symposium on "Planning-Programming-Budgeting System," *Public Administration Review* 27, no. 4 (December 1966); Dwight Waldo, ed., symposium on "Planning-Programming-Budgeting System Re-examined," *Public Administration Review* 29, no. 2 (March-April 1969); Edwin L. Harper, Fred A. Kramer, and Andrew M. Rouse, "Implementation and Use of PPB in Sixteen Federal Agencies," *Public Administration Review* 29, no. 6 (November-December 1969); Stanley B. Botner, "Four Years of PPB: An Appraisal," *Public Administration Review* 30, no. 4 (July-August 1970); Fremont J. Lyden and Ernest J. Miller, *Planning, Programming, Budgeting* (Chicago: Markham, 1967); Guy Block, "Externalities and Structure in PPB," *Public Administration Review* 31, no. 6 (November-December 1971); Robert E. Millward, "PPBS: Problems of Implementation," *Journal of the American Institute of Planners* (March 1968); Jesse Burkhead and Jerry Miner, *Public Expenditure* (Chicago: Aldine-Atherton, 1971).

21. Some of the literature already cited bears upon the matters referred to in the latter part of this paragraph. Consult also: Raymond A. Bauer, ed., *Social Indicators* (Cambridge, Mass.: M.I.T. Press, 1966); Raymond D. Gastil, "Social Indicators and Quality of Life," *Public Administration Review* 30, no. 6 (November-December 1970); Robert S. Weiss and Martin Rein, "The Evaluation of Broad-Aim Programs: Experimental Design, Its Difficulties, and an Alternative," *Administrative Science Quarterly* 15, no. 1 (March 1970); Francis E. McGilvery, "Program and Responsibility Cost Accounting," *Public Administration Review* 28, no. 2 (March-April 1968); Alice M. Rivlin, *Systematic Thinking for Social Action* (Washington, D.C.: Brookings Institution, 1970).

22. Lynton K. Caldwell, ed., symposium on "Environmental Policy: New Directions in Federal Action," *Public Administration Review* 28, no. 4 (July-August 1968); Daniel H. Henning, "Natural Resource Administration and the Public Interest," *Public Administration Review* 30, no. 2 (March-April 1970); Harvey Lieber, "Public Administration and Environmental Quality," *Public Administration Review* 30, no. 3 (May-June 1970); Lynton K. Caldwell, "Environment: A Short Course in Semantics," *Public Administration Review* 31, no. 6 (November-December 1971); Lynton K. Caldwell, "Environmental Quality as an Administrative Problem," THE ANNALS 400 (March 1972).

23. While there is a vast popular and semi-popular literature on consumerism, and even considerable scholarly writing, as suggested it is still little reflected in the literature of Public Administration. See: Thomas L. Eovaldi and Joan E. Gestrin, "Justice for Consumers: The Mechanism of Redress," *Northwestern University Law Review* 66 (July-August 1971); Senate Committee on Government Operations, Subcommittee on Executive Reorganization, *To Establish a Consumer Protection Agency: Hearings*, 92d Congress, First Session, 4 vols. (Washington, D.C.: U.S. Government Printing Office, 1969). On administrative regulation see: Marver Bernstein, ed., "The Government as Regulator," THE ANNALS 400 (March 1972); Michael Reagan, ed., symposium on "Administrative Regulation," *Public Administration Review* 31, no. 4 (July-August 1972).

24. See: Jameson W. Doig, ed., symposium on "The Police in a Democratic Society," *Public Administration Review* 28, no. 5 (September-October 1968); Edward C. Gallas and Nesta M. Gallas, eds., symposium on "Judicial Administration," *Public Administration Review* 31, no. 2 (March-April 1971); Leslie T. Wilkins, ed., symposium "Five Pieces on Penology," *Public Administration Review* 31, no. 6 (November-December 1971).

25. Helene S. Markoff, "The Federal Women's Program," *Public Administration Review* 32, no. 2 (March-April 1972); W. Henry Lambright, "Womanpower: The Next Step

in Manpower Policy," *Public Personnel Review* 31 (January 1970); John J. Corson, "Sex and the Public Service," *Public Personnel Review* 31 (July 1970).

26. Frederick C. Mosher, *Democracy and the Public Service* (New York: Oxford University Press, 1968); Frederick C. Mosher, "The Public Service in the Temporary Society," *Public Administration Review* 31, no. 1 (January-February 1971); Emmette S. Redford, *Ideal and Practice in Public Administration* (University, Ala.: University of Alabama Press, 1958). See also forthcoming monograph of the American Academy of Political and Social Science on *Public Service Professional Organizations and the Public Interest.*

27. Many of the above citations, such as those pertaining to participation, are relevant here. See also: Orion F. White, Jr., "The Dialectical Organization: An Alternative to Bureaucracy," *Public Administration Review* 29, no. 1 (January-February 1969); Herbert G. Wilcox, "Hierarchy, Human Nature, and the Participative Panacea," *Public Administration Review*, no. 1 (January-February 1969).

28. "Reorganization Plan No. 2 of 1970," the Plan with accompanying explanation and Executive Order, *Public Administration Review* 30, no. 6 (November-December 1970); William D. Carey, "Reorganization Plan No. 2; Remarks," *Public Administration Review* 30, no. 6 (November-December 1970); Selma Mushkin and John F. Cotton, *Sharing Federal Funds for State and Local Needs* (New York: Praeger, 1969); Henry S. Reuss, *Revenue Sharing: Crutch or Catalyst for State and Local Government?* (New York: Praeger, 1970); Congressional Research Service, *Departmental Reorganization, and General and Special Revenue Sharing: Some Issues They Raise* (Library of Congress, June 1971).

29. Note 20 introduces the voluminous literature on PPBS. While much of what is cited bears upon the limitations and problems of PPBS, "retrospection" has only begun. In this connection see Allen Schick, "A Death in the Bureaucracy," *Public Administration Review*, forthcoming.

30. The literature of "ferment" in American education is voluminous and of course outside the scope of this review. Chiefly with foreign readers in mind, I cite the following as an introduction: Nevitt Sanford, ed., *The American College* (New York: Wiley, 1967); Christopher Jencks and David Riesman, *The Academic Revolution* (Garden City, N.Y.: Doubleday, 1968); Jacques Barzun, *The American University; How It Runs, Where It Is Going* (New York: Harper and Row, 1968); George B. Leonard, *Education and Ecstasy* (New York: Dell, 1968); Carl Rogers, *Freedom to Learn* (Columbus, Ohio: Merrill, 1969); Charles E. Silberman, *Crisis in the Classroom* (New York: Random House, 1970). More focused for present purposes is: Clyde J. Wingfield, ed., symposium on "The American University: A Public Administrative Perspective," *Public Administration Review* 30, no. 2 (March-April 1970).

31. Again, a large, "unfocused" literature on these matters. But see: Robert Brown, *Explanation in Social Science* (Chicago: Aldine, 1963); Peter L. Berger and Thomas Luckman, *The Social Construction of Reality; A Treatise in the Sociology of Knowledge* (Garden City, N.Y.: Doubleday, 1967); Maurice Mandelbaum, *Phenomenology of Moral Experience* (Baltimore: Johns Hopkins Press, 1969); Eugene S. Meehan, *Value Judgment and Social Science* (Homewood, Ill.: Dorsey, 1969); S. M. Lyman and M. B. Scott, *A Sociology of the Absurd* (New York: Appleton-Century- Crofts, 1970); Charles Hampden-Turner, *Radical Man* (New York: Doubleday, 1971); William J. Filstead, *Qualitative Methodology* (Chicago: Markham, 1971).

32. A discussion of these matters will be found in: James C. Charlesworth, ed., *Theory and Practice of Public Administration: Scope, Objectives, and Methods,* Monograph 8 in a series sponsored by The American Academy of Political and Social Science; Cosponsor for this volume: The American Society of Public Administration (Philadelphia, 1968). This is, generally, a very useful source on the recent period in Public Administration.

33. The new currents in political science have been evident mainly in journals, but are manifested also in some books. Consult: Henry S. Kariel, *The Promise of Politics* (Englewood Cliffs, N.J.: Prentice-Hall, 1966); Peter Bachrach, *The Theory of Democratic Elitism; A Critique* (Boston: Little, Brown, 1967); Charles McCoy and John Playford, eds., *Apolitical Politics; A Critique of Behavioralism* (New York: Crowell, 1967); Marvin Surkin and Alan Wolfe, eds., *An End to Political Science* (New York: Basic Books, 1970).

34. See: Anthony Downs, *An Economic Theory of Democracy* (New York: Harper, 1957); Anthony Downs, *Inside Bureaucracy* (Boston: Little, Brown, 1967); Gordon Tullock, ed., *Public Choice* (Blacksburg, Va.: Center for Studies in Public Choice, Virginia Polytechnic Institute, 1968); Gordon Tullock, *Private Wants, Public Means; An Economic Analysis of the Desirable Scope of Government* (New York: Basic Books, 1970); Gordon Tullock and James M. Buchanan, *The Calculus of Consent* (Ann Arbor, Mich.: University of Michigan Press, 1967); Gordon Tullock, *The Politics of Bureaucracy* (Washington, D.C.: Public Affairs Press, 1965); Walter W. Heller, *New Dimensions of Political Economy* (Cambridge, Mass.: Harvard University Press, 1966); William A. Niskanen, Jr., *Bureaucracy and Representative Government* (Chicago: Aldine-Atherton, 1971); William C. Mitchell, "The Shape of Political Theory to Come: From Political Sociology to Political Economy," *American Behavioral Scientist* 11, no. 2 (November-December, 1967); William C. Mitchell, *Public Choice in America* (Chicago: Markham, 1971); L. L. Wade, "Political Science and Public Policy: A Review Essay," *Policy Sciences* 2, no. 3 (Summer 1971); Marver H. Bernstein, "Understanding the Political Economy of Public Regulation," *Polity* 4, no. 4 (Summer 1972).

35. The reference is to a book by Vincent Ostrom; and a book co-authored by Gary Wamsley (political scientist) and Mayer Zald (economist). See also: Vincent Ostrom and Elinor Ostrom, "Public Choice: A Different Approach to the Study of Public Administration," *Public Administration Review* 31, no. 2 (March-April 1971).

36. This is certainly indicated by a Delphi exercise conducted at the Maxwell School, Syracuse University (by Emanuel Wald). A Delphi exercise conducted by the National Academy of Public Administration suggests this conclusion; but the data do not bear directly on the point.

37. For a discussion of these developments see: "Training MBAs for the Public Sector," *Business Week*, June 10, 1972, pp. 82–84.

38. The central document of the new Public Administration is: Frank Marini, ed.,*Toward a New Public Administration; The Minnowbrook Perspective* (Scranton, Penna.: Chandler, 1971). A collection of pieces concerning the movement and responses from administrators may be found in: *Public Management* 53, no. 11 (November 1971). Several essays in the following are relevant: Dwight Waldo, ed., *Public Administration in a Time of Turbulence* (Scranton, Penna.: Chandler, 1971). See also: Richard S. Page, "A New Public Administration?" *Public Administration Review* 29, no. 3 (May-June 1969); Wesley E. Bjur, "The 'New' Public Administration," *Public Administration Review* 30, no. 2 (March-April 1970); Lyle J. Sumek and Franklin D. Reinow, "New Public Administration: For a Time of Crisis—In a Time of Change," *Midwest Review of Public Administration* 4, no. 2 (August 1970); Robert F. Wilcox, "The New P.A.: Have Things Really Changed That Much?" *Public Management* 54 (March 1971).

39. See: Abraham Maslow. *Eupsychian Management* (Homewood, Ill.: Irwin Dorsey, 1965); Abraham Maslow, *Toward a Psychology of Being* (New York: Van Nostrand Reinhold, 1968): Douglas McGregor, *The Human Side of Enterprise* (New York: McGraw-Hill, 1960); Douglas McGregor (edited—posthumously—by Warren G. Bennis and Caroline McGregor), *The Professional Manager* (New York: McGraw-Hill, 1967); Rensis Likert, *New Patterns for Management* (New York: McGraw-Hill, 1961);

Rensis Likert, *The Human Organization* (New York: McGraw-Hill, 1967); Warren G. Bennis, *Changing Organizations* (New York: McGraw-Hill, 1966); Warren G. Bennis and Philip E. Slater, *The Temporary Society* (New York: Harper and Row, 1969); Warren G. Bennis, Kenneth D. Benne, and Robert Chin, *The Planning of Change*, 2nd ed. (New York: Holt, Rinehart and Winston, 1969); Chris Argyris, *Integrating the Individual and the Organization* (New York: Wiley, 1964); Chris Argyris, *Intervention Theory and Method* (Reading, Mass.: Addison-Wesley, 1970). The reflection of organizational humanism is prominent in new Public Administration, but it is more extensive: see, for example, the writings of Robert T. Golembiewski, for example, his *Men, Management, and Morality; Toward a New Organizational Morality* (New York: McGraw-Hill, 1965).

40. This paragraph represents a point of view reflected in an unpublished paper (dated March 1972) by M. E. McGill, "Discarding the Monolithic Myth: Assumptions about Personal and Interpersonal Relationships Underlying Approaches to OD." Some proponents and practitioners, as the following paragraph suggests, would reject McGill's "broad spectrum" definition; they would identify the earlier techniques not with OD, but with management science.

41. As indicated, there is much overlapping between organizational humanism and OD, and some of the preceding citations are relevant here as well. See also: J. K. Fordyce and Arthur Weil, *Managing With People* (Reading, Mass.: Addison-Wesley, 1971); Harvey A. Hornstein et al., *Social Intervention: A Behavioral Science Approach* (New York: Free Press, 1971); Richard Walton, *Interpersonal Peacemaking; Confrontations and Third Party Consultation* (Reading, Mass.: Addison-Wesley, 1969); Robert T. Golembiewski and Arthur Blumberg, eds., *Sensitivity Training and the Laboratory Approach* (Itaska, Ill.: Peacock, 1970); Edgar Schein and Warren G. Bennis, eds., *Personal and Organizational Change Through Group Methods* (New York: Wiley, 1965); Leland Bradford, Jack R. Gibb, and Kenneth D. Benne, eds., *T- Group Theory and the Laboratory Method* (New York: Wiley, 1964). *The Journal of Applied Behavioral Science* is the central journal of OD and should be consulted for further information. *The Administrative Science Quarterly* is also a useful source on OD, as well as various other matters, such as management science. On impact in public administration, see, for example: Robert T. Golembiewski, "The 'Laboratory Approach' to Organizational Change: Schema of a Method," *Public Administration Review* 27, no. 3 (September 1967); Robert T. Golembiewski, "Organizational Development in Public Agencies: Perspectives on Theory and Practice," *Public Administration Review* 29, no. 4 (July-August 1969); William B. Eddy and Robert J. Saunders, "Applied Behavioral Science in Urban Administrative/Political Systems," *Public Administration Review* 32, no. 1 (January-February 1972); William B. Eddy, "Beyond Behavioralism? Organization Development in Public Management," *Public Personnel Review* 31 (July 1970). See also: George E. Berkley, *The Administrative Revolution; Notes on the Passing of Organization Man* (Englewood Cliffs, N.J.: Prentice-Hall, 1971).

42. The documentation for this review has presented unusual difficulties: of "target," level of assumed knowledge, and so forth. With this in view, the following suggestions for further exploration and explanation are made; some may find them useful: Claude E. Hawley and Ruth G. Weintraub, eds., *Administrative Questions and Political Answers* (New York: Van Nostrand, 1966); Alan A. Altshuler, ed., *The Politics of the Federal Bureaucracy* (New York: Dodd, Mead, 1968); Francis E. Rourke, *Bureaucratic Power in National Politics*, 2nd ed. (Boston: Little, Brown, 1972). All three of these are useful collections—and all are broader in scope than their titles suggest. Gerald E. Caiden, *The Dynamics of Public Administration; Guidelines to Current Transformations in Theory and Practice* (New York: Holt, Rinehart and Winston, 1971) is recent, intelligent, and provocative. Finally, recent editions of textbooks should not be overlooked, both because they review what is presently happening and because they at-

tempt to project emerging perspectives. See: John M. Pfiffner and Robert V. Presthus, *Public Administration* (Ronald); Herbert A. Simon, Donald W. Smithburg, and Victor A. Thompson, *Public Administration* (Knopf); Felix A. Nigro, *Modern Public Administration* (Harper and Row); Marshall E. and Gladys O. Dimock, *Public Administration* (Holt, Rinehart and Winston); Ira Sharansky, *Public Administration; Policy-Making in Government Agencies* (Markham); Robert T. Golembiewski, Frank Gibson, and Geoffrey Y. Cornog, eds., *Public Administration; Readings in Institutions, Processes, and Behavior* (Rand McNally). Purposely, I have omitted dates. My information is that all but two of these books are being revised: consult the latest edition.

The Pornography of Everyday Life

WARREN BENNIS

When the Pentagon Papers were published, what disturbed me more than the deceits, the counter-deceits, the moral numbness and ethical short-circuiting of our leaders, was the pornography of it all. The hubris of those men, thousands of miles away, making life-and-death decisions for others, manipulating the most modern tools of technology, using game theory with models so abstract they could reproduce one another in one joyless, screamless parthenogenetic act. But not once, these men, not once could they experience the epiphany of childbirth—or the smell of burning flesh.

I thought of pornography because that, also, is distance from reality, from direct experience. Actors in porn films are not real people making love, but appendages of sexual organs engaged in mechanical acts. These appendages are so without personalities or identifiable social characteristics that, as one movie critic pointed out, they are more about physical engineering than love—so many pistons and valves. Loveless sex. Distant, remote, calculated, vicarious.

The "war room" at the Pentagon is as distant from the reality of war as downtown Boston's so-called "combat zone," the festooned, free area for porno sales, is from the reality of sex.

In those now yellowing Papers, we see Secretary of Defense Robert S. McNamara busying himself with the minutiae of war planning because lists of numbers and cost estimates have a distracting if illusory moral neutrality.

Toward the end of his tenure, he stops questioning the military or political significance of sending 206,000 more troops into Indochina, into a war he now knew could not be won and concentrates, instead, on the logistical problems of getting them there. That's administration. And as he fulfilled the requirements of efficiency and effectiveness, during his own final days, his wife reports that he began to grind his teeth—every night—while tossing fitfully.

Albert Speer elevated the promises of Hitler's "technocracy" to a point where these promises quickly became shields against any inclination to think of the human and social consequences of his actions. The challenges, the deadlines, the deadly routines of the Third Reich—as of the Defense Department, or any large bureaucracy—become tasks to be performed, power to be exercised, problems to be solved, monuments to be designed (or demolished).

Is it the nature of large-scale organizations to make it possible for an ethical person such as a McNamara—or unethical Watergaters—to work toward an ultimately immoral end—without an immediate sense of personal responsibility or guilt? Bureaucracies are, by definition, systems of increased differentiation and specialization, and thus the ultimate morality of bureaucracy is the amorality of segmented acts.

Coming home:

On the first real day of spring, two beautiful trees in the infancy of bloom are chopped down to make more room for cars to turn down a campus driveway. Everybody is outraged. Students pack into my office to tell me about it. A few are hysterical and crying. I leave my office and walk over to the little grass plot—there is so little green on our campus—to see a man with a small hand power saw, cleaning and stacking up the milk-white wood into neat piles.

A crowd of some 200 students and faculty stand around and hiss me as I break through the circle to speak to him. "Man, am I glad you're here. They're ready to crucify me." It turns out he's not employed by the university. He works for a local contractor. I could never find out who was responsible: the landscape artist who designed the new plot with poodle hedges, or his boss, the landscape architect; the director of planning, or his boss the head of the physical plant; the vice president for management and finance, the university building committee, the executive vice president the committee reports to . . .

When I called them all together they numbered twenty, and they were innocents all. All of us. Bureaucracies are beautiful mechanisms for the evasion of responsibility and guilt.

Too far from the classroom, from the munitions plant, from the battlefield, from the people, from love. That's pornography.

There are no easy answers—or options. The problem is immense and invades all of our lives. Recently the Bureau of Census reported that only 1.5 percent of our employment rolls are made up of the "self-employed"; the rest work, as you and I do (if we work), in large organizations. Less than 75 years ago, that ratio was the opposite.

And it's far too simple (and unrealistic) to talk about "small is beautiful." Smallness helps only if it prevents the episodic, disconnected experience that characterizes so many of our leaders and administrators. And it does no good to pretend closeness and a direct relationship with "the people," displaying the candidate or governor wearing saffron robes, walking to work, eating vegetarian dinners to a recording of Fritz Perls reading Zen Haiku. The "simple" life—through a technotronic, quadraphonic TV tube. That's "soft porn" for the intellectual, falsely lulling, and just as corrupt as the hard kind.

What's important, it seems to me, is the capacity to see things in wide perspective, to receive impressions and gain experiences directly—not vicariously—that point beyond the experiences and data themselves. Continuity and purpose.

To the pornographic leader, things and events of the world appear as portable fragments. The long view is replaced by shortsightedness. Detail, but no pattern. The fresh outlook yields to a stereotyped and biased one. Experiences and impressions, what there are of them seen through the lucite gray of a limousine window, cannot be fully valued and enjoyed because their character is lost.

Our leaders must learn to embrace error and take risks, to explore in the presence of others. Almost like learning how to play the violin in public.

Unless they do (and we permit them to), they will continue to sound as if they are talking through a plate-glass window, distant, isolated, removed from the complex lives of living people on the other side.

ACKNOWLEDGMENTS (continued from page iv)

Richard Marvel, Robert J. Parsons, Winn Sanderson, and N. Dale Wright, "Legislative Intent and Oversight." Reprinted with permission from *State Government* (Winter 1976) published by the Council of State Government, Lexington, Kentucky.

Roger C. Cramton, "Judicial Law Making and Administration." Reprinted by permission from *Public Administration Review* (Sept./Oct. 1976). Copyright © 1976 by American Society for Public Administration, 1225 Connecticut Avenue N. W., Washington, D. C. 20036. All rights reserved.

James W. Fesler, "The Basic Theoretical Question: How to Relate Area and Function." Reprinted by permission from *The Administration of the New Federation*, ed. Leigh E. Grosenick (ASPA, 1973). Copyright © 1973 by American Society for Public Administration, 1225 Connecticut Avenue N.W., Washington, D. C. 20036. All rights reserved.

Deil S. Wright, "Intergovernmental Relations: An Analytical Overview." Reprinted from volume no. 416 (November 1974) of *The Annals* of The American Academy of Political and Social Science. © 1974 by The American Academy of Political and Social Science. All rights reserved.

Peter M. Blau and Marshall W. Meyer, "The Concept of Bureaucracy." From *Bureaucracy in Modern Society*, Second Edition, by Peter M. Blau and Marshall W. Meyer. Copyright © 1956, 1971 by Random House, Inc. Reprinted by permission of the publisher.

Douglas M. McGregor, "The Human Side of Enterprise." Reprinted by permission of the publisher from *Management Review*, November 1957, © 1957 by American Management Association, Inc. All rights reserved.

Melvin L. Kohn, "Bureaucratic Man." Reprinted by permission from *New Society* (October 28, 1971). This article first appeared in *New Society*, London, the weekly review of the social sciences.

Fred E. Fiedler, "Style or Circumstance: The Leadership Enigma." Reprinted from *Psychology Today* Magazine (March 1969). Copyright © 1969 Ziff-Davis Publishing Company.

Robert B. Denhardt and Jan Perkins, "The Coming Death of Administrative Man." Reprinted by permission from *Public Administration Review*, 36 (July/August 1976). Copyright © 1976 by American Society for Public Administration, 1225 Connecticut Avenue N. W., Washington, D. C. 20036. All rights reserved.

Adam W. Herbert, "The Minority Administrator: Problems, Prospects and Challenges." Reprinted by permission from *Public Adminis-*

tration Review, 34 (Nov./Dec. 1974). Copyright © 1974 by American Society for Public Administration, 1225 Connecticut Avenue, N. W., Washington, D. C. 20036. All rights reserved.

Rufus E. Miles, Jr., "Considerations for a President Bent on Reorganization." Reprinted by permission from *Public Administration Review* (March/April 1977). Copyright © 1977 by American Society for Public Administration, 1225 Connecticut Avenue N.W., Washington, D. C. 20036 All rights reserved.

Herbert Kaufman, "Reflections on Administrative Reorganization," reprinted from Joseph A. Pechman, ed., *Setting National Priorities: The 1978 Budget*. Copyright © 1977 by The Brookings Institution.

Martin Landau, "Redundancy, Rationality, and the Problem of Duplication and Overlap." Reprinted by permission from *Public Administration Review*, 29 (July/August 1969). Copyright © 1969 by American Society for Public Administration, 1225 Connecticut Avenue N. W., Washington, D. C. 20036. All rights reserved.

David T. Stanley, "What's Happening to the Civil Service?" Reprinted from *Good Government*, 91 (Summer 1974). Copyright © 1974 National Civil Service League, *Good Government* Magazine.

E. S. Savas and Sigmund G. Ginsburg, "The Civil Service: A Meritless System?" Reprinted with permission of the authors from *The Public Interest*, No. 32 (Summer 1973). © by National Affairs, Inc.

Catherine Lovell, "Three Key Issues in Affirmative Action." Reprinted by permission from *Public Administration Review*, 34 (May/June 1974). Copyright © 1974 by American Society for Public Administration, 1225 Connecticut Avenue N. W., Washington, D. C. 20036. All rights reserved.

Richard L. Schott, "Public Administration as a Profession: Problems and Prospects." Reprinted by permission from *Public Administration Review*, 36 (May/June 1976). Copyright © 1976 by American Society for Public Administration, 1225 Connecticut Avenue N. W., Washington, D. C. 20036. All rights reserved.

Jerry Wurf, "Merit: A Union View." Reprinted by permission from *Public Administration Review*, 34 (September/October 1974). Copyright © by American Society for Public Administration, 1225 Connecticut Avenue N. W., Washington, D. C. 20036. All rights reserved.

Raymond D. Horton, David Lewin, and James W. Kuhn, "Some Impacts of Collective Bargaining on Local Government: A Diversity Thesis" is reprinted from *Administration & Society*, Vol. 7, No. 4 (February 1976), 497–516 by permission of the Publisher, Sage Publications.

Aaron Wildavsky, "The Budgetary Process." From "Toward a Radical Incrementalism" by Aaron Wildavsky in *Congress: The First Branch of Government*, ed. Alfred De Grazia (Washington: American Enterprise Institute, 1966). Reprinted with permission.

Jimmy Carter, "Jimmy Carter Tells Why He Will Use Zero-Based Budgeting." Reprinted by permission from *Nation's Business*, January 1977. Copyright 1977 by *Nation's Business*, Chamber of Commerce of the United States.

James Q. Wilson, "Zero-Based Budgeting Comes to Washington" reprinted from *The Alternative* (February 1977). Copyright 1977, *The Alternative* Magazine, Bloomington, Indiana 47401. Reprinted with permission.

Herbert Simon, "Decision Making." Reprinted by permission from *Public Administration Review*, 25 (March 1965). Originally entitled "Administrative Decision Making." Copyright © 1965 by American Society for Public Administration, 1225 Connecticut Avenue N. W., Washington, D. C. 20036. All rights reserved.

Alice M. Rivlin, "Making Federal Programs Work Better," (Brookings Research Report No. 112, 1971). Copyright © 1971 by the Brookings Institution.

James R. Schlesinger, "Systems Analysis and the Political Process," Rand Corporation Paper No. P-3464. Reprinted by permission of James R. Schlesinger and The Rand Corporation.

Joseph S. Wholey, "What Can We Actually Get From Program Evaluation?" reprinted from *Policy Sciences*, 3 (1972), 361–369. By permission of Elsevier Scientific Publishing Company.

Peter F. Drucker, "Managing the Public Service Institution," Copyright Peter F. Drucker 1973, Reprinted by permission from *Public Interest*, Fall 1973.

Charles Peters, "How to Take Over the Government." Reprinted with permission from *The Washington Monthly* (September 1974). Copyright 1974 by The Washington Monthly Co., 1028 Connecticut Avenue, N. W., Washington, D. C. 20036.

George S. Odiorne, "MBO in State Government." Reprinted by permission from *Public Administration Review*, 36 (January/February 1976). Copyright © 1976 by American Society for Public Administration, 1225 Connecticut Avenue N.W., Washington, D. C. 20036. All rights reserved.

Nancy S. Hayward, "The Productivity Challenge." Reprinted by permission from *Public Administration Review*, 36 (September/October 1976). Copyright © by American Society for Public Administration, 1225 Connecticut Avenue N. W., Washington, D. C. 20036. All rights reserved.

Brian W. Rapp, "You Can't Manage City Hall the Way You Manage General Motors." Reprinted by permission from *Good Government*, Summer 1975. Copyright © 1975 National Civil Service League, *Good Government* Magazine.

Caspar W. Weinberger, "Do More Public Programs Equal Less Private Freedom?" from *The Chronicle of Higher Education*, August 4, 1975. Reprinted with permission from The Chronicle of Higher Education.

Robert Nisbet, "Leviathan and Laissez-Faire." From *The New York Times*, Sept. 23, 1975. © 1975 by the New York Times Company. Reprinted by permission.

Charles A. Reich and Burke Marshall, "Needed: A Government that Governs." From *The New York Times*, Dec. 23, 1973. © 1973 by The New York Times Company. Reprinted by permission.

George Cabot Lodge, "Top Priority: Renovating Our Ideology," *Harvard Business Review*, September-October 1970. Copyright © 1970 by the President and Fellows of Harvard College; all rights reserved.

Charles L. Schultze, "The Public Use of Private Interest." This article appeared in the September/October 1977 issue of *Regulation*. It was adapted from *The Public Use of Private Interest* by Charles L. Schultze. Copyright © 1977 by The Brookings Institution.

Anthony Downs, "Increasing Bureaucratization, Social Efficiency and Individual Freedom." From *Inside Bureaucracy*. Copyright © 1967, 1966 by The Rand Corporation. Reprinted by permission of the publisher, Little, Brown and Company and The Rand Corporation.

Herbert Kaufman, "Administrative Decentralization and Political Power." Reprinted by permission from *Public Administration Review*, 29 (January/February 1969). Copyright © 1969 by American Society for Public Administration, 1225 Connecticut Avenue N. W., Washington, D. C. 20036. All rights reserved.

James L. Sundquist, "Reflections on Watergate: Lessons for Public Administration." Reprinted by permission from *Public Administration Review*, 34 (September/October 1974). Copyright © 1974 by American Society for Public Administration, 1225 Connecticut Avenue N. W., Washington, D. C. 20036. All rights reserved.

Allen Schick, "Let the Sunshine In." Published by permission of Transaction, Inc. from *The Bureaucrat*, Vol. 1, no. 2 (Summer 1972). Copyright © 1972 by Transaction, Inc.